THE GENESIS
OF THE WORLD WAR

THE
GENESIS OF THE
WORLD WAR

AN INTRODUCTION TO THE
PROBLEM OF WAR GUILT

by

HARRY ELMER BARNES

*Professor of Historical Sociology, Smith College;
William Bayard Cutting Fellow in History,
Columbia University (1916-17); Bibliographic Editor of "Foreign Affairs"
(1922-25).*

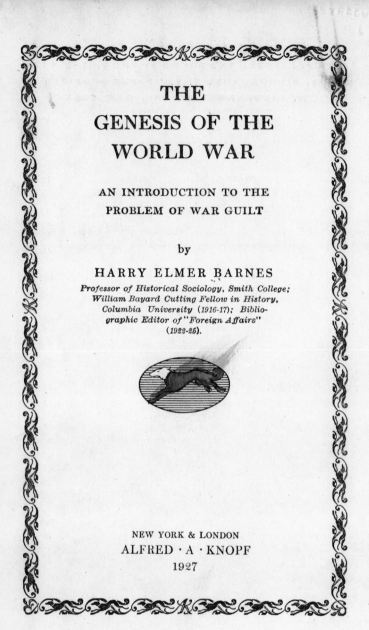

NEW YORK & LONDON
ALFRED · A · KNOPF
1927

TO
HERBERT CROLY
GEORGE W. OCHS-OAKES
CHARLES CLAYTON MORRISON
AND
OSWALD GARRISON VILLARD

Distinguished American Editors, whose courage
and public spirit in opening their columns to a
discussion of the causes of the World War have
been primarily responsible for such progress as
has been made in dispelling war-time illusions and
laying the basis for an intelligent approach to
contemporary international problems.

PREFACE

This book is frankly what the title implies: an *introduction* to the study of the problem of the responsibility for the World War. It aims to present the subject as it now stands on the basis of the secret documents published since 1917 and of the monographic literature which has appeared in this same period, analyzing and assessing the significance of this new documentary material. It is the purpose of the writer to arouse interest in the subject and to create a general conviction that there is here a major international problem, the nature and importance of which are scarcely realized by even the average educated American. If this primary purpose of the book is realized, it is hoped that it will serve a second function equally well, namely, to act as a guide to the study of the more technical and voluminous literature.

It is the contention of the author that the book is a fair assessment of the facts and issues as they appear on the basis of the evidence at present available. The facts are collected and presented here in such a fashion as to indicate their bearing upon the views on war guilt which were entertained by most historical scholars in Entente countries during the War, and still guide and control the thinking of most educated persons and newspaper editors in these same states. The book is frankly controversial in tone, and for a number of reasons. Among them are the nature of the subject, the fact that this approach is probably the best procedure for the first book of the sort published, the belief of the author that such a method will do the most to arouse interest and demolish prevalent error, and the undoubted fact that the controversial method is the one which the writer can personally exploit most forcefully in this field. The writer offers no apology whatever for the style and tone of the book. Facts of this order of importance are worthy of clear and decisive statement. Taken by themselves alone, timidity of attitude and obscurity of statement are scarcely invariable proof of historical erudition or scholarly command of the subject. Nor is it less "emotional" and more "dispassionate" to cling desperately to old myths than to assume an open-minded attitude towards newly revealed facts.

As far as possible, the writer has attempted to anticipate the objections to his particular formulation of the revisionist position on war guilt, and to answer such objections in the text of the present work. The writer has carefully followed most of the controversial literature on the subject for several years and is fully acquainted

with the nature of the attacks upon the revisionist statement of the case.   He believes that these
are satisfactorily answered in the present work.
Throughout there is consistent effort to refute
the apologies for the war-time illusions, particularly the apologetic efforts of leading Entente
statesmen and of the "die-hards" and "straw-
clutchers" among the historians.

The author has especially endeavored to present what he believes to be the broad conclusions
to which we are forced by the newer material.
This he has done not only for the convenience of
the general reader, but also to challenge the more
timid revisionists: (1) to indicate wherein the
facts upon which such conclusions are based are
erroneous; or (2) to expose the fallacious nature
of the reasoning whereby such conclusions are
drawn from generally accepted facts.   The
writer has felt that, in general, the revisionist
cause has suffered more than anything else from
the excessive timidity or interpretative incapacity of many revisionist scholars who appear to the
writer to be unwilling to draw the inevitable conclusions from the facts which they present.   In
this book he offers a good-natured invitation to
more conservative scholars to show why they regard their views as more sound and tenable than
those which are here brought together.   The
same privilege is obviously extended to the equal
number of writers who believe that the present

writer does not go far enough in his departure from the conventionally accepted views.

The writer has often been accused of being "too extreme" in his interpretation of the revisionist viewpoint. This has usually meant that he has departed too far from the conventional notions for the peace of mind of his readers. Obviously, there can be no validity to this charge unless it can be proved that the statements of fact are unreliable or the conclusions unwarranted. Facts themselves, and the interpretations which justly grow out of such facts, can never be too extreme, no matter how far they depart from popular convictions in the premises. Moderation is an excellent slogan in the abstract, but it has been used for the most part with respect to recent studies of war guilt as a commendable ideal under which writers have disguised their unwillingness completely to surrender their own war-time illusions. The writer has never had it satisfactorily explained to him why it should be more scholarly to be fifty per cent short of the truth than to be one per cent beyond it.

The chapters on the countries involved in the diplomacy leading to the World War have been prepared so that each is, in a certain sense, a unit by itself, though introduced and clarified by reference to previous material. This accounts for the existence of some repetitions, and the citing of particularly important documents in sev-

eral places.   It is believed that such a procedure
is desirable for the sake of emphasis, as well as
being indispensable for the guidance of the
reader who is for the first time attempting a systematic mastery of the problem.

The author has prepared this book with the
definite conviction that the problem of responsibility for the World War is not primarily an
esoteric matter of erudite historical scholarship
isolated from the world of affairs.   The writer
would have no time to waste upon this subject if
he did not believe that the truth about the causes
of the World War is one of the livest and most
important practical issues of the present day.
It is basic in the whole matter of the present European and world situation, resting as this does
upon an unfair and unjust Peace Treaty, which
was itself erected upon a most uncritical and
complete acceptance of the grossest forms of
war-time illusions concerning war guilt.   The
facts in this case are also of the greatest significance as an aid in attacking the whole problem of
the future of war—the chief menace to the inhabitants of our planet to-day.   Never was any previous war so widely proclaimed to have been
necessary in its origins, holy in its nature, and
just, moderate and constructive in its aims.
Never was a conflict further removed in the actu-
alities of the case from such pretensions.   If we
can learn the great lesson here embodied we shall

have a powerful argument with which to meet the propaganda of those who will announce the necessity and idealism of the next war.

Like most other human beings the writer is not free from all animus or convictions, but his animus is not the pro-Germanism of which he is frequently accused. He has no traces of German ancestry and all of his cultural and educational prejudices are strongly pro-British and pro-French. The "LaFayette, we are here!" attitude toward France was from the beginning an integral part of his education, and he accepted thoroughly in 1917–18 the conventional mythology in the Entente epic. While early becoming sceptical of the pure and lofty idealism of the bullet-manufacturers who wrote brave tracts for the National Security League and the American Defense Society, he was actually first awakened from his "dogmatic slumbers" by Professor Fay's articles in the summer of 1920. Professor Fay's demolition of the myth of the Potsdam Conference was a shock almost equivalent to the loss of Santa Claus in his youth. (If Germany is here cleared of any significant amount of direct guilt in producing the War in 1914, it is because the writer believes that the facts lead one inevitably to that conclusion.) There is no effort in this book to free Germany of her mutual share in the responsibility for the general international system which inclined Europe towards war, though the writer does not believe that it can be demonstrated that Germany was more at fault here than any other major European nation. And in placing the guilt upon "France" and "Russia" the writer obviously uses these terms in a purely conventional sense, and actually means the guilt of a few men like Izvolski, Sazonov, the Grand Duke Nicholas, Poincaré, Delcassé, Paul Cambon, Viviani *et al.* One cannot accurately indict a nation for the acts and policies of a half dozen temporary leaders. No one recognizes better than the author that France under men like Caillaux, Herriot, Painlevé and Combes is quite a different thing from France under Poincaré and Delcassé, or that the mass of French people were for peace in 1914.

The main animus and *tendenz* motivating the writer in preparing this book is a hatred of war in general and an ardent desire to execute an adequate exposure of the authors of the late World War in particular. The World War was unquestionably the greatest crime against humanity and decency since the missing link accomplished the feat of launching *homo sapiens* upon his career. Yet the authors of this crime have not only for the most part escaped censure but the majority of them have even continued to be regarded as men of high nobility of character and as valiant crusaders for peace. Their reputations for unselfish human service have been actually enhanced by the War. Still they were the means of sending more individuals prematurely to the angels than all the individual murders since eolithic days. Nevertheless, we cannot put men like Sazonov, Izvolski, Poincaré and Delcassé in the same category as the man who shoots down the paying-teller in a bank and makes off with a roll of bills. They were all men with reasonably high standards of personal honor and morality and were doubtless convinced that they were high-minded and unselfish servants of the state. Therefore, it is an adequate cause for reflection upon the type of ethical criteria and social system which makes it possible for a half dozen men to plunge the great majority of civilized mankind into mental and moral debauchery, physical slaughter and economic ruin, and escape with immaculate reputations.

It has been charged that in placing the guilt for the World War upon a few individuals such as Poincaré, Delcassé, Cambon, Izvolski, Sazonov and Grand Duke Nicholas, the writer has departed from his fundamental historical philosophy which stresses the primary significance of great intellectual currents, economic influences and social forces in determining the course of historical events. The writer has never pretended to believe that general historical forces operate independent of the individual actors in the historic drama. The individuals above mentioned

would never have been able to bring about a
European war in 1914 if the general situation in
Europe had not been shaping up for such an
event for some years before 1914. Poincaré
and Izvolski were successful because the general
orientation of European society and politics was
favorable to the realization of their program
through an appeal to economic envy, nationalism, secret diplomacy and military force.

Several noble souls have complained that the
writer has but substituted one set of devils for
another. " ' 'Twas the Kaiser did it!' then 'No!
'Twas Poincaré!' " wails Dr. Mack Eastman,
for example. The writer frankly admits that *a
priori* this might seem to constitute a valid logical charge against his thesis. He regrets that
the facts compel this substitution of a set of truly
responsible agents for the mythical group that
we believed responsible in 1914–1918. But he is
not here arbitrarily selecting arguments with a
view to winning an inter-collegiate debate. He
does not propose to dodge crucial facts and conclusions, even though they may seem to present a
casual and specious objection to his position.

The writer has attempted to make the statements of fact as accurate as possible, and to
present only conclusions which are the logical
outgrowth of the facts presented. He has further profited by the critical aid and advice of
experts, not only in regard to the present book

but also in every stage of his work in this field.
Each chapter has been read by one or more of
the chief specialists on the subject-matter of that
particular chapter. Yet the author does not
pretend that the present book represents any
final statement of the matter of war guilt as regards minor details. In so vast a field many
slips are possible and new evidence may require
the modification of certain statements. The
author feels sure, however, that the general outlines of the picture and the basic conclusions will
remain unshaken, and that subsequent additions
to our information will only serve to make the
case against the Entente even more decisive.

Many critics held that the writer's article in the
New York *Times Current History Magazine*
for May, 1924, was extreme in its statements,
but the progress of investigation in this field since
that time has already served to make many of the
details and some of the conclusions of that article
seem highly conservative if not archaic.

In the light of these facts this book has been
printed directly from type with the assumption
that the publication of additional documents and
further travel and conference with eminent authorities on war guilt abroad will render desirable
the revision of some matters of detail. Suceed-
ing editions of this book, then, will await the results of such developments, as well as the critical
reviews to which the work will be subjected. In-

tellectually adult readers will not need to be reminded that the detection of a few minor errors
and the statement of open differences of opinion
do not constitute the basis for a refutation of the
major conclusions of the work as a whole. (The
most determined efforts to discredit the first edition of this book by reviews in the *Outlook* for
June 23, 1926, the London *Times* for September
30, 1926, *Foreign Affairs* for October, 1926, the
London *Observer* for October 3, 1926, and the
American Historical Review for January, 1927,
afford ample proof of the unwillingness of critics
even to attempt to grapple with the outstanding
issues and contentions contained in the book and
of the necessity of disingenuous concentration on
irrelevant details.

Because of the fact that the chapter on England's part in the diplomatic crisis of 1914 is
much longer than that on any other state it might
be assumed that the author has a special griev-
ance against Great Britain, but this is in no sense
the case. As we indicate at length in that chapter, the direct guilt of England does not compare
with that of France and Russia. But there is
to-day more need for realistic education on the
matter of the relation of Great Britain to the
World War than on any other subject connected with the general problem of war guilt.
The attitude of Canadian and English writers
towards the brief and almost eulogistic discus-

sion of Grey's diplomacy, which was published
in the writer's articles in the *Christian Century,*
as well as the objections of Mr. Percy Ashley to
the equally mild and courteous characterization
of Grey in the writer's concluding chapter to
Ashley's *Europe from Waterloo to Sarajevo,*
served to convince the writer of the almost un-
believable need for education on this subject
in British quarters, in spite of Morel, Gooch,
Conybeare, Loreburn, Ewart, Dickinson and
Beazley. The British illusions, as well as the
perpetuation of the British epic, are just at present being vigorously inflated and nursed along
by the phenomenally popular memoirs of Viscount Grey. Hence, it has seemed to the writer
that the time is highly opportune for a thorough
demolition of the Grey fiction. Reviews of the
first edition of this book in the London *Outlook*
for September 18, 1926, in the London *Times*
for September 30, 1926, and in the London *Observer* for October 3, 1926, show that many Englishmen are still bent upon confirming my thesis
as to their essential illiteracy with respect to the
facts about war guilt.

In my work on war guilt my indebtedness to
specialists has been heavy, and I can only mention the few who have been of the greatest assistance. Most of all I am indebted to Professor William L. Langer of Clark University who
has read and criticized everything of any signif-

icance which I have written on the subject of the
causes of the World War. His wide and precise knowledge of the facts and literature of contemporary diplomatic history has saved me from
innumerable slips in matters of detail, and his
sound judgment has often added much in way of
interpretation. I am also heavily indebted to
the courageous and illuminating writings of Professor Sidney Bradshaw Fay and to many helpful conversations with him during which he has
given me the benefit of his enviable knowledge
of the facts regarding the diplomatic crisis of
1914. He is not, however, to be held in any
sense responsible for any interpretations.

Professor Langer has read and criticized the
proof of the entire volume. The first chapter
was read in proof by Professor Harry J. Carman of Columbia University; the second by Professor Parker T. Moon of Columbia University;
the third with special care by Professor William
L. Langer; the fourth by Professor Bernadotte
Everly Schmitt of the University of Chicago;
the fifth by Dr. Joseph V. Fuller of the Department of State and Mr. William C. Dreher of Amherst, Massachusetts; the sixth by Dr.
John S. Ewart of Ottawa, Canada; the seventh
by Judge Frederick Bausman of Seattle, Professor Lindsay Rogers of Columbia University
and Professor Graham H. Stuart of Leland
Stanford University; the eighth by Professor

Manley O. Hudson of the Harvard Law School and by Dr. Ewart; the ninth by Professor E. M. Borchard of the Yale Law School and Mr. James Kerney of Trenton, New Jersey; the tenth by Professor Lawrence Packard of Amherst College; and the eleventh by Professor Carl Becker of Cornell University. All of these men have made extremely valuable suggestions and criticisms, most of which have been embodied in the book. In no case, however, is any one of these scholars to be held in any sense responsible for any statements in the book or for any errors of fact or interpretation which may still remain.

In preparing the copy for the second revised edition of the book it was the great good fortune of the writer to be able to use the results of a two days' criticism of the work by a conference of more than a dozen of the foremost European authorities on war guilt, drawn from all the leading European countries. He has also been able to utilize most valuable and detailed criticisms on the entire text by Professor Raymond Beazley of the University of Birmingham.

I am also indebted to Mr. William C. Dreher of Amherst, Mass., for a critical reading of the page proofs of the whole book. His wide knowledge of European affairs and his extensive acquaintance with the European literature of war guilt have been of great assistance to me in checking up on matters of detail.

HARRY ELMER BARNES.

Northampton, Mass.
February 22, 1927.

CONTENTS

xxi

THE GENESIS
OF THE WORLD WAR

Why Forget?

A movement backed by more than 100 prominent British citizens, among them H. G. Wells, Bernard Shaw and Maynard Keynes, has been launched to eliminate sections 227 and 231 of the Versailles treaty. These sections charge Germany with responsibility for the war, for the violation of international law and for serious offenses against the sanctity of treaties and the customs of war. These, the sponsors of this movement declare, are "manifestly unjust and constitute a grave obstacle to international understanding."

But are they unjust? Have any facts been brought to light since the peace conference to reduce Germany's responsibility for the war or to mitigate her violation of the neutrality of Belgium, or to justify such an offense against civilization as the torpedoing of the Lusitania?

From some points of view it doubtless would be better if these war incidents were forgotten. The recent Locarno compact looks definitely in the direction of mutual understanding between Germany and her late enemies. But in forgetting them, is there any obligation upon England, France and Belgium to salve Germany's feeling and write out of the treaty the articles which place the blame for the war definitely on her shoulders?

If Germany was not responsible, who was? And if her war practices were defensible why did the United States take up arms against her and help to drive from Europe the Hohenzollerns and all they stood for? If they were wrong, why not invite old Kaiser Wilhelm and the crown prince back to Berlin with the humble apologies of the allied governments?

The millions of soldiers who bore arms against Germany, remembering their comrades who made the great sacrifice at Verdun, Ypres and in the Argonne, have no sympathy with sentimentalists who would erase the war blame sections of the treaty. If Germany was not the offender, and is now to be given a clean bill, how are they going to justify the war they fought to their children and grandchildren?

Editorial in Cleveland *Plain Dealer*, December 26, 1925.

CHAPTER I

THE BASIC CAUSES OF WARS

I. NECESSITY OF EXAMINING THE FUNDAMENTAL CAUSES OF WAR

No adequate consideration of the causes and lessons of the late World War could well be limited to a discussion of diplomatic exchanges between June 28 and August 3, 1914. We must not only deal with the general diplomatic and political situation in Europe from 1870 to 1914, but also go back of diplomatic history to the fundamental causes of war in general. The World War could not have come in the summer of 1914 if the system of international relations prevailing at the time had not been one which invited armed hostilities. But likewise it may be held that a system of international relations making for war could not well exist unless there were certain deeper causes which have made war the usual method of solving international disputes. There can be no hope of ending war unless we understand thoroughly the basic and complex forces which lead mankind to continue this savage and archaic method of handling

1

the relations between states. War will disappear, not through petty and sporadic treatment of its symptoms, but only through an understanding of, and a consistent attack upon, those material conditions and those attitudes of mind which make wars possible in contemporary society.[1]

II. BIOLOGICAL FACTORS PROMOTING WAR

First in order we may consider the biological causes of war, both those which represent biological realities and those which rest upon a false application of biological and pseudo-biological principles to social processes.[2] The most important potential biological cause of war is to be found in that tendency, perceived by Malthus a century ago, on the part of mankind to increase more rapidly than the means of subsistence. In other words, there is a propensity for the population to outrun the possibility of being maintained in a state of comfort or prosperity within its political boundaries, with the resulting necessity of looking elsewhere for new homes.[3] As Dr. Thompson and others have convincingly demonstrated, the population changes since 1750 throughout the western world have amply confirmed Malthus's main generalizations.[4] There has been, however, up to the present time a vast amount of relatively unoccupied area on the earth's surface to which the surplus populations of the more congested districts of the world might freely migrate. Hence, there has been no truly biological cause of war inherent in population increases.

Yet there can be no doubt that population pressure was a contributing cause in producing the late world catastrophe. This was because a certain biological principle had become inseparably linked with a dangerous psychological attitude and political fetish. It was commonly believed disastrous to the mother country and emigrants alike for any large number of people to leave their native land and take up residence under the political authority of another country. It was held that migrating citizens should retain their citizenship and carry the glories of the fatherland overseas. Such an aspiration was possible of execution only in conjunction with the development of colonies.[5] While much of the earth's surface was still an area for free and legitimate occupation, relatively little remained at the close of the nineteenth century as land available for colonial dominion, England, Russia and France having appropriated the larger portion of the earth's surface not already under the domination of independent sovereign states. There thus inevitably came a clash between this desire to obtain colonies for outlet and the fact that potential colonial area was continually diminishing in extent. This struggle for colonies, particularly on the part of Germany, Italy and Japan, helped to precipitate many of the international crises which constituted the diplomatic background of the World War. It will be seen, however, that the cause was not primarily biological but rather psychological and political. Had not the patriotic and colonial psychosis existed, population increases up to the present date would in no important sense have produced an international situation making for war.[6]

Though it may be held that up to the present time specific biological factors in the way of population increase may not have constituted a vital cause of conflict, we can scarcely hold that this constitutes a reason for neglecting the possible importance of population pressure as a cause of war in the future. If the present rate of population increase goes on for another century and a half, the world will have reached a degree of density of population which will constitute the maximum capable of subsistence without a progressive lowering of the standards of living. If such conditions are allowed to develop it may well be that the more powerful nations will prefer to attempt to despoil their weaker neighbors and deprive them of their lands and resources rather than to reduce their own level of comfort and prosperity.[7] If this is the case it means that various methods for the artificial and conscious limitation of population should be embodied in any comprehensive and far-sighted scheme for the elimination of war, and it is here that advocates of pacific international relations may well link hands with the proponents of birth control.[8]

Another important biological factor which must be considered is the fact that man has, during a considerable portion of his existence on the planet, obtained a large part of his livelihood and prestige through war. In other words, he has been differentiated from the other animals and developed to his present state of ascendency in part as a fighting animal. War and physical struggles have unquestionably played a most important selective part in the biological history of man and have left their impress upon him in a hundred different ways in both instinctive tendencies and physiological processes.[9] It would be nonsense to contend, as some have done, that man is wholly or even primarily a fighting animal,[10] but it is equally absurd to maintain that he is wholly pacific and characterized chiefly by a spirit of brotherly love.[11] The sensible thing is to recognize that man is biologically oriented for both physical struggle and social coöperation, and that the sane procedure for the friends of peace is to advocate an educational and institutional system which will do everything possible to promote the pa-

cific and coöperative tendencies of man and to
sublimate or divert and discourage his warlike
proclivities.[12]   Any scheme for peace which ig-
nores the inherent human capacity for blind rage
and passion toward citizens of other states is
likely to be wrecked when faced by the practical
realities which to-day lead to war. This was well
exemplified in the case of the international Socialists of the various European countries who
before the war had sworn to an eternal brotherhood based on the international solidarity of the
working classes, but who rallied to the standards
of the fatherlands in the summer of 1914 with
a gusto which in many cases exceeded that evi-
denced by the monarchists and capitalists.[13]

Among the most potent causes of war has undoubtedly been one which, while drawn from
alleged biological data, is really primarily psychological or cultural, namely, the doctrine that
war in human society is the social analogue of
the biological struggle for existence in the realm
and processes of organic evolution. This is the
doctrine which is sometimes known as "social
Darwinism." [14] It is, of course, incorrect to
hold Darwin responsible for any such position,
as he frankly admitted that he did not know how
far the processes of individual biological evolution could be applied to the problems of social
development. But a number of biologists and
sociologists have warmly espoused the view that

the chief factor in social and cultural progress has been the wars between human groups from the days of tribal society to the world wars of the present age.[15] The fallacies underlying this view, so relentlessly exposed by such writers as Novicow, Nicolai and Nasmyth, are so obvious that we need scarcely delay to reveal them.[16] In the first place, the theory is not valid in a strictly biological sense, as the active struggle for existence in the biological world is rarely a battle within the same species but a struggle between different species. The selective process that goes on within the same species is normally one which simply leads the weaker members of the species to succumb more quickly than their more vigorous associates in the joint struggle for food and protection. In fact, the human animal is almost the only animal that preys upon his own species, and this he has come to do, not because of any inherent biological necessity, but primarily because of false and perverted mental attitudes and cultural traditions which have made him look upon war as the only honorable method of adjusting his difficulties.

But even if the theory of nature "red in tooth and claw" were valid in a biological sense, it would not by any means follow that this doctrine is sound sociologically. Biological processes are not normally directly transferable to the social realm, but must be modified in the light of the widely different factors and conditions which distinguish society from the biological organism.

Hence, while we may well recognize the possible services of war in primitive society as an integrating and disciplinary factor making possible the origins of orderly political society, we may correctly contend that at the present time war is both an anachronism and an unmitigated menace to culture and social welfare.[17]   Particularly is this true in contemporary society where the progress in the technology of war has made modern warfare in no sense a test of biological supremacy but rather a test of technical efficiency and capacity for organization.[18]   As Nicolai and Jordan have well shown, war is today biologically counter-selective, the better types being selected and decimated as "cannon-fodder," while the task of procreation is passed on to the inferior types which remain safely preserved at home.[19]   Added to this are the biological ravages of disease, suffering, starvation and mutilation which war inevitably brings in its train.[20]

It is one of the pressing tasks of the rational and constructive exponents of world peace to recognize both the realities and the fallacies in these biological factors involved in war or potential war, and to carry on a campaign of education designed to eliminate as far as possible both the real and the pseudo-biological causes of conflict, realizing that a fallacious dogma may be quite as dangerous in causing war as a biological reality. We need no less to refute the doctrines of social Darwinism than to safeguard against the possibilities of such an overcrowding of the planet as to invite a world struggle for habitations and food resources.[21]

III. PSYCHOLOGICAL CAUSES OF WAR

The second main type of the fundamental causes of war, as we shall classify them here, is the psychological. We may first mention one psychological cause of war which is very closely related to social Darwinism as mentioned above. This is the so-called cult of war which represents military and naval achievements as the most noble of the activities to which a people may devote themselves, and which elevates the military classes to a position of both social and psychological ascendency.[22] It is held that war brings forth the highest and most unselfish of human sentiments, as well as the most heroic expressions of devotion to the group. The great heroes in the country's past are looked upon as those who have done most to bring glorious victories in time of war. Inseparably related to this war cult is pride in territorial aggression.[23] It emerges in what has been called the "mapitis psychosis." Maps of the national states and of the world are so drawn as to indicate in impressive coloration territory wrested from neighboring or enemy states. The main technique exploited by exponents of the war cult in securing popular support is the alarmist bogy, and the allegation that we must "prepare" against ominous and imminent threats of aggression. This was a basic apology for the great armaments of the decade before the World War which were alleged to be merely preparation for peace, but which Professor Sumner correctly prophesied would inevitably lead to war.[24]

As all readers have lived through the World War it will not be necessary to take space to refute the fundamental contentions of the exponents of the war cult. War, instead of promoting the noblest of our emotions, brings forth, for the most part, the most base and brutal factors and processes in human behavior. Lust, cruelty, pillage, corruption and profiteering are among the attitudes invariably generated by military activity. Yet, fallacious as the theory of the war cult may be, it is unquestionably still powerful among us to-day and it constitutes one of the chief obstacles to sane discussion and practical achievement in the cause of peace.[25]

Akin to the cult of war is the sentiment which is usually denominated patriotism. In discussing this matter we must distinguish between two altogether different concepts. One is that noble ideal of devotion to the community which was first thoroughly developed by the ancient Greek philosophers and expounded more thoroughly by the modern Idealists. This is, perhaps, the highest of human socio-psychological achievements and is one of the things which most distinctly separates us from the animal kingdom.[26]

On the other hand, we have that savage sentiment of group aggression and selfishness known conventionally at present as "Hundred Percentism." This is but a projection into modern civilization of the psychology of the animal hunting-pack and the savagery of primitive tribesmen. It is certainly one of the lowest, most brutal and most dangerous of contemporary psychic attitudes and behavior patterns.[27] It has become a world menace chiefly since the Scientific and Industrial Revolutions have given it a technological basis for nation-wide operation. Down to the middle of the eighteenth century there could be little national patriotism because the majority of mankind knew of little or nothing beyond their neighborhood or local group. Suddenly the telephone, the telegraph, the cable, the railroad, the printing press, the cheap daily newspaper and free city and rural delivery of mail made it possible to spread this neighborhood superstition, narrow-mindedness, provincialism and savagery throughout the entire limits of a great national state. Thus it has come about that we

may all practically simultaneously pick up our
morning papers at the breakfast table and have
our group pride inflated by the record of the doings of the American Marines in Nicaragua or
Shanghai, or have our passions aroused by an
alleged insult to our national honor in Persia or
Timbuctoo.[28]   The citizens of an entire state
may now be stirred as effectively by the press as
a neighborhood might have been aroused a century ago by the return of a messenger from the
battle front.   The potentialities of the "movies"
and the "radio" in the service of patriotic fanat-
icism almost transcend imagination.   Until we
are able to deflate and obstruct patriotism, as it
is conventionally understood, and to substitute
for it the constructive sentiment of civic pride
and international good-will, there can be little
hope of developing those coöperative agencies
and attitudes upon which the program of world
peace necessarily depends.[29]

A powerful stimulant of savage patriotism
has been national history and literature.   In the
first place, our histories have been filled primarily
with records of battles and the doings of military
and naval heroes.   A country's importance has
been held to depend primarily upon its warlike
achievements.   The activities of scientists, inven-
tors, artists and others who have been the real architects of civilization receive but scant notice.[30]
Hence, it is not surprising that as children we

develop the view that after all war is the most significant and important of human activities.

Even worse, the history of wars and diplomatic intrigues, which makes up the larger portion of the subject-matter of the majority of our historical works, has been most notoriously and inaccurately distorted in our school textbooks. The country of the writer is always represented as having been invariably right in all instances of international dispute, and all wars are represented as having been gloriously-fought defensive conflicts. In this way fear, hatred and intolerance of neighboring states are generated in the minds of school children, to be continued later through perusal of the biased and prejudiced presentation of international news in the subsidized press.[31] No training is afforded in the development of a judicious and reflective consideration of international issues and inter-state relations, though a few textbook writers have of late attempted to improve both the subject-matter and the tone of our school textbooks. Their efforts have, however, been savagely attacked by innumerable patriotic and hyphenated societies which endeavor to stir up international hatreds and prejudices. Such attention as is given in many textbooks to the questions of national culture is usually devoted to a demonstration of the superiority of the culture of the state of the writer to that of any adjoining political group.

In the last few years we have had our attention
called rather sharply to the dangers in the form
of the super-patriotic teachings in the textbooks
in the United States, but it is unfortunately true
that the school textbooks in the majority of the
European states are even more chauvinistic and
bigoted to-day than were the worst of the school
texts in this country a generation ago.   When
the minds of children are thus poisoned with suspicion, fear, arrogance, bigotry and intolerance
there is little hope that they will develop, along
with physical maturity, a sense of calmness and
justice in their scrutiny of international affairs.[32]
These psychological causes of war are viewed by
the writer as of transcendent importance because
all other factors, biological, social, economic or
political, become active and significant only
through their psychological expression.

IV. SOCIOLOGICAL CAUSES OF WAR

Of the alleged sociological causes of war the
most important is that which rests upon the tendency of groups to develop conflicting interests
and to struggle for their realization by physical
force if necessary.   It is alleged by many that
this inevitable conflict of interests in human society will always remain as a permanent incentive to war, there being many forms of conflicting interests which can scarcely be eliminated by

any degree of social progress.[33] Further, struggle or conflict is regarded as a great social discipline and a highly significant impulse to social progress. The inaccuracies in this position are apparent at once upon analysis. As Ratzenhofer, Small, Bentley and others have so convincingly shown, the struggle of conflicting interest-groups is even more prominent within each state than between different states.[34] Yet this struggle of groups within the state does not take the form of physical conflict but tends rather towards adjustment, compromise and intellectual competition. If we were able to develop the same degree of legal control and juristic adjustment in world society as now prevails within the boundaries of each state, there would no longer be any need or justification for the struggle of national groups to obtain their legitimate desires.[35] Again, while social struggles and conflicts may be an important means of progress, Novicow and other penetrating writers have long since demonstrated that purely physical struggle has become a disastrous anachronism in society. The constructive forms of social conflict must become in the future more and more distinctly economic, cultural and intellectual. This sort of competition may indeed prove a stimulant to progress, but physical combat will inevitably throw mankind back toward primitive barbarism and misery.[36]

The remaining sociological cause of war is one which was dealt with above in connection with the biological factors, namely, the struggle of groups for areas into which increasing populations may migrate. It was earlier pointed out that, short of a complete filling up of the earth's surface by increasing populations, the migration of emigrants is not necessarily a cause of war, except when accompanied by various psychological and political attitudes, such as imperialism and colonialism, which invite a clash of political systems. Shorn of these fetishes, international migration might proceed peacefully and constructively.[37]

V. THE ECONOMIC ORIGINS OF WAR

Among the most potent causes of war are the economic.[38] The Industrial Revolution produced an enormous increase in commodities available for sale. The old local and home markets proved inadequate for this increasing flood of goods. It was deemed necessary to find new markets overseas.[39] In part these markets might be discovered among highly developed peoples in distant lands, but for the most part the industrial countries endeavored to develop or exploit colonies as potential customers for goods manufactured in the mother country. This led to what has been called modern economic imperialism or the struggle for markets, raw materials and investment areas overseas. Probably the most dynamic incentive to imperialism, particularly in the last generation, has been the struggle for control over the sources of raw materials. The zeal exhibited to-day in the effort to get command of the oil and rubber supply is but the most conspicuous contemporary manifestation of this tendency. As a result, most of the areas which were not already under the dominion of independent modern states in 1870 have been parcelled out among the British, French, Russians and Americans.[40]

This scramble for overseas territory was one of the most potent causes of international disputes in the fifty years before 1914.[41] England and Germany clashed in Africa over Walfisch Bay and over the German attitude toward the British policy in dealing with the Boers; in Oceania concerning the Samoan and other islands; and in Asia Minor over the attempt of Germany to secure a port and naval base on the Persian Gulf. England and Russia were led by jealousy over territory in the Near East into a bloody war in the middle of the century and to the brink of another in 1878; and mutual aggression in Afghanistan and Persia ended without war only through a parcelling out of the territory between them. England and France, after earlier friction over northern Egypt, came near to

war over the Fashóda incident in the Sudan in
1898, and hostility was here averted solely by a
redistribution of colonial possessions and ambitions. Germany and France twice threatened
the peace of Europe over Morocco before the
matter was even temporarily adjusted. The rivalry of Germany and Russia in Asia Minor was
not wholly settled by the "Willy-Nicky" correspondence or the convention of 1911, and the
conflict between the "Mittel-Europa" and Pan-
Slavic plans, and the mutual rivalry over Turkey helped to create the diplomatic crisis which
precipitated the war. Germany and the United
States clashed over the Samoan Islands and in
regard to the American conquest of the Philippines. Italy broke her long friendship with
France over the latter's annexation of Tunis
and made war on Turkey to secure Tripolitania
after being sharply obstructed in Abyssinia.
Russia and Japan fought over eastern Siberia
and Manchuria. Finally, the "glory" of the war
with Spain and the rise of "the American Empire" served the better to prepare the United
States to enter upon the World War.

Not only has there been a struggle for overseas dominions for markets and raw materials;
the Industrial Revolution in due time produced
an enormous supply of surplus capital that
sought investment in overseas dominions.[42]
This in itself was legitimate enough. But the in-

vestors sought special protection and unique
rights independent of the laws and customs of
the country in which the investments were made.
Extra-territorial rights were demanded which
made the investors free from the laws and courts
of the exploited country. Each state, in ad-
ministering its laws, was, naturally, biased in
favor of its own nationals.[43] In many cases,
when the exploited state was weak enough in a
political or military sense to allow such oppression, foreign investors have induced their home
governments to impose severe economic handicaps upon the country undergoing economic
penetration. A notorious representative example of such procedure is the limitation of the customs duties which may be imposed by the
Chinese government. Chinese merchants shipping goods into foreign countries are compelled
to pay the extortionately high customs duties
imposed, while the Chinese are themselves limited to notoriously low customs rates on imports.[44] The Boxer Revolution of 1900 and the
recent uprisings in China have been very largely
caused by the oppressive activities of foreign investors supported by the armed forces of their
home governments.[45] Such procedure makes
for nothing but international hatred and a desire to throw off the oppressor. Nothing has
done more to align the yellow race against the
white than the economic exploitation of China

by European countries and the United States.

Even more serious has been the intimidation or the military or naval occupation of weaker states at the behest of investors.[46] The investor of capital in some weak state may believe that his interests are not adequately protected by the laws and institutions of the state in which he is carrying on business, or may find it difficult to collect his debts in this same country. He then hastens at once to the state department or foreign office of his home government and demands that his economic and financial interests be protected by the army or marines of his mother country. This has led to notorious intervention on the part of various states and the forceful occupation of weaker or dependent states in order to collect the debts due to private citizens.[47] This procedure is a direct repudiation of the established practice within each state. An investor at home would never for a moment dream of requesting so preposterous a thing as the use of the standing army to enable him to collect a debt, but the investor abroad demands exactly this form of special protection and intervention. This has produced a large number of irritating and oppressive incidents in modern international relations, perhaps the most notorious of which have been our own relations with various Latin-American countries, where our foreign policy has been very extensively dictated by the wishes and interests of our investors, the vigorous disclaimers of ex-Secretary Hughes notwithstanding. Nothing else has done so much to produce international discord on the western hemisphere, but our American examples of this practice are only representative illustrations of a well-nigh universal practice on the part of the more powerful states of the modern world as exemplified by the recent activities of the British in Egypt, China and Persia, or the French in Morocco and Syria.[48]

The international menace inherent in many modern economic conditions, particularly imperialism and foreign investments, has been intensified by the differential and discriminatory system of protective tariffs which has evolved parallel with the rise of modern industry and world commerce. In the late eighteenth and early nineteenth centuries there was a steady movement toward free-trade, but the rise of modern industrialism, nationalism and imperialism produced a strong reaction in favor of that form of economic nationalism which is known as the protective tariff.[49] Even the most extreme exponents of this policy in the earlier days contended that it was desirable only when helping a developing industrial state to establish itself in a condition of relative economic equality with more advanced states. As Friedrich List himself admitted, there is no valid justification for a protective tariff on the part of a well developed industrial state.[50]   Yet modern politicians and special economic interests have secured a well-nigh universal adoption of the protective tariff system, which is nothing else than a form of economic warfare continuing during the periods of assumed political peace. Particularly has this been true of the discriminatory tariff systems which were common in Europe before the World War and have in some cases been continued in an even more irritating form since that conflict has officially terminated.   We shall never be able to eliminate the economic causes of war so long as the archaic principle of the protective tariff remains an unabated nuisance.[51]   Unfortunately, there is little prospect at present for relief in this direction.   Even England has believed herself compelled to revert to the tariff system after nearly a century of approximately free trade, while the United States now finds itself laboring under the most atrocious tariff law in the history of our country.

But the basest and most vile of all the forms of the economic causes of war are those which are related to the propaganda of various firms engaged in the manufacturing of armor, explosives, and various other types of munitions used in warfare, both on land and water.[52]   Such organizations subsidize the militaristic propaganda, support patriotic societies and contribute

enthusiastically to the maintenance of speakers
and periodicals which emphasize the value of
citizen training camps and other forms of effort
to keep the military cult forcefully before the
people. In the period before the late European
war it was not uncommon for munitions manufacturers to bribe foreign newspapers to print
highly alarmist news in a rival country in order
to stir up reciprocal fear in the state of the munitions manufacturers and hence make it possible
to secure larger appropriations for armament
and munitions.[53]   Then there is the lust of those
economic vultures who see in war an opportunity
for unique pecuniary profit, and are willing to
urge a policy which will lead to enormous loss of
life and an increase of general misery in order
that they may accumulate additional revenue
over the dead bodies of their fellow-citizens.[54]

Though these very real and potent economic
causes of war exist, it has long since been apparent to the intelligent and penetrating econ-
omists that modern economic society is becoming more and more a world society in every
important sense. Modern methods of communication and transportation have tended to make
the world ever more an economic unit characterized by interdependence and the necessity for
coöperation.[55] Only the foolhardy psychological attitudes which have come down from an
earlier age serve as pseudo-economic motives for

division and discord. Further, as Norman Angell warned before the War and still further proved upon the basis of the results of the recent World War, no war can to-day be a profitable one, even for the victors.[56] The main hope for the mitigation of the economic forces making for war are, on the one hand, the development of an educational program designed to reveal the menace of economic imperialism and the high protective tariff system, and, on the other hand, the gradual recognition on the part of the more intelligent and forward-looking bankers and investors that the old system was wrong-headed in its notions and must be modified if ultimate disaster is to be averted.[57]

VI. THE POLITICAL CAUSES OF WAR

Among the most important of the political causes of war is the modern national state system, the psychological results of which were mentioned above in connection with the military cult and conventional patriotism. Largely as a result of the rise of modern capitalism and the Protestant Reformation, the benign dream of a united political entity comprehending all Europe was replaced by the hard actuality of the modern national state.[58] This system was first thoroughly legalized in European public law in the Treaty of Westphalia of 1648. The

independence of nationalities in a political sense
was at first confined primarily to the greater
European states, but the aspiration to such independence soon spread to the lesser peoples, and
the nineteenth century was in part taken up with
their struggles for emancipation. Owing to the
fact that subject nationalities were frequently
oppressed within the greater states, these oppressed peoples came to regard nationality as
something which required political independence
for adequate expression.[59]

In this way there grew up that disastrous tendency to confound the purely cultural fact of
nationality with political autonomy and sovereignty. The acceptance of this view has promoted the creation of a large number of small
national states which constitute just so much
greater invitation to war unless brought within
some world organization or some European fed-
eration.[60] The Peace of Versailles carried to its
logical extreme this recognition of political nationalism, without at the same time adequately
safeguarding the process by a strong international organization. It is perfectly true that
nationalism may be adjusted to world order and
organization, but it will need to be a nationalism
much more tempered and conciliatory than that
which motivated and conditioned European psychology in the century before the World War.[61]

Aside from its psychological expression in

fanatical patriotism the chief reason why the
national state has been a menace to peace and
world order has been the fact that nationalism
has been linked with the conception of absolute
political sovereignty. This was a notion de-
rived vaguely from Roman law, but primarily
developed by political philosophers from Bodin
in the sixteenth century, through Hobbes, Black-
stone, Bentham and Austin to Burgess in our
own day. In the words of Burgess it means the
"original, absolute, universal and unlimited
power of the state over any subject or group
of subjects." [62]   Such a political concept, held
to be the very key and core of the modern political order, has naturally proved a nasty theoretical stumbling-block to any movement for world
organization. It has been maintained that any
such plan would involve some sacrifice of sovereignty and independence, and would therefore
pull down the whole edifice of modern political
society in its wake. Added to this metaphysical
fetish has been the even more absurd notion of
"national honor"—a phrase used normally to
cover supposedly non-judicable topics and disputes.[63]

It is easy to show that this view of absolute
political sovereignty is a purely metaphysical
fiction, the power of the state being in both
theory and practice limited by every treaty and
international arrangement, as well as by the so-

cial power exerted by various groups within the state.[64] The concepts and practices of political pluralism are already severely challenging the theory of the omnipotent sovereign state, and we may safely hold that there is nothing in sound political science of the present time which constitutes any obstacle to the plans for an effective society of states.[65] Yet the fetish of the sovereign state still persists to give pathological sensitivity to many contemporary statesmen and politicians when a program of world unity is brought up for discussion. The view that there are subjects which a state cannot submit to adjudication without a lesion of national honor is as misleading as it is to contend that there are matters which a private individual should not submit to the courts of law. The concept of "national honor" is not an adjunct of national dignity or world order but a criterion and a stigma of international lawlessness, comparable to duelling and lynch law within the state.[66]

VII. CONCLUSIONS

The above brief discussion of some of the more obvious fundamental causes of war should be useful, if for no other reason, because it makes plain the necessary breadth of any adequate program for securing world-peace. The pacifist has normally been a single-track reformer, putting his trust in some *one* alleged panacea, such as disarmament, international arbitration, international conferences, international discussion clubs, religious unity, leagues of nations, free-trade, non-resistance, and so on. While every one interested in the cause of peace should be allowed to affiliate himself with whatever branch of the general peace movement is able to claim his most enthusiastic support, he should understand that his particular pet scheme will be helpful only as a part of a larger whole comprehending the consistent assault upon each and every one of the factors making for war in contemporary society. When we shall have eliminated the causes of international friction, the symptoms of this world malady will no longer be present to harass us.[67]

SELECTED REFERENCES

Bakeless, J., *The Economic Causes of Modern Wars; The Origins of the Next War;* Bryce, J., *International Relations;* Buell, R. L., *International Relations;* Culbertson, W. S., *International Economic Policies;* Duggan, S. P., *The League of Nations;* Dunn, R. W., *American Foreign Investments;* East, E. M., *Mankind at the Crossroads;* Enock, A. G., *The Problem of Armaments;* Hobson, J. A., *Imperialism;* Moon, P. T., *Imperialism and World Politics; A Syllabus of International Relations;* Muir, R., *Nationalism and Internationalism;* Nearing, S., and Freeman, J., *Dollar*

Diplomacy; Nicolai, G., *The Biology of War;* Novicow, J., *War and Its Alleged Benefits;* Page, K., *War: Its Causes, Consequences and Cure;* Partridge, G. E., *The Psychology of Nations;* Playne, C. E., *The Neuroses of the Nations;* Potter, P. B., *An Introduction to the Study of International Organization;* Scott, J. F., *Patriots in the Making;* Swinburne, J., *Population and the Social Problem;* Young, A. A., "Economics and War," in *American Economic Review,* March, 1926.

FOOTNOTES AND FURTHER REFERENCES

[1] As a syllabus and bibliography on the underlying causes of war the most useful book in English is Edward Krehbiel, *Nationalism, War and Society.* The most profound discussion of the problem is to be found in Thorstein Veblen, *The Nature of Peace and the Terms of Its Perpetuation.*

[2] The literature and the various biological and pseudo-biological theories involved in the biological causation of war are surveyed by the present writer in a series of articles on "Representative Biological Theories of Society," in the *Sociological Review,* 1924–26. The most effective attack on the biological determinists and social Darwinists is contained in G. Nicolai, *The Biology of War.*

[3] J. Bonar, *Malthus and His Work.*

[4] W. S. Thompson, *Population: a Study in Malthusianism.*

[5] M. S. Wertheimer, *The Pan-German League;* A. Megglé, *La Domaine coloniale de la France;* A. G. Keller, *Colonization;* H. C. Morris, *A History of Colonization;* S. P. Orth, *The Imperial Impulse;* P. S. Reinsch, *World Politics; Colonial Government;* D. S. Jordan, *Imperial Democracy;* S. Nearing, *The American Empire;* L. Verlane, *La Méthode de colonisation;* H. Robinson, *The Development of the British Empire;* L. Vignon, *Un Programme de politique coloniale;* E. Lémonon, *La Politique coloniale de l'Italie;* A. Zimmermann, *Geschichte der deutschen Kolonialpolitik;* A. Krausse, *Russia in Asia;* I. Bowman, *The New World.*

[6] C. J. H. Hayes, *Political and Social History of Modern Europe,* Vol. II, Part V; H. A. Gibbons, *Introduction to World Politics;* R. L. Buell, *International Relations;* G. L. Dickinson, *The Causes of International War;* L. Woolf, *Empire and Commerce in Africa;* W. Lippmann, *The Stakes of Diplomacy.*

7 E. M. East, *Mankind at the Crossroads.*

8 M. Sanger, *The Pivot of Civilization.*

9 Carveth Read, *Natural and Social Morals; The Origin of Man and of His Superstitions;* P. Bovet, *The Fighting Instinct;* L. Gumplowicz, *Der Rassenkampf.*

10 E.g., Bovet, op. cit.

11 As by Tolstoi and others.

12 G. Wallas, *Our Social Heritage;* P. Kropotkin, *Mutual Aid: a Factor of Evolution;* G. Nicolai, *The Biology of War.*

13 E. Bevan, *German Social Democracy during the War;* G. Demartial, *La Guerre de 1914. Comment on mobilisa les consciences;* C. E. Playne, *The Neuroses of the Nations.*

14 See the positive statement in the writings of Gumplowicz; and the critical expositions in J. Novicow, *La Critique de darwinisme social;* and Nasmyth, G. W., *Social Progress and Darwinian Theory.*

15 See H. E. Barnes, *Sociology and Political Theory,* pp. 52–55. Gumplowicz's *Der Rassenkampf* is the most important work of this sort.

16 Novicow and Nicolai as cited; and D. S. Jordan, *War and the Breed; War and Manhood.*

17 Cf. Novicow, *Les Luttes entre sociétés humaines.*

18 W. Irwin, *The Next War;* J. B. S. Haldane, *Callinicus, a Defence of Chemical Warfare;* B. H. L. Hart, *Paris, or the Future of War;* J. F. C. Fuller, *The Reformation of War;* J. Bloch, *The Future of War.*

19 Works cited; and D. S. Jordan, *The Human Harvest.*

20 D. S. Jordan, *War's Aftermath;* S. Dumas and K. O. Vandel-Petersen, *Losses of Life Caused by War.*

21 J. Novicow, *La Critique du darwinisme social;* G. Wallas, *Our Social Heritage.*

22 F. N. Maude, *War and the World's Life;* H. Maxim, *Defenceless America;* A. T. Mahan, "The Place of Force in International Relations," in *North American Review,* January, 1912; H. Lea, *The Valour of Ignorance;* R. M. Johnston, *Arms and the Race;* J. A. Cramb, *Germany and England;* F. von Bernhardi, *Germany and the Next War;* and the various writings of Paul Déroulède and Léon Daudet.

23 J. A. Cramb, *The Origins and Destiny of Imperial Britain;* H. Lea, *The Day of the Saxon;* S. Grumbach, *Germany's Annexationist Aims;* T. Roosevelt, *The Winning of the West.*

24 W. G. Sumner, *War and Other Essays;* E. D. Morel, *Military Preparation for the Great War.*

25 G. Wallas, *Our Social Heritage;* J. K. Turner, *Shall It Be Again?;* Z. Chafee, *Freedom of Speech;* L. Post, *The Deportations Delirium;* N. Thomas, *The Conscientious Objector;* E. P. Oppenheim, *Profiteers.*

[26] E. Barker, *Political Thought in England from Spencer to the Present Day*, Chaps. i–iii; J. Royce, *The Philosophy of Loyalty; The Hope of the Great Community*.

[27] Graham Wallas, *Our Social Heritage;* B. Russell, *Why Men Fight;* C. Read, op. cit.; L. Perla, *What is National Honor?;* A. E. Stevenson, *Revolutionary Radicalism in America;* S. Howard, "Our Professional Patriots," in *New Republic,* 1924. For an inevitably unsuccessful, but suggestive, attempt to combine these two conceptions of patriotism, see F. H. Giddings, *The Responsible State.*

[28] F. S. Chapin, *An Historical Introduction to Social Economy*, Chap. xvi; C. H. Cooley, *Social Organization*, Part II. The best brief histories of nationalism are J. H. Rose, *Nationality in Modern History;* R. Muir, *Nationalism and Internationalism;* S. Herbert, *Nationality and Its Problems;* and C. J. H. Hayes, *Nationalism.*

[29] The best work on the relation of patriotism to war is C. E. Playne, *The Neuroses of the Nations*, Vol. I, on Germany and France; Vol. II, on England. See also G. E. Partridge, *The Psychology of Nations;* and W. B. Pillsbury, *The Psychology of Nationalism and Internationalism.* The best criticism of patriotism in relation to war is J. H. Holmes, *Patriotism Is Not Enough.* See also L. Le Fur, *Races, nationalités, états.*

[30] C. Altschul, *The American Revolution in Our School Textbooks;* J. B. Scott, *Patriots in the Making;* H. E. Barnes, *History and Social Intelligence*, Parts I–II; *The New History and the Social Studies*, Chap. i; J. Langdon-Davies, *Militarism in Education.*

[31] Scott, op. cit.; W. Lippmann, *Liberty and the News;* L. M. Salmon, *The Newspaper and Authority; The Newspaper and the Historian.*

[32] B. L. Pierce, *The Control of History Teaching; Public Opinion and the Teaching of History;* Barnes, *History and Social Intelligence*, Chap. i.

[33] This thesis is defended by Gumplowicz and his followers, and attacked by Novicow.

[34] G. Ratzenhofer, *Wesen und Zweck der Politik;* A. W. Small, *General Sociology;* A. F. Bentley, *The Process of Government.*

[35] Cf. Monroe Smith, "The Nature and Future of International Law," in *American Political Science Review*, February, 1918.

[36] Cf. Novicow, *Les Luttes entre sociétés humaines.*

[37] For a presentation of the case for population pressure as a cause of war see C. Gini, *Problemi sociologici della guerra.*

[38] The best brief survey is J. Bakeless, *Economic Causes of Modern Wars.* For an extreme but striking statement of the case for economic determinism in regard to war see A. Loria, *Aspetti sociali ed economici della guerra mondiale.*

[39] L. Woolf, *Economic Imperialism;* J. A. Hobson, *Imperialism;* the best guide to a study of imperialism is P. T. Moon, *Syllabus of International Relations.*

[40] A. Viallate, *Economic Imperialism and International Relations;* P. T. Moon, *Imperialism and World Politics;* E. Fueter, *World History, 1815–1920;* W. S. Culbertson, *Raw Materials and Food Stuffs in the Foreign Policies of Nations.*

[41] H. A. Gibbons, *Introduction to World Politics;* Moon, op. cit.; R. L Buell, *International Relations;* J. S. Ewart, *The Roots and Causes of the Wars, 1914–1918.*

[42] J. A. Hobson, *Imperialism;* L. Woolf, *Economic Imperialism;* S. Nearing and J. Freeman, *Dollar Diplomacy;* P. l'E. de la Tramerye, *The World Struggle for Oil;* E. H. Davenport, and S. R. Cooke, *The Oil Trusts and Anglo-American Relations;* H. Withers, *International Finance;* R. Luxemburg, *Die Akkumulation des Kapitals.*

[43] P. M. Brown, *Foreigners in Turkey;* C. S. Labingier, *Extraterritorial Cases;* Shih Shun Liu, *Extra-territoriality, Its Rise and Decline.*

[44] M. J. Bau, *The Open Door Doctrine in Relation to China;* M. T. Z. Tyau, *Treaty Obligations between China and Other States.*

[45] P. H. Clements, *The Boxer Rebellion;* T. F. Millard, *The Conflict of Policies in Asia;* T. W. Overlach, *Foreign Financial Control in China.*

[46] Cf. S. Nearing, *The American Empire;* Nearing and Freeman, *Dollar Diplomacy;* Hobson, *Imperialism;* Woolf, *Economic Imperialism; Empire and Commerce in Africa.*

[47] References as in footnotes 42 and 46 above; and C. L. Jones, *The Caribbean Interests of the United States;* R. W. Dunn, *American Foreign Investments;* and E. Kimpen, *Die Ausbreitungspolitik der Vereinigten Staaten.*

[48] E.g. our intervention in Santo Domingo, Nicaragua and Cuba, and our recent recognition policy in regard to Mexico.

[49] P. Ashley, *Modern Tariff History;* G. M. Fisk and P. S. Pierce, *International Commercial Policies.*

[50] Gide and Rist, *History of Economic Doctrines,* pp. 264–88.

[51] R. R. Bowker, *Economic Peace.*

[52] The existence of such propaganda on the part of the great munitions plants in Europe before the World War has been well established, and it is alleged to be true of this country as well. N. Angell, *Arms and Industry;* H. N. Brailsford, *The War of Steel and Gold.*

[53] For literature on this subject see the bibliography in Krehbiel, op. cit., pp. 55–56.

[54] J. K. Turner, *Shall It Be Again?*

[55] J. L. Garvin, *Economic Foundations of Peace;* J. W. Hughan,

A Study of International Government; Friedman, *International Finance;* L. Woolf, *International Government;* W. S. Culbertson, *International Economic Policies.*

56 N. Angell, *The Great Illusion; The Fruits of Victory.*

57 E.g. F. Vanderlip, *What Next in Europe?;* D. W. Morrow, *The Society of Free States;* H. Croly, *Willard Straight.*

58 Muir, *Nationalism and Internationalism;* C. J. H. Hayes, *Political and Social History of Modern Europe,* Vol. I; P. Smith, *The Age of the Reformation.*

59 J. H. Rose, *Nationality in Modern History;* F. Schevill, *History of the Balkan Peninsula;* A. Toynbee, *Nationality and the War.*

60 A. E. Zimmern, *Nationality and Government;* I. Zangwill, *What is Nationality?;* P. S. Mowrer, *Balkanized Europe.*

61 S. P. Duggan, Ed., *The League of Nations;* R. Muir, *Nationalism and Internationalism,* S. Herbert, *Nationality and Its Problems;* I. Fisher, *League or War.*

62 C. E. Merriam, *A History of the Theory of Sovereignty since Rousseau.*

63 Cf. C. E. Merriam and H. E. Barnes, Eds., *A History of Political Theories: Recent Times,* Chaps. iii–iv.

64 Cf. H. J. Laski, *Studies in the Problem of Sovereignty; A Grammar of Politics.*

65 Laski, *Grammar of Politics,* Chap. xi; J. B. Scott, *Sovereign States and Suits before Arbitral Tribunals and Courts of Justice.*

66 A view for which I am indebted to Professor J. T. Shotwell. Cf. also Perla, *What is National Honor?*

67 G. L. Dickinson, *War, Its Causes and Cure;* K. Page, *War: Its Causes, Consequences and Cure;* P. M. Brown, *International Society;* P. Kerr and L. Curtis, *The Prevention of War.*

CHAPTER II

THE GENERAL HISTORICAL BACKGROUND OF 1914

I. THE NEW DOCUMENTARY EVIDENCE

ARTICLE 231 of the Treaty of Versailles, signed on June 28, 1919, reads as follows:

The Allied and Associated Governments affirm, and Germany accepts, the responsibility of herself and her allies, for causing all the loss and damage to which the Allied and Associated Governments and their nationals have been subjected as a consequence of the war imposed upon them by the aggression of Germany and her allies.

On the basis of this assertion the Entente Powers specifically and concretely erected their claim to reparations from Germany, and by implication the general nature of the entire treaty. Some have supposed that Germany, by apparently acquiescing in this charge of full and complete guilt in regard to the outbreak of the war, finally and for all time clinched the argument of the Allied Powers in regard to her sole responsibility. Such a position could hardly be held, however, by any one familiar with the

34

methods of the Allies during the Peace Conference. Germany occupied the situation of a
prisoner at the bar, where the prosecuting at-
torney was given full leeway as to time and presentation of evidence, while the defendant was
denied counsel or the opportunity to produce
either evidence or witnesses. Germany was confronted with the alternative of signing the confession at once or having her territory invaded
and occupied, with every probability that such
an admission would be ultimately extorted from
her in any event. In the light of these obvious
facts it is plain that the question of the responsibility for the outbreak of the World War must
rest for its solution upon the indisputable documentary evidence which is available in the premises.[1] To quote Elbridge Colby: "Treaties
signed at the point of a gun do not necessarily
tell the truth or do justice."

Under the circumstances which ordinarily
follow a war, we should still be as ignorant of
the real causes of the World War as we were in
1914. It has been a general rule that the
archives, or repositories of the public documents
of the States involved, have been closed to non-
official readers until from forty to eighty years
after the events and negotiations which these
documents describe. Hence we should normally
have been required to wait until about 1975 for
as great a volume of documentary evidence as

we now possess, and two generations of students would have passed away without progressing beyond dubious guesses and intuitive approximations to the truth.   The explanation of our good fortune in this regard is to be found in the revolutionary overturns in Germany, Austria and Russia before the close of the World War.   The new governments were socialistic in character and hypothetically opposed to war and militarism, despite the fact that the Socialists had for the most part remained loyal to their capitalistic or landlord governments in the World War. Desiring to make their tenure more secure by discrediting the acts and policies of the preceding régimes, the new governments believed that they might help to advance this end by throwing open the national archives in the hope that historical editors might discover therein evidence of responsibility on the part of the former governing groups for the inundation of blood, misery and sorrow which swept over Europe after 1914.[2]   In addition to these voluntarily opened archives, the Germans seized the Belgian archives during the War and published collections of extracts.   Then B. de Siebert, Secretary to the Russian Embassy at London in the period before the War, had secretly made copies of the important diplomatic exchanges between London and St. Petersburg from 1908 to 1914, and later gave or sold many of them to the Germans.

The nature of the European diplomatic and military alignments in 1914 accounts for the fact that these revelations are reasonably adequate to settle the problems concerning the declarations of war in 1914, despite the further fact that France, Italy and Serbia refused to make their archives accessible to scholars. Inasmuch as Italy was technically allied with Germany and Austria in the Triple Alliance, the nature of much of her foreign policy and many of her diplomatic engagements may be gleaned from the German and Austrian archives. But she was at the same time secretly negotiating with France, and, after 1914, with the members of the Triple Entente. This material is, in part, available in the documents in the Russian archives and in those which have been published from the French archives. England and France having been the other members of the Triple Entente, the secret diplomacy of this group is reasonably covered in the Russian archives and the Siebert documents, the latter of which are now duplicated in part in the publications from the Russian archives, though it would be desirable to know of any possible secret Franco-British exchanges not revealed to Russia. The French have, of course, published some of their documents in the various *Livres Jaunes*— the most important of which is that on the Balkan policy (1922), but they are officially edited and many incriminating documents are, naturally, suppressed. England is now allowing Gooch and Temperley to edit eleven volumes of pre-war material in the English archives. The volume on the crisis of 1914 has just appeared.

Although a vast number of documents in the archives of Germany, Austria and Russia have not yet been published, the collections thus far available are impressive. Many diplomatic documents covering the broad historical background of the Austrian crisis of 1914 are presented in the admirable collection of Professor A. F. Pribram.[3] The documents in the Austrian archives dealing with the month preceding the outbreak of the World War have been edited by the publicist and scholarly journalist, Roderich Goos, in the three volumes of the Austrian *Red Book*.[4] In Germany an even more voluminous collection on the diplomacy of Germany and related countries from 1871 to 1914 has been published under the editorship of J. Lepsius, A. Mendelssohn-Bartholdy and F. Thimme. This embraces all the important diplomatic documents in the German Foreign Office; some fifty bulky volumes have already appeared. It is the most extensive publication of this sort yet undertaken in any country.[5] The documents dealing with the antecedents of August, 1914, were extracted from the German archives by the German Socialist,

Karl Kautsky, and published in four volumes under the editorship of the eminent scholars, W. Schücking, M. Montgelas and A. Mendelssohn-Bartholdy.[6] A supplementary collection has been more recently published which embodies: (1) The testimony of leading Germans in military, diplomatic and business life before a committee appointed by the German post-war government to investigate the responsibility for the War; (2) the records of the reaction of Germany to Mr. Wilson's peace note of December, 1916; and (3) the negotiations between Germany and her allies, and Germany and the United States concerning submarine warfare and the policies which produced the entry of the United States into the World War.[7]

No Russian documents have been made available as yet which cover so ample an historical background as the work of Pribram and the published volumes of the *Grosse Politik*. The Siebert documents [8] deal only with the period from 1908–1914. The *Livre Noir* (Black Book) is another important publication of the Russian documents. It was collected by René Marchand, a scholarly French publicist and journalist thoroughly familiar with the Russian language and with Russian public life and politics. It presents many of the Russian diplomatic documents of the years 1910–1914, particularly stressing the correspondence of Izvolski. A much more thorough collection of the Russian documents has been edited by Dr. Friedrich Stieve in five large volumes. These are the most important published collections of Russian source material.[9] The diary of Baron M. F. Schilling, Chief of the Chancellery in the Russian Foreign Office in 1914, is invaluable for many details.

This newly accessible archival material has enabled scholars to check up on the collections of apologetic or extenuating documents published by the great powers in the early days of the War. A step in this direction has been taken by G. von Romberg, who has brought out a publication of the actual exchanges between Paris and St. Petersburg following the submission of the Austrian ultimatum to Serbia on July 23, 1914. This lays bare the serious and important suppressions in the original Russian *Orange Book,* which eliminated all the damaging evidence regarding conciliatory German proposals or aggressive Franco-Russian aims and policies.[10] Also from the Russian archives has come the recently published collection revealing Italy's dickering with the Entente for territorial cessions from 1914 to the time of her entry into the World War in May, 1915.[11] The Belgian documents published by Germany embrace chiefly the dispatches and opinions of the Belgian ambassadors in the major European capitals following 1886, playing up especially those which express fear of

Entente collusion and aggression. Highly selected and one-sided, the collection is yet of real
value as proving that the Belgians were alarmed
at the policies of the states other than Germany
and incidentally vindicating beyond any doubt
the neutrality of official Belgian opinion as a
whole before 1914.[12]   Finally, we have the depressing Secret Treaties of the Entente, which
eliminate once and for all any basis for the hypothesis of idealism underlying the military activities of either side in the World War, and convict
the Allies of aggressive aims as thoroughly as
Grumbach's *Das Annexionistische Deutschland*
proves Germany and Austria guilty of similar
ambitions.[13]

These collections of documents have been supplemented by a vast number of apologetic and
controversial memoirs, reminiscences and auto-
biographies which possess highly varied value
and relevance, and by infinitely more important
scholarly monographs analyzing in detail one or
another of the many diplomatic and political
problems and situations lying back of the World
War.[14]

It is upon such material as this that we are
able to construct a relatively objective and definitive estimate of the causes of and responsibility for the great calamity of 1914–18 and its
aftermath.   It is quite evident that if any account written prior to 1919 possesses any validity

whatever or any approximation to the true picture of events, this is due solely to superior guessing power or good luck on the part of the writer, and in no sense to the possession of reliable or pertinent documentary evidence.

In his recent defense in *Foreign Affairs* for October, 1925, Poincaré has made the absurd insinuation that this new material bearing on war guilt is German and Bolshevik propaganda. An examination of the facts will put this preposterous charge forever at rest. The German documents were made public by the Socialistic government which hoped thereby to discredit the Kaiser and the imperial régime. If the documents had been garbled they would have been altered in the direction of attempting to emphasize German guilt. As an actual matter of fact, they were carefully edited under the direction and scrutiny of both liberal and conservative scholars. No informed person can question their authenticity. The same holds true of the Austrian documents. Of the Russian documents the exchanges between London and St. Petersburg were edited by Siebert, a Russian landlord and an enemy of the Bolsheviks, years before the Bolsheviks came into power. Those between Paris and St. Petersburg were edited in the first instance by two French scholars, Laloy and Marchand. An even more complete edition was later prepared by D. F. Stieve, a German scholar. There is no discrepancy of significance between these editions, and the Bolsheviks have in no sense interfered with the editing. Further, if Poincaré knew that these documents were false, he had an admirable opportunity to clear himself by ordering a full publication of the French documents, as he was premier of France after the appearance of the *Livre Noir* which contains the damaging evidence against him. He made no such move. It is even more significant that while Poincaré makes a general and blanket charge that these new documents are untrustworthy he has seen fit to deny the truth of only one important incriminating document or statement of Izvolski. The whole question of the authenticity of the collections of Russian documents made by Marchand and Stieve has recently been settled by Sazonov. In his foreword to Baron Schilling's diary, *How the War Began,* he admits their complete authenticity.

II. GERMANY AND EUROPE, 1870–1914

Without undertaking to make a detailed summary of the diplomatic history of Europe from 1870 to 1914, we can at least present in its major outlines the picture of the European system which made possible the great calamity of 1914. Such an attempt is not only important in preparing the ground for an understanding of the im-

mediate causes of the World War, but also as
a refutation of a most significant phase of the
Entente propaganda—a phase which has developed chiefly since 1919.   During the War the
conventional propaganda in the Allied countries
tended to rest content for its proof of full and
complete German responsibility upon the alleged
Potsdam Conference of July 5, 1914, where the
Kaiser and his war-lords were supposed to have
revealed their determination to precipitate the
European struggle, urging Austria on in her
policy of threatening Serbia for the primary purpose of bringing Russia into the struggle and
thus setting off a general European conflagration.[15]

The further documentary evidence which has
recently come out with respect to the immediate
causes of the War has decisively demonstrated
that the German civil government not only did
not will war in 1914 but was distinctly opposed
to its outbreak.   It has been impossible for any
honest and unbiased student of the documents
to deny these facts.   Hence, some who are unwilling to adjust their conceptions fully and
freely to the new facts, have turned from the
immediate diplomatic events of June–August,
1914, to the general European setting from 1870–
1914 as proof of the primary German responsibility for the World War.   They admit that the
evidence shows that Germany was specifically

opposed to the War in the summer of 1914, and that the aggression came from the side of France and Russia. Yet they contend that if Germany did not will the War in 1914, she was persistently the most active and menacing bully in the general European situation from 1870 onward, and really forced France and Russia into their aggressive acts of 1912–1914 as a matter of self-protection.[16] We shall here examine the actual facts in the situation with the aim of discovering how much truth there is in this common allegation of contemporary Entente propagandists that if Germany did not specifically bring on the World War, nevertheless she created that system of militarism and bullying which made the war inevitable.

III. ECONOMIC RIVALRY: ENGLAND AND GERMANY

The general underlying causes of the European military menace may be summarized under four main headings: economic and commercial rivalry, nationalism and patriotism, military and naval preparations, and the two great systems of counter-alliances. In regard to the first of these, the greatest guilt, if it may be thus called, falls unquestionably upon Great Britain and Germany. From the close of the War of 1812

onward Great Britain had been far and away
the most powerful industrial and commercial
country in the world. During the late '70's and
'80's Germany experienced the Industrial Revolution which brought to her the mechanical
technique and the factory system. A stu-
pendous industrial and commercial transformation ensued which, in rapidity and extent, has
only been rivalled by the development of American industry since the Civil War and the parallel
transformation of Japanese industry. Particularly in the textile industry, the iron and steel
industry and the new chemical industry did
Germany rapidly forge ahead, to become a notable contender with Great Britain for the industrial primacy of Europe. Likewise Germany
developed rapidly a great merchant marine which
struggled with England for the carrying trade
of the oceans, and she sought territory overseas
for colonial empire and areas of investment to
afford markets for her surplus products and outlet for her capital accumulations. And, in the
same way that Great Britain had developed a
great navy to protect her colonies and merchant
marine, so toward the close of the nineteenth
century Germany also began to lay plans for
a real navy.[17]

Many, including the present writer, have referred to the German naval plans as "foolish" or
worse. Doubtless this is true in an absolute

sense, as all forms of military and naval preparedness must be viewed as fundamentally
idiotic. Yet the German naval plans were only
a natural and normal outgrowth of the general
spirit of the times and of the particular circumstances of German development following 1890.
No modern state has yet developed a colonial
empire, extensive world trade and a great merchant marine without feeling that it is desirable
to secure protection through the provision of
an adequate navy. The German naval expansion was unquestionably a psychological, diplomatic and pecuniary liability, but the same may
be said of all navies. The German naval plans
formulated by Von Tirpitz were insane only in
the sense that the whole preparedness race was
imbecilic. Further, as will be apparent from the
statistics of armaments given below, the German
navy was never any real challenge to the naval
supremacy of Great Britain alone, to say nothing
of the combined navies of Great Britain, France,
Russia and Japan. Finally, the German naval
policy cannot be regarded as a direct cause of the
war as Germany and England had reached a
satisfactory, if informal, understanding before
1914 on the 16:10 basis.

These developments in commerce and naval
plans greatly alarmed Great Britain and led her
to look upon Germany rather than France as
the chief menace to her interests and safety in

the west. Up to this time she had regarded France as the chief danger in this area, but shortly after the beginning of the present century France was supplanted by Germany as the chief object of British concern in the traditional British policy to maintain England free from danger from any power on the coasts of the North Sea.[18]

Added to this British jealousy of German industrial and commercial progress and her fear of the German menace to her safety on the North Sea, due to the development of German naval plans, was the growing influence of Germany in the Near East which was involved in the German plans for the railroad from Berlin to Bagdad, with the resulting desire to exploit the great resources of Mesopotamia. During the nineteenth century Great Britain had looked upon Russia as the great menace to her interests in the Near East, but with the launching of the German plans for the railroad from Hamburg to the Persian Gulf England became more and more fearful about the possible results of German advances in Turkey and Mesopotamia.[19] Dr. John S. Ewart, a most distinguished Canadian jurist, whose recent book *The Roots and Causes of the Wars, 1914–1918* is the most thorough book in English on the subject, presents the following admirable summary of these causes of Anglo-German rivalry: [20]

1. Germany's rivalry in manufactures, in commerce, in finance, in mercantile shipping, and in war-navy, added to her predominance in military power, aroused British apprehension, and created British antagonism. That was one root of the war between the United Kingdom and Germany.

2. British policy in western Europe had for many years pivoted upon the determination to maintain freedom from menace on the North Sea coasts. While France was the danger in this regard, France was the potential enemy. As Germany waxed, and France relatively waned, British apprehension became fixed on the power to the east of Belgium and Holland, instead of, as formerly, on the power to the west. That was another root of the war between the United Kingdom and Germany.

3. British traditional policy in eastern Europe and the Near East had been the protection of Constantinople and India against the advances of Russia. The advent of Germany as a competitor for domination at Constantinople, and for political as well as economic expansion in Asia Minor, Persia and Mesopotamia, diverted British apprehension from Russia to Germany. That was another root of the war between the United Kingdom and Germany.

It is also undoubtedly true that the American willingness to enter the World War was considerably enhanced by the American jealousy of German commercial and industrial expansion, but this certainly played no part whatever in precipitating the World War, and may thus be dismissed without any further mention as a cause of the War.[21] Many historians believe that there was no inconsiderable economic basis for the rivalry between Germany and Russia particularly due to the German economic conquest of Russia, which was so complete that by 1913 fifty per cent of Russia's imports came from Germany and thirty-five per cent of her exports went into Germany. Along with this German industrial penetration went a tariff war which was based upon the discriminatory and differential tariff system common to the European states before the World War.[22]

But unquestionably the chief economic and commercial cause of the War lay in the rivalries which developed between the industry, commerce, imperialistic policies and naval armaments of Great Britain and Germany. It is probably inaccurate to apply the term "guilt" in any sense to either Great Britain or Germany in this connection. It was but natural that each country should do all it could to further its industrial and commercial development and, granting the existence of the prevailing economic and commercial policies of the time, it was equally inevitable that there should be a clash between these two powers. Certainly there was nothing in the situation which would justify one in holding Germany primarily responsible for this Anglo-German economic antagonism.

IV. NATIONALISM AND PATRIOTISM

With respect to the spirit of nationalism and arrogant patriotism, none of the Great Powers can here show a clean bill of health. All were afflicted with this chief psychological cause of hatred and suspicion. Probably the most virulent expression of this patriotism was to be found in France under the leadership of Déroulède, Barrès and other apostles of revenge and Gallicanism. But certainly the difference between France and other major European states was chiefly one of degree rather than of kind. The Germans were exuberant over their successes in 1870 and the subsequent marvelous development of the united German Empire. The Russians were busy with Pan-Slavic programs designed to make Russia the most powerful state in the eastern hemisphere and the natural leader of all the Slavic peoples in Europe. A most vigorous patriotism flourished in the naval clique in Great Britain, and no more obsessed organ was published anywhere in Europe than the bellicose and chauvinistic *National Review* edited in London by Mr. L. J. Maxse. Likewise, the enthusiasm of the Italian patriots, led by men like D'Annunzio, knew no bounds either in ambition or literary expression.[23]

During the War the Entente propaganda represented Germany as almost unique and alone in

this patriotic literature and lust for world-domin-
ion, basing their assertions chiefly upon the publications of the Pan-German League and the
books of writers like Nietzsche and Bernhardi.[24]
Dr. Mildred S. Wertheimer, in a recent thorough
and painstaking study [25] of the Pan-German
League, executed under the direction of Professor C. J. H. Hayes of Columbia University, has
shown that the Pan-German League was but a
small organization of fanatical patriots, comparable to our own National Security League
and American Defense Society, and having less
influence over the German government than our
American societies had over the foreign policy
of Woodrow Wilson from 1913–1916. Even in
official circles the Pan-German League was
laughed at as a noisy nuisance. Nietzsche fiercely
hated the Prussian military bureaucracy and
could in no sense be regarded as their spokesman,
while Bernhardi was simply the German ex-
positor of the military cult common to certain
classes and groups throughout Europe in the
half century before the War. His *Germany
and the Next War* had not been read by anybody
in the German Foreign Office in 1914. It can be
matched readily by comparable and synchronous
publications in England, France and Russia.
Fully as uncompromising adulations of the military cult are to be found in the writings of

Maude, Cramb, Lea, Wyatt, Maxim, Mahan, Déroulède, Daudet and Barrès.[26] The sane view of this matter is one which makes no attempt at either a special condemnation or whitewashing of Germany. She was, in general, as bad as the other countries with respect to patriotic propaganda and national pride, but certainly no worse.

Least of all can it be contended that it was Germany which gave birth to the ardent patriotic sentiments of the European states in the nineteenth century. In large part they were the product of general historical and cultural conditions, but in so far as they came from any particular country the responsibility must be assigned to the military tradition of the French Bourbons, and, above all, to the traditions of military glory and patriotic pride developed in France during the period of the Revolution and of Napoleon Bonaparte and revived with vigor by Napoleon III in the era of the second French Empire. German patriotism itself had its birth as a reaction against the indignities perpetrated upon the Prussians by Napoleon during the French occupation following 1806.[27] Ewart presents the following statesmanlike conclusions with respect to this whole problem of the alleged unique German responsibility for obsessed patriotism and national arrogance: [28]

From what has been said, the following conclusions may safely be drawn:

1. That Germany sought to dominate the world is a very ridiculous assertion.

2. That Nietzsche, Treitschke, or Bernhardi advocated world-domination is untrue.

3. That Germany desired to be able to exercise the chief influence in world affairs is as true as that the United Kingdom has occupied that position for the last hundred years.

4. Germany's desire for a strong navy was based upon the same reasons as those which actuated the United Kingdom, namely, (1) protection of coasts, (2) protection of commerce, (3) protection of colonies, and (4) diplomatic influence.

5. Of imperialism, all virile nations have been guilty. The victors in the recent war, and their friends, made the most of their opportunities. Previous to her defeat, Germany was no exception to the general rule.

6. The prose and poetry of all nations boastfully assert superiorities, and reveal imperialistic proclivities. German authors were and are as foolish as the others.

V. ARMAMENTS AND PREPAREDNESS

In no other respect has there been more general unanimity of opinion in our country than in the assumption that the military preparedness of Germany was far superior to that of any other European country with respect to both the number and quality of troops and the equipment of cavalry, infantry and artillery. Germany has been pictured as the one country overrun with soldiers armed to the teeth and trained to the minute, while the other European states have been represented as but conducting feeble and imperfect defensive programs in lame and fearful imitation of Germany.[29]   Direct recourse to the facts quickly dispels this persistent and misleading illusion.   The following table presents the effective peace strength of the various major world powers in 1899, 1907 and 1914: [30]

	1899	1907	1914
Germany	604,000	629,000	806,000
Austria	346,000	382,000	370,000
Italy	258,000	284,000	305,000
France	574,000	559,000	818,000
Russia	896,000	1,254,000	1,284,000

Professor Moon makes practically the same estimate, with the addition of the population of the states involved:

	1895	1910	1914	Population 1914
Germany	585,000	634,000	812,000	68,000,000
Austria-Hungary	349,000	327,000	424,000	52,000,000
Italy	238,000	288,000	318,000	36,000,000
Russia	910,000	1,200,000	1,300,000	174,000,000
France	572,000	634,000	846,000	40,000,000
Great Britain	369,000	255,000	250,000	46,000,000
Japan		230,000	250,000	54,000,000
United States		81,000	105,000	99,000,000

General Buat, a leading French military expert, contends that the active French army in 1914 numbered 910,000 with 1,325,000 reservists, while the active German army he holds to have been at this time 870,000 with 1,180,000 reservists.[31] The distinguished French historian, Charles Seignobos, has recently pointed out in Lavisse's *Histoire de France contemporaine* how, in instituting the new three-year service act in 1913–14, the French military authorities, in addition to calling up two new classes, also retained the one which would have ordinarily been released. Thus, in the summer of 1914, France had the unique and wholly temporary advantage of having four classes with the colors.

In the decade from 1905–1914 the expenditures for arms on the part of the four major powers were the following: [32]

Russia	£495,144,622
France	£347,348,259
Germany	£448,025,543
Austria	£234,668,407

In equipment, likewise, Russia and France were overwhelmingly superior to Germany and Austria-Hungary with the sole exception of heavy batteries. Some readers, while accepting the inevitable proof of these concrete statistics that quantitatively speaking the Austro-German forces were immensely inferior to the land forces of Russia and France combined, may quite likely assert that at least the German army was much more thoroughly drilled and much more competent in its manœuvres than the armies of the Entente. To dispel this mistaken notion we may cite the opinion of Colonel Repington, a distinguished British military expert, who closely observed German manœuvres in 1911: [33]

The writer has not formed a wholly favorable opinion of the German army, which appears to him to be living on a glorious past and to be unequal to the repute in which it is commonly held. There was nothing in the higher leading at the manœuvres of a distinguished character, and mistakes were committed which tended to shake the confidence of foreign spectators in the reputation of the command. The infantry lacked dash, displayed no knowledge of the use of ground, entrenched themselves badly, were extremely slow in their movements, offered vulnerable targets at medium range, ignored the service of security, performed the approach marches in an old-time manner, were not trained to understand the connection between fire and movement, and seemed totally unaware of the effect of modern fire. The cavalry was in many ways exceedingly old-fashioned. The artillery, with its out-of-date material and slow and ineffective methods of fire, appeared so inferior that it can have no pretension to measure itself against the French in anything approaching level terms, and finally, the dirigibles and aeroplanes presented the fourth arm in a relatively unfavorable light. A nation which after all gives up little more than half its able-bodied sons to the army has become less militarist than formerly.

Some might contend that though this was true in 1911, it was not an accurate description of the state of affairs in 1914. As an actual matter of fact, however, it is well known that the French and Russians made much more progress in military preparations between 1911 and 1914 than did the Germans.

It will be noted that in the above estimates we have left out entirely the large potential army which England was able to raise when war actually came. This should be added to the already overwhelming odds possessed by Russia and France as against Germany and Austria in a land war. In comparing the military preparations of Germany and France it must be remembered that the German population was nearly double that of France in 1914, so the fact that the French army was slightly larger than the German at this time indicates far heavier preparedness per capita in France than in Germany.

When we turn to naval expenditures we find that here in the ten years before the War the joint expenditures of France and Russia were much greater than those of Germany and Austria, in spite of the fact that we are commonly led to believe that, aside from England, Germany was the only European country which contemplated extensive naval preparations. Here, in particular, we have to add to the Franco-Russian appropriations for navies the enormous and unparalleled British expenditures during the same period which amounted to more than those of France and Russia combined. The following tables indicate the comparative naval expenditures from 1904 to 1914: [34]

```
France .......................£161,721,387
Russia .......................£144,246,513
                             ──────────────
                              £305,967,900
Germany .........£185,205,164
Austria-Hungary ...£ 50,692,814  £235,897,978
                             ──────────────
Excess of France and Russia for 10
    years .......................£ 70,069,922
                             ──────────────
During the same period the British
    naval expenditure was..........£351,916,576
```

Many critics will cite the remarkable German successes in the World War as proof that Germany was more adequately prepared than any other European state, and that Repington was notoriously wrong in his estimate of the German army. No one realizes better than the writer the fact that the mere counting of noses or the footing up of expenditures does not constitute a final and complete statement of the military fitness or preparations of a modern state. But they do prove that, as far as drafting a nation's man power and draining a nation's pecuniary resources for war preparations are concerned, the Entente efforts were far in excess of those of

Germany and Austria. What the German successes proved was that Germany was more efficient than the other states in this field of endeavor and got more for her money. There was not the same amount of graft that there was in France, and, particularly, Russia. The German successes were also in part due to the unexpected ease with which the Belgian forts yielded to modern heavy artillery, and to the strategic value of von Hindenburg's unique knowledge of the East Prussian area where he dealt the Russians the decisive blow that saved Germany in 1914.

A common argument brought up by those who admit the superiority of preparations for war on the part of the Entente as compared to Germany and Austria is that if the German preparations were inferior to those of her enemies, at least she was responsible for the aggressive system and military tradition in the western world. One could trace primary responsibility for militarism in one period or another back to the ancient Assyrians and earlier. As Fyffe has shown, the modern Prussian military system was developed following 1806 as a defense against Napoleon. It was kept alive from 1815 to 1866 chiefly through the autocratic and reactionary policy of Metternich and his successors who refused to sanction a pacific union of the German states and forced Bismarck into the policy of union through "blood and iron." At the time of the War of 1870 it was the almost universal opinion of historical and military experts that the second French Empire was the chief concrete embodiment of the military tradition and procedure.[35] It was the French insistence upon war in 1870 which enabled Bismarck to carry out his forceful policy in the way of unifying the German Empire through a victorious war against France in 1870–71.[36]

Even if it were to be admitted, though it is obviously untrue, that it was German militarism prior to 1910 which forced France and Russia into their extensive preparations, it might be held with equal validity that it was the militarism of Austria, and the Second Empire in France which produced the Prussian military preparations of 1860–71. The practice of military conscription originated in the French Revolution,[37] but the system of extensive armaments cannot be said to be the invention of any single modern power. Specifically, the greatest incentives to the extensive military preparations on the part of the European powers before the War were the revenge aspirations of France, Germany's fear of being encircled, and the frequently recurring imperialistic crises. Second to these three major motives was the Russian desire for a strong army and navy which would enable her ultimately to control the Near East.[38]

Nothing could be more absurd than to hold that it was Germany which forced the system of universal military service upon Europe. As the French writer, Gustave Dupin, has correctly and courageously stated: [38a]

There are three important facts which we must recall to ourselves unless we are to lay ourselves open to the charge of not having approached the study of the causes and responsibilities of the last war with adequate candor: (1) It is we French who have contributed to Europe the practice of conscription (Law of the 18 Fructidor, Year VI) ; (2) it is we French who have inaugurated the system of universal and obligatory military service, without exemptions or exceptions (Law of 27 July, 1872) ; (3) it is we French who have brought into existence the latest development and, in conjunction with our English allies, have imported tens of thousands of colored troops for service in Europe.

Those who plead for Germany and her justification of a large army are certainly correct in their contention that the German geographical position was unique in that she was surrounded by powerful enemies who could combine overwhelming odds against her on both land and sea. And, as we shall see later, the events of the summer of 1914 proved that she was correct in contending that she was subject to a very real danger of attack by these encircling powers. No one could be more contemptuous of the military system than the present writer, but it is difficult to see how any fair-minded student of the situation can deny that Germany possessed better reasons for desiring a large army for protection than any other major European state—a fact freely admitted by Lloyd George in his famous interview of January 1, 1914.

There was certainly as much justification for German militarism as for English navalism, for the Germans were as much in jeopardy from land attacks as England was from sea power. But the German militarism never approximated the proportions of British navalism. The British desired a navy twice the size of her nearest contender or as large as that of her two nearest rivals. Germany's army was smaller than that of either France or Russia, though by English naval precedents she would have been justified in maintaining an army as large as that of Russia and France combined. The "encirclement" conception was not a myth concocted in Germany, but was recognized by the most reputable of Entente authorities. J. Holland Rose, writing even after the World War had begun, agreed that:

We who live behind the rampart of the sea know but little (save in times of panic) of the fear which besets a state which has no natural frontiers. . . . Germany accomplished a wonderful work in unifying her people; but even so she has not escaped from the disadvantages of her situation; by land she is easily assailable on three sides.

The distinguished French writer, Marcel Sembat, agrees that:

The German has grown up under the overshadowing threat of a formidable avalanche suspended over his head; an avalanche always ready to become detached, to roll down upon him; an avalanche of immense savagery, of barbarous and brutal multitudes threatening to cover his soil, to swallow up his civilisation and his society.

Sir Thomas Barclay, an ardent exponent of the Anglo-French Entente, frankly admitted that:

Wedged in between France and Russia, with England dominating all her issues to the outer world, her frontiers open to all the political winds that blow, Germany has a geographical position which forces her statesmen to listen with an anxious ear to any movements, projects, or combinations of her neighbors.

In the light of these facts and the great armies of France and Russia the German precautions in the way of military preparedness tend to appear, in a quantitative sense, at least, careless and inadequate almost to the point of levity.[39]

Again, some writers have recently maintained that even though France and Russia precipitated the World War, the situation which enabled them to do so was one which was forced upon them by the German military increases provided in the army bill of 1913. The assumption is that Germany initiated this policy of great military increases just before the War, and that the other states unwillingly followed her merely in terror-stricken self-defense. As an actual matter of fact no one country was solely responsible for the great increases in military preparations in 1913–14. They grew out of the general feeling of uneasiness and tension generated by the Balkan wars and near eastern difficulties. Indeed, the French bill providing for the great increases in the French army was framed before the French knew the terms of the German bill and was introduced in the Chamber of Deputies before the comparable German bill was introduced in the Reichstag, though the German bill was actually passed before the French bill. One of the strongest factors in leading the French to the army increases of 1913 was the insistence of Izvolski that the French revive the three-year service practice to forward the war plans of Poincaré and himself.[40]

The salient facts in regard to the French and German army bills of 1913 have been well summarized by Professor Fay in the *New Republic* for January 6, 1926:

We are still too apt to accept the old myths. For instance, an editorial in the New York *Times* of December 14, commenting on Marx's article (in *Foreign Affairs* for January, 1926), indicated that it was Ger-

many's fault—German sabre-rattling—which changed
the situation for the worse in the two years before the
War. It implies that the French army law introduc-
ing the three-year service "passed by the Chamber of
Deputies on July 9, 1913," was in consequence of, and
in reply to, "the fact that in March, 1913, the Bundes-
rat approved a bill adopted in the Reichstag on May 1,
raising the peace effectives of the German Army from
544,000 men to somewhere between 835,000 and 875,000
men." In reality the new French Army Law was announced in the *Temps* of February 17, 1913, discussed
by Izvolski in a despatch of February 27, and laid before the Chamber of Deputies on March 10—eighteen
days before the German law was laid before the Reichstag on March 28. In both countries there were some
newspaper guesses concerning new military laws prior
to these dates, but it is almost certain that neither was
the French military increase caused by the German,
nor vice versa. In both countries the increase of armaments originated with the increasing suspicion and political tension growing out of the Balkan crisis.

VI. THE GREAT ALLIANCES

Unquestionably one of the chief diplomatic
causes of the World War was the existence of the
great counter-alliances that had come into being between 1878 and 1914. Ostensibly planned
in the interests of defense and peace, they
actually produced suspicion, fear and aggression.
A forceful exposition of the part played by these
alliances in producing the political and psycho-

logical background of the War is contained in the following citation from Professor Schmitt: [41]

The causes of the great war have been analyzed from many points of view. The explanation usually offered is the vaulting ambition of this or that great power, Germany being most often selected as the offender. Persons internationally minded insist that rabid nationalism was a universal disease and draw vivid pictures of the European anarchy. The pacifist points to the bloated armaments, and the Socialist can see only the conflict of rival imperialisms. Facts galore can be cited in support of each thesis. Yet no one of these explanations is entirely satisfactory, or the lot of them taken together. Why should the different kinds of dynamite explode simultaneously in August, 1914? Why, for instance, should a war break out between Great Britain and Germany at a moment when their disputes were seemingly on the verge of adjustment? There must have been some connecting link which acted as a chain of powder between the various accumulations of explosive material. And so there was ; as one peruses the innumerable memoirs by politicians, soldiers and sailors, from the German Emperor to obscure diplomatists, or tries to digest the thousands of documents published since 1918 fom the German, Austrian, Serbian, Russian, French, Belgian and British archives, the conviction grows that it was the schism of Europe in Triple Alliance and Triple Entente which fused the various quarrels and forces into one gigantic struggle for the balance of power; and the war came in 1914 because then, for the first time, the lines were sharply drawn between the two rival groups, and neither could yield on the Serbian issue without seeing the balance pass definitely to the other side.

It would be misleading and unfair, however, to regard the Triple Alliance and the Triple Entente as equally vigorous in 1914 and as equally a menace to the peace of Europe. The Triple Alliance of Germany, Austria and Italy had been formed by 1882. It possessed some degree of strength and unity up to 1900, when Italy began negotiations with France that ended in a secret agreement in 1902 which meant for practical purposes the withdrawal of Italy from the Triple Alliance, though after 1910 the Italian Foreign Minister, the Marquis of San Giuliano, made a vain effort to revive Italian ardor. From 1908 onward Austria also became more and more of a liability to Germany by her truculent attitude towards Serbia. Several times the Austrian aggressiveness provoked tension between Berlin and Vienna, and in 1914 it was the Austrian initiative which dragged Germany into disaster by allowing Austria to lead her into the Franco-Russian trap. Hence, during the decade before the War, the Triple Alliance had become an empty shell, inadequate even for defense.

The Triple Entente began with the Franco-Russian Alliance cemented between 1891 and 1894 under the direction of Freycinet. Bismarck had negotiated a re-insurance treaty with

Russia, but the Kaiser allowed it to lapse. This left Russia free to be exploited by France, and Freycinet was quick to seize the opportunity. This loss of Russia was probably the chief diplomatic blunder of the Kaiser's régime. England and France drew together after the Fashoda crisis of 1898, and, by the time of the second Morocco crisis, presented a united front against Germany. This Anglo-French Entente was carefully nursed through by Delcassé. In 1907 England and Russia patched up their long-standing dispute over the Near East by dividing Persia between them, and the Triple Entente had come into being. Though both of these great alliances were avowedly purely defensive, they were, as Professors Dickinson, Gooch and Schmitt have indicated, in reality a menace to the peace of Europe, for when any major crisis presented itself neither organization could well back down without losing some prestige.

Two of the leading "bitter-enders" and "straw-clutchers," Bernadotte Schmitt and Heinrich Kanner, have assumed to discover a dark plot against the peace of Europe in a secret military convention, alleged to have been concluded between von Moltke, the German Chief of Staff, and Conrad von Hötzendorf, the Austrian Chief of Staff, early in 1909. This exchange of letters is held by these writers to have superseded the formal diplomatic alliance and to have been

much more dangerous to European peace than
the Poincaré-Izvolski arrangements of 1912–14.
Professor Fay and Count Montgelas have recently riddled this "Schmitt-Kanner Myth," and
have shown it to have no substantial foundation
in fact.[42]

VII. GERMANY AND THE HAGUE
CONFERENCES

In this connection, one should consider the
matter of the attitude of Germany at the Hague
Conferences. Writers with a strong anti-German bias have contended that it was Germany
and Germany alone which prevented the Hague
Conferences from bringing about universal
European disarmament and compulsory arbitration of all international disputes.[43] In reality,
northing of the sort was the case. Germany certainly did not conduct herself during the Hague
Conferences as an outspoken supporter of either
disarmament or general arbitration, but her conduct in this respect was certainly no worse than
that of either France or England. The Germans at the Hague were simply more honest in
expressing their opinions, and, hence, in a diplomatic sense, just that much more incompetent.

The Russian proposals for disarmament at the
first conference were not made in good faith. As
Count Witte has confessed, the Russian proposal
that the peace strength of the various European
armies should not be increased for five years was

basic to his scheme of a continental alliance of
France, Germany and Russia against England.
He felt that such an alliance would enable the
continental powers to save the money expended
for arms to protect themselves against each other
and they would thus be able to construct a joint
navy capable of contending against that of Great
Britain. The first great extension of Russian
naval preparations actually came in 1898. There
was also a special reason for the Russian proposal in 1899, namely, the fact that Russia did
not possess resources to match the proposed Austrian increase in artillery. Further, the Russian
proposal for army limitation made an exception
of the Russian colonial troops, thus making the
proposal unacceptable to any of the other powers.
Instead of Germany alone opposing the Russian
plan, all the other members voted against the
Russian representative. Great Britain, led by
Sir John Fisher, resolutely refused to accept any
proposal for naval limitations; and, while the
first Hague Conference was still sitting, the
British admiralty requested an additional appro-
priation of approximately twenty-five million
pounds for the completion of new warships. At
the second Hague Conference the matter of disarmament was not seriously discussed, its introduction having been opposed strenuously by
both Germany and France.[44] The humanita-
rian movement in England forced the English

leaders to bring up the matter of disarmament, but it was tabled without a vote.

As to the relation of Germany to the proposals for arbitration at the Hague Conferences, Germany ultimately withdrew her opposition to the proposal of a permanent court of arbitration, though she did oppose making arbitration obligatory. At the second Hague Conference Germany had special reason for being opposed to compulsory arbitration as England had refused to abide by the terms of the Anglo-German arbitration treaty of 1904. As a literal matter of fact the international prize court, which was the main achievement in the matter of arbitration at the second Hague Conference, was really the product of the coöperative endeavor of England and Germany. Further, it must be remembered that the proposals for arbitration in the Hague Conferences were *not* such as involved the compulsory arbitration of the major causes of war. The compulsory clauses were to apply only to legal disputes, and in no sense to political disputes which usually constitute the occasion of war. The most that can be said against the Germans at the Hague is that diplomatically speaking they were extremely stupid to go on record as opposing the irrelevant arbitration proposals. These meant nothing anyway, but by taking a public stand against them the Germans put at the disposal of their enemies material which seemed extremely damaging to their pacific claims when maliciously distorted by Entente propagandists.

Hence, it will quickly be seen that the common allegation that Germany's action at the Hague Conferences was mainly responsible for the perpetuation of the military system in Europe is pure nonsense. Germany was no more opposed to the plan for limiting land armament than was France. England remained unalterably opposed to the proposals for the protection of commerce and the immunity of private property at sea, the absence of which was believed by the United States and other powers to be the chief reason for the existence and expansion of naval armament. In the very year of the second Hague Conference England and Russia were parcelling out Persia between them and cementing the Triple Entente.   In the two years before 1907 England had, during the first Morocco crisis, aligned herself with France.   In the light of these circumstances it was scarcely to be expected that Germany would show any great enthusiasm for a proposal of limitation of armaments which did not carry with it adequate guarantees of safety. The charge of encirclement seemed vindicated as never before in 1907.[45]

In short, the Russian proposals for armament

limitation were not made in good faith, but were
a piece of selfish and temporizing Russian strategy; the arbitration proposals in no sense covered
the basic causes of war; Germany was no more
opposed to limitation of land armament than
France, though she had far greater need of extensive preparations; England was unalterably
opposed to any naval limitation; and Germany
took as prominent a part as any major European
state in bringing about such achievements in arbitration as were secured at the Hague Conferences.[46]

VIII. PRE-WAR DIPLOMACY TO 1912

1. The Franco-Prussian War

All discussions of the diplomatic background
of the World War must necessarily begin with
reference to the Franco-Prussian War of 1870
and its aftermath, as the French desire for revenge and the recovery of Alsace-Lorraine is admitted by all competent students to have been
the most powerful and persistent single force
in keeping Europe in a continual state of anticipation of, and preparation for, war. As
Ewart has well said on this point: [47]

Not France only, but all Europe, kept in mind, between 1871 and 1914, with varying intensity, the prospect—one might say the assumed certainty—of the re-
currence of the Franco-Prussian war. Every change in
the European situation raised apprehension of its im-

minence, and the most important of the international occurrences had direct reference to its anticipated arrival. If, for example, we were to select from Bismarck's foreign policy his principal purpose, it would be that France should be kept isolated; while, on the other hand, the endeavor of French statesmen (generally speaking) was to secure alliances without which France would be helpless. For forty-three years, Germany and France believed that the fate of Alsace-Lorraine would be settled by war (they still think so) and both countries arranged for the struggle as best they could, by alliances, by understandings, and by military preparations.

We do not have space now to go into the problem of the responsibility for the Franco-Prussian War, but it should be pointed out here that no informed scholar in any country, not even excepting France, holds to the conventional notion that it was forced by the brutal Prussian bullying of a weaker and pacific state.[48] Writing in the *Saturday Evening Post* for October 24, 1914, Clemenceau frankly admitted that:

In 1870 Napoleon III, in a moment of folly, declared war on Germany without even having the excuse of military preparedness. No true Frenchman has ever hesitated to admit that the wrongs of that day were committed by our side. Dearly have we paid for them.

France had invited war even before Bismarck published the condensed "Ems telegram."

Again, in 1870 France was a much larger, supposedly more powerful, and more militaristic state than Prussia and the French leaders expected an easy victory. The public opinion of both Great Britain and the United States was overwhelmingly on the side of Prussia, and believed the Prussian victory was a salutary rebuke to military autocracy and aggression.[49]

2. Alsace-Lorraine

The annexation of Alsace-Lorraine by Germany after the war has proved disastrous to both Germany and Europe, but it was only the natural outcome of events. Nations, particularly victorious nations, have never yet guided their conduct on the basis of the ultimate good of mankind, and certainly the terms of the peace of 1871 were most magnanimous to France as compared to the terms imposed by France upon Germany in 1919. The greater part of Alsace and Lorraine had originally been German territory, wrested from her by force by the French. Neutral opinion at the time agreed that Germany would be foolish not to take advantage of the situation to rectify her frontiers and protect herself against the further aggression of France, though many European statesmen recognized the danger to the future peace of Europe inherent in the probable undying ambition of the French for revenge.[50]   The latter were right; the Alsace-Lorraine problem blocked every move for successful *rapprochement* between France and Germany after 1870.   Not even men like Caillaux were able to overcome the French lust for retaliation.   It became a veritable obsession with Déroulède and his followers after 1871, and later with men like Foch and Poincaré who came into control of French policy after 1912.   Foch confesses that: [51]

From the age of 17, I dreamed of revenge, after having seen the Germans at Metz.   And when a man of ordinary capacity concentrates all of his faculties and all of his abilities upon one end, and works without diverging, he ought to be successful.

Poincaré himself stated in an address to university students: [52]

When I descended from my metaphysical clouds I could discover no other reason why my generation should go on living except for the hope of recovering our lost provinces.

Of all the underlying political and diplomatic causes of the World War the French hope of avenging 1870 must be held to be, beyond all comparison, the most important.   Next to it came the Russian ambition for the Straits.

3. The Near East

The other main root of the War lay in the near eastern problem. From the time of Catherine the Great, Russia had entertained an ambition to control Constantinople and the Straits in order to have a warm-water port and an unrestricted naval outlet on the Mediterranean. After the conquest of India the interest of England in the Near East enormously increased, as the country which was ascendant in Asia Minor and Mesopotamia was a potential menace to British India. This British sensitiveness to near eastern developments was still further intensified by the British occupation of Egypt following the '70's. Russia and England became traditional enemies over the near eastern issue, fighting the Crimean War over this and nearly coming into armed conflict again in 1878. At the very close of the nineteenth century Germany became a factor in the Near East with the successful inauguration of her plan to build a railway to the Persian Gulf and exploit Mesopotamia.[53] Though instigated by Cecil Rhodes, this alarmed Great Britain, paralleling as it did the German commercial rivalry and the beginnings of the German navy; and, when Holstein persuaded Bülow to reject the British proposals for an adequate understanding with Germany,[54] Great Britain suppressed her ancient hatred for Rus-

sia and came to a temporary agreement over the
Near East in the partition of Persia in 1907.[55]
Germany in the meantime continued her work on
the Bagdad railroad and became the most influential of the great powers at Constantinople.[56]

This greatly excited Izvolski, Sazonov and
other Russian expansionists, who entertained an
ardent hope of ultimately securing control of
the Straits. Poincaré and the French militarists were able to exploit this Russian fear in
return for Russian sympathy with the cause of
the recovery of Alsace-Lorraine. After 1909,
Austria had little or no economic or imperialistic
interest in the Near East. Her program only
involved preserving order among the diverse
nationalities inhabiting her polyglot empire, thus
maintaining the political integrity of the Dual
Monarchy. This included the repression of the
Jugo-Slav nationalistic movement in so far as it
threatened the existence of Austria-Hungary.
Germany supported her in the moderate phases
of this policy, for Austria-Hungary was essential
to Germany as her only strong ally and as a link
in the territory keeping open the Bagdad railroad. Austrian antipathy towards the Jugo-
Slavs gave Russia an ever-present excuse for
alertness in the Balkans as the assumed protector
of all Slavic peoples, though she never hesitated
to betray them (as in 1908 and 1911) when her
interests dictated such action. Russia was active

in forming the Balkan League in 1912. In
November, 1912, Poincaré gave Russia a free
hand in the Balkans, promising aid in the event
of war. After 1912 Russia initiated a systematic program of encouraging leading Serbian
statesmen and plotters to keep alive the intrigues
against Austria.[57]

Between 1912 and 1914 the earlier Russian
aspiration merely to secure unimpeded use of the
Straits for her warships and commerce was transformed into a determination to get actual control of the Straits through an occupation of this
area.

4. Morocco

Added to Alsace-Lorraine and the Near East
as major factors in the diplomatic background
of the War was the Morocco question. Entente
propagandists have represented this as a situation where, in 1905 and 1911, the Kaiser brought
Europe to the verge of war through wanton
and illegal bullying of France. In reality
Bülow merely insisted in 1905 that France could
not proceed with the disposition of northern
Africa without submitting the question to an
international conference.[58] Ewart has effectively disposed of the allegation of Thayer and
Bishop that President Roosevelt *forced* the
Kaiser to accept the Algeciras settlement, as
well as of Count Witte's palpable fabrication

that it was he who persuaded the Kaiser to accept this solution.[59] Even Poincaré has admitted that it was Germany who forced France to accept the submission of the problem to the concert of Europe. In 1911 Germany intervened to get compensation for French advances into Africa and to weaken Anglo-French relations. Erudite German writers, such as Montgelas, do not attempt to defend all the details of German diplomacy in the Morocco crises, but we may admit with Ewart that, in the major issues involved, both moral and legal rights were very distinctly on the side of Germany: [60]

Germany was within her rights in insisting in 1905 upon a reference of her dispute with France concerning Morocco to an international conference. President Roosevelt was of that opinion. He warmly congratulated the Kaiser on his success in that regard. And the result of the proceedings of the conference—the act of Algeciras—was to a large extent a declaration in favor of the German contention for international equality in Morocco, and a denial of the claim of France and Spain to exclusive domination.

French and Spanish military operations in 1911 were subversive of the chief principle of the act of Algeciras, namely, "the sovereignty and independence of his majesty, the sultan." France so regarded the Spanish actions, and Spain so regarded the French. Germany, as a party to the act, was within her rights in objecting to these proceedings.

In some ways Great Britain emerges with the least credit from the Morocco crises. In 1905, without consulting Germany, she made a secret treaty with France, giving the latter a free hand in Morocco, and she exhibited, particularly in 1911, an unwarranted and gratuitous bellicosity towards Germany which did much to alarm the latter and increase the European tension.[61]

Much has been made by some writers of the alleged national insult to France in a specific German demand for the resignation of the anti-German minister Delcassé in 1905. As a matter of fact, the German suggestion was an indirect and quasi-official one, and the result of coöperation with Rouvier and the French opponents of the bellicose policies of Delcassé.[62] In his recent defense of himself in *Foreign Affairs* for October, 1925, Poincaré makes a dramatic reference to France's signing the treaty of November 4, 1911, concerning Morocco, "under the very cannon of the *Panther*." It so happens that the *Panther* was an insignificant little German gunboat carrying a crew of 125 men—about as much of a ship of war as the Kaiser's private yacht. Poincaré apparently fails to see that it is chiefly a reflection upon French policy if France had to be kept up to her treaty obligations concerning Morocco by even a symbolic show of German naval power.

The Morocco crisis of 1911 markedly increased

the European unrest. The French jingo press capitalized the alleged French "defeat" and used it to discredit Caillaux and the friends of peace in France. Germany was alarmed by the attitude of England and regarded encirclement by the Entente as now complete.[63]

IX. GENERAL DEVELOPMENTS, 1908–1914

The years from 1908 to 1914 were ominous ones for the future of Europe.[64] We have already mentioned the second Morocco crisis and the tension in the Near East caused by the Berlin-Bagdad railroad. In September, 1908, at Buchlau, Izvolski, then Russian Foreign Minister, and Count Aehrenthal, the Austrian Foreign Minister, secretly agreed that Austria should annex the two Serb provinces of Bosnia and Herzegovina, in return for which Austria was to support the Russians in securing from Turkey the freedom of the Straits. Aehrenthal, urged on by Burian and the Turkish Revolution, forthwith annexed these provinces, thus enraging the Serbians, while Great Britain blocked the Russian plan in regard to the Straits, to the exasperation of Izvolski.[65] The latter, after more fruitless negotiation, decided that Russia could gain her objective only by a general European war, and he set to work to bring into being those forces and circumstances which actually precipitated the World War in the summer of 1914. He secured the appointment as Russian Ambassador to France, and was soon in collaboration with the French *Revanchards* led by Delcassé, Poincaré, Jonnart and the military clique.[66]

His two intimates in diplomatic collusion were Poincaré and Delcassé. The former was born in Lorraine, and his one life-long obsession, like that of Foch, was the recovery of Alsace-Lorraine from Germany.[67] Poincaré and Izvolski decided that their joint program—the Russian seizure of the Straits and the French recovery of Alsace-Lorraine—could be realized only by war, and they came to the conclusion that the Balkans were the most favorable area in which to foment or seize upon a crisis suitable for provoking the desired conflict. Poincaré gave Russia a free hand in the Balkans, provided he have general supervisory control to see that France would not be involved in a way which would not advance the recovery of Alsace-Lorraine, and Izvolski obtained large sums of money from Russia to bribe the French press to print such news, articles and editorials as would convince the French people that they possessed a grave concern and vital interest in Balkan problems. This money was distributed to the French papers under the direction of Poincaré, Tardieu, Berthelot and others. Izvolski also secured financial aid for the campaign of Poincaré for the French presidency in 1912.[68]

The Balkan Wars of 1912–13 created great uneasiness throughout Europe, and were the chief factor in promoting the great military and naval increases of 1913–14. There was a war scare throughout Europe. The anti-Austrian feeling in Serbia grew. Austria was twice prevented from attacking Serbia by German and Italian opposition. Poincaré expressed great disappointment about the relative lack of Russian concern over this fact. But the Russians were not asleep. On December 8, 1913, Sazonov informed the Tsar that the Russian ambitions in regard to the Straits could only be realized by a European war. In December, 1913 and February, 1914, the Russians held Crown Councils in which they debated the wisdom of suddenly pouncing upon Constantinople and risking the consequences. They concluded that it would be best to await the outbreak of a world war which they believed imminent. In the late spring of 1914 Great Britain and Russia began negotiations for joint naval action, and the Russians proudly boasted that they were ready for war.[69]

The setting was, thus, ideal for the precipitation of a general European conflagration, and it was in this atmosphere that the Serbian fanatics laid the plot for the assassination of the Archduke Franz Ferdinand, which was executed on June 28, 1914.[70] The only ray of hope on the

horizon was the successful Anglo-German negotiations over the Bagdad railroad, which were
concluded in June, 1914, and brought better relations between these two states than had previously existed since 1901.[71]   But before this
could bear any fruit, Grey had allowed Britain
to be drawn into the conflict to pull the Franco-
Russian chestnuts out of the fire.[72]

Ewart presents the following admirable summary of the nature and outcome of the system of
European international relations from 1870–
1914: [73]

Alsace-Lorraine was the cause of the maze of military
combinations and counter-combinations which had perplexed European diplomats for over forty years.   During the latest ten, reasons for anxiety had rapidly ac-
cumulated; the combinations had hardened; the work
of the diplomats had become more difficult, more complicated, more continuous, more urgent; the general
staffs of the allied nations, in conference with each
other, had diligently elaborated their plans of campaign; every year had witnessed an increased expenditure upon war preparations, of many millions of money;
almost every year had witnessed a narrow avoidance of
hostilities; no effort had been made, by removal of
fundamental disagreements, to escape from the ever-
quickening rapids which were certain to tumble into
maelstrom; indeed, well-informed statesmen knew that
many of the international rivalries could not be peaceably adjusted; all were well aware that some incident
might at any moment produce general war.

Before we pass on to the assassination of Archduke Franz Ferdinand, we must, however, devote a separate chapter to the details of the collusion between Izvolski and Poincaré from 1912 to 1914, as this is by all odds the most important phase of the genesis of the World War.

X. CONCLUSIONS

(1) The whole question of the responsibility for the World War and the antecedent diplomacy must be reëxamined in the light of the new documentary evidence which has recently been made available by the publication of the material in the Foreign Offices of Austria, Germany and Russia.

(2) It is generally assumed that Germany not only deliberately provoked the World War in 1914, but was also responsible for the system of arrogant nationalism, imperialism, armament and secret diplomacy that predisposed Europe to war in the generation prior to 1914.

(3) The chief factors which inclined Europe towards war from 1870 to 1914 were economic rivalry, nationalism and patriotism, extensive armaments on land and water, and secret alliances.

(4) Germany was inseparably involved in this system of European relations, but was certainly no worse in any respect than the others. Eco-

nomic rivalry was chiefly Anglo-German, was inevitable, and in no way involved direct war guilt. German patriotism was no more highly developed or obtrusive than that of France or Italy. Germany was far inferior to France and Russia in regard to land armament, and equally inferior to England in naval preparations. The German navy was never any real menace to Great Britain's naval supremacy, and, more than a year before the War broke out, the two countries had arrived at a working arrangement as to future building plans. Germany did not initiate the system of compulsory universal military service, actually introduced by France in 1872. Nor was she responsible for the French Army Bill of 1913.

(5) The chief roots of the War in diplomatic tension were Alsace-Lorraine and the French revenge aspirations, the Near East, and Morocco.

(6) The Franco-Prussian War was desired by both France and Prussia. France desired it to bolster up the fortunes of the Bonapartist dynasty, and Bismarck wished it to forward the cause of German unity. The opinion of the neutral world was heavily on the side of Prussia. The War left a fatal desire for revenge on the part of France, which remained to 1914 the main obstacle to European amity and the chief menace to the continuance of peace.

(7) German progress in the Near East

alarmed England and Russia, and led them to bury their ancient rivalries and form a combination against Germany. Germany and England, however, arrived at a satisfactory diplomatic settlement of their near eastern problems in June, 1914, but it was too late to keep England from joining France and Russia in the World War. Russia realized that she could oust Germany from her control of Turkey only by a general European war in which Germany would be defeated.

(8) In the Morocco crises Germany was in the right legally and morally, but sadly bungled matters in diplomatic procedure. The chief disastrous result was that the German diplomacy aided the French militarists and chauvinists in driving Caillaux and the pacific French group from office and led to the substitution of the aggressive anti-German and revenge clique headed by Poincaré, Delcassé, Millerand, Jonnart, Paléologue and the Cambons.

(9) In the Hague Conferences Germany was no more opposed to the vital proposals as to disarmament than France or England. She took as active a part as any country in bringing about the constructive achievements of the Conferences, but by foolishly going on record against the irrelevant arbitration proposals she put at the disposal of her enemies a powerful instrument in propaganda.

(10) The years from 1908 to 1914 were threatening ones for the peace of Europe. Izvolski was blocked in his plan to open the Straits by diplomatic means, and was convinced that a European war must be provoked. In 1912 he was joined in this program by Raymond Poincaré as Prime Minister of France. Sazonov was converted to the scheme at the end of 1913, and before June, 1914, it was practically assured that Great Britain would enter any war on the side of France and Russia against Germany. An incident was awaited in the Balkans which would serve as an adequate excuse for war. Meanwhile Franco-Russian military preparations proceeded, and the French republic was prepared for war over the Balkans by a press bribed with Russian gold.

SELECTED REFERENCES

Bausman, F., *Let France Explain;* Dickinson, G. Lowes, *The International Anarchy, 1904–1914;* Durham, E., *Twenty Years of Balkan Tangle;* Earle, E. M., *Turkey, the Great Powers and the Bagdad Railway;* Enock, A. G., *The Problem of Armaments;* Ewart, J. S., *The Roots and Causes of the Wars, 1914–1918;* Fabre-Luce, A., *La Victoire;* Fisk, G. M., and Pierce, P. S., *International Commercial Policies;* Gooch, G. P., *Modern Europe, 1878–1920;* Herbert, S., *Nationality and Its Problems;* Hobson, J. A., *Imperialism;* Hull, W. I., *The Two Hague Conferences;* Montgelas, M., *The Case for the Central Powers;* Morel, E. D., *Ten*

Years of Secret Diplomacy; The Secret History of a Great Betrayal; Playne, C. E., *The Neuroses of the Nations;* Rose, J. H., *Nationality in Modern History;* Schmitt, B. E., *England and Germany, 1740–1914;* "Triple Alliance and Triple Entente," in *American Historical Review,* April, 1924; Stieve, F., *Isvolsky and the World War; Deutschland und Europa, 1890–1914;* Toynbee, A. J., *Nationality and the War;* Woolf, L., *Economic Imperialism.*

FOOTNOTES AND FURTHER REFERENCES

[1] A. Pevet, *Les Responsables de la guerre,* p. 518; V. Margueritte, *Les Criminels,* pp. 347ff.

[2] See K. Kautsky, *Wie der Weltkrieg entstand.*

[3] *The Secret Treaties of Austria-Hungary, 1879–1914.* The American edition was supervised by Profesor A. C. Coolidge and published by the Harvard University Press, 1920. It should be pointed out that Pribram's work is not yet finished. He is waiting for the complete publication of the German documents in the *Grosse Politik.*

[4] *Diplomatische Aktenstücke zur Vorgeschichte des Krieges,* 1914, three volumes, Vienna, 1919. These are now available in English translation by Allen and Unwin.

[5] *Die Grosse Politik der Europäischen Kabinette, 1871–1914.* Berlin, 1923–1927. An indispensable guide to this collection is provided in the *Wegweiser* of Dr. Bernhard Schwertfeger. See *Die Kriegsschuldfrage,* December, 1926.

[6] *Die Deutschen Dokumente zum Kriegsausbruch,* four volumes, Charlottenburg, 1919. They are now available in English translation by the Oxford University Press.

[7] *Official German Documents Relating to the World War.* Carnegie Endowment for International Peace. Two volumes, New York: Oxford University Press, 1923.

[8] Edited by George Schreiner as *Entente Diplomacy and the World, 1909–1914.* New York: Knickerbocker Press, 1922. It is now known that Siebert has held out many documents most incriminating to the Entente. There are over a thousand in his collection awaiting publication.

[9] *Un Livre Noir: Diplomatie d'Avant-Guerre d'après les Documents Russes, Novembre, 1910, Juillet, 1914.* Two volumes, Paris, 1922–23. *Der Diplomatische Schriftwechsel Iswolskis, 1911–1914.* Five volumes, Berlin, 1924. A brief collection of

these Russian documents was published in Paris as early as 1919 under the editorship of Emile LaJoy. It is important as containing the secret Russian conference in February, 1914, on the desirability of seizing the Straits.

[10] *Falsifications of the Russian Orange Book.* New York: Huebsch, 1923. Herr Wegerer has done much the same thing with the French *Yellow Book* of 1914.

[11] *L'Intervento dell' Italia nei Documenti Segreti dell' Intensa.* Rome, 1923.

[12] *Belgische Aktenstücke 1905–1914.* Berlin, 1915. *Zur Europäischen Politik.* 1886–1893, 1897–1914. Five volumes, Berlin, 1919–22. These collections are edited by B. H. Schwertfeger. Some of them (1905–14) have appeared in English translation.

[13] These treaties were courageously printed by Mr. Villard in the New York *Evening Post* early in 1918 as a result of their revelation by the Bolsheviki. They are printed in F. S. Cocks, *The Secret Treaties.* They are analyzed by R. S. Baker in his work, *Woodrow Wilson and the World Settlement.* Mr. Baker defends the truly astonishing assertion that Mr. Wilson left for the Peace Conference nearly a year later with no knowledge of their nature or contents.

[14] The best summary of this literature is contained in G. P. Gooch's "Recent Revelations on European Diplomacy," *Journal of the British Institute of International Affairs,* January, 1923. See also below Appendix I.

[15] H. Morgenthau, *Ambassador Morgenthau's Story,* esp. Chap. vi; see the slashing critique of this legend by S. B. Fay in the *Kriegsschuldfrage,* May, 1925, pp. 309 ff.

[16] See the editorials in the New York *Times* for May 4, 1924, May 3, 1925, and September 15, 1925; and the review of the book by the Crown Prince, *Ich Suche die Wahrheit,* by Simeon Strunsky, Ibid., August 30, 1925.

[17] B. E. Schmitt, *England and Germany, 1740–1914;* T. Veblen, *Imperial Germany and the Industrial Revolution;* W. H. Dawson, *The German Empire; The Evolution of Modern Germany; Industrial Germany;* E. D. Howard, *The Causes and Extent of the Recent Industrial Progress of Germany;* J. S. Ewart, *The Roots and Causes of the Wars, 1914–1918,* Chaps. v, xix–xxi, xxv; A. Hurd and H. Castle, *German Sea Power;* E. Protheroe, *The British Navy;* Viscount Haldane, *Before the War;* A. von Tirpitz, *My Memoirs;* W. S. Churchill, *The World Crisis.*

[18] Ewart, op. cit., Chap. v.

[19] E. M. Earle, *Turkey, the Great Powers and the Bagdad Railway,* Ewart, op. cit., Chap. xxi.

[20] Ewart, op cit., p. 876.

[21] J. K. Turner, *Shall It Be Again?;* C. E. Schieber, *The*

Transformation of American Sentiment towards Germany, Chap. iv.

22 P. Ashley, *Modern Tariff History;* W. S. Culbertson, *International Economic Policies;* Fisk and Pierce, *International Commercial Policies;* V. Wittchewsky, *Russlands Handels-Zoll-und-Industrie Politik;* A. Zimmermann, *Handelspolitik des deutschen Reiches.*

23 C. J. H. Hayes, "The War of the Nations," in *Political Science Quarterly,* December, 1914; H. A. L. Fisher, *Studies in History and Politics,* pp. 146–61 (on French nationalism); C. E. Playne, *The Neuroses of the Nations;* M. Wertheimer, *The Pan-German League;* A. D. Fischel, *Der Pan-slawismus bis zum Weltkrieg;* A. Mayer, *Der Italienische Irredentismus.*

24 R. G. Usher, *Pan-Germanism;* A. Chéradame, *The Pan-German Plot Unmasked;* E. E. Sperry, *The Tentacles of the German Octopus in America;* C. Andler, *Le Pangermanisme.*

25 M. S. Wertheimer, *The Pan-German League, 1890–1914.*

26 See the outline and references in E. Krehbiel, *Nationalism, War and Society,* pp. 16–25.

27 J. H. Rose, *Nationality in Modern History;* R. Muir, *Nationalism and Internationalism.*

28 Ewart, op. cit., pp. 477–78.

29 C. D. Hazen, *Fifty Years of Europe;* W. S. Davis, *The Roots of the War.*

30 M. Montgelas, *The Case for the Central Powers,* pp. 25, 27, 104 ff., 235; Ewart, op. cit., Chap. xvii; Moon, *Syllabus on International Relations,* p. 75.

31 General Buat, *L'Armée allemande pendant la guerre de 1914–18,* pp. 7–9.

32 Bausman, *Let France Explain,* p. 165; Ewart, op. cit., p. 508.

33 Cited by Bausman, op. cit., p. 168.

34 Ewart, op. cit., p. 512.

35 Ibid., Chap. xviii, esp. pp. 662 ff.; C. E. Schieber, op. cit., Chap. i.; D. N. Raymond, *Contemporary British Opinion during the Franco-Prussian War.*

36 Ewart, op. cit., Chap. xviii; R. H. Lord, *The Origins of the War of 1870;* and Richard Fester, works cited by Lord, op. cit., p. 286; B. E. Palat (Lehautcourt), *Les Origines de la guerre de 1870;* H. Oncken, *Die Rheinpolitik Kaiser Napoleons III.*

37 F. M. Cutler, "Military Conscription," in *Historical Outlook,* May, 1923, and references appended.

38 Ewart, op. cit., Chaps. xvi–xvii; Moon, *Syllabus on International Relations,* Part IV.

38a G. Dupin, *Conférence sur les responsabilités de la guerre,* p. 17.

39 Ewart, op. cit., pp. 494–7, 500–504, 716–17.

[40] Stieve, *Isvolsky and the World War,* pp. 167ff.

[41] B. E.. Schmitt, "Triple Alliance and Triple Entente," in *American Historical Review,* April, 1924, pp. 449–50. Cf. Schmitt, loc. cit., passim; Stieve, op. cit.; Gooch, op. cit.; H. Friedjung *Das. Zeitalter des Imperialismus;* E. Brandenburg, *Von Bismarck zum Weltkriege;* F. Rachfahl, *Deutschland und die Weltpolitik;* A. F. Pribram, *The Secret Treaties of Austria-Hungary, 1879–1914.*

[42] B. Schmitt, *Recent Disclosures Concerning the Origins of the War,* pp. 21 ff.; H. Kanner, *Die Schlüssel zur Kriegsschuldfrage;* S. B. Fay, in *American Historical Review,* January, 1927, pp. 317–19; M. Montgelas in *Revue de Hongrie,* November 15, 1926.

[43] E.g., C. D. Hazen, *Europe since 1815,* pp. 639–40; E. R. Turner, *Europe since 1870,* p. 427. Even Gooch repeats the traditional view in more moderate fashion.

[44] For a brief demolition of the Entente propaganda concerning the Hague Conferences see Montgelas, *The Case for the Central Powers,* pp. 23–30, and S. B. Fay, in *American Historical Review,* October, 1925, p. 133.

[45] Cf. Brandenburg, op. cit.

[46] A. W. Ward and G. P. Gooch, *Cambridge History of British Foreign Policy,* Vol. III, pp. 258 ff., 349 ff.

[47] Ewart, op. cit., pp. 671–2.

[48] Lord, Palat, Oncken and Fester as cited; and E. M. Carroll, in *American Historical Review,* July, 1926, pp. 679–700.

[49] Miss Schieber and Mrs. Raymond, as cited.

[50] Ewart, op. cit., pp. 666 ff.

[51] Ibid., p. 671.

[52] M. Morhardt, *Les Preuves. Le crime de droit commun. Le crime diplomatique,* p. 135; also cited by Langer, *New Republic,* October 15, 1924, p. 179.

[53] Schmitt, op. cit., Earle, op. cit.; Ewart, op. cit., Chap. xxi.

[54] J. Haller, *Die Ära Bülow;* E. Fischer, *Holsteins grosses "Nein."*

[55] *Cambridge History of British Foreign Policy,* Vol. III, pp. 356 ff.; H. A. Gibbons, *The New Map of Europe,* Chap. v.

[56] Earle, op. cit., Chaps. iii–iv.

[57] Friedjung, op. cit.; M. Bogitshevich, *The Causes of the War;* Stieve, op. cit.; E. Durham, *The Serajevo Crime;* Ewart, Chap. xxiii.

[58] Ewart, Chap. xxii; E. D. Morel, *Ten Years of Secret Diplomacy; Cambridge History of British Foreign Policy,* Vol. III, pp. 338 ff.

[59] Ewart, op. cit., pp. 800 ff.

[60] Ibid., p. 877; cf. Lord Loreburn, *How the War Came,* pp. 86–111; Montgelas, op. cit., pp. 41 ff.; J. Caillaux, *Agadir, ma*

politique extérieure. P. Albin, *La Querelle franco-allemande: le coup de Agadir.*

61 Ewart, op. cit., 776 ff., 846 ff.; Morel, op. cit.; Loreburn, op. cit.

62 Ewart, op. cit., pp. 781–2. On Delcassé and the Morocco crises see Gooch, in the *Contemporary Review,* April, 1923; and Ewart, op. cit., pp. 769 ff., 836 ff. The facts in regard to Germany and Delcassé's resignation are revealed in the *Grosse Politik.*

63 Perhaps the best summary and estimate is contained in Gooch, op. cit., Chap. xiv. See Caillaux's masterly exposition, "Les Responsables," in *Les Documents Politiques,* March, 1926, translated in the *American Monthly,* January, 1927.

64 Montgelas, op. cit., Part II.

65 Friedjung and Stieve, as cited.

66 Stieve, op. cit.; F. Gouttenoire de Toury, *Jaurès et le parti de la guerre.*

67 Ibid.; and Morhardt, op. cit.

68 Stieve, op. cit.; and Morel, *The Secret History of a Great Betrayal.*

69 Stieve, op. cit.; and Gooch, op. cit., Chap. xv.

70 See the articles by Professor Fay in the New York Times *Current History Magazine,* October and November, 1925; and E. Durham, *The Serajevo Crime.*

71 Earle, op. cit., pp. 258 ff.

72 Morel, *The Secret History of a Great Betrayal.*

73 Ewart, op. cit., p. 1001.

CHAPTER III

THE FRANCO-RUSSIAN PLOT THAT
PRODUCED THE WAR

I. "TWO HEADS ARE BETTER THAN ONE"

IN a remarkable article in the New York Times
Current History Magazine for November, 1925,
Professor Sidney B. Fay describes the plan to
assassinate the Archduke in Bosnia as "The
Black Hand Plot that Led to the World War."
While agreeing entirely with Professor Fay in
his interpretation of the Serbian responsibility
for the assassination of Franz Ferdinand, the
present writer believes that behind the local plot
to assassinate a member of the Austrian royal
family there was a much larger and more far-
reaching plot, without which the murder of June
28, 1914, could never have brought about the
World War. This was the plot carefully laid
and elaborated by Alexander Petrovitch Izvolski and Raymond Poincaré between 1912 and
1914, on the basis of Izvolski's previous schemes
and machinations.

We have already pointed out how Izvolski in
1908 treacherously betrayed the Serbians by suggesting that Austria annex Bosnia and Herze-

govina in return for Austrian support of the
Russian plan to open the Straits.   We indicated
that Izvolski was blocked in this plan by the
evasive opposition of England to Russian access
to the Straits.   Foiled in this first plan to secure
the chief object of his *Politik*, Izvolski turned to
the scheme he brought to success in the summer
of 1914, namely, using the Balkan situation as
the basis for European complications which
would secure the Straits for Russia.   He made a
speech to the Russian Duma urging the federa-
tion of the Balkan states, and immediately put
himself behind the Greater Serbia movement.[1]
In December, 1909, he proposed a secret military
treaty with Bulgaria, the fifth article of which
declared that: [2]

The realization of the high ideals of the Slav peoples
in the Balkan peninsula, which are so close to Russia's
heart, is only possible after a fortunate issue of the
struggle of Russia with Germany and Austria-Hungary.

On September 28, 1910, Izvolski resigned as
Russian Foreign Minister and became the Russian Ambassador to Paris.   Many have regarded
this as a sign of his displacement as the leader
of Russian foreign policy.   Lord Grey holds
that this fact in itself proves that Izvolski is not
to be held primarily responsible for Russian
foreign policy after 1910.   We know that this
view is wholly incorrect.   Izvolski was not de-

moted or reduced in rank. As Count Muraviev, the distinguished Russian diplomat, explained, Izvolski voluntarily resigned and chose the Paris portfolio because he felt that he could work better in Paris than in St. Petersburg. "To bring the healing crisis, to direct European politics to a breach, can be more effectively achieved in Paris than in St. Petersburg." [3] There was another and special reason why Izvolski could do better work in Paris than St. Petersburg after 1909, namely, that his bungling of the Bosnian matter had made things rather hot for him in certain circles at the Russian capital. During the remainder of 1910 and 1911 Izvolski was not able to accomplish much of significance in strengthening and Balkanizing the Franco-Russian Alliance, as Caillaux and the more pacific French group were still in control. But they were weakened through the reaction of the second Morocco crisis upon French politics, and were soon to be replaced by Poincaré and the military clique.[4]

On January 14, 1912, a revolutionary change took place. There came to the premiership M. Raymond Poincaré, one of the ablest Frenchmen since Jules Ferry, and the man who has confessed that he could see no reason for existing unless Alsace-Lorraine could be recovered, knowing well that it could not be restored except by force. Russian and French foreign policy had now come under the control of two men who espoused programs which obviously could only be realized as the result of a military victory over Germany and Austria-Hungary.   Izvolski immediately noted the change in the reception of his policy, and reported that he felt like a new man after Poincaré's accession to the office of Prime Minister.[5]   In his apology in *Foreign Affairs* Poincaré represents himself as having disapproved of Izvolski and his policy, and invites his readers to consult Dr. F. Stieve's elaborate edition of Izvolski's correspondence to discover this fact.   It happens that Professor W. L. Langer, an expert on contemporary diplomatic history, and bibliographic editor of the very journal in which Poincaré writes, has carefully examined this same collection, and tells us in the following words of the close collaboration of Poincaré and Izvolski in preparing Russia, France and the Balkans for the oncoming conflict: [6]

But the gods were with Izvolski and against humanity.   Everything changed as in a dream when, in 1912, Poincaré succeeded to the premiership.   It was a disastrous event, for Poincaré, convinced of the inevitability of war with Germany, agreed entirely with Izvolski that the entente must be strengthened and that the central powers must be shown that the days of their dictation were over.   After the first conversations with the new premier Izvolski felt like a new man.   Life was

138845

once more worth living. . . . Both Poincaré and Izvolski were determined to succeed, and the chronicle of the two years preceding the war is the story of their victory over all opposition. They were not particular as to means, nor considerate of persons. Every opportunity was seized to revivify the entente and develop it, and the utmost care was taken to replace the European concert by two opposing coalitions.

The story is a long one and not very edifying. Poincaré seems to have disliked Izvolski personally, and both appear to have distrusted each other. But in political matters they made an ideal team. There was no divergence in their views. And so they were able to coöperate, supporting and assisting each other in the attainment of the "great solution." Together they intrigued against the pacific French ambassador of St. Petersburg, Georges Louis, and Russian funds were put at the disposal of Poincaré and Klotz to enable them to silence the opposition and even to bring about Poincaré's election as president. And where they could not coöperate, they supplemented each other. It was Poincaré's opposition that wrecked the agreement between England and Germany and it was Poincaré who effected the naval arrangement between England and Russia in 1914, after Izvolski had brought about the Russian-French naval pact in 1912.

The same impression of Poincaré's enthusiastic coöperation with Izvolski was also carried away by the distinguished Russian scholar, Baron Serge Korff, from his careful reading of the *Livre Noir:* [7]

We find new light thrown upon the pre-war attitude of France, strangely but constantly connected with one big name—Poincaré.   Pichon, Barthou and many other familiar names are frequently mentioned, but none seems to have played any such prominent rôle in the building up and strengthening of the Franco-Russian alliance as Poincaré; and besides, with a very evident object—steady preparation for the coming conflict with Germany.   The reader will put aside this volume with the inevitable conviction that Poincaré long before 1914 had one idea on his mind, the war with Germany. . . . These documents give a most vivid picture of the French pressure exerted on Russia with that one object in view, a war with Germany.   At times the Russians were even losing patience with the French, so little did the latter mind the Russian interests; they were willing to lend the Russians money, but only on condition that Russia would increase her army and build new strategic, but otherwise quite useless, railways.

Even Professor Bernadotte E. Schmitt, one of the most ardently pro-Entente of our students of contemporary European diplomacy, would really assign to Poincaré the dominant part in the strengthening of Franco-Russian relations between 1912 and 1914.   He writes on this subject: [8]

The credit belongs in the first instance to M. Raymond Poincaré, who became Premier of France in January, 1912.   Under his masterly care, Franco-Russian relations, which had become somewhat tenuous, while one ally was absorbed in Morocco and the other in Persia and the Far East, were soon exhibiting the closest harmony. In the liquidation of the Tripolitan war and throughout the Balkan wars, Paris and St. Petersburg devised and applied a common policy, carrying London with them if possible. M. Poincaré repeatedly assured Izvolsky, now Ambassador to France, that the republic would fulfil all the obligations of the alliance; Izvolsky took the Paris press into pay to create a sentiment for Russia and to strengthen the position of the Premier whom he recognized as most useful to Russia. The French statesman urged the Czar to proceed with the construction of strategic railways in Poland and sent Delcassé as his representative at the Russian court; the Russian Ambassador, at least according to some persons, demanded that France revive the three years' military service. The French and Russian General Staffs, in annual conferences, perfected their plans for war, which were based on a joint offensive against Germany. A naval convention was concluded. Finally, M. Poincaré went to Russia, and M. Sazonov, the Foreign Minister, expressed to the Czar his hope that "in the event of a crisis in international relations there would be at the helm in France if not M. Poincaré, at least a personality of the same great power of decision and as free from the fear of taking responsibility." The elevation of M. Poincaré to the Presidency of the republic in no way interrupted the newly developed intimacy. Indeed, from 1912 to the outbreak of the war, the Dual Alliance presented a solid front at every turn to the rival diplomatic group.

It is probably impossible to over-emphasize the importance of this union of Poincaré and Izvolski for the future of Franco-Russian and European international relations.   While the Franco-Russian military Alliance had possessed impressive strength on paper from 1893 onward, it had little real power until 1912.   It had no real "punch" in European diplomacy until Poincaré and Izvolski were able to bring into a joint program the recovery of Alsace-Lorraine and the seizure of the Straits, and were also successful in giving this ambition a definite practical bent and feasible area for probable realization through the "Balkanizing" of the Alliance.   Up to 1912 the Russians were irritated at the French conciliation of Great Britain, who blocked Russian ambitions regarding the Straits, and the French were unwilling to risk alienating England by openly backing Russia in her near eastern program. Several times between 1893 and 1912 Russia was on as good terms with Germany as with France. Izvolski and Poincaré first turned the trick and made the Franco-Russian program the dynamic and pivotal element in European affairs from 1912–1917.

II. FRANCO-RUSSIAN MILITARY AND NAVAL
UNDERSTANDINGS

The Franco-Russian military arrangements had been perfected by 1893, and Poincaré and Izvolski now turned their attention to the conclusion of a naval convention which was formulated on July 16, 1912, in the following terms: [9]

Article 1. The naval forces of France and Russia operate jointly in all eventualities in which the Alliance foresees and provides for the co-operation of the land forces.

Article 2. Provision is made in time of peace for the joint operation of the naval forces.

To this end the Chiefs of the two Naval Staffs are henceforth empowered to correspond direct with one another, to exchange all news, to study all possibilities of warfare, and to agree together on all strategic plans.

Article 3. The Chiefs of the two Naval Staffs confer personally together at least once a year; they draw up minutes of their conferences.

Article 4. This convention is to be identical with the military convention of August 17, 1892, and the treaties arising out of it, in regard to its duration, elaboration, and secrecy.

Paris, *July* 16, 1912.

On August 5, 1912, Poincaré left for Russia for a conference with Sazonov, the Russian Foreign Minister. The terms of the naval convention of July 16th were confirmed at once. Poincaré urged upon Sazonov the immediate construction of better railroad facilities to transport Russian troops to the German frontier: [10]

M. Poincaré also spoke of the protocol of the last sitting of the Chiefs of General Staffs, and said that he

attached great importance to the realization of the desire expressed therein by the French General Staff for
an increase in the efficiency of our railway system leading to our western frontier by the construction of a
second track on the lines indicated in the protocol.   I
[Sazonov] replied that I was aware of these desires and
that they would probably be taken into consideration
as far as possible.

Most important of all, Poincaré revealed to
Sazonov the existence of the verbal British agreements to aid France on land and sea in the event
of a war with Germany, which Grey and Asquith
were later to deny before the House of Commons, and urged Sazonov during his anticipated
journey to England to propose to the British authorities an agreement for joint naval action between Russia and Great Britain against Germany.   Sazonov thus reports to the Tsar: [11]

British-French relations were the subject of a specially candid exchange of views between M. Poincaré
and myself.

The French Premier mentioned that latterly, under
the influence of Germany's aggressive policy towards
France, these relations had assumed the character of
quite special intimacy, and he confided to me that while
no written agreement between France and Great
Britain was in existence, the General and Naval Staffs
of the two States were nevertheless in close touch with
one another, and were uninterruptedly and with entire
openness consulting one another on matters of mutual

interest. This continual exchange of ideas had led to a verbal agreement between the Governments of France and Great Britain, in which Great Britain had declared her readiness to come to the aid of France with her land and naval forces should the latter be attacked by Germany. Great Britain had promised to support France on land by a detachment 100,000 strong sent to the Belgian frontier, in order to ward off an invasion of the German army through Belgium, which was expected by the French General Staff.

M. Poincaré begged me urgently to preserve absolute silence about this information, and not to give even the British ground for suspicion that we were informed of it.

When we spoke of the mutual assistance which Great Britain and France contemplated rendering to one another at sea, M. Poincaré touched on the possibility of simultaneous coöperation between the Russian and British naval forces.

Under our naval convention, France has undertaken the obligation to help us by diverting the Austrian fleet in the Mediterranean from us and preventing its penetration into the Black Sea. In Poincaré's view the British naval forces could undertake the same rôle in the Baltic, to which the French fleet is unable to extend its activity. Accordingly, he asked me whether I would not take advantage of my impending journey to England to raise in my conversations with the leaders of British policy the question of joint operation of the Russian and British fleets in the event of a conflict with the Powers of the Triple Alliance.

I replied to M. Poincaré that this question required close consideration.

How well Sazonov carried out Poincaré's suggestion, as well as the cordial reception of the idea by Grey and the King, is revealed in the following report to Sazonov to the Tsar concerning his reception at Balmoral in September, 1912: [12]

As a favourable opportunity occurred I felt it useful, in one of my conversations with Grey, to seek information as to what we might expect from Great Britain in the event of a conflict with Germany.   What the director of British foreign policy said to me as to this, and King George himself later, I think is very significant.

Your Majesty is aware that during M. Poincaré's stay in St. Petersburg last summer he expressed to me a wish that I would clear up the question of the extent to which we might count on the co-operation of the British fleet in the event of such a war.

I informed Grey confidentially of the main points of our naval convention with France, and remarked that under the treaty concluded the French fleet would endeavour to safeguard our interests in the southern theatre of war by preventing the Austrian fleet from penetrating into the Black Sea; and I then asked whether Great Britain for her part could perform the same service for us in the north, by keeping the German squadrons away from our Baltic coasts.   Grey declared unhesitatingly that should the anticipated conditions arise Great Britain would make every effort to strike a crippling blow at German naval power.   On the question of military operations he said that negotiations had already taken place between the competent authorities concerned, but in these discussions the con-

clusion had been reached that while the British fleet
could easily penetrate into the Baltic, its stay there
would be very risky. Assuming Germany to succeed
in laying hands on Denmark and closing the exit from
the Baltic, the British fleet would be caught in a
mousetrap. Accordingly Great Britain would have to
confine her operations to the North Sea.

On his own initiative Grey then gave me a confirmation of what I already knew through Poincaré—an
agreement exists between France and Great Britain,
under which in the event of war with Germany Great
Britain has accepted the obligation of bringing assistance to France not only on the sea but on land, by
landing troops on the Continent.

The King touched on the same question in one of his
conversations with me, and expressed himself even more
strongly than his Minister. When I mentioned, letting
him see my agitation, that Germany is trying to place
her naval forces on a par with Britain's, His Majesty
cried that any conflict would have disastrous results
not only for the German navy but for Germany's overseas trade, for, he said, "We shall sink every single
German merchant ship we shall get hold of."

These words appeared to me to give expression not
only to His Majesty's personal feelings but also to the
public feeling predominant in Great Britain in regard
to Germany.

That Poincaré made an excellent impression
on Sazonov during his visit to St. Petersburg is
shown by the following excerpt from the Sazonov's report to the Tsar: [13]

Finally, I feel bound to mention that I was very glad of the opportunity to make the acquaintance of M. Poincaré, and to get into personal touch with him; all the more since our exchange of views left me with the feeling that in him Russia has a true and trustworthy friend, gifted with uncommon statesmanly intelligence and unbending strength of will. In the event of a crisis in international relations it would be very desirable that there should stand at the head of our ally's Government, if not M. Poincaré himself, at all events a personality as resolute as the French Premier, and as entirely unafraid of responsibility.

On December 5, 1912, Izvolski confirmed Sazonov's judgment in a telegram to the latter:

In a recent talk with me, Poincaré remarked that opinion in France is strongly pro-peace, and that he has always to keep this in mind. We are, it seems to me, all the more indebted to him for his fixed resolve most loyally to fulfil his duties as an ally in case of need. . . . If the crisis comes, the decision will be made by the three strong personalities who stand at the head of the Cabinet—Poincaré, Millerand and Delcassé. And it is a piece of good fortune for us that we have to deal with these personalities and not one or another of the opportunist politicians who have succeeded one another in the course of recent years in the Government of France [i. e. Combes, Caillaux, Herriot, Painlevé et al., the opponents of the war policy—Author].

The significance of what had been accomplished by Izvolski, Poincaré and Sazonov even before the outbreak of the Balkan Wars has been admirably summarized by Dr. Stieve: [14]

It is evident from all this how comprehensive were already the war preparations of the Entente Powers. A close network had been placed around the Central Powers. In the North Sea, British and French fleets were to act together. On top of this a British land army of 100,000 men was to join on in Belgium to the left wing of the French army, which had to carry out from there to Lorraine the speediest possible advance against Germany. In the Mediterranean the French fleet recently transferred thither aimed at holding the Austrian naval forces in check, and on the Russian frontier all conceivable measures were to be taken to expedite as far as possible the advance of the troops of the enormous Tsarist empire if the emergency arose. These were, indeed, gigantic plans, covering all Europe, which, as we have just seen, were in important respects developed and promoted by Poincaré's initiative in Russia.

III. THE BALKANIZING OF THE PLOT

Russia was primarily responsible for the Balkan War of 1912, as the Balkan League was to no small degree a creation of Izvolski, who hoped to use it as an instrument to drive the Turk out of Europe. The hostilities broke out rather earlier than was desired by Poincaré, for, while a Balkan War by itself might secure the Straits for Russia, it would not return Alsace-Lorraine

to France.   There was still a faint hope in 1912
that a struggle in the Near East might secure for
Russia what Izvolski had been aiming at, but
Poincaré's ambition quite obviously could only
be realized by a general European war.   Therefore, when trouble seemed imminent in the Balkans in 1912 Poincaré endeavored to keep the
situation under control and to prevent the outbreak of hostilities.   He was not yet ready to
use the Balkans as the pretext for a general war.
Russia was not prepared for war in a military
sense, and the French people had not yet been
converted by the bribed press to take an active
interest in Balkan matters.   It was best to lie
low in this crisis, as the time was not yet ripe to
execute his plan.   Peace was maintained primarily because Sir Edward Grey at that time refused to allow England to be drawn into any conflict to forward the Russian ambitions, and co-
operated with Germany in localizing the conflict.
If he had done the same in 1914, as Germany
urged him to do, there would have been no European war.

Izvolski was, of course, only interested in the
Balkans in so far as Balkan disturbances might
secure the Straits, and advance the Russian
hegemony in this area.   To Poincaré this was
wholly secondary.   To him the Balkans were important as the one area over which a European
war might be provoked and at the same time in-

sure the Russian attack upon Germany which would provide the only possible method for the French to recover Alsace-Lorraine. Hence, he determined to adopt a policy which would prevent Russia from gaining her ends without the European war so indispensable to the French program. The Balkan situation must be so manipulated as to bring about a European war. The famous "Millerand conversation" amply confirms this interpretation of Poincaré's attitude during the Balkan crisis of 1912–13. (Cf. Stieve, op. cit., p. 124; and Judet, *Georges Louis*, p. 143.) On the 12th of September, 1912, Poincaré told Izvolski that France would probably refuse to follow him in a war over the Balkans unless Germany should support Austria: [15]

Should, however, the conflict with Austria result in armed intervention by Germany, the French Government recognizes this in advance as a *casus foederis*, and would not hesitate a moment to fulfil the obligations which it has accepted towards Russia. "France," continued M. Poincaré, "is beyond question entirely peaceful in disposition, and neither desires nor seeks a war; but German intervention against Russia would at once bring about a change in public feeling, and it may be taken as certain that in such an event Parliament and public opinion would entirely support the decision of the Government to give Russia armed support."

M. Poincaré also told me that in view of the critical

situation in the Balkans the superior French military authorities are examining with increased closeness all the military eventualities which might occur, and that he knows that well-informed and responsible personalities are very optimistic in their judgment of the prospects of Russia and France in the event of a general conflict.

The outbreak of hostilities in the Balkans in the autumn of 1912 still further emphasized to Poincaré the necessity of his preventing Russia from obtaining her ambitions short of a European war. On November 17, 1912, he gave Izvolski and the Russians what practically amounted to a blank cheque in regard to the Balkans, promising Russia that if she went to war France would follow.   It was deemed better to go to war prematurely than to take a chance that France would lose out on the possibility of regaining her lost provinces: [16]

"It is," said Poincaré, "for Russia to take the initiative in a matter in which she is the most closely interested party.   France's task is to accord to Russia her most emphatic support. Were the French Government to take the initiative, it would be in danger of forestalling the intentions of its Ally."   In order to leave him no doubt whatever as to the degree of our co-operation, I felt it necessary to acquaint him with a passage in M. Sazonov's instructions to the Russian ambassador in Belgrade, in which it is stated that France and Great Britain have declared openly that they have no intention at all of joining issue with the Triple Alliance over the conflict. "Broadly," added M. Poincaré, "it all comes to this: if Russia goes into the war, France will do the same, as we know that in this matter Germany would stand at Austria's back." I asked whether he knew the British standpoint in the matter; Poincaré replied that according to his information the London Cabinet would confine itself for the moment to promising Russia its full diplomatic support, but that this would not exclude more substantial assistance in case of necessity.

The effect of Poincaré's vigorous policy upon the attitude of the French government towards Russia's conduct in the Balkans is admirably summarized by Izvolski in his letter of December 18, 1912, to Sazonov: [17]

It is still only a short time since the French Government and Press were inclined to suspect us of egging Serbia on, and one was constantly hearing people say that France has no desire to go to war about a Serbian port (*France ne veut pas faire la guerre pour un port Serbe*). Now, however, there is astonishment and unconcealed dismay at our indifference to Austria's mobilization. Anxiety in this regard is finding expression not only in the conversations of French Ministers with me and with our military attaché, but is reaching the general public and newspapers of very varying political tendency. The French General Staff is so concerned that, as I reported in my telegram No. 445, the War Minister thought fit to draw Poincaré's attention to the fact. Poincaré showed me Millerand's letter, which he had put before a Council of Ministers called specially for this purpose. French astonishment has been anything but dissipated by the telegram from Georges Louis containing the reply of our general staff to General de la Guiche. I was shown the text of the telegram. According to this, General de la Guiche was told that we not only regard Austria's arming as a purely defensive measure, but that Russia would not strike even in the entirely improbable event of an Austrian attack on Serbia. At this information Poincaré and all the Ministers were utterly astonished.

Poincaré's insistence that he should have knowledge of, and a veto upon, Russian conduct in the Balkans, lest it result in some form of exploitation of the situation which would advance Russian interests and not those of the French, is expressed in a telegram of Izvolski on January 30, 1913: [18]

Under present conditions, and in view of the existing system of alliances and agreements, any isolated action in Balkan affairs on the part of one Power or another may very quickly lead to a general European war. The French Government fully realizes and recognizes the special situation of the Russian Government, which has to take account of nationalist feeling and of all-powerful historic traditions; the French Government is making no attempt to rob Russia of her freedom of action or to throw doubt on her moral obligations towards the Balkan States. Russia is therefore assured by France not only of armed assistance in the event defined in the Franco-Russian agreement, but also of the most decided and energetic support of all measures adopted by the Russian Government in the interest of those States. But precisely in order that France may be able at any moment to extend to Russia her friendly help as an Ally in the fullest degree, the French Government earnestly asks us to take no steps on our own account without a prior exchange of views with France, our Ally; for only on this condition can the French Government successfully prepare public opinion in France for the necessity of participating in a war.

IV. POINCARÉ BECOMES PRESIDENT OF FRANCE

Because of the uncertainty in French political life, due to the group or *bloc* system, Poincaré concluded to resign as Prime Minister and become a candidate for the French presidency, an office with a term of seven years, which would give him much greater certainty of maintaining a definite and consistent foreign policy. A powerful French President like Poincaré would be able to control appointments to the cabinet. As President for seven years, with subservient foreign ministers, he knew that he had a far better prospect of continuing the French policy he had marked out in conjunction with Izvolski than he would have in the precarious position of Premier and Foreign Minister in a French cabinet. Matters were headed right and he did not desire to take any chances on having everything upset by so likely an eventuality as an overthrow of a French cabinet.[19]

Izvolski well understood the importance of making Poincaré's election certain and he telegraphed home frantically for large sums of Russian money to bribe the French press and members of the Senate and Chamber of Deputies in order to further Poincaré's candidacy and election. In particular was it necessary to combat the *Radical,* the organ of M. Perchot, which was vigorously attacking Poincaré's foreign policy and the closer relations with Russia.[20] The following is a representative telegram asking for Russian financial aid. It was sent on January 3, 1913: [21]

Poincaré asked me to draw your attention again to the Perchot affair, which continues to be a source of anxiety to him. He says that the arrangement with the Russian banks mentioned in Perchot's letter to V. N. Kokovtsov is at present under consideration in the Finance Ministry, and that he hopes that you will make a point of working for a satisfactory settlement. I learn from an entirely trustworthy source that it is very important to Poincaré that the affair shall be disposed of by January 4 (old style), the date of the Presidential election, for Perchot can do a great deal of harm in this election. I am of opinion that it is greatly to our interest to give Poincaré's candidature this assistance.

The Russian aid proved adequate and Poincaré was easily elected on the 17th of January, 1913.   About two weeks after the election Izvolski tells of a long conference with Poincaré, during which the latter gave assurance of his ability to maintain personal control of French foreign policy during his seven years as President, and urged Izvolski to come to him directly in case he desired to discuss important matters in this field: [22]

I have just had a long talk with Poincaré.   He told me that in his capacity of President of the Republic it would be perfectly possible for him directly to influence France's foreign policy.   He will not fail to take advantage of this during his seven years of office to assure the permanence of a policy based on close harmony with Russia.   He also expressed the hope that he would continue to see me often, and asked me to go direct to him in every case in which I felt this desirable.   In regard to current affairs he spoke in much the same vein as Jonnart yesterday.   As he put it, it is of the greatest importance to the French Government to have the opportunity of preparing French public opinion in advance for participation in any war which might break out over the Balkan question.   This is why the French Government asks us not to take any separate action which might result in such a war without a prior understanding with France.

In another place Izvolski tells us that after he became President Poincaré went to the Foreign

Office almost daily, and that no important step was taken without his full knowledge and approval. (*Livre Noir,* II, pp. 19–20.) This presents an illuminating contrast to Poincaré's hypocritical and dishonest implication in his *Foreign Affairs* article (loc. cit., p. 15), where he represents himself to have been but the merest ornamental figure-head as the French President, and suggests that all matters of foreign policy were handled responsibly and exclusively by the Foreign Minister, who was in this case Viviani.

V. THE BRIBERY OF THE FRENCH PRESS

Not only was it necessary to get money from Russia to aid Poincaré in becoming President of France; Russian gold was also essential in the campaign to bribe and corrupt the French press so that the French people might come to have the same enthusiasm for a war over the Balkans as that possessed by Poincaré and his associates. Consistently through 1912 and 1913 Izvolski wrote or telegraphed home for Russian money to bribe the French editors and writers to prepare articles, news and editorials designed to frighten or incense the French public.[23]

The following memorandum of Izvolski to Sazonov on July 21, 1913, telling of an interview with Poincaré and of the need of more money for the bribery of the Paris papers, is representative of these insistent demands for Russian pecuniary aid in the corruption campaign. It is to be noted that Izvolski was astute enough to put the "kept" Paris editors on a monthly installment basis so that they would consistently deliver the goods. This particular communication was first printed by C. L. Hartmann in the *Deutsche Rundschau* in the summer of 1924. It was believed by Dr. von Wegerer to be either spurious or altered (*Kriegsschuldfrage,* August, 1924), but it has been identified under oath by former Russian Prime Minister, Kokovtzov, in the libel suit of the *Matin* against *Humanité*. It is printed in *Behind the Scenes in French Journalism,* by "A French Chief Editor," and reproduced in large part in *The Progressive* for February 1, 1926:

No. 348.   Strictly confidential.

DEAR SERGEI DIMITRIEVITCH:

From this interview I was convinced that M. Poincaré is in every respect in accord with us, considers the moment has finally arrived to realize the century-old aims of our traditional policy (the seizure of the Straits), and therewith restore the European balance of power by the return of the stolen provinces of Alsace-Lorraine.

Poincaré did not conceal the great difficulties which we have to overcome yet. The principal trouble he expects from the radical Socialists who are opposed to any war caused by financial or commercial reasons, especially when its origin is in the Balkans.   This party has some highly intelligent men: Caillaux, Herriot, Painlevé, and disposes of a considerable number of deputies and newspapers.   Of the latter, some have only few readers—*Le Radical, La Lanterne, Le Rappel, L'Action, L'Aurore, La Dépêche de Toulouse*—but they have much influence.   They are the mouthpiece of some prominent leader and accorded by his partisans unflinching political obedience.   Each of these publishers and leaders is backed by a group of deputies and senators who want to rise with him and submit themselves without contradiction . . . M. Poincaré shares my opinion that a very large sacrifice on our part is necessary for this purpose.   I hardly dare to mention the amount: *three million francs*, of which 250,000 francs alone is for the *Radical*, the organ of Senator Perchot. If we consider, that the Turkish Government has spent five millions to influence the French press and bought even one of their most prominent authors (Pierre Loti) and if we also contemplate the relative insignificance of this amount in comparison to the world-changing program which we can bring closer to realization therewith, you may want to undertake to submit this proposition to the cabinet for their immediate consent.

I propose that the subsidy be paid in monthly installments as heretofore in order to be sure every minute of the zeal of the newspapers.   I consider it advantageous this time not to use Lenoir but Laffon.   Laffon has considerable influence with the *Matin*, whose financial director he was, as well as with the great dailies.

Izvolski.

Sazonov made the following reply to this request for funds:

No. 2155.   To be kept strictly secret.
                                          July 15/28, 1913.

In consequence of your Excellency's letter of July 8/21 (No. 348), I have not failed to submit your proposition and the report of your conversation to the cabinet, *presided over by His Majesty.* It is a great joy to be able to communicate to you *that the request of the President of the Republic regarding the amounts to be put by us at the disposition of the press,* has, after some natural hesitations (quelques hesitations bien compréhensibles), *been granted by His Majesty* with the condition that, as heretofore, Privy-Counselor Raffalovitch will be entrusted with the financial part of the transaction. The State-Counselor Davidov will start for Paris immediately with the most far-reaching instructions.

                                          SAZONOV.

The report of A. Raffalovitch, Paris representative of the Russian Ministry of Finance for many years before the World War, rendered on November 19, 1913, setting forth the nature of his second series of bribery payments for the month, gives a fair idea of the nature and extent of this press campaign:

Le Radical (Perchot's paper) second installment
.... 120,000 francs.
La Lanterne (Millerand's paper) ...   35,000 "
Le Figaro ....   25,000 "

Le Temps	50,000	francs.
La Libre Parole	80,000	"
L'Aurore (Clemenceau's paper) second installment		
....	45,000	"
La Gaulois	25,000	"
La Liberté	30,000	"

The personal part taken by Poincaré in supervising the distribution of these funds is indicated in a telegram of Izvolski on October 23, 1912, asking for a subvention of 300,000 francs to lubricate the French political machinery: [24]

It is important to do nothing without informing M. Poincaré and securing his consent, for good results can only be expected subject to this being done. French statesmen are very adept in deals of this sort. My conversation with M. Poincaré has convinced me that he is ready to lend us his assistance in this matter, and to let us know the most suitable plan of distribution of the subsidies. . . . He expressed to me his liveliest gratitude for my discussion of the matter with him in all candor, and added that he would himself have approached me to ask me to do nothing without prior agreement with him.

This bribery was productive of violently anti-German and anti-Austrian articles written by Tardieu, Chéradame and others in the semi-official *Temps* and elsewhere. Tardieu also aided Poincaré and Izvolski in distributing the Russian money. This shows how inadequate is Poincaré's characterization of Tardieu as a "mere journalist." The joint campaign of bribery and publicity was wholly successful in "Balkanizing" the Franco-Russian Alliance and arousing a most active and solicitous French interest in Balkan problems, towards which they had been indifferent before 1912. The French by 1914 were more willing to support Poincaré in a war over the Balkans and the Near East. In the meantime the Russian military preparations had proceeded apace, financed by supervised French loans which the Russians were compelled to expend chiefly for military purposes. By June, 1914, the preparatory program outlined by Poincaré and Izvolski was much nearer completion than in November, 1912.

VI. DELCASSÉ REPLACES GEORGES LOUIS

In the spring of 1913 there were but three important unfulfilled desires in the joint policy of Izvolski and Poincaré. The first was the fact that the French Ambassador at St. Petersburg, Georges Louis, was sympathetic with the group in Paris who desired to delay war over the Balkans and to check the dangerous collusion between Poincaré and Izvolski.[25] Hence, he was no man to handle the French case at the Russian capital. Sazonov, Izvolski and Poincaré were all agreed upon this, and on February 17, 1913, M. Louis was dismissed and replaced by M. Theophile Delcassé, a man who was scarcely

second to Poincaré in his desire to avenge 1870.
In fact, Delcassé had been the most tireless of all
French diplomats in the generation preceding
1912 in working toward the diplomatic isolation
of Germany, and the organization of an effective
coalition against her.   The failure of his aggressive policy in the first Morocco crisis had led
to his resignation from the ministry at that time.
He had also had a distinguished part in further-
ing the Franco-Russian Alliance, as in August,
1899, he had been the man who went to St.
Petersburg and effected what amounted to a
transformation of the Franco-Russian Alliance
from a purely defensive to an offensive basis.
To promote an aggressive policy between France
and Russia no man short of Poincaré himself
could have been more appropriately chosen for
the Russian post. When Delcassé had completed his mission he returned to Paris to collaborate with Poincaré and Izvolski at home.
He was succeeded by Maurice Paléologue, one
of the most ardent members of the Poincaré
clique.   It was he who had worked out with Izvolski the Franco-Russian naval convention of
July 16, 1912.[26] During this same period the
moderate French Ambassador at Vienna, M.
Crozier, was replaced by the bellicose puppet, M.
Dumaine.

In his recent defense in *Foreign Affairs* for
October, 1925, Poincaré has attempted to defend

himself in the Louis case by a discreditable attack upon M. Louis and his deadly memoirs.[27] Poincaré's defense of himself in this episode has been subjected to merciless, if dignified, criticism by Professor Sidney B. Fay in the *New Republic* for October 14, 1925 (pp. 199–200). In his memoirs Poincaré continues his defense, but he is utterly unsuccessful in explaining the chief point in the case against him, namely, the replacing of the moderate Louis by the firebrand, Delcassé. Izvolski's complete understanding of the character of Delcassé, as well as of what was expected of him during his mission to Russia, is well manifested in communications of February 17 and March 13, 1913: [28]

Jonnart has also asked me to transmit to you the request to obtain the All-Highest approval of the appointment of M. Delcassé as ambassador in St. Petersburg. He added the following information: The French Government has been moved to this choice mainly by the circumstance that in the eyes of leading French circles and of public opinion M. Delcassé is regarded, in the present exceedingly grave international situation, which may call for the application of the Franco-Russian Alliance, as a personality of quite special authority, a sort of personification of the Alliance. From this point of view it is very important that when appointed ambassador M. Delcassé shall be able to retain his mandate as Deputy. The legal obstacle to this, arising from the principle that Deputies may only be entrusted with temporary commissions, is purely formal in character and can be overcome by periodical renewals of the decree by the President, for which precedents exist. I venture to add on my own account that M. Delcassé, whose past political career is familiar to you, is entirely devoted to the idea of the very closest association between Russia and France, and, as one of the most influential parliamentarians in France, may play, if the critical moment should come, a decisive part in overcoming any hesitation on the part of the Government, which is always exposed to pressure from various quarters. I know that it is desired here to proceed as quickly as possible with Delcassé's appointment.

As you are aware, M. Delcassé is specially competent not only in questions of foreign politics but in all that concerns military and especially naval matters. Our military attaché has learned that he is specially commissioned to persuade our military administration of the necessity of increasing the number of our strategic lines, in order to enable our army to be more rapidly concentrated on the western frontier. M. Delcassé is so well informed on this matter and is so familiar with the views of the French General Staff that he can discuss the question quite independently with our military authorities. He is also empowered to offer Russia all the financial assistance required, in the form of railway loans.

The Russian government was in need of money for the building of railroads, the increase of armament, and other general purposes. The French refused to make these loans except on the condition that Russia use a considerable proportion of the money in the building of strategic railroads to the German frontier and in greatly increasing the size of the Russian army. This fact is well brought out in the letter of Kokovtsov, Russian Minister of Finance, to Sazonov on June 27, 1913: [29]

The chairman of the Paris Stock Exchange, M. de Verneuil, has told me that while in St. Petersburg he is commissioned to communicate to us the standpoint of the French Government in regard to the floating in France of Russian Government loans, guaranteed by the State. This he has defined to me as follows:

"I have been authorized to tell you that the French Government is ready to allow Russia to obtain in the Paris market every year from 400 to 500 million francs in the form of a State loan, or of a loan guaranteed by the State, for the realization of a national programme of railway construction, subject to two conditions:

"1. That the construction of the strategic lines planned out in collaboration with the French General Staff is begun at once;

"2. That the effective peace strength of the Russian army is considerably increased."

Morel, in his *Secret History of a Great Betrayal,* thus summarizes the Russian military preparations:

(a) Passing by the Duma of a law extending the term of service with the colors from three to three and a half years, involving an increase of the Russian Army of about 450,000 men for six months in the year

(October-April); (b) passing by the Duma of a law providing for an increase of the annual contingent of recruits by 130,000 men; (c) loan of £20,000,000 contracted in Paris for improvements in strategic railways and roads in Russian Poland; (d) immense accumulation of stores of all kinds—the estimates for war expenditures for 1914 jumping to £97,500,000 from £87,000,000 in 1913, the 1913 figures showing an increase of £13,000,000 over 1912; (e) a complete mobilization (May, 1914) of all the reserves of the three annual contingents of 1907 to 1909, ordered for the whole empire under the form of "exercises" at an expenditure of £10,000,000 sterling; the "exercises" were to take place in the autumn, but the war turned them into real practice.

That Poincaré was willing to recognize the joint responsibility for Franco-Russian military increases is well borne out by the fact that he at once took the lead in putting through the great French army bill of 1913, reviving the three-year service practice, a policy urged by Izvolski.[30]

VII. ENGLAND IS TAKEN IN TOW

The second major achievement still in part unfulfilled early in 1913 was to bring England into thorough accord with the Franco-Russian policy and to provide for an Anglo-Russian agreement upon joint naval action. By 1910 Lord Haldane (*Before the War*, pp. 31 ff.) had worked out complete plans, in consultation with the French, as to how and where the British were to land 160,000 men in France near the Belgian frontier (the Belgians had refused the British request to land them on Belgian soil) to aid the French, in coöperation with the "assistance of Russian pressure in the east." Thus, even the military basis of the encirclement policy had been laid no less than four years before the War. We have already seen how Poincaré on his visit to Russia in August, 1912, had revealed the existence of this verbal agreement between France and England as to joint action. This was reduced to writing in a letter of Sir Edward Grey to Paul Cambon, French Ambassador at London, on the 22nd of November, 1912, five days after Poincaré had given Russia a free hand in the Balkans: [31]

MY DEAR AMBASSADOR,—From time to time in recent years the French and British naval and military experts have consulted together. It has always been understood that such consultation does not restrict the freedom of either Government to decide at any future time whether or not to assist the other by armed force. We have agreed that consultation between experts is not and ought not to be regarded as an engagement that commits either Government to action in a contingency that has not yet arisen and may never arise. The disposition, for instance, of the French and British Fleets respectively at the present moment is not based upon an agreement to co-operate in war.

You have, however, pointed out that, if either Government had grave reason to expect an unprovoked attack by a third Power, it might become essential to know whether it could in that event depend upon the armed assistance of the other.

I agree that if either Government had grave reason to expect an unprovoked attack by a third Power, or something that threatened the general peace, it should immediately discuss with the other whether both Governments should act together to prevent aggression and to preserve peace, and, if so, what measures they would be prepared to take in common.

If these measures involved action, the plans of the General Staffs would at once be taken into consideration, and the Governments would then decide what effect should be given to them.

After the outbreak of the Balkan Wars Poincaré put still more pressure on Great Britain for more explicit arrangements as to joint military action in the event of a European war. Izvolski thus describes these efforts and their results in a dispatch of December 5, 1912:

Since the beginning of the present crisis M. Poincaré has not ceased, on every occasion, to invite the London cabinet to confidential conversations, with the object of clearing up the position which would be adopted by England in the event of a general European conflict. On the British side no decision has been taken hitherto. The London cabinet invariably replies that this would depend upon circumstances and that the question of peace or war will be decided by public opinion. On the other hand, not only has the examination of all eventualities which may present themselves not been interrupted between the French and British headquarters staffs, but the existing military and naval agreements have quite recently undergone a still greater development, so that at the present moment the Anglo-French military convention is as settled and complete (*a un caractere aussi achevé et complet*) as the Franco-Russian convention; the only difference consists in the fact that the former bear the signature of the chiefs of the two headquarter staffs, and on this account are, so to speak, not obligatory upon the Government. These last few days General Wilson, the English chief of staff, has been in France, in the most rigorous secrecy, and on this occasion, various complementary details have been elaborated; moreover, apparently for the first time, it is not only military men who participated in this work, but also other representatives of the French Government.

Early in 1912 Lord Haldane, who had two years earlier completed his plans for crushing Germany between France and England on the west and Russia on the east, visited Berlin in the effort to bring about better relations between Germany and England. He was favorably received and certainly might have been able to promote a definite accord had it not been for Poincaré, who heard of the pacific developments and warned Sir Edward Grey that to confirm the

Haldane negotiations would be to terminate the existing Franco-British relations. Grey, with humiliating docility, rejected the German proposal. Izvolski reveals this fact, together with the extent of the Anglo-French military plans in a letter of December 5, 1912: [32]

England's views are incomparably more important. In my conversations with Poincaré and Paléologue I was informed, in strict confidence, that, during Lord Haldane's well-known visit to Berlin (in February), Germany made Great Britain a very definite proposal to the effect that the British Cabinet should give a written undertaking to remain neutral if Germany became involved in a war not provoked by her. The British Cabinet informed M. Poincaré of this proposal which Great Britain apparently hesitated either to accept or reject. Poincaré expressed himself most emphatically against any such undertaking. He pointed out to the British Government that the signing by Great Britain of such a treaty with Germany would, with one blow, put an end to the present Franco-British relations. This objection had its due effect: the British Cabinet declined Germany's proposal.

Since the commencement of the present crisis, Poincaré has never failed to draw the British Cabinet into confidential conversations in order to obtain certainty as to the attitude which Great Britain proposed to adopt in the event of a general European conflict. . . . Not only has the examination of all conceivable possibilities by the French and British general staffs not been interrupted, but the existing military and naval agreements have quite recently been extended in such a manner that, at present, the Anglo-French Military Convention is just as thoroughly and exhaustively worked out in detail as is the Franco-Russian. . . .

Sazonov was not satisfied, however, with the Anglo-French agreement. He felt that there must be greater assurance of English participation in the prospective war. In a secret Russian conference of December 31, 1913, he expressed himself as follows:

In reality a Russian initiative supported only by France would not appear particularly dangerous to Germany. The two States would hardly be in a position to deal Germany a mortal blow, even in the event of military successes, which can never be predicted. A struggle, on the other hand, in which Great Britain participated might be disastrous to Germany, who clearly realizes that if Great Britain were drawn in, the result might be social disturbances of a catastrophic nature within her frontiers in less than six weeks. Great Britain is dangerous to Germany, and in the consciousness of this is to be found the explanation of the hatred with which the Germans are filled in the face of Great Britain's growing power. In view of this it is essential that before taking any decisive steps the Tsar's Government shall assure itself of the support of the London Cabinet, whose active sympathy does not seem, in the Minister's view, to be certain.

The next step was to bring about an Anglo-Russian naval convention. Poincaré and Izvolski seized upon the opportunity provided by the visit of Sir Edward Grey and the British King to Paris in April, 1914. In a conference between Sir Edward Grey and M. Doumergue, the French Prime Minister, the former expressed himself as heartily in favor of this naval convention and promised to attempt to win over Asquith to this arrangement: [33]

When the discussion of the various questions of current politics on the order of the day had come to an end, M. Doumergue came to the question of Russo-British relations, and made to Sir Edward Grey the representations which he and I [Izvolski] had agreed on. He brought into the field two main arguments in favour of a closer Russo-British agreement:

1. The German efforts to detach us from the Triple Entente, as a weak and unreliable political combination, and

2. The opportunity afforded by the conclusion of a naval convention between us and Great Britain of releasing part of the British naval forces, not only as regards active operations in the Baltic and North Sea, but also in the Mediterranean.

(M. Doumergue mentioned to Sir Edward Grey, among other things, that in two years' time we should have a strong Dreadnought squadron in the Baltic.)

Sir Edward Grey replied to M. Doumergue that he was personally entirely in sympathy with the ideas which he had expressed and was quite ready to con-

clude an agreement with Russia in the form of that
in existence between Great Britain and France.   But
he did not conceal from M. Doumergue that there
were, not only in the Government party but even
among the members of the Cabinet, persons who were
prejudiced against Russia and very little inclined to
any further approach to her.   However, he expressed
the hope that he would be able to bring over Mr.
Asquith and the other members of the Government to
his view. . . . Sir Edward Grey's idea is that only a
naval convention could be concluded between us and
Great Britain, and not a land convention, since all the
British land forces are already distributed in advance and they obviously could not co-operate with the
Russian forces.   He added that on his return to London he would at once submit the above plan to Mr.
Asquith and his other colleagues for examination.

On the 12th of May Sir Edward Grey summoned Count Benckendorff, the Russian Ambassador at London, and told him with enthusiasm of how he had won over Asquith to the plan
for a naval arrangement with Russia: [34]

On this occasion Grey spoke with a warmth unusual
for him, showing that he has a solid basis for his conclusions.   It is evident what led him to send for me to
make such a communication.   He wanted to let me
know that a new phase of still closer approach to
France was beginning.   This intention was still more
evident to me when he went straight on to remark that
I had no doubt been informed of the discussion which
he had had with Doumergue about Russia.   He told

me that in Paris, away from his colleagues, it had been impossible for him to do more than express his own personal agreement with the plan that the Governments of Great Britain and France should inform the Russian Government of all the existing military agreements between Great Britain and France. To-day, he said, he was able to tell me that immediately after his return to London he had discussed this with the Prime Minister, and that the latter had agreed with his view and had had no objections to offer to the proposed plan.

These arrangements were carried forward until the outbreak of the World War rendered them superfluous. The naval convention between England and Russia was not actually signed, but we do know that before England entered the War she had begun active coöperation with Russia in the joint Anglo-Russian naval plans and manœuvres. The actual signing of the Anglo-Russian naval convention was temporarily delayed because of a "leak" which alarmed the Germans and made Grey cautious. But the Russian representative was in London awaiting the favorable moment when the War actually broke out and made such action unnecessary. It is an interesting commentary upon the diplomacy of Sir Edward Grey that at this very time he was also carrying on negotiations with Germany designed to settle Anglo-German tension over the Near East and Africa, and to promote a general Anglo-German understanding which would render any military or naval coöperation with France and Russia quite unnecessary.[35]

While subsequent events proved that England was thoroughly involved in the military and naval plans of France and Russia and felt herself honor-bound to enter any war waged by France against Germany, it is quite true that Russia and France were never sure of the degree to which they could count upon British aid until August 2, 1914. As late as July 31, 1914, Poincaré went so far as to telegraph George V, urging England to declare herself openly as on the side of France and Russia, and both Sazonov and Poincaré were worried from July 24th to August 2nd about England, though they felt fairly certain that they could count on her aid. Whatever their doubts, however, they were without any foundation. Not even the German proposal to keep out of Belgium or the German promise not to attack France in 1914 was adequate to secure English neutrality. Thus, England was safely "hooked" by April, 1914, if not by November, 1912, even if France and Russia were not convinced of the certainty of their "catch."

VIII. THE CONVERSION OF SAZONOV TO THE WAR POLICY

The third element in the policy of Poincaré and Izvolski was to convert Sazonov to the view that the Straits were absolutely essential to a successful Russian foreign policy and could be obtained only by a European war. The failure of the Balkan League, with the resulting struggles among the Balkan allies, put a disastrous end to the hope which Sazonov had entertained that the Straits might be secured for Russia through the Balkan Wars. By the close of 1913 Sazonov had become converted to the war policy, and from that time on he presented a united front with Izvolski and Poincaré. In a famous memorandum to the Tsar, sent on December 8, 1913, he frankly confesses to his conversion to the war program: [36]

Our doubts of the continued vitality of Turkey bring again to the fore the historic question of the Straits and of their political and economic importance to us. . . . Can we permit any other country to obtain entire control of the passage through the Straits? To ask the question is to answer it—"No." To give up the Straits to a powerful State would be equivalent to placing the whole economic development of Southern Russia at the mercy of that State. . . .

Moreover, *I must repeat that the question of the Straits can hardly be advanced a step except through European complications.* To judge from present conditions, these complications would find us in alliance with France and possibly, but not quite certainly, with Great Britain, or at least with the latter as a benevolent neutral. In the event of European complications, we should be able to count in the Balkans on Serbia and perhaps also on Roumania.

In December, 1913, and February, 1914, were held the famous secret Russian Crown Councils, at which the question was considered as to whether Russia should seize Constantinople and the Straits suddenly and unaided, or should await the expected World War. It was decided that the latter alternative was much the most attractive. Sazonov explicitly remarked that "it could not be assumed that our operations against the Straits could take place without a general European war, and that it was to be assumed that under such circumstances Serbia would direct all her forces against Austria-Hungary." Plans were accordingly drawn up dealing in great detail with the military activities which Russia would execute in the campaign against Turkey in the event of the World War.[37] On the 23d of March, 1914, the Tsar reported, to use his own words, "I entirely approve of the resolutions of the Conference." [38]

Nothing remained now but to wait for the spark which would kindle the fire in the Balkans. But the Russian delay was not an idle one. Morel, in his *Secret History of a Great Betrayal* (see full report in Bogitshevich, *Causes of the War*, pp. 126–134), tells how

In February, 1914, the Tsar received Serbia's "Minister President," M. Paschitsch. There ensued between these two worthies an alluring conversation, in the course of which Paschitsch congratulates the Tsar that "Russia had armed herself so thoroughly," following up the compliment by a modest request for 120,000 rifles, munitions and howitzers, the Tsar replying that Sazonov shall be furnished with a list of Serbia's requirements, plus a polite inquiry as to the number of men "Serbia can put in the field." "Half a million," answers Paschitsch. The Tsar is delighted. "That is sufficient, it is no trifle, one can go a great way with that." They part with mutual esteem. "For Serbia," remarks the Tsar, "we shall do everything. Greet the King and tell him. For Serbia we shall do all."

Russian gold was poured into Serbia to aid and encourage the Serbian plotters against the Austrian throne. We also have evidence of direct complicity on the part of Russian authorities in the specific plot for the assassination of the Archduke. Colonel Bozine Simitch and Dr. Leopold Mandl have now shown that there is conclusive evidence that Dragutin Dimitrijevitch, Chief of the Intelligence Division of the Serbian General Staff, who laid the plot for the assassination of the Archduke, worked in collusion with Artamanov, the Russian military attaché at Belgrade.[39] The French nationalists also encouraged the Serbian intrigues. As early as 1909 the distinguished French writer, E. Lémonon, had declared that "Serbia must be made a dagger in the flank of Austria." [40] France also made extensive loans to the Balkan States and defeated proposed loans to Austria.

IX. FRANCO-RUSSIAN WAR AIMS

It has been frequently stated by French apologists and their American advocates, such as Bernadotte Schmitt, that there is absolutely no documentary evidence that France insisted on the recovery of Alsace-Lorraine as her reward for participation in the Franco-Russian Alliance. Georges Louis makes it clear that there was no need for mentioning this in the diplomatic communications of Izvolski, for, before Izvolski left for Paris, the French program of recovering 'Alsace-Lorraine in the event of a European war had become axiomatic in all discussions of the objectives of the Franco-Russian Alliance. To mention it continually would have been as foolish and unnecessary as for a writer on modern astronomy to preface his book with his allegiance to the Copernican system. As early as August, 1910, Georges Louis committed to writing the universally accepted objectives of the Franco-Russian Alliance: [41]

In the Alliance, Constantinople and the Straits form the counterpart of Alsace-Lorraine.

It is not specifically written down in any definite agreement, but it is the supreme goal of the Alliance which one takes for granted.

If the Russians open the question [of the Straits] with us, we must respond: "Yes, when you aid us with respect to Alsace-Lorraine."

I have discovered the same idea in the correspondence of Hanotaux with Montebello.

We now know that this "same idea" was rein-
forced by Delcassé while on his mission to Russia
in 1913.[42]

The unmitigated hypocrisy and dishonesty in
Sazonov's contention that France and Russia
promised Turkey territorial integrity in return
for Turkish neutrality is well revealed in Izvolski's telegram of August 11, 1914, in which he
states that the French Foreign Minister recommended that Russia attempt to purchase Turkish
neutrality by promising Turkey inviolability of
her territory. He was careful to state, however,
that any such promise to Turkey made in 1914
.would not in any way prevent Russia "from deciding the Dardanelles question according to her
own wishes at the close of the war." [43] As early
as September 2, 1915, we know that there existed
between Russia and France "a political agreement which recognized Russia's right to the final
possession of Constantinople after the conclusion
of peace," later embodied in the Secret Treaties.[44]

After the War had begun under such auspi-
cious circumstances, with England safely in on
the side of France and Russia, the French added
to the return of Alace-Lorraine the demand that
German economic power should be destroyed.
This is revealed in a telegram of Izvolski to
Sazonov on October 13, 1914.[45]

Continuation. Personal. Very confidential. Del-

cassé then referred to the negotiations which took place
in St. Petersburg in 1913, and earnestly asked me to
draw your attention to the fact that the demands and
aspirations of France remain unaltered, with the addition only of the necessary destruction of the political
and economic power of Germany.

As the War went on the French demands as to
German humiliation grew more severe. By
February 14, 1917, they included not only the
return of Alsace-Lorraine but also the seizure of
the Saar Basin and the disintegration of the German Empire through the detachment of the Rhine
Provinces. These demands were embodied in an
exchange between Sazonov and the French Ambassador in St. Petersburg on February 14, 1917.
How much earlier they had been formulated we
cannot say. These French war aims follow: [46]

1. Alsace-Lorraine to be restored to France.

2. The frontiers (of this territory) to be extended
so as to include at least the former Duchy of Lorraine
and to be fixed according to the wishes of the French
Government, the strategic requirements being taken
into account, so that the whole iron ore district of Lorraine and the whole coal basin of the Saar shall be included in French territory.

3. The remaining districts on the left bank of the
Rhine which now form part of the German Reich, are
to be detached from Germany and to be freed from all
political and economic dependence upon Germany.

4. The districts on the left bank of the Rhine which
are not incorporated in the French territory shall form
an autonomous and neutral state and shall remain oc-

cupied by French troops until the enemy countries shall
have finally fulfilled all the conditions and guarantees
to be enumerated in the Treaty of Peace.

Here we have the vital facts in the historical
indictment of France and Russia, and it does not
rest for its evidence upon any of that "micro-
scopic document-chopping" of which Mr. Simeon
Strunsky is so contemptuous.[47]   The documents
which support the case against France and
Russia are not chips and pieces but great
heaps of consistent and incontrovertible source-
material, and we invite Mr. Strunsky to chew on
this material for a few months.   The same type
of cerebro-gastronomic exercise might prove edifying to the learned archivist who wrote the New
York *Tribune* editorial of May 6, 1925, declaring that all of the material upon which the revisionists base their evidence is some chance remarks and casual asides of Izvolski which were
completely ignored by the St. Petersburg government and wholly misrepresented the French
attitude and policies.   As the present writer
pointed out in the *Progressive* for December 1,
1926, Poincaré's efforts to clear himself in his
memoirs have been totally inadequate and unsuccessful.

In the light of the material brought forward in
this chapter the following quotations from Sir
Edward Grey's speech of August 3, 1914,
and his recent memoirs are at least mildly amusing: [48]

I can say this with the most absolute confidence—no
Government and no country has less desire to be involved in a war over a dispute with Austria and Serbia
than the Government and the country of France. . . .

France, indeed, dreaded war, and did all she could to
avoid it.   French minds were probably more preoccupied with the awful peril of war to France than with the
dread of war as a general catastrophe.   The immense
growth and strength of Germany had smothered all
French intention to attempt a *revanche*.   The idea of
recovering the lost provinces of Alsace and Lorraine
had tacitly been dropped, though the French Government might not have dared to say in public that it had
been forever abandoned.   The Franco-Russian Alliance
did not contemplate or cover a French *revanche*. . . .
That the Tsar, or Sazonof, or anyone who had a decisive word in Russia was planning to provoke or to make
war I do not believe.   Perhaps it may be true to say,
of Russia, that she was like a huge, unwieldy ship,
which in time of agitation kept an uncertain course;
not because she was directed by malevolent intentions,
but because the steering-gear was weak.

X. CONCLUSIONS

(1) The original or basic thread in the immediate causes of the World War is to be found
in the Russian desire to secure control of the
Straits leading out of the Black Sea.   The man
who manipulated this program was Alexander
Izvolski, Russian Foreign Minister and later
Russian Ambassador to Paris.

(2) In 1908 he made an effort to open the
Straits through diplomacy.   He consented to

Austrian annexation of Bosnia and Herzegovina, in return for which Austria was to support
Russia in her program for the Straits.   Austria
agreed, and annexed Bosnia and Herzegovina,
but England blocked Russia in her attempt to
open the Straits.   After some more futile diplomatic manœuvring, Izvolski became convinced
that the Straits could only be secured by a European war—"the road to Constantinople is
through Berlin"—and he set about it so to direct
the European situation that when the time came
Russia would be in a position where victory
would be probable.

(3)   Hence, in 1910 he went to Paris.   In 1912
his plans were notably furthered by the entry of
Raymond Poincaré, a leader of the revenge and
military group in France, into the office of Premier and Foreign Minister of France.   Poincaré's dominating ambition was the restoration of
Alsace-Lorraine.   Izvolski quickly saw that he
could exploit Poincaré's desire to recover the
Lost Provinces in the interest of getting French
support for Russia's aspirations in regard to the
Straits.   He received cordial support from Poincaré.   Though the two men disliked each other
personally, and distrusted each other to some degree, they worked together with unwavering persistence and consistency to advance their joint
program of a European war which would accomplish the dual result of returning Alsace-Lorraine
to France and securing the Straits for Russia.

(4) Franco-Russian military coöperation had been assured by 1893. A naval agreement was worked out in July, 1912. Poincaré was opposed to war in the Balkans in 1912, because the Russians were not yet ready for war and the minds of the French people had not yet been prepared for the prospect of a war over the Balkans. Yet he feared a premature war less than he did the prospect of Russia's getting the Straits without the European war which was essential to the recovery of Alsace-Lorraine. Hence, he promised that if Russia went to war with Germany over the Balkans France would follow and make the struggle a general European conflict. Poincaré further safeguarded his scheme by insisting that he have full knowledge of Russian diplomatic activity in the Balkans, lest events might take some turn which would secure the Russian ambitions without realizing the aims of France.

(5) While awaiting the satisfactory incident in the Balkans over which war might be precipitated, French and Russian military preparations were to be hastened, and the French people made ready for war by a campaign of anti-German and anti-Austrian propaganda in the French papers, whose editors and writers were bribed by Russian funds obtained by Izvolski for that purpose and disbursed under the direction of Poincaré, Klotz, Berthelot and Tardieu.

(6) In order to insure permanence in his for-

eign policy, Poincaré resigned as Premier and Foreign Minister and became President of France. He retained his control over foreign policy, however, and informed Izvolski that all important matters in foreign policy were to be discussed with him directly.

(7) The moderately inclined French Ambassador in St. Petersburg, Georges Louis, was recalled and was replaced by the leader of the anti-German sentiment in France, Delcassé, who pressed the French war aims at St. Petersburg, and supervised the disbursement of the French loans to Russia, which were mainly directed to financing the army increases and the building of strategic railroads to the German frontier.

(8) England was brought into line with the program of Izvolski and Sazonov through the Grey-Cambon correspondence of November, 1912, and the preliminary arrangements for the Anglo-Russian naval convention in the spring of 1914. While the French and Russians did not feel thoroughly sure of British aid until August 2, 1914, subsequent events proved that Grey felt that his promises and British interests bound him to support France in any war with Germany.

(9) By December, 1913, Sazonov, the Russian Foreign Minister, announced his conversion to the war policy in regard to the Straits.

(10) On December 31, 1913, and February 8, 1914, the Russians held secret Crown Councils

in which they considered the proposition of suddenly pouncing upon Turkey and seizing Constantinople and the Straits. They rejected this proposal in favor of awaiting a general European war.

(11) The Tsar, having promised Serbia Russian protection in the summer of 1913, received the Serbian Premier early in 1914, heartily encouraged the Serbian nationalist ambitions, and promised the Serbians arms and ammunition for their army.

(12) The crux of the whole matter was admirably stated by Colonel House in his letter of May 29, 1914, to President Wilson: "Whenever England consents, France and Russia will close in on Germany and Austria."

SELECTED REFERENCES

L'Alliance franco-russe: troisième livre jaune; Bausman, F., *Let France Explain;* Becker, O., *Bismarck;* Ewart, J. S., *The Roots and Causes of the Wars, 1914–1918;* Fabre-Luce, A., *La Victoire;* Friedjung, H., *Das Zeitalter des Imperialismus;* Gooch, G. P., *Modern Europe, 1878–1914;* Huddleston, S., *Poincaré;* Judet, E., *Georges Louis; Les Carnets de Georges Louis;* Laloy, E., *Les Documents secrets des archives du ministère des affaires étrangères de Russie;* Langer, W. L., "The Franco-Russian Alliance, 1890–1894," in *Slavonic Review,* 1925; "Poincaré, Avenger of France," *New Republic,* October 15, 1924; "Izvolski and Poincaré," Ibid., April 15, 1925; Earl Loreburn, *How the War Came;* Marchand, R., *Un Livre noir; La Condamnation d'un régime;* Morel, E. D., *The Secret History of a Great Betrayal;* Poincaré, R., *The Origins of the War; Au Service de la France;* Schmitt, B., "Triple Alliance and Triple Entente," in *American Historical Review,* April, 1924; Schreiner, G., *Entente Diplomacy and the World, 1909–1914;* Seeger, C. L., *The Memoirs of Alexander Iswolsky;* Stieve, F., *Der Diplomatische Schriftwechsel Iswolskis, 1911–1914; Im Dunkel der Europäischen Geheim-diplomatie; Isvolsky and the World War; Deutschland und Europa 1890–1914.*

FOOTNOTES AND FURTHER REFERENCES

1 Friedrich Stieve, *Isvolsky and the World War,* pp. 15–16.

2 Ibid., p. 16.

3 Ibid., p. 17. Cf. E. Judet in *Humanité,* January 17, 1924.

4 Stieve, op. cit., Chap. ii.

5 Ibid., pp. 54 ff.

6 W L. Langer, in the *New Republic,* April 15, 1925, Part II, pp. 13–14.

7 *American Historical Review,* July, 1923, pp. 747–8.

8 Ibid., April, 1924, pp. 457–8.

9 Stieve, op. cit., p. 83. The reader may well be reminded here that Dr. Stieve is the world's foremost authority on the Russian documents involved in the question of the pre-war diplomacy. His five volume edition of these documents, *Der Diplomatische Schriftwechsel Iswolskis, 1911–1914,* has superseded the earlier collections by Laloy and Marchand. In this chapter the references to the documents are made to those in Professor Stieve's analytical volume based on his collection of documents. He here reproduces the most relevant documents, and they are thus available in English translation. In each case he gives in brackets the number of the document in his five volume collection. It is to be hoped that this collection will be translated into English as the Kautsky Documents and the Austrian *Red Book* have already been. It has been charged that American and English publishers and foundations have been singularly unwilling to undertake this because they desire to keep these incriminating documents from American and English readers as long as possible.

10 Stieve, op. cit., p. 87.

11 Ibid., p. 88.

12 Ibid., pp. 89–90.

13 Ibid., pp. 91, 118.

14 Ibid., p. 90.

15 Ibid., p. 106.

16 Ibid., p. 113. In his memoirs (see English edition, pp. 310–

313) Poincaré attempts to clear himself in relation to this blank check of November, 1912, but the best he can do is to prove that he insisted upon knowing the Russian plans and policies, something which Izvolski himself fully emphasized in many telegrams.

[17] Stieve, op. cit., pp. 122–3.

[18] Ibid., p. 135.

[19] Cf. Lindsay Rogers, "The French President and Foreign Affairs," in *Political Science Quarterly*, December, 1925; R. H. Soltau, *French Parties and Politics*, p. 17; Joseph Barthélemy, *The Government of France*, Chaps. vi, viii; *Le Président Poincaré;* R. Poincaré, *How France is Governed*.

[20] Stieve, op. cit., pp. 129 ff.

[21] Ibid., p. 132.

[22] Ibid., p. 134.

[23] Ibid., pp. 117 ff., 134 ff.; the *New Republic* and the New York *Nation*, February 6 and 20, 1924.

[24] Stieve, op. cit., p. 117.

[25] Ernest Judet, *Carnets de Georges Louis; Georges Louis*.

[26] *L'Alliance Franco-Russe: troisième livre jaune français*, No. 93–5. Cf. J. Debrit, in *Vers la verité* pp. 114–19.

[27] loc. cit., pp. 11–2.

[28] Stieve, op. cit., pp. 137–8.

[29] Ibid., pp. 169–70.

[30] Ibid., pp. 167 ff.

[31] J. S. Ewart, *The Roots and Causes of the Wars, 1914–1918*, pp. 117–18.

[32] *Russia and France on the Road Towards War*, p. 16; E. D. Morel, *The Secret History of a Great Betrayal*, p. 12.

[33] Stieve, op. cit., pp. 197–8.

[34] Ibid., p. 199.

[35] Cf. E. M. Earle, *Turkey, the Great Powers and the Bagdad Railway*, pp. 266 ff.

[36] Stieve, op. cit., pp. 180–81, 187–9.

[37] The full minutes of these Crown Councils are contained in the appendix to Stieve, pp. 219 ff.

[38] Ibid., p. 194.

[39] Ibid., p. 209; and *Clarté*, May, 1925.

[40] André Chéradame was particularly active in this sort of intrigue.

[41] Ernest Judet, *Georges Louis*, p. 143.

[42] Stieve, op. cit., pp. 247–8.

[43] *France and Russia on the Road Towards War*, p. 22.

[44] Ibid., p. 23.

[45] Stieve, op. cit., p. 248.

[46] F. Stieve, *Iswolski im Weltkriege*, p. 213.

[47] See editorial in New York *Times*, September 15, 1924.

[48] Grey of Fallodon, *Twenty-Five Years, 1892–1916*, Vol. II, pp. 22–3, 313.

CHAPTER IV

THE ASSASSINATION OF THE
ARCHDUKE AND THE AUSTRO-
SERBIAN CRISIS

I. THE POLITICAL DEVELOPMENT AND INTER-
NATIONAL RELATIONS OF SERBIA

In no respect has the newly revealed information been more startling or revolutionary than with regard to the explicit and direct guilt of Serbia in precipitating the immediate causes of the World War. Down to 1919 it was very generally believed that Serbia was an oppressed and innocent little country, wholly lacking in responsibility for the assassination of the Archduke, and desirous of doing everything within the bounds of reason to satisfy the utterly unjustifiable and insulting demands of Austria-Hungary. The Commission appointed by the Peace Conference at Paris in 1919 to investigate the responsibility for the War reported that "a crime committed by an Austro-Hungarian subject within territory of the Dual Monarchy can in no way compromise Serbia," and contended that "the war had arisen in consequence of Austria-Hungary's deliberate intention to destroy this brave little country." [1]

Recent evidence has, however, proved the full guilt of the Serbian civil and military authorities. The facts in this matter are brought together with force, clarity and the most thorough scholarship by Professor Sidney B. Fay in the New York Times *Current History Magazine* for October and November, 1925. Readers may be referred to these articles, to Victor Serge's article in *Clarté* for May, 1925, and to Miss Edith Durham's book, *The Serajevo Crime,* and her article in *Current History* for February, 1927, for the details of the murder plot and the revelations of Serbian responsibility.

No examination of the guilt of Serbia could be adequate which is not based upon an initial understanding of the rudimentary political development of the Balkan states in general as well as of Serbia in particular. The prevailing technique of government in this area has been a mixture of tyranny, intrigue and assassination. In 1903 the entire royal family of Serbia and most of their ministers were assassinated in one of the most brutal murders in the annals of political history. Edward VII of England ostentatiously blacklisted the dynasty which was brought in by the wholesale murders. The present dynasty of Serbia was thus installed, and it was one of the members of the band of assassins of 1903 who took the lead in the plot of 1914. It must be made clear that however natural may have been the Serbian aspirations for the hegemony of the Balkans and the realization of a Greater Serbia, there was nothing in the political life and institutions of Serbia which would have justified intrusting Serbia with political leadership and control.   By 1914 she had not yet learned the lessons of orderly self-government at home, to say nothing of possessing the capacity to bring adjacent peoples under her dominion. Whatever the defects in the political methods of the Austro-Hungarian Dual Monarchy, there can be no doubt that Austria was far better fitted to govern the Jugo-Slav peoples within her boundaries than was Serbia to emancipate them and bring them under her administration. Nothing could be more misleading than Professor Slosson's comparison of the Serbian intriguers with the Italian followers of Mazzini and Cavour.   Serbian nationalism had been inflamed by the Austrian annexation of Bosnia and Herzegovina in 1908, the menacing attitude of Austria in the period of the Balkan Wars of 1912–1913, and petty Austrian oppression in such instances as the so-called "Pig War." [2]

The Serbian plots and intrigues against Austria were encouraged by Russian approval and by Russian support of Serbian officials and plotters.   The latter were given a feeling of assurance and security by the Russian promises of protection against Austria in the summer of 1913 and in February, 1914.   In other words, Russia encouraged a type of Serbian activity which was bound sooner or later to bring about an acute Austro-Serbian crisis, and in 1914 intervened in behalf of Serbia in this crisis which she had herself helped to create.[3]

II. SERBIA AND THE SARAJEVO PLOT

1. *The Plot and Its Authors*

In 1913–1914 the Serbian plotting against Austria for the emancipation of Bosnia and Herzegovina and the independence and unification of Jugo-Slavia exceeded all previous developments, and among these intrigues was the "Black Hand" plot which actually brought on the World War.   The background of the plot to assassinate the Archduke Franz Ferdinand, heir apparent to the Austrian throne, must be found in the general plotting of the "Black Hand," the most aggressive and active of the various groups which were busy organizing intrigues in Serbia against the Austrian government.   Among the membership of about one hundred thousand were many important officials in the Serbian army and administrative force.   They were encouraged in their activity by Russian funds, the instigation of secret Russian agents, and the definite understanding between the Serbian and Russian governments that Russia would intervene to protect

Serbia against any just punishment by the Austro-Hungarian Dual Monarchy. The Russian minister at Belgrade, von Hartwig, who handled the relations between the Russian and Serbian governments in 1914, was one of the most notorious and corrupt characters among the unscrupulous Russian diplomats of the pre-War period.[4]

Even before January, 1914, the "Black Hand" had decided that their great stroke should be the assassination of Franz Ferdinand, and they awaited an appropriate and suitable time for the execution of the plot. In March of 1914 it became known that Franz Ferdinand was to inspect the army manœuvres at Sarajevo in Bosnia during the following June. The conspirators seized upon this as the opportunity for which they had been waiting, and plans were quickly matured for the execution of the plot.[5] The leader was Colonel Dragutin Dimitrijevitch, the Chief of the Intelligence Division of the Serbian General Staff, and one of the leaders in the wholesale murders of 1903 which established the reigning Serbian dynasty.[6] Seton-Watson, nevertheless, calls him "an attractive personality." [7] The three volunteers who were chosen to carry out the actual assassination were Tchabrinovitch, Printsip and Grabezh. By some these men have been represented as pure and noble-minded patriots, who, like Nathan

Hale, regretted that they had only one life to give for their country. As a matter of fact they were actually rattle-brained adventurers. Even R. W. Seton-Watson, whose hatred of Austria and whose love of the Serbians amounts to a veritable obsession, has described them in the following words: "All three were consumptive and neurasthenic and found it hard to make ends meet, and were ready for any deviltry." [8]   They were taken into tow by Dimitrijevitch and his aides, Tankositch and Tsiganovitch. Tsiganovitch was the friend and confidant of Premier Pashitch of Serbia. These men gave the three prospective assassins elaborate training in the use of revolvers, furnished them with automatic pistols, ammunition and bombs from the Serbian arsenal, and arranged the details of the process of smuggling them into Bosnia where they awaited the coming of the Archduke.[9]

These facts were revealed by a courageous professor of history at Belgrade, Stanoje Stanojevitch, a member of the *Narodna Odbrana,* another Serbian nationalistic and revolutionary society. It had been charged by some that the *Narodna Odbrana* had been responsible for the plot to assassinate the Archduke, and Stanojevitch appears to have written his brochure incriminating Dimitrijevitch in order to clear his own society. This pamphlet [10] was written in 1923, and revealed the complicity of the Serbian

army officers in the assassination plot. We did
not at that time know that the Serbian civil government possessed any information about the
plot before the assassination, and the Serbian
Premier, Mr. Pashitch, in 1914 repeatedly denied any knowledge whatever of the plot or the
plotters. Since 1923 we have, however, received
the startling revelation that in 1914 the Serbian
cabinet knew about the plot nearly a month before the assassination took place. In 1924 an
exuberant volume was published in Belgrade
celebrating the tenth anniversary of the outbreak of the World War which had brought
such glorious results to the Serbians in the way
of the realization of the Greater Serbia aspirations. To this volume, entitled *The Blood of
Slavdom,* one article was contributed by Mr.
Ljuba Jovanovitch, Minister of Education in the
Pashitch cabinet in July, 1914.[11] He reveals the
full knowledge of the plot possessed by the cabinet by the end of May, 1914: [12]

At the outbreak of the World War, I was Minister
of Education in M. Nikola Pashitch's Cabinet. I have
recently written down some of my recollections and
some notes on the events of those days. For the
present occasion I have chosen from them a few extracts, because the time is not yet come for everything
to be disclosed.

I do not remember whether it was at the end of
May or the beginning of June, when one day M.

Pashitch said to us (he conferred on these matters more particularly with Stojan Protitch, who was then Minister of the Interior; but this much he said to the rest of us): that certain persons (neki) were making ready to go to Sarajevo to murder Franz Ferdinand, who was to go there to be solemnly received on St. Vitus Day. As they told me afterward, this plot was hatched by a group of secretly organized persons and by patriotic Bosno-Herzegovinian students in Belgrade. M. Pashitch and the rest of us said, and Stojan agreed, that he should issue instructions to the frontier authorities on the Drina to prevent the crossing over of the youths who had already set out from Belgrade for that purpose. But the frontier "authorities" themselves belonged to the organization, and did not carry out Stojan's instructions, but reported to him (as he afterward told us) that the instructions had reached them too late, because the youths had already crossed over.

In spite of this information in the possession of the Serbian cabinet, the Serbian government took no active steps either to frustrate the plot or to warn the Austrian government of the danger to the Archduke in his prospective visit to Sarajevo. As Professor Fay puts it: "The Austrian Foreign Office never received any 'warning' of any kind from the Serbian government." [13] There is some evidence that Jovan Jovanovitch, the Serbian Minister in Vienna, passed on a hint to Bilinski, the Austrian Minister of Finance, that some Bosnian soldier at Sarajevo

might substitute a ball cartridge for a blank cartridge. It would appear that Bilinski, if he received such information, never handed it on to
the Archduke or Count Berchtold.[14]

From reliable Serbian sources the writer
learned in the summer of 1926 that the Serbian
King and Crown Prince were also thoroughly acquainted with the plot before its execution, and
that the Crown Prince gave valuable presents to
the plotters and helped support their chief publication.

2. The Execution of the Plot

A number of authorities, most notably Mr. H.
Wickham Steed, author of the notorious myth
concerning the plot supposed to have been
hatched between the Kaiser and Franz Ferdinand for the conquest and redistribution of
Europe at their meeting at Konopischt in June,
1914,[15] have stated that Austrian authorities
made no effort whatever to protect the Archduke
on his visit, thus indicating that many in the
Austrian government itself desired to see the
Archduke assassinated. There is no ground
whatever for this assertion. In the first place,
the Austrian authorities did not possess any
definite knowledge of the plot, and, in the second
place, what seemed to be thoroughly adequate
provisions for the protection of the Archduke
had been made. The great defect in the ar-

rangements for the defense of the Archduke lay
in the fact that the detectives sent to protect
him at Sarajevo were strangers in the locality
and, hence, extremely ineffective in their protective measures. The only remaining precaution which might have been taken would have
been to bring a large detachment of troops into
Sarajevo, but such procedure would never have
been tolerated by a man of the personal bravery
of Franz Ferdinand.[16] One of the conspirators,
Mr. Jevtitch, tells of the seeming elaborateness
but practical helplessness of the precautionary
measures taken by the Austrians to protect the
Archduke in Sarajevo: [17]

The preparations made by the Austrian police for
guarding the Archduke were as elaborate as they were
ineffective. On the day before the arrival of the Archduke a complete cordon enveloped the city. Hundreds
of detectives came from Vienna in order to make the
surveillance more complete. . . . But all these new
agents, possibly even more zealous than those of
Bosnia, appeared at a great disadvantage. They
knew neither the language nor the identity of those
they were expected to watch. They examined the pass
of Printsip and let him enter Sarajevo, imagining,
doubtless, that they had passed a rural Bosnian going
to see the sights. In the same way they passed as
"merchandise" the bombs and arms coming from Tuzla.

The plot for the assassination of the Archduke
was so perfectly planned that there was no

chance whatever of his escaping. The details
of the assassination were thus revealed to Mr.
Clair Price in 1924 by one of the conspirators of
1914: [18]

Prinzip first learned of the Archduke's intended
visit to Serajevo in a paragraph which appeared in a
Zagreb paper in April, 1914. Somebody cut out the
paragraph and mailed it to Prinzip, who was then in
Belgrade, having been expelled from Serajevo by the
Austrian police. There was only the clipping in the
envelope, nothing else. Prinzip found all the help he
needed at Belgrade. The arms were smuggled in a
single package from Belgrade direct to Serajevo, and
were delivered to a man named Ilitch, who was the
head of the organization here. Prinzip himself, along
with Gabrinowitsch and the other volunteers, were
smuggled across the frontier and into Serajevo by a
chain of Orthodox families, all of whom belonged to
the organization.

On the night before the assassination Prinzip suddenly appeared at his home in the country near here.
His people had supposed he was still in Belgrade, but
they asked no questions and he told them nothing.
He put his arms round his father, his mother and his
sister and kissed them good-bye. In five minutes he
was gone. At 7 o'clock the next morning he went to
a coffee house near the Hotel Central, where Ilitch was
distributing the arms to the six volunteers. Given
the complete lack of protection which the Austrian
military authorities afforded to the Archduke that
morning, nothing on earth could have saved him. Six
men were waiting for him, and if Prinzip had missed

him, there was another ready a few yards further along
in the street and another a few yards still further.

As it happened, only two of the six were needed.
The Archduke's train reached the station from his
general headquarters at Ilidja, a fashionable watering
place about ten miles from Serajevo, at 9:50 o'clock.
An inspection of the guard delayed him at the station
until 10. The two and a half miles between the station and the quay took him about fifteen minutes.
There were only three cars in the procession, the
Archduke, his wife and the Austrian Governor in the
first and the Archduke's staff in the two following.
The Mayor was to make an address of welcome at the
Town Hall, that big pink and yellow building further
up the quay above the corner here.

They passed Gabrinowitsch about 10:15, and, as
everybody knows, Gabrinowitsch's bomb was tipped out
of the car by the Archduke himself and exploded under the car behind, injuring the Chief of Staff, who
was hurried away to the hospital at once, while the
Archduke's car continued along the quay to the Town
Hall without stopping. At the Town Hall the Mayor,
who knew nothing of the attack, began his address of
welcome, but the Archduke burst out, "What is the
good of your speeches? I come to Serajevo on a visit
and get bombs thrown at me. It is outrageous."
With that burst of temper the Archduke went back to
his car, intending to go to the hospital to see how
badly his Chief of Staff had been injured. At the
rate of speed at which his car traveled it took only
two minutes to return to this corner from the Town
Hall, but here his car had to slow down to make the

turn. You can see for yourself that the turn is a
sharp one and the street is not very wide.

Prinzip and the rest of them were waiting here just
around the corner, and Prinzip himself jumped on
the running board of the car before it had time to
resume its speed. What he did is history. Both the
Archduke and his wife were dead almost before the
car could be stopped. It happened just here, on this
patch of new pavement on which we are standing.

It is interesting to follow briefly the career
of Dimitrijevitch, who led the plot. If the culpable members of the Serbian civil government
have remained to gloat over the assassination,
such was not the good fortune of Dimitrijevitch.
By 1916 it began to appear that there was a
reasonable prospect that the Central Powers
would win the War, and particularly that Austria
would conquer Serbia. Pashitch and his associates were panic-stricken, lest in such an eventuality the Austrian government should take up
once more the question of the responsibility for
the murder plot of 1914 and discover the complicity of the Serbians. Hence it was decided
that Dimitrijevitch must be removed. The
plans for his murder were put under the general
supervision of General Zivkovitch and this same
Ljuba Jovanovitch, who has more recently revealed the prior knowledge possessed by the
Serbian cabinet concerning the plot. They were
aided by the renegade, Tsiganovitch. At first

an attempt was made to assassinate Dimitrijevitch, but this failed. The Serbian government
then resorted to a faked-up charge of treason,
and condemned Dimitrijevitch to death by what
was a most notorious and obvious process of judicial murder. He was shot at Saloniki in June,
1917. It is one of the most curious ironies of
fate in all history that the very information which
the Serbian government hoped would pass out of
existence with the death of Dimitrijevitch was
actually later revealed to the world by the same
man who was in general charge of the plans to
put Dimitrijevitch out of the way.[19]

3. Serbian and Russian Responsibility

In the light of these facts we must certainly
agree with Professor Fay that the full responsibility for the immediate crisis, which ultimately
was manipulated into the origins of a general
European war, falls entirely upon Serbia: [20]

From what has been said above it will be seen that
the Serbian Government was doubly responsible for
the crime which became the occasion of the World
War. It was responsible for permitting, in spite of
its promises of 1909, the subversive nationalistic agitation of the Narodna Odbrana and its affiliated agents,
which tended to encourage a series of political assassinations of Austrian personages, of which the Sarajevo crime was but the culmination. It also was responsible for the Serbian officers who directly aided

in the preparation of the plot in Belgrade and the successful smuggling of the assassins and their weapons across the frontier from Serbia into Bosnia. Furthermore, the Pashitch Cabinet was aware of the plot for nearly a month, but took no effective steps to prevent its execution or to warn the Archduke of the impending danger.

Even Professor Seton-Watson admits that unless new facts can be brought forth to disprove the assertions of Stanojevitch, Jovanovitch and Simitch, the Serbian government must be held responsible for having plotted an assassination designed to advance Serbian national aspirations through provoking a European war: [21]

Public opinion in Europe and America is more interested than ever in the problem of responsibility for the Great War, and is entitled to demand a full and detailed explanation from Ljuba Jovanovitch and from his chief, Mr. Pashitch. Failing that, it will henceforth be necessary for the historian, while exposing the aggressive Balkan policy of the Ballplatz and emphasizing the criminal negligence of the Austro-Hungarian authorities in Bosnia, to convict the Serbian Government of the calculation that the assassination might serve their national ends and in oblivion of the fact that "murder will out." The crime of Sarajevo is an indelible blot upon the movement for Jugoslav unity.

As yet no evidence has been forthcoming to alter the facts so thoroughly and competently

amassed by Fay and Miss Durham.   The anti-
Austrian group eagerly awaited Seton-Watson's
Sarajevo, but the book proved a distressing failure.   The best the author could do was to attempt to divert the reader's attention from Serbia by suggesting who might have shot the Archduke if he had not been assassinated by the Black
Hand.

It is important to note, however, that both
Fay and Seton-Watson deny that these facts
justified the action of Austria following June
28, 1914.[22]   We shall examine this matter more
thoroughly later, but it would seem that whatever the element of unwisdom in the Austrian
policy, in an absolute or cosmic sense, there can
be no doubt whatever that any other modern
state placed in Austria's position in the summer
of 1914 would certainly have acted as severely
and harshly in the circumstances as did Austria;
and, if we may judge from their activities in the
past, many would certainly have behaved in a
much more rash and precipitate fashion.   Austria's action was unjustifiable and unpardonable
only in the sense that pacific diplomatic negotiations must be viewed by all rational beings as superior to the test and arbitrament of force.   But
in 1914 no powerful state or group of states had
ever set the precedent for behaving in this rational fashion when confronted by an international crisis as serious as that which faced Austria

after June 28, 1914. As Lowes Dickinson has well said (*International Anarchy,* p. 463): "I do not believe there was a State in existence that would not, under similar circumstances, have determined, as Austria did, to finish the menace, once for all, by war."

As to the degree of the direct responsibility of Russia for the assassination plot, and the problem of whether Russian as well as Serbian officials knew of the plot before it was executed we cannot make any final statement as yet. Russian encouragement of the general plotting is fully established. The Russian minister in Belgrade, Hartwig, was informed of the plot long before its execution. Colonel Bozine Simitch, Bogitshevich, and Leopold Mandl have shown that Dimitrijevitch worked in collusion with Artamanov, the Russian military attaché in Belgrade. Izvolski reports that just after the assassination he received a messenger from the King of Serbia to the effect that "we (the Serbians) have just done a good piece of work." This would seem to indicate that Izvolski must have been informed of the plot in advance of the assassination. Early in June, 1914, after the assassins had left for Bosnia, Sazonov at Constantza inquired of the Rumanians as to what they would do in the event that the Archduke was assassinated on his visit to Bosnia. Miss Durham concludes that "there are indications that at least an influential section of the Russian military were cognizant and approved of the plot." It is asserted by Col. Simitch and Mandl that Dimitrijevitch held up the plans for the plot until the Russian military attaché got into touch with Minister Hartwig and with St. Petersburg, and received Russian approval, a Russian subsidy and the promise of Russia to intervene to protect Serbia from Austria.[23] The complicity of Hartwig and Artamanov in the Sarajevo Plot was fully and independently confirmed to the writer by informed Serbians in the summer of 1926.

4. Serbian Neglect in the Punishment of the Plotters

The conduct of the Serbian government after the assassination was as remiss as it had been in its failure to warn the Austrian government before the commission of the crime. During nearly a month which intervened between the assassination of Franz Ferdinand and the Austrian ultimatum to Serbia, the Serbian government undertook no independent investigation of the responsibility for the murder on June 28th. Two days after the murder the Austrian Minister at Belgrade inquired from the Serbian government as to the measures already taken or proposed to investigate the responsibility for the double assassination and to punish the guilty.

The Serbian government replied that "up till now the police have not occupied themselves with the affair." [24] Nor did they so occupy themselves in the weeks that followed. During this same period the Serbian press glorified the assassins, and proclaimed the act to be a noble patriotic achievement.[24a] In estimating the significance of such an attitude we must remember that the Serbian government had, in 1909, made a solemn promise to the Austrian government that it would curb the intrigues and plots against Austrian authority and punish those guilty of such activity. Even the historical counsel and advocate of the Jugo-Slavs, Mr. Seton-Watson, can find little to excuse the conduct of the Serbian government in the weeks following the assassination: [25]

The Serbian Government was, however, guilty of a grave blunder in not immediately forestalling Vienna's demands by instituting a searching inquiry of its own. This omission is only very partially explained by absorption in the electoral campaign. The complicity of Major Tankositch and Tsiganovitch became known at a very early stage, and it would at least have been good tactics, if nothing else, to take some action against two notoriously suspect characters. Inaction was all the more inexcusable, in view of the frank warning administered by Herr von Zimmermann, the German Foreign Under-Secretary, to the Serbian Chargé d'Affaires in Berlin as early as July 1. He emphasized the grave consequences of any failure of Serbia "to do her duty" by proceeding against suspect persons: in that case "one could not tell what would happen." It is indeed impossible to deny Herr von Jagow's plea that the Belgrade Government, though giving official expression to its horror at the crime, took no serious steps either to search for its authors or to check propagandist excesses. Disregarding the advice of its Minister in Vienna, Jovan Jovanovitch, it remained inactive for three weeks, and when at last on July 20 it presented at Berlin a note formally inviting the German Government to use its good offices at the Ballplatz, and affirming a desire to meet Austria's demands wherever possible, it was already far too late to produce any effect either in Berlin or Vienna, and in point of fact merely brought down a severe snub from Jagow upon the head of the Chargé d'Affaires. . . .

Energetic action by Mr. Pashitch during the week or even fortnight following the murder would not of course have led the war party in Vienna to renounce its aims, but it would undoubtedly have deprived it of its tactical position and increased the chances of friendly mediation from the outside. To this extent, then, the Pashitch Cabinet must share the responsibility for what befell. It could no doubt plead absorption in an electoral campaign which threatened the whole future of the Radical Party, but a true grasp of European realities should have shown that infinitely more was at stake.

Serbian apologists have attempted to extenuate the action of Pashitch and his cabinet in 1914 on the ground that there were so many plots and rumors of plots against Austria rife in Serbia that the Serbian government would have had little time for anything else if it had taken seriously the reports of every plot and attempted to run it down and punish its instigators, but this seems to the writer a naïve and self-condemnatory excuse. If true, it would be a striking reflection upon the degree to which Serbia had made good its promises of 1909 to suppress the plots against Austria. Further, it is apparent from Jovanovitch's article that the Serbian cabinet in early June, 1914, well understood that the plan to murder the Archduke was no bogus or merely rumored plot, and that they further recognized the seriousness of the plot and the results which might be expected to follow its execution. Much more honest and plausible was the statement of a Serbian student to Miss Edith Durham, a leading English authority on Jugo-Slavia: "Yes, it is a pity so many men were killed (in the World War), but you see our plan has succeeded. We have made Great Serbia." [26] As Miss Durham has convincingly shown, it is as certain that the Serbian plotters planned to make the assassination of the Archduke the means of precipitating a European war as that the Austrian army and civil government determined to make the same deed the justification for the long delayed punishment of Serbia. The question is merely as to which was the more base and dangerous plan.[27]

Much has been made of a savage attack upon Miss Durham's book, *The Serajevo Crime,* by R. W. Seton-Watson in the *Slavonic Review* for December, 1925. The anti-Austrian group of historians in this country and England have hailed it with delight and proceeded upon the easy assumption that it leaves her book without a leg to stand on. Quite the opposite is the case. Seton-Watson does not upset or disprove a single vital assertion in this book or in Professor Fay's erudite articles with regard to the complicity of the Serbian government. It is one of those facile and clever reviews, which, by a deadly assault upon errors in minor details, endeavors to leave the reader with an impression of having over-thrown the major theses of the work. And certainly nothing of which he accuses Miss Durham with respect to her characterization of books or sources of information could be more misleading or unscholarly than his own characterization of Herr von Wegerer's *Kriegsschuldfrage.* Pertinent here is Dr. Bogitshevich's and Herr von Wegerer's criticism of Seton-Watson's own recent discussion of the Sarajevo crime in the *Kriegsschuldfrage* for January, February and October 1926. As Miss Durham and Professor Fay have shown, Seton-Watson's own work, *Sarajevo,* has proved a pathetic failure as an effort to clear the Serbs.

III. AUSTRIA'S DETERMINATION TO
PUNISH SERBIA

1. *The Jeopardy of Austria-Hungary*

The essential background for any comprehension of the Austrian attitude and conduct following the assassination must be found in an understanding of the composition and organization of the Austro-Hungarian Dual Monarchy. It was made up in part of a large number of Slavic peoples held together by the domination of the Germans in Austria and Magyars in Hungary. Any serious and successful revolt of one of those subject nationalities would have been a signal for similar efforts on the part of the others, with the resulting disintegration of the whole political structure of the Dual Monarchy. We need not necessarily take the view that the preservation of the Dual Monarchy was a matter of great moral import for the world at large, but we can readily understand how Austro-Hungarian statesmen would naturally have regarded it as the most vital necessity in their whole political policy. For some time the greatest menace to the integrity of the Austrian Empire had been the plotting of Serbia for the emancipation of the Jugo-Slavs under Austrian domination.[28] Serbia was continually an irritating nuisance to Austria—worse than the Mexican menace to the United States in the palmiest days of Francesco Villa.   Judge Bausman has well stated this parallel between Serbia and Mexico: [29]

The relation of Serbia towards Austria was like that of Mexico to us at its worst, multiplied tenfold. Let us imagine that in the United States there were several millions of Mexicans, and that a constant intrigue went on between Mexico and this body of our citizens.   To make the illustration simpler, suppose that Mexico was a negro republic and that it was in constant agitation of the negroes of the United States against our government.   Is not this a question which we would insist upon settling ourselves, and if some great Power like Russia resolved upon supporting Mexico in any such course of conduct or upon taking out of our hands the right of private settlement of our disputes with Mexico, would we not regard that other Power as aiming at our destruction?

American readers can perhaps get some idea of the Austrian feeling by imagining the attitude of the United States if Theodore Roosevelt and his wife had been assassinated at El Paso, Texas, on July 4, 1901, while watching a review of the Rough Riders; their assassins having been members of a notorious Mexican secret society which had plotted for years against the United States, with the Mexican papers acclaiming the assassination as a noble and heroic act.   There is little probability that under these circumstances the United States would have delayed even long enough to send an ultimatum to Mexico. In all probability American military forces would have been rushed into Mexico without any formal diplomatic exchanges whatever. Certainly our conduct in initiating the Spanish-American War was less provoked than that of Austria and no more creditable in the details of its execution.

With the assassination of the Archduke the Austrian statesmen believed that a final and definitive solution of the Serbian menace could no longer be postponed with safety. The long record of Serbian broken promises as to the cessation and punishment of plots against Austria convinced the statesmen of the Dual Monarchy that decisive steps must now be taken against Serbia. Great stores of arms had been secreted in Bosnia, and the Serbs expected a national uprising after the assassination. Even Sir Edward Grey frankly admitted the situation justified a definite humiliation of Serbia.[30] If Serbia was not properly punished, other plots and assassinations might take place subsequently in other parts of the Dual Monarchy with results wholly disastrous to its existence. Even Count Berchtold, the Austrian Foreign Minister, was aroused from his political lethargy and interest in sports to a determined attitude in the situation, and the

Hungarian Premier, Count Tisza, was also soon won over to the policy of strong action against Serbia.[31]

2. The Real Plans of Austro-Hungary with Respect to Serbia in the Crisis of 1914

As is the case with most other phases of the pre-War diplomacy, little dependence can be placed in the veracity of the Austrian or Serbian public pronouncements, demands and promises of 1914, and we must seek in the secret telegrams, conferences and minutes of ministerial councils the truth as to the real purposes and plans of Austria in the crisis. Not having at our disposal as yet the Serbian archives we cannot arrive with such certainty as to the secret decisions of Serbia in this period. The chief source for the discovery of the basic Austrian policy is the minutes of the Austro-Hungarian ministerial council held in Vienna on July 7, 1914.[32] From this we quickly discern the fact that Berchtold and the Austrian ministers desired a sudden surprise attack upon Serbia, but were prevented from this foolhardy policy by the opposition of the Hungarian Premier, Count Tisza. He insisted that the first move should be adequate diplomatic demands upon Serbia. If these

were refused he would approve a war upon
Serbia, provided the Austrian ministers would
agree in advance not to annex any part of Serbia.
Tisza expressed himself as believing that territorial aggrandizement at the expense of Serbia
would surely bring in Russia and provoke a
European war. Berchtold and his group
sharply maintained the opposite position, and
contended that even the most thorough-going
diplomatic victory over Serbia would be useless,
as Serbia could not be trusted to fulfil her promises. War was necessary, and the quicker the
better. The longer it was postponed the more
dangerous would become the Serbian nuisance,
the more overwhelming the military strength of
France and Russia and the larger the probability that they would interfere in any local punitive war of Austria upon Serbia. Tisza, nevertheless, refused to yield, and the council came
to the following decision: [33]

1. All present wish for a speedy decision of the controversy with Servia, whether it be decided in a warlike
or a peaceful manner.

2. The council of ministers is prepared to adopt the
view of the Royal Hungarian Premier according to
which the mobilization is not to take place until after
concrete demands have been addressed to Servia and
after being refused, an ultimatum has been sent.

3. All present except the Royal Hungarian Premier

hold the belief that a purely diplomatic success, even
if it ended with a glaring humiliation of Servia, would
be worthless and that therefore such stringent demands must be addressed to Servia, that will make a
refusal almost certain, so that the road to a radical
solution by means of a military action should be
opened.

Tisza not only opposed the war plans at the
outset in the ministerial council, but also expressed the same views in a letter to the Austrian
Emperor on July 8th. Within the next ten
days, however, Tisza yielded in some degree to
the pressure of Berchtold, Krobatin, Bilinski,
Stürgkh, Forgach, Hoyos and others of the
war party and, at a second ministerial council
held on July 19th, consented to sending an ultimatum so severe that it could scarcely be expected
that Serbia would accept it, with the result that
Austria would then intervene through a military
invasion of Serbia.[34] Tisza still insisted, however, that the military action must be preceded
by diplomatic action, and that there be a public
declaration at the beginning of the actual warfare that Austria intended no annexations or
dismemberment at the expense of Serbia. He
forced the council to make the following declaration: [35]

The Common Council of Ministers at the proposition of the Royal Hungarian Premier votes that as
soon as the war begins, the monarchy declares to the

foreign powers that no war for conquest is intended, nor is the annexation of the kingdom (of Servia) contemplated.

The Austrian Chief of Staff, Conrad von Hötzendorf, in his unusually frank and illuminating memoirs, candidly reveals the fact that the army group in Austria were from the first for quick and decisive military action against Serbia, and were greatly irritated by the necessity of awaiting prior diplomatic activities purely for the purpose of making a favorable influence upon European public opinion.[36]

Some writers have quite legitimately pointed out the fact that in his letter to the Kaiser, drafted on July 2, 1914, the Austrian Emperor had stated that "my government's efforts must in the future be directed to isolating Serbia and reducing its size." The Austrian war party was undoubtedly in favor of this policy. But Tisza quickly emphasized the fact that such a program would, in all probability, bring about the intervention of Russia and produce a European war. He, therefore, forced the change of policy which we have just described above. After Austria had proclaimed before Europe that she would respect Serbian territory there was little probability that she would attempt to violate this promise. Even Sazonov admitted that he believed Austria on this point. Hence, what the Emperor may have stated on July 2nd, or what Berchtold and his group may have wished for before being blocked by Tisza, can in no sense be regarded as the basis of Austrian policy after July 23rd. Likewise, the marginal note of the Kaiser, stating that Austria must become ascendant in the Balkans at the expense of Russia and Serbia, cannot be held to be his dominating attitude after he later changed his mind when Serbia made her apparently conciliatory reply to Austria.

From the above it will be quickly discernible that only in the light of these secret documents can we approach intelligently the policies and communications of Austria-Hungary in 1914 in regard to Serbia. Without these we might naturally suppose that Austria desired a diplomatic and juristic adjustment, when she actually aimed at nothing of the kind. The ultimatum of Austria to Serbia was to be purely a ruse to create a more favorable impression upon European opinion than might be expected to follow a precipitate military occupation of Serbia. This stratagem, it was believed, would make France and Russia less likely to intervene to prevent a local punitive war, particularly when coupled with the promise to respect the territorial integrity of Serbia. In other words, the Austrian ultimatum had a purpose identical in character with that of the French frontier withdrawal order of July 30th.   On the other hand, this proof that Austria from the beginning intended war, and that the ultimatum was not only severe but not made in good faith, does not in itself demonstrate that Austria was wrong or immoral in her conduct.   Such a conclusion could be arrived at only by proving that anything less than war would have been adequate to clear up the Serbian menace, and by showing that Austria could have proceeded to a war with Serbia in some manner less likely to incite Russia and France to legitimate intervention.   No one, to the writer's knowledge, has yet been able to bring forward conclusive evidence to establish either of these two potential indictments of Austrian procedure.[37]

Professor Schmitt has contended that Austria might have solved the Jugo-Slav problem by a more liberal policy in regard to the Slavic peoples within the Austrian Empire, but he apparently overlooked the fact that it was the Archduke's plan to give the Austrian Slavs greater freedom in a tripartite monarchy which was a chief reason for the Serbian determination to assassinate Franz Ferdinand.   There was nothing which the adherents to the Greater Serbia idea more feared than a change of Austrian policy which would make Serbians contented with Austrian rule and reluctant to fight for independence.

3. Germany Agrees to Support Austria in Punishing Serbia

Two steps were essential before launching upon the scheme of punishment.   One was to obtain the consent of Germany to the punitive policy, and the other was to carry out a careful investigation of the assassination plot and of the responsibility of the Serbian government in the premises. Down to June 28, 1914, Germany had consistently opposed forcible Austrian intervention against Serbia.   As late as July 1, 1914, Count Tisza, the Hungarian Prime Minister, accused the Kaiser of special fondness for Serbia.[38] But Berchtold and Hötzendorf believed that the Kaiser would be so horrified by this last Serbian outrage that he would at last give his consent to strong Austrian measures against Serbia.   They counted rightly upon the Kaiser's change of heart.   Berchtold formulated a personal letter from the Austrian Emperor to the Kaiser, calling attention to the imminent dangers which threatened the Dual Monarchy as the result of the Serbian plots which had culminated in the assassination of Franz Ferdinand, and asking for German approval of such punitive action against Serbia as Austria might find necessary.[39]   One of Berchtold's subordinates, Hoyos, was sent from Vienna to Berlin with this message, which was presented to the Kaiser on July 5 by the

Austrian Ambassador in Berlin, Count Szögyény.[40] The next day Bethmann-Hollweg, the German Chancellor, transmitted to Szögyény the official statement of the policy of supporting Austria which the Kaiser and his ministers had decided upon.[41]

Austria must judge what is to be done to clear up her relation to Serbia; whatever Austria's decision may turn out to be, Austria can count with certainty upon it, that Germany will stand behind her as an ally and friend.

Bethmann-Hollweg also telegraphed to Tschirschky, the German Ambassador at Vienna: [42]

As far as concerns Serbia, His Majesty, of course, cannot interfere in the dispute now going on between Austria-Hungary and that country, as it is a matter not within his competence. The Emperor Franz Joseph may, however, rest assured that His Majesty will faithfully stand by Austria-Hungary, as is required by the obligations of his alliance and of his ancient friendship.

This is the famous blank cheque which Germany gave to Austria. That this reversal of the previous restraining policy of Germany was foolish and ill-advised cannot be denied. The Kaiser himself, later in the month, frankly admitted this to be the case, and remarked in high irritation that he and Bethmann-Hollweg had thereby inserted their necks into a noose,[43]—the complete truth of which assertion he very imperfectly understood in 1914. Yet it must be kept clearly in mind that on July 5th the Kaiser felt certain that Austria would be able to take all necessary steps against Serbia without bringing on a European war. It should also be pointed out that Poincaré had given Russia what amounted to a free hand in the Balkans in the fall of 1912; and, on his trip to St. Petersburg later in July, 1914, he apparently gave Russia the same blank cheque in regard to the Austro-Serbian crisis that the Kaiser had extended to Austria on July 6, 1914.[44] And while the Kaiser only hastily and in a state of unusual excitement permitted his ally to undertake a program which was deemed essential to the integrity of the Dual Monarchy, with the firm belief that such punitive policy would not bring about a general European war, Poincaré calmly and deliberately encouraged Russia so to act, where her national safety and territorial integrity were in no sense at stake, that a general European war would be inevitable.[45]

4. The Austrian Investigation of the Assassination Plot

The secret investigation of Serbian responsibility for the assassination of the Archduke, which was ordered by Count Berchtold, was entrusted to Dr. Friedrich von Wiesner, who spent the three days from July 11 to July 13 at Sarajevo investigating the evidence which had been brought together for his scrutiny. His general conclusion was that while the Serbian government could not be proved to have instigated the plot, nevertheless the plot had originated in Serbia and had been carried out by secret societies whose activity had been tolerated by the Serbian government.[46]

On April 4, 1919, the experts of the American delegation to the Paris Peace Conference, Secretary of State Robert Lansing, and Dr. James Brown Scott, cited as the only essential part of the von Wiesner report to Count Berchtold the following paragraph: [47]

Herr von Wiesner to the Ministry of Foreign Affairs in Vienna:

Serajevo, July 13th, 1914. 1.10 P. M.

Nothing to show or even to lead one to conjecture the complicity of the Serbian Government or that it directed or prepared the crime or that it supplied the weapons used. On the contrary there is evidence that would appear to show that such complicity is out of the question.

How far this single paragraph, torn from its context is in reality from being the gist of von Wiesner's report may be seen from the following complete statement of von Wiesner's memorandum to Berchtold: [48]

That Pan-Serbian propaganda is being carried on here from Serbia as a centre, not only through the press but also through Clubs and other organizations, and further that this is taking place with the encouragement as well as with the knowledge and approval of the Serbian Government, is the conviction of authoritative circles here.   The material that has been laid before me by the civil and military authorities as the basis on which they have formed their conviction may be characterized as follows: the material belonging to the period preceding the assassination offers no evidence that would lead me to suppose that propaganda was encouraged by the Serbian Government. There is, however, material which though sparse is sufficient to show that this movement with Serbia as a centre was fostered by Clubs with the toleration of the Serbian Government.

Investigation of the crime:

There is nothing to show the complicity of the Serbian Government in the directing of the assassination or in its preparation or in the supplying of weapons. Nor is there anything to lead one even to conjecture such a thing.   On the contrary, there is evidence that would appear to show that such complicity is out of the question.   From the statements of the persons charged with the crime, it has been ascertained in a manner hardly controvertible that the crime was resolved upon in Belgrade and that it was prepared with the assistance of a Serbian state official named Ciganovic and of Major Tancosic, these two men providing the bombs, ammunition and cyanide of potassium. The participation of Pribicevic has not been proven and the first reports on this point are due to a re-grettable misunderstanding on the part of the police authorities investigating the case. It has been proved objectively and beyond all doubt that the bombs origi-nally came from the Serbian army magazine at Kragu-jevac, but there is no evidence to show that they had only recently been taken from this magazine for the special purpose for which they were employed, as the bombs may have belonged to the war stores of the Comitatschis.

Judging by the statements made by the accused, we can scarcely doubt that Princip, Cabrinovic and Grabez were secretly smuggled across the frontier into Bosnia with bombs and arms by Serbian organs at the instigation of Ciganovic. These organized transports were conducted by the Frontier Captains at Schabatz and Loznica and carried out by organs of the excise guards. Even though it has not been ascertained whether these men were aware of the purpose of the journey, they must surely have assumed the mysterious nature of the mission. Other investigations made sub-sequent to the assassination throw light upon the or-ganization of the propaganda of the Narodna Od-brana. The material obtained is valuable and can be turned to account. It has yet to be carefully exam-ined. Investigations are being made with all speed.

In the event of intentions which prompted my de-parture still remaining unchanged, the demands could be still further extended:

(a) The suppression of co-operation of Serbian government organs in the smuggling of persons and articles across the frontier.

(b) Dismissal of Serbian Frontier Captains at Schabatz and Loznica, as well as of the excise guard organs concerned.

(c) Prosecution of Ciganovic and Tankosic.

I leave this evening, arriving Vienna Tuesday evening. Will come straight to the Ministry. It is necessary that I should supplement my remarks with verbal report.

5. The Austrian Ultimatum and the Serbian Reply

Austria delayed ten days more before sending her ultimatum to Serbia. Up to July 14th the delay had been chiefly to have time to convert Count Tisza to vigorous action against Serbia, and to await the report of Dr. von Wiesner. The ten days' delay between July 14th and July 23rd, when the ultimatum was ultimately dispatched, was due to the Austrian desire to allow time for Poincaré to leave St. Petersburg and be on his way back to France before the ultimatum was delivered.[49] Austria preferred to have Poincaré out of Russia before she made her demands upon Serbia, for she quite correctly feared that Poincaré would incite the Russians to intervention, which would make it all the more difficult to

localize the Austrian punishment of Serbia.[50]
This demonstrates, however, that Austria desired,
above all, to avoid a European war; otherwise
she would have wished to submit her ultimatum
while Poincaré was in St. Petersburg, in order
to make the world conflict that much more
certain and inevitable. We now know that
Austria's precautions in this respect were all in
vain. Though Poincaré did not know of the
terms of the Austrian ultimatum when he was
in St. Petersburg, he urged the Russians to take
a strong stand in regard to whatever action
Austria decided upon, and promised complete
French aid to the Russians in whatever policy
they decided upon. This promise was subsequently confirmed by Paléologue, and by Viviani
from Reval on July 24th.[51] In his defense of
his alleged innocence as to war guilt in *Foreign
Affairs* for October, 1925, Poincaré naïvely suggests that Austria desired to have him out of
Russia before sending the ultimatum, because she
felt that if he were on his way home there would
be much greater probability of localizing the
punitive action against Serbia. He does not
seem to realize that this statement is a boomer-
ang, and one of the best bits of evidence which
we have that Austria ardently desired to avoid a
general European war.

In formulating the specific terms of the ultimatum Austria acted entirely independently of

Germany.   Bethmann-Hollweg did not receive a copy of the ultimatum until the evening of July 22, the night before its delivery, and the Kaiser first learned of the terms through a newspaper account which he read while on his vacation cruise.[52] Both Bethmann-Hollweg and von Jagow, the German Foreign Minister, believed the ultimatum too harsh,[53] but made no effort to protest, as they still adhered to the policy they had enunciated on July 6th of allowing Austria a free hand in the premises.   The actual text of the Austrian ultimatum to Serbia here follows:[54]

On the 31st March, 1909, the Servian Minister in Vienna, on the instructions of the Servian Government, made the following declaration to the Imperial and Royal Government:

"Servia recognizes that the fait accompli regarding Bosnia has not affected her rights, and consequently she will conform to the decisions that the Powers may take in conformity with Article 25 of the Treaty of Berlin. In deference to the advice of the Great Powers Servia undertakes to renounce from now onward the attitude of protest and opposition which she has adopted with regard to the annexation since last Autumn. She undertakes, moreover, to modify the direction of her policy with regard to Austria-Hungary and to live in the future on good neighborly terms with the latter."

The history of recent years, and in particular the painful events of the 28th June last, have shown the existence of a subversive movement with the object of detaching a part of the territories of Austria-Hungary from the monarchy. The movement, which had its birth under the eye of the Servian Government, has gone so far as to make itself manifest on both sides of the Servian frontier in the shape of acts of terrorism and a series of outrages and murders.

Far from carrying out the formal undertakings contained in the declaration of the 31st March, 1909, the Royal Servian Government has done nothing to repress these movements. It has permitted the criminal machinations of various societies and associations directed against the monarchy and has tolerated unrestrained language on the part of the press, the glorification of the perpetrators of outrages, and the participation of officers and functionaries in subversive agitation. It has permitted an unwholesome propaganda in public instruction. In short, it has permitted all manifestations of a nature to incite the Servian population to hatred of the monarchy and contempt of its institutions.

This culpable tolerance of the Royal Servian Government had not ceased at the moment when the events of the 28th June last proved its fatal consequences to the whole world.

It results from the depositions and confessions of the criminal perpetrators of the outrage of the 28th June that the Serajevo assassinations were planned in Belgrade, that the arms and explosives with which the murderers were provided had been given to them by Servian officers and functionaries belonging to the Narodna Odbrana, and, finally, that the passage into Bosnia of the criminals and their arms was organized and effected by the chiefs of the Servian frontier service.

The above-mentioned results of the Magisterial investigation do not permit the Austro-Hungarian Government to pursue any longer the attitude of expectant forbearance which it has maintained for years in face of the machinations hatched in Belgrade, and thence propagated in the territories of the monarchy. The results, on the contrary, impose on it the duty of putting an end to the intrigues which form a perpetual menace to the tranquility of the monarchy.

To achieve this end the Imperial and Royal Government sees itself compelled to demand from the Royal Servian Government a formal assurance that it condemns this dangerous propaganda against the monarchy; in other words, the whole series of tendencies, the ultimate aim of which is to detach from the monarchy territories belonging to it, and that it undertakes to suppress by every means this criminal and terrorist propaganda.

In order to give a formal character to this undertaking the Royal Servian Government shall publish on the front page of its Official Journal of the 26th June (13th July) the following declaration:

"The Royal Government of Servia condemns the propaganda directed against Austria-Hungary—i. e., the general tendency of which the final aim is to detach from the Austro-Hungarian monarchy territories belonging to it, and it sincerely deplores the fatal consequences of these criminal proceedings.

"The Royal Government regrets that Servian officers and functionaries participated in the above-mentioned propaganda and thus compromised the good neighborly relations to which the Royal Government was solemnly pledged by its declaration of the 31st March, 1909.

"The Royal Government, which disapproves and repudiates all idea of interfering or attempting to interfere with the destinies of the inhabitants of any part whatsoever of Austria-Hungary, considers it its duty formally to warn officers and functionaries, and the whole population of the kingdom, that henceforward it will proceed with the utmost rigor against persons who may be guilty of such machinations, which it will use all its efforts to anticipate and suppress."

This declaration shall simultaneously be communicated to the royal army as an order of the day by his Majesty the King and shall be published in the Official Bulletin of the army.

The Royal Servian Government further undertakes:

1. To suppress any publication which incites to hatred and contempt of the Austro-Hungarian Monarchy and the general tendency of which is directed against its territorial integrity;

2. To dissolve immediately the society styled Narodna Odbrana, to confiscate all its means of propaganda, and to proceed in the same manner against other societies and their branches in Servia which engage in propaganda against the Austro-Hungarian Monarchy. The Royal Government shall take the necessary measures to prevent the societies dissolved from continuing their activity under another name and form;

3. To eliminate without delay from public instruc-

tion in Servia, both as regards the teaching body and also as regards the methods of instruction, everything that serves, or might serve, to foment the propaganda against Austria-Hungary;

4. To remove from the military service, and from the administration in general, all officers and functionaries guilty of propaganda against the Austro-Hungarian Monarchy whose names and deeds the Austro-Hungarian Government reserves to itself the right of communicating to the Royal Government;

5. To accept the collaboration in Servia of representatives of the Austro-Hungarian Government in the suppression of the subversive movement directed against the territorial integrity of the monarchy;

6. To take judicial proceedings against accessories to the plot of the 28th June who are on Servian territory.   Delegates of the Austro-Hungarian Government will take part in the investigation relating thereto;

7. To proceed without delay to the arrest of Major Voija Tankositch and of the individual named Milan Ciganovitch, a Servian State employe, who have been compromised by the results of the magisterial inquiry at Serajevo;

8. To prevent by effective measures the co-operation of the Servian authorities in the illicit traffic in arms and explosives across the frontier, to dismiss and punish severely the officials of the frontier service at Schabatz and Loznica guilty of having assisted the perpetrators of the Serajevo crime by facilitating their passage across the frontier;

9. To furnish the Imperial and Royal Government

with explanations regarding the unjustifiable utterances of high Servian officials, both in Servia and abroad, who, notwithstanding their official position, did not hesitate after the crime of the 28th June to express themselves in interviews in terms of hostility to the Austro-Hungarian Government; and, finally,

10. To notify the Imperial and Royal Government without delay of the execution of the measures comprised under the preceding heads.

The Austro-Hungarian Government expects the reply of the Royal Government at the latest by 6 o'clock on Saturday evening, the 25th July.

A memorandum dealing with the results of the magisterial inquiry at Serajevo with regard to the officials mentioned under heads (7) and (8) is attached to this note.

As to the nature and justifiability of this ultimatum there is ample opportunity for the widest variety of opinions.[55] From the standpoint of the Austrian statesmen, however, who had as their background the long period of intrigues and broken promises on the part of Serbia, and who were faced on the immediate occasion with the hideous murder of their prospective monarch, it can scarcely be held that they could have been expected to adopt a more moderate or conciliatory tone.[56] It is true that the fifth and sixth demands of Austria, to the effect that Serbia should accept the collaboration of Austrian authorities in suppressing Serbian intrigues against Austria, was scarcely compatible with the rights and dignity of a sovereign state. The vital question at issue is as to whether, in the light of her conduct towards Austria, Serbia was really entitled to be treated as an independent and civilized political community. On this point the Manchester *Guardian* for August 3, 1914, said: "If one could tow Serbia to the edge of the ocean and swamp it, the atmosphere of Europe would be cleared." The reactionary British journal, *John Bull,* expressed itself in a similar vein on August 8, 1914: "Serbia ought to disappear. Let us efface it from the map of Europe." [57]

It is certain that the total failure of Serbia's past promises to put down intrigues against Austria within her boundaries had made it quite apparent to the Vienna statesmen that Serbia could not be trusted to carry out her promises in this regard. If there was to be any prospect of a suppression of the nationalistic plots, this would have to be achieved under Austrian supervision, however much this might intrude upon the sovereignty of Serbia. It must be clear then that point five was the real core of the Austrian ultimatum. For Serbia to reject this meant for all practical purposes the rejection of the whole ultimatum; but this was exactly the point which Serbia refused to concede. This demonstrates the fallacy in the easy remark of many commentators to the effect that Serbia acceded to all of the Austrian demands save one.[58]

Nevertheless, our knowledge that the Austrian civil authorities shaped their policy wholly with the aim in view of forcing a situation where war with Serbia would be inevitable, and with a complete determination not to rest satisfied with even sweeping diplomatic and juristic triumphs, makes it impossible for the informed reader to take very seriously the Austrian defense of the ultimatum as a document designed to effect a pacific adjustment of the crisis with Serbia. One may forgive the Austrians for desiring a war with Serbia, but he can have little respect for their quibbling and pretensions about a willingness to settle the dispute by diplomatic negotiations and juristic processes. The Austrians would have been as much disappointed if the Serbians had fully accepted their ultimatum as Sir Edward Grey would have been if Germany had not invaded Belgium.[59]

The Serbian reply to the Austrian ultimatum can only be understood when viewed in the light of the plans of France and Russia. If Austria hypocritically planned her diplomatic approach to the Serbian problem in order to make the proposed punitive war more palatable to European opinion, so did France and Russia similarly utilize the opportunity afforded by the Serbian answer better to prepare Europe for the initiation of the European conflict involved in their program. France and Russia desired to avoid, above all, either a truculent and arrogant attitude or an actual declaration of war on the part of Serbia. European opinion was still on the side of Austria on account of the murder of the Archduke. For Serbia to have made a haughty and insulting reply to the Austrian demands would have made matters still worse. For her to have declared war on Austria would not only have affected European opinion very unfavorably, but would have precipitated hostilities before Russia could have mobilized over her vast area.

The first efforts of France and Russia were, therefore, directed towards securing an extension of time for the Serbian reply, so as to give France, and particularly Russia, more time for their military preparations before Austria declared war on Serbia. We know from Dobrorolski that the Russian army officials assumed that the European war was *on* when they heard of the terms of the Austrian ultimatum. Baron Schilling has recently revealed the fact that Sazonov expressed the same opinion. In fact, on reading the Austrian ultimatum he specifically exclaimed: *"C'est la guerre européenne."* If France and Russia were to precipitate a European war in the guise of protectors of Serbia, it was necessary to do everything possible to make such intervention attractive before European and world opinion. Serbia must be made to appear a "brave and innocent little country" who had gone to extreme limits in surrendering to the Austrian demands—but had not quite acquiesced. For Serbia to have acceded to all of the Austrian demands would have been as embarrassing to France and Russia as to Austria.

To carry out this program of putting the "soft-pedal" on Serbia, the Russian Ministerial Council of July 24, 1914, decided to advise Serbia to avoid above everything else declaring war on Austria, and to make a response conciliatory in tone and content alike. France went even further. Philippe Berthelot, deputy political director of the French Foreign Office, and an influential person with Poincaré, once boasted to Jacques Mesnil that he got hold of M. Vesnitch, Serbian Minister in Paris, and drafted in outline the Serbian reply to Austria. This reply, as we shall see, was formulated in very conciliatory language, feigned great friendliness for and humility toward Austria, and seemed to consent to everything of significance in the Austrian ultimatum, while actually rejecting the only really important item in it. In this way, Serbia, as well as France and Russia later, were put in a good light before world opinion and Austria in an equally disadvantageous position when she proceeded to carry out the secret plans of the Austrian ministers and attack Serbia. In the diplomatic ruses of the Entente before the War there was no more clever bit of subterfuge than the planning of the Serbian response to Austria. As we shall learn later it sufficed completely to deceive even the Kaiser. These facts about the Serbian responsibility for the assassination and about the Serbian and Entente designs in the Serbian reply to Austria expose with deadly thoroughness the preposterous implications of naïve Serbian innocence and pacific expectations contained in Mr. Armstrong's article in Foreign Affairs (American) for January, 1927. The Serbian reply, submitted on July 25th, follows: [60]

The Royal Servian Government have received the communication of the Imperial and Royal Government of the 10th (i.e. 23rd, N. S., Author) instant, and are convinced that their reply will remove any misunderstanding which may threaten to impair the good neighborly relations between the Austro-Hungarian Monarchy and the Kingdom of Servia.

Conscious of the fact that the protests which were made both from the tribune of the national Skupshtina and in the declarations and actions of the responsible representatives of the State—protests which were cut short by the declaration made by the Servian Government on the 18th March, 1909—have not been renewed on any occasion as regards the great neighboring Monarchy, and that no attempt has been made since that time, either by the successive Royal Governments or by their organs, to change the political and legal state of affairs created in Bosnia and Herzegovina, the Royal Government draw attention to the fact that in this connection the Imperial and Royal Government have made no representation except one concerning a school book, and that on that occasion the Imperial and Royal Government received an entirely satisfactory explanation. Servia has several times given proofs of her pacific and moderate policy during the Balkan crisis, and it is thanks to Servia and to the sacrifice that she has made in the exclusive interest of European peace that that peace has been preserved. The Royal Government cannot be held responsible for manifestations of a private character, such as articles in the press and the peaceable work of societies—manifestations which take place in nearly all countries in the ordinary course of events, and which as a general rule escape official control. The Royal Government are all the less responsible in view of the fact that at the time of the solution of a series of questions which arose between Servia and Austria-Hungary they gave proof of a great readiness to oblige, and thus succeeded in settling the majority of these questions to the advantage of the two neighboring countries.

For these reasons the Royal Government have been pained and surprised at the statements according to which members of the Kingdom of Servia are supposed to have participated in the preparations for the crime committed at Serajevo; the Royal Government expected to be invited to collaborate in an investigation of all that concerns this crime, and they were ready, in order to prove the entire correctness of their attitude, to take measures against any persons concerning whom representations were made to them. Falling in, therefore, with the desire of the Imperial and Royal Government, they are prepared to hand over for trial any Servian subject, without regard to his situation or rank, of whose complicity in the crime of Serajevo proofs are forthcoming, and more especially they undertake to cause to be published on the first page of the "Journal officiel," on the date of the 13th (26th) July, the following declaration:

"The Royal Government of Servia condemn all propaganda which may be directed against Austria-Hungary, that is to say, all such tendencies as aim at ultimately detaching from the Austro-Hungarian Monarchy territories which form part thereof, and they sincerely deplore the baneful consequences of these criminal movements. The Royal Government regret that, according to the communication from the Imperial and Royal Government, certain Servian officers and officials should have taken part in the above-mentioned propaganda, and thus compromise the good neighborly relations to which the Royal Servian Government was solemnly engaged by the declaration of the 31st March, 1909, which declaration disapproves and repudiates all idea or attempt at interference with the destiny of the inhabitants of any part whatsoever of Austria-Hungary, and they consider it their duty formally to warn the officers, officials, and entire population of the kingdom that henceforth they will take the most rigorous steps against all such persons as are guilty of such acts, to prevent and to repress which they will use their utmost endeavor."

This declaration will be brought to the knowledge of

the Royal Army in an order of the day, in the name of his Majesty the King, by his Royal Highness the Crown Prince Alexander, and will be published in the next official army bulletin.

The Royal Government further undertake:

1. To introduce at the first regular convocation of the Skupshtina a provision into the press law providing for the most severe punishment of incitement to hatred or contempt of the Austro-Hungarian Monarchy, and for taking action against any publication the general tendency of which is directed against the territorial integrity of Austria-Hungary. The Government engage at the approaching revision of the Constitution to cause an amendment to be introduced into Article 22 of the Constitution of such a nature that such publication may be confiscated, a proceeding at present impossible under the categorical terms of Article 22 of the Constitution.

2. The Government possess no proof, nor does the note of the Imperial and Royal Government furnish them with any, that the "Narodna Odbrana" and other similar societies have committed up to the present any criminal act of this nature through the proceedings of any of their members. Nevertheless, the Royal Government will accept the demand of the Imperial and Royal Government and will dissolve the "Narodna Odbrana" Society and every other society which may be directing its efforts against Austria-Hungary.

3. The Royal Servian Government undertake to remove without delay from their public educational establishments in Servia all that serves or could serve to foment propaganda against Austria-Hungary, when-

ever the Imperial and Royal Government furnish them with facts and proofs of this propaganda.

4. The Royal Government also agree to remove from military service all such persons as the judicial inquiry may have proved to be guilty of acts directed against the integrity of the territory of the Austro-Hungarian Monarchy, and they expect the Imperial and Royal Government to communicate to them at a later date the names and acts of these officers and officials for the purposes of the proceedings which are to be taken against them.

5. The Royal Government must confess that they do not clearly grasp the meaning or the scope of the demand made by the Imperial and Royal Government that Servia shall undertake to accept the collaboration of the organs of the Imperial and Royal Government upon their territory, but they declare that they will admit such collaboration as agrees with the principle of international law, with criminal procedure, and with good neighborly relations.

6. It goes without saying that the Royal Government consider it their duty to open an inquiry against all such persons as are, or eventually may be, implicated in the plot of the 15th (28th) June, and who happen to be within the territory of the kingdom. As regards the participation in this inquiry of Austro-Hungarian agents or authorities appointed for this purpose by the Imperial and Royal Government, the Royal Government cannot accept such an arrangement, as it would be a violation of the Constitution and of the law of criminal procedure; nevertheless, in concrete cases communications as to the results of the investigation

in question might be given to the Austro-Hungarian agents.

7. The Royal Government proceeded, on the very evening of the delivery of the note, to arrest Commandant Voislav Tankossitch. As regards Milan Ziganovitch, who is a subject of the Austro-Hungarian Monarchy and who up to the 15th June was employed (on probation) by the directorate of railways, it has not yet been possible to arrest him.

The Austro-Hungarian Government are requested to be so good as to supply as soon as possible, in the customary form, the presumptive evidence of guilt, as well as the eventual proofs of guilt which have been collected up to the present time, at the inquiry at Serajevo, for the purposes of the latter inquiry.

8. The Servian Government will reinforce and extend the measures which have been taken for preventing the illicit traffic of arms and explosives across the frontier. It goes without saying that they will immediately order an inquiry and will severely punish the frontier officials on the Schabatz-Loznitza line who have failed in their duty and allowed the authors of the crime of Serajevo to pass.

9. The Royal Government will gladly give explanations of the remarks made by their officials, whether in Servia or abroad, in interviews after the crime, and which, according to the statement of the Imperial and Royal Government, were hostile toward the Monarchy, as soon as the Imperial and Royal Government have communicated to them the passages in question in these remarks, and as soon as they have shown that the remarks were actually made by the said officials,

although the Royal Government will itself take steps to collect evidence and proofs.

10. The Royal Government will inform the Imperial and Royal Government of the execution of the measures comprised under the above heads, in so far as this has not already been done by the present note, as soon as each measure has been ordered and carried out.

If the Imperial and Royal Government are not satisfied with this reply, the Servian Government, considering that it is not to the common interest to precipitate the solution of this question, are ready, as always, to accept a pacific understanding, either by referring this question to the decision of the International Tribunal of The Hague, or to the Great Powers which took part in the drawing up of the declaration made by the Servian Government on the 18th (31st) March, 1909.

Belgrade, July 12 (25), 1914.

As to the adequacy of the Serbian reply there can be as much difference of opinion as over the justice of the Austrian ultimatum. If Serbia had been a highly cultured, truly civilized, and politically developed state, with an excellent record as to the fulfillment of her promises to neighboring nations, it would most certainly have to be admitted that the Serbian reply was relatively adequate in content. In the light of the actual facts concerning Serbian politics and diplomacy, and the history of her relations with Austria in the decade before 1914, it can

scarcely be maintained that Austria could have
been satisfied short of Serbian acquiescence in
the two Austrian demands concerning Austrian
participation in the investigation of the responsibility for the plot to assassinate the Archduke
and other similar intrigues in Serbia.[61] That
the Serbians themselves recognized the truth of
this assertion is to be seen in the fact that three
hours before dispatching the messenger with her
reply to Austria the Serbian government ordered the mobilization of the 400,000 men in the
Serbian army, and made provision for the abandonment of Belgrade and retirement to Nish.[62]
It must be admitted, however, that the Austrian
complaints and arguments as to the unsatisfac-
tory nature of the Serbian reply would be far
more convincing if we did not possess the notes
of the secret Austrian ministerial councils where
it had been decided to attempt to force a war
upon Serbia, however great the degree of
Serbian diplomatic capitulation and humiliation.
Likewise, we should have more respect for the
reply of Serbia if we were unacquainted with the
plans of France and Russia and with the part
that they played in determining, not merely the
nature, but even the phraseology of the Serbian
response.

In short, in spite of the large part which the
Austrian ultimatum and the Serbian reply have
played in the discussions of war guilt, and in

spite of the space we have devoted to them here, they really have little or no real bearing upon the actual plans and motives of either Austria or Serbia in the crisis. Austria was insistent upon a punitive war no matter what the Serbian attitude, and Serbia was equally determined to resist Austria and enter the local war which she hoped would bring Russia to her rescue and set off the European conflagration that would at its close bring into being Greater Serbia. Before Austria sent the ultimatum she had made full military plans for the invasion of Serbia, and before Serbia sent her reply she had directed the mobilization of her army against Austria, six hours before the Austrian mobilization was ordered. She had been preparing for the conflict actively for more than a year, and for several months had been receiving shipments of arms from Russia in anticipation of the ultimate struggle with Austria.

The Kaiser, as we shall point out more thoroughly later, regarded the Serbian reply as a quite unexpected and complete concession to Austria, and as removing any justification for Austrian military intervention in Serbia.[63] On the other hand, the Austrians refused to accept this view, and, thoroughly in keeping with their previous secret arrangements, decided upon military activity against Serbia. On the evening of July 25th, some six hours after the mobilization

of the Serbian army, Austria ordered the mobilization of a part of the Austrian forces against
Serbia.[64]

Germany, impressed by the extensive submission of Serbia, alarmed at the prospect of Russian
intervention, and urged on by Sir Edward Grey,
began on the 27th of July to press Austria for
suspension of military activities and the opening
of negotiations with Russia on the Serbian issue.[65] To forestall further progress in this
policy Berchtold declared war on Serbia at noon
on July 28, and then contended that negotiations
concerning the Austrian policy in Serbia were
no longer possible on account of the outbreak
of war.[66]   Austria was, thus, determined not to
let the crisis of 1914 pass without what seemed
to be adequate punitive treatment of Serbia.
This she did in spite of the fact that Germany
was, after July 27, opposed to her conduct, but
she could allege justification in the original blank
cheque which Germany had handed her on the
6th of July. The rest of the story as to the
strenuous but vain efforts of Germany to restrain her ally and prevent the development of a
general European war will be reserved for a
subsequent chapter upon the rôle of Germany
in the crisis of 1914. It will be apparent, however, in spite of the misleading writings of Heinrich Kanner, that, as far as the decision upon the
policies to be followed in regard to Serbia, both

before and after July 25, is concerned, the responsibility falls almost entirely upon the statesmen and diplomats of the Dual Monarchy, though they may have been encouraged by von Moltke's precautionary telegrams.[67]

IV. AUSTRIA REJECTS DIPLOMATIC NEGOTIATIONS

There is no more misleading myth about war guilt than the once popular theory that Austrian policy towards Serbia was decided upon and forced by Germany against the better judgment and wishes of Austria, and that, when Austria in terror decided to back down before Russian pressure, Germany stepped into the breach and prevented the success of pacific negotiations by a rash, hasty and unjustifiable declaration of war on Russia. As Gooch states the case, "the readiness of Austria for an eleventh-hour compromise, of which we heard so much at the beginning of the war, proves to be a legend." [68]

The facts about the Austrian attitude towards mediation and negotiations are the following: At the time of sending the ultimatum to Serbia Austria on the same day informed the other powers that her relations to Serbia were a matter which could not be submitted to negotiation or conferences: [69]

We cannot allow the demands which we have addressed to Servia, and which contain nothing that would not be considered natural between two neighbors, living in peace and harmony, to be made the subject of negotiations and compromises.

This is in tone and content surprisingly like Sazonov's statement on July 27th that the Russians would not submit the Russian policy towards Austria to any outside parties or mediative processes: [70]

If there is any question of exercising a moderating influence on St. Petersburg, we reject it in advance.

Germany disapproved of Sir Edward Grey's proposal for a conference of powers on the Austro-Serbian issue, as she knew this would be rejected by Austria, but she suggested the opening of direct negotiations between Vienna and St. Petersburg. Sir Edward Grey heartily approved this plan.[71] Berchtold, as we have pointed out above, desired to avoid even this and declared war on Serbia on July 28th to provide the excuse that the opening of hostilities precluded the possibility of discussing Austro-Serbian relations. Recognizing the increasing prospect of a general European war, Germany became ever more insistent that Austria should open negotiations with Russia concerning Serbia. Berchtold remained adamant, if evasive, until the 31st. On that day we learn from Sazonov that the Austrian Ambassador at St. Petersburg informed him that Austria was will-

ing to discuss the contents of the ultimatum to
Serbia: [72]

> The Austrian Ambassador called on me and told me
> that his Government are ready to enter into an ex-
> change of opinions in reference to the contents of the
> ultimatum sent to Serbia.   I expressed my gratification
> and remarked to the Ambassador that it would be
> preferable to have these negotiations in London under
> participation of the Great Powers.   We hope that the
> English Government will accept the management of
> this conference, whereby it would oblige all Europe
> to gratitude.   To assist these negotiations to a suc-
> cessful end it is most desirable that Austria discon-
> tinue her military operations on Serbian territory.

On July 31st (telegram left Vienna at 1 A. M.
August 1st) Berchtold communicated to Count
Szögyény, the Austrian Ambassador in Berlin,
the following statement of his alleged willingness
to accept Sir Edward Grey's proposal of mediation between Austria and Serbia, copies of which
were also sent to the Austrian Ambassadors in
London and St. Petersburg: [73]

> I beg your Excellency to thank the Imperial Chancel-
> lor very much for the information forwarded to us
> through Herr von Tschirschky and to declare to him
> that we, in spite of the change of the situation occa-
> sioned by the mobilisation of Russia, and fully appreci-
> ating the efforts of England for the maintenance of the
> world's peace, are ready to approach the proposal of
> Sir Edward Grey of a mediation *between us and Serbia.*

We pre-suppose of course that our military action against the kingdom shall meanwhile continue and that the English Cabinet shall make the Russian Government stop the mobilisation directed against us, in which case we would of course also stop the defensive military counter-measures in Galicia, which the Russian mobilisation has forced us to undertake.

That this assumed acceptance of mediation by Berchtold was scarcely reliable or made in good faith is apparent from the fact that earlier on July 31st the Emperor of Austria had telegraphed the Kaiser that Austria would not hold up her military activities in Serbia on account of the Russian threat, that he recognized the serious implications of this decision, and that he counted upon the armed assistance of Germany in the probable European war which might follow continued Austrian hostilities in Serbia: [74]

The action my army is involved in at this moment against Servia cannot be interrupted by the threatening and insolent attitude of Russia.

A renewed rescue of Servia by Russian intervention would have the most serious consequences for my countries and I can therefore in no case admit of such an intervention.

I am fully aware of the importance of my decisions and have made them, confiding in the justice of God, with the absolute certainty that your army, as an unfailingly true ally, will stand by my country and the Triple Alliance.

It is, thus, quite obvious that neither Sazonov
nor Berchtold was acting in good faith in their
discussions of a diplomatic settlement on July
31st. Berchtold insisted on defying the Kaiser
by continuing the campaign against Serbia, instead of resting satisfied with the occupation of
Belgrade. Any talk by Sazonov at this time
about negotiations was likewise pure hypocrisy,
as the Russian general mobilization had been going on for twenty-four hours, and hence Sazonov
knew that the European war was *on* and could
not be stopped.

Austria, therefore, steadfastly refused to respond to German pressure for negotiation with
Russia concerning the Serbian crisis until after
Russia had ordered and proclaimed her fatal general mobilization which meant an inevitable and
unavoidable European war. Her apparent willingness to discuss the Serbian affair at this late
date was in all probability a fake and ruse, like
the ultimatum itself, though we cannot be sure that
this was the case, as Russia, England and France
refused to "call her bluff" and went ahead with
their war plans.[75] It was the premature Russian
general mobilization which made it impossible
for Germany to bring her pressure upon Austria
to a logical completion and for Europe to test
the genuineness or falsity of the avowed Austrian
capitulation on July 31st. It was not, as some
have contended, the German ultimatum to Rus-

sia, which came surprisingly late and was as justifiable as it was inevitable. As to whether Austria would have persisted in her stubborn determination to continue her Serbian campaign if she had been sure that she and Germany would be attacked by Russia, France, England and Italy, we cannot be certain, but it does seem that she was willing to risk a war between herself and Germany and France and Russia rather than hold up the Serbian invasion. Grey's evasiveness also certainly encouraged Austria. On July 27th Grey informed the Russians that they ought to see in the mobilization of the British fleet evidence of British intervention, while on the same day he told the Austrian Ambassador that "if Austria could make war on Serbia and at the same time pacify Russia, well and good."

V. AUSTRIAN AND RUSSIAN OBJECTIVES IN THE SERBIAN CRISIS OF 1914

The part played by Russia in the Austro-Serbian crisis is a complicated but important aspect of the case. It was the Russian intervention which transformed the local punitive war into a conflict of European proportions. This much is certain, namely, that Austria was far more justified in military intervention to punish Serbia than was Russia in the military intervention to protect Serbia, particularly as even Rus-

sian officials fully admitted that they were satisfied that Austria did not contemplate depriving
Serbia of any of her territory. Nothing could
well be more misleading than the conventional
notion that Russia was bound by either the
dictates of international morality or the obligations of a treaty to intervene to protect Serbia. The fact is that the Serbian affair of 1914
was merely the incident for which France and
Russia had been waiting in the Balkans for at
least two years in the hope of a fortunate time
for the precipitation of general European hostilities.[76] Russia had betrayed Serbia in 1908
when she believed that she could secure the
Straits by this action. Perhaps most astonishing
of all is the fact that in the secret negotiations
with Turkey from October to December, 1911,
Russia offered to protect Turkey from the Balkan states if Turkey would give Russia the freedom of the Straits. Russia had, further, encouraged the Balkan League as a means of getting the Turk out of Europe, but this failed.
Izvolski had long been convinced that war was
the only solution of the Russian program, and
Sazonov had been converted to this position by
December, 1913, and so informed the Tsar.
Even more, the Russian encouragement of Serbian plots against Austria, with the promise of
aid against Austria, removed any moral justification for Russian intervention to protect Ser-

bia from the just punishment which her actions merited. As far as the writer knows, Russia was under no treaty obligation to protect Serbia. Yet Premier Pashitch has told us that he was definitely promised Russian protection for Serbia against any attack by Austria in the summer of 1913, and we know that this was confirmed and extended at his interview with the Tsar in February, 1914.[77]

But whatever attitude one may take concerning the justification of the Austrian response to the Serbian reply to her ultimatum, this much is clear, namely, that Austria did not at any time plot or desire a general European conflict. What she was determined upon was purely a punitive invasion of Serbia. She was apparently willing to risk bringing on a European war rather than desist from her Serbian foray, but she certainly did not desire to have general complications arise out of her policy. A European war would naturally divert her forces away from Serbia toward a protection of her frontiers against the Russians, and possibly the Italians, the latter of whom had gradually slipped away from the Triple Alliance after the beginning of the present century. When the World War broke out later there was actually great confusion as a result of the necessity of transferring Austrian troops from Serbia to the Russian frontier. *There is here a difference of the ut-*

most significance for assessing the responsibility of Austria on the one hand, and France and Russia on the other, for the outbreak of the World War.

Without keeping in mind this vital distinction between the type of war desired by Austria and unwillingly tolerated by Germany, and that worked for by France and Russia from July 23rd to August 1st, it is as impossible to assess the degree of war guilt shared by the various powers as it would be to make the attempt to do so without consulting the collections of documents published since 1919. While the very existence of Austria was at stake, the safety and territorial integrity of Russia were in no sense directly involved in the Serbian crisis. Nothing could be more erroneous than to hold that Russia was as much justified in intervening to protect Serbia as was Austria in intervening to punish her.

VI. CONCLUSIONS

The following conclusions as to the Austro-Serbian crisis and its bearing upon the genesis of the World War seem justified:

(1) There was an intense nationalistic spirit among the Serbians, who desired to unite the southern Slavic peoples into a great Serbian kingdom. This aspiration was encouraged by

Russia, and was obstructed by Austria-Hungary. The Austrian annexation of Bosnia and Herzegovina in 1908 had been a severe blow to this Serbian aspiration and to Serbian pride. At this time Serbia promised to cease plotting against Austria, but this date actually marks the beginning of more active and widespread Serbian intrigues against Austria.

(2) The Serbian plans for a Greater Serbia could not be harmonized with the interests and territorial integrity of Austria-Hungary. They were still further menaced by the proposal of Franz Ferdinand, once he became Emperor of Austria, to unite all the Slavs in the Dual Monarchy into a Slavic kingdom to be federated with Austria and Hungary in a triple union.

(3) The Serbians decided that Franz Ferdinand must be assassinated to forestall this plan and also to provoke a general European war in which, through the aid of Russia, they hoped to bring to realization the Greater Serbia program.

(4) The assassination of the Archduke was planned by a high-ranking officer of the Serbian army, who furnished the assassins with arms and ammunition, trained them in pistol shooting, and smuggled them into Bosnia to await the coming of the Archduke. The Serbian civil government was fully aware of the plot a month before its execution, but did little to prevent it from being carried out and failed adequately to warn the

Austrian government as to the peril of the Archduke.

(5) Serbia undertook no independent investigation of the responsibility for the assassination, made no effort to suppress the intriguers, and the Serbian press praised the assassination as a patriotic act and a glorious national achievement.

(6) The assassination was a real challenge to the continued existence of the Dual Monarchy, and demanded severe retaliation. Even Sir Edward Grey conceded the fact that the Serbians would have to be humiliated.

(7) Austria-Hungary decided that nothing short of a punitive war would suffice to put the Serbian situation under safe control, but Count Tisza forced the Austrian authorities to go through the form of prior diplomatic pressure on Serbia. Hence, the Austrian ultimatum was deliberately framed in such fashion that the Serbians were likely to refuse certain points. The Serbian reply, drafted in outline, if not in detail, in the French Foreign Office, was designed so as to create a favorable impression on European opinion, through its combination of a conciliatory tone and seeming capitulation to Austria with actual rejection of the very core of the Austrian demands. In the light of our present knowledge of Serbian complicity in the

murder of the Archduke, Austria would appear to have been justified in her determination upon war, but this fact does not constitute a full justification of her procedure in detail in 1914.

(8) Germany gave Austria a blank cheque in regard to her settlement of the Serbian problem, but she did not have any part in framing the ultimatum, regarded it as too harsh, held the Serbian reply adequate, and disapproved the Austrian declaration of war on Serbia.

(9) When the prospect of Russian intervention threatened to precipitate a general European war, Germany severely pressed Austria to begin conversations with St. Petersburg in regard to the Austro-Serbian dispute, but Austria refused to yield at all for three days, and when she simulated consent on the 31st of July it was too late, as the fatal Russian mobilization, which meant an unavoidable European war, had then been decided upon and proclaimed.

(10) Austria was as eager to avoid a European war as she was to wage a punitive war on Serbia, and all of her plans in regard to the method of initiating the war with Serbia were determined by this basic desire to avoid a general conflict.

(11) Russia had no moral right to intervene to protect Serbia, as she had encouraged the Serbians in the very intrigues which had necessi-

tated their punishment. She had very slight diplomatic or juristic grounds for intervention, as Austria steadfastly proclaimed her determination to respect the sovereignty and territory of Serbia from July 28th on.

(12) The Austrian war on Serbia did not in itself involve or necessitate a European war. It was the unjustifiable and indefensible intervention of Russia, urged on by France, which produced the wider conflict.

SELECTED REFERENCES

Bogitshevich, M., *Causes of the War;* Durham, E., *Twenty Years of Balkan Tangle;* "Why I Believe the Serbians Deliberately Precipitated the War," in the *Kriegsschuldfrage,* July, 1925; "The Guilt of the Serb Government in 1914," in *Foreign Affairs* (English), December, 1924; "More Light on Sarajevo," in *The Progressive,* February 1, 1925; *The Serajevo Crime;* "The Sarajevo Murder Plot," in New York *Times Current History Magazine,* February, 1927; Earle, E. M., *Turkey, the Great Powers, and the Bagdad Railway;* Fay, S. B., "New Light on the Origins of the World War," in *American Historical Review,* July and October, 1920; "Serbia's Responsibility for the World War," in New York *Times Current History Magazine,* October, 1925; "The Black Hand Plot that Led to the World War," Ibid., November, 1925; Reply to A. V. Seferovitch, Ibid., December, 1925; Goos, R., *Das Wiener Kabinett und die Entstehung des Weltkrieges;* (Editor) *The Austrian Red Book* (English edition, Allen and Unwin): Jovanovitch, L., *The Murder of Serajevo;* Kanner, H., *Kaiserliche Katastro-*

phenpolitik; Montgelas, M., *The Case for the Central Powers;* Morhardt, M., *Les Preuves. Le Crime de droit commun. Le Crime diplomatique;* Renouvin, P., *Les Origines immédiates de la guerre;* Seton-Watson, R. W., *The Southern Slav Question and the Hapsburg Monarchy;* "The Murder at Sarajevo," in *Foreign Affairs,* April, 1925; review of Durham E., *The Serajevo Crime,* in *Slavonic Review,* December, 1925, pp. 513–20; *Sarajevo;* Szilassy, J. von, *Der Untergang der Donaumonarchie;* Temperley, H. W. V., *A History of Serbia;* Wendel, H., *Der Kampf der Südslawen um Freiheit und Einheit;* Wiesner, F. von, "The Forged and the Genuine Text of the 'Wiesner Documents,'" in the *Kriegsschuldfrage,* October, 1925; "Der Sarajevoer Mord und die Kriegsschuldfrage," in *Das Neue Reich* (Vienna), August 2, 1924; Berchtold, L., *Count Berchtold's Own Story.*

FOOTNOTES AND FURTHER REFERENCES

[1] F. von Wiesner, "The Forged and the Genuine Text of the 'Wiesner Documents,'" in the *Kriegsschuldfrage,* October, 1925, p. 649.

[2] The most elaborate work on this subject is H. Wendel, *Der Kampf der Südslawen um Freiheit und Einheit.* See also his *Die Habsburger und die Südslawenfrage.* The best books in English are R. W. Seton-Watson, *The Southern Slav Question and the Hapsburg Monarchy;* and E. Durham, *Twenty Years of Balkan Tangle.* Seton-Watson writes from a distinctly anti-Austrian angle. The relation of these issues to the causes of the World War is well presented in M. Bogitshevich, *The Causes of the War.* There is a realistic brief summary of the question in M. Morhardt, *Les Preuves,* pp. 20–70. The most recent and complete summary of the Austro-Serbian problem in its relation to the World War is contained in Edith Durham's book, *The Serajevo Crime.* See the review of this by R. W. Seton-Watson in the *Slavonic Review,* December, 1925, pp. 513–20.

[3] Bogitshevich, op. cit., Annex, xxi; F. Stieve, *Isvolsky and the World War;* and footnote 23 below.

[4] References as in previous footnote; and E. D. Morel, *The*

Secret History of a Great Betrayal, Senate Document No. 40, 68th Congress, 1st Session, pp. 20–21, 28; S. B. Fay, "The Black Hand Plot that Led to the World War," in New York *Times Current History Magazine,* November, 1925; and V. Serge, in *Clarté,* May, 1925.

[5] Fay, loc. cit., pp. 203–4.

[6] S. B. Fay, "Serbia's Responsibility for the World War," in *Current History,* October, 1925, pp. 42–3.

[7] R. W. Seton-Watson, "The Murder at Sarajevo," in *Foreign Affairs* (American), April, 1925, p. 500.

[8] Ibid., pp. 505–6. *Cf.* A. Mousset, in *Le Figaro,* May 2, 1924; E. Durham, *The Serajevo Crime,* pp. 75 ff.

[9] Seton-Watson, Ibid., pp. 500 ff.; Fay, in November *Current History, passim.*

[10] S. Stanojevitch, *Die Ermordung des Erzherzogs Franz Ferdinand;* Durham, op. cit., pp. 96 ff.

[11] *The Murder of Sarajavo,* published in English by the British Institute of International Affairs, 1925.

[12] Ibid., p. 3; and Fay, in October *Current History,* pp. 44–5; Durham, op. cit., pp. 127 ff. Pashitch's alleged denials consist only in his assertion that he talked over the assassination with the cabinet members individually rather than in a cabinet meeting.

[13] Fay, in November *Current History,* p. 207.

[14] Ibid., pp. 206–7. Cf. L. Mandl, in the *Kriegsschuldfrage,* April, 1924, translated in *Humanity and Its Problems,* September-October, 1924, pp. 358–62; Durham, op. cit., pp. 148 ff.

[15] H. W. Steed, *The Pact of Konopischt.* See the characterization of this preposterous fabrication by Professor Fay in *Current History* for December, 1925, pp. 385–6.

[16] Fay, in November *Current History,* p. 205.

[17] Ibid.

[18] C. Price, "Serajevo Ten Years After," in New York *Times,* June 22, 1924, Section 4, p. 2.

[19] E. Durham, "More Light on Serajevo," in *The Progressive,* February 1, 1925; *The Serajevo Crime,* pp. 158 ff.; M. Bogitshevich, "Weitere Einzelheiten über das Attentat von Serajewo," in the *Kriegsschuldfrage,* January 1925, pp.. 15–21; and Ibid., July, 1925, pp. 437–44; January, 1926, pp. 21–8. The chief source on both the plot and the Salonika trials is a Serbian work, *Tajna Prevratna Organizatzia,* about to be rendered into English by Bogitshevich.

[20] Fay, in November *Current History,* pp. 205–6.

[21] Loc. cit., pp. 508–9.

[22] Fay, in November *Current History,* p. 207; Seton-Watson, loc. cit., *passim.*

[23] References above in footnotes 2 and 3; Stieve, op. cit., p. 209; L. Mandl, in Wiener, *Neues Act-Uhr Blatt,* July 27–28, 1924; Robert Dell, in London *Nation and Athenæum,* September 19, 1925, p. 723; Bogitshevich, in the *Kriegsschuldfrage,* July, 1925,

pp. 437–44, September, 1926 pp. 664 ff.; Durham, op. cit., pp. 196 ff.; Victor Serge, in *Clarté*, May, 1925.

24 Morel, op. cit., pp. 28–9; Morhardt, op. cit., pp. 73, 292.

24a See S. Ruppricht, in *Kriegsschuldfrage*, September, 1925, pp. 618 ff.

25 Seton-Watson, loc. cit., pp. 497–99.

26 In *Kriegsschuldfrage*, July, 1924, p. 258.

27 Ibid., pp. 255–8; *The Serajevo Crime* and "The Serajevo Murder Plot," in New York *Times Current History Magazine*, February, 1927.

28 References as in footnotes 2, 4 and 23 above.

29 *Let France Explain*, p. 174.

30 Ewart, *Roots and Causes of the Wars*, Vol. II, pp. 1018–19.

31 Fay, "New Light on the Origins of the World War," in *American Historical Review*, July, 1920, pp. 626–39.

32 *The Austrian Red Book* (edited by R. Goos), English edition published by Allen and Unwin, three volumes. Vol. I, pp. 22–33.

33 Ibid., p. 30.

34 Ibid., pp. 35–9, 53–58.

35 Ibid., p. 58.

36 Conrad von Hötzendorf, *Aus meiner Dienstzeit, 1906–1918*, four volumes.

37 The Austrian policy is condemned by R. W. Seton-Watson, *Sarajevo;* and defended by Hans Delbrück in *Der Stand der Kriegssuldfrage*, and M. Morhardt, *Les Preuves*.

38 *Austrian Red Book*, Vol. I, p. 15.

39 Ibid., pp. 1–13.

40 Fay, in *American Historical Review*, July, 1920, pp. 626–7.

41 Ibid., p. 627; *Red Book*, pp. 20–21.

42 *The Outbreak of the World War*. German Documents Collected by Karl Kautsky and edited by Max Montgelas and Walther Schücking. Translated and published by the Carnegie Endowment for International Peace, 1924, p. 79.

43 Fay, in *American Historical Review*, July, 1920, p. 628, footnote 38.

44 Stieve, op. cit., pp. 106, 113, 209 ff.; A. Fabre-Luce, *La Victoire*, pp. 208 ff.

45 Fabre-Luce, *La Victoire*, pp. 208 ff.; Morhardt, *Les Preuves*, pp. 117 ff.

46 *Red Book*, Vol. I, pp. 44–5; F. R. von Wiesner, "The Forged and the Genuine Text of the 'Wiesner Documents,'" in the *Kriegsschuldfrage*, October, 1925, pp. 649–57.

47 Wiesner, loc. cit., p. 650.

48 Ibid., pp. 653–4.

49 *Red Book*, Vol. I, pp. 48–50.

50 See Poincaré's own naïve and damaging admission on this point in *Foreign Affairs* (American), October, 1914, p. 15.

51 Fabre-Luce, op. cit., pp. 205 ff.; Morhardt, op. cit., pp. 139 ff.

52 *The Outbreak of the World War*, pp. 152, 227.

53 Fay, in *American Historical Review,* July, 1920, p. 636.

54 *Red Book,* Vol. I, pp. 58–63. The text reproduced here is taken from *International Conciliation Pamphlet,* No. 83, October, 1914.

55 Compare the bitter criticism of A. Dumaine, *La dernière ambassade de France en Autriche* with the defense in M. Morhardt, *Les Preuves;* and both with the moderate view in P. Renouvin, *Les Origines immédiates de la guerre,* pp. 38 ff.; and Ewart, op. cit., Vol. II, p. 1000 ff.

56 The authoritative Austrian defense is contained in *Count Berchtold's Own Story.*

57 Cf. Morhardt, *Les Preuves,* pp. 20 ff., 106 ff.; M. Bogitshevich, "Die Balkanstaaten," in *Schweizerische Monatshefte für Politik und Kultur,* March, 1925, pp. 721–32.

58 The writer regards the whole matter as of no vital significance in the light of the actual plans and motives of both Austria and Serbia.

59 Cf. *Red Book,* Vol. I, *passim;* Ewart, op. cit., pp. 134 ff.

60 R. Viviani, *As We See It,* pp. 267–8; R. C. Binkley, "New Light on Russia's War Guilt," in *Current History,* January, 1926, pp. 531–3; P. Renouvin, *Les Origines immédiates de la guerre,* p. 60; G. Dupin, "M. Raymond Poincaré se défend en Amérique," in *La Revue de Hongrie,* December 15, 1925, p. 174; *International Conciliation Pamphlet,* No. 83, October, 1914.

61 Cf. Renouvin, op. cit., pp. 58 ff.

62 Morhardt, op. cit., pp. 106 ff.

63 *The Outbreak of the World War,* p. 254.

64 Fay, loc. cit., July, 1920, p. 637; H. Lutz, in *Current History,* May, 1925, p. 267; and *Lord Grey und der Weltkrieg,* pp. 207–8.

65 Ewart, op. cit., Vol. II, pp. 1073 ff.

66 Fay, loc. cit., p. 638; Ewart, pp. 1097–8.

67 Ewart, pp. 1080 ff.

68 *Recent Revelations on European Diplomacy,* p. 18.

69 *Red Book,* Vol. I, p. 111.

70 *Falsifications of the Russian Orange Book* (New York edition, Huebsch), p. 17.

71 Ewart, pp. 1084 ff.

72 *Falsifications of the Russian Orange Book,* p. 56.

73 *Red Book,* Vol. III, pp. 59–60.

74 Ibid., pp. 44–45.

75 Montgelas, op. cit., pp. 184 ff.

76 See above Chap. iii.

77 Stieve, op. cit., *passim;* Ewart, op. cit., pp. 930 ff., 1026 ff.; Edith Durham, "The Sarajevo Murder Plot," in *Current History,* February, 1927, p. 660; M. Bogitshevich, *Causes of the War,* pp. 126–134; V. Serge, in *Clarté,* May, 1925.

CHAPTER V

THE RÔLE PLAYED BY GERMANY IN THE CRISIS OF 1914

I. THE ENTENTE MYTHOLOGY AND THE INDICTMENT OF VERSAILLES

In the Entente propaganda of 1914–18 Germany has been uniformly represented as the unique aggressor of 1914. She is reputed to have determined upon war for years before 1914, to have driven the other European states into the military system against their will and in self-defense, and to have seized upon the Sarajevo murder as "Der Tag" for which she had been waiting for a decade. This bellicose decision is supposed to have been revealed by the Kaiser to German and Austrian statesmen and officers at a conference at Potsdam on July 5, 1914. Austria is held to have been intimidated by Germany into taking her strong stand against Serbia and prevented by Germany from backing down, thus drawing the fire of Russia and precipitating the long desired struggle.

On the threat of a complete military occupation of Germany the German representatives were compelled at Versailles to subscribe to this indictment, as embodied in Article 231 of the Treaty of Versailles:

The Allied and Associated Governments affirm, and Germany accepts, the responsibility of herself and her allies, for causing all the loss and damage to which the Allied and Associated Governments and their nationals have been subjected as a consequence of the war imposed upon them by the aggression of Germany and her allies.

We shall here set forth the well-established facts and observe how much remains of this war-time romance of the Entente.

II. GERMANY AND THE EUROPEAN SYSTEM

It is necessary at the outset to summarize briefly the material embodied in the second chapter, namely, Germany's part in the menacing system of European relations which prevailed before the World War. This is essential on account of the fact that, while many educated persons have come to see that the obvious facts compel them to give up the idea that Germany was solely guilty for the World War, they still cling to the illusion that it was Germany which produced the system of nationalism, imperialism, militarism, navalism and secret diplomacy which challenged the peace of the world for decades before the great explosion came in 1914. And even ostensibly intelligent citizens of the United States are willing to arrive at this conclusion and cling doggedly to it on the basis of "general impressions" in the face of undeniable historical and statistical facts.[1]

We have already made it clear that Germany shared in these reprehensible and ominous characteristics of the pre-War system. She was nationalistic, imperialistic, militaristic, ambitious as to naval plans, and given to secret diplomacy. But she was not as nationalistic as France, not as imperialistic as Great Britain, France or Russia, not as militaristic as France or Russia, not as devoted to navalism as Great Britain, and not engaged in as dangerous or extensive a system of secret diplomacy as that which France and Russia were developing from 1911 to 1914. Germany was certainly not a lamb in the midst of the pack of European wolves, but it is just as apparent that she was not the unique wolf in the fold. And the fact that Germany was less adequately prepared on either land or sea than her potential foes is all the more striking, in the light of the fact that her position was the most precarious of all major European states. She was surrounded on land and sea by powerful enemies whose combined land and sea forces overwhelmingly outnumbered the armies and navies of Germany, Austria and Italy, the latter of which could not, moreover, be counted upon with any certainty.

Another matter to examine is the question as to whether Germany had any basic policy or objective that she could gain only by war, and which was supported by any large body of citizens or by responsible persons in power before 1914. Austria felt that a war was necessary to punish the Serbians and furnish a salutary warning to the other subject nationalities within the polyglot Dual Monarchy. Serbia knew that she would have to await a European war to realize the Greater Serbia aspiration. Russia recognized that only by a European war could she secure the Straits, and France was well aware that Alsace-Lorraine could be recovered only by the successful outcome of a general European conflict. Did Germany have any similar ambition? It may be categorically stated that she did not. Everything was going smoothly. She was capturing yearly an ever greater percentage of the world's trade, her phenomenal industrial development was proceeding apace, and her chief area of imperialistic expansion was coming under her control, with the general success of the Berlin to Bagdad railway scheme, and her triumph at Constantinople. The success of the negotiations with England over the Near East, Africa and naval construction by June, 1914, removed the basis for acute Anglo-

German rivalry. The leaders of Germany in economics and politics well understood that she stood to win what she desired by the continuation of existing tendencies, while a war against the overwhelming odds she would have to face would put her whole future in jeopardy. To be sure, there were a few terrified autocrats who were alarmed at the growth of German socialism and were willing to risk a war in the hope of reviving in radicals a new-born loyalty to the reigning dynasty, and there were a few chauvinistic fools who desired a war on Great Britain because of commercial and naval rivalry; but no large group in Germany wanted war, and the responsible members of the German civil government, from the Kaiser down, were thoroughly opposed to war in the spring of 1914, though they were alarmed at the bellicose utterances of Russia and the rumors of an Anglo-Russian naval convention. Though the Kaiser was often rash and irresponsible in his utterances, full of military symbolism and rhetoric, and in his personal behavior, even Colonel House admits his underlying pacific intentions.[2]

No myth in contemporary history is more difficult to down than the contention that the overwhelming mass of the German people were slavish worshippers of militarism and eager for the first opportunity for war. A fair measure of German opinion in this matter can be secured in the popular vote for members of the Reichstag in the election of 1912. The distribution of votes among the main parties was as follows:

Conservatives 1,149,916
National Liberals 1,671,297
Centre 2,012,990
Radicals 1,556,549
Social Democrats 4,238,919

Of these parties the last three, containing an overwhelming majority of the German people, were unalterably against war and militarism. The National Liberals were about equally divided on the subject. Only the Conservatives could claim a majority for militarism.

It has been frequently contended that though the German civil government in 1914 did not desire a European war, yet the military classes did do so and felt that 1914 was the ideal moment for such a conflict. There seems little ground for such conclusion. We know that von Moltke secretly telegraphed to the Austrian Chief-of-Staff urging him to stand firm in his plan to punish Serbia and advising mobilization, but there is no evidence that von Moltke desired to provoke a general European war. His telegrams were purely precautionary. It is known that von Tirpitz, the leader of the most bellicose element in Germany, was greatly disappointed that the War came in 1914 before his naval plans had been completed. Ewart says on this point: [3]

Grand Admiral von Tirpitz, the creator of the German navy, has been particularly pointed at as a chief of the militarist class who dominated the German government and precipitated the war. Had not he been waiting for the completion of the Kiel canal, and, now that it could pass his big warships, was he not eager for hostilities? He was not. He was building a formidable navy, but it was still far from competent for war with the United Kingdom, and few people were more disappointed by its outbreak than Tirpitz.

It would seem that the most that can be said against the military group in Germany in 1914 is that once they became convinced that war with Russia and France was inevitable they clamored for immediate action in order to avert dangerous delay in the face of the overwhelming Russian numbers. But Poincaré has openly confessed to a similar degree of chafing and impatience upon the part of General Joffre and his associates in their desire to get at Germany.

III. THE LEGEND OF THE POTSDAM CROWN COUNCIL OF JULY 5, 1914

In the later years of the World War the most important element in the Entente case against Germany as the unique instigator of the conflict and the sole war criminal was the allegation that on July 5, 1914, the Kaiser called together a great council of the economic, political and military leaders of Germany and Austria and told them that he had decided to plunge Europe into war. The financiers protested that they needed a few days in which to call in their loans, and the Kaiser granted them two weeks' delay for this purpose. The next morning the Kaiser left for a vacation cruise to prepare himself for the strenuous times which he knew were to follow his return, as well as to lull Europe into a wholly deceptive sense of security and continued peace. The Austrian ultimatum to Serbia, which he had drawn up in such a manner as inevitably to produce a general European war, was to be delayed in presentation during these two weeks needed by the bankers to put the country in complete readiness for war.

This myth was first spread on a large scale in July, 1917. It had its origin with a waiter in the Kaiserhof Hotel in Berlin, who overheard and misinterpreted some gossip passed between subordinate officers of the German army and some members of the Austrian Embassy in military uniform who were dining at the hotel. It may have been spread by a correspondent of the *Frankfurter Zeitung,* though the correspondent accused has denied this allegation.[4] But the legend burst into full bloom only with the publication in 1918 of a book by Henry Morgenthau, the American Ambassador to Turkey from 1913 to 1916, entitled *Ambassador Morgenthau's Story.* It is somewhat strange that he withheld so important a bit of evidence against Germany for more than three years! Mr. Morgenthau thus describes how he learned of this foul plot from Wangenheim, the German Ambassador to Turkey, very early in the World War: [5]

In those early days the weather for the German Ambassador was distinctly favorable. The good fortune of the German armies so excited him that he was sometimes led into indiscretions, and his exuberance one day caused him to tell me certain facts which, I think, will always have great historical value. He disclosed precisely how and when Germany had precipitated this war. To-day his revelation of this secret looks like a most monstrous indiscretion, but we must remember Wangenheim's state of mind at the time. The whole world then believed that Paris was doomed and Wangenheim reflected this attitude in his frequent declarations that the war would be over in two or three months. The whole German enterprise was evidently progressing according to programme. I have already mentioned that the German Ambassador had left for Berlin soon after the assassination of the Grand Duke, and he now revealed the cause of his sudden disappearance. The Kaiser, he told me, had summoned him to Berlin for an imperial conference. This meeting took place at Potsdam on July 5th. The Kaiser presided and nearly all the important ambassadors attended. Wangenheim himself was sum-

moned to give assurance about Turkey and enlighten
his associates generally on the situation in Constantinople, which was then regarded as almost the pivotal
point in the impending war. In telling me who attended this conference Wangenheim used no names,
though he specifically said that among them were—
the facts are so important that I quote his exact words
in the German which he used—"die Häupter des Gen-
eralstabs und der Marine"—(The heads of the general
staff and of the navy) by which I have assumed that
he meant Von Moltke and Von Tirpitz. The great
bankers, railroad directors, and the captains of German industry, all of whom were as necessary to German war preparations as the army itself, also attended.

Wangenheim now told me that the Kaiser solemnly
put the question to each man in turn: "Are you ready
for war?" All replied "yes" except the financiers.
They said that they must have two weeks to sell their
foreign securities and to make loans. At that time few
people had looked upon the Sarajevo tragedy as something that would inevitably lead to war. This conference, Wangenheim told me, took all precautions
that no such suspicion should be aroused. It decided
to give the bankers time to readjust their finances for
the coming war, and then the several members went
quietly back to their work or started on vacations.
The Kaiser went to Norway on his yacht, Von
Bethmann-Hollweg left for a rest, and Wangenheim
returned to Constantinople.

In telling me about this conference Wangenheim, of
course, admitted that Germany precipitated the war.

I think that he was rather proud of the whole performance, proud that Germany had gone about the
matter in so methodical and far-seeing a way, and
especially proud that he himself had been invited to
participate in so epoch-making a gathering. I have
often wondered why he revealed to me so momentous
a secret, and I think that perhaps the real reason was
his excessive vanity—his desire to show me how close
he stood to the inner counsels of his emperor and the
part that he had played in bringing on this conflict.
Whatever the motive, this indiscretion certainly had
the effect of showing me who were really the guilty
parties in this monstrous crime. The several blue,
red and yellow books which flooded Europe during
the few months following the outbreak, and the hundreds of documents which were issued by German
propagandists attempting to establish Germany's innocence, have never made the slightest impression on
me. For my conclusions as to the responsibility are
not based on suspicions or belief or the study of circumstantial data. I do not have to reason or argue
about the matter. I know. The conspiracy that has
caused this greatest of human tragedies was hatched
by the Kaiser and his imperial crew at this Potsdam
conference of July 5, 1914. One of the chief participants, flushed with his triumph at the apparent success of the plot, told me the details with his own mouth.
Whenever I hear people arguing about the responsibility for this war or read the clumsy and lying ex-
cuses put forth by Germany, I simply recall the burly
figure of Wangenheim as he appeared that August
afternoon, puffing away at a huge black cigar, and giv-

ing me his account of this historic meeting. Why waste any time discussing the matter after that?

This imperial conference took place July 5th and the Serbian ultimatum was sent on July 22nd. That is just about the two weeks' interval which the financiers had demanded to complete their plans. All the great stock exchanges of the world show that the German bankers profitably used this interval. Their records disclose that stocks were being sold in large quantities and that prices declined rapidly. At that time the markets were somewhat puzzled at this movement but Wangenheim's explanation clears up any doubts that may still remain. Germany was changing her securities into cash for war purposes. If anyone wishes to verify Wangenheim, I would suggest that he examine the quotations of the New York stock market for these two historic weeks. He will find that there were astonishing slumps in prices, especially on the stocks that had an international market. Between July 5th and July 22nd, Union Pacific dropped from 155½ to 127½, Baltimore and Ohio from 91½ to 81, United States Steel from 61 to 50½, Canadian Pacific from 194 to 185½, and Northern Pacific from 111⅜ to 108. At that time the high protectionists were blaming the Simmons-Underwood tariff act as responsible for this fall in values, while other critics of the Administration attributed it to the Federal Reserve Act—which had not yet been put into effect. How little the Wall Street brokers and the financial experts realized that an imperial conference, which had been held in Potsdam and presided over by the Kaiser, was the real force that was then depressing the market!

This luxuriant and voluptuous legend was not only the chief point in the Allied propaganda against Germany after the publication of Mr. Morgenthau's book, but it has also been tacitly accepted by Mr. Asquith in his apology, and solemnly repeated by Bourgeois and Pagès in the standard conventional French work, both published since the facts have been available which demonstrate that the above tale was a complete fabrication. The myth has been subjected to withering criticism by Professor Sidney B. Fay in the *Kriegsschuldfrage* for May, 1925: [6]

The contemporary documents now available prove conclusively that there is hardly a word of truth in Mr. Morgenthau's assertions, either as to (a) the persons present, (b) the Kaiser's attitude toward delay, (c) the real reasons for delay, or (d) the alleged selling of securities in anticipation of war. In fact his assertions are rather the direct opposite of the truth.

a) As to the persons present, it is certainly not true that "Nearly all the important ambassadors attended." They were all at their posts with the exception of Wangenheim, himself, and it is not certain that even he saw the Kaiser. Moltke was away taking a cure at Karlsbad, and Tirpitz was on a vacation in Switzerland. Jagow was also in Switzerland on a honeymoon and did not return until July 6. Ballin, the head of the Hamburg-American Line, who was absent from Berlin in the early part of July at a health resort, does not appear to have had any information until July 20, that there was a possible danger of warlike complications. Krupp v. Bohlen-Halbach, the head of the great munition works, was not at Potsdam on July 5, but saw Emperor William next day at Kiel as the Emperor was departing for his Northern cruise. Nor is there any evidence that there were gathered at Potsdam on July 5 any of the others who were "necessary to German war preparations." The only person with whom the Kaiser conferred on July 5, at Potsdam after his lunch with the Austrian Ambassador, were Bethmann-Hollweg, the Chancellor, Falkenhayn, the Prussian Minister of War, and certain subordinate routine officials.

b) It is certainly not true that the Kaiser wished Austria to delay for two weeks whatever action she thought she must take against Serbia in order to give the German Bankers time to sell their foreign securities. There is abundant proof to indicate that Emperor William wished Austria to act quickly while the sentiment of Europe, shocked by the horrible crime at Sarajevo, was still in sympathy with the Hapsburgs and indignant at regicide Serbs. As he wrote in a marginal note, "Matters must be cleared up with the Serbs, and that soon."

c) The real reasons for the delay of two weeks between July 5 and 23, were not to give the German bankers two weeks to sell their foreign securities. The real reasons for delay were due wholly to Austria, and not to Germany. They were mainly two, and are repeatedly referred to in the German and Austrian documents which were published in 1919. The first was that Berchtold, the Austro-Hungarian Minister of Foreign Affairs, could not act against Serbia until he had secured the consent of Tisza, the Premier of Hungary. It took two weeks to win Tisza over from his original attitude of opposition to violent action against Serbia. The second, and by far the most important reason for the final delay, was the fact that Berchtold did not want to present the ultimatum to Serbia until it was certain that Poincaré and Viviani had left Petrograd and were inaccessible upon the high seas returning to France. For otherwise Russia, under the influence of the "champagne mood" of the Franco-Russian toasts and the chauvinism of Poincaré, Iswolski, and the Grand Duke Nicholas gathered at Petrograd, would be much more likely to intervene to support Serbia with military force, and so Austria's action against Serbia would less easily be "localized."

d) In regard to Germany's alleged selling of securities in anticipation of war, if one follows Mr. Morgenthau's suggestion and examines the quotations on the New York Stock Exchange during these weeks, and reads the accompanying articles in the New York *Times*, one does not find a shred of evidence, either in the price of stocks or the volume of sales, that large blocks of German holdings were being secretly unloaded and depressing the New York market during these two weeks. The stocks that he mentioned declined only slightly or not at all; moreover, such declines as did take place were only such as were to be naturally expected from the general trend downward which had been taking place since January, or are quite satisfactorily explained by local American conditions, such as the publication of an adverse report of the Interstate Commerce Commission. Here are the facts. The amazing slump in Union Pacific from 155½ to 127½ reported by Mr. Morgenthau represented in fact an actual rise of a couple of points in the value of this stock. Union Pacific sold "ex-dividend" and "ex-rights" on July 20; the dividend and accompanying rights were worth 30⅝, which meant that shares ought to have sold on July 22nd at 125¾. In reality they sold at 127½; that is, at the end of the two weeks' period during which it is asserted that there was "inside selling" from Berlin, Union Pacific, instead of being depressed, was actually selling two points higher.

Baltimore and Ohio, Canadian Pacific, and Northern Pacific did in fact slump on July 14, and there was evidence of selling orders from Europe. But this is to be explained, partly by the fact that Baltimore and Ohio had been already falling steadily since January, and partly to the very depressing influence exercised on all railroad shares by the sharply adverse report on the New York, New Haven and Hartford Railroad, which was published by the Interstate Commerce Commission. The comment of the New York *Times* of July 15, is significant: "Stocks which had lately displayed a stable character in the face of great weakness of particular issues could not stand up under such selling as occurred in New Haven and some others today. There were times when it looked as though the entire market was in a fair way to slump heavily, and only brisk short covering toward the close prevented many sharp net declines. . . . For its own account, or on orders from this side, Europe was an unusually large seller of stocks in this market. The cable told that a very unfavorable impression had been created abroad by the Commerce Commission's New Haven report. The European attitude toward American securities is naturally affected by such official denunciations of the way in which an important railway property has been handled."

Most extraordinary is Mr. Morgenthau's assertion about United States Steel Common. He says that between July 5th and 22nd it fell from 61 to 51½. The real fact, as any one may verify from the Stock Market reports for himself, is that Steel during these two weeks never fell below 59⅝, and on July 22nd was almost exactly the same as two weeks earlier.

When the facts are examined, therefore, it does not appear that the New York Stock Market can afford much confirmation to Mr. Morgenthau's myth of German bankers demanding a two weeks' respite in which to turn American securities into gold in preparation for a world war which they had already plotted to bring about.

In his apology in *Foreign Affairs* even Poincaré has been compelled to admit that there was no Potsdam Conference and that Germany and Austria had not decided upon a world war from the beginning of the 1914 crisis. He makes the following startling and revolutionary admission: [7]

I do not claim that Austria or Germany, in this

first phase, had a conscious thought-out intention of provoking a general war. No existing document gives us the right to suppose that, at that time, they had planned anything so systematic.

Thus disappears the whole Entente case against Germany as it was presented during the war period and utilized to arouse the sympathy of the United States for the Allied cause, which was represented to us as the battle for civilization against the Central Powers, who had willed from the very beginning an unprovoked and brutal war.[8]

As Mr. Morgenthau has persistently refused to offer any explanation or justification of his "story" or to answer written inquiries as to his grounds for believing it authentic, we are left to pure conjecture in the circumstances. It appears highly doubtful to the present writer that Mr. Morgenthau ever heard of the Potsdam legend while resident in Turkey. It would seem inconceivable that he could have withheld such important information for nearly four years. The present writer has been directly informed by the Kaiser that Wangenheim did not see him in July, 1914. We know that Mr. Morgenthau's book was not written by himself, but by Mr. Burton J. Hendrick, who later distinguished himself as the editor of the Page letters. We shall await with interest Mr. Hendrick's explanation of the genesis of the Potsdam fiction as it was composed for *Ambassador Morgenthau's Story.*

IV. THE KAISER'S RESPONSE TO AUSTRIA'S APPEAL FOLLOWING THE ASSASSINATION OF THE ARCHDUKE

Having now cleared the field of the legend of the Potsdam Conference, we may examine the facts as to the reaction of the Kaiser to the assassination of Franz Ferdinand, and his response to the appeal of the Austrian Emperor for support of the Austrian program of punishing Serbia. In the first place, it is necessary to bear in mind the fact that, up to the assassination, the Kaiser had been a moderating influence in regard to the belligerent attitude of Austria toward Serbia. Twice in 1912–13 he had prevented Austria from attacking Serbia.[9] As late as July 1, 1914, Count Tisza had accused the Kaiser of a special fondness for Serbia, and he wrote to Emperor Franz Josef that the Kaiser's expected visit to Vienna to attend the funeral of the Archduke should be utilized to convert the Kaiser to the Austrian view of the Serbian problem:[10]

I considered it my duty to approach Your Majesty with the submissive request to graciously make use of Emperor William's presence in Vienna for combating that monarch's preference for Servia, a thing that should not be difficult in the view of the recent revolting events and to induce him to support us energetically in our intended Balkan policy.

The murder of the Archduke wrought a complete transformation in the Kaiser's attitude towards Serbia. The reasons were personal and political. The Kaiser was a warm personal friend of the Archduke and they had been together at Konopischt only a couple of weeks before the assassination. Quite naturally, as the head of a reigning dynasty, the Kaiser did not relish assassinations. He had been greatly perturbed at the time of the assassination of President Carnot of France and King Humbert of Italy. This time it had come closer home with the murder of the Hapsburg next in succession to the throne. He, himself, might be the next victim. The Kaiser, indeed, cancelled his visit to Vienna because of fear of assassination.[11] Berchtold was clever enough to play upon this fear. On July 3rd he reported to Tschirschky that he had just learned that twelve assassins were on their way to murder the Kaiser.[12] The political reason for the Kaiser's alarm was his recognition that the murder was a challenge to Austrian dominion over her subject Slavs, which, if successful, would lead to the weakening or destruction of his only important ally, and to serious interference with German plans in the Near East.

The Kaiser's change of attitude towards Serbia appears clearly in his marginal comments on the communications of his ambassadors to von Jagow and Bethmann-Hollweg. On July 2nd or 3rd he wrote on the margin of Tschirschky's telegram to Bethmann-Hollweg to the effect that the former was trying to exert a moderating influence upon Austria: [13]

This is none of his (Tschirschky's) business, as it is solely the affair of Austria what she plans to do in this case. Let Tschirschky be good enough to drop this nonsense! The Serbs must be disposed of and that right *soon!*

In his letter of July 10th to von Jagow, Tschirschky suggested that it might be well to attempt to influence the British press against Serbia, but that this should be done cautiously, so as not to alarm the Serbians. The Kaiser commented on this: [14]

To act like "gentlemen" to murderers after what has happened! Idiocy!

In a letter to Franz Josef on July 14th he wrote: [15]

The dreadful crime of Serajevo has thrown a blazing light on the pernicious agitations of mad fanatics and on the mischievous Panslavic disturbances that threaten the structure of the state.

He wrote "Bosh!!!" "Bosh!" and "Hot Air!" in the margin of the telegram of his minister in Belgrade sent on July 8th and telling of a conference with Pashitch, in which the latter emphasized the difficulty of holding in check the Serbian agitators and plotters, and his determination to deal with them as severely as possible.[16] In his telegram of July 14th to Bethmann-Hollweg Tschirschky informed the Chancellor of Tisza's decision to support a firm attitude towards Serbia, and the Kaiser's marginal comment was: "Well, a real man at last!"[17] It is interesting to contrast this remark with Tisza's complaint of two weeks earlier that the first step in the Austrian policy would have to be the conversion of the Kaiser from his excessive fondness for Serbia! On July 23rd von Jagow sent to the Kaiser an account of the attitude of Sir Edward Grey, as reported by the German Ambassador in London. The Kaiser remarked on the margin:[18]

Grey is committing the error of setting Serbia on the same plane with Austria and other Great Powers! That is unheard of! Serbia is nothing but a band of robbers that must be seized for its crimes!

In the margin of the telegram of Tschirschky to von Jagow on July 24th, the Kaiser wrote:[19]

Austria must become preponderant in the Balkans as compared with the little ones, and that at Russia's expense; otherwise there will be no peace.

The German Minister at Belgrade telegraphed to von Jagow that the harsh tone and severe terms of the Austrian ultimatum were a surprise to the Serbians.   The Kaiser commented: [20]

Bravo! One would not have believed it of the Viennese!

In short, up to the time he learned of the nature of the Serbian reply to the Austrian ultimatum, the Kaiser was enthusiastically for a severe and rapid movement of Austria against Serbia.   He was quite willing to see this take the form of a punitive war, though, unlike the Austrians, he did not insist that the Austrian policy *must* involve war to be successful.   He was from the first, however, unalterably against letting a local war grow into a European war which would bring in Russia, France and England against Germany.   The Kaiser's impatient desire that Austria should deal with Serbia quickly was not due to a wish to start a European war, but to the very opposite motive, namely, the feeling that the quicker the move the greater the prospect of localizing the conflict.

We have already pointed out that,[21] on July 5th, the Kaiser received the letter from Franz Josef asking for support of the premeditated action against Serbia, and that on the next morning Bethmann-Hollweg communicated to the Austrian Ambassador in Berlin the German decision to stand back of Austria in whatever policy Austria should adopt towards Serbia. The Chancellor also confirmed this in a telegram to Tschirschky the same day, and the Kaiser repeated the same promise in his letter to Franz Josef on July 14th. These constituted the famous blank cheque to Austria, which was in its later developments to prove the undoing of both empires.

The Kaiser has been severely, and perhaps justly, criticized for giving his *carte blanche* to Austria in the Serbian crisis. But it must be remembered that this was essentially what Poincaré had already given to Russia in regard to the Balkans in 1912, and was exactly what he soon gave to Russia concerning the Austro-Serbian dispute of July, 1914, on his visit to St. Petersburg before he was fully aware of the terms of the Austrian ultimatum. Further, the offense of Poincaré in the circumstances was a far more grievous one. The Kaiser merely gave consent to a purely localized punitive action essential to the preservation of an ally; Poincaré consented to the wanton waging of a war which would necessarily involve all Europe. When the Kaiser saw that his action in regard to Austria threatened to bring Europe to war he made every effort to restrain Austria; when Poincaré saw that his encouragement of Russia meant certain war he secretly urged Russia to proceed more rapidly with her fatal preparations.

Far from announcing his determination to precipitate a European war on July 5th, the Kaiser left the next morning with the conviction that there was but the slightest probability of a general conflict developing out of any punitive policy which Austria might employ against Serbia. What were his reasons for holding this view? In the first place, he believed that the Tsar would be even more alarmed and horrified than himself at the assassination of the Archduke, and would be willing to see the Serbian plotters severely punished. As late as July 28th the Kaiser exclaimed: [22]

I could not assume that the Czar would place himself on the side of bandits and regicides, even at the peril of unchaining a European war. Germans are incapable of such a conception. It is Slavic or Latin.

Further, he knew from his military attaché in St. Petersburg and other sources that the Russians had shown no apparent alarm over the threats of Austria against Serbia in the two preceding years.[23] Indeed, Henry Lützow, former Austrian Ambassador to Italy, in a letter published in the London *Times* Literary Supplement for December 31, 1925, states that after the

assassination of the Serbian Royal Family in
1903, the Russian government confidentially informed the Austrian government that it would
not interfere if Austrian troops occupied Belgrade.   Finally, he counted upon the sending of
Lichnowsky to England and upon the successful
negotiations with England during the previous
months to secure the neutrality of England,
which, he believed, would keep France and Russia from intervening in behalf of Serbia.   Professor Fay has well summed up the Kaiser's pacific intentions and anticipations as he left for his
vacation cruise on July 6, 1914: [24]

He expected military action by Austria against Serbia, but on July 5 he did not think it probable that the
Austro-Serbian dispute would lead to a European war;
he could safely start next morning as had long been
planned, and as Bethmann advised, on his northern
cruise.   This he would hardly have done, if he had expected that the early action, which he hoped Austria
would take at once instead of delaying more than two
weeks, would certainly involve serious European complications.   Nevertheless, he realized that while it was
not probable that Austria would kindle a European
war, it was possible.   Therefore, early on July 6, before leaving Potsdam at quarter past nine for Kiel, he
had brief separate interviews with subordinate representatives of the army and navy.   He informed each
of his interview with Szögyény.   He told them pri-
vately to inform their chiefs, who were absent on
furlough from Berlin, but added that they need not cut

short their furloughs to return to Berlin, and that no
orders for military preparations need be given, as he
did not expect any serious warlike complications.

Much has been made by some of von Jagow's
denial that he had read the Austrian ultimatum
to Serbia before July 23, 1914, but it would seem
that the most that can be said on this point is that
he hedged like any honorable diplomat. The
matter has little bearing on war guilt, as he
neither inspired nor approved the Austrian ultimatum.

V. GERMANY AND THE AUSTRO-SERBIAN CRISIS

1. The Kaiser and the Serbian Reply

The Kaiser's attitude towards the Austro-
Serbian crisis underwent a marked transformation as soon as he read of the nature of the Serbian reply to the Austrian ultimatum. Not
knowing that the ultimatum was a faked ruse of
Austria, behind which lay the determination to
make war upon Serbia, he took the ultimatum
and the reply seriously, and regarded the latter
as wholly adequate and as removing all justification for a punitive war of Austria against Serbia. On his copy of the Serbian reply he made
the following note: [25]

A brilliant performance for a time-limit of only
forty-eight hours. This is more than one could have
expected! A great moral victory for Vienna; but with

it every reason for war drops away, and Giesl (Austrian minister to Serbia) might have remained quietly in Belgrade! On the strength of this I should never have ordered mobilization!

In his letter to von Jagow of July 28th, setting forth the essentials of his "pledge plan" for the occupation of Belgrade by Austria, he renders an almost identical opinion: [26]

After reading over the Serbian reply, which I received this morning, I am convinced that on the whole the wishes of the Danube Monarchy have been acceded to. The few reservations that Serbia makes in regard to individual points could, according to my opinion, be settled by negotiation. But it contains the announcement *orbi et urbi* of a capitulation of a most humiliating kind, and as a result, *every cause for war* falls to the ground.

This is the definitive answer to those who, like Poincaré,[27] charge that the Kaiser urged the Austrians into a precipitate declaration of war on Serbia. On the contrary, the Austrians actually declared war to escape from the Kaiser's pressure for a pacific settlement of the Serbian dispute after the receipt of the Serbian reply.[28]

2. The Kaiser's Plan to Avert War

The Kaiser was not only convinced that the Serbian reply removed all cause for war, but he was also determined that Austria should be prevented from developing her plans so as to involve Europe in war. It has often been stated that the Kaiser showed no solicitude about war until he heard the early reports of Russian mobilization. This is not true. He became alarmed for the peace of Europe the moment he heard of the rumored Serbian mobilization at the time of handing in the Serbian reply to Austria. On Bethmann-Hollweg's telegram of July 25th he wrote relative to the Serbian mobilization: [29]

This may result in mobilization by Russia; will result in mobilization by Austria!

Learning the next day of Austrian mobilization, as well as the Serbian, he wrote on the margin of Bethmann-Hollweg's telegram advising calmness: [30]

Calmness is the first duty of a citizen! Keep calm—only keep calm! But a calm mobilization is something new, indeed!

By the 27th of July Russian protests and the rumors of Russian military preparations against Austria convinced the Kaiser, Bethmann-Hollweg and von Jagow that Germany must give up her plan of allowing Austria a free hand with Serbia, in the expectation that the Austro-Serbian affair could be kept purely localized, and must resume her policy of the two previous years in the way of restraining Austria.

The solution of the problem which he proposed was for Austria to occupy Belgrade as a guaranty that the Serbians would fulfil their promises, and then hold up further military activity against Serbia. This, together with Austria's declaration that she would respect the sovereignty and territorial integrity of Serbia, he believed should satisfy both Russia and the Austrian army. He summarized this plan in a letter to von Jagow on July 28th: [31]

Nevertheless, the piece of paper (Serbian reply), like its contents, can be considered as of little value so long as it is not translated into *deeds*. The Serbs are Orientals, therefore liars, tricksters, and masters of evasion. In order that these beautiful promises may be turned to truth and facts, a *douce violence* must be exercised. This should be so arranged that Austria would receive a *hostage* (Belgrade), as a guaranty for the enforcement and carrying out of the promises, and should occupy it until the *petita* had *actually* been complied with. This is also necessary in order to give the army, now unnecessarily mobilized for the third time, the external *satisfaction d'honneur* of an ostensible success in the eyes of the world, and to make it possible for it to feel that it had at least stood on foreign soil. Unless this were done, the abandonment of the campaign might be the cause of a wave of bad feeling against the Monarchy, which would be dangerous in the highest degree. In case Your Exellency shares my views, I propose that we say to Austria: Serbia has been forced to retreat in a very humiliating manner, and we offer our congratulations. Naturally, as a result, *every cause for war has vanished.* But a *guaranty* that the promises *will be carried out* is unquestionably necessary. That could be secured by means of the temporary military occupation of a portion of Serbia, similar to the way we kept troops stationed in France in 1871 until the billions were paid. *On this basis,* I am ready to *mediate for peace* with Austria. Any proposals or protests to the contrary by other nations I should refuse regardless, especially as all of them have made more or less open appeals to me to assist in maintaining peace. This I will do in my own way, and as sparingly of Austria's *nationalistic feeling,* and of the *honor of her arms* as possible. For the latter has already been appealed to on the part of the highest War Lord, and is about to respond to the appeal. Consequently it is absolutely necessary that it receive a visible *satisfaction d'honneur;* this is the *prerequisite* of my mediation. Therefore Your Excellency will submit a proposal to me along the lines sketched out; which shall be communicated to Vienna. I have had Plessen write along the lines indicated above to the Chief of the General Staff, who is entirely in accord with my views.

It is worth while to emphasize in this place that this so-called "pledge-plan" was the one which was also independently suggested with enthusiasm by Sir Edward Grey and King George as the procedure best suited to the preservation of the interests of both Austria and Russia, and as a sufficient concession and guaranty to Russia to

justify the cessation of military preparations by
the latter.[32]

3. *Germany and the Diplomatic Proposals*
of 1914

We may now turn to the measures proposed
by the various European countries to bring
about a peaceful settlement of the disputes between Austria and Serbia, and Russia and Austria. Here we shall be able to show the complete falsity of what has been, next to the
alleged Potsdam Conference, the chief point in
the Entente propaganda representing Germany
as primarily responsible for the initiation of hostilities in 1914, namely, the charge that she not
only offered no plans for pacific settlement herself, but resolutely rejected all the plans for
mediation and negotiation suggested by other
states. We shall find that exactly the reverse
was the case. Germany was as fertile as any
other state in suggesting plans for mediation
and negotiation, and warmly coöperated with
England in advancing the two pacific modes
of adjustment and accommodation which were
agreed upon by both England and Germany as
the most feasible and desirable under the circumstances. Ewart has thus briefly summarized the
facts: [33]

We are now to examine the negotiations with reference to the various proposed methods for arriving at a peaceful solution of the quarrel, keeping in view the frequently repeated statement that Germany declined every proposal for accommodation. Four methods were proposed:

1. A Conference at London of the Ambassadors of France, Italy and Germany with Sir Edward Grey.

2. Mediation between Austria-Hungary and Russia.

3. Direct conversations between Austria-Hungary and Russia.

4. Mediation between Austria-Hungary and Serbia.

Of these, Germany and Russia declined the first with Sir Edward Grey's approval. Germany concurred in the second, and actively assisted in it; and eventually proposed the third. The fourth was not suggested until the 27th, and Germany immediately and persistently pressed acceptance of it upon Austria-Hungary.

The first plan listed above, namely, a conference of ambassadors at London, was suggested by Sir Edward Grey on July 26th, when he put forward the proposal that the German, French and Italian ambassadors should meet with him in London to discuss appropriate methods for a peaceful solution of the diplomatic conflict existing between Austria and Serbia. This was rejected by Germany and Austria. Germany and Austria were opposed to a conference to adjust the Austro-Serbian dispute. But France and

Russia were rigidly opposed to any proposal for a conference which would deal with the Austro-Russian difficulties.[34]

On the 27th Italy made the most constructive proposition as to a conference of powers which was brought forward during the whole crisis of 1914.[35] This was the proposal that there be a conference of England, Italy, Germany and France which would be committed to the complete acceptance by Serbia of the Austrian ultimatum, but would save the face of Serbia by allowing her to make this capitulation before a European conference rather than to Austria directly. France ignored the proposal, Grey forwarded it without enthusiasm and Sazonov hypocritically evaded the issue. Germany urged it upon Austria, but the latter rejected it. Morhardt holds that this is the most damaging reflection upon the Entente during the whole period of the negotiations.

The second plan was one of mediation between Austria-Hungary and Russia. This was proposed by Grey on the 24th and 25th of July. Germany at once assented and agreed to mediation between Russia and Austria as soon as an occasion arose which would permit of such action.[36] This procedure was not followed, however, as it was superseded by the method of promoting direct conversations between Vienna and St. Petersburg—the method originally proposed by Grey on July 20th, rejected by Poincaré as early as July 22nd, later suggested by Germany.

On the 28th Sir Edward Grey admitted cheerfully that this third plan was the best method, after all: [37] "As long as there is a prospect of a direct exchange of views between Austria and Russia, I would suspend every other suggestion, as I entirely agree that this is the most preferable method of all." This expedient of direct conversations was urged upon Austria by Germany with great earnestness, but it proved unsuccessful because Russia insisted upon discussing the relations between Austria and Serbia, and Austria maintained that this was her own affair, in spite of vigorous statements to the contrary by Germany after July 28th. As we have seen above, Austria deliberately declared war on Serbia to forestall negotiations. She did not give in and even ostensibly assume to be willing to discuss her Serbian policy with Russia until after the declaration of the Russian general mobilization, which meant an unavoidable general conflict.[38]

The fourth method of pacific accommodation attempted was mediation between Austria-Hungary and Serbia. This proposal came from England and was quickly accepted by Germany. Some of Bethmann-Hollweg's most insistent telegrams to Vienna dealt with the matter of the necessity of Austria's accepting media-

tion.[39] We have indicated earlier that on this
point Berchtold did not even feign to accede until the telegram sent out of Vienna early in the
morning of August 1st, in which he agreed to
accept the mediation of England in regard to
the Serbian issue.   There is little reason to believe that this capitulation was made in good
faith, but even if it had been it would have
availed nothing, as Sir Edward Grey took no
action on the basis of the telegram, Russia had
mobilized, and France had just informed Russia
of her declaration for war.[40]

The above facts are an adequate commentary
upon the accuracy and reliability of Kautsky
and Lichnowsky, and upon the honesty of Mr.
Asquith who, long after the German and Austrian documents were available, quoted approv-
ingly the following from Kautsky: [41]

Austria rejected all mediation proposals that were
made, none of which emanated from Germany. The
latter was satisfied with simply transmitting the proposals of others, or else refusing them at the very outset as incompatible with Austria's independence.

And also the following even more preposterous
misrepresentation from Lichnowsky: [42]

It had, of course, needed but a hint from Berlin to
induce Count Berchtold to be satisfied with a diplomatic success. But this hint was not given. On the
contrary, the war was hurried on.

4. The German Pressure Telegrams

To give some impression of the tension and anxiety at Berlin over the increasing danger of a general European war after the 27th of July, as well as of the severity of the German telegrams to Vienna urging conversations and the acceptance of mediation, we shall quote from some of the representative telegrams of this period and from the Kaiser's personal comments.

On July 30th Bethmann-Hollweg telegraphed to Tschirschky to convey to Berchtold the following appeal to Austria to accept mediation: [43]

As a result we stand, in case Austria refuses all mediation, before a conflagration in which England will be against us; Italy and Roumania to all appearances will not go with us, and we two shall be opposed to four Great Powers. On Germany, thanks to England's opposition, the principal burden of the fight would fall. Austria's political prestige, the honor of her arms, as well as her just claims against Serbia, could all be amply satisfied by the occupation of Belgrade or of other places. She would be strengthening her status in the Balkans as well as in relation to Russia by the humiliation of Serbia. Under these circumstances we must urgently and impressively suggest to the consideration of the Vienna Cabinet the acceptance of mediation on the above-mentioned honorable conditions. The responsibility for the consequences that would otherwise follow would be an uncommonly heavy one both for Austria and for us.

On the same day Bethmann-Hollweg induced the Kaiser to send the following telegram to the Austrian Emperor: [44]

I do not feel myself able to refuse the personal plea of the Czar that I undertake to attempt mediation for the prevention of a world conflagration and the maintenance of world peace, and had proposals submitted to your Government yesterday and today through my Ambassador. Among other things, they provide that Austria should announce her conditions after occupying Belgrade or other places. I should be honestly obliged to you, if you would favor me with your decision as soon as possible.

Later in the day Bethmann-Hollweg sent the following urgent telegram to Tschirschky, insisting that Austria accept mediation upon the basis of the "pledge-plan" as suggested by Germany and Sir Edward Grey: [45]

If Vienna declines to give in in any direction, especially along the lines of the last Grey proposal, as may be assumed from the telephone conversation of Your Excellency with Mr. von Stumm, it will hardly be possible any longer to place the guilt of the outbreak of a European conflagration on Russia's shoulders. His Majesty undertook intervention at Vienna at the request of the Czar since he could not refuse to do so without creating the incontrovertible suspicion that we wanted war. The success of this intervention is, of course, rendered difficult, inasmuch as Russia has mobilized against Austria. This we have announced to

England today, adding that we had already suggested in a friendly tone, both at Paris and Petersburg, the cessation of French and Russian war preparations, so that we could take a new step in this direction only through an ultimatum, which would mean war. We suggested to Sir Edward Grey, nevertheless, that he work energetically along this line at Paris and Petersburg, and have just received through Lichnowsky his assurance to that effect. If England's efforts succeed, while Vienna declines everything, Vienna will be giving documentary evidence that it absolutely wants a war, into which we shall be drawn, while Russia remains free of responsibility. That would place us, in the eyes of our own people, in an untenable situation. Thus we can only urgently advise that Austria accept the Grey proposal, which preserves her status for her in every way.

Your Excellency will at once express yourself most emphatically on this matter to Count Berchtold, perhaps also to Count Tisza.

5. The Alarm of the Kaiser

The state of mind of the Kaiser at this time is admirably reflected by his long note appended to the telegram of Count Pourtalès, the German Ambassador to St. Petersburg, on July 30th telling of the Russian decision to take the fatal step of mobilization: [46]

.If mobilization can no longer be retracted—*which is not true*—why, then, did the Czar appeal to my mediation three days afterward without mention of the issuance of the mobilization order? That shows plainly that the mobilization appeared to him to have been precipitate, and that after it he made this move *pro forma* in our direction for the sake of quieting his uneasy conscience, although he knew that it would no longer be of any use, as he did not feel himself to be strong enough to *stop* the mobilization. Frivolity and weakness are to plunge the world into the most frightful war, which eventually aims at the destruction of Germany. For I have no doubt left about it: England, Russia and France have *agreed* among themselves —after laying the foundation of the *casus foederis* for us through Austria—to take the Austro-Serbian conflict for an *excuse* for waging a *war of extermination* against us. Hence Grey's cynical observation to Lichnowsky "as long as the war is *confined* to Russia and Austria, England would sit quiet, only when we and France *mixed into it* would he be compelled to make an active move against us (") ; i. e., either we are to shamefully to betray our allies, *sacrifice* them to Russia— thereby breaking up the Triple Alliance, or we are to be attacked in common by the Triple Entente for our *fidelity to our allies* and punished, whereby they will satisfy their jealousy by joining in totally *ruining* us. That is the real naked situation *in nuce*, which slowly and cleverly set going, certainly by Edward VII, has been carried on, and systematically built up by disowned conferences between England and Paris and St. Petersburg; finally brought to a conclusion by George V and set to work. And thereby the stupidity and ineptitude of our ally is turned into a snare for us.

So the famous *"circumscription"* of Germany has finally become a complete fact, despite every effort of our politicians and diplomats to prevent it. The net has been suddenly thrown over our head, and England sneeringly reaps the most brilliant success of her persistently prosecuted purely *anti-German world-policy*, against which we have proved ourselves helpless, while she twists the noose of our political and economic destruction out of our fidelity to Austria, as we squirm *isolated* in the net. A great achievement which arouses the admiration even of him who is to be destroyed as its result! Edward VII is stronger after his death than am I who am still alive! And there have been people who believed that England could be won over or pacified, by this or that puny measure!!! Unremittingly, relentlessly she has pursued her object, with notes, holiday proposals, scares, Haldane, etc., until this point was reached. And we walked into the net and even went into the one-ship-program in construction with the ardent hope of thus pacifying England!!! All my warnings, all my pleas were voiced for nothing. Now comes England's so-called gratitude for it! From the dilemma raised by our fidelity to the venerable old Emperor of Austria we are brought into a situation which offers England the desired pretext for annihilating us under the hypocritical cloak of justice, namely, of helping France on account of the reputed "balance of power" in Europe, i. e., playing the card of all the European nations in England's favor against us! This whole business must now be ruthlessly uncovered and the mask of Christian peaceableness publicly and brusquely torn from its face in public, and

the pharisaical hypocrisy exposed on the pillory!!
And our consuls in Turkey and India, agents, etc.,
must fire the whole Mohammedan world to fierce rebellion against this hated, lying, conscienceless nation
of shop-keepers; for if we are to be bled to death,
England shall at least lose India.

The same day he made the following comment
on an article in the London *Morning Post* on
"Efforts towards Peace": [47]

The only possible way to ensure or enforce peace is
that England must tell Paris and Petersburg—its
Allies—to remain quiet, i. e., neutral, to the Austro-
Serbian conflict, then Germany can remain quiet too.
But if England continues to remain silent or to give
lukewarm assurances of neutrality; that would mean
encouragement to its Allies to attack Austro-Germany.
Berlin has tried to mediate between Petersburg and
Vienna on the appeal of the Czar. But His Majesty
silently had already *mobilized* before the appeal; so
that the mediator—Germany—is placed *"en demeure"*
and his work becomes illusory. Now only *England*
alone can stop the catastrophe by restraining its
Allies, by clearly intimating that—as Sir E. Grey declared—it had nothing to do with the Austro-Serbian
conflict, and that if one of its Allies took an active
part in the strife it could not reckon on the help of
England. That would put a stop to all war. King
George has communicated England's intention to remain neutral to me by Prince Henry. On the other
hand the Naval Staff have this morning—July 30—
received a telegram from the German military attaché

in London, that Sir E. Grey in a private conversation with Prince Lichnowsky, declared that if Germany made war on France, England would immediately attack Germany with a fleet! Consequently Sir E. Grey says the direct contrary to what his Sovereign communicated to me through my brother and places his King in the position of a double-tongued liar *vis-à-vis* to me.

The whole war is plainly arranged between England, France and Russia for the annihilation of Germany, lastly through the conversations with Poincaré in Paris and Petersburg, and the Austro-Serbian strife is only an excuse to fall upon us! God help us in this fight for our existence, brought about by falseness, lies and poisonous envy!

As Ewart remarks: [48] "The attitude here revealed is not that of a man who finds himself, at his own selected moment, in the situation for which he has secretly prepared for forty years." It is a striking indication of the progress in our knowledge of war guilt in the last six years that even so calm and judicious a student of the problem as Professor Fay could in 1920 designate the above statements of the Kaiser as a "raving philippic," [49] while to-day we must recognize that they are a fairly accurate and concise description of the actual facts as they have been established by the documents published since 1919, and especially the Russian and British documents published since 1921.

The "die-hards" contend that these German efforts to restrain Austria were not genuine but were made only to save appearances in the event of war. This is patently absurd, though, of course, if war broke out, Germany wanted her case to be as good as possible before European opinion.

6. Did Germany Decide for War on the 30th of July?

A very important point in connection with the above is the question as to whether Germany gave up hope of diplomatic negotiations and decided upon war before she learned of the Russian general mobilization, ordered late in the afternoon of July 30th and announced the following day. If it can be demonstrated that she did, then the basic argument that Germany was driven into the decision upon war by the Russian mobilization falls to the ground, though, of course, it would still be true that the Russian mobilization long preceded the German. A distinguished student of the problem of war guilt has made this assertion, namely, M. Pierre Renouvin, in his important work *Les Origines immédiates de la guerre*.[50] Professor Fay has, however, pointed out clearly the obvious falseness of this contention.[51] It is based primarily upon the fact that at 11.20, on the night of July

30th, Bethmann-Hollweg wired Tschirschky, cancelling a restraining telegram sent somewhat earlier that day. Renouvin, and Poincaré, who has breathlessly followed him in this, contend that this is proof that by this time Bethmann-Hollweg had surrendered to Moltke and the militarists.

Such an interpretation is preposterous in the light of what we know to have been the real reasons of Bethmann-Hollweg for this action. As Fay and Ewart point out from the documents,[52] there were two reasons why this was done. The first was the receipt of information from the army that the Russians were mobilizing on the German frontier, and he desired to get further information on this point before proceeding with diplomatic pressure. The second cause of his action was the receipt, late on the 30th, of a telegram from George V to Prince Henry of Prussia, stating that England was attempting to restrain France and Russia, and asking Germany to press Austria more vigorously to accept the "pledge-plan" for the occupation of Belgrade alone. Bethmann-Hollweg desired to examine this telegram and its implications before continuing with his own pressure plans. How far the Chancellor was from desisting in his peace pressure is evident from the fact that at 2.45, on the morning of July 31st, he sent the telegram of George V on to Vienna with his approval and a forceful appeal for an immediate decision from Vienna. As Professor Fay describes his action: [53] "Bethmann grasped at this telegram from George V as another chance for peace. He sent it on with a last urgent appeal 'for a definite decision in Vienna within the course of the day'." By the next day Germany learned of the Russian general mobilization, and from that time on her diplomatic activities were chiefly directed towards the futile effort to induce Russia to suspend her mobilization, without which there was no chance of averting war. Germany, then, remained firm for pacific negotiations until the end. What prevented her from success in these endeavors were the stubbornness and evasion of Austria, encouraged, perhaps, by Moltke's precautionary telegrams to Hötzendorf, the precipitate and unjustifiable Russian mobilization, encouraged by Poincaré and the announced mobilization of the English fleet.

7. The Szögyény Telegram, and Bethmann-Hollweg's Inquiry concerning the Attitude of England

This will be as appropriate a place as any to dispose of two specious criticisms of German efforts to settle the July crisis by diplomacy which are still tenaciously adhered to by the "straw-clutchers" and "bitter-enders" among the "old guard," namely, the *Szögyény Telegram* of July 27, 1914, and Bethmann-Hollweg's attempt to discover the attitude of Great Britain in the crisis on July 29th. The telegram sent to Vienna by Count Szögyény, the Austrian Ambassador at Berlin, was held by the American delegation at Versailles to be conclusive proof of the insincerity of Germany in supporting Grey's diplomatic efforts. This telegram, with Montgelas' reflections, follows:

"The Foreign Secretary informed me, in the strictest confidence, that the German Government would shortly acquaint Your Excellency with possible English proposals of mediation.

"The German Government give the most positive assurance that they do not identify themselves in any way with the proposals, they are even decidedly against their being considered, and they only forward them, in compliance with the English request.

"In doing so they are guided by the view that it is of the utmost importance that England should not make common cause with Russia and France at the present moment. Consequently everything must be avoided that would break off the communications between Germany and England which have hitherto worked so well. If Germany were to tell Sir Edward Grey plainly that she would not forward the wish to Austria-Hungary, which England thinks more likely to be considered if it comes through Germany, this would lead to the very state of affairs it is so essential to avoid.

"Moreover, whenever England made a request of this

kind in Vienna, the German Government would state most explicitly that they did not in any way endorse such requests for intervention, and only passed them on in compliance with England's wish."

"The English Government, it appears, had already approached him (the Foreign Secretary) yesterday through the German Ambassador in London, and through their representative here, with a view to inducing him to support England's wish that we should modify the note to Serbia. He, von Jagow, replied that he would certainly comply with Sir Edward Grey's wish that he should forward England's request to Your Excellency, but he could not second it, as the Serbian dispute was a question of prestige for the Austro-Hungarian Monarchy, in which Germany had an interest.

"He, the Foreign Secretary, had therefore forwarded Sir Edward Grey's Note to Herr von Tschirschky, but without instructing him to submit it to Your Excellency; he had been able to inform the English Cabinet that he did not directly reject the English wish, and had even passed it on to Vienna.

"In conclusion the Secretary of State repeated his view of the case, and begged me, in order to avoid any misunderstanding, to assure Your Excellency that his having acted as intermediary in this instance does not at all mean that he is in favor of the English proposal being considered."

The American delegation at Versailles only published the two first paragraphs of this telegram, which, taken by themselves, must give an impression of Machiavellism. But if the fourth paragraph is correctly read, it does away with this impression. In it the Berlin Gov-

ernment state that whenever an English proposal is
made which they do not think suitable, they will inform
the Cabinet in London that they do not support the
proposal, and are merely forwarding it to Vienna, in
compliance with England's request. This would have
been a perfectly frank and honorable course, and it is
what the German Government really did. With regard
to the purport of the telegram, it should be noted:
(1) that England never proposed that Austria should
"modify the Note to Serbia." The Ambassador was
probably referring to the proposal which reached Berlin on the evening of July 25, that Germany should try
to induce Vienna to consider the Serbian answer satisfactory. (2) This proposal was forwarded to Vienna,
and at the same time the British Chargé d'Affaires was
told that it had only been passed on, and that the Government did not see their way to going beyond this.
(3) Both Herr von Bethmann Hollweg and Herr von
Jagow have stated most positively that they never made
any communication to the Austrian Ambassador, which
would coincide with the two first paragraphs.

To Montgelas' convincing remarks the writer
would add the following considerations. The
telegram referred to a time and events before
Germany had become convinced of the danger to
Europe in the Austro-Serbian dispute and when
she still clung to the view that this struggle could
be localized. Germany's determination upon
restraint of Austria only developed after the 27th
and 28th. The telegram did not refer to any of
the five plans of diplomatic settlement actually

proposed or utilized in the crisis. The telegram is completely out of accord with all of the actual achievements of Germany in regard to diplomatic pressure. Neither Berchtold nor Hoyos, in their post-war efforts to put the blame for war on Germany, has ever invoked the *Szögyény Telegram* in their defence, and Hötzendorf has shown us that after July 29th Berchtold had no doubt as to the sincerity of German pressure on Austria. The French writer, Fabre-Luce, completely repudiates the view of the *Szögyény Telegram* held by the American delegation at Versailles and concludes that the evidence "is sufficient to show that the Ambassador's telegram did not refer to the endeavors to mediate on the 29th and 30th of July, and that, if it faithfully describes the German Government's feelings on the 27th, it merely helps to measure the extent and rapidity of the change [in the attitude of Germany after the 27th]."

The allegation that Bethmann-Hollweg's attempt on July 29th to discover the position of England in the event of a war proves the German decision upon war by that time is even more silly than the Potsdam Conference Myth and the *Szögyény Telegram* accusation. It was a matter of great importance for Germany to learn whether or not England intended to remain neutral. The ineffectiveness of Bethmann-Hollweg's intervention in Vienna and the rumors of Russian mobilization made the outlook dark. Germany certainly had as much justification in being interested in British neutrality as France and Russia had in investigating her likelihood of intervening to aid them. And whereas Bethmann did not inquire until July 29th, Sazonov attempted to force the hand of England as early as the 24th when he stated to Buchanan that he "hoped that his Majesty's Government would not fail to proclaim their solidarity with Russia and France." On the 29th Sazonov was telegraphing to Izvolski: "We have no alternative but to hasten our military preparations and to assume that war is probably inevitable. . . . It is much to be desired that England, without losing time, join France and Russia."

8. *Was German Diplomatic Pressure Exerted too Late?*

It has often been held that German pressure was applied to Austria "too late" to achieve any effective results. It is essential to examine in just what sense and just why it was "too late." [54] It was such because of the combined stubbornness of Austria and the overprecipitate and deliberately provocative general mobilization of the Russian army. Germany was from the first alert as to any symptoms that the proposed punitive war might develop into a

European war, and eager to prevent any such
disaster. She acted as soon as it became at all
evident that localization might not be successful.
It might be said that she should have deserted
Austria in the light of the latter's refusal to accept the German advice, but Germany never
had any opportunity to bring Austria to her
senses in this fashion, for, before she had ceased
exerting pressure on Austria, Russia had intervened with her general mobilization which put
an end forever to any hope of a pacific solution
of the crisis of 1914. Indeed, Russia, following
the advice of France, saw to it that Germany was
afforded no opportunity to desert Austria.
Russia mobilized directly against Germany, and
after the outbreak of hostilities hurled half a million men against the German frontier.

Certainly, the guilt of Russia was incomparably greater.[55] Austria insisted on a local war
for reasons which involved her most vital interests, and under conditions which made Russian
intervention unnecessary and unjustifiable,
namely, the promise to respect the territory and
sovereignty of Serbia. Even more, Russia
knowingly took the fatal step before it was in
any sense certain that Germany's pressure on
Austria would not lead her to accept the pledge-
plan favored by the Kaiser, George V and Sir
Edward Grey. Indeed, at the time of proclaim-
ing the mobilization, there seemed more proba-

bility of Austrian capitulation than at any other period in the crisis up to that moment.[56]   Therefore, if Germany was "too late" with her pressure for peace, it was not her fault but that of Austria and, particularly, Russia.   And certainly neither France nor England can criticize Germany on this ground, as France made no effort whatever to restrain Russia, and England made but the most feeble, if not utterly faked and deceptive, efforts to restrain Russia, and none at all to restrain France.[57]   Nor can the Russians complain about Austrian stubbornness in accepting mediation, as Sazonov, having been given a blank cheque by Poincaré in St. Petersburg, warned the other powers at the outset that Russia rejected in advance any proposals for moderation with respect to Russia's policy towards Austria.[58]

VI. THE KAISER AND THE OUTBREAK OF HOSTILITIES

We shall reserve a detailed consideration of the Russian mobilization which produced the World War for the next chapter, limiting ourselves here to a discussion of Germany's reaction to the military preparations of Russia.   During the 27th and 28th of July there were repeated rumors brought to Berlin of extensive military preparations on the part of the Russians, rumors which we now know to have been founded upon

substantial facts.[59]   Late in the evening of July
28 the Kaiser sent the following telegram to the
Tsar, urging him to keep the Russian situation
under control:[60]

It is with the gravest concern that I hear of the impression which the action of Austria against Serbia
is creating in your country. The unscrupulous agitation that has been going on in Serbia for years has
resulted in the outrageous crime to which Archduke
Franz Ferdinand fell a victim. The spirit that led
Serbians to murder their own king and his wife still
dominates the country. You will doubtless agree with
me that we both, you and me, have a common interest,
as well as all Sovereigns, to insist that all the persons
responsible for the dastardly murder should receive
their deserved punishment. In this politics play no
part at all.

On the other hand I fully understand how difficult it
is for you and your Government to face the drift of
your public opinion. Therefore, with regard to the
hearty and tender friendship which binds us both from
long ago with firm ties, I am exerting my utmost influence to induce the Austrians to deal straightly to
arrive at a satisfactory understanding with you. I
confidently hope you will help me in my efforts to
smooth over difficulties that may still arise.

On the morning of July 29 the Tsar signed an
order for the general mobilization of the Russian army, and during the day General Dobrorolski, chief of the mobilization division, made his

preparations for sending out the announcements and orders involved.[61]   But at 6.30 in the afternoon of July 29 the Kaiser sent the following telegram to the Tsar: [62]

I received your telegram and share your wish that peace should be maintained.   But as I told you in my first telegram, I cannot consider Austria's action against Serbia an "ignoble" war.   Austria knows by experience that Serbian promises on paper are wholly unreliable.   I understand its action must be judged as tending to get full guarantee that the Serbian promises shall become real facts.   Thus my reasoning is borne out by the statement of the Austrian Cabinet that Austria does not want to make any territorial conquests at the expense of Serbia.   I therefore suggest that it would be quite possible for Russia to remain a spectator of the Austro-Serbian conflict without involving Europe in the most horrible war she has ever witnessed.   I think a direct understanding between your Government and Vienna possible and desirable and as I already telegraphed to you, my Government is continuing its exertions to promote it.   Of course military measures on the part of Russia which would be looked on by Austria as threatening would precipitate a calamity we both wish to avoid and jeopardize my position as mediator which I readily accepted on your appeal to my friendship and my help.

This made a strong impression upon the Tsar, who, between 9 and 11 P. M., ordered the Russian Minister of War to stop the general mobilization and remain content with a partial mo-

bilization.[63] But on the afternoon of the 30th
Sazonov persuaded the Tsar to consent once
more to the ordering of the general mobilization.
Sazonov telephoned this information to the Chief
of Staff about 4 P. M. on the 30th.[64] By 7 P. M.
the announcement of the general mobilization
had been telegraphed throughout the Russian
Empire. At 2 P. M. on the 31st the Kaiser made
a last desperate appeal to the Tsar: [65]

In my endeavors to maintain the peace of the world
I have gone to the utmost limit possible. The responsibility for the disaster which is now threatening the
whole civilized world will not be laid at my door. In
this moment it still lies in your power to avert it. Nobody is threatening the honor or power of Russia who
can well afford to await the result of my mediation.
My friendship for you and your Empire, transmitted
to me by my grandfather on his deathbed, has always
been sacred to me and I have honestly often backed up
Russia when she was in serious trouble, especially in
her last war.

The peace of Europe may still be maintained by
you, if Russia will agree to stop the military measures
which must threaten Germany and Austria-Hungary.

These telegrams prove how eager the Kaiser
was to avert hostilities. Moreover, his deeds at
the time agree with his words, something which
cannot be claimed for Sazonov, Poincaré, Grey
or George V. In spite of the fact that French,
Russian and British authorities had long assumed

that Russian mobilization was equivalent to a
Russian declaration of war upon Germany, and
would in all probability be followed by an immediate declaration of war by Germany, the
Kaiser did not actually declare war upon Russia
until two days after Russian general mobilization had been determined upon, and after all of
his efforts to induce the Tsar to suspend mobilization had completely failed.   At 1 P. M. on July
31st Germany proclaimed "the state of imminent
danger of war."   At 3.30 on the afternoon of
the 31st she warned Russia that she would mobilize unless Russia suspended mobilization
within twelve hours.   At 5 P. M. on the next day
(August 1), after more than twenty-four hours'
delay, instead of twelve, to receive the Russian
answer which never came, Germany ordered
mobilization, and an hour later declared war on
Russia.[66]   Judge Bausman comments in the following manner on the Kaiser's moderation and
hesitation with respect to mobilization and the
declaration of war:

To me the patience of the Kaiser is incredible. . . .
The fact is that if we look at this thing purely from
the standpoint of German safety, the Kaiser should
have ordered general mobilization a week sooner than
he did, or at least have served upon Russia his ultimatum that her military preparations cease.

Sazonov and Poincaré, in their attempts to
defend their action, have contended that Russian

mobilization was not equivalent to war, but this is pure quibbling and misrepresentation. The French and Russian military authorities from 1893 onward definitely operated on the candid assumption that this mobilization was equivalent to war, and expected a German declaration of war to follow immediately. When the English arranged their military conventions with France and Russia they fully accepted this view. Further, as Morhardt demonstrates, the Tsar, George V, the Kaiser and most of the leading statesmen and diplomats of 1914 frankly admitted this to be the fact.[67] Viviani openly proclaimed the first to mobilize as the aggressor, and tried to demonstrate that Germany had been the first.[68] Further, on July 25th, Sir George Buchanan, the British Ambassador at St. Petersburg, solemnly warned Sazonov that Russian mobilization would inevitably bring on a European war.[69]

Another war-time myth should be mentioned here, namely, the allegation that Russia determined upon general mobilization because of the publication of a false report of German mobilization in the Berlin *Lokalanzeiger* at 1 P. M. on July 30th.[70] How preposterous this assertion is will be fully demonstrated in the next chapter.[71]

The "straw-clutchers," in their effort to sustain their thesis of German responsibility for the

precipitation of the World War, fall back upon
Moltke's telegrams to Conrad on July 31st, urging the latter to stand firm in his military plans
and to hasten Austrian mobilization. This, they
allege, proves that Moltke was determined
upon war from the beginning and deliberately
"double-crossed" the Kaiser and Bethmann-
Hollweg.

Count Montgelas and Herr von Schäfer have
thoroughly disposed of this fiction, supported by
Bernadotte Schmitt, Heinrich Kanner and others, in masterly articles in the *Kriegsschuldfrage* for August, 1926, and in the *Revue de
Hongrie* for November 15, 1926. On July 27th
Moltke telegraphed to his wife to remain at the
opera festival as he did not expect any military
crisis before August 15th, if at all. This remained his attitude until the arrival in Berlin of
frequent and credible rumors of Russian mobilization. As late as the 31st Moltke stated that
the civil government was in full control in Berlin and that he could assume no control of the
situation until the rumored Russian mobilization
was fully confirmed. Further, Moltke demanded three independent and reliable confirma-
tions of the Russian mobilization before he would
consent to request German mobilization.[72]

When Germany found herself unavoidably
involved in war with Russia she attempted to
secure the neutrality of France and England.

The futility in any hope of inducing France to remain neutral is now well known since the publication of the Russian documents.[73]   Poincaré had firmly bound himself anew to fulfil the promises he made to Russia in 1912 which we described in an earlier chapter.[74]   But, more important than this, we now know that late in the evening of July 31st the French government had firmly and irrevocably decided upon war, and that, at 1 A. M. on the morning of August 1st, Izvolski telegraphed this information to Sazonov.[75]   Hence, France had decided upon war at least sixteen hours before Germany declared war on Russia.   Technically France was not bound by the terms of the alliance with Russia to come to her aid in 1914, in the light of the priority of the Russian mobilization to that of the German.[76]

It was equally impossible to persuade England to remain neutral.   As early as the 25th of July Sir Edward Grey had envisaged Russian mobilization, and he steadfastly refused to put any firm pressure on Russia to compel her to suspend her fatal military preparations.   How misleading is the conventional assertion that England entered the War because of the invasion of Belgium may be seen from the fact that on August 2nd, long before the German invasion, Grey assured Paul Cambon, the French Ambassador in London, that England would enter the War on the side of France and Russia.[77]   Germany would very probably have kept out of Belgium if Grey had promised neutrality on this basis, but he refused to commit himself.[78] Germany even proposed not to attack France if England would remain neutral, but the offer availed her nothing. The German declaration of war on France was a mere formality, and the English declared war on Germany.

We might here also discuss briefly the attitude of the German officials and diplomats at the time of the outbreak of the World War. The French, Russians and British, fighting for their lives on the defensive, and hypothetically terror-stricken, should have been much downcast at the prospect, while the Germans, at last realizing the prelude to their plans of a generation for world dominion, should have been enormously elated. It is surprising that the reverse seems to have been the case. Paléologue tells us of the great enthusiasm of the Russians (excepting the Tsar) for war,[79] and Izvolski tells of the "hearty, high spirits" with which the French informed him of their decision for war.[80] While Grey and Asquith took their decision for war with some gravity, there was enormous enthusiasm on the part of Churchill, Bonar Law, Maxse and Nicolson.[81] Yet, von Tirpitz and the British military attaché in Berlin tell us of the distress of the Kaiser when war was determined upon; the British Ambassador in Berlin has given us a graphic picture of Bethmann-Hollweg as near a collapse during his last interview with him; and Buchanan, Paléologue and Baron Schilling have recounted how Pourtalès, the German Ambassador to Russia, broke down and wept when he handed the declaration of war to Sazonov.[82]

VII. THE GERMAN INVASION OF BELGIUM
AND THE GERMAN ATROCITIES

There is no doubt whatever that the German invasion of Belgium was a diplomatic blunder of the first magnitude, but that it was a unique crime never contemplated by other powers is pure nonsense. The Franco-British military plans of 1911, 1912, and 1913 contemplated an Anglo-French movement through Belgium to the German frontiers.[83] France and Great Britain were not surprised by the German invasion of Belgium, as they knew of the plan by 1906. For a period of ten years before the War England had periodically approached Belgium to secure Belgian consent to the landing of British troops in Belgium in the event of a war with Germany.[84] The Belgian King expressed himself in 1914 as more fearful of the French than the Germans.[85] In 1914 Germany simply "beat them to it." France did not dare to move into Belgium before the British entry into the War, because this would have turned British opinion against France. Hence in 1914 the French plan of advance in the west was shifted to Alsace.[86]   Grey could not swing British opinion for war until after the Germans had invaded Belgium.[87]   Again, Germany had the candor at once to admit that the invasion of Belgium was a violation of neutral rights, but England defended as legal her atrocious and numerous violations of neutral rights on the seas during the War. The bull-dozing of Greece by Great Britain to force her into the War is highly comparable to the conduct of Germany towards Belgium in 1914.[88]   As Alcide Ebray has shown in his *Chiffons de Papier,* treaty violation was a major recreation of all the European powers in the century before the World War; and it is ironically amusing to consider the Entente indictment of Germany for violating the Treaty of 1839, in the light of the Entente violation of the Fourteen Points by the Treaty of Versailles and of the French violation of the Treaty of Versailles by the Ruhr invasion.

Further, what Germany did after the War began obviously has little or no bearing whatever upon her responsibility for its origin. Hence the absurd nonsense in any such statement as the following from the pen of a "bitter-ender," Mr. Simeon Strunsky, which appeared in the New York *Times* for August 30, 1925: [89]

The telegrams of the diplomats were belied by common sense and experience and utterly refuted by the final event of the German guns against Liége. All the carefully edited citations from telegrams, reports, conversations, letters and speeches, despite their precision of year, day and minute, will not avail to establish Germany's innocence against her record as written in the general impressions of half a century—and in the light of the final event.

It would also be useful here to destroy for all time a phase of Entente propaganda which successfully aroused world opinion against Germany —namely, that of the alleged atrocities of Germany during the War. While war itself is an atrocity, and the Germans may have been guilty of as many acts of misconduct as any other major power, with the possible exception of Russia, the stories which passed current during the War have been utterly repudiated by both Entente and neutral investigators. Even Belgian authorities themselves have denied the truth of such charges of German atrocities in Belgium as those embodied in the Bryce Report and other similar publications. Lloyd George and Nitti have admitted that no one has ever seen a Belgian child with its hands cut off by the Germans. Likewise, in regard to the submarine warfare, Admiral Sims has challenged anyone to produce evidence of more than one German atrocity in the period of submarine activity, and the officers guilty of this were punished by the German government. The astonishing falsification of "atrocity" pictures by the French and the

British has recently been revealed by Ferdinand Avenarius.[90] The following example is one of thousands of similar character: Certain German officers early in June, 1914, had been given prizes for superior riding and manœuvring. They had been photographed proudly exhibiting these trophies. The French took this picture, removed the verbal explanation from beneath it, and replaced it by a new and falsified description representing these officers as defiantly displaying spoil taken from ravaged Polish homes and churches. Likewise, the pictures purporting to exhibit German atrocities in Poland have been shown to be actually pictures of the Russian *pogroms* against the Jews in Poland and elsewhere in 1905 and subsequent years.

Much interest has also been recently aroused by the revelations of General J. V. Charteris, who was, during the War, Chief of the Intelligence Division of the British General Staff.[91] At a speech before the National Arts Club in New York City on October 19, 1925, he naïvely revealed how he had switched the title of the picture of a train-load of dead German horses being taken to a fertilizer plant to a picture of dead German soldiers being taken to the rear. This picture was sent to China, a country believing in ancestor worship, and hence outraged by this picture of the desecration of the dead. The photograph had a great deal of influence

in inducing the Chinese to enter the World
War on the side of the Allies. The picture was
then sent back to England where the dead,
headed for the fertilizer plant, were represented
as in part dead British soldiers. This aroused
great indignation among the British, stimulating
contributions and enlistments in the British Isles.
Charteris still further revealed how he had endeavored to give the fabrication still greater
plausibility by faking a diary to be put in the
pocket of a dead German soldier describing his
horrible experiences while at work in one of these
"corpse factories." An English friend of the
writer reproached Lord Bryce for his part in
spreading the false atrocities stories, but he dismissed the matter with a shrug of his shoulders
and the cynical remark: "Anything goes in
wartime!"

In the recent sensational book, *Behind the
Scenes in French Journalism,* the author, "A
French Chief Editor," thus describes the organi-
zation of propaganda in France during the
World War: [91a]

If you reduce the lie to a scientific system, put it on
thick and heavy, and with great effort and sufficient
finances scatter it all over the world as the pure truth,
you can deceive whole nations for a long time and drive
them to slaughter for causes in which they have not
the slightest interest. We have seen that sufficiently
during the last war and will see it in the next one by

which a kind providence will clumsily try to solve the problem of over-population.

We concluded immediately and very correctly that it is not sufficient to inflame the masses for war, and, in order to escape the accusation of the war-guilt, to represent the enemy as a dangerous disturber of the peace and the most terrible enemy of mankind.

We did not wait for Lord Northcliffe's procedure. On the spur of the moment we appreciated the great importance to enthuse public opinion for our more or less just cause. As early as three days after the outbreak of the war, Viviani promulgated a law which on the same day was passed by the Chamber and the Senate, and which provided as the first installment of a powerful propaganda the trifling amount of 25 million francs in gold for the establishment of *La Maison de la Presse*, a gigantic building, Francois Street, 3, five stories high, without the basement, where the printing presses are located, and the ground floor, with its large meeting hall. A busy, lively going and coming, as in a beehive; trucks arriving, elegant autos with pretentious looking persons. The two hundred rooms contain the work-shops, offices, parlors, and reception-rooms, where those war-mad heroes are domiciled, whose courage grows with the degree of distance from the trenches. From the basement, up to the fifth story, covered with a glass roof—all is the embodiment of concentrated propaganda. In the basement stood the machinery necessary for printing and reproduction, under the glass roof operated the photo-chemigraphic department. Its principal work consisted in making photographs and cuts of wooden figures with cut-off hands, torn-out

tongues, gouged-out eyes, crushed skulls and brains laid
bare.   The pictures thus made were sent as unassailable evidence of German atrocities to all parts of the
globe, where they did not fail to produce the desired
effect.   In the same room fictitious photographs were
made of bombarded French and Belgian churches, violated graves and monuments and scenes of ruins and
desolation.   The staging and painting of those scenes
were done by the best scene-painters of the Paris Grand
Opera.

That bombardment of cities famous for their
antiquities or art treasures is not a unique
German crime or military procedure one may
discover from reflecting upon the fate, during the
last few years, of Damascus, a city far more
precious in the historic traditions of humanity
than Rheims.   The air-bombardment of non-
combatants during the recent Riffian War in
Morocco is also a pertinent case at this point.

Many will doubtless allege that this chapter
constitutes a well-nigh complete "white-washing"
of Germany as far as immediate responsibility
for the World War is concerned, and the writer
frankly admits that such is the case.   But if the
facts lead us to this conclusion we must be willing to accept it, however distasteful it may be.
Of course, no one in his right mind would contend that Germany hereby escapes her due share
of responsibility for the European system of nationalism, imperialism, militarism, navalism and
secret diplomacy which predisposed that conti-

nent towards war, but even here we must completely abandon the idea that Germany was any more guilty in this respect than any of the other major states in Europe after 1870. The writer doubts if it can be proved that she was even as much responsible for the system as France or Russia during this same period. And it must further be recognized that, far from deliberately plunging Europe into war in 1914, the Kaiser acted as vigorously and consistently as any other person in Europe during the acute crisis of 1914 in the effort to avert the development of the general conflict. He may not have written more charmingly during this period than Sir Edward Grey, but he backed up his pretensions to the desire for peace by important concrete acts of restraint, something which cannot be claimed for Grey and his supporters. We, of course, recognize that the speeches and personal traits of the Kaiser had often raised apprehensions prior to 1914, but so had the acts and words of Edward VII and the diplomacy of Delcassé and Izvolski.

This chapter must not, of course, be interpreted in any sense as an argument for or against the German system of government in 1914, or for the superiority or inferiority of German culture. To hold Germany relatively guiltless as far as the immediate precipitation of the World War is concerned does not prove Cologne Cathedral superior to Rheims or Notre Dame,

Rhine wine more delectable than sparkling Bur-
gundy, Goethe more seductive than Rabelais, or
Eucken more abstruse and profound than Berg-
son. Nor are we assuming high idealism on the
part of Germany at the close of July, 1914.
Her restraint of Austria was certainly intensified by the increasing fear of English intervention and of Italian defection.

Some have contended that even if Germany
did not cause the War in 1914, her policies and
conduct would sooner or later have plunged
Europe into general warfare. Taking the situation as it existed before June 28, 1914, there is no
ground whatever for such a view. She was on
better terms with England than at any previous
period for some fifteen years, and had reached
a working agreement with England concerning
naval construction. It is highly probable that
von Tirpitz would have been dismissed after the
ratification of the treaty with England over the
Near East. There was bitter antagonism between him and Bethmann-Hollweg, and events
were shaping up in favor of the policies of the
latter. Aside from the possible development of
greater Franco-Russian bellicosity, there is no
reason to think that Germany would have grown
more militaristic after 1914, if the War had not
come, and there are many reasons for believing
that she would have become less warlike.
Hence, if she did not desire war in 1914, there
is little probability that she would have wanted

a war in 1916, 1918 or 1925.   On the other hand,
Lowes Dickinson contends (*International Anarchy*, p. 466) that the documents on the period
from 1912 onward are ample to convince one
that Russia would have started a European war
as soon as her military preparations were complete, namely, in 1915 or 1916.

VIII. CONCLUSIONS

(1) Germany was in no sense uniquely responsible for the system which divided Europe
into "two armed camps" by 1912.   In 1914 she
had no reason for desiring war, as all of her ambitions were being more effectively realized by
peace than they could have been by war.

(2) There is no basis in fact for the myth of
the Potsdam Crown Council of July 5, 1914,
at which the Kaiser is supposed to have revealed
his foul plot to throw Europe into universal
carnage.

(3) The Kaiser, severely shocked and alarmed
by the assassination of the Archduke, was in favor of rapid and severe action by Austria against
Serbia, though he was quite content that the humiliation of Serbia should be diplomatic rather
than military.   He agreed on July 6th to stand
back of Austria in whatever policy she should
take in regard to Serbia.   This was a risky promise, but at the time the Kaiser had no expectation
that the possible punitive war of Austria on Serbia would lead to a general European war.   And

his blank cheque to Austria cannot form the basis for holding him directly responsible for the War, because the policies and action of Austria in regard to Serbia prior to July 25th, which were tacitly encouraged by the Kaiser, furnished no adequate moral or legal reasons for the Russian mobilization.

(4) The Serbian reply, in the light of the severity of the Austrian demands, greatly pleased the Kaiser, and he believed that it removed all justification for even Austrian mobilization against Serbia. He was distinctly opposed to the Austrian declaration of war on Serbia.

(5) Austria did not declare war on Serbia because of German incitement, but to create a situation which would allow her to escape from the pressure which Germany was beginning to put on her to compel her to submit her dispute with Serbia to mediation and to begin conversations with Russia.

(6) When the Kaiser saw that a European war was possible because of the threatening attitude of Russia towards Austria, he pressed Austria to accept mediation and conversations. This pressure was "too late" only because of Austrian obstinacy, and, above all, because his efforts were cut short by the premature, unprovoked and indefensible Russian general mobilization. Neither the *Szögyény Telegram* nor Bethmann-Hollweg's interrogation of England on the 29th affords any foundation whatever for

doubting the extent, intensity or sincerity of the German pressure of Austria for peace after July 27th.

(7) Germany did not decide to resort to war on the night of July 30th. The Moltke telegrams to Conrad were purely precautionary and were provoked by well-founded rumors of Russian mobilization. There is no ground whatever for the assertions of Poincaré and Sir Edward Grey that the militarists were in control of the situation in Germany before late in the afternoon of July 31st, when the Russian action had made it practically impossible to avert hostilities.

(8) In spite of the fact that the Russian, French and British authorities had for years agreed that Russian general mobilization was equivalent to a Russian declaration of war on Germany, and had expected it to be answered immediately by a German declaration of war, the Kaiser, though gravely threatened by war on two fronts against overwhelming odds, did not declare war until exactly forty-eight hours after the final issuance of the Russian mobilization order, and after he had waited for more than twenty-four hours to receive an answer from Russia to an ultimatum with a twelve-hour limit.

(9) He then tried to localize the war in the East and secure French and British neutrality, but the French sixteen hours before had telegraphed to Russia their declaration for war upon

Germany. The next day (August 2nd), and two days before Germany invaded Belgium, Sir Edward Grey gave his promise to the French Ambassador which implied that England would join France in making war on Germany.

(10) The Belgian question has nothing whatever to do with the question of the responsibility for bringing on the World War. The British and French had similar plans for meeting the Germans in Belgium, but the peculiar circumstances of getting England into the War in 1914 compelled them to modify these plans at that time. This fact does not excuse Germany, and she has never tried to pretend that the invasion was legal, but it does show that her act was not one of unique perfidy never contemplated by another state.

(11) There is no evidence that Germany resorted to a war of "frightfulness" or was guilty of "atrocities" to a greater degree than any of the other states involved, not even excepting the United States. The falsity of the major charges against Germany in this respect have been completely exposed by Entente and neutral, as well as German, investigators.

(12) There is no evidence that any responsible element in Germany in 1914 desired a world war, and the Kaiser worked harder than any other European statesman during the crisis to avert a general European conflagration.

We may accept as an accurate estimate of the

whole problem of Germany's rôle in 1914 the conclusions of Dr. John S. Ewart: [92]

Publication of the foreign office records of Germany and Austria-Hungary makes perfectly clear not only that Germany did not select 1914 for a European war, but that she was strongly opposed to its outbreak. Unquestionably, she agreed to the Austro-Hungarian pressure upon Serbia, and urged expedition in its prosecution; for, in her view, punishment of Serbia was necessary for the maintenance, unimpaired, of the integrity of the Dual Monarchy, and, consequently, for Germany's own military security. But it is equally unquestionable that when Serbia, in her reply to the Austro-Hungarian demands, made extensive submission, and when it became apparent that a local war would take on European proportions, Germany endeavored to effect accommodation of the difficulty. . . .

When, on the 27th–28th, Germany became aware of the character of the Serbian reply to the Austro-Hungarian note, her attitude changed, and from that time she persistently urged, even to the extent of threat of non-support, conciliatory methods on her ally. Recognition of the probability that a local war would immediately become one of European dimensions probably deepened Germany's desire for conciliation. . . .

This view is also confirmed by the personal letter of Sir Edward Goschen, British Ambassador to Germany, written to Sir Arthur Nicolson on July 30, 1914, in which he says:

I have a stronger conviction than Cambon that both the Chancellor and Jagow would like to avoid a general war—whatever may be the opinion of the hot-headed division and the general staff. This is not only my opinion but the opinion of most diplomats and many Germans. . . . I hear from all sides that the financial and industrial classes are dead against a war in any shape—but particularly against a war which in its origins does not touch German interests."

SELECTED REFERENCES

Avernarius, F., *How the War Madness was Engineered;* Bausman, F., *Let France Explain;* Brandenburg, E., *Von Bismarck zum Weltkriege;* Bülow, B. von, *Die Krisis; Die ersten Stundenschläge des Weltkrieges;* Delbrück, H., *Kautsky und Harden; Der Stand der Kriegsschuldfrage;* Dobrorolski, S., *Die Mobilmachung der russischen Armee, 1914;* Ewart, J. S., *The Roots and Causes of the Wars;* Fay, S. B., "New Light on the Origins of the World War," *American Historical Review,* July and October, 1920; "Morgenthau's Legend of the Potsdam Council," in *Kriegsschuldfrage,* May, 1925; Goos, R. (Ed.), *The Austrian Red Book;* Grelling, R., *La Campagne "Innocentiste" en Allemange et le Traité der Versailles;* Hammann, O., *Um den Kaiser; Deutsche Weltpolitik, 1890–1912;* Kautsky, K., *Wie der Weltkreig entstand;* Lichnowsky, K. M., *My London Mission;* Marx, W., "Responsibility for the War," in *Foreign Affairs* (American), January, 1926; Montgelas, M., *The Case for the Central Powers; The Outbreak of the World War,* edited by Max Montgelas and Walther Schücking; Renouvin, P., *Les Origines immédiates de la guerre;* Schilling, M. F., *How the War Began;* Wilhelm, Kronprinz, *Ich suche die Wahrheit.*

FOOTNOTES AND FURTHER REFERENCES

[1] E.g. Simeon Strunsky in New York *Times*, August 30, 1925, Section 3, pp. 1, 25; and editorial Ibid., September 14, 1925.

[2] Cf. C. P. Gooch, *Germany*, Chap. vi; Ewart, op. cit., pp. 451 ff.; C. Seymour, *The Intimate Papers of Colonel House*, Vol. I, p. 261. E. Ludwig's book on the Kaiser is little more than a caricature, deplored even by German liberals.

[3] Ewart, op. cit., p. 569. See also von Wegerer in *Current History*, July, 1926.

[4] Montgelas, *The Case for the Central Powers*, p. 207.

[5] Henry Morgenthau, *Ambassador Morgenthau's Story*, pp. 83–87.

[6] Fay, loc. cit., pp. 309–15; and P. Renouvin, *Les Origines immédiates de la guerre*, pp. 13 ff.

[7] Loc. cit., October, 1925, p. 14.

[8] Cf. Sir Edward Grey, *The Conflict for Human Liberty;* W. S. Davis. *The Roots of the War;* J. M. Beck, *War and Humanity*.

[9] H. Friedjung, *Das Zeitalter des Imperialismus*, Vol. III; E. Brandenburg, *Von Bismarck zum Weltkriege*.

[10] *Austrian Red Book*, Vol. I, p. 15.

[11] *Outbreak of the World War* (i.e., Kautsky collection of German documents), pp. 59–60.

[12] *Austrian Red Book*, Vol. I, p. 15.

[13] *Outbreak of the World War*, p. 61.

[14] Ibid., p. 93.

[15] Ibid., p. 90.

[16] Ibid., p. 96.

[17] Ibid., p. 113.

[18] Ibid., p. 163.

[19] Ibid., p. 182.

[20] Ibid., p. 186. On this same telegram from the German Minister at Belgrade he also commented in regard to the Serbians: "Just tread hard on the heels of that rabble."

[21] See above, pp. 184 ff.

[22] *Outbreak of the World War*, p. 266.

[23] See also the remarks of Izvolski, above, pp. 114–15, as to the alarm of the French over Russia's apparent indifference.

[24] *American Historical Review*, July, 1920, p. 629.

[25] *Outbreak of the World War*, p. 254.

[26] Ibid., p. 273.

[27] In *Foreign Affairs*, October, 1925, pp. 14–15.

[28] Ewart, op. cit., Vol. II, pp. 1097–8.

[29] *Outbreak of the World War*, p. 201.

[30] Ibid., p. 208.

[31] Ibid., pp. 273–4.

32 Ewart, op. cit., pp. 1081, 1156.

33 Ewart, p. 1073; cf. Renouvin, op. cit., pp. 66 ff., 120 ff.

34 Ewart, pp. 1073 ff.

35 Morhardt, *Les Preuves,* Part II, Chap. vii.

36 Ewart, pp. 1077–8.

37 Ibid., p. 1084.

38 See above, pp. 211–13; and Ewart, pp. 1091 ff., 1110 ff.

39 See below, pp. 265 ff.

40 Montgelas, op. cit., pp. 1:65–9, 176, 184–7.

41 H. H. Asquith, *The Genesis of the War,* pp. 280.

42 Ibid., p. 290.

43 *Outbreak of the World War,* p. 345.

44 Ibid., p. 371.

45 Ibid., pp. 372–3.

46 Ibid., pp. 349–50.

47 Ibid., p. 351.

48 Ewart, op. cit., p. 1083.

49 *American Historical Review,* October, 1920, p. 50.

50 Op. cit., pp. 138–41, 162, 259–61; followed by Fabre-Luce.

51 *American Historical Review,* October, 1920, pp. 50–51; and, especially, in *The Political Quarterly,* December, 1925, pp. 628–9.

52 Fay, loc. cit.; and Ewart, p. 1109.

53 *American Historical Review,* October, 1920, p. 51.

54 Fay, in *American Historical Review,* July, 1920, p. 639; October, 1920, p. 52; cf. Ewart, pp. 1123 ff.

55 Ewart, pp. 1123 ff.; G. Frantz, *Russlands Eintritt in den Weltkrieg.* The new evidence completely invalidates Gooch's statement to the contrary in his *History of Modern Europe,* p. 547.

56 Ewart, pp. 1112–13; 1122–23; Montgelas, op. cit., pp. 156–65.

57 Montgelas, pp. 169 ff.; Loreburn, *How the War Came;* Morel, *The Secret History of a Great Betrayal;* Morhardt, *Les Preuves.*

58 *Falsifications of the Russian Orange Book* (American edition), p. 17.

59 Cf. S. Dobrorolski, *Die Mobilmachung der russischen Armee;* and Frantz, op. cit.; and in *Current History,* March, 1927.

60 *Outbreak of the World War,* pp. 296–7.

61 Dobrorolski, op. cit.; and in French, Morhardt, op. cit., pp. 154 ff.

62 *Outbreak of the World War,* p. 315.

63 M. F. Schilling, *How the War Began,* p. 50; Fay, in *American Historical Review,* January, 1921, p. 246; and references in footnote 61.

64 As above, and Schilling, pp. 65–6.

65 *Outbreak of the World War,* p. 399.

66 Montgelas, op. cit., pp. 167, 170, 172, 187, 192; Morhardt, op. cit., pp. 160–61.

67 Morhardt, pp. 295–6.

68 Ewart, op. cit., Vol. I, p. 107; Montgelas, pp. 182, 187, 189, 202.

69 Hermann Lutz, in New York *Times Current History,* May, 1925, p. 266; *British Blue Book,* No. 17.

70 M. F. Schilling, *How the War Began,* Foreword, p. 9.

71 See below, pp. 365 ff.

72 M. Montgelas, loc. cit., pp. 121–125; and von Schäfer in *Die Kriegsschuldfrage,* August, 1926.

73 Schilling, pp. 113 ff.; *Falsifications of the Russian Orange Book.*

74 *Falsifications of the Russian Orange Book,* p. 53; Morhardt, pp. 117–161.

75 *Falsifications of the Russian Orange Book,* pp. 60–61.

76 G. Dupin, *Conférence sur les responsabilités de la guerre,* pp. 33–5.

77 Ewart, pp. 140, 194–5; Montgelas, pp. 197–8.

78 Ewart, pp. 134 ff., 140, 413 ff.

79 M. Paléologue, *An Ambassador's Memoirs,* Vol. I; cf. also F. Stieve, *Isvolsky and the World War.*

80 *Falsifications of the Russian Orange Book,* p. 61.

81 W. Churchill, *The World Crisis, 1911–1914,* Vol. I; L. J. Maxse, "Retrospect and Reminiscence," in *National Review,* August, 1918.

82 F. Bausman, *Let France Explain,* pp. 26–7; Schilling, *How the War Began,* pp. 76–8.

83 Montgelas, *The Case for the Central Powers,* pp. 224–5; A. Pevet, "De Serajevo à Bruxelles," in *Kriegsschuldfrage,* July, 1924, pp. 261 ff.; E. L. Fox, *Behind the Scenes in Warring Germany,* Chap. XV.

84 Viscount Haldane, *Before the War;* C. A. Beard, *Cross-Currents in Europe Today,* pp. 50–55; Fox, op. cit., Chap. XV.

85 Montgelas, p. 225, and footnote 3.

86 Pevet, loc. cit.

87 Ewart, Vol. I, pp. 131 ff.

88 M. Caracciolo, *L'Intervento della Grecia nella guerra mondiale e l'opera della diplomazia alleata;* S. Cosmin, *L'Entente et la Grèce pendant la grande guerre.*

89 Loc. cit., Section 3, p. 25.

90 F. Avenarius, *How the War Madness was Engineered.* Cf. P. Gibbs, *Now It Can Be Told,* p. 521; R. J. Thompson, *England and Germany in the War,* pp. 48–56; G. Karo, *Der geistige Krieg gegen Deutschland; Truth,* by "Verax" Chap. VII.

91 New York *Times,* October 20, 1925; cf. *Nation,* November 18, 1925.

91a *Hinter den Kulissen des Französischen Journalismus,* pp. 224 ff.

92 Ewart, pp. 569, 1164, 1165.

CHAPTER VI

THE RUSSIAN MOBILIZATION PRECIPITATES THE WORLD WAR

I. THE RUSSIAN SITUATION UP TO THE ASSASSINATION OF THE ARCHDUKE

WE have already set forth in detail in the third chapter of the present work the description of how the French and Russians, under the leadership of Izvolski and Poincaré, drew together in the plan to exploit the Balkan situation as the most suitable and probable basis for realizing a European war which would secure the Straits for Russia and Alsace-Lorraine for France. The plans for joint military action, which had been concluded by 1894, were supplemented by a Franco-Russian naval convention in 1912.[1] The French public had been prepared for the prospect of a war over Balkan problems, hitherto a highly unpopular proposal, by corrupting the French press through the influx of Russian gold feverishly demanded by Izvolski for this purpose, and dispensed under his direction according to suggestions offered by Poincaré and his clique.[2] England had made plans for joint naval action with France against Germany as early as 1905, and these were given a definite form in the correspondence between Grey and Cambon on November 22, 1912.[3] From 1906 onward the British laid plans with the French for the landing of a British expeditionary force on the Continent for coöperation with the French in the west and the Russians in the east to crush Germany between them. By 1912 the Franco-British plans for joint military action were as detailed as those between the French and Russian general staffs. In the spring of 1914 the circle had become complete through the negotiations for an Anglo-Russian naval convention.[4]

We have also called attention to the fact that Poincaré and Izvolski had successfully completed their campaign for the conversion of Sazonov to the war policy by December, 1913. In his famous memorandum to the Tsar on December 8, 1913, he had stated that Russia must have the Straits, and that they could not be obtained without invoking European complications which would lead to a general European war.[5] Izvolski reported in 1912 that Poincaré had told him that the French General Staff felt that Russia and France together could defeat Germany and Austria, but Sazonov took the opposite view.[6] At a secret conference on December 31, 1913, he argued that it would be necessary to make sure of English coöperation in the event of war to make a victory certain and rapid: [7]

In reality a Russian initiative supported only by France would not appear particularly dangerous to Germany. The two states would hardly be in a position to deal Germany a mortal blow, even in the event of military successes, which can never be predicted. A struggle, on the other hand, in which Great Britain participated might be disastrous to Germany, who clearly realizes that if Great Britain were drawn in, the result might be social disturbances of a catastrophic nature within her frontiers in less than six weeks. Great Britain is dangerous to Germany, and in the consciousness of this is to be found the explanation of the hatred with which the Germans are filled in the face of Great Britain's growing power. In view of this it is essential that before taking any decisive steps the Tsar's government shall assure itself of the support of the London Cabinet, whose active sympathy does not seem, in the Minister's view, to be certain.

This doubt and uncertainty was diminished, as we have seen, by the descent of Izvolski, Poincaré and the French ministers upon Sir Edward Grey during the latter's visit to Paris in the spring of 1914.[8] From then on there was little to fear, particularly in the light of Russia's having a strong representative at London in Sir Arthur Nicolson who was Grey's right-hand man in the Foreign Office.[9] As Paléologue tells us, however, the Tsar was still worried in

July, 1914; and laid stress on making absolutely sure of English adherence to the Entente.[10]

It was earlier shown that in February, 1914, the Tsar warmly received Premier Pashitch of Serbia, inquired how many men Serbia could put in the field against Austria, promised to supply Serbia with rifles, cannon and ammunition, and told the Premier to convey his highest regards to the King of Serbia and tell him that Russia would do everything for Serbia.[11] We likewise referred to the secret Crown Council of February 8, 1914, at which it was decided that Russia would be wiser not to strike Turkey unaided, but should await the outbreak of the anticipated European war. Definite plans were made for the campaign against Turkey as soon as the war should come. The Tsar approved the decision of the Council on March 23, 1914.[12] The negotiation of the naval convention with Great Britain was a practical step in preparing for the alignment of powers essential before the conflict should burst forth. We have also summarized the Franco-Russian war aims, which had been mutually agreed upon and officially approved by October, 1914, providing that Russia should have the Straits, and France Alsace-Lorraine. Finally, we made it clear that Russia had been putting forth heroic efforts to increase her army and navy, particularly the former, between 1912 and 1914. Delcassé, during his mission to St. Petersburg in 1913, had encouraged this military program, and France had insisted that the French loans to Russia be spent in large part for the arming of the Russians and the building of strategic railroads to the German frontier.[13]   By the beginning of the summer of 1914 the Russians were "feeling their oats" as a result of the success of their unparalleled military efforts.   During the second week in June the Russian Minister of War, W. A. Sukhominlov, inspired the following article in the semi-official Russian paper, the *Birshewija Wjedomosti,* which was obviously published to help Poincaré and his group in their campaign to increase the French army, and discredit enemies of the army bill of 1913: [14]

Russia does not permit herself to mix into the internal affairs of a foreign nation, but cannot remain merely an unconcerned onlooker during a crisis in a friendly and allied country.   If the French parliament feels itself at liberty to comment on such internal affairs of Russia as army contracts, which are connected with certain economic advantages to the contractors, Russia can certainly not remain indifferent in the face of a purely political question, such as the three-year service term, which constitutes a cause of dissension between the parties of the French parliament.   In Russia there is no divided opinion in regard to this matter.   Russia has done everything to which her alliance with France obligates her, and she now

expects that her ally will perform her obligations as
well. It is known all over the world, what colossal
sacrifices have been made by Russia to bring the
Franco-Russian alliance to the point of the ideal.
The reforms made in the Russian military departments
during the training of Russia's armed forces exceed
anything that has ever been done before in this line.
The recruit contingent this year has, by the latest
ukase of His Majesty, been raised from 450,000 to
580,000 men, and the period of service has been length-
ened by six months. Thanks to these measures there
are in service every winter in Russia four contingents
of recruits under arms, making an army of 2,300,000
men. Only the great and mighty Russia can permit
herself such a luxury. Germany has at her command
over 880,000, Austria somewhere over 500,000 and
Italy rather more than 400,000 men. It is thus quite
natural that Russia should expect from France 770,-
000 men, which is only possible under the three-year
term of service. It must be remarked that these army
increases in time of peace are exclusively for the purpose of effecting rapid mobilization. Russia is at the
same time moving on toward new reforms, to the construction of a whole network of strategic railways,
for the most rapid concentration of the army in case
of war. Russia wants the same thing from France,
which she can only do by realizing the three-year term
of service. Russia and France want no war, but Russia is ready and France must be ready also.

As we indicated in the fourth chapter, we
are not yet certain as to the degree to which the

Russians were informed concerning the plot to assassinate the Archduke, or the extent to which they coöperated in it. The Russians have not yet published the Russo-Serbian dispatches of this period. As Mandl, Simitch and Bogitshevich have shown, there is no longer any doubt that the Russian Minister at Belgrade, N. von Hartwig, and the Russian military attaché at Belgrade, Artamanov, were thoroughly aware of the plot before its execution. Hartwig was very powerful in Serbia.[15]   Franz Josef remarked to Tschirschky on July 2, 1914, that "von Hartwig is master at Belgrade, and Pashitch does nothing without consulting him." [16]   While this may be an exaggeration, there can be no doubt that Pashitch and Hartwig must have discussed a matter of such great importance to the future of both countries as the plot, and certain Russian authorities seem to have given assurances of approval and support.   Certainly the Russians had encouraged and bribed the Serbian plotters in wholesale fashion after 1912.[17]   The distinguished British publicist, Robert Dell, goes even further and alleges that he possesses confidential information to the effect that the plot was laid at the instigation of the Russian authorities: [18]

The complicity of the Serbian government in the assassination is now admitted, or rather triumphantly claimed.   The assassins have become Serbian national heroes.   I believe that we shall sooner or later have convincing proof of the complicity of the Russian government, of which I have already strong evidence from an inside source.   According to my information the Tsar was kept in ignorance of the design.   The late M. Izvolski, at any rate, seems to have known all about it.   How else can one explain his report about the visit to him in Paris, just ,after the assassination, of a diplomatist coming from Belgrade, who brought him the message from the King of Serbia that, "*We* have done a good piece of work"?   My theory of the origin of the War, based on considerations and evidence into which I have not now space to enter, is that the Russian government had decided on war in June, 1914, and that the assassination of Serajevo was deliberately planned to provoke it.

Whether or not we go as far as Mr. Dell, it is certain that the Russian encouragement and financing of the Serbian intrigues and plots against Austria removed any justification for Russian intervention to protect Serbia against the just wrath of Austria.

II. RUSSIA FROM THE MURDER AT SARAJEVO
TO THE GENERAL MOBILIZATION

1. Poincaré at St. Petersburg in July, 1914

There was much excitement in St. Petersburg after the assassination of the Archduke, though just how much and of what kind we shall never

know with full certainty until we possess more
information as to the degree of complicity and
knowledge on the part of St. Petersburg in the
plot of Sarajevo. The long delay of Austria in
taking any action with respect to making demands upon Serbia seemed ominous. As we
have seen above, the delay after July 14th was
chiefly due to the Austrian desire to postpone
submitting the ultimatum to Serbia until after
President Poincaré had left Russia.[19]

It has been charged that Poincaré planned this
visit after the assassination in order to lend encouragement to the Russian militarists and make
a general war certain. Whatever may have
been his intentions and achievements in July,
1914, the visit was planned during the previous
January. He arrived in Russia at 2 P. M. on
July 20th and left at 10 P. M. on July 23rd.[20]
In his defense in *Foreign Affairs* he represents
himself as but a ceremonial figurehead who went
to Russia as a mere symbolic representative of
Franco-Russian friendship and took no part
whatever in discussing foreign policy and
Franco-Russian relations, full charge of which
was left to his Foreign Minister, Viviani.[21] Paléologue and others have presented an altogether
different picture of the situation.[22] If anybody
was a figurehead it was Viviani. All the Russian
attentions were showered upon Poincaré, and he
took full charge of all negotiations and conver-

sations with the Russian court and with the diplomats at St. Petersburg.

Only the more significant aspects of Poincaré's visit can be dealt with here. At the banquet given to him by the Tsar on July 20th, the evening of his arrival, Poincaré made the following reply to the Tsar's toast: [23]

Sire! I thank your Majesty for your hearty reception and beg you to believe that it has been a great pleasure to me to pay to-day another visit to the sublime Ruler of this friendly and allied nation. True to the path followed by my honourable predecessors, I have desired to bring to your Majesty here in Russia solemn evidence of the unalterable feelings dwelling in every French heart. Nearly twenty-five years have passed since our countries with clear vision have united the efforts of their diplomacy, and the happy effects of these enduring associations are daily made apparent in the world balance. Founded upon community of interests, consecrated by the peaceful desires of the two Governments, supported by armed forces on land and sea which know and value each other and have become accustomed to fraternize, strengthened by long experience and augmented by valuable friendships, the alliance to which the sublime Tzar Alexander III and the lamented President Carnot gave the initiative has ever since constantly afforded proof of its beneficial activity and its unshakable strength. Your Majesty can be assured that France in the future, as always in the past, will in sincere and daily co-operation with her ally pursue the work of peace

and civilization for which both the Governments and
both the peoples have never ceased to labour. I raise
my glass in honour of your Majesty, of the Tzarina, of
Her Majesty the Imperial Mother, of His Imperial
Highness the Grand Duke, the heir to the Throne, and
of the whole Imperial Family, and I drink to the
greatness and welfare of Russia.

On the afternoon of the 21st Poincaré met
the assembled diplomats in the Winter Palace.
He ignored all discussions with the German Ambassador, appealed to the Japanese Ambassador
to remain faithful to the Triple Entente, attempted to impress upon the English Ambassador the moderation of the Tsar's policy in
Persia, then scolded the Austrian Ambassador
for Austria's past policy in regard to Serbia and
threatened him in case Austria took a strong
stand in the 1914 crisis, after which he turned
and expressed sympathy to the Serbian Minister.[24]   Paléologue thus describes Poincaré's conversation with the Austrian Ambassador: [25]

After a few words of condolence over the assassination of the Archduke Francis Ferdinand, the President
asked Szápáry,

"Have you had any news from Serbia?"

"The judicial investigation is going on," replied
Szápáry coldly. Poincaré replied, "I cannot but fear
the results of this inquiry, M. l'ambassadeur. I remember two earlier investigations, which did not improve your relations with Serbia. . . . You will re-

member, M. l'ambassadeur . . . the Friedjung affair
and the Prohaska affair."

Szápáry answered drily, "We cannot, M. le Président, permit a foreign Government to prepare assassinations of our sovereigns on its territory."

Poincaré tried, in the most conciliatory tone, to
point out to him that in the present condition of feeling in Europe every Government must act with re-
doubled caution. "With a little good will this Serbian
affair can easily be settled. But it can also easily
develop dangerously. Serbia has very warm friends
among the Russian people. And Russia has an Ally,
France. What complications are to be feared here!"

It has been held by William Stearns Davis and
others that this conversation of Poincaré with
Szápáry proves the former's desire to preserve
peace. In the light of Poincaré's behavior
throughout the crisis of 1914, it would seem far
more probable that he was merely "feeling out"
Szápáry in order more intelligently to arrive
at a final understanding with Russia before
leaving.

Even more significant is Paléologue's descrip-
tion of the attitude of the Grand Duchesses
Anastasia and Melitza, wives of Grand Duke
Nicholas and Grand Duke Peter, respectively, at
a dinner given to Poincaré by Grand Duke
Nicholas on July 22nd. It indicates the great
enthusiasm for war engendered in the Grand
Duke's circle by Poincaré's visit, as well as show-

ing that the war group felt that the Tsar was still opposed to their policy: [26]

"Do you know, we are passing through historic days, blessed days! . . . At to-morrow's review the bands will play nothing but the *Marche Lorraine* and *Sambre et Meuse.* . . . I have had a telegram from my father [King of Montenegro] to-day, in a code we agreed on; he tells me we shall have war before the month is out. . . . What a hero, my father! He is worthy of the Iliad. . . . Stop a minute, look at this little box— it never leaves me; it has Lorraine soil in it, Lorraine soil, which I brought over the border when I was in France two years ago with my husband. And now look at that table of honor! It is decorated entirely with thistles; I would not have any other flowers put on it. Now then! They are thistles from Lorraine! I picked a few stalks from close where I was, brought them here and had the seeds sown in my garden. . . . Melitza, go on telling the ambassador; tell him all to-day means to us, while I go and receive the Tsar."

During the meal I was sitting next the Grand Duchess Anastasia and the dithyrambics continued, mixed with prophecies:

"War is going to break out. . . . There will be nothing of Austria left. . . . You will get Alsace-Lorraine back. . . . Our armies will meet in Berlin. . . . Germany will be annihilated. . . .

Then suddenly—"I must control myself, the Tsar is looking at me."

Poincaré not only stiffened the Russian militarists; before he left he had also blocked Grey's first precautionary proposals for preserving peace. Grey had telegraphed Buchanan on July 20th (*British Documents* No. 67): "It would be very desirable that Austria and Russia should discuss things together if they become difficult." Poincaré's adamant opposition to anything which would be likely to divide the French and Russians and make a pacific adjustment possible is shown by Buchanan's telegram to Grey on the 22nd (*British Documents,* N. 76), stating that Poincaré had sharply disapproved of discussions between St. Petersburg and Vienna: "His Excellency (Poincaré) expressed the opinion that a conversation *à deux* between Austria and Russia would be very dangerous at the present moment." Poincaré suggested putting pressure on Vienna, something which even Nicolson recognized would only make matters worse. This inflexible determination of Poincaré to have France and Russia present a rigid front against Germany and Austria, in order to make any diplomatic adjustment difficult if not impossible, is the real key to his *Politik* throughout the whole crisis of 1914, and completely belies his ostensibly conciliatory conversation with Szápáry.

As his farewell toast on July 23rd Poincaré offered the following: [27]

"Sire! I do not wish to leave this shore without once more declaring to your Majesty how deeply touched I am by the moving cordiality manifested

towards me by your Majesty during my stay, and by
the warm reception accorded to me by the Russian
people. In these proofs of attention with which I
have been overwhelmed, my country will see a new
guarantee for the sentiments which your Majesty has
always manifested towards France and an emphatic
affirmation of the indissoluble alliance which unites
Russia and my native France. With regard to all
the problems which daily confront the two Governments and which demand the concerted activity of their
united diplomats, there has always been agreement and
always will be, and all the more readily because both
countries have frequently experienced the advantages
accruing to each from regular coöperation, and because they are both animated by the same ideal of
peace combined with strength, honour and dignity.

That this speech had a very great effect
on the Tsar is evident from Nicholas' statement
to Cruppi a year later that Poincaré's words of
July, 1914, still rang in his ears. Paléologue regarded Poincaré's Russian speeches as binding
diplomatic documents.[28]

The specific agreements reached are summarized in a telegram which was deliberately
omitted from the British *Blue Book* in 1914:[29]

Minister of Foreign Affairs and French Ambassador
told me confidentially result of visit of President of
French Republic had been to establish the following
points:

1. Entire community of views concerning the various questions facing the Powers, so far as concerns

the maintenance of the general peace and balance of power in Europe, and especially in the East.

2. Resolve to take steps in Vienna to prevent a request for explanation, or any demand equivalent to an interference in Serbia's internal affairs, which Serbia might legitimately regard as an attack on her sovereignty and independence.

3. Solemn confirmation of the obligations laid by the Alliance on the two countries.

This is confirmed by a dispatch sent to Bienvenu-Martin by Viviani from Reval on July 24th: [30]

In the course of my conversation with the Russian Minister for Foreign Affairs we had to take into consideration the dangers which might result from any step taken by Austria-Hungary in relation to Servia in connection with the crime of which the Hereditary Archduke has been a victim. We found ourselves in agreement in thinking that we should not leave anything undone to prevent a request for an explanation or some *mise en demeure* which would be equivalent to intervention in the internal affairs of Servia, of such a kind that Servia might consider it as an attack on her sovereignty and independence.

We have in consequence come to the opinion that we might, by means of a friendly conversation with Count Berchtold, give him counsels of moderation, of such a kind as to make him understand how undesirable would be any intervention at Belgrade which would appear to be a threat on the part of the Cabinet at Vienna.

The British Ambassador, who was kept informed by

M. Sazonov, expressed the idea that his government would doubtless associate itself with a *démarche* for removing any danger which might threaten general peace, and he has telegraphed to his government to this effect.

It is particularly significant that all of these conversations and the Franco-Russian agreements were made before Poincaré, by his own confession, was fully aware of the terms of the Austrian ultimatum to Serbia.[31]   It shows that the French and Russians had firmly determined to take an aggressive stand against Austrian action in Serbia, no matter what it turned out to be.   Poincaré explicitly informed Paléologue that Sazonov should be kept from weakening in the crisis by prompt and persistent promises of French support.   As Dr. Stieve well summarizes this matter: [32]

It proves irrefutably that, in full accord with what has already been established here in regard to the attitude of the French and Russian Governments, an assurance of mutual armed assistance was given before there was any occasion for it arising out of the course of events.   The French and Russian will to war came together here at a critical moment, and from this moment on the Government of the Tsar knew that it had its Ally at its back if in the acute Austro-Serbian conflict it resorted to force.   The blank cheque for world war signed first by Poincaré in 1912 was now signed again.

Poincaré's evil influence upon Russia continued during his homeward voyage. He had instructed Paléologue to keep Sazonov firm. On the 25th Paléologue gave Sazonov a reassurance of French support which was important in leading to the Russian decision upon war on this same day. Buchanan telegraphed to Grey on July 25th (*British Documents* No. 125):

French Ambassador (Paléologue) said he had received a number of telegrams from Minister in charge of Ministry of Foreign Affairs, that no one of them displayed the slightest sign of hesitation, and that he was in a position to give His Excellency (Sazonov) formal assurance that France placed herself unreservedly on Russia's side.

An extremely severe indictment of Poincaré for inciting the Russians at this critical time comes from the pens of two distinguished French publicists. M. Mathias Morhardt of the Paris *Temps,* and one of the most active French leaders in the movements for justice and truth since the days of the Dreyfus Case, thus summarizes the significance of Poincaré's visit to Russia for the subsequent development of events in the crisis of July, 1914: [33]

If one consults the diplomatic records during the first few weeks following June 28, one sees only hesitations and uncertainty. No Foreign Office knew exactly what steps to take. Confusion was general.

The situation required direction and a leader. This leader was M. Raymond Poincaré. In the midst of the European crisis he set out resolutely for St. Petersburg.

The fact alone of undertaking such a trip at such a time meant a plan for war. How could there be any doubt on this matter? If M. Raymond Poincaré wanted peace, a letter to St. Petersburg would have sufficed. If Russia had been warned that France was resolved not to espouse, before the world, the cause of the assassins at Serajevo, the whole matter would have been solved. Peace would have been maintained. . . . Never, if he had not gone to preach savagely the war crusade in St. Petersburg, as M. Maurice Paléologue has told us, would the cowardly Nicholas II have dared to take the aggressive initiative.

The brilliant young French publicist, Alfred Fabre-Luce comes to essentially identical conclusions: [34]

There is, then, no possible doubt about the attitude taken by Poincaré at St. Petersburg between the 20th and the 23rd of July. Without any knowledge whatever of the Austrian demands or of the policy of Germany in the circumstances, he assumed a position of energetic opposition to the Central Powers, gave this opposition a very specific character, and never modified it in the slightest degree to the very end. Such a policy rests upon the assumption that the program of one's adversary is a blind force, incapable of change or modification, and hence does away with any temptation to attempt a pacific adjustment of the situation. From that time on there was a very slight chance indeed of averting war; and, moreover, Poincaré had given Russia *carte blanche* to initiate hostilities any time she wished to do so, as we know from the fact that two days after Poincaré's departure from St. Petersburg, Paléologue, following his instructions, promised Sazonov, without any reservations after the delivery of the Austrian ultimatum, that France would fulfil all the obligations of the alliance. Further, Viviani, who accompanied Poincaré, declared to Nekludof at Stockholm on July 25th that "if it is a war for Russia, it will be, most certainly, a war for France also."

The material just presented as to the part played by Poincaré in inciting the Russians to action in the crisis of 1914, together with the more thorough analysis of the rôle of France in 1914, which will be presented later, makes it necessary to modify somewhat the severe judgment passed upon Russia by Ewart and others holding that state to be the chief culprit in the precipitation of the World War in 1914. While it is entirely true that Russia took the specific steps which made the War inevitable, and the *only* steps which made it unavoidable, yet she would never have dared to act as she did except for the preliminary encouragement of Poincaré and his persistent promises of full French aid in the event of hostilities. Though the decisions of the Russian Crown Council and military authorities on July 25th were made upon the assumption that they were going through with a war program, yet there is evidence that on several occasions Sazonov wavered and could have been turned for peace by French restraint. In every instance of this sort Poincaré resolutely and promptly forced Sazonov into line with his inflexible policy to present an unyielding front to Germany and Austria.[35] Poincaré also boasted to a prominent French publisher after the war that he felt safe in taking his belligerent stand in St. Petersburg because he had in his pocket a letter from George V, promising British support in the impending crisis.

2. *The Austrian Ultimatum and the Russian Decision for War*

The effect of the French assurances upon Russia were quickly apparent. On July 22nd Sazonov sent a telegram to the Russian Minister in Vienna apprising him of the fact that Russia proposed to take a strong stand against any Austrian humiliation of Serbia.[36] This, it will be remembered, was the day before the Austrians handed their ultimatum to Serbia. On the 24th, after he learned the terms of the Austrian ultimatum, he threatened Count Pourtalès, the German Ambassador, concluding his interview with the statement that "if Austria gobbles up Serbia, we shall make war upon her." [37] He told Buchanan and Paléologue on the 24th that he thought Russia would mobilize.[38]   In fact, as early as the 18th he had stated that he would never permit Austria "to use menacing language or military measures against Serbia." [39] The news of the nature of the Austrian ultimatum had stiffened his belligerent attitude still more, as the Austrian demands were sufficiently severe to allow him to use them as the basis for a menacing policy towards Austria and as an excuse for the beginning of military preparations.[40]

There has been a general tendency among revisionist students of war guilt in late years to date the real turning point of the crisis of 1914 from the decision for the general Russian mobilization on July 30th, but it seems to the writer that it is far more accurate to date it from the moment the Russians learned of the terms of the Austrian ultimatum, remembering that the Russians possessed no knowledge whatever of the secret Austrian decision to attack Serbia, even if the latter gave a relatively conciliatory reply to the ultimatum.   The military clique in Russia, led by the Grand Duke Nicholas, and supported by Sazonov, a fanatic apostle of Panslavism and Greek orthodoxy, immediately discerned that the ultimatum was of the sort which would furnish Russia an admirable screen behind which to hide the fact that she had been deter-

mined to seize the first satisfactory opportunity
to turn a Balkan crisis into a European war to
secure the Straits.   According to Schilling and
Buchanan, Sazonov's first words upon learning
the terms of the Austrian ultimatum were:
"This means a European war." [41]   The European complications which Sazonov had foreseen
and longed for on December 8, 1913, and the prospective British adherence to the Franco-Russian
Alliance were now realized.   And Poincaré, who
had assured Izvolski in 1912 that it only remained
for Russia to seize upon an appropriate incident
in the Balkans to bring Germany and France
into a European war, had, before he left Russia,
given Sazonov explicit assurance that the particular "incident in the Balkans" which had been
created by the assassination of the Archduke was
a satisfactory one, quite adequate to evoke the
fulfilment of his promise of two years before.
The "European complications" could now be
manipulated in such a manner as certainly to
bring Europe to war, while Sazonov could mask
his intentions under the pretense of protecting
"a brave and innocent little country" against
wanton bullying, if not complete extinction.

There were very special reasons why 1914 was
a crucial year for France and Russia.   Many
in the British Liberal Party were becoming
alarmed at Grey's commitments to France and
Russia.   The symptoms of a growing *rap-*

prochement between Germany and England in
the early part of 1914 had thrown Paris and St.
Petersburg into a panic, and had stirred Paul
Cambon to heroic efforts in opposition.   In another year Grey's policy might be repudiated.
Further, in June and July, 1914, Russia was
threatened with an economic and social revolution which could probably be averted by war.
The French situation was likewise one which
made 1914 a most favorable year for war.
There were four classes with the colors, and the
radicals might soon develop sufficient strength
under the leadership of Jaurès to abolish the
three-year service act of 1913.[42]

The militarists in Russia were thoroughly
with Sazonov. As early as July 25th, says
Professor Fay: [43]

They were probably convinced that war was "inevitable," and that here was Russia's heaven-sent opportunity to have her final reckoning with Germany
and to acquire Constantinople and the Straits.   Therefore, the sooner full mobilization was declared the
better.

From the 24th onward the Russians carried their
military preparations steadily and unhesitatingly forward, well knowing that they must inevitably plunge the whole Continent into war.
The 30th of July is important only as the date on
which the preparations had been carried so far
that a general mobilization was necessary to

avoid obstructing the plans preparatory to war. In fact, the military crowd argued that the 28th was the desirable day for the order, and secured the Tsar's consent on the 29th, only to have their premature joy cut short by the Tsar's countermanding order after he had received an appeal from the Kaiser.[44] A secret partial mobilization was in operation from the 26th onward in both France and Russia.

The Tsar was unquestionably desirous of preserving peace, once war imminently and concretely faced him, in spite of his approval of the war plans in the preceding March. But the preliminary military plans did not call for his express sanction, and were carried out in part without his knowledge. By the time he was thoroughly aware of what was going on, he found himself quite unable to stem the tide of military zeal in the court, the ministry and the army. His telegram to the Kaiser on the 28th practically confesses his helplessness before the military crowd: [45]

Am glad you are back. In this most serious moment I appeal to you to help me. An ignoble war has been declared on a weak country. The indignation in Russia, shared fully by me, is enormous. I foresee that very soon I shall be overwhelmed by the pressure brought upon me, and be forced to take extreme measures which will lead to war. To try and avoid such a calamity as a European war, I beg you

in the name of our old friendship to do what you can
to stop your allies from going too far.

Upon this telegram the Kaiser quite appropriately commented: "A confession of his own
weakness, and an attempt to put the responsibility on my shoulders. . . . Instead of summoning us to check our allies, His Majesty
should turn to the Emperor Franz Josef and
deal with him in order to learn His Majesty's
intentions." [46]

The one thing which was needed on July 25th
—the day Paléologue gave him formal assurance
of unconditional French aid—to make Sazonov
relatively sure of his ground in deciding upon
war was to have reasonable assurance that England would rally to the cause of France and Russia. This assurance was implicitly given on July
25th. On this day—the day before he proposed
a European conference to Germany—Sir Edward Grey telegraphed Buchanan and remarked
to Benckendorff that he felt that the Austrian
action towards Serbia would involve Russian
mobilization. Benckendorff immediately telegraphed this ominous and all-important statement to Sazonov, and to make doubly certain
that Sazonov would get this information and recognize its significance he telegraphed it to Sazonov a second time on the same day.[47] This encouraged Sazonov in the hope and belief that

England could be counted upon, and, as he had himself previously stated, he felt that a war of France, Russia and England against Germany and Austria, would rapidly end disastrously for the Central Powers, and would enable the Entente to "strike a death blow" at Germany.[48] As Sir Edward Grey-at no time after the 25th made any effort to obstruct the Russian mobilization, there was never any specific or concrete reason for Sazonov's suspecting that England could not be counted upon. As we shall see, the trend of events bore out his expectation to the full. Grey's statements on the 25th were peculiarly significant, as Buchanan had taken pains to remind Sazonov on this very day that Russian mobilization would inevitably produce a European war.[49] On this same 25th of July Grey was telling the German Ambassador that "with reference to the Austrian note he recognized the good right of Austria to obtain satisfaction, as well as the legitimacy of the demand for the punishment of the accomplices in the assassination."[50] As late as the 29th he wrote to the British Ambassador in Paris:[51]

In the present case the dispute between Austria and Servia was not one in which we felt called to take a stand. . . . If Germany became involved and France became involved, we had not made up our minds what we should do; it was a case that we should have to consider.

As Grey was admittedly an ignoramus in regard to military matters, it may well be that he did not technically mean "mobilization" in his note to Buchanan and his interview with Benckendorff, but Benckendorff and Sazonov assumed that he knew what he was talking about, and they acted accordingly. Sazonov's belief in English coöperation was increased on July 26th by the information that the English fleet was mobilized. That Grey encouraged Sazonov to take this as an implication of probable British aid is stated in his telegram to Buchanan on July 27th. We know from many reliable contemporary sources that Grey's remarks about the English fleet had an enormous influence in encouraging Russian mobilization.[52]

3. The Steps in the Fatal Russian Military Measures

The first step was taken at a council of ministers held at 3 P. M. on the afternoon of July 24th.[53] It was here planned to mobilize the four military districts of Odessa, Kiev, Moscow and Kazan (1,100,000 men), as well as the Black and Baltic Sea fleets, and "to take other military measures should circumstances so require." It was decided that all this military preparation should, for the time being, be directed exclusively against Austria. The mobilization of the

fleets proves, however, that at even this early
date action against Germany was contemplated.
The Minister of War was also authorized "to
proceed immediately to gather stores of war
material." The Minister of Finance was directed to do all he could at once to call in all
Russian money in Germany and Austria. To
prevent Serbia from confusing the plans and
"messing" the military and diplomatic program
of Russia by premature military activity, it was
decided to direct Serbia not to resist by military
force an Austrian invasion. It is suggested by
some competent students of the July crisis that
this strange and novel plan of a partial Russian
mobilization was suggested to Sazonov by Poincaré or Paul Cambon. It was quite evidently a
diplomatic ruse, like the French ten kilometer
withdrawal order, designed to create a favorable
impression on European and English opinion,
as well as to deceive the Austrians and Germans.
The Russian army officials protested from the
beginning as to the impractical nature of any
such thing as a "partial mobilization." [54]

The military measures were carried still further at another Crown Council held the next
afternoon—the 25th—before Austria had mobilized against Serbia. The council determined
to recall the troops throughout the Russian Empire from their summer camps to their regular
quarters, so that they could be equipped for

war. All military manœuvres throughout the Empire were called off. It was further agreed that preparation should be made for the mobilization of thirteen army corps, at a date to be determined by Sazonov.[55] The army group now took matters into their own hands, apparently not with the approval of the Tsar, but with the connivance of Sazonov. Dobrorolski frankly states that:

On the evening of July 25th, 1914, a meeting of the Committee of the General Staff took place at which it was decided to declare at once a preparatory mobilization period and further to declare a state of war over all fortresses and frontier stations. War was already decided on.

The military officials proceeded to put the frontier districts adjoining Austria and Germany on a war footing just as rapidly as possible. They were able to do this without the sanction of the Tsar, as the Minister of War had the authority to call out the reservists and militia for service in the frontier districts. "It was by these measures," says Professor Fay, "that Sukhomlinov and Janushkevich really began secret mobilization measures against Germany on July 26th and when war actually came surprised Germany and the world by the rapidity with which the Russian troops poured into East Prussia."[56] July 26th was the day, it will be recalled, when Sir Edward Grey suggested to Germany a European Conference to settle the Austro-Serbian dispute,[57] Germany's refusal of which in favor of direct conversations between Austria and Russia is repeatedly stated by Grey in his memoirs to have been the cause of the World War.[58] It was also the same day that Sazonov assured Count Pourtalès that "no mobilization orders of any kind had been issued." [59]

On the 28th it was decided to mobilize the thirteen army corps against Austria, as had been determined at the Crown Council of July 25th.[60] The Russian Chief of Staff, Janushkevich, urged Sazonov to promise him at this time that the Russians would make war solely on Austria, and refrain from hostilities against Germany. Sazonov refused. Janushkevich then pointed out the necessity of supplanting the order for partial mobilization by one for general mobilization.[61] Sazonov felt quite safe in pressing the Tsar for the general mobilization, as Paléologue had called on him on the 28th to assure him once more that France would stand by Russia,[62] and Izvolski had telegraphed him on the same day that the French government "does not for a moment admit the possibility of exercising a moderating influence in St. Petersburg." Dobrorolski makes out an even more damaging case against Sazonov's action on the 28th by stating that it was Sazonov who took the initiative in deciding to recommend general mobilization.[63]

On the morning of the 29th the Tsar was persuaded to sanction the order for general mobilization, apparently without fully knowing what he was really doing. "This information," says Baron Schilling, "was received with great enthusiasm by the small circle of those acquainted with what was in progress." [64]   Telegrams were at once sent to London and Paris informing the Russian Ambassadors of the ominous decision which had been made.   The French government was to be thanked for its promise of support, and it was ordered that a telegram should be sent to the British government requesting it "to range itself alongside of Russia and France without delay in order to prevent the European balance from being destroyed." [65]   Dobrorolski, as chief of the mobilization division of the Russian General Staff, was instructed to prepare for the telegraphing of this order throughout Russia.   Just as he was ready to send it out that evening, the Tsar, on account of the Kaiser's moderating telegram which he had received after ordering the general mobilization, directed the cancellation of the sending of the general mobilization order.   The order for partial mobilization of 1,100,000 men was sent out instead.[66]

Sazonov had dispatched a telegram to the

French government asking for final and explicit
approval of the decisive Russian military measures. Poincaré, Viviani and Messimy held a
secret night conference at Poincaré's official residence, and Viviani later telegraphed to Paléologue stating that France was fully resolved "to
fulfil all the obligations of the alliance," and advising him to tell the Russians to proceed as secretly as possible in their military preparations,
so as not to afford the Germans any excuse for
mobilization.[67] Izvolski telegraphed an almost
identical statement to Sazonov, laying special
stress upon the French advice as to preserving
the utmost secrecy in the Russian military preparations. He added that the French were quite
willing to have these speeded up, provided the
necessary secrecy was maintained.[68] Izvolski
telegraphed again that Paul Cambon had been
informed as to the Russian military plans and
the support promised by France, and that he
would press Grey for a final answer as to England's position as soon as the crisis had advanced
far enough.[69] As will be pointed out later, he
secured Grey's implicit promise to come into the
war on August 2nd, the day before Grey's
speech in the House of Commons, and two days
before the Germans invaded Belgium.[70] Sazonov was further reassured by a telegram from
the Russian Ambassador at Berlin. He stated
to Sazonov that on July 29th he had been to see

Jules Cambon, the French Ambassador in Berlin, with the following results: [71]

He [Jules Cambon] said to me [Sverbeiev] that, in his opinion, the situation was very serious and that there was scarcely any hope of a peaceful issue. He added that at any rate, judging by a telegram from his brother, Paul Cambon, the French Ambassador in London, in consequence of the refusal of the Vienna Cabinet to accept the more than conciliatory reply of Servia to the Austro-Hungarian ultimatum, France and Russia were assured of the actual support of England in the event of war.

These assurances apparently satisfied Sazonov, though there is no doubt that he would have pressed the Tsar again for the general mobilization order without them, as he had done so on the 29th without having these repetitions of the assurances of Poincaré on his visit, and of Paléologue on the 25th and the 28th. Sharp refusals to sanction the Russian mobilization coming from Paris would, however, have prevented Sazonov from taking the fatal step. Instead came the exhortations to hasten the military preparations but to be as secretive about them as possible. Therefore, Morhardt quite correctly states that the secret conference of Poincaré, Viviani and Messimy, in consultation with Izvolski, on the night of the 29th of July, marks the moment when the horrors of war were specifically unchained upon Europe. After that there was no chance whatever of preserving peace, and the French President and ministers knew this as well as did Izvolski and Sazonov.[72] Hence, the complete hypocrisy in all diplomatic pretensions of both France and Russia after midnight of July 29th to any desire or efforts to avert war!

The details as to the process of persuading the Tsar to give his consent to the final issuance of orders for the general mobilization are recounted with thoroughness in the invaluable diary of Baron Schilling. His account proves how very reluctant the Tsar was to take the fatal step, but how powerless he was before the persistent pleading and importuning of Sazonov and Janushkevich on July 30th: [73]

Between 9 and 10 A. M. the Minister for Foreign Affairs [Sazonov] spoke to the Minister for Agriculture by telephone. Both of them were greatly disturbed at the stoppage of the general mobilization, as they fully realized that this threatened to place Russia in an extremely difficult position in the event of relations with Germany becoming acute. S. D. Sazonov advised A. V. Krivoshein to beg an audience of the Tsar in order to represent to His Majesty the dangers called forth by the change.

At 11 A. M. the Minister for Foreign Affairs again met the Minister for War [Sukhomlinov] and the Chief of the General Staff [Janushkevich]. Informa-

tion received during the night still further strengthened the opinion which they all held that it was im-
perative to prepare for a serious war without loss of
time. Accordingly, the Ministers and the Chief of
Staff adhered to the view which they had expressed
yesterday to the effect that it was indispensable to
proceed to a general mobilization. Adjutant-General
Sukhomlinov and General Janushkevich again endeavored to telephone to persuade the Tsar to revert
to his decision of yesterday to permit a general mobilization. His Majesty decidedly refused to do so, and
finally shortly declared that the conversation was at
an end. General Janushkevich, who at this moment
was holding the telephone receiver, only succeeded in
reporting that the Minister for Foreign Affairs was
there with him and asked to be allowed to say a few
words to His Majesty. A somewhat lengthy silence
ensued, after which the Tzar expressed his willingness
to hear the Minister. S. D. Sazonov requested His
Majesty to receive him to-day, to enable him to
present a report concerning the political situation
which admitted of no delay. After a silence, the Tsar
asked: "Is it all the same to you if I receive you at
3 o'clock, at the same time as Tatistchev, as otherwise
I have not a free minute to-day?" The Minister
thanked his Majesty and said that he would present
himself at the hour named.

The Chief of Staff warmly pleaded with S. D.
Sazonov to persuade the Tsar without fail to consent
to a general mobilization in view of the extreme danger
that would result for us if we were not ready for
war with Germany should circumstances demand the

taking of decisive measures by us after the success of a general mobilization had been compromised by recourse to a partial mobilization. General Janushkevich requested the Minister that in the event of his succeeding in persuading the Tsar he would telephone to him to that effect from Peterhof, in order that he might immediately take the necessary steps, as it would be requisite first of all to stop as soon as possible the partial mobilization which had already been commenced and substitute fresh orders for those which had been issued. "After that," said Janushkevich, "I shall go away, smash my telephone and generally adopt measures which will prevent anyone from finding me for the purpose of giving contrary orders which would again stop our general mobilization."

On his return to the Foreign Office, S. D. Sazonov had an interview with the French Ambassador.

Meanwhile A. V. Krivoshein informed S. D. Sazonov that in reply to his request that the Tsar would receive him he was told that His Majesty was so extremely occupied to-day that he could not see him. Krivoshein then expressed a desire to see S. D. Sazonov before the latter went to Peterhof. It was decided that they should breakfast together at Donon's, and at 12.30 they and Baron Schilling met in a private room there. The general state of mind was tense and the conversation was almost exclusively concerned with the necessity of insisting upon a general mobilization at the earliest possible moment, in view of the inevitableness of war with Germany, which momentarily became clearer. A. V. Krivoshein expressed the hope that S. D. Sazonov would succeed in persuading the Tsar, as otherwise, to use his own words, he would be marching towards a certain catastrophe.

At 2 P. M. the Minister for Foreign Affairs left for Peterhof, together with Major-General Tatistchev, and both of them were received together there in the Alexander Palace by His Majesty. During the course of nearly an hour the Minister proceeded to show that war was becoming inevitable, as it was clear to everybody that Germany had decided to bring about a collision, as otherwise she would not have rejected all the pacificatory proposals that had been made and could easily have brought her ally to reason. Under these circumstances it only remained to do everything that was necessary to meet war fully armed and under the most favorable conditions for ourselves. Therefore it was better to put away any fears that our warlike preparations would bring about a war, and to continue these preparations carefully rather than by reason of such fears to be taken unawares by war.

The firm desire of the Tzar to avoid war at all costs, the horrors of which fill him with repulsion, led His Majesty in his full realization of the heavy responsibility which he took upon himself in this fateful hour to explore every possible means for averting the approaching danger. Consequently he refused during a long time to agree to the adoption of measures which, however indispensable from a military point of view, were calculated, as he clearly saw, to hasten a decision in an undesirable sense.

The tenseness of feeling experienced by the Tzar at this time found expression, amongst other signs, in the irritability most unusual with him, with which His

Majesty interrupted General Tatistchev. The latter, who throughout had taken no part in the conversation, said in a moment of silence: "Yes, it is hard to decide." His Majesty replied in a rough and displeased tone: "I will decide"—in order by this means to prevent the General from intervening any further in the conversation.

Finally the Tzar agreed that under the existing circumstances it would be very dangerous not to make timely preparations for what was apparently an inevitable war, and therefore gave his decision in favour of an immediate general mobilization.

S. D. Sazonov requested the Imperial permission to inform the Chief of the General Staff of this immediately by telephone, and this being granted, he hastened to the telephone on the ground floor of the palace. Having transmitted the Imperial order to General Janushkevich, who was waiting impatiently for it, the Minister with reference to their conversation that morning, added: "Now you can smash your telephone."

In great contrast to this gusto, buoyancy and enthusiasm of Sazonov was the attitude of the Tsar. Paléologue tells us how, after unwillingly granting Sazonov's request for the general mobilization, he broke down and protested:

Think of the responsibility you advise me to take! Remember that it is a question of sending thousands upon thousands to their death.

The execution of the order for general mobilization which was to block any subsequent move for peace, is admirably described by General Serge Dobrorolski, who was in 1914 chief of the mobilization division of the Russian General Staff. After frankly admitting that general mobilization meant irrevocable war—"this once fixed there is no way backwards. This step settles automatically the beginning of war"—he presents the following graphic account of the fatal decision and the sending out of the crucial telegram to all parts of the Russian Empire: [74]

About 11 o'clock on the morning of the 30th of July, General Janushkevich telephoned me: "It is to be hoped that the situation will clear up" (i. e Tsar's opposition to general mobilization overcome). "Bring me all the documents immediately after my afternoon conference."

Janushkevich had persuaded Sazonov to point out to the Tsar the great danger of a partial mobilization in its political implications, it being an obstacle to our fulfilling our obligations in the alliance with France. A partial mobilization would permit William II to demand of the French government a promise of neutrality, and if we should remain in a state of partial mobilization, he would declare war upon us and would have the advantage of the fact that we would not be prepared.

About 1 o'clock in the afternoon, Janushkevich was

called to the telephone by Sazonov who declared to him that the Tsar thought it necessary because of the latest news from Berlin, to proclaim the general mobilization of the entire Russian army and navy.

Then Sazonov added, "Give your orders and keep out of sight for the rest of the day."

Immediately afterwards, Janushkevich called me to him and informed me of this conversation. It was then necessary immediately to send out another telegram ordering a general mobilization. The 31st of July was designated as the first day of the mobilization in all the military districts and throughout all Russian territory.

It was now necessary once more to go to the three ministers to have the telegram signed which fixed the general mobilization for the 31st of July. The telegram of the preceding day was now worthless. At this moment a special meeting of the Council of Ministers was in session at the Palace of Marie presided over by President Gorémykine. Janushkevich was on his way there. He suggested to me that I accompany him in his carriage, for, in view of the fact that all of the Ministers were there, the required signatures could be obtained immediately. Thus matters were brought to a conclusion. The telegram was finished. About 5 o'clock in the afternoon I deposited it at the central telegraph office. It was a repetition of the acts of the preceding day.

Involuntarily I reflected: Would I succeed this time in dispatching the telegram without any obstruction? I thought of Sazonov's words "Remain out of sight for the rest of the day." Finally, by evening, all the instruments were ready to receive the telegram announcing mobilization.

I entered the office. All the operators, men and women, maintained an impressive silence. Each one was seated near his instrument and awaited the copy of the telegram which was to dispatch to all the corners of Russia the important news of the summoning of the Russian people for the great conflict. A few minutes afterward, while absolute silence reigned in the room, all the instruments began to tick. It was the beginning of a great epoch.

Towards 7 o'clock in the evening from all points which were linked with St. Petersburg by direct telegraph lines, came answers announcing that the mobilization telegram had been safely received. The thing was irrevocably begun. It was already known in all the large cities of our vast country. A change was no longer possible. The prologue of the great drama had commenced!

In spite of all this, and of the fact that the Russian military authorities recognized that the War was "on" from this minute, both technically and actually, the Tsar sent the following telegram to the Kaiser after the mobilization order had been announced publicly the next day: [75]

I thank you heartily for your mediation, which begins to give one hope that all may yet end peacefully. It is technically impossible to stop our military preparations, which were obligatory owing to Austria's mobilization. We are far from wishing war. So long as the negotiations with Austria on Serbia's account are taking place my troops shall not take any provocative action. I give you my solemn word for this. I put all my trust in God's mercy and hope in your successful mediation in Vienna for the welfare of our countries and for the peace of Europe.

The Tsar promised the Kaiser that he would send his aide, General Tatistchev, to Berlin with explanations and instructions, but he never came, for Sazonov had him arrested and detained just as he was about to enter his compartment on the Berlin train—another link in the case against Sazonov.

III. THE PROBLEM OF RUSSIAN RESPONSIBILITY FOR THE WORLD WAR

1. *The Deliberate and Unjustifiable Aggression of Russia in 1914*

All of the military preparations described in the preceding section were determined upon and put into effect before there had been any counter military measures against Russia by either Austria or Germany. The Austrians mobilized twenty-two divisions against Serbia on July 25th at 9.30 P. M., after Serbia had mobilized her whole army against Austria at 3 P. M. that afternoon. Austria declared war upon Serbia on the 28th at noon, first explicitly stating to Russia that she bound herself to respect the territory

and sovereignty of Serbia. Austria did not mobilize against Russia until July 31st at 12.23
P. M. Germany did not mobilize against Russia
until August 1st at 5 P. M.[76] This proves the
inaccuracy in the Entente claims that the general mobilization was proclaimed as defense
against previous military measures initiated by
Germany and Austria. And it is also significant that, though Russia has tried to justify her
mobilization on the ground of her danger at the
hands of Austria, she yielded to French advice
and paid little attention to Austria, throwing all
her forces against Germany. It has been held
by some, like Professor Schmitt, that it was the
Austrian bombardment of Belgrade that provoked the Russian mobilization and the war, but
Dobrorolski has admitted that the Russians had
decided upon war on the 25th, three days before.

We may now survey the state of diplomatic
negotiations for a pacific settlement on the 29th
of July. This was the date on which Sazonov
secured the first order for the general mobilization, which proves that by this time he had decided upon a European war. Were the diplomatic efforts so demonstrably a failure by the
29th that Sazonov was justified in assuming that
there was no way out except through war? It
may be categorically denied that they were.[77]
In the first place, Austria had explicitly informed Sazonov that she "had no intention of

annexing Serbian territory, nor did she contemplate infringing Serbian sovereignty." As
Montgelas says with entire accuracy, "This was
all that Russia could legitimately ask." [78] It
assured Sazonov that Serbia would not be "gob-
bled up" as he had affected to fear. Sazonov
was careful to conceal the Austrian assurances as
to Serbian sovereignty from his Allies in July
and August, 1914. The Austrian Ambassadors
in Paris and London, however, revealed these
facts as to Austrian assurances and the concealment of them by Sazonov. Number 223 in the
complete Russian *Orange Book* indicates the
consternation and discomforture of Izvolski and
Poincaré when this news leaked out in Paris and
London, and their immediate decision to offset
this information by declaring it untrue. They
recognized that this lie was necessary to save
their case at London. Further, as both the Tsar
and Sazonov were fully aware at the time, the
German pressure on Austria to accept the British proposals was at its height on the 29–30th of
July, when Russia took the fatal steps towards
mobilization.

Sazonov cannot escape guilt by asserting that
he knew that the German efforts to curb Austria
would not succeed. Nobody then knew they
would not succeed, and no one can say that they
would not have succeeded if Russia had refrained from mobilization. It seems more than

probable that they would have been successful if
Russia had given Germany time enough, even
though the symptoms of Austrian wavering on
the 31st of July and August 1st may have been
fictitious. Germany was certainly prepared to
go to great lengths against Austria to avert a
European war if she had not been threatened by
the Russian mobilization. It may also be recalled that Grey expressed himself as satisfied
with the trend of diplomatic efforts on the 29th.[79]

It may, then, be stated with absolute assurance that there was nothing in either the military
or diplomatic situation on July 29, 1914, to justify the Russian determination upon general
mobilization. It was a precipitate and bellicose
act, which can be explained only on the ground
that Sazonov and the military crowd, encouraged
by Poincaré, had determined to exploit the
Austro-Serbian crisis as the incident over which
to precipitate the anticipated European war.[80]

2. Sazonov and Russian Mobilization

It is desirable to emphasize here that the more
recent material on the Russian situation has
proved that we must revise our views of the
relative responsibility of Sazonov for the mobilization.[81] As Baron Schilling and Dr. G.
Frantz have proved beyond any doubt, we can no
longer regard Sazonov as a trembling diplomat
bull-dozed by the army officials. He was at

every step the leader in St. Petersburg.[82] And it was he who wrung the mobilization order from the reluctant Tsar on both the 29th and the 30th. He had in July, 1914, the courage of his convictions expressed on December 8 and 31, 1913, and February 8, 1914. Janushkevich was his right-hand man at St. Petersburg. Sukhomlinov, the Minister of War, was such a notorious liar that we can place little confidence in his voluminous memoirs, but it seems that he lost his nerve at the last, and that Sazonov took full responsibility among the ministers for railroading the mobilization order through.[83] Izvolski was, of course, looking after matters at Paris, and his egoistic nature led him to attempt to snatch the credit for precipitating the War away from Sazonov. Lord Bertie, the British Ambassador at Paris, tells how Izvolski boasted about Paris early in August, 1914, that *"c'est ma guerre!"* [84]

It will not be necessary in this place to discuss in detail the question as to whether the Russian mobilization was equivalent to war. We made it clear above that the Franco-Russian military convention of 1893 was very specific in declaring that the first to mobilize must be held the aggressor, and that general mobilization *"is war."* All responsible persons in France, Russia and England had subsequently acted on that supposition, and Sazonov was fully aware of the fact. No person informed on matters of military strategy had suggested for a generation that Germany should lose the incalculable advantage of speed as against the overwhelming Russian numbers by simply answering the Russian general mobilization by an order for counter-mobilization and awaiting results.[85]

3. Relative Guilt of Russia and Austria

Next to the fact that the Russian general mobilization blocked every possible road to peace, it seems to the writer that the most important aspect of the question of the relative guilt of Russia in bringing on the war is the enormous difference in the degree of justification for the Russian intervention against Austria as compared with the merits of the Austrian action against Serbia, even in the light of the information possessed by Austria in 1914. Even if Austria had planned to annihilate Serbia in 1914, Russia would have had slight justification for intervention in the light of her incitement of Serbia against Austria. When Austria gave assurance that she would not annex any part of Serbian territory or violate Serbian sovereignty, all cause for Russian intervention disappeared. When the Kaiser, in addition, promised Russia that he would press Austria sternly to compel her to cease military operations and remain satisfied with the temporary occupation of Belgrade, only an implacable Russian determination upon war can explain the subsequent Russian action. In short, while Austria may have lacked complete justification for her policy towards Serbia in 1914, Russia had no justification whatever for her aggressive action towards Austria. Austrian integrity and national existence were at stake; Russia had nothing at stake except her prestige, already sadly impaired in the Balkans, and her ambition to secure Constantinople and the Straits.

Further, Russia had shown herself willing to abandon Serbia when Russian interests were to be advanced thereby, as was proved in 1908 by the case of Bosnia and Herzegovina, the annexation of which had been suggested by Izvolski in return for Austrian approval of prospective Russian access to the Straits. An even more flagrant case of Russian abandonment of Serbian interests in advancing her own program is afforded by the Russian proposal to Turkey during the secret Russo-Turkish negotiations of October–December, 1911, that Russia should act as the protector of Turkey against the Balkan states in return for Turkish consent to Russian freedom of the Straits. Finally, even if one were to hold that her policy in regard to Serbia had no justification whatever in 1914, *Austria never planned or desired a general*

European war, while this was what Russia aimed at from her first military preparations.

One of the most forceful statements of the threadbare nature of the Russian pretensions in 1914 comes not from a German nor an Austrian, but from no less a person than Lord Bertie, the British Ambassador in Paris in 1914. Writing in his diary on July 26, 1914, he said: [86]

I was to have gone to Martigny to-day. I had arranged with Grey to do so, subject to returning in the event of a crisis. When the Austrian Note appeared I made up my mind to give up Martigny. It seems incredible that the Russian Government should plunge Europe into war in order to make themselves the protectors of the Servians. Unless the Austrian Government had proofs of the complicity of Servian officials in the plot to murder the Archduke they could not have addressed to the Servian Government the stringent terms which the Austrian Note contained. Russia comes forward as the protectress of Servia; by what title except on the exploded pretension that she is, by right, the protectress of all Slavs? What rubbish! And she will expect, if she adheres to her present attitude, France and England to support her in arms. Public opinion in England would never sanction such a policy, but unfortunately we might be dragged into a war through reverses to French arms and the necessity to prevent the annihilation of France.

4. *Bogus Nature of Sazonov's Diplomatic Proposals*

Some may hold that the writer has been unfair to Sazonov, because the latter at times seemed to favor a pacific adjustment of the disputes between Russia and Austria and Austria and Serbia, but the good faith of all of these proposals is belied by his specific acts, the nature and dates of which cannot be denied or evaded. Nowhere in this book have we or shall we give any credence to words which do not agree with acts. But, for the sake of thoroughness, we shall examine his alleged efforts for peace. On the 24th it is held that he counselled moderation on the part of Serbia, and advised her not to open hostilities with Austria. He later stated that he would be satisfied if Austria would withdraw points four and five of the ultimatum. On the 30th he told Pourtalès that if Austria ceased hostilities against Serbia and submitted the dispute to a European Conference, Russia would cease military preparations. On the 31st he requested Grey to initiate negotiations for a settlement in London. And the Tsar suggested that Austria and Serbia submit their dispute to the Hague Court.[87]

What validity have these proposals as the basis for the assertion of Sazonov's pacific intent in 1914, as over against his acts in leading Russia straight to the general mobilization? It was but natural that he should advise Serbia against war on the 24th, as a Serbian declaration of war at that date would have greatly hastened matters at the outset, and have led Russia, with its great area and few railroads, into a serious disadvantage as compared with the more compact and better equipped countries such as Germany and Austria. It was also desirable from the standpoint of influencing European opinion to have Serbia assume a humble and conciliatory attitude towards Austria. The insistence on the removal of points four and five of the ultimatum would, as we made clear in an earlier chapter, have robbed the document of any real significance. No country ever had up to 1914, and no country ever has since then, submitted a matter of the type of the Austro-Serbian dispute to the Hague Court. Further, as Montgelas has pointed out, Sazonov was himself primarily responsible for the failure of any effort to submit the dispute to the Hague Court. On the 29th it was rather too late to act on the suggestion without seriously obstructing the Russian military operations, but on the 27th, as we have learned from the recently published Russian documents, the Tsar made the same suggestion in writing to Sazonov, but the latter disregarded the advice absolutely. Likewise, he made no effort to promote the proposition on the 29th.[87a] The pro-

posal to Count Pourtalès was obviously made in
bad faith, as the general mobilization had already
been determined upon.

But the most convincing proof of the complete bankruptcy of Sazonov's claim to basic
pacifism is to be found in his proposal of July
31st. On this day, twenty-four hours after the
ordering of the general mobilization which all
the Russians knew blocked every road to peace
and meant that Europe was virtually at war, he
telegraphed to Izvolski that the Austrian Ambassador had just told him that Austria was
willing to discuss the ultimatum to Serbia, that
he (Sazonov) was much gratified, and had told
the Ambassador that he would like to have London take charge of the negotiations.[88] He also
had the obvious effrontery to telegraph to Benckendorff in London: [89]

I have requested the British Ambassador to express
to Grey my deep gratitude for the firm and friendly
tone which he has adopted in the friendly discussions
with Germany and Austria, thanks to which the hope
of finding a peaceful issue to the present difficulties
need not yet be abandoned. I also requested him to
inform the British Ministry that in my opinion it was
only in London that the discussions might still have
some faint chance of success and of rendering the necessary compromise easier for Austria.

It is obvious that Sazonov knew that it was too
late to preserve peace, but by a new suggestion

as to negotiations he would gain more time for the execution of the Russian mobilization before hostilities commenced.[90] He would also give Grey additional material with which to dupe the English public by pointing to the apparent pacific intent of Russia at this late date.

The final and definitive proof of the faked-up nature of Russian diplomatic suggestions in 1914 is to be found in the military plans from November, 1912, to August, 1914, and in the scheme for using diplomatic proposals and negotiations as a barrage to cover the aggressive military preparations designed to lead to war. In a long article in *Current History* for June, 1926 (pp. 391–97), Mr. Charles Altschul has attempted to demonstrate that the Russian general mobilization did not mean war, in spite of Professor Gooch's clear pronouncement that "it was well understood between the French and Russian experts that mobilization was equivalent to a declaration of war." Mr. Altschul met a crushing reply from Dr. Ernest F. Henderson in the August number of the same journal (Chronicles, pp. viii ff.) in which Henderson refuted Altschul by citing the relevant sections of the very documents used by Altschul (cf. Frantz in *Current History,* March, 1927.)

The essential facts are the following: The Franco-Russian military alliance of 1893 was based upon the assertion that "mobilization is war," and the French military representative, General Boisdeffre, and the Russian Tsar both expressed themselves at the time as thoroughly understanding this interpretation. In the Russian secret Military Protocol of November 8, 1912, the plan was definitely laid for a diplomatic barrage to cover these fatal and decisive mobilization measures. It was there stated:

Mobilization does not necessarily mean the immediate beginning of hostilities because it may be of advantage to complete the marshalling of our troops without beginning hostilities, in order that our opponent may not be entirely deprived of the hope that war may still be avoided. Our military measures will then have to be masked by clever pretended diplomatic negotiations in order to lull the fears of the enemy as completely as possible. If by such measures we can gain a few days they absolutely must be taken.

We have already indicated in the summary of the Russian military preparations that the procedure in 1914 fitted in exactly with these plans of 1912. Further, we have Dobrorolski's frank confession that Russian diplomacy in 1914 was actually a barrage for the mobilization. He says that by July 25, 1914, "war was already decided upon and the whole flood of telegrams between the Governments of Russia and Germany represented merely the *mise en scène* of an historical drama." In his now famous letter of July 31, 1914, to his chief of staff on the political situ-

ation (*Die Kriegsschuldfrage,* November, 1926),
Premier Pashitch confirms this interpretation:

> The reports received from our [Serbian] Minister at
> St. Petersburg state that Russia is now negotiating and
> is prolonging the negotiations in order to gain time
> for the mobilization and concentration of her army.
> When her mobilization is finished she will declare war on
> Austria.

Writing in 1915 General Palizyn, the Russian
chief of staff at that time, complained that events
had made it impossible for the Russians completely to carry out their mobilization plans under cover of their diplomatic subterfuges, but
expressed great satisfaction that the Russians
through their diplomatic ruse had gained twelve
days for their secret military measures and were
able to surprise their enemies by the degree of
their preparations:

> Just think what would have occurred if the Austrians
> had thrown their troops solidly against us. Our march
> to the frontier would not have succeeded, and the Aus-
> trians would have inflicted partial defeats upon us.
> But for a long time they did not believe we would de-
> clare war. They devoted all their attention to Serbia
> in the full conviction that we would not stir. Our mo-
> bilization struck them like a thunder-bolt. It was then
> too late for them. They had become involved with Ser-
> bia. The Germans too permitted the first days to
> elapse without action. Altogether we gained twelve

days. Our enemies committed a huge blunder [by crediting Russian diplomatic efforts as sincere] and conceded to us at the same time an incalculable advantage.

In 1916 Sazonov apparently forgot for a moment that he was a diplomat and indulged in some amazing frankness. In a communique to the *Russkoe Slovo* he said at this time of his motives for entering the war: [91]

Herr Bethmann-Hollweg maintains that France and Russia would never have dared to accept the challenge of Germany if they had not been sure of the support of England. But the real political situation was the following, even if the Chancellor will not admit it: In reality, France and Russia, notwithstanding their profound love for peace and their sincere efforts to avoid bloodshed, had decided to break the pride of Germany at any price, and to make her stop, once for all, treading on the toes of her neighbors.

The above constitutes a sufficient rejoinder to the naïve article of Mr. Binkley in the New York *Times Current History Magazine* for January, 1926, attempting to prove from the minutes of the Russian ministerial council of July 24, 1914, that Russia did not want war.[92]

5. Sazonov in Apology and Retreat

Another method of dealing with Sazonov is to examine his defense of his action made in the leisure of his exile from Russia since the War. It would appear obvious that if he had been really working for peace in 1914 he would be vindicated by a calm statement of the case, without any necessity for flagrant and easily detected falsification of readily verifiable facts. At least twice since the spring of 1923 he has attempted to clear himself. In order to offset the effect of the present writer's article in *Current History* for May, 1924, the New York *Times* obtained an interview with Sazonov, which was published in the *Times* for May 11, 1924. The former Foreign Minister here says that on the 29th of July Austrian mobilization was almost complete, that the German mobilization had begun, and that as an answer he ordered the mobilization of four Russian military districts. The facts are that the decision to mobilize these districts was made on the 24th, and that the Austrian mobilization did not begin until the 31st and the German not until the 1st of August. He further states that on the 29th Pourtalès demanded that Russia cease mobilizing on the Austrian frontier without promising that Germany would order Austrian mobilization to cease on the Russian frontier, but Austrian mobilization did not begin until two days later. Sazonov then resurrects the ancient myth of the *Lokalanzeiger* article. He states that he was unwillingly brought to the order for general mo-

bilization by the publication of a false report of
the German mobilization in the Berlin *Lokalanzeiger* at 2 P. M. (Russian time) on July
30th. This is a most transparent falsehood.
Sazonov had asked for the general mobilization
on the 28th, had obtained it on the 29th, only to
have it cancelled later. On the 30th he had extracted the Tsar's consent for the renewal and
had given the new order to Janushkevich and
Dobrorolski long before the Russian Ambassador in Berlin had telegraphed the news of the
Lokalanzeiger article. Dobrorolski says he got
the order for mobilization at 1 P. M. on the 30th,
but from Baron Schilling's diary it would appear
to have been about 4 P. M. that Sazonov informed
Janushkevich to issue the order and "smash his
telephone." We now know that the Russian
Ambassador's telegram about the article was not
handed to the telegraph office in Berlin until
4.28 P. M. (Russian time). The excessive demands on the St. Petersburg wires, in large part
due to the telegraphing of the Russian mobilization order, prevented this telegram from reaching
St. Petersburg until 12.20 A. M. This was over
five hours after the remote Russian districts had
telegraphed back to St. Petersburg that they had
received the mobilization order as sent out by
Dobrorolski late that afternoon. Therefore,
Sazonov could not have learned of the article
until at least nine hours after he had informed

Janushkevich to go ahead with the order which the Tsar had approved, and to smash his telephone and keep out of sight for the rest of the day. Most important of all is the fact that in 1914 the Russians never mentioned this *Lokalanzeiger* article as justification for Russian mobilization. It was a pure fiction invented by Sir Edward Grey from an inaccurate remark made by Bethmann-Hollweg. It was not until 1916, after Grey had again revived the myth, that the Russians stooped to exploit it in their defense.[93]

Sazonov mentions the absurd proposal of the Tsar to refer the Austro-Serbian issue to the Hague Tribunal, a matter we shall not comment on further in this place. He contends that Russia had an honorable and unbroken record as the protector of Serbia for one hundred and fifty years. Yet in 1908 Russia had actually been the instigator of the annexation of Bosnia and Herzegovina, and in 1911 offered Turkey an alliance. In 1912–13, when the Russians were as yet unprepared for war, they offered no objection to the Austrian threats against Serbia. He contends that Russia had to act to prevent the annihilation of Serbia, though he himself admitted on July 29, 1914, that he was fully convinced that Austria intended to respect the integrity of Serbian territory.[94] Finally, he makes the atrocious misstatement that "Germany proclaimed her intention to exercise her influence in the direction of moderation in Vienna but did nothing." If this is all that Sazonov has to offer, we may well conclude that he has no defense.

Some might claim in extenuation of the above that Sazonov was careless in this interview and did not take time to present a carefully prepared vindication. He was given a second chance. Early in the year 1925 he consented to prepare a foreword to the diary of the Russian Foreign Office kept in 1914 by Baron Schilling. Apparently Sazonov had nothing new to offer. The following citation from this foreword reveals the same old "chestnuts" of the *Times* interview: [95]

Referring to the question of the Russian mobilization, to which German writers attach such importance, stated briefly the facts which preceded it or coincided with it were as follows: (1) On the 30th of July the Russian mobilization was decided upon about five o'clock P. M., and proclaimed on the 31st, after Belgrade had been bombarded by the Austrians; (2) Austria's mobilization was in full swing; (3) the semiofficial *Local Anzeiger* had published in a special edition the decree of the German mobilization, which was afterwards denied, but not before it had time to reach St. Petersburg; (4) Count Pourtalès had, on the 29th, in the name of his Government, presented the demand that Russia should stop all military preparations on her western frontiers without any reciprocal undertaking on the part of Austria; (5) the Emperor

Nicholas had proposed to the Kaiser to submit the Austro-Serbian conflict to The Hague Tribunal; (6) the "Kriegsgefahrzustand," which is equivalent to a decree of mobilization in any other country, "mobilization" being inseparable in Germany, according to Count Pourtalès, with the commencement of hostilities, had been announced in Berlin on the 31st of July, i. e. simultaneously with the announcement of the Russian mobilization.

I conclude these brief introductory lines by mentioning the accusation often addressed by Germany to France and Russia, that they desired war in order that France might recover her lost provinces and Russia acquire the Straits and Constantinople.

As regards the latter, I feel bound to state that shortly after Germany had declared war upon the Dual Alliance, and before the Berlin Government had sent its warships through the Straits into the Black Sea and had thus drawn Turkey into a war with Russia, the Russian Government, together with its Allies, had offered Turkey to guarantee her territorial integrity on the sole condition of her remaining neutral.

This fact, officially announced in the Russian *Orange Book*, speaks for itself, putting an end to the accusations piled up in Berlin against Russian diplomacy.

As we have just shown the preposterous and misleading nature of the first five of these points, we shall not repeat the refutation here. His attempt to clear himself by contending that the German announcement of the "imminence of war" was equivalent to mobilization and came synchronously with the announcement of the Russian general mobilization, is of a piece with his other fabrications. This German announcement was not made until after Berlin had been informed by Pourtalès of the Russian general mobilization, namely, two days after the Tsar had signed the first order for general mobilization, and a day after the final order had been issued. Germany then waited more than twenty-four hours before ordering mobilization, in spite of the fact that the Franco-Russian military plans had been formulated on the assumption that she would declare war the minute she learned of the Russian mobilization. As to his remarks about the Straits, we pointed out in the third chapter that this was simply a ruse to deceive the Turkish government. Izvolski and the French authorities had discussed the wisdom of proposing a guaranty of Turkish integrity, and concluded that it would be desirable and would in no sense interfere with the plans of the Entente in disposing of Constantinople and the Straits as they saw fit at the close of hostilities. And we know that an explicit agreement between France and Russia that the latter should get the Straits had been made before Turkey entered the War.[96]

While Russia executed the acts which led to the outbreak of the War, France and England cannot be exonerated from their share of the blame for the calamity. Russia would never have taken the deliberate steps to provoke war without Poincaré's incitement on his St. Petersburg trip. The French obligation to aid Russia in 1914 was based solely upon Poincaré's personal promises, as the fact of the priority of the Russian general mobilization to that of either Austria or Germany released France from the obligations imposed by the military convention of 1893. As early as July 22nd Poincaré blocked Grey's pacific plan for direct discussions between Vienna and St. Petersburg, and on July 25th Paléologue informed the Russians that France placed herself "unreservedly on Russia's side" (*British Documents,* Nos. 76, 125). And England was both directly and indirectly involved in the Russian mobilization. By telling Buchanan and Benckendorff on July 25th that England envisaged without protest the possibility of Russian mobilization as an answer to the Austrian ultimatum to Serbia, and by calling Sazonov's attention to the mobilization of the British fleet on July 27th, Sir Edward Grey made Sazonov feel that England had implicitly committed herself to the support of Russia in the event of war. Moreover, Grey's statement to Buchanan on July 27th that the mobilization of the British fleet ought to disabuse Sazonov of the idea of British neutrality was probably the deciding point in leading to the fatal Russian mobilization.[97]

IV. CONCLUSIONS

(1) For several years previous to the outbreak of the World War, Izvolski had become convinced that the most important point in Russian foreign policy was the securing of the Straits, and that they could only be obtained by a European war. Sazonov was converted to this view by December, 1913, and he expressed himself as believing that, with British help, France and Russia could easily dispose of Germany and put an end to her existence as a first-class European power. A secret Russian Crown Council, held on February 8, 1914, decided that Russia could not afford to strike Turkey through a surprise attack unaided, but must await a European war. English adherence to the Franco-Russian plans was practically assured by the negotiations concerning an Anglo-Russian naval convention in May, 1914.

(2) Poincaré had assured Izvolski in 1912 that as soon as Russia was prepared in a military way, and the bribed French press had reconciled the French people to the idea of a war over the Balkans, he would join with Russia in any incident in the Balkans which might be used as the basis for precipitating the war which would restore Alsace-Lorraine, as well as capture the Straits. To prepare for such an incident, the Russians had encouraged Serbian plots against

Austria, supplied the Serbians with arms, and twice promised them Russian aid against Austria. Russian army, and possibly diplomatic, circles knew of the Sarajevo plot in advance and gave it their approval.

(3) Poincaré visited St. Petersburg late in July, 1914, fired the Russian militarists with new zeal and hope, and even stirred the Tsar. He gave the Russian extremists assurance of full support against Austria before he fully knew of the terms of the Austrian ultimatum, and gave them to understand that the prospective Austro-Serbian crisis would be satisfactory to him as the "incident in the Balkans" over which the Russians might kindle a European war and count upon finding France at their side.

(4) Even before Poincaré had left St. Petersburg, and two days before he learned of the contents of the Austrian ultimatum, Sazonov informed the Russian Ambassador at Vienna that Russia proposed to take a strong stand against any Austrian move against Serbia. Two days later Viviani dispatched a telegram from Reval to the French acting Foreign Minister telling him that France must likewise be prepared to move against Austria in her prospective dispute with Serbia. Sazonov's early advice to Serbia to adopt a conciliatory attitude towards Austria and, above all, not to declare war, cannot be taken as in any sense a proof of his desire for

peace. It is belied by all of his subsequent procedure, and was paralleled at the very moment by a decision upon measures designed to lead to war. This advice is to be accounted for on the basis of Sazonov's desire to secure as much time as possible for Franco-Russian military preparations and to put Serbia and her protectors in as favorable a light as possible before world opinion.

(5) From the 24th of July, the day they learned of the Austrian ultimatum, the Russians began steady and unabated military preparations in anticipation of war, and carried these to their logical and fatal culmination in the general mobilization order of July 30th. The 24th of July, then, marks the turning-point in the history of contemporary Europe which transformed the European system from one which invited war into one which was based upon a determination to precipitate war. Neither the French nor the British offered any objections to these Russian military measures, and the French explicitly advised greater haste, coupled with more complete secrecy. Consciously or unconsciously, on July 25th, Sir Edward Grey led Sazonov to understand that Great Britain would countenance Russian mobilization.

(6) Personal responsibility for the provocative Russian military preparations rests mainly upon the Grand Duke Nicholas, Sazonov and

Izvolski, but chiefly on Sazonov, who led on the militarists rather than being bull-dozed by them. The Tsar was pacific, but confused and helpless.

(7) In 1916 Sazonov, in a moment of indiscreet candor, admitted that the war was brought on in 1914 through the determination of France and Russia to humiliate Germany. His recent attempts to clear himself of the charges against him, which have been summarized in this chapter, have consisted solely of the most obvious and flagrant misstatements of easily verifiable and incontestable facts. He has not been able to offer one valid fact in extenuation of his conduct.

(8) Sazonov's suggestions as to a diplomatic settlement were not made in good faith, but, following the Protocol of November 8, 1912, were designed purely to gain more time for the execution of the Russian military preparations. His most definite and comprehensive suggestions as to a diplomatic settlement were made after the general mobilization order had been issued, which he well knew blocked every possible road to peace. At the time of the issuance of the mobilization order the movement for a diplomatic settlement of the crisis, which had been initiated by Germany and England, was at its height. Moreover, Austria had weakened and agreed to discuss her dispute with Serbia before the expiration of the German ultimatum to Russia.

(9) The article in the Berlin *Lokalanzeiger* of July 30th inaccurately announcing German mobilization had no influence upon the Russian decision to order a general mobilization. The news of this article did not reach St. Petersburg until nine hours after Sazonov had secured the Tsar's consent to general mobilization and had turned over this order to the chief of staff. Dobrorolski tells us frankly that Russia decided upon war on July 25th, and that Sazonov's diplomatic manœuvres were only the protective barrage for the military preparations, carried out strictly according to the secret military protocol of November 8, 1912.

(10) The first German and Austrian military action against Russia came long after the Russian general mobilization, and neither country had made a move against Russia until after the Russian general mobilization order had been telegraphed throughout Russia. Germany did not even then move hastily, but vainly waited twenty-four hours for a reply to a twelve-hour ultimatum to Russia before ordering mobilization.

SELECTED REFERENCES

Bogitshevich, M., *Causes of the War;* Buchanan, G., *My Mission to Russia;* Bülow, B. von, *Die Krisis;* Dobrorolski, S., *Die Mobilmachung der russischen Armee, 1914;* "Noch einiges von der russischen Mobilmachung im Jahre 1914," in *Kriegsschuldfrage,* April,

1924; "Die Kriegsbereitschaft der russischen Armee im Jahre 1914," Ibid., January, 1925; Ewart, J. S., *The Roots and Causes of the Wars;* Fay, S. B., "New Light on the Origins of the World War," in *American Historical Review*, January, 1921; Frantz, G., *Russlands Eintritt in den Weltkrieg;* Gouttenoire de Toury, F., *La Politique russe de Poincaré;* Höniger, R., *Russlands Vorbereitungen zum Weltkriege;* Lutz, H., "Lord Grey's Responsibility for Russian Mobilization," in New York *Times Current History Magazine*, May, 1925; Montgelas, M., *The Case for the Central Powers;* Morel, E. D., *Tsardom's Part in the War;* Morhardt, M., *Les Preuves;* Nansen, F., *Russland und der Friede;* Paléologue, M., *An Ambassador's Memoirs;* Pourtalès, F., *Am Schcidewege zwischen Krieg and Frieden;* Renouvin, P., *Les Origines immédiates de la guerre;* Romberg, B., *Falsifications of the Russian Orange Book;* Schilling, M. F., *How the War Began;* Seeger, C. L. (Ed.), *The Memoirs of Alexander Iswolsky;* Siebert, B. de, and Schreiner, G. A., *Entente Diplomacy and the World: the Matrix of the History of Europe, 1909–1914;* Stieve, F., *Isvolsky and the World War; Die diplomatische Schriftwechsel Iswolskis, 1911–1914;* Südland, L. von, *Die südslawisische Frage und der Weltkrieg;* Sukhomlinov, W. A., *Erinnerungen;* Tönnies, F., *Die Schuldfrage; Der Zarismus und seine Bundesgenossen 1914;* Trubetzkoi, G. N., *Russland als Grossmacht;* Wegerer, A., von (Ed.) *Das Russische Orangebuch von 1914; Les Allies contre la Russie,* foreword by V. Margueritte.

FOOTNOTES AND FURTHER REFERENCES

1 W. L. Langer, "The Franco-Russian Alliance, 1890–1894," in *Slavonic Review*, 1925.

2 F. Stieve, *Isvolsky and the World War, passim;* the *New Republic,* and the New York *Nation,* February 6 and 20, 1924.

3 E. D. Morel, *The Secret History of a Great Betrayal;* Earl Loreburn, *How the War Came.*

4 Ibid., and Stieve, op. cit.

5 Stieve, op. cit., pp. 186 ff.

6 Ibid., p. 106.

7 Ibid., pp. 195–6.

8 Ibid., pp. 195 ff.

9 B. de Siebert and G. A. Schreiner, *Entente Diplomacy and the World,* p. 525.

10 Stieve, op. cit., p. 110.

11 M. Bogitshevich, *Causes of the War,* pp. 127–34 and Annex xxi.

12 Stieve, op. cit., pp. 230 ff.

13 Ibid., pp. 136 ff., 168 ff. Cf. S. Dobrorolski, "Die Kriegsbereitschaft der russischen Armee im Jahre 1914," in the *Kriegsschuldfrage,* January, 1925.

14 *The Outbreak of the World War,* pp. 53–4.

15 L. Mandl, in Vienna *Neues Acht-Uhrblatt,* July 27, 28, 1924; M. Bogitshevich, "Weitere Einzelheiten über das Attentat von Sarajevo," in *Kriegsschuldfrage,* July, 1925. See also references in footnotes 2, 4 and 27 in Chap. iv above.

16 *Outbreak of the World War,* p. 62.

17 Bogitshevich, *Causes of the War;* E. Durham, *Twenty Years of Balkan Tangle;* and *The Serajevo Crime.*

18 In London *Nation and Athenæum,* September 19, 1925, p. 723. Cf. V. Serge, in *Clarté,* May, 1925.

19 *Austrian Red Book,* Part I, pp. 47–8.

20 *Outbreak of the World War,* p. 147.

21 *Foreign Affairs* (American), October, 1925, p. 15; and more in detail in his *Origins of the War.* See the withering criticism in Lazare, *A l'Origine du Mensonge,* pp. 159–92.

22 M. Paléologue, *The Memoirs of an Ambassador.* See the brilliant review by W. L. Langer, in the *New Republic,* June 25, 1924.

23 M. F. Schilling, *How the War Came,* pp. 114–15. For Paléologue's view of the significance of these speeches of the Tsar and Poincaré see Schilling, p. 32.

24 Stieve, pp. 211 ff.; Lazare, pp. 167 ff.

25 Stieve, pp. 211–12.

26 Ibid., pp. 212–13.

27 Schilling, p. 115.

28 A. Fabre-Luce, *La Victoire,* p. 209; and Schilling, pp. 31–2.

29 Stieve, p. 214; *British Documents,* No. 101.

30 S. B. Fay, "New Light on the Origins of the World War," in *American Historical Review,* January, 1921, p. 229; M.

Morhardt, *Les Preuves*, pp. 139 ff.; *French Yellow Book*, No. 22.

31 *Foreign Affairs*, October, 1925, p. 15.

32 Op. cit., pp. 214–15.

33 *Les Preuves*, pp. 299–301, 305.

34 *La Victoire*, pp. 209–10.

35 Cf. *British Documents, passim;* Morhardt, 117 ff., 297 ff.; Fabre-Luce, op. cit., pp. 208 ff.; Lazare, op. cit., *passim;* A. Pevet, *Les Responsables de la guerre.* See the Russian documents in *Les Allies contre la Russie.*

36 *Das russische Orangebuch von 1914*, p. 4.

37 *Outbreak of the World War*, p. 187.

38 Fay, loc. cit., pp. 230–31.

39 Ibid., p. 229 and *Outbreak of the World War*, p. 162.

40 Fay, loc. cit., pp. 229 ff.; Schilling, pp. 28 ff.

41 Schilling, p. 28–9; *British Documents*, No. 101.

42 Morel, *Secret History of a Great Betrayal*, pp. 21–2; Fay, loc. cit., p. 233; E. Judet, *Carnets de Georges Louis* Vol. II, pp. 178–9.

43 Fay, pp. 229 ff.

44 Schilling, op. cit., pp. 15–17, 47 ff.

45 *Outbreak of the World War*, p. 295.

46 Ibid.

47 H. Lutz, "Lord Grey's Responsibility for Russian Mobilization," in *Current History*, May, 1925, pp. 265 ff.

48 Stieve, op. cit., pp. 194–5.

49 *British Blue Book*, No. 17.

50 Ewart, *Roots and Causes of the Wars*, p. 1018; *Outbreak of the World War*, p. 200.

51 Ewart, op cit., pp. 103, 114; *British Blue Book*, Nos. 87, 90.

52 *British Blue Book*, No. 47. Count Pourtalès has furnished the writer with much information on this point.

53 Schilling, p. 30; R. C, Binkley, "New Light on Russia's War Guilt," in New York *Times Current History Magazine,* January, 1926. Beyond all comparison the best account of the development of the Russian military preparations is G. Frantz, *Russlands Eintritt in den Weltkrieg.* See also Frantz in *Current History*, March, 1927.

54 Schilling, pp. 16–17, 49–50, 62–3; cf. S. B. Fay, in *American Historical Review*, April, 1925, p. 646.

55 Fay, *American Historical Review*, January, 1921, pp. 232–5.

56 Ibid., p. 236.

57 *British Blue Book*, No. 36.

58 Viscount Grey, *Twenty-Five Years*, 1892–1916, Vol. I, pp. 308–9, 311, 314.

59 *Outbreak of the World War*, p. 233.

60 Fay, loc. cit., pp. 240–41.

61 Schilling, p. 16.

62 Ibid., p. 50.

63 *Falsifications of the Russian Orange Book,* p. 30; Montgelas, op. cit., p. 161; Dobrorolski, *Die Mobilmachung der russischen Armee,* p. 23.

64 Schilling, p. 50.

65 Ibid.

66 Ibid.; Dobrorolski, *Die Mobilmachung der russischen Armee, 1914,* pp. 23–8, 45–6.

67 Morhardt, pp. 275 ff. This telegram was falsified when published in the *French Yellow Book.* Cf. G. Demartial, *L'Evangile du Quai d'Orsay.*

68 *Falsifications of the Russian Orange Book,* p. 53.

69 Ibid., p. 52.

70 Montgelas, *The Case for the Central Powers,* p. 198.

71 Schilling, pp. 56–7.

72 Morhardt, pp. 287–9; *Vers la verité,* pp. 89–95

73 Schilling, pp. 62–6.

74 Dobrorolski, op. cit., pp. 10, 27–29. There is a French translation in Morhardt, pp. 154–9. There is a brief and more recent German description by Dobrorolski in the *Kriegsschuldfrage* for April, 1924. In the latter Dobrorolski takes up the matter of the discrepancy between his account and that of Schilling as to just when the final order for general mobilization was given. Dobrorolski puts it as 1 P. M., and Schilling at some time after 3 P. M., probably as late as 4 P. M. Dobrorolski contends that he is right. If this is so, the order was given before the Berlin *Lokalanzeiger* of July 30th was even issued.

75 *Outbreak of the World War,* pp. 402–3.

76 Morhardt, pp. 160–61; Ewart, pp. 1067–8, 1124 ff.

77 See the excellent summary of this matter in Ewart, pp. 1073 ff., and especially pp. 1117 ff. Cf. Renouvin, *Les Origines immédiates de la guerre,* Chaps. vi, vii, ix.

78 Montgelas, p. 162.

79 Ewart, p. 1084.

80 As in footnote 42.

81 Professor Fay, loc. cit., p. 233, was able to hold in 1921 that Sazonov was for peace, a view shared by the present writer in his article in *Current History* for May, 1924. It is now necessary to abandon that view completely. Cf. Fay, in *American Historical Review,* April, 1925, p. 646; and Schilling, op. cit., *passim.*

82 See especially G. Frantz, *Russlands Eintritt in den Weltkrieg;* and Schilling, *passim;* and W. A. Sukhomlinow, in *Kriegsschuldfrage,* November, 1925, pp. 753–4

83 Frantz, op. cit.; and Fay, *American Historical Review,* April, 1925, p. 646.

84 *The Diary of Lord Bertie, 1914–1918* (Edited by Lady Algernon Gordon Lennox), Vol. I, pp. 16, 66. By November

Izvolski had changed his tune with the increased disasters for the Entente. Bertie notes in his diary for November 10th: "What a fool Iswolsky is! He said a few days since:—'J'ai des rivaux et il y a des hommes dont je me sers.' At the beginning of the war he claimed to be its author:—'C'est ma guerre!' Now he says:—'Si j'étais responsable en quoi que ce soit pour cette guerre je ne me pardonnerais jamais.'" Ibid., p. 66.

85 Langer, loc. cit.; Montgelas, pp. 165 ff.

86 Bertie, op. cit., Vol. I, p. 1.

87 Schilling, pp. 30–31, and *passim;* Ewart, pp. 1087–8, 1093, 1113–15, 1122.

88 *Falsifications of the Russian Orange Book,* p. 56.

89 Ewart, p. 1123.

90 Montgelas, pp. 177–8.

91 Ewart, pp. 76, 154.

92 Loc. cit., January, 1926; See also the editorial by the present writer in the New York *Nation,* January 27, 1926, p. 77.

93 Montgelas, pp. 215–17; Renouvin, op. cit., pp. 147 ff.

94 *Austrian Red Book,* Part III, pp. 17–19.

95 Schilling, pp. 9–10.

96 See above pp. 142–3; and *France and Russia on the Road Towards War,* pp. 22–3.

97 Morhardt, op. cit., pp. 275 ff., Lutz, op. cit.; Ewart, Chap. v; A. Pevet, *Les Responsables de la guerre,* pp. 211 ff., 861 ff.; E. F. Henderson, *The Verdict of History: the Case of Sir Edward Grey; British Documents,* Nos. 112, 177; the writer has been personally informed by Count Pourtalès that Grey's telegram about the British fleet on the 27th had a revolutionary effect on the Russian psychology and was probably the deciding factor in encouraging Sazonov to go ahead with mobilization.

CHAPTER VII

POINCARÉ AND HIS CLIQUE
INCITE THE RUSSIANS IN
THE CRISIS OF 1914

I. THE WAR OF 1870 AND THE WORLD WAR

ANY intelligent and adequate discussion of the
relation of France to the World War must begin
with a consideration of the Franco-Prussian
War, for, as Ewart has well expressed the situation: "Alsace-Lorraine was the cause of the
maze of military combinations and counter-
combinations which had perplexed European
diplomats for over forty years." [1]   We need here
do nothing more than briefly summarize what
was pointed out in an earlier chapter concerning
this question.   The conflict was a needless and
fundamentally immoral war.   It was produced
primarily by: (1) the desire of Bismarck to use
the Germanic patriotism, which might be generated through a war against France, as the means
of bringing the unification of the German Empire to completion, and (2) by the aspiration of
the politicians and diplomats of the Second Empire in France to exploit a war in the interest of
bolstering up for a time the tottering Bonaparte

dynasty. Of the two ambitions that of Bismarck was doubtless the more constructive and laudable. The War was actually precipitated through the foolhardy aggressive diplomacy of the Duke of Gramont, the French Foreign Minister. Writing to Countess Louise de Mercy-Argenteau on March 2, 1871, Napoleon III said: "I acknowledge that we were the aggressors." [2]

The only important point with reference to the problem at hand in this chapter is to emphasize the fact that the popular impression that the Franco-Prussian War was a wanton war waged by a powerful and aggressive military state against a weaker, reluctant and pacific neighbor is pure illusion. France was a much larger and more powerful state than Prussia in 1870, was fully as eager for war as Prussia, and expected to win a quick and decisive victory over Prussia, to be followed by a triumphant entry into Berlin, thus repeating the glorious feat of the first Napoleon. In fact, the great majority of prominent Englishmen and Americans, and the greater part of the influential press in both countries, looked upon France as the most menacing military state in Europe in 1870, viewed her as the aggressor in 1870, and welcomed the early decisive victories of von Moltke's armies. [3]

The Franco-Prussian War has a direct bearing upon the causes of the World War chiefly because at its close Bismarck, against his own best judgment and at the behest of the Prussian King and the extremists, annexed a part of the former German provinces of Alsace-Lorraine to Germany. The Germans could allege with entire accuracy that these provinces had originally been German for centuries, and had been ruthlessly torn from Germany by Louis XIV and other French autocrats. In 1870 Alsace-Lorraine was still more German than French in language and culture, but many Frenchmen found the idea of their permanent surrender to Germany absolutely intolerable. It is true that the annexation was rather generally approved in England and America, though many at the time foresaw the danger of the development of a French movement for revenge, but it proved the most disastrous act in the history of contemporary European diplomacy.[4] From 1871 onward there was a strong group in France which was determined never to rest until a victorious war over Germany should have restored the "Lost Provinces." The early leader of this group of *Revanchards* was Paul Déroulède, who created the League of Patriots for the purpose of keeping alive an unceasing agitation for the recovery of Alsace-Lorraine. He even visited foreign countries, seeking aid for the movement and agitating against Germany. His place was taken after his death by Maurice Barrès, a distinguished writer and an equally fanatical apostle of revenge.

These men had great influence on French sentiment and opinion, and no little influence on
French politics—certainly much more than that
exerted on the German government by the Pan-
German League.[5] The same spirit permeated
the army officers. Marshal Foch has stated:[6]

From the age of 17, I dreamed of revenge, after
having seen the Germans at Metz. And when a man
of ordinary capacity concentrates all of his faculties
and all of his abilities upon one end, and works without
diverging, he ought to be successful.

In general, the chief Republican leaders of
France were only lukewarm over the movement
for the recovery of Alsace-Lorraine, however
much they may have desired to regain these provinces. Most of the prominent *Revanchards*
prior to 1900 were, in differing degrees, enemies
of the Third Republic, as they felt that a monarchy would be more easily manipulated for war.
After the final victory of the Republicans in the
Dreyfus Case, there was a general movement
away from revenge and towards better relations
with Germany which was led by Caillaux,
Combes, Painlevé, Herriot and others.[7] Unfortunately, these men allowed the foreign policy of
France to be dominated by Delcassé, who was
one of the foremost apostles of revenge and the
ultimate defeat of Germany. His activities
more than offset all that the pacific group could

accomplish to mitigate the revenge spirit, and his attitude in regard to the Franco-Russian Alliance, the Anglo-French Entente and the Morocco question did more than anything else to alarm Germany and prevent Franco-German relations from assuming a tranquil tone. When he was compelled to resign it was too late to repair the damage, and Poincaré later took up Delcassé's work where it had been laid down.[8]

Raymond Poincaré was a French lawyer of very great ability who had taken a fairly active part in French politics from early years. He was a Lorrainer by birth, and had always entertained an almost fierce determination to do all in his power to recover his Fatherland.[9] In an address to university students in October, 1920, he confessed that he had been unable to see any real reason for existence except in the hope of recovering Alsace and Lorraine: [10]

In my years at school, my thought, bowed before the spectre of defeat, dwelt ceaselessly upon the frontier which the Treaty of Frankfort had imposed upon us, and when I descended from my metaphysical clouds I could discover no other reason why my generation should go on living except for the hope of recovering our lost provinces. Could life present any more satisfactory spectacle than to witness the reunion in Strasbourg of the youth of Alsace and the rest of France?

In a similar vein, M. Colrat, an intimate personal friend of Poincaré, wrote in *L'Opinion* for

December 14, 1918, with the approval of Poincaré: [11]

We must recognize that the recovery of Metz and Strasbourg is not only the magnificent work of our soldiers, living and dead, of the dead more than the living—it is the final culmination of a definite political policy. It is the achievement of M. Raymond Poincaré who has worked for it with an ingenious perseverance which sacrificed, when it was necessary, the accessory to the principal, the means to the end, men to the task.

These statements constitute the basis for some rather serious qualifications upon Poincaré's assertion in *Foreign Affairs* for October, 1925, that by 1912 the French had given up all hope of fighting for the recovery of the lost provinces: "The fact that she continued to think sorrowfully of those who had been torn from her did not mean that she dreamed for a single moment of delivering them by force of arms." [12]

Mathias Morhardt, a distinguished French publicist, has concisely described Poincaré's obsession in regard to the recovery of Alsace-Lorraine, with its decisive effect upon his policies: [13]

Let one take, one by one, the acts of his political life during these twelve long and terrible years! Let one analyze even the secret intentions! One always will find there the same spirit, the same will, the same methods. M. Raymond Poincaré—he has solemnly affirmed it in the *Manifeste aux Étudiants* which we have cited—had no other ambition than to recapture Alsace-Lorraine. His policy was invariably directed against Germany. It was a narrow policy full of violence and hate. But it was a policy of reparation. To satisfy it, he consented to the worst sacrifices and we have seen him putting France, the blood of two million of her children, even her fortune, to the service of the imperialistic ambitions of the Russian autocracy, the least compatible of governments with the genius and with the democratic aspirations of our own country. . . .

The plan created by M. Raymond Poincaré was all-embracing. Let a spark be lighted in the Balkans and the world war would be certain—for Russia coveted Constantinople and the Straits; and, like Austria, who was opposed to this dream and who was allied with Germany, France would undertake the struggle, because Germany would also enter. The conflict was so certain that M. Raymond Poincaré would do nothing either to eliminate it or even to avert it. . . . With an oriental fatalism he awaited serenely the hour of the realization of his program.

We have pointed out how the French chauvinists exploited the second Morocco crisis to discredit Caillaux and the pacific group, and came into power themselves with the accession of Poincaré to the office of Premier of France and Foreign Minister on January 14, 1912.[14] There had been plenty of vigorous activity on the part of the revenge group before this time, but they had been opposed by the majority of the Republican leaders. Now, for the first time, the Republic itself became committed to the *Revanchard* cause. Poincaré cannot escape, as he has tried to do, by calling attention to the fact that there were pacifically minded persons in his cabinet and that he became President in 1913.[15] He, Delcassé and Paléologue kept full control of foreign policy while he was Prime Minister, and, after he became President, he likewise maintained a whiphand over his Foreign Ministers and directed all important negotiations with Russia and England.[16] This fact demonstrates the misleading nature of his comparison of the theoretical constitutional and parliamentary control of foreign policiy in France with the autocratic domination over foreign affairs in pre-War Germany.

The danger to European peace inherent in the attitude and policies of the French firebrands was well expressed in January, 1914, by Baron Guillaume, the Belgian minister in Paris:

I have already had the honor of informing you that it is M.M. Poincaré, Delcassé, Millerand and their friends who have invented and pursued the nationalist, boastful and jingoistic policy whose revival we have witnessed. It is a danger for Europe and for Belgium. I see in it the greatest peril which threatens the peace of Europe today.

II. THE TRIPLE ENTENTE AND THE PREPARATION FOR THE WORLD WAR

In the third chapter we summarized the various stages in the development of the *Politik* of Poincaré and Izvolski. We shall here pass it in review, merely to emphasize the significance of these achievements for an understanding of the European situation in June, 1914. The Franco-Russian Alliance, negotiated between 1890 and 1894, was at the outset a purely defensive arrangement, though much was done to give it a more aggressive turn during Delcassé's mission in the summer of 1899. It was provided in the military convention of 1893 between the two countries that one was required to come to the aid of the other *only* in the event of a prior mobilization against one of them by Germany or Austria. In the Morocco crises Russia took no aggressive part in supporting France. Likewise, the Franco-Russian Alliance was, to 1912, based upon the provision for military coöperation alone. On July 16, 1912, a naval convention was completed which provided for coöperation by sea. The scheme for land coöperation was also greatly strengthened between 1912 and 1914 by Delcassé's mission, which dealt with the French loans to Russia, with their employment to increase the railroad facilities for transporting Russian troops to the German frontier, and with the necessity for enormous increases in the Russian army. The plans worked out by the general staffs of the two countries became more precise, and the interchange of views more intimate and frequent. Russian practice manœuvres in Poland became more comprehensive and scientific. The French also provided for great military increases in their army bill of 1913. As early as 1912 Izvolski reported that Poincaré had stated that French military experts believed France and Russia had a good chance against Germany and Austria in the event of war.

Diplomatic developments paralleled the naval and military increases.[17] The moderate and far-sighted Georges Louis was recalled as Ambassador to Russia, to be replaced by the belligerent arch-enemy of Germany, Théophile Delcassé. Poincaré and Izvolski agreed that the Balkans were the most promising area to be exploited for the purpose of inviting a general European war to secure the Straits and recover Alsace-Lorraine, but the French people were strongly opposed to a war over the Balkans. Hence, they had to be scared and deluded into a favorable attitude towards the Franco-Russian Balkan policy of 1912–14. This was achieved through the bribery of the French press by Russian money, obtained by Izvolski and dispersed by him with the advice of Poincaré and his associates. In this way the Franco-Russian Alliance

was "Balkanized." [18]   Poincaré was at the outset opposed to the Balkan Wars of 1912–1913,
for he felt that the conflict over the Balkans
should not be precipitated before Russia had advanced further with her military increases and
the French public was better prepared for war
by the bribed press.   But after war had broken
out in the Balkans he was willing to take a chance
on a prematurely initiated European war rather
than to let the Balkan situation develop in such a
fashion that Russia would get the Straits without the general European war necessary for the
recovery of Alsace and Lorraine.   Therefore, in
the fall of 1912, he made arrangements with Izvolski to the effect that France would willingly
follow Russia into a European war over the Balkan question, and did all he could to prevent
Russia from any possibility of gaining her ends
without a reciprocal advantage to France.   H
thus insisted upon a supervisory knowledge of
Russian policies in the Balkan area.   Throughout the Balkan Wars Poincaré and Izvolski
actively coöperated to oppose the interests of
Germany and Austria at every turn. [19]   By December, 1913, Sazonov was converted to the plan
of a European war to obtain the Straits, and even
the Tsar approved the scheme in March, 1914. [20]
Poincaré had from the first recognized that a general war was necessary to recover the lost provinces, and rejected in 1912 German advances for

better relations with France on the basis of far-reaching autonomy for Alsace-Lorraine. The French willingness for war is well described by no less a personage than Count Benckendorff in a report to Sazonov on February 25, 1913: [21]

Recalling his [M. Cambon's] conversations with me, the words exchanged, and, adding to that, the attitude of M. Poincaré, the thought comes to me as a conviction that, of all the Powers, France is the only one which, not to say that it wishes war, would yet look upon it without great regret. . . . The situation, as I regard it, seems to be that all the Powers are sincerely working to maintain peace. But of all of them, it is France who would accept war the most philosophically. As has been said, France "stands erect once more." Rightly or wrongly, she has complete confidence in her army; the old ferment of animosity has again shown itself, and France would very well consider that the circumstances to-day are more favorable than they will ever be later.

The transformation of the millenniumlong Anglo-French animosity and antipathy into active diplomatic coöperation between the two countries was begun when Delcassé seized the opportunity to exploit the Fashoda Incident of 1898 for the purpose of making a bid for English good-will and support.[22] By 1905 the Conservative government in England had laid specific and direct plans for coöperation with the French navy, and more nebulous plans for military co-

operation.   In 1906 Grey, as Foreign Secretary
of the new Liberal government, participated in
initiating in earnest the direct conversations between France and England, providing for joint
military action between England, France and
Russia against Germany.   Before the close of
1906 these plans had assumed a highly specific
character, and were progressively worked over by
the general staffs of the countries involved until
the outbreak of the World War.   At the time of
the second Morocco crisis, in 1911, England
took the opportunity to announce through Lloyd-
George her firm and aggressive association with
France against Germany in the case of a war between the latter and France.   In 1912 Poincaré
compelled Sir Edward Grey to renounce the arrangements discussed by Lord Haldane during
his visit to Germany to improve relations between Germany and England.   On November
22, 1912, Paul Cambon, French Ambassador to
England, induced Grey to agree to a plan of
naval coöperation with France, according to
which the French navy could be concentrated in
the Mediterranean to coöperate with the Russian
Black Sea fleet and hold in check the Austrian
navy, while the English bound themselves to protect the French coasts against any attack by the
German fleet.[23]   This meant that for all practical purposes England was actually committed
to make war on Germany whenever France did,

for, as Cambon well expressed it, a nation does not make war by halves, its navy fighting while its army remains inactive.[24]   The plans for military coöperation assumed a much more detailed and explicit form under the direction of Generals Wilson and French between 1912 and 1914, until they were as explicit and thorough as those existing between the French and Russian general staffs.   In November, 1912, Sazonov wrote to the Tsar that both Grey and Poincaré had assured him that England had bound herself by a verbal agreement to come to the aid of France if the latter were attacked by Germany.[25]

We have indicated above that Sazonov held that France and Russia could not risk a war with any assurance except on the assumption that England could be counted upon.   We have traced above the development of the understandings between France and Russia and between France and England.   England and Russia had been rivals for a century over the Near East, but better relations between these countries began with the partition of Persia in 1907, though there was friction over Persia right down to the outbreak of the World War.   One of the conspicuous acts of Poincaré on his visit to St. Petersburg in 1914 was to reassure the British Ambassador as to Russian policy in Persia.[26] From 1907 onward the British military plans were framed in contemplation of coöperation

with France in the west and Russia in the east
against Germany.   In 1910 another step was
taken when Sir Arthur Nicolson was recalled
from his post as Ambassador to St. Petersburg
and made permanent under-secretary at the British Foreign Office.   Grey frankly admitted that
he had been appointed to improve the relations
between Russia and England.[27]   In the spring
of 1914 Grey had persuaded Asquith and others
in the British cabinet to consent to negotiations
for an Anglo-Russian naval convention.   This
was advancing successfully when the crisis of
1914 came on, the Russian representative being
in London at the time.[28]   It is thus apparent
that by June, 1914, the ring around Germany
and Austria was practically complete.

It has been held by some that Poincaré's policy
was purely defensive and produced by a mortal
fear of German aggression.   This is, quite obviously, nonsense.   In 1912 Poincaré himself
wrote: "The German Government seems obsti-
nately bent on a *rapprochement* which nothing
but complete reparation for the past would render possible."   The truth of the matter has been
admirably summarized by Fabre-Luce: [29]

In short, with variations in their tactics, the German
government aimed at reconciliation until 1913, when,
finding all their proposals rejected, they were persuaded that France wanted war, and turned their whole

attention to strengthening their armaments to insure their defence.

III. POINCARÉ AND HIS CLIQUE IN THE CRISIS OF 1914

1. *Responsibility that of Poincaré rather than of French People*

In treating the responsibility of France in the July crisis of 1914 it should be understood at the outset that the responsibility was that of scarcely more than a half-dozen men, including Poincaré, Viviani, Messimy, Delcassé, Paul Cambon and Paléologue. The final decision upon war was officially made on the nights of July 29th and 31st by only three men—Poincaré, Viviani and Messimy. As Messimy, the Minister of War, was called in as an expert from an important department involved, and as Viviani was not a militarist at heart,[30] it may almost be held that the complete responsibility for this momentous responsibility rests upon the shoulders of Poincaré alone. It may safely be said that there was more autocratic action in deciding upon entering the World War in France than in Russia, Germany or Austria. In no case did the legislative branches have anything to do with the decisions in these countries, and a larger group of ministers coöperated in making the decisions in Russia, Austria and Germany than in France. The nearest resemblance was the case of Sazonov in Russia, but he was less the master of the situation than was Poincaré. Poincaré had no Tsar to cancel mobilization orders or to resist the issuance of new orders. He was himself complete master of the policy of Paris. Therefore, when we speak of the responsibility of France for the great cataclysm, we do not mean the responsibility of the French people, but the responsibility of Raymond Poincaré, and his willing servants in the ministry and diplomatic service.

It is certain that the French people were not clamoring for war in 1914, and they had admittedly been overwhelmingly pacific in 1912. Nothing is more frequently mentioned in Izvolski's reports to Sazonov concerning his interviews with Poincaré than the insistence of the latter upon the fact that the French people were peace-loving and opposed to war over the Balkan issue. Poincaré very often emphasized with Izvolski the fact that it would require a long campaign of corruption of the French press by the employment of Russian funds in order to delude the French people into feeling that they were in danger from the Austro-German policy in the Balkans, thereby rendering them willing to follow Poincaré into war.[31] Even two years of persistent efforts in this respect were not adequate to lead the French populace into a belligerent attitude. When the war crisis came in 1914 it was found necessary to break up all pacifist meetings in Paris for days before the outbreak of war, to print false statements concerning the German Ambassador in Paris, to misrepresent flagrantly the facts about the German attitude towards a diplomatic settlement of the crisis, to publish obvious lies about the relative state of the Russian and German military preparations and activities, to assassinate the great leader of the Socialists, to delay the formal mobilization order and to fake defensive military gestures, to develop a most rigid censorship of the news, to initiate the most thorough campaign of propaganda, and to refuse to submit the decision upon war to debate in the Chamber of Deputies. Only by deceiving the French people in these ways and leading them thereby to accept the fiction that France was waging a desperate war of defense was Poincaré and his group able to drag the French people into the conflict.   As the most astute of all French students of war guilt, Georges Demartial, has well expressed the matter: "France was thrown into the war as helpless as a bound chicken destined for the spit." [32]

Therefore, when we proceed to indict Poincaré and his clique for the French responsibility in the launching of the World War, we are not in any sense attempting to indict France.   We well recognize that the French people were the unconscious but tragic victims of their unscrupulous

masters, and that they have suffered more than
any others from their delusion. We simply use
the term "France" with respect to war responsibility as a blanket term in ordinary usage. And
we have to recognize that it was all France which
ultimately went into the War, even though a narrow political oligarchy controlled her policy and
relentlessly pushed her into the bloody contest.
Least of all, would we hold that the indictment
of Poincaré and his policies from January, 1912,
to August, 1914, constitutes in any sense an indictment of French culture, in his admiration of
which the present writer yields to no one. And,
further, it may be pointed out here that there
have been written in France more creditable
books attacking Poincaré and his group as responsible for the War than there have been in
Germany and Austria combined.[33] Finally, the
first organized movement in any Entente country
to repudiate the old lies about war guilt was in-
stituted in France late in 1925 by Victor Margueritte and his associates, though Morel Beazley
and others had protested far earlier in England.[34]

2. The Myth of "Defenseless France"

There is a most persistent myth which we have
already shown to be highly absurd, but which
still crops up as one of the most frequently cited
proofs of the innocence of France in 1914,

namely, the allegation that the Triple Entente was hopelessly outnumbered by Germany and Austria, and that France was timid and fearful on the defensive. Very recently indeed, in his popular book *France and the French,* Mr. Sisley Huddleston regaled us with this perennial illusion after the following fashion: [34a]

I have had the privilege of some personal acquaintance with the private sentiments of such outstanding French soldiers as Marshal Foch and General Gouraud, and I affirm emphatically that no greater pacifists could anywhere be found. It was with trepidation that France entered the War in 1914; neither M. Poincaré, the President, nor M. Viviani, the Prime Minister, who were on the high seas when the fatal step was taken, would have deliberately dared to face the consequences of a new struggle with Germany with the recollection of the defeat and humiliation of 1870 in their minds and with no certainty of English or American aid. The odds against France were far too great. As for the French people, they were, as anybody who had any acquaintance with them at that time will concede, altogether pacific in their intentions. Much praise has been rightly bestowed on the tenacity and the bravery of the French, but on several occasions during the War the so-called *défaitistes* nearly brought about a catastrophic surrender. Men like Clemenceau, when once the War began, were determined to see it through at any cost, and doubtless, though not seeking, they welcomed the opportunity, as they supposed, of shattering once and for all the German peril.

The statistics of comparative armaments which we cited in the second chapter are adequate to refute this. The truth is contained in the statement of former Chancellor Marx that "The Entente was so much stronger than the Central Powers that an aggressive scheme on the part of Germany and Austria would have been almost suicidal." And we know that Poincaré was fully aware of the facts. As early as 1912, before the enormous increases in the Russian and the French armies, he told Izvolski that the French military experts believed that France and Russia alone had an excellent chance against Germany and Austria. In a speech at Nantes in October, 1913, Poincaré declared: "France does not want war, but she does not fear it." Now Sir Edward Grey tells us that in the spring of 1914 the French and British military experts held that France and England unaided would be able to withstand the Central Powers. Poincaré further knew in July, 1914, that he could certainly count on Serbia, and probably on Italy and Roumania. In the light of these facts the thesis of a cringing and terror-stricken France in 1914 is utterly ridiculous.

3. *Aftermath of the St. Petersburg Visit*

In the preceding chapter we indicated at some length how the initial impulse to the aggressive action on the part of the Entente that produced the World War came from Poincaré's visit to St. Petersburg from July 20th to 23rd, 1914. He put new vigor into the Russian militarists, stirred the Tsar, incited the Russians to take a strong stand against Austria, and gave the Russians to understand that France would stand firmly behind them in whatever action they took in the premises.[35] On the 24th he had Viviani send a telegram from Reval telling the acting Foreign Minister at Paris that France must be prepared to act decisively in the Austro-Serbian crisis. The Russians were encouraged to make their crucial decision upon war on the 25th through Paléologue's statement to Sazonov on the 25th that he was "in a position to give his Excellency formal assurance that France placed herself unreservedly on Russia's side." Between the Reval Dispatch and Poincaré's arrival in Paris (specifically July 24–27) Paul Cambon secretly rushed from London to Paris lest Bienvenu-Martin might become too conciliatory in his discussions of the crisis with the German Ambassador. Cambon thus stiffened up the policy of the French Foreign Office until the return of Poincaré and Viviani. Berthelot also contributed very clever and competent assistance to the Franco-Russian program at this time through his extremely astute outlining of the Serbian reply to the Austrian ultimatum. For weeks before war broke out Clemenceau urged the French on to a war of conquest by his writings in *L'Homme Libre*.

Poincaré's attitude at the end of his Russian trip is illustrated by the following anecdote narrated by Armand Charpentier. When he landed at Dunkirk at noon on July 29th Poincaré was asked by Senator Trystram: "Do you believe, Mr. President, that the war can be averted?" To this Poincaré replied: "To do so would be a great pity, for we shall never witness more favorable circumstances!"

Upon his return to Paris, where he was greeted with a great patriotic demonstration and cries of "on to Berlin," Poincaré continued his aggressive policy without flinching. The acting Foreign Minister, Bienvenu-Martin, and the German Ambassador in Paris, Baron von Schoen, had discussed the Austro-Serbian affair in a friendly manner. This was a poor beginning for a policy of war, so Poincaré's henchman, Berthelot, published in the *Echo de Paris* grave distortions of the conversations between Schoen and Bienvenu-Martin, designed to inflame the French public; and this in spite of the fact that Poincaré affects great indignation at Bismarck's alleged distortion of the Ems telegram of 1870.[36] Active steps in the way of military preparations began to be taken by the French military authorities from the 24th of July onward, though for purely diplomatic reasons the French delayed the order for general mobilization until after the German proclamation of a state of imminent war.

Poincaré was quickly faced with the responsibility incurred by his inflammatory policy while in St. Petersburg. On the very night of his return to Paris he received a telegram from Sazonov announcing the Russian mobilization plans, the Russian decision that war was probable, and the Russian assumption that France could be counted upon to fulfil all the obligations of the alliance with Russia.[37] We have already shown how Poincaré, Viviani and Messimy took up this crucial matter in a secret conference on the night of July 29th, and made the fatal decision for war. Though they did not actually announce their formal declaration for war until late on the night of the 31st, they well knew that their decision on the night of the 29th would lead the Russians to continue those steps which would make a general European war inevitable. On the morning of July 30th Poincaré told a friend of the Spanish Ambassador that he regarded a European war as inevitable.[38]

Viviani telegraphed the next morning to the French Ambassadors at London and St. Petersburg that France was determined to fulfil all the obligations of her alliance with Russia, and that he had advised Russia to carry on her military preparations in such a manner as to keep

Germany as much in the dark as possible and not afford the latter any pretext for counter-mobilization. He also added that he had assured the German Ambassador in Paris that the French had taken no steps towards preparation for war and were eagerly supporting every diplomatic effort being made to preserve peace.[39]

Izvolski at once informed Sazonov of the contents of Viviani's telegrams, and also of the fact that Cambon had been put to work on Grey to induce him to line up England with France and Russia in the crisis.[40]

Perhaps Izvolski's most important telegram was one to the effect that France was not opposed to the Russian military preparations, but that Russia should be as secretive as possible about them. The French suggested that the Russian government issue a public declaration that they were willing to curtail their mobilization activities in the interest of peace, and then, under the cover of this announcement, actually speed up these mobilization measures. The insistence upon secrecy was, of course, dictated by the desire to gain as much time as possible on Germany and not to alarm England. By the early morning of the 30th of July, then, France was urging Russia to hasten the steps which would make war inevitable, but was instructing her to screen them behind public declarations of a desire to preserve the peace of Europe through

negotiations. This famous telegram of Izvolski, one of the most important during the whole
July crisis, was excluded wholly from the original Russian *Orange Book,* as, indeed, were the
two previous ones just mentioned. It reads as
follows: [41]

Margerie [Director of the French Foreign Office]
with whom I just spoke tells me that the French Government do not wish to interfere with our military
preparations, that, however, they would consider it
most desirable on account of the still continuing negotiations for the preservation of the peace, if these
preparations were carried on in the least open, least
provocative manner possible. For his part, the Minister of War expressed the same idea to our Military
Attaché, and said we might declare that, in the higher
interests of peace, we were willing to slow down for the
time being our preparations for mobilization, which
would not hinder us to continue and even accelerate
these preparations, but on so doing we would have to
refrain as much as possible from the transportation of
troops on a larger scale.

These undeniable facts as to the French encouragement of the aggressive Russian acts from
the very first constitute a most illuminating commentary upon the honesty of Poincaré in telegraphing George V on July 31st that France
had from the beginning of the crisis offered
counsels of restraint and moderation to Russia,
and that Russia had uniformly heeded such ad-

monition.[42] The reverse was, of course, the truth. As early as July 27th Sazonov hastened to inform the French that "regarding counsels of moderation, we reject these at the outset." [43] And Bienvenu-Martin was equally prompt in informing Sazonov that he did "not for a minute admit the possibility of exercising a moderating influence in St. Petersburg." [44]

4. Diplomatic Subterfuges of "Reluctant France"

Having thus committed themselves to an inevitable European war the French considered with acumen the possible diplomatic ruses and subterfuges which might be employed to deceive the Germans as to the state of the Franco-Russian diplomatic agreements and military preparations, and to dupe the English, French and Italian peoples into thinking that France was steadfastly working for peace until the last hope of averting war had vanished. The impression was also to be spread abroad that when the French finally accepted the necessity of war, they entered upon hostilities in a purely defensive and reluctant attitude. The most famous and ambitious gesture in this direction was the order given on July 30th for the withdrawal of the French troops on the frontier to a distance of ten kilometers from the boundary. This, as General Joffre was fully informed at the time,

and as Viviani and Messimy frankly admitted in
speeches before the Chamber of Deputies on
January 31, 1919, was purely and simply a diplomatic ruse to impress the peoples of England,
France and Italy with the apparent fact that
France was doing everything in her power to
avert even the appearance of wishing war.[45]   In
this manner Poincaré and Viviani hoped to rally
the French people to the support of their government, to put British opinion behind Sir Edward Grey in coming to the assistance of France,
and to help to detach Italy from the Triple Alliance. Of the greatest importance was the
hoped-for effect upon British opinion. This is
well brought out in a telegram from Messimy
(the Minister of War) to General Joffre on the
afternoon of August 1st: [46]

In order to secure the coöperation of our English
neighbors, it is still essential not to allow patrols and
detachments to go beyond the general line fixed in
telegram No. 129 of the 30th of July.

The bluff worked perfectly, not only in the case
of England, but also with respect to France and
Italy.

Since the secret purpose of the order has been
revealed, Poincaré has attempted to defend himself by alleging that this move was assuredly a
serious effort to demonstrate the pacific intentions of France because it was a dangerous act

from a military point of view, and was fiercely opposed by Joffre and the military authorities.[47] This is an obvious falsehood. Viviani stated in his speech of January 31, 1919, before the Chamber of Deputies, that the withdrawal order was not opposed by Messimy. Messimy immediately arose in the Chamber, confirmed this statement, and added that the withdrawal order was not opposed by the French General Staff.[48] We now know that there was no reason why it should have been. In some places the order was only for a four kilometer withdrawal. On those sections of the frontier where even temporary evacuation of posts might have been dangerous the order was not executed. The order was given before the Germans had taken any steps towards military preparations for imminent war. The patrols were left in the border posts to report the advance of any German troops, and the French troops could have been marched back over the ten kilometers in two hours. The ten kilometer limitation was removed on August 2nd, the day that Grey gave Cambon his promise that England would come into the War on the side of France. This was twenty-four hours before the German declaration of war. Hence, the withdrawal order was in no sense a military menace or a handicap to the French General Staff. Indeed, it was a positive advantage, as it provided a screen behind which even more extensive secret military preparations could be carried on by the French.[49]   The new British documents (No. 319 and enclosure) reveal the fact that Viviani informed Cambon and Grey that the withdrawal order was given solely to influence British opinion.

The most striking and startling information concerning the withdrawal order is the alleged revelation that the suggestion came to the French from London as the result of collusion between Paul Cambon and Grey who, as Benckendorff tells us, understood the importance of preparing English opinion for the coming conflict.[50]   This information that the withdrawal order was given at the instigation of England has come from Mr. Gerald Campbell of the London *Times*.[51]   The new British documents furnish no confirmation of Campbell's allegation. They do prove that Grey had certainly not decided as early as the 30th that war was inevitable and that England must enter on the side of France.   Nevertheless, Grey fully realized that the French withdrawal order was absolutely a diplomatic subterfuge and he coöperated fully with Cambon and Viviani in using this ruse to deceive his own countrymen as to the acts and policies of Russia and France.[52]

An amusing but utterly discreditable bit of stage-play appears in the telegrams exchanged between France and England over the with-

drawal order. It will be remembered that all
of these communications took place after France
had decided, on the night of July 29th, to
support the Russian activities which were certain to bring on a European war, after Poincaré
had told the friend of the Spanish Ambassador
that he believed a European war inevitable, and
after Grey was completely aware of both the
Russian intentions and the French support of
these Russian military measures. On July 30th
Viviani telegraphed to Paul Cambon that the
withdrawal order had been carried out, and
asked him to inform Grey to that effect.[53] On
the same day Viviani again telegraphed to London to emphasize the necessity of informing the
King as to the withdrawal order.[54] On the 31st
Poincaré blithely telegraphed the King that:[55]
"We have ourselves, since the beginning of the
crisis, recommended to our allies a moderation to
which they have adhered." The King gallantly
expressed his "appreciation" of these pacific
measures by replying:[56] "I admire the con-
straint that you and your Government are exercising in abstaining from taking, on your frontiers, the final military measures, and in adopt-
ing an attitude that can in no sense and in no way
be interpreted as a provocation."

In his conversation with Lord Bertie on July
30th and 31st (*British Documents,* Nos. 318,
373) and in his telegram to the King on July 31st

Poincaré included another ruse, namely, an effort
to get Grey and George V to declare specifically
that England would range herself on the side of
France and Russia. He argued for this action
on the ground that it would restrain Germany
from making war: "He [Poincaré, writes
Bertie] is convinced that the preservation of
peace between the Powers is in the hands of England, for if His Majesty's Government would
announce that, in the event of a conflict between
Germany and France, resulting from the present
differences between Austria and Serbia, England
would come to the aid of France, there would be
no war, for Germany would at once modify her
attitude." Poincaré himself knew well enough
at the time that it was Russia and not Germany
which needed restraint if war was to be avoided.
If Grey and George V had openly assented to
this, the actual result would have been to make
St. Petersburg even more defiant and aggressive. What Sazonov had been wishing for ever
since the 29th was absolute and explicit written
assurance that Russia could count on England.
It having already been determined by Russia and
France that Germany was going to be attacked,
such a declaration as Poincaré attempted to obtain from England could not have kept Germany
from going to war unless she had been unwilling
to fight for her existence. After this can one
accept the good faith of the French suggestions

of diplomatic measures for peace any more than he can the proposal of Sazonov on July 31st for a conference at London?

In his apology in *Foreign Affairs* Poincaré attempts to establish his own innocence and that of France on the basis of an assertion that the German Ambassador in Paris reported to Berlin on July 29th that Viviani still hoped for peace and was taking every diplomatic step to bring it about. What this statement proves is not the pacific intent of Viviani and Poincaré, but their success in pulling the wool over the eyes of Baron Schoen.[57]

It is, perhaps, worth while to emphasize once more that the French decision, on the night of the 29th, to support the Russians in making war, and the withdrawal order of the 30th, were both determined upon when the German pressure upon Austria to negotiate and accept mediation was at its height and when there was every prospect and opportunity for a successful diplomatic settlement of the whole crisis.

Another phase of Poincaré's plan for misleading public opinion as to French military measures was his refusal to grant Joffre's initial request for mobilization on July 31st. Poincaré represents this as having been due to his determination to act on the defensive as long as possible.[58] In a telegram to Sazonov on August 1st Izvolski tells of his conference with the

French authorities on the matter of the French
mobilization, and explains the real reason for the
French delay:[59] "It is very important for
France on account of political considerations
relative to Italy and most especially England,
that the French mobilization should not pre-
cede the German one, but form the answer to
the latter." The French did not, of course, wait
for the German general mobilization, but used
the German proclamation of a state of imminent
war as the justification for the French mobilization order. In spite of their delay with the formal mobilization order, the French had proceeded
with their military preparations in a thorough
fashion without resorting to formal mobilization.
For example, it was announced on August 1st,
when the French mobilization was finally ordered
(at 3.30 P. M.), that the five French army corps
on the frontier were absolutely prepared for
war.[60]

5. France Declares for War on July 31st

Poincaré lays much stress upon the statement
that the purely formal move for a declaration
of war was taken first by Germany, in spite of
the fact that he says it was of no significance
whatever that France was the first to declare
war in 1870.[61] "The aggressor is the one who
renders inevitable the first shot, in other words
the nation who first declares war."[62] This

opinion, of course, diverges entirely from the terms of the Franco-Russian military convention of 1893, which stated that the aggressor is the one who first mobilizes, namely, Russia in 1914.[63]   As every one knows, who is at all informed as to the details of the diplomatic crisis and military preparations in 1914, the German declaration of war upon France was a pure formality which the French expected long before it came.[64]   The important matters are as to who first ordered the general mobilization that made war inevitable and as to which state was the first to announce that it was through with diplomacy and determined to resort to war.   It is incontestable that Russia was the first to order general mobilization.[65]   Poincaré and Renouvin have tried to shoulder Germany with the responsibility of having been the first to decide to resort to war.[66]   We have already indicated the utter lack of any factual foundation for this thesis.   The Russians were the first to take steps which they knew must lead to war, but the French were the first to declare themselves through with diplomacy and determined upon war.   This decision was arrived at in a ministerial conference held under the supervision of Poincaré at his official residence on the evening of July 31st.[67]   At 1 A. M. on the morning of the 1st of August Izvolski telegraphed as follows to Sazonov: [68]

The French Minister of War disclosed to me with
hearty high spirits that the French Government have
firmly decided upon war, and begged me to confirm the
hope of the French General Staff that all our efforts
will be directed against Germany and that Austria will
be treated as a *quantité négligeable.*

The Russians, for all practical purposes,
carried out this wish of the French General
Staff, and turned most of their forces against
Germany; and this in spite of the fact that
Sazonov originally tried to justify his early
steps in mobilization on the basis of his alleged
fear of the Austrian mobilization against Russia, which did not take place until two days after
the Russian partial mobilization was initiated!
*France was, thus, the first country in the
European crisis officially to announce her determination upon war.* This announcement
came sixteen hours before Germany declared war
on Russia and two and a half days before
Germany declared war on France.   Many of the
revisionist school are inclined to lay the greatest
stress upon this French announcement of the
31st, but the writer is inclined to regard as
even more damaging Poincaré's decision forty-
eight hours earlier to support the Russian war
measures at a time when Germany had not even
taken any preliminary steps towards mobilization, and when the diplomatic negotiations,
formally approved by the representatives of the

Entente, were in full and uninterrupted swing.
Even if the false charge of Poincaré and
Renouvin were true, namely, that Germany decided upon war just before midnight on the
30th, this would furnish no alibi for the French,
as they had decided to support the measures
which they knew must mean war more than
twenty-four hours earlier.

6. *Autocratic Methods and Personal Responsibility of Poincaré*

Poincaré has contended that France could
not have avoided taking the action that she did
on July 31st unless she had been willing to "tear
up her defensive alliance" with Russia,[69] but he
knew well enough that this was not true, even
if the French Chamber of Deputies was in ignorance of the facts in the situation. We have
pointed out a number of times that the terms of
the Franco-Russian military convention of 1893
required French intervention only in case Russia
was mobilized against by a member of the
Triple Alliance before Russia had mobilized.
The Chamber of Deputies first discovered this
fact in 1918, but Poincaré was fearful lest they
might discover it before hostilities commenced
in 1914.[70] Hence, he persistently refused to
declare war on Germany, because, as he explained to Izvolski, to do so would mean that

he would have to summon the Chamber of Deputies. This would invite a debate upon the question of whether the Treaty of 1893 really required French intervention under the circumstances which existed in 1914.[71] He waited for Germany to declare war, and then exploited the psychology of fear generated by false propaganda to secure the approval of war by the Chamber.

In spite of his explicit knowledge to the contrary at the time, Sir Edward Grey gave expression to the same falsehood in his speech of August 3, 1914, requesting the House of Commons to approve his promise to aid France: [72]

I can say this with the most absolute confidence— no Government and no country has less desire to be involved in a war over a dispute with Austria and Serbia than the Government and country of France. They are involved in it because of their obligation of honour under a definite alliance with Russia.

Sir Edward Grey was here guilty of a double error, for not only was France not required in 1914 to fulfil the agreement of 1893 with Russia, but the real reason why she was bound to aid Russia was Poincaré's promise in 1912 that if Russia would pick a suitable diplomatic crisis in the Balkans, presumably a struggle between Austria and Serbia, France would come to her aid. It

was Poincaré's assurance to Russia, at the time
of his visit to St. Petersburg, that the assassination of the Archduke had created a satisfactory
incident for French intervention, together with
his subsequent promises to Russia after July
23rd, which furnished the grounds for his insistence upon throwing France into the War in support of the Russian general mobilization. These
circumstances relative to Poincaré's refusal to
submit the question of the declaration of war to
the Chamber of Deputies before the German
declaration, and his concealment of the fact that
the terms of the Alliance of 1893 did not apply
to the situation in 1914, offer an illuminating
commentary upon his more recent statement in
Foreign Affairs for October, 1925, to the effect
that: [73]

The republican institutions of France are indeed
conceived in such a manner that no one man can substitute his will for that of the people. No President of
the Republic can act without the counter-signature of
a minister and every minister is responsible to the
Chamber for his actions. It would be a simple matter
to show, year by year and point by point, that, before
the war as since, the foreign policy of France has been
carried on in the open and in complete accord with
Parliament.

We shall only casually mention in passing the
additional interesting reflection occasioned by

Poincaré's above cited remarks, namely, the method he followed of lubricating the political machinery of republican France by the gold imported for the purpose from autocratic Russia.

7. *Deluding the French Public*

One other matter remains to be discussed in this connection, namely, the methods employed by Poincaré to mislead the French people about the facts of the crisis of 1914, and to bring them to accept the fiction that France had done everything in her power to avert war, that she was obligated to go to the aid of Russia, that she had been wantonly attacked by Germany, and that she was fighting a strictly defensive war. We have already indicated how the French were being brought around to the view of the imminence and inevitability of a war over the Balkans through the bribery of the French press with that end in view. We have also called attention to the distortion of the conversations between the German Ambassador in Paris and the French acting Foreign Minister, prior to the return of Poincaré and Viviani from Russia, by Poincaré's confidant and henchman, Berthelot, as well as to the mode of concealing the facts and deceiving the French people in 1914 about the obligations of France under the Russian treaty of 1893. A definite manipulation of the French press began early in the crisis. Information as to the diplomatic activities and pacific efforts of Germany was carefully concealed from the people, as was likewise the date and implications of the precipitate and unjustifiable mobilization measures of Russia.

On the other hand, utterly false reports were circulated as to the date and priority of the German and Austrian mobilization and other military activities, while the avowed pacific intentions of France were emphasized by such impostures as the ten kilometer withdrawal order, the delay of the formal mobilization order, and the insistence of Poincaré that he await the German declaration of war to avoid the necessity of a debate on the French obligations under the terms of the Russian Alliance. The friends of peace in France in 1914 were obstructed by the government at every turn, and long before France was in any danger of attack. As early as July 29th Izvolski telegraphed to Sazonov that he had been assured by the French government that they would take sharp and decisive measures to break up any pacifist meetings, and later in the same day telegraphed Sazonov that Viviani had forbidden the holding of such meetings. Finally, the one outstanding French leader who might have organized a large body of Frenchmen for peace, Jean Jaurès, was assassinated by a member of the military party at the instigation of Izvolski and the Russian secret police before he could take

any active steps to obstruct the war policy of
Poincaré. Just before his assassination he remarked: "That scoundrel Izvolski has now got
his war!" The despicable assassin was acquitted
as a public benefactor of France.[74]

IV. POINCARÉ AND VIVIANI IN RETREAT

1. The Modesty of Poincaré

In his article in *Foreign Affairs,* among the
various ways in which Poincaré attempts to
wriggle out from under the conviction of guilt
which has been fastened irrevocably upon him
is to ask the question as to whether it could have
been possible for one man to perpetrate a deception of such proportions upon the whole
world.[75] His countryman, Mathias Morhardt,
answers the query in a positive fashion, and contends that Poincaré has achieved more to change
the face of the world and the course of history
than any other individual in human history, not
even excepting the first Napoleon:[76]

If we examine his rôle, not, indeed, from the point of
view of morality and reason, but from the standpoint
of historic events, he takes the first place among the
men who have exercised a decisive influence upon the
world. Take, for example, Napoleon I; the great
Corsican adventurer did not succeed, after fifteen years
of the most absolute power in accomplishing results at
all comparable to those which M. Raymond Poincaré

can glory in having achieved. No one before him ever upset the world with more cold-blooded enthusiasm.

Morhardt raises the further question as to why Poincaré not only refuses to take credit for such a magnificent achievement, but even insists upon his being held entirely innocent in 1914. The answer is, of course, that Poincaré expected a very short war in 1914, having expressed himself as believing that either France and Russia or France and England could defeat Germany and Austria. With France, England and Russia all in against Germany and Austria, he believed that the Central Powers would be quickly crushed. Few realize how sound *a priori* were his convictions in this respect, though they seem reasonable enough as soon as one consults the statistics of armaments in 1914. If the Belgian defenses had not yielded to the German bombardment far sooner than the French and English had expected, and if von Hindenburg had not won one of the greatest and most striking victories in the history of warfare through his defeat of the Russians in the Battle of Tannenberg in August, 1914, it is probable that the Central Powers would have been compelled to sue for peace in the winter of 1914–15. The length of the war upset all Poincaré's calculations, and even the recovery of his Lorraine and the temporary humiliation of Germany could not provide him with enough courage to face the

relatives of the millions of dead and maimed
Frenchmen and admit his primary responsibility
for their decease and all the attendant suffering.

It should also be pointed out here that, during his term of office as Premier since the War,
the conduct of Poincaré was strictly conformable
to that from 1912 to 1918. By insisting upon
continuing the policy of utterly crushing Germany, according to the French war aims of
1914, he alienated England and much of the
rest of the world. By financing the aggressive
occupation policy in Germany as well as the
great armies of the new French allies against
Germany, he doubled the French debt and put
French finances in a state from which it will be
difficult to escape short of the most crushing
taxation for generations, if, indeed, bankruptcy
and repudiation can be avoided. Since 1918 as
before, Poincaré proved himself far more an
enemy of Germany than a friend of France.[77]

2. Poincaré in the Quicksand

As we suggested above with respect to the
case of Sazonov, if the Entente statesmen and
diplomats were actually in favor of peace in
1914 and were doing all in their power to bring
it about, it should not be necessary for them to
falsify and evade on the main issues when defending their acts and policies. We shall not

devote space here to a discussion of the striking
falsifications and alterations of the original
French *Yellow Book,* as this question can be
dealt with more adequately after the French
documents are published in full. It may be remarked in passing, however, that even at the present time most significant attempts at falsification
have been detected, and have been made the subject of a highly important chapter in M. Morhardt's book on war guilt, and of an entire book
by M. Demartial.[78] We shall here limit ourselves to a few observations on the attempts of
Poincaré and Viviani to defend their conduct of
office in 1914.

Poincaré has been assailed for his guilt in
precipitating the War in 1914 by a number of
French scholars and publicists from 1919 onward. This led him to publish an attempted
defense, *The Origins of the War,* in 1922.
This contains so many errors of fact and interpretation that a French scholar, Lazare, has
been compelled to write an even longer book in
order carefully but scathingly to refute it point
by point.[79] During the summer of 1925 Poincaré was induced by the editor of the important
American periodical, *Foreign Affairs,* to prepare another defense, directed particularly
against such American students of war guilt as
Professor Fay, Judge Bausman and the present
writer.[80] It has been our privilege to refute
this statement by Poincaré at length and in a

number of periodicals, and we shall not repeat that performance in this place.[81]   It will suffice to enumerate a few of Poincaré's errors of fact in positive statement, ignoring here his errors of omission and interpretation.   It is significant at the outset to note that even Poincaré no longer dares to repeat the fiction of the Potsdam Conference.   He makes the following startling and revolutionary admission: [82]

I do not claim that Austria or Germany, in this first phase, had a conscious thought-out intention of provoking a general war.   No existing document gives us the right to suppose that, at that time, they had planned anything so systematic.

Poincaré does not pause to point out that this admission completely destroys the cornerstone of the Entente epic as it was unfolded during the war period.   The Entente peoples and many neutrals were primarily inflamed by the oft-repeated assertion that the Central Powers had from the beginning deliberately willed a brutal and unprovoked war.

Poincaré attempts to establish his innocence by citing the unscholarly and intemperate book by the completely discredited German renegade, Richard Grelling, unmindful of the fact that there are a score of infinitely better French books by much more reputable authors which proclaim his own guilt.   Poincaré proceeds un-blushingly to assert that the Russian documents are for the most part forgeries; that the French entertained no thought of a conflict for the recovery of Alsace-Lorraine; that he was the merest ornamental figurehead on his Russian trip; that Germany encouraged Austria in her determination to declare war on Serbia, and did not seriously advise restraint or moderation; that "by their common action on July 27 Germany and Austria did everything to make a European war possible"; that Germany decided to abandon diplomatic efforts on July 30th and to adopt the policy of resorting to war; that the Russian mobilization did not constitute an act of aggression or justify the German counter-measures; that the ten kilometer imposture was really a serious effort of the French to mollify the Germans and was a risky military venture opposed by the French General Staff; that France could not have failed to join Russia in the hostilities of 1914 without tearing up her sacred defensive treaty obligations; and that he could not have been responsible personally for the acts of France in 1914, as he could only act through his ministry, and his ministry could not act except with the consent of the Chamber of Deputies. These assertions require no comment!

Within the last year Poincaré has begun the publication of his voluminous memoirs designed to clear himself of the charges levelled against him. His case is worse, however, than before the appearance of the three volumes which have been published. Until now it had been believed by some that he actually had something vital and relevant to present in his defense. His memoirs constitute an amazing but ineffective exhibit of Jesuitry, and have been riddled by Fay, Fabre-Luce, Margueritte, Dupin and Charpentier. The best characterization is contained in Fabre-Luce's brilliant reply in *Europe* for April 15, 1926: "In this last bit of pleading, as in his earlier efforts to clear himself, Poincaré has contented himself with the effort to conceal highly significant omissions under a luxuriant mass of explanations dealing with wholly secondary issues." His *Au Service de la France* is convincing only to writers like Bernadotte Schmitt, possessed of an implacable "will to believe" all which supports the war-time myths.

3. The Futile Rhetoric of Viviani

Viviani's misrepresentations during the 1914 crisis are well known from such acts as his reprehensible effort to represent the German mobilization as preceding the Russian; as well as from his circular note of August 1st in which he contended that Russia had agreed to stop her mobilization measures, but had been forced to resume them by the German ultimatum.[83] In 1922 he brought out a lengthy defense, directed in part against the *Memoirs* of the Kaiser.

This book is entitled *As We See It,* and is a much more absurd performance than Poincaré's *Origins of the War.*

The myth of the unique, malicious and unparalleled German militarism is once more spread before us with the greatest thoroughness, together with the fiction of defenseless and innocent France. He holds at the outset that Germany's guilt is established and sealed for all time because of Germany's acceptance of the charge in the Paris Peace Treaty, and because the Reichstag voted to accept the Treaty.[84] The legend of the Potsdam Conference is solemnly repeated, with the attendance slightly reduced. The Kaiser is represented as having determined upon a European war on the 5th of July, and his departure for a vacation cruise is designated a "deceiving alibi." [85] Germany is represented as having known the terms of the Austrian ultimatum before July 10th (before it was even formulated by the Austrians) and von Jagow is said to have lauded it at this early date.[86] He contends that the Austrian *Red Book* contains absolute proof that the Germans spurred the Austrians on in their determination to declare war on Serbia.[87] He presents the abridged and falsified Wiesner Report as the full report made by Wiesner to the Austrian government.[88] His account of the visit to St.

Petersburg in 1914 would awaken suspicion,
even if one possessed no knowledge of what
actually happened there.   Here we have it: [89]

M. Poincaré and I left our country on the morning
of July 16, 1914.   Rocked lightly between the blue
skies and the blue waters, in that isolation which, for a
man in public office, is the reward of action, the President of the French Republic and I sat chatting with
each other.   We were journeying with heads held high
and clean of heart, toward peace, toward the strengthening of our alliance with Russia, toward the establishment of friendly relations with other lands, toward that
fusion of general sympathies wherein the privileged
friendship caused by the existence of an alliance does
not preclude additional knitting together of thoughts
and interests. . . .

What can I say of our conversations?   The head of
the French Republic spoke alone for almost an hour
with the Tsar, as was proper.   I too conversed with the
Tsar; also, naturally, with the Premier, and, above all,
with M. Sazonoff.   We were in agreement, as other
Ministers had been before me, in 1912, and at all times,
regarding the necessity for maintaining the alliance in
dignity and peace.

Shall I speak of celebrations, reviews, parades, of the
reception by the Empress, so magnificent in her beauty,
with her blue eyes as piercing as sapphires?   How long
ago it all is!   The soil of Russia, a shroud that is always frozen, hides the horrors of hecatombs, to escape
from which neither rank, age nor sex availed.

This is all he has to tell us of the diplomatic significance and agreements on this momentous journey.

The Kaiser's pledge-plan, openly and warmly approved by Grey and George V, is condemned as a brutal and wanton scheme: [90]

Is this not outrageous? What more could insatiable Austria want beyond almost total occupation of an innocent country which, by its moderation, was making itself deserving of glory in the annals of history, since it was acting in the interest of peace?

The Austrian Ambassador is denounced for leaving Belgrade after the Serbian reply to the ultimatum, ignoring the fact that before a messenger had been dispatched from Belgrade with this reply the Serbian government had ordered the mobilization of the Serbian army and the removal of the Serbian government from Belgrade to Nish.[91] He once more repeats the demonstrable falsehood of 1914, to the effect that Austria and Germany mobilized before Russia, and, most discreditable of all and in spite of the fact that he had read Dobrorolski's memorandum, he devotes page after page to the preposterous allegation that the Russian general mobilization was caused by the publication of the false report of the German mobilization in the Berlin *Lokalanzeiger* on July 30th.[92]

Viviani attempts to make Bethmann-Hollweg

more of a war criminal than the Kaiser, and
holds that his efforts to restrain Austria were not
in any sense made in good faith because he cancelled a moderating telegram just before midnight on July 30th.[93]   Viviani neglects to tell us
that this cancellation was due to the fact that
information was leaking into Germany concerning the Russian mobilization upon which France
had set its stamp of approval twenty-four hours
earlier.   The 1914 fiction that France and England worked for diplomatic adjustment from the
first, and that Russia followed their suggestions
meekly, is valiantly reaffirmed.[94]   The ten kilometer withdrawal is played up as a genuine effort to demonstrate pacific French intentions,
and is represented as a move which was dangerous to French defensive strategy and opposed
by the military authorities, forgetful of the fact
that he and Messimy had both denied that such
was the case in their speeches to the French
Chamber in 1919.[95]   Finally, he insists that
France was obligated in 1914 to come to the aid
of Russia by the explicit terms of the Franco-
Russian Alliance.[96]

It has been frequently stated that no leading
French statesman has ever admitted the responsibility of the French leaders in 1914 for egging
on Russia and making a European war inevitable.   This is not so.   In a long memoir, com-
piled during his trial and published in *Les Docu-*

ments Politiques, Diplomatiques et Financiers for March 1926 (translated in the *American Monthly* for January, 1927), Joseph Caillaux indicts Poincaré at great length, and shows how, if the French had adopted in 1914 a policy comparable to that taken by Caillaux in the last Morocco crisis, there would have been no World War following the Sarajevo murder. Subsequent documentary revelations have fully confirmed Caillaux's general contention (Cf. G. Demartial, in *Evolution,* June 15, 1926, pp. 14–21).

4. Difficulties in Historical Apologetic

Perhaps even more significant than these efforts of Poincaré and Viviani to squirm out of their responsibility are the misrepresentations of which even distinguished French scholars have been guilty in their effort to clear France. Two eminent French students of diplomatic history, Bourgeois and Pagès, in the standard conventional French work on war origins,[97] even stoop to accepting in its entirety the myth of the Potsdam Conference, though it had been demonstrated to be a pure fiction long before they wrote their book. Their work is so full of obvious misrepresentations that the German ex-Crown Prince has actually been able to riddle it.[98] Equally illuminating is the case of Pierre Renouvin, the best informed Frenchman who has written on the question of war guilt and a man free from the war psychology. Renouvin has found it necessary to avoid specifically stating that the Russian general mobilization meant war, though he knows such to be the case.[99] He maintains the indefensible thesis that Germany hoped to localize the Austro-Serbian conflict to the very end. He tries to prove, in obvious defiance of the facts, that the German government abandoned its diplomatic efforts on July 30th and determined to resort to war.[100] He very inadequately emphasizes the French diplomatic subterfuges involved in the ten kilometer withdrawal order, the delay in issuing the mobilization order, and the awaiting of the German declaration of war.[101] Finally, he presents a very conventional interpretation of the alleged pacific policy of Sir Edward Grey, at obvious variance with the facts assembled by Lutz, Loreburn, Morel and Ewart.[102] Montgelas, Dupin and Margueritte have criticized Renouvin in detail.

V. UNIQUE GUILT OF FRANCE AND RUSSIA

We may thus say that the main, in fact the only, direct and immediate responsibility for the general European War falls upon Russia and France. It is difficult to say which should be put in the first place. Unquestionably there had been the closest collaboration between Izvolski and Poincaré from 1912 to August, 1914, and

the program of both was inseparably connected
with the encouragement of a European war. Izvolski proudly boasted in August, 1914, that the
war which had just broken out was *his* war, but
we may safely say that without the ardent and
persistent coöperation of Poincaré he would
never have been able to lead his government into
actual warfare. We may thus hold that France
and Russia share about equally the responsibility
for the great calamity and it is unquestionably
true that no other European power, except Serbia, desired a general European conflict in the
summer of 1914.

The writer, in coming to this conclusion of the
sole and direct responsibility of Russia and
France for the European War in 1914, does so in
full knowledge of the fact that many authorities
contend that there was no plan about the events
of 1914, and that all "stumbled" into the war.[103]
He has also read all of the literature counselling
caution in regard to an indictment of Poincaré
as overtly guilty. It is the opinion of the writer
that the thesis of "stumbling" is as far from the
truth as the older Entente mythology of wilful
and malicious German determination upon war
from July 5, 1914. Even cautious scholars like
Professor Fay are now admitting that the more
Poincaré writes the more obvious his guilt becomes.[104] Likewise, with regard to the theory
that, whatever the truth, one ought to defend the

thesis of divided responsibility because this would make it so much easier to woo people away from the old myth of full German responsibility, the writer is fully aware of the fact that it would be far more easy to convince people of the truth of divided responsibility than it is to prove to them the primary responsibility of France and Russia. But the writer is not running for Congress on the issue of war guilt; he is only interested in expounding what appears to him to be the truth before an honest and intelligent group of readers. It seems to him better to make slow progress in advancing the cause of truth than to be quickly successful in disseminating a benign illusion.*

VI. CONCLUSIONS

(1) Alsace-Lorraine was the one important root of the War as far as the policy of France was involved. Up to 1912 the chief apostles of revenge had been monarchists or conservatives: enemies of the Third Republic. The accession of Poincaré to the premiership in 1912 for the first time committed the Republic to the policy of revenge and the program of recapturing the "Lost Provinces." Poincaré openly confessed that the hope of restoring them had long been his only real reason for existence.

* The new British documents fully substantiate my indictment of Poincaré.

(2) To advance this ambition he transformed the Franco-Russian Alliance into an aggressive union, and by August, 1914, had been able to make England congenial to its general program of closing in on Germany at the opportune moment.

(3) During the autumn of 1912 Poincaré agreed to aid Russia in any war precipitated over the Balkans, provided this would involve Germany and lead to a world war that would result in Russia's securing the Straits and France's recovering Alsace-Lorraine. The French war aims, many of which were approved by Russia as early as October, 1914, involved not only the restoration of Alsace-Lorraine, but also the annexation of the Saar region and the creation of an independent Rhenish state under French protection. The French were highly confident of success in a European war, as they felt that either France and England or France and Russia would be able to cope successfully with Germany and Austria. With England, France and Russia joined against the Central Powers, an easy and rapid victory was expected. With Italy also in, Germany and Austria would have no chance at all. The chief thing which upset the plan was Hindenburg's colossal defeat of the Russians.

(4) The French people were pacifically inclined in 1912, but from 1912 to 1914 had been gradually prepared for the idea of a war over

the Balkans through the propaganda carried on
in the French papers, which was financed by
Russian gold secured by Izvolski and disbursed
with the advice of Poincaré and his henchmen.

(5) Even as late as 1914 the French people
were sufficiently opposed to war so that it was
necessary to resort to every form of deceit, censorship, force and diplomatic chicanery in order
to dupe the French populace into accepting the
fiction of a defensive war. The obligations of
France under the Russian Alliance were not
even allowed to come up for debate in the Chamber of Deputies. Hence, the responsibility of
France means the responsibility of Poincaré and
a half-dozen trusted lieutenants. There was
more autocracy in controlling French foreign
policy in the crisis of 1914 than prevailed in the
same period in either Russia, Germany or Austria. This completely refutes Poincaré's continual reference to French democracy as a safeguard against war and a guaranty of French
innocence in 1914.

(6) Poincaré first gave a belligerent turn to
the crisis of July, 1914, through his visit to St.
Petersburg. He encouraged the military group
at the Russian court, gave them to understand
that France would fulfil all the obligations of the
Franco-Russian Alliance, and blocked Grey's
first plan for peace before he left St. Petersburg.
Viviani warned the French Foreign Office on
July 24th to be prepared for decisive action in

regard to the Austro-Serbian dispute. On July 25th, just before the crucial Russian decision upon war in the council meeting of that day, Paléologue informed the Russians that "France places herself unreservedly on Russia's side." Paul Cambon made a secret trip from London during Poincaré's absence to stiffen up the action of Bienvenu-Martin and Berthelot in the Foreign Office pending the return of Poincaré and Viviani. As early as the 27th Sazonov had informed the French that he would not tolerate any French restraint on his policies, and the French acting Minister of Foreign Affairs assured him that none would be attempted. By the time Poincaré had returned to Paris Sazonov had determined upon the mobilization policy which inevitably meant a European war.

(7) On July 29th, after the first Russian general mobilization order had been issued and before the Tsar cancelled it, Sazonov informed the French of his military plans and inquired if he could count on full French aid. He also requested that France attempt at once to force Grey's hand and get England committed to the aggressive plans.

(8) Poincaré, Viviani and Messimy took up this matter in conference on the night of July 29th, and decided to support the Russian policy, though they were perfectly conscious of the fact that this would mean a general European war

and the end of all diplomatic efforts to settle the crisis. Viviani telegraphed the promise of full French aid, and counselled the Russians to be as secretive as they could in their preparations, so as to gain the utmost possible advantage of time over the Germans. Izvolski telegraphed that Messimy had informed him that the French would be glad to have the Russians speed up their military preparations, but that they should be cautious about them and also issue a public declaration that they were willing to slow down these preparations in the interest of peace. He also informed Sazonov that Paul Cambon would immediately approach Sir Edward Grey and obtain his reaffirmation of the agreement of November 22, 1912.

(9) In spite of the above facts, Poincaré informed George V on July 31st that France had from the beginning counselled moderation upon Russia, and that Russia had uniformly accepted this advice. Poincaré tried to trick George V into promising English aid to France under the guise of restraining Germany. France also supported Sazonov's fake proposal of the 31st to submit the crisis to a European conference. But on the night of the 31st France decided upon war "with hearty high spirits," and so informed Izvolski. France was, thus, the first country officially to announce her decision to abandon diplomatic efforts and resort to war.

(10) Having decided upon war the French government executed a number of diplomatic manœuvres to lead the French, Italian and British peoples to believe that they were preparing for a strictly defensive war. Among these were the ten kilometer withdrawal imposture of July 30th, the delay in ordering mobilization, and the determination to await the German declaration of war in order to impress the English and to avoid a debate on the obligations to Russia under the alliance. In spite of the delay in the mobilization order, French military preparations advanced steadily from the 24th onward.

(11) While it was the Russian mobilization which actually precipitated the World War, France was as responsible as Russia, because Poincaré gave the initial encouragement to Russian aggression on his St. Petersburg visit, and confirmed this attitude by his decision on the night of July 29th to support the Russian mobilization plans. France was not bound by treaty obligation to aid Russia in 1914, as Russian priority in mobilization released France from the terms of the military convention of 1914. Poincaré carefully concealed this fact from the French Chamber of Deputies in 1914, and refused to allow the matter to be submitted to debate.

(12) The French *Yellow Book* of 1914 was more atrociously falsified than any other state papers of the period. Neither Poincaré nor Vi-

viani has been able to defend himself except by
resorting to the most obvious and flagrant falsifications of facts or evasions of vital issues.[105]

In the light of the facts about war origins
which we have brought together in this and preceding chapters, the following message of Poincaré to the French Parliament on August 4,
1914, presents an almost unique combination of
heroic tragedy and light humor:

France has just been the object of a violent and premeditated attack, which is an insolent defiance of the
law of nations. Before any declaration of war had
been sent to us, even before the German Ambassador
had asked for his passports, our territory has been
violated. The German Empire has waited till yesterday evening to give at this late stage the true name to a
state of things which it had already created.

For more than forty years the French, in sincere love
of peace, have buried at the bottom of their heart the
desire for legitimate reparation.

They have given to the world the example of a great
nation which, definitely raised from defeat by the exercise of will, patience and labour, has only used its renewed and rejuvenated strength in the interest of
progress and for the good of humanity.

Since the ultimatum of Austria opened a crisis which
threatened the whole of Europe, France has persisted in
following and recommending on all sides a policy of
prudence, wisdom and moderation.

To her there can be imputed no act, no movement,

no word, which has not been peaceful and conciliatory.

At the hour when the struggle is beginning, she has
the right, in justice to herself, of solemnly declaring
that she has made, up to the last moment, supreme efforts to avert the war now about to break out, the
crushing responsibility for which the German Empire
will have to bear before history. (*Unanimous and repeated applause.*)

On the very morrow of the day when we and our allies
were publicly expressing our hope of seeing negotiations which had been begun under the auspices of the
London Cabinet carried to a peaceful conclusion, Germany suddenly declared war upon Russia, she has invaded the territory of Luxemburg, she has outrageously
insulted the noble Belgian nation (*loud and unanimous
applause*), our neighbour and our friend, and attempted treacherously to fall upon us while we were in
the midst of diplomatic conversation. (*Fresh and repeated unanimous applause.*)

But France was watching. As alert as she was
peaceful, she was prepared; and our enemies will meet
on their path our valiant covering troops, who are at
their post and will provide the screen behind which the
mobilisation of our national forces will be methodically
completed.

Our fine and courageous army, which France to-day
accompanies with her maternal thought (*loud applause*), has risen eager to defend the honour of the
flag and the soil of the country. (*Unanimous and repeated applause.*)

The President of the Republic, interpreting the unanimous feeling of the country, expresses to our troops, by land and sea, the admiration and confidence of every Frenchman (*loud and prolonged applause*).

Closely united in a common feeling, the nation will persevere with the cool self-restraint of which, since the beginning of the crisis, she has given daily proof. Now, as always, she will know how to harmonise the most noble daring and most ardent enthusiasm with that self-control which is the sign of enduring energy and is the best guarantee of victory (*applause*).

In the war which is beginning France will have Right on her side, the eternal power of which cannot with impunity be disregarded by nations any more than by individuals (*loud and unanimous applause*).

She will be heroically defended by all her sons; nothing will break their sacred union before the enemy; to-day they are joined together as brothers in a common indignation against the aggressor, and in a common patriotic faith (*loud and prolonged applause and cries of "Vive la France"*).

She is faithfully helped by Russia, her ally (*loud and unanimous applause*); she is supported by the loyal friendship of Great Britain (*loud and unanimous applause*).

And already from every part of the civilised world sympathy and good wishes are coming to her. For to-day once again she stands before the universe for Liberty, Justice and Reason (*loud and repeated applause*). "Haut les coeurs et vive la France!" *(unanimous and prolonged applause)*.

SELECTED REFERENCES

Barnes, H. E., "Poincaré's Guilt in the War," in New York *Nation,* October 7, 1925; "A Rejoinder to M. Poincaré," in *American Monthly,* December, 1925; also in the *Kriegsschuldfrage,* December, 1925; and the *Nuova Revista Storica,* November–December, 1925; Bausman, F., *Let France Explain;* Bourgeois, E., and Pagès, G., *Les Origines et les Responsabilités de la grande guerre;* Converset, Colonel, *Les trois ans de diplomatie secrète qui nous menèrent à la guerre de 1914;* Demartial, G., *L'Evangile du Quai d'Orsay; La Guerre de 1914. Comment on mobilisa les consciences;* Dupin, G., *Considérations sur les responsabilités de la guerre; Conférence sur les responsabilités de la guerre;* Ewart, J. S., *The Roots and Causes of the Wars;* Fabre-Luce, A., *La Victoire;* Fay, S. B., "M. Poincaré and War Responsibility," in *New Republic,* October 14, 1925; "Who Started the War?" Ibid., January 6, 1926; Gouttenoire de Toury, F., *Jaurès et le parti de la guerre; Poincaré a-t-il voulu la querre?* Judet, E., *Georges Louis; Carnets de Georges Louis;* Lavisse, E. (Ed.), *Histoire de France contemporaine,* Vol. X; Lazare, *A l'origine du mensonge;* Marchand, R., *La Condamnation d'un régime;* Margueritte, V., *Les Criminels;* Marx, W., "The Responsibility for the War," in *Foreign Affairs* (American), January, 1926; Montgelas, M., *The Case for the Central Powers;* Morhardt, M., *Les Preuves;* Pevet, A. H., *Les Responsables de la guerre;* Poincaré, R., *Origins of the War;* "The Responsibility for the War," in *Foreign Affairs,* October, 1925; *Au Service de la France;* Reinach, J., *Histoire de douze jours;* Renouvin, P., *Les Origines immédiates de la guerre;* Rogers, L., "The French President and Foreign Affairs," in *Political Science Quarterly,* December, 1925; Schoen, F. von, *Memoirs of an Ambassador;* Stieve, F., *Isvolsky and the World War;* Viviani, R., *As We See It.*

FOOTNOTES AND FURTHER REFERENCES

1 *The Roots and Causes of the Wars,* p. 1001; cf. Earl Loreburn, *How the War Came,* Chap. iii.

2 J. H. Rose, *The Development of Modern European Nations;* H. Oncken, *Die Rheinpolitik Kaiser Napoleons III,* Vol. I., p. 114.

3 Ewart, op. cit., Chap. xviii; D. N. Raymond, *Contemporary British Opinion during the Franco-Prussian War;* C. E. Schieber, *Transformation of American Sentiment towards Germany,* Chap. i.

4 In *Foreign Affairs* for October, 1925, p. 5, Poincaré makes the astonishing statement that the culture of the Alsace-Lorraine area has no real bearing upon the morality of political control and possession. He holds that even though the Germans had made the district thoroughly Teutonic in culture and politically contented within the German Empire, it would still have been a moral mistake for France to allow it to remain under German control. It is obvious that this argument would, in reality, constitute a complete vindication of the German seizure of the provinces in 1870.

5 H. A. L. Fisher, *Studies in History and Politics,* pp. 146–61; C. E. Playne, *The Neuroses of the Nations,* Part II; E. Dimnet, *France Herself Again.* V. Margueritte, *Les Criminels,* pp. 113 ff.

6 Ewart, op. cit., p. 671.

7 G. P. Gooch, *Franco-German Relations, 1870–1914;* cf. A. Fabre-Luce, *La Victoire,* pp. 109 ff., 134 ff.; and *Caillaux's* famous memoir in the *American Monthly,* January, 1927.

8 Ibid.; also Gooch, in *Contemporary Review,* April, 1923; and Ewart, pp. 769–73.

9 S. Huddleston, *Poincaré;* M. Morhardt, *Les Preuves;* F. Guttenoire de Toury, *Jaurès et la parti de la guerre.*

10 Morhardt, *Les Preuves,* pp. 135–6.

11 Ibid., p. 135.

12 Loc. cit., p. 5.

13 Morhardt, op. cit., pp. 297–9.

14 Ewart, op. cit., pp. 746 ff.; Stieve, op. cit., Chaps. ii–iii; Fabre-Luce, *La Victoire,* pp. 133 ff.

15 *Foreign Affairs,* October, 1925, pp. 4–5.

[16] Morhardt, op. cit., pp. 117 ff.; Stieve, op. cit., *passim;* B. Schmitt, "Triple Alliance and Triple Entente," in *American Historical Review,* April, 1924, pp. 457–8.

[17] Stieve, op. cit.; Colonel Converset, *Les trois ans de diplomatie secrète qui nous menèrent à la querre de 1914;* Fabre-Luce, op. cit., pp. 140 ff.; E. Judet, *Georges Louis.*

[18] Fabre-Luce, op. cit., pp. 179–91; Stieve, op. cit.; Chaps. iv–v.

[19] Stieve, Chaps. iii–v.

[20] Ibid., pp. 186 ff.

[21] *Un Livre noir,* Vol. II, pp. 303, 306; on the Alsace-Lorraine issue see Montgelas, *The Case for the Central Powers,* p. 52.

[22] C. J. H. Hayes, *Political and Social History of Modern Europe,* Vol. II, p. 702; Earl Loreburn, *How the War Came,* p. 72.

[23] Earl Loreburn, *How the War Came,* Chap. iv; E. D. Morel, *The Secret History of a Great Betrayal.*

[24] E. F. Henderson, *The Verdict of History: the Case of Sir Edward Grey,* p. 204; see *La Revue de France,* July 1, 1921.

[25] Schmitt, loc cit., p. 460; Stieve, op. cit., pp. 88–90.

[26] Stieve, p. 211.

[27] Siebert and Schreiner, *Entente Diplomacy and the World,* p. 525.

[28] Stieve, Chap. vi; Henderson, op. cit., p. 184.

[29] *La Victoire,* pp. 112–113.

[30] See the obituary article by Robert Dell in the London *Nation,* September 19, 1925, p. 723.

[31] Stieve, Chaps. iii–iv; also New York *Nation,* February 20, 1924; *The Progressive,* February 1, 1926, pp. 182 ff.

[32] G. Demartial, *La Guerre de 1914. Comment on mobilisa les consciences.*

[33] See below, pp. 720 ff.

[34] The views here expressed agree fairly consistently with those of Fabre-Luce. Gouttenoire de Toury, Morhardt, Lazare, Pevet, Converset, Dupin and Demartial are far more severe in their criticisms of Poincaré. The utmost that can be said by a scholar in his defense is contained in the valuable work by Renouvin.

[34a] *France and the French,* pp. 37–38.

[35] Fabre-Luce, op. cit., pp. 206 ff.; Stieve, Chap. vii; Lazare, *A l'Origine du mensonge,* pp. 161 ff.; *British Documents,* No. 101.

[36] B. W. von Bülow, *Die Krisis; Die ersten Stundenschläge des Weltkriegs;* Freiherr von Schoen, *Erlebtes,* pp. 162 ff.; *Foreign Affairs,* October, 1925, p. 4.

[37] *Falsifications of the Russian Orange Book,* pp. 38–40.

[38] Ibid., pp. 50–51; Morhardt, pp. 275 ff.; Fabre-Luce, pp. 211 ff.; *Vers la verité,* pp. 89–95; *British Documents.* No. 320 (b).

[39] *French Yellow Book,* No. 101. Compare the true text, and

the false text as published in the *Yellow Book*, in Morhardt, pp. 275 ff.; cf. Fabre-Luce, pp. 211 ff.; 227; and Demartial, *L'Evangile du Quai d'Orsay.*

[40] *Falsifications of the Russian Orange Book*, pp. 50–52; see *British Blue Book*, No. 105, for evidence that Cambon got busy at once.

[41] *Falsifications of the Russian Orange Book*, pp. 53–4.

[42] Fabre-Luce, p. 227; G. Dupin, *Conférence sur les responsabilités de la guerre*, p. 21.

[43] *Falsifications of the Russian Orange Book*, p. 17.

[44] Ibid., p. 30.

[45] Montgelas, op. cit., pp. 217–20; *Vers la verité*, pp. 65–70; Renouvin, op. cit., pp. 177 ff. The texts in English with Viviani's explanations are contained in R. Viviani, *As We See It*, pp. 191 ff. See also the *Kriegsschuldfrage* December, 1925; pp. 833–4.

[46] Montgelas, p. 219; Viviani, p. 197.

[47] *Foreign Affairs*, October, 1925, p. 18.

[48] Montgelas, p. 218.

[49] Ibid., pp. 217–20; Dupin, op. cit., pp. 30–33.

[50] Dupin, op. cit., p. 32.

[51] Ibid.; and *Kriegsschuldfrage*, December, 1925, p. 834.

[52] *British Documents*, No. 319 and enclosure; Dupin, pp. 32–3.

[53] *French Yellow Book*, No. 106; Viviani, op. cit., pp. 192–3.

[54] Dupin, p. 31.

[55] Poincaré, *The Origins of the War*, pp. 238–9; G. L. Dickinson, *International Anarchy*, pp. 454–5.

[56] Poincaré, op. cit., pp. 249–50; Dickinson, op. cit., p. 455.

[57] *Foreign Affairs*, October, 1925, p. 2; Viviani, pp. 215 ff.

[58] *Foreign Affairs*, pp. 17–18.

[59] *Falsifications of the Russian Orange Book*, pp. 64–5.

[60] Ibid., pp. 58, 63.

[61] *Foreign Affairs*, p. 4.

[62] Ibid., p. 19.

[63] *Livre jaune de l'alliance Franco-Russe*, Nos. 53 and 71.

[64] Montgelas, op. cit., pp. 193–4; *Falsifications of the Russian Orange Book*, pp. 69–72; Renouvin, op. cit., pp. 197 ff.

[65] See above, pp. 335 ff.

[66] *Foreign Affairs*, pp. 16–17; Renouvin, op. cit., pp. 138 ff., 162, 259 ff.

[67] *Falsifications of the Russian Orange Book*, pp. 59–60.

[68] Ibid., pp. 60–61.

[69] *Foreign Affairs*, p. 18.

[70] Dupin, op. cit., pp. 33–5; *Livre jaune de l'alliance Franco-Russe*, Nos. 28–92.

[71] *Falsifications of the Russian Orange Book*, p. 69.

72 *Twenty-five Years,* Vol. II, Appendix D, p. 313.

73 Poincaré, loc. cit., p. 3; cf. Pevet, op. cit., pp. 387 ff.

74 Demartial, op. cit.; *Hinter den Kulissen des Französichen Journalismus; Falsifications of the Russian Orange Book,* pp. 45, 48; Henderson, op. cit., p. 188; *The Diary of Lord Bertie,* Vol. II, p. 245; G. Dupin, in *Vers la verité,* pp. 136–7. On the French Socialist opposition to the bellicose aims of the Triple Entente see B. J. Horde, "French Socialism and the Triple Entente," in *Journal of Political Economy,* August, 1922. The complicity of Izvolski in the assassination of Jaurès has been established by Jacques Mesnil.

75 Loc. cit., p. 3.

76 Morhardt, op. cit., pp. 301–2.

77 Fabre-Luce, *La Victoire;* and, by the same author, *La Crise des alliances;* H. G. Moulton and C. Lewis, *The Financial Problem of France.*

78 Marhardt, *Les Preuves,* pp. 162 ff. See also *Vers la verité,* pp. 13–8; and G. Demartial, *L'Evangile du Quai d'Orsay.*

79 *A l'Origine du mensonge.*

80 Loc. cit. p. 1, footnote, and p. 3.

81 New York *Nation,* October 7, 1925; *The American Monthly,* December, 1925; the *Kriegsschuldfrage,* December, 1925; and the *Nuova Revista Storica,* November–December, 1925; cf. also S. B. Fay, in the *New Republic* for October 14, 1925; and January 6, 1926; and G. Dupin, "M. Raymond Poincaré se defend en Amerique," in *La Revue de Hongrie,* December 15, 1925.

82 Loc. cit., p. 14.

83 Montgelas, op. cit., pp. 180–82, 202; Demartial *L'Evangile du Quai d'Orsay,* pp. 70 ff.

84 Op. cit., p. 104. For a French criticism of Viviani see G. Dupin in *Vers la verité,* pp. 9–13.

85 Viviani, op. cit., pp. 111–13.

86 Ibid., pp. 88, 101.

87 Ibid., p. 104.

88 Ibid., p. 124.

89 Ibid., pp. 89–92.

90 Ibid., pp. 143–4.

91 Morhardt, op. cit., pp. 45 ff., 293–4.

92 Viviani, pp. 160 ff.

93 Ibid., pp. 186 ff.; 201 ff.

94 Ibid., pp. 205 ff.

95 Ibid., pp. 191 ff.

96 Ibid., p. 211.

97 *Les Origines et les responsabilités de la grande guerre.*

98 *Ich suche die Wahrheit;* cf. Hans Delbrück, in the *Kriegsschuldfrage,* September, 1925, pp. 604–8.

99 *Les Origines immédiates de la guerre*, pp. 261 ff.; on Renouvin see M. Montgelas in the *Kriegsschuldfrage*, July, 1925 and January, 1926; in the New York *Nation*, November 18, 1925; S. B. Fay in *Political Science Quarterly*, December, 1925, pp. 626–9; G. Dupin, in *Revue de Hongrie*, May–June, 1926; and V. Margueritte, in *Evolution*, April 15, 1926.

100 Op. cit., pp. 138–41; 162; 259–61.

101 Ibid., pp. 175 ff.

102 Ibid., pp. 209 ff.

103 Gooch, *Modern Europe*, p. 559.

104 *New Republic*, October 14, 1924, p. 200. Cf. Bausman in *Foreign Affairs* (London), January, 1926; and *The Progressive*, February 1, 1926 and December 1, 1926.

105 With this set of conclusions may be compared the summary of Viviani's defense of France (*As We See It*, pp. 267–8):

1. As far back as July 24, 1914, at one o'clock in the morning I telegraphed, while on my way from Cronstadt to Stockholm, to the French Ministry of Foreign Affairs, asking that it seek through our ambassador to Austria, to calm down Austria and suggest to England that mediation be attempted by the four nations in order that the dispute might be arranged peacefully.

2. France supported Sir Edward Grey's proposal.

3. The French Government supported the request for extension of the time allowed Serbia (*Yellow Book*, No. 29).

4. It renewed its request on July 27th (*Yellow Book*, No. 61).

5. Same request, July 29th (*Yellow Book*, No. 85).

6. On July 29th (No. 97) France urgently asked London that Sir Edward Grey renew the proposal of mediation by the four nations, in whatever form he might deem best.

7. On July 30th (No. 101) the French Government suggested to Russia that, if she adopted defensive measures against the mobilization already carried out by Austria, she would give Germany no excuse for meddling.

8. On July 30th a telegram was sent to England to inform the latter that the French Government had just given the order to have the French troops drawn back from the frontier a distance of ten kilometers.

9. On July 31st (No. 112) the French government urged all ambassadors to support the English proposal of mediation by the four nations.

10. August 1, 1914 (No. 122), France renewed her declaration that she would respect Belgian neutrality.

It may be pointed out that the first five of the above were obviously designed to gain time for Serbia, Russia and France in their military preparations. Grey admitted that mediation and direct conversations between Vienna and St. Petersburg were better methods of handling the problem than a conference of powers, and Germany was exerting herself to the fullest degree in this direction on the 29th, 30th and 31st of July when France approved the Russian military measures which were sure to produce war, and indulged in the diplomatic ruses designed to deceive Europe as to her real intentions. All diplomatic gestures of France after the morning of July 30th were obviously irrelevant and purely deceptive. The French promise to respect Belgian neutrality on August 1st is no proof of French pacific intent. The French and British were in the closest collusion by August 1st as to measures which must be taken to avoid alienating the British public, and neither would have countenanced for a moment so fatal a step as the French invasion of Belgium. Further, by this time it was evident that the circumstances surrounding the bringing of England into the War in 1914 were to be such that it would be impossible to execute the Franco-British plans of 1911, 1912, 1913 to march into Germany through Belgium. The French plan was altered to provide for an advance through Alsace.

CHAPTER VIII

SIR EDWARD GREY AND THE
RESPONSIBILITY OF ENGLAND

I. ENGLAND AND FRANCE TO 1914

THERE can be no intelligent understanding of the
reasons for the British entry into the World War
unless we have a definite knowledge of the nature
and development of Anglo-French relations as
they existed on June 28, 1914. While England
was involved in Entente relations with Russia,
the Russian alliance was never popular in England, and until six months after the World War
had been declared England steadfastly refused
to accede to the chief aim of Russian foreign
policy, the seizure of the Straits and Constantinople. As we shall see later, Sir Edward Grey
had to resort to shady measures sufficiently to influence British opinion to make a war with
Russia as an ally at all palatable.[1] Grey persistently refused to make the Austro-Serbian
dispute a direct issue with England, and in the
midst of the last stage of the crisis of 1914 even
the chauvinistic Bottomly journal, *John Bull*,
published a leading article under the heading
"To Hell With Servia . . . once more, to Hell

453

with Servia!"[2]   Nor did England enter the war primarily because of the invasion of Belgium. Grey had committed himself in writing to enter the war on August 2, 1914, before Germany had made any move to invade Belgium; even before she had sent Belgium an ultimatum.   Grey refused the German proposal to respect Belgian territory on condition that England remain neutral.   Neither was Grey bound to come to the aid of France by his note of August 2nd, for, between that time and the declaration of war by England, Germany had offered to make concessions which entirely removed the conditions for joining France which were stipulated in Grey's letter to Paul Cambon on August 2nd.

It cannot be held that Grey wanted war for war's sake or even to humiliate and weaken Germany, much as he desired the latter.   The real reason why Grey threw England into the war was because he had brought England into such a condition of written and verbal promises to France that he felt obliged to drag his country into any war in which France was engaged against Germany.   In his memoirs Grey represents himself as regarding the obligation to aid France as resting more upon the conviction of the interests of England than upon the debt of honor to France which was emphasized at the time of the outbreak of the War.   Doubtless both factors played a large part in his decision.   This

obligation was alleged to be so acute and specific
that he has openly confessed that he would have
resigned if he had not been able to bring England into the conflict.[3]   Being from the outset
informed as to Franco-Russian intentions and
preparations, and yet unwilling to curb his allies
after he knew of their belligerent plans, he was
drawn into the conflict without having wished
war in the abstract at the beginning of the crisis.
In other words, England entered the war because Grey was determined to stand by an ally
who was herself determined upon war.   As the
former Lord Chancellor of England, Earl Loreburn, well expressed it: "We went to war
unprepared in a Russian quarrel because we were
tied to France in the dark." [4]   In the Anglo-
French understandings, then, is to be found the
key to British responsibility for the World War.
The master architects were Théophile Delcassé
and Paul Cambon. We have in this chapter
the interesting story of how a country which
was theoretically against war came to be the one
whose assured participation alone made the
World War almost inevitable.

Except for coöperation in the abortive Crimean War, France had been the most persistent
and important rival of England for five hundred
years.   Prior to the Fashoda Incident of 1898
there was bitter feeling between England and
France.   France had been vigorously opposed

to British policy in South Africa. Even during the Boer War France, in spite of Delcassé and Fashoda, was much more hostile to England than was Germany, welcoming President Kruger with ostentatious cordiality.[5] The beginning of definite Anglo-French engagements came with the treaty negotiated by the Conservative government in 1904, dealing with Franco-British procedure in Egypt, Newfoundland and elsewhere, and giving France a free hand in Morocco.[6] The next year the Conservative government, still in power, laid the basis for direct naval conversations with France and for indirect military conversations.[7] It also is held to have promised France aid in the event of war with Germany during the first Morocco crisis.

Sir Edward Grey continued the same policy with enthusiasm after he entered the Cabinet of Campbell-Bannerman in December, 1905. The significance of Grey's entry into the Foreign Office with respect to the attitude of England towards Germany and France is well stated by Lord Loreburn in the following passage: [8]

On the formation of the Liberal Government on 12th December, 1905, three Ministers, Mr. Asquith, Mr. Haldane, and Sir Edward Grey, laid the foundation for a different policy, namely, a policy of British intervention if Germany should make an unprovoked attack on France. They did this within a month, probably within

a few days of taking office, by means of communications
with the French Ambassador and of military and naval
conversations between the General Staffs of the two
countries, who worked out plans for joint action in war
if Great Britain should intervene.   They did it behind
the back of nearly all their Cabinet colleagues, and,
what really matters, without Parliament being in any
way made aware that a policy of active intervention between France and Germany was being contemplated.

Grey admits that in his childhood his pro-
French father and grandfather attempted, we
may guess with great success, to develop in him
a sentimental love for France and hatred for
Germany through instilling into his mind the
conventional French view of the Franco-Prussian
War.[9]   We shall not press the potential Freu-
dian interpretation of the 1914 crisis in the
British Foreign Office.   The British promise of
aid to the French in the first Morocco crisis was
kept secret, Grey's statements after he came
into office having been kept from the knowledge
of the majority of the Cabinet.   But in the second Morocco crisis the British defiance of Germany was openly uttered by Lloyd George in
his Mansion House speech of July 21, 1911.[10]
There is doubtless much truth in the contention of certain authorities that Grey's original
purpose was more to establish a balance of power
in Europe than to organize an alliance against

Germany or even to be a party to such an alliance. It was to no small degree the rather unwise policy of Germany, particularly in Morocco, which led Grey further along the path of an alliance with France and Russia than he would originally have chosen to go. While the German cause was legally just in both the Morocco crises, Germany was more interested in breaking the Anglo-French entente than in securing her rights in Morocco. This forced Grey into decisive support of France unless he was willing to abandon his plan of reëstablishing the balance of power.

The Balkan Wars which broke out in 1912 threatened the peace in Europe. Poincaré was fearful lest Russia might secure the Straits without a European war. Hence, he gave Russia his promise that France would follow Russia into a European war over the Balkans. It was desirable that English participation should be assured, and Paul Cambon had been instructed to approach Grey and obtain from him the limit which England would promise at the time. After much negotiation the English agreement was expressed in the following form in Grey's letter to Cambon on November 22, 1912. The plan referred to was that England would protect the northern coast of France and allow the French fleet to be concentrated in the Mediterranean: [11]

Nov. 22nd, 1912.

MY DEAR AMBASSADOR,—From time to time in recent years the French and British Naval and Military experts have consulted together. It has always been understood that such consultation does not restrict the freedom of either Government to decide at any future time whether or not to assist the other by armed force. We have agreed that consultation between experts is not and ought not to be regarded as an engagement that commits either Government to action in a contingency that has not yet arisen and may never arise. The disposition, for instance, of the French and British fleets respectively at the present moment is not based upon an engagement to coöperate in war. You have, however, pointed out that if either Government had grave reason to expect an unprovoked attack by a third Power it might become essential to know whether it could in that event depend upon the armed assistance of the other. I agree that if either Government had grave reason to expect an unprovoked attack by a third Power, or something that threatened the general peace, it should immediately discuss with the other whether both Governments should act together to prevent aggression and to preserve peace, and, if so, what measures they would be prepared to take in common. If these measures involved action, the plans of the General Staffs would at once be taken into consideration and the Governments would then decide what effect should be given to them.

EDWARD GREY

So important was this arrangement that Grey, in his famous speech of August 3, 1914, admitted that it was the "starting-point for the Government with regard to the present crisis." [12]   It was literally so, because it was his confirmation of this document on August 2, 1914, which made him feel irrevocably bound to bring England into the War.   Cambon well understood that this agreement would bring England into a war in a wholehearted fashion, as it was unthinkable that a state would allow its navy to participate without its army.[13]   This correspondence also had a most important effect on the British navy. Winston Churchill, First Lord of the Admiralty, frankly admits that from this time on the naval authorities assumed the inevitability of a war with Germany and steadily prepared for it in both a physical and psychological fashion.[14]

While we cannot be certain in this matter until the publication of the French and British archives, it would seem that there must have been more than mere chronological coincidence between Poincaré's definite promise to aid Russia in the case of a European war over the Balkans, which was made on November 17, 1912, and the letter from Grey to Cambon on November 22, 1912.   At any rate, November, 1912, was a crucial period in European diplomacy.   It was the time when real teeth were at last put into the Franco-Russian Alliance and when England was definitely committed in principle to the program of supporting France.   It was also when (on

November 8th) the Russians laid their plan for the secret mobilization of their army under cover of a diplomatic barrage. *The diplomatic background of the World War is to be found in the diplomacy of this month quite as much as it is in the two weeks following July 23, 1914.*

Army preparations paralleled the development of arrangements for naval coöperation. In January, 1906, Grey and Lord Haldane, Minister of War, secretly arranged for the continuous collaboration of the French and British General Staffs, including explicit plans for coöperation with Russia in the East. By the end of 1910 these plans had taken on an elaborate development involving completed arrangements for the landing of a British expeditionary force on the Continent, if necessary in Belgium with or without the consent of the Belgian authorities.[15] Mr. Morel, taking his facts from Lord Haldane's own book, *Before the War,* thus describes the situation as it existed in 1910: [16]

Within five years, "by the end of 1910," the detailed "plans," the existence of which Lord Grey was so anxious to conceal from the House in August, 1914, had been "worked out." Lord Haldane had solved his "problem" of how to mobilize and concentrate "at a place of assembly to be opposite the Belgian frontier," "which had been settled between the staffs of France and Britain," a force of 160,000 men to operate with the French armies, "with the assistance of Russian pressure in the East." Note that the coöperation of the armies of the Czar was part of the "problem," an integral part of the "plans" from the very beginning, *i. e.,* from 1906, and ask yourselves what the progressive forces in the country would have said had they known of it, and how long the Government would have lasted had these "plans" been disclosed! British and French staff officers had thoroughly reconnoitered the ground upon which the allied armies were to fight in Belgium and in France; Sir Henry Wilson had been all over it on his bicycle. So comprehensive had the "plans" become by that time that at the first conference of the French and Russian headquarters' staffs, held subsequent to their completion—at Krasnoe-Selo, in August, 1911—General Dubail, the French chief of staff, was able to assure his Russian colleagues that the French Army would "take the offensive against Germany, with the help of the British Army on its left flank," on the tenth day after mobilizing. In December of that year (1911) Lord French with his staff visited the French headquarters. Thus was the second milestone silently erected while the British people went about their daily business, in blissful ignorance of everything but the fact that they were in the proud position of enjoying a democratic constitution, and, unlike their benighted continental neighbors, were the masters and not the servants of their rulers.

In his report of December 5, 1912, Izvolski pointed out that the Franco-British military convention was as explicit and thorough as the Franco-Russian: [17]

Since the beginning of the present crisis M. Poincaré has not ceased, on every occasion, to invite the London cabinet to confidential conversations, with the object of clearing up the position which would be adopted by England in the event of a general European conflict.   On the British side no decision has been taken hitherto.   The London cabinet invariably replies that this will depend upon circumstances, and that the question of peace or war will be decided by public opinion. On the other hand, not only has the examination of all eventualities which may present themselves not been interrupted between the French and British headquarters staffs, but the existing military and naval agreements have quite recently undergone a still greater development, so that at the present moment the Anglo-French military convention is as settled and complete (*a un caractère aussi achevé et complet*) as the Franco-Russian convention; the only difference consists in the fact that the former bear the signatures of the chiefs of the two headquarters staffs, and on this account are, so to speak, not obligatory upon the Government. These last few days General Wilson, the English chief of staff, has been in France, in the most rigorous secrecy, and on this occasion various complementary details have been elaborated; moreover, apparently for the first time, it is not only military men who participated in this work, but also other representatives of the French Government.

Lord Haldane himself indicates the bearing of these preparations upon the rapidity with which the expeditionary force was mobilized and shipped across the Channel in 1914: [18]

After the war was over, Lord Haldane explained with considerable and pardonable pride, how as minister of war from 1905 to 1912 he had reorganized the department and prepared for "eventualities" on the continent. This was done on the occasion of the coal inquiry. We may quote the question of the Chairman and the answers of Lord Haldane from the minutes of the commission:

"Chairman. Am I right in thinking that during that time you organized the territorial forces of the crown and that also you provided for a speedy mobilization of our forces in the event of the nation being called upon to go to war? (Lord Haldane) That is so.

"I think as a result of your efforts, a very speedy mobilization of our forces was effected when war was declared against Germany?—Yes. The thing we concentrated upon was extreme rapidity of mobilization and concentration in the place of assembly, and that we carried out.

"I suppose it is no longer a secret, but war was declared on Tuesday, August 4th, 1914, and I think within a matter of twelve or fourteen hours, under the scheme of mobilization which you had prepared, some of our troops were already in France?—Yes, within a very short time; within a very few hours troops were in France.

"How long was it before the whole of the British Expeditionary Force was placed in the field at the appointed place?—On Monday, August 3rd, 1914, at the request of the Prime Minister, I, as Lord Chancellor, went back to the War Office and mobilized the machine with which I was familiar. That was done at 11 o'clock upon Monday, August 3rd, and the giving of the orders took only a few minutes; everything was prepared years before."

The details of the plans for military coöperation with France, as well as the anticipation of imminent war in the British War Office long prior to the assassination of Franz Ferdinand, are admirably illustrated by the following revelation by Major W. Cyprian Bridge, official translator to the War Office in 1914: [19]

But what perhaps impressed me more than all was the fact that about an hour after we declared war on the fatal 4th of August there was taken out of its hiding place a big document marked "very secret." It was drawn up in French and was entrusted to me for translation. It proved to be an elaborate agreement between the British and French Governments regarding the manner in which payments on behalf of the British Expeditionary Force *operating in North France* were to be adjusted. It went into details, for instance as to the rate of exchange at which calculations were to be made, such as any military officer of experience would know could only be useful or necessary *if the plan was expected to be put into almost immediate execution. The document was dated and signed early in February* (I think the 4th) *1914.*

The Northcliffe (Harmsworth) press was solidly behind these military plans. Indeed, these papers in England presumed to influence French opinion by ardently supporting the French army bill of 1913, which greatly increased the land armament of France, and by violently attacking the opponents of the bill. Clemenceau, next to Northcliffe the greatest of pre-war propagandists, reciprocated by supplying much incendiary material for Maxse's notorious *National Review.*[20]

While the agreements between England and France were kept secret, hidden even from the majority of the members of the Cabinet, and known only to Asquith, Grey, Haldane and Lord Crewe, nevertheless suspicions developed that something more than amiable relations existed between England and the country across the Channel. Consequently, Asquith and Grey were openly questioned on the matter by members of the House of Commons. On March 10, 1913, Lord Hugh Cecil put the following question to Asquith in the House of Commons:[21]

There is a very general belief that this country is under an obligation, not a treaty obligation, but an obligation arising out of an assurance given by the Ministry, in the course of diplomatic negotiations, to send a very large armed force out of this country to operate in Europe. This is the general belief.

Mr. Asquith answered: "I ought to say that is not true." On March 24th he went even further to say:[22]

As has been repeatedly stated, this country is not under any obligation, not public and known to Parlia-

ment, which compels it to take part in a war.   In other
words, if war arises between European Powers, there
are no unpublished agreements which will restrict or
hamper the freedom of the Government or Parliament
to decide whether or not Great Britain should participate in a war.

On April 28, 1914, just after Grey had returned from Paris, where he had agreed to try
to force an agreement upon a naval convention
with Russia, he was asked: [23]

Whether he is aware that demands have recently
been put forward for a further military understanding
between the Powers of the Triple Entente with a view to
concerted action on the Continent in the case of certain
eventualities, and whether the policy of this country
still remains one of freedom from all obligations to engage in military operations on the Continent.

Grey replied: [24]

The answer to the first part of the question is in the
negative, and as regards the latter part, the question
now remains the same as stated by the Prime Minister in
answer to a question in this House on March 24, 1913.

On June 11, 1914, within less than two months
of the outbreak of the War, Grey was asked a
similar question by Mr. King.   He answered
more at length: [25]

The hon. Member for North Somerset asked a similar
question last year with regard to military forces, and

the hon. Member for North Salford asked a similar
question also on the same day, as he has again done to-
day.   The Prime Minister then replied that if war arose
between European Powers, there were no unpublished
agreements which would restrict or hamper the freedom
of the Government or of Parliament to decide whether
or not Great Britain should participate in a war.
That answer covers both the questions on the Paper.
It remains as true to-day as it was a year ago.   No
negotiations have since been concluded with any Power
that would make the statement less true.   No such negotiations are in progress, and none are likely to be
entered upon so far as I can judge.   But if any agreement were to be concluded that made it necessary to
withdraw or modify the Prime Minister's statement of
last year, which I have quoted, it ought, in my opinion,
to be, and I suppose that it would be, laid before Parliament.

When Grey made his notable speech of August
3, 1914, asking the approval of Parliament for
his promise to aid France, he faced the difficult
situation of having to request consent to fulfil an
obligation which he had said did not exist.   He
had denied that there were any explicit written
arrangements such as the letter to Cambon, to
say nothing of the plans of the general staffs of
the two countries.   It was what Professor Beard
has designated as an "astounding" and "amazing" revelation to admit the existence of even the
general commitments of the Cambon letter.

Grey could not summon up courage enough to admit that a military and naval convention existed between the two countries. Hence, in reading the letter to Cambon in the House of Commons, he left off the damning concluding sentence. We follow Morel in giving in parallel columns the significant part of the letter, as originally written to Cambon, and as read in the House by Grey: [26]

The Conclusion of the Grey-Cambon Letter as read to the House of Commons	*The Conclusion of the Letter as actually written to M. Cambon.*
I agree that if either Government have grave reason to expect an unprovoked attack by a third power, or something that threatened the general peace, it should immediately discuss with the other whether both Governments should act together to prevent aggression and to preserve peace; and if so, what measures they would be prepared to take in common.	I agree that if either Government had grave reason to expect an unprovoked attack by a third power, or something that threatened the general peace, it should immediately discuss with the other whether both Governments should act together to prevent aggression and to preserve peace, and, if so, what measures they would be prepared to take in common. If these measures involved action, the plans of the general

staffs would at once be taken into consideration and the Governments would then decide what effect should be given to them.

In his memoirs Grey offers the following illuminating and amusing explanation of his omission of the vital concluding sentence: [27]

It was not until 1923, nine years later, that a charge of having omitted the last sentence of that letter was brought to my notice. My first impulse was to deny the thing as impossible; but it is so: the last sentence of the letter does not appear in the report of the speech.

A question, according to the report, was interjected about the date of the letter and it may be that the interruption in the reading of the letter, so near the end, caused an accidental omission, or perhaps I thought the last sentence unimportant, as it did not affect the sense and main purport of what had already been read out. I cannot say. The letter was published in full in the White Paper two or three days later; the proof of that Paper was submitted to me before publication; I certainly did not raise any question of how the letter should appear in the White Paper, and so I must either have attached no importance to the omission of a sentence in the speech, or have been unconscious of there having been any omission.

It may be observed that it was most convenient for Sir Edward to omit accidentally the sentence that most obviously demonstrated the falsehood in his replies to the House of Commons in April and June, 1914; and that it was most curious for him to attach no significance to the most important and damaging feature of the Cambon correspondence. We may further suggest that a cogent reason why he did not object to its publication in full in the *White Paper* was that on August 4th Viviani read the letter in full in the French Chamber of Deputies.[28]

It might be pointed out that Grey's diplomatic undertakings with France and his explanations of these present some of the finest illustrations of what Theodore Roosevelt described in derision as "weasel words" when criticizing the diplomatic communications of Woodrow Wilson. They were extremely evasive and nebulous, though when the test came Grey stood firmly by the most extreme interpretation of his commitments to the Entente.

II. ENGLAND AND RUSSIA

While Anglo-Russian rivalry did not have as long an historic past as Anglo-French antipathy, it had been much more acute in the half century prior to 1914. England and Russia fought one war over the Near East and were close to a second in 1878 and a third in 1884. England looked upon Russian expansion in Asia as a menace to India, and the Russian aspiration for the Straits was believed to be inimical to English interests in Egypt and the Suez Canal. It was England which, in 1908–9, even after the partition of Persia, blocked Izvolski's plan for the Russian occupation of the Straits which he had coupled with the Austrian annexation of Bosnia and Herzegovina.[29] After the German advances in Turkey and Mesopotamia the British became somewhat less alarmed over the Russian menace in Asia, and in 1907 came a temporary understanding with Russia through the partition of Persia.[30] Still England remained evasive upon the Straits question, not only blocking the 1908–9 scheme, but also refusing to sanction the plan when Russia brought it up again during the second Morocco crisis.[31]

England made another definite bid for Russian good-will in 1910 by the recall of Sir Arthur Nicolson, the Ambassador to Russia, and his appointment as permanent under-secretary in the British Foreign Office. The purpose of this transfer is stated in a telegram of Benckendorff to Izvolski on June 15, 1910: [32]

In connection with the probable recall of Nicolson from St. Petersburg, Grey told me last evening that he hoped the St. Petersburg Cabinet would be convinced that the appointment of the Viceroy of India, and the Ambassadorial change at St. Petersburg, were intended chiefly to strengthen the ties between Russia and Eng-

land. It is his opinion that the situation demanded
that somebody should be in office in London who is as
well acquainted with the current questions as Hardinge
and Nicolson. Grey told me that he insisted upon the
arrangement, because the Emperor, perhaps, would not
like to part with an Ambassador to whom he had always given so gracious a reception.

From this time on Nicolson exercised an influence
over Grey in strengthening the English entente
with Russia comparable to that exerted by Cambon in promoting Anglo-French accord. Moreover, Grey was not familiar with the details of
European diplomacy, and was wont to rely heavily upon Nicolson and his assistant, Sir Eyre
Crowe, for advice.

From 1911 onward the triangular military
plans of the general staffs of England, France
and Russia grew more explicit and intimate.
General Foch visited both London and St.
Petersburg endeavoring to coördinate and unify
the military plans of the Entente. Sazonov
visited England in the late summer of 1912, and
was able to write to the Tsar in September to the
following effect with respect to the English sympathy with Russia and her animus towards
Germany: [33]

As a favorable opportunity occurred I felt it useful,
in one of my conversations with Grey, to seek information as to what we might expect from Great Britain in

the event of a conflict with Germany. What the director of British foreign policy said to me as to this, and King George himself later, I think is very significant.

Your Majesty is aware that during M. Poincaré's stay in St. Petersburg last summer he expressed to me a wish that I would clear up the question of the extent to which we might count on the co-operation of the British fleet in the event of such a war.

I informed Grey confidentially of the main points of our naval convention with France, and remarked that under the treaty concluded the French fleet would endeavor to safeguard our interests in the southern theatre of war by preventing the Austrian fleet from penetrating into the Black Sea; and I then asked whether Great Britain for her part could perform the same service for us in the north, by keeping the German squadrons away from our Baltic coasts. Grey declared unhesitatingly that should the anticipated conditions arise Great Britain would make every effort to strike a crippling blow at German naval power. On the question of military operations he said that negotiations had already taken place between the competent authorities concerned, but in these discussions the conclusion had been reached that while the British fleet could easily penetrate into the Baltic, its stay there would be very risky. Assuming Germany to succeed in laying hands on Denmark and closing the exit from the Baltic, the British fleet would be caught as in a mousetrap. Accordingly Great Britain would have to confine her operations to the North Sea.

On his own initiative Grey then gave me a confirmation of what I already knew through Poincaré—an agreement exists between France and Great Britain, under which in the event of war with Germany Great Britain has accepted the obligation of bringing assistance to France not only on the sea but on land, by landing troops on the Continent.

The King touched on the same question in one of his conversations with me, and expressed himself even more strongly than his Minister.   When I mentioned, letting him see my agitation, that Germany is trying to place her naval forces on a par with Britain's, His Majesty cried that any conflict would have disastrous results not only for the German navy but for Germany's overseas trade, for, he said, "We shall sink every single German merchant ship we shall get hold of."

These words appeared to me to give expression not only to His Majesty's personal feelings but also to the public feeling predominant in Great Britain in regard to Germany.

We pointed out above in some detail how in the spring of 1914 the French and Russians seized the opportunity afforded by Sir Edward Grey's visit to Paris to initiate proceedings for an Anglo-Russian naval convention.   Grey secured Asquith's consent, but the negotiations progressed slowly because of a "leak" regarding them which greatly alarmed Germany and caused Grey vigorously to deny the existence of any such arrangements.   Sazonov heatedly contended that the naval convention existed only "in the mind of the *Berliner Tageblatt* and in the moon."   Plans were made, however, for their

resumption at an opportune moment, and the
Russian delegation was still in London when the
War broke out.[34]

In spite of these ever closer relations with Russia, the Russian entente was never popular in
England, and the British public could never have
been induced directly to sanction intervention in
a war designed to advance Russian interests.
There was still bad feeling over Persia in 1914,
and there was no enthusiasm in the British government for the Russian occupation of the
Straits. Even Grey had to put the soft pedal on
the Russian aspects of the crisis of 1914, and to
hold that England in no sense entered the War
to aid the Serbian cause. English acquiescence
in the Russian demand for the Straits after hostilities commenced had to be embodied in the Secret Treaties. The reason that England supported the Entente in a "Russian quarrel" was
that the Russian quarrel was linked with a
French quarrel, and England under Grey was
sure to support France against Germany.[35]
The French and Russians were clear enough
about the import of those European "complications" of which Sazonov wrote on December 8,
1913. A Serbian insurrection in the Balkans
would bring in Austria, and a Russian attack on
Austria would cause German intervention. This
would afford France an excuse for entering the
conflict, and the French entry would bring the

English in its train. This was what the French
and Russians expected from 1912 to 1914, and it
was essentially what happened in 1914. It was
the Anglo-French accord and that alone, which
made the Anglo-Russian entente a positive force
in the crisis of 1914.[36]

III. ENGLAND AND GERMANY

About 1900 Joseph Chamberlain, desiring a
strong Continental ally, made a real effort to improve relations with Germany, but without success. The blame for this failure to bring about
an Anglo-German *rapprochement* has been usually laid at the door of Baron von Holstein.
This interpretation has been based chiefly upon
the views of Baron Eckardstein, but it would
seem that it is now time to take the opinions of
von Eckardstein *cum grano*. He was a sort of
German Walter Hines Page, and his account has
been shown to be sadly lacking in intellectual
honesty. Holstein actually appears to have been
an astute but short-sighted diplomat, whose chief
mistake in his negotiations with England lay in
the fact that he allowed England to struggle too
long for an arrangement with Germany. This
was due to his belief that an agreement between
England and Russia and England and France
was out of range of probabilities. Hence, he
preferred to place these countries off against one

another. The English proposition to Germany
was also one which did not appeal to many Germans. England demanded a defensive agreement to include the whole British Empire, imply-
ing even the obligation to defend India against
Russia. Yet England was quite unwilling to
accept a reciprocal obligation concerning Germany's closest allies. The negotiations fell
through, and with their failure passed the possibility of an Anglo-German entente.[37] The
Conservative government turned a favorable ear
to France, and when Grey assumed office the
Germans had to face a less sympathetic figure
than Chamberlain or Lansdowne. Britain became progressively more worried after 1899 by
the German naval increases.

The first Morocco crisis further estranged
Germany and England, but following the
Kaiser's visit to England in 1907 better feeling
developed. The prospect for an understanding
was greatly diminished, however, by the publication in the London *Daily Telegraph* on
October 28, 1908, of an interview with the Kaiser
in which he declared his personal friendship for
England, but admitted that it was not wholly
shared by his subjects or appreciated by England. L. J. Maxse, in the *National Review,* together with the majority of the Northcliffe press,
violently denounced Germany, and Sir John
Fisher proposed that England seize and scuttle

the whole German fleet. King Edward VII encouraged the Anti-German encirclement movement and did his best in 1908 to disrupt the Triple Alliance.[38]

The most important element in arousing British antipathy was, however, the revelation in 1909 of plans for a somewhat larger German navy. This was, unquestionably, a foolish move for Germany, but Great Britain greatly exaggerated its significance. The German naval plans never in any serious degree challenged the naval power of Great Britain alone, to say nothing of the combined navies of Great Britain, France and Russia, to which were potentially added those of Japan and Italy. Negotiations for a mutual understanding on naval construction seemed well under way in the summer of 1911, when the second Morocco crisis broke out. The strong stand of England against Germany at this time alarmed the Kaiser and his ministers, and made the Kaiser lose his confidence in England altogether.[39]

In February, 1912, Lord Haldane visited Berlin to promote a better understanding with Germany. Except for the psychological results of the affair the significance of this Haldane "mission" has been greatly exaggerated, for Haldane had little to offer Germany and apparently had no power whatever to carry through any definite agreement. He found Bethmann-

Hollweg favorable to a naval arrangement, but Tirpitz was opposed. Finally, it was decided that a general benevolent neutrality pact should be agreed upon, with the assumption that Germany would in return hold up her proposed naval increases.[40] But the Haldane negotiations had no chance of success, as Benckendorff assured the Russian Foreign Office at the time. Grey stated that he would resign rather than see any arrangements made with Germany which would weaken the Triple Entente.[41] Poincaré heard of the proposed neutrality arrangement with Germany, and induced Grey to refuse the proposition. Izvolski reveals this fact in his letter of December 5, 1912: [42]

In my conversations with Poincaré and Paléologue I was able to learn in strict confidence that on the occasion of the well-known journey of Lord Haldane to Berlin (in February of the present year) Germany made to Great Britain a quite definite proposal, as follows: the London Cabinet should engage itself in writing to maintain neutrality should Germany be drawn into a war which was not provoked from her side. The London Cabinet informed M. Poincaré of this, and apparently delayed sending either an acceptance or a refusal of this proposal. M. Poincaré expressed himself most emphatically against such an undertaking. He pointed out to the British Government that the signature of such a treaty with Germany by Great Britain would end at a blow the existing Franco-British relations, since no written agreement of a general political character existed between France and Great Britain. This objection had its result: the London Cabinet declined Germany's proposal, to the lively dissatisfaction of Berlin.

This was one of the most humiliating moments in the entire history of British foreign policy, but, as Mr. Morel has pointed out, it was the inevitable outcome of Grey's relations with France and Russia: [43]

Can one criticise Poincaré? I hardly think so. Humiliating as was his veto, the humiliation had been invited. Could a more contemptible record be imagined? The very minister who, after the war, tells us that by the end of 1910 he had, after four years' labour, reorganized the British Army for the express purpose of participating in a war with Germany in fulfilment of our "contract" with France, goes over to Germany in 1912 to discuss the possibility of our remaining neutral in a war between Germany and France! And the Government which sent him over actually consults Poincaré as to whether it shall accept, or reject, a German offer of conditional neutrality! Small blame to Poincaré for making it peremptorily clear that he would not allow us to run with the hare and hunt with the hounds! But thenceforth British foreign policy was directed not from London, but from Paris and Petrograd. We had become, in effect, impotent to exercise a decisive influence over events.

The British government could not, of course, admit the reason for the failure of the Haldane mission, so they preferred to keep secret the fact that it had failed.   On July 25, 1912, Mr. Asquith spoke of Anglo-German relations before the House of Commons in the following terms: [44]

Our relations with the great German Empire are, I am glad to say, at this moment, and I feel sure they are likely to remain, relations of amity and good-will. Lord Haldane paid a visit to Berlin early this year; he entered upon conversations and an interchange of views there which have been continued since in a spirit of perfect frankness and friendship, both on one side and the other.

Instead of an Anglo-German understanding, the year 1912 ended with the Grey-Cambon correspondence of November 22, 1912, which spelled the end of complete English independence in foreign policy until the break-down of the Anglo-French Entente after the World War.

In spite of the failures in the year 1912, Anglo-German relations grew steadily better from the close of 1912 to the outbreak of the World War.   In March, 1912, Winston Churchill, first Lord of the Admiralty, announced that England would be satisfied with an arrangement whereby Germany agreed not to build more than ten battleships to each sixteen constructed by Great Britain.   On February 7, 1913, Von Tirpitz announced that Germany would not exceed that ratio.[45]   England had thus secured her ambition in the Haldane proposals without Germany's obtaining the reciprocal advantage of a guaranty of British neutrality. In spite of repeated statements to the contrary by Grey, Asquith, and the mythologizing historians, German naval rivalry cannot, therefore, be designated as an important immediate cause of the World War in 1914.

Still greater progress was made in 1914. Early in this year a large group in the British Liberal Party, even though most incompletely informed as to the lengths to which the negotiations with France had actually gone, became alarmed concerning the degree to which England had apparently become involved in the Entente. Efforts were initiated to improve relations with Germany. On New Year's Day, 1914, Lloyd-George gave out his famous interview in the London *Daily Chronicle* in which he declared that the rumored increases in the German army were "vital, not merely to the existence of the German Empire, but to the very life and independence of the nation itself, surrounded, as Germany is, by other nations, each of which possesses armies as powerful as her own." The King announced the satisfactory progress of negotiations regarding Mesopotamia and the Bagdad Railway.[46] These negotiations proceeded successfully. By June 15th an agreement satisfactory to both parties had been reached, and thus was

settled the most important dispute, indeed the
only significant source of contention, between
Germany and Great Britain.[47] As Lloyd
George expressed it, even after war had been declared in August, 1914, Anglo-German relations
in July, 1914, were better than they had been for
fifteen years. He might have said for twenty
years. There was no longer any significant
cause for tension between these two states, and
there is little validity in the efforts of anti-British
or anti-German historians to refer to acute
clashes before 1912 as active causes of the World
War. The fly in the ointment lay in the fact
that, with characteristic duplicity, Sir Edward
Grey was at this very time arranging the naval
convention with Russia which would close the
ring about Germany and give Sazonov and Poincaré that assurance of British aid to the Franco-
Russian military alliance which they deemed
necessary in order to deal Germany the "mortal
blow" mentioned by Sazonov in the secret ministerial conference of December 31, 1913.[48]

There is no doubt that this development of
better relations between Germany and England
was the determining factor in convincing Russia
and France that the desired European war must
be fought, if possible, in 1914; in other words,
before England could be detached from the
Entente. Georges Louis quotes Paul Deschanel
as stating that the French leaders were also im-

patient to initiate hostilities before the French radicals could secure the repeal of the French three-year service act.[49] At any rate, the Anglo-German negotiations and the expression of sympathy for Germany in England threw Paul Cambon, Poincaré, Izvolski and Sazonov into a panic, and they hastened to regain control of the situation before their efforts of eight years had been undone. Mr. Morel has in the following passages admirably summarized the effect of the progress towards an Anglo-German *rapprochement* upon the Franco-Russian authorities and upon their determination to force the European war before England could be detached from the Entente: [50]

The anxiety caused by these manifestations of improved relations between Britain and Germany at the very moment when the conspirators in Petrograd, Belgrade, and elsewhere were reckoning that the plum was almost ripe enough for plucking, is evident in the Russian dispatches we now possess. Thus the Russian ambassador in Berlin, reporting to Sazonov, February 13, 1914, remarks that Cambon (French ambassador in Berlin, and brother of the French ambassador in London) "is very much worried by these constant rumors of an improvement in Anglo-German relations, since he agrees that there is a possibility of *rapprochement* between these two countries in the future." Cambon's Russian colleague did not "fully share these fears," yet his dispatches show that he was disturbed and uneasy.

But the uneasiness of the French and Russian ambassadors in Berlin was as nothing compared with that which reigned in Petrograd and Paris. (Note that the warlike announcements in the Russian press, the chief war measures taken in the Duma, and, especially, the great war council at Petrograd followed hard upon the King's speech.) We obtain corroboration from totally different sources of this deep disquiet, lest Britain slip from the meshes of the net so patiently and closely drawn around her. Mr. Page, American ambassador to Britain, in a letter to Colonel House (January 11, 1914) explains how, as the result of Mr. Lloyd George's speech, "the French allies of the British went up into the air. They raised a great howl. Churchill went to see them to soothe them. They would not be soothed!" Sazanov had been almost equally disquieted a year before, when Tirpitz (the head of the German Admiralty) had made a speech in the Reichstag, which was a virtual recognition of British naval superiority. On that occasion Sazanov wired to Benckendorff about this "alarming symptom" and his uneasiness at the "effort of German diplomacy to bring about a *rapprochement* with England." He wanted to know "in what degree machinations of that sort might find a favorable soil in London!"

But now something obviously had to be done, and quickly, to grip the British nation still more tightly in the vise into which certain British Ministers by their secret actions had placed us. The entire policy of eight laborious years was trembling in the balance. Was there consciousness of this among the protagonists of that policy in London? Read carefully the inspired

Times throughout the months of February to June. Assuredly was there consciousness of it at Krasnoe-Selo and at the Quai d'Orsay. If the inconceivable happened and the British salmon should slip out of the net at the last moment, the fishers in troubled waters were down and out. If a section of the British cabinet should clearly perceive almost at the last moment the rocks ahead, and force the hands of the other section by some public reference that would suddenly electrify the British public into a sense of imminent peril leading to insistent inquiry as to their true relationship with the rival continental groups—then, indeed, all might be lost. For, without Britain, Sukhomlinoff might shout through his newspaper that he was ready till all was blue—there would be nothing doing. Something had to be done—and this is what was done, in the silence and secrecy of the diplomatic closet.

Sazonov led off with a series of dispatches to the Russian ambassadors in London and Paris, urging that "a further reinforcement and development of the so-called triple entente, and, if possible, its transformation into a new triple alliance appears to me to be a demand of the present situation." Lord Grey and King George were going to Paris; Poincaré and Doumergue (French foreign minister) should urge upon the former a "closer agreement between Russia and England." Doumergue agreed. He thought the task would be easy, "because it is most obvious that, inasmuch as France has special military and naval understandings with Russia and England, this system must be co-ordinated and completed by corresponding understandings between Russia and England." The scheme as finally worked out was this. When Lord Grey reached Paris the French Government would urge him to (a) communicate officially to the Russians, the text of the Grey-Cambon exchange notes, of November 22, 1912, and the text of the military and naval conventions; (b) draw up a naval convention with Russia, active co-operation between the British and Russian armies being obviously impracticable.

Such were the events which preceded Lord Grey's visit to Paris three and a half months before the outbreak of war.

When Lord Grey reached Paris he went off to Versailles to attend the French military manœuvres. The next day the conference met. Its members were Doumergue (French foreign minister), Paul Cambon (French ambassador to Britain), De Margerie (head of the permanent staff at the French Foreign Office), Lord Grey and Sir William Tyrrel, his private secretary. The results of the conference, which were duly reported in great detail by Isvolsky to Sazonov, exceeded the expectations of the French negotiators:

"All three of those present at the conference— Messrs. Doumergue, Cambon, and De Margerie—told me they were astonished at the clearly stated and definite readiness to enter upon a closer approach to Russia, which Sir Edward Grey had expressed."

Lord Grey, indeed, may be fairly said to have leaped at the bait, and to have swallowed it without a moment's hesitation, merely pointing out that there were certain elements in the cabinet prejudiced against Russia. But he hoped to win over Mr. Asquith and the whole cabinet. Thereupon he returned to London. The fish was fairly landed.

Sazanov was naturally delighted at his success:

"The readiness of the British Government to begin without delay negotiations regarding the conclusion of an agreement between Russia and England, which would concern joint operations of our naval forces in the event of a common military action, has been received, on our part, with a feeling of the greatest satisfaction. Quite apart from the fact that such an agreement is desirable from a special military standpoint, we attach great importance to it in a general political sense."

And with reason! Had not *Le Temps*, the official organ of the French Foreign Office, remarked (April 20), of the short official communiqué sent out to the press at the end of the conference, that it "says enough to make it unnecessary to insist that the Entente is the Triple Entente, and more than ever prepared for united action." . . .

But how can one explain the fact that Lord Grey, at the very time that he was negotiating a "colonial" agreement with Germany, was secretly fastening the Russo-French noose tighter around our necks, and denying right and left that he was doing anything of the sort? In the present state of our knowledge only surmise is possible. And surmise in this particular connection is fruitless.

But there can be no doubt whatever as to the effect of the British Mesopotamian negotiations with Germany, in which oil played a substantial but by no means exclusive part, upon the men who were directing Russian and French diplomacy. If they did not know the exact nature of the negotiations, they were aware that negotiations of some kind had been going on for months,

and had recently been accelerated, and they probably
had a pretty good idea of their tenor.

M. Cambon always took care to be well informed.

They first sought to counterbalance them by an
Anglo-Russian naval convention which would complete
the circuit of triple military and naval conventions, and
produce the conditions of a triple alliance in everything but name. But the actual conclusion of the convention was hanging fire, while negotiations with Germany continued. Then they made up their minds to
strike, and they struck with the certain knowledge that
the leading members of the Liberal cabinet—notably
and above all the Foreign Secretary and the Prime Minister—had placed themselves in a position from which
they could extricate neither themselves nor the country. It was a gamble. But they held the trumps.
And they won.

IV. SIR EDWARD GREY IN THE CRISIS OF 1914

1. Grey Theoretically for Peace in 1914

It is of real importance at the outset to have
in mind what seems to have been the dominating
attitude of Sir Edward Grey towards throwing England into a general European war.
There are some who contend that from the first
Grey was determined to make use of the crisis
to crush German commerce and sea power.
They cite as evidence his negotiation of the Russian naval convention at the same time he was

concluding the arrangement with Germany concerning the Bagdad Railway; his suggestion on July 25th to Benckendorff that he could see the necessity of Russian mobilization; his telegram to Buchanan on July 27th to the effect that any Russian fear about British neutrality should have been dispelled by the order for the concentration of the British fleet at Portland; Campbell's allegation that the French withdrawal imposture of July 30th was suggested by Grey and Cambon; his refusal to formulate any terms on which England would remain neutral; his persistent refusal to attempt to put any restraint on Russia; his refusal to guarantee English neutrality if Germany would not invade Belgium or attack the coast of France; his commitment of England to war on August 2nd before Germany had even sent an ultimatum to Belgium; and his insistence upon coming into the conflict after Germany had offered not to attack the Channel ports of France, which had been the condition on which he had promised France support the preceding day (cf. J. W. Burgess, *The European War*).

Damaging as this indictment is, we cannot yet accept the thesis that Grey was for war from the moment of the assassination of the Archduke and pursued a Machiavellian policy, even more skilful and subtle than that displayed by Poincaré, Viviani, Sazonov and Izvolski. The thesis which

will be maintained throughout this chapter is that
Grey was for peace in the abstract in the crisis
of 1914, however much he had done from 1906 to
1914 to encourage a European situation favorable to war.   Yet it seems equally certain that he
was determined to enter the Continental war if
France was involved, no matter how justifiable
or unjustifiable the French entry, and irrespective of Belgium or any concessions which Germany might make to England.*   It is true that
on July 31st Grey announced that, if France and
Russia refused reasonable concessions by Germany and Austria, England would stand aside,[51]
but he did not act consistently with this promise,
and, moreover, it was of no significance at the
time since the Russian mobilization was in full
swing.   This basic assumption is that held also
by Lord Loreburn: [52]

The answer to this question [why England entered
the War], in a single sentence, is that we have brought
into the war because Mr. Asquith and Sir Edward Grey
and their confidants, by steps some of which are known
while others may be unknown, had placed us in such a
position towards France, and therefore towards Russia,
that they found they could not refuse to take up arms
on her behalf when it came to the issue, though till the

---

* This estimate of Grey's attitude in 1914 is fully vindicated
by the complete British documents.

end they denied it to Parliament, and probably even to themselves. They were driven from point to point because they would not realize that they had so committed themselves, and accordingly would not take any decisive attitude. Nothing breeds irresolution more certainly than a sense that you are in a false position which you will not bring yourself to recognize.

On July 31st, having found himself about to be involved in an actual war in behalf of France, Grey was faced with the grave necessity of discovering some great moral issue which would put the English public solidly behind him and help obscure the fact of his deception of people and Parliament when the great revelation had to be made, as it was on August 3rd. This "moral issue" was the German invasion of Belgium, and so important in Grey's program was this potential lever on English opinion that he resolutely refused to promise France that England would surely intervene until he had assured himself: (1) that Germany would invade Belgium unless England promised to remain neutral, and (2) that Belgium would resist this invasion by force of arms. After he had promised France English aid on August 2nd, he desired above all other things that Germany would invade Belgium, and he practically coerced Belgium into issuing an appeal to the Entente to save her from Germany.[53]

2. Grey's Disastrous Policy of Evasion and Indecision

This dilatory, evasive and indecisive policy pursued by Grey in 1914, while far less criminal in a positive sense than the persistent determination of Poincaré and Sazonov upon war from the first, was most certainly the worst possible attitude which England could have taken in 1914 if she desired to maintain the peace of Europe. It was probably fully as dangerous a position as it would have been if she had come out for intervention on the side of France and Russia from the beginning. This policy of vacillation, non-commitment and indiscriminate encouragement made France and Russia feel that they could count on England's support, while it made Germany and Austria equally certain that England would remain neutral. Loreburn has well stated the results of this fatal procedure on the part of Grey: [54]

According to the despatches, Sir Edward Grey is often asked, What will you do? What will be your attitude? Will you be neutral, and on what conditions will you be neutral? Will you at once declare that you will support us in arms? Sir Edward refuses to give an answer either way. He hints at what we may do, but will not say what we will do. . . . (On July 29th) All the Great Powers were still at peace with one another. If Germany and Austria even now learned for

certain that in the event of a general war England would
fight against them, they could still accept some submission from Serbia without any stain on that code of
military honour which both of them so highly prize.
Or if Russia even now learned definitely that England
would not join her and France in arms over a Servian
quarrel, if she mobilized prematurely, she might have
stayed for a few days the military steps which Sir Edward Grey was constantly urging her to pretermit,
and which ultimately brought on the rupture.   But
such are the penalties of indecision and of the ambi-
guities which it begets, that at this very time not only
was Austria reckoning on our sympathy, but Russia
was counting on our support. . . . Both sides construed an ambiguous attitude as an attitude favorable
to their own hope, of British neutrality on the one side,
of British support on the other.

3. Grey's Indifference to the Austro-Serbian Quarrel

In analyzing the specific acts of Sir Edward
Grey in the crisis of 1914 it is desirable at the
outset to show that he was from the first opposed
to making the Austro-Serbian issue the acknowledged cause of British intervention.   In his first
statement on the subject in a telegram to the
British Ambassador in Berlin on July 20, 1914,
he said that he "hated the idea of a war between
any of the Great Powers, and that any of them
should be dragged into a war by Serbia would be

detestable." [55]   In the official introduction to the
British *White Book* of 1914 it was stated by the
authority of Grey, if not in his own words: [56]

The dispute between Austria and Servia was a dispute
between two Governments with which Great Britain had
nothing to do.   Sir E. Grey, therefore, consistently
stated that he had no concern in the dispute; that he
had no title to intervene between Austria and Serbia;
that he would express no opinion on the merits of the ultimatum.

On the 29th of July he stated that "there must,
of course, be some humiliation of Servia, but
Austria might press things so far as to involve
the humiliation of Russia." [57]   Again on the 29th
he expressed himself as follows: [58]

The Austrian Ambassador told me today he had
ready a long memorandum, which he proposed to leave,
and which he said gave an account of the conduct of
Servia toward Austria, and an explanation of how necessary the Austrian action was.   I said that I did not
wish to discuss the merits of the question between Austria and Servia.

In his memoirs Grey continues his 1914 position
that England had little interest in Serbia: [59]

The notion of being involved in war about a Balkan
quarrel was repugnant.   Serbia, to British people, was
a country with which a few years ago we had severed
diplomatic relations, because of a brutal murder of the
King and Queen; and, though that was over, and we

were now on good terms, there was no sentiment urging us to go into a war on Serbia's behalf.

At the same time that Grey was refusing to take any part in the Austro-Serbian dispute he was directly or by implication encouraging Austria. On July 27th Grey told the Austrian Ambassador that "if Austria could make war on Serbia and at the same time pacify Russia, well and good." On July 28th the British Ambassador in Vienna was assuring Berchtold that there was no lack of sympathy for the Austrian cause in England, and Grey let this assurance stand without any qualification.[60] At other times Grey expressed himself as thinking that the Austrian ultimatum was far too severe. In a telegram to the British Ambassador at Vienna he stated on July 24th that "I had never before seen one State address to another independent State a document of so formidable a character."[61] In fact, on July 25th he telegraphed Buchanan in St. Petersburg that he regarded the Austrian ultimatum of such a type as to invite Russian mobilization.[62] In this way, while not at any time taking a definite stand on the Serbian problem, he helped to make it a cause of European complications through leading the Austrians to feel sure of British sympathy and the Russians positive of British indignation.[63] And whether or not he was willing to go to war directly over the Serbian issue, he allowed France and Russia to use the Serbian incident as the means of provoking the War, and then refused to stand aside.

4. Grey's Refusal to Restrain Russia or to Promise English Neutrality

It was once rather widely held, and the present writer at one time subscribed to this view, that Grey's great mistake was that he did not inform Germany and Austria promptly on July 24th or 25th that, in the event of a general European war, England would be found on the side of France and Russia. It was once believed that if Grey had done this Germany and Austria would have restrained themselves and the general conflict would have been averted. It would seem that we must now abandon this view in the light of our present knowledge of the determination of France and Russia to force a Continental war in 1914. The old theory rested on the assumption that it was Germany which required restraint, while we now know that it was France and Russia which needed to be held in leash. Had Grey declared himself for France and Russia at the outset these two powers would have been even more eager for war and more cocksure in their procedure.* They understood this well enough at the time, and under the cover of the allegation that it would advance the cause of

* Fully proved by the new British documents.

peace, their statesmen made repeated efforts
to get England to declare openly that she would
support France and Russia. Poincaré even
went so far as to telegraph his appeal directly to
the King on July 31st.[64]   How much good faith
there was in their appeals may be seen from the
fact that their most insistent demands in this respect were made after the Russian general
mobilization had been ordered.   An early statement by England of her decision to stand by
France could not have prevented the War unless
Germany had been unwilling to fight in self-
defense.

The only way whereby Grey could have prevented war, if at all, in 1914 would have been by
declaring that England would remain neutral if
Germany did not invade Belgium, or by warning
Russia before July 30th that England would not
aid France and Russia unless Russia ceased her
preparations for mobilization.   Both of these
things Grey refused to do.   After Grey had refused to promise the German Ambassador that
England would remain neutral in the event of
Germany's agreeing not to invade Belgium, the
German Ambassador asked Grey to formulate
the conditions according to which England would
remain neutral; but Grey refused point-blank to
do so, though he afterwards falsely informed the
House of Commons that he had stated these con-

ditions.[65]   Equally definite was Grey's refusal to attempt to restrain the Russian military measures in spite of earnest German appeals.   Sazonov had, as early as July 27th, informed the French and English governments that he would tolerate no counsels of moderation, and Grey refused to call his bluff.[66]   In his memoirs Grey even expresses himself as unsympathetic with the very idea of restraining Russia: [67]

> I felt impatient at the suggestion that it was for me to influence or restrain Russia.   I could do nothing but express pious hopes in general terms to Sazonov. . . .
> Nor can the Russian mobilization be fairly construed as evidence of a desire for war.   After the veto of a Conference, with Austria mobilized and Germany ready to strike, what counselor could have honestly advised the Tsar that mobilization in Russia was a premature, unnecessary precaution?

Grey discussed the German neutrality proposals with France, who curtly rejected them.[67a]

It was once supposed that Grey's failure to restrain Russia might have been due to his ignorance of Russian military preparations, but the new British documents refute this thesis.   Grey was thoroughly informed at all stages.   On July 25th Buchanan telegraphed that the Russian Crown Council had authorized Sazonov to mobilize 1,110,000 men.   Early in the evening of the 30th Buchanan promptly warned Grey that: "It has been decided to issue orders for [Rus-

ˊsian] general mobilization." On the 31st Grey telegraphed to Bertie: "The latest news was that Russia had ordered a complete mobilization of her fleet and army. This, it seemed to me, would precipitate a crisis, and would make it appear that German mobilization was being forced by Russia." Grey was fully aware in 1914 that the Russian mobilization preceded not only the Austrian and German mobilizations, but also the German proclamation of a "state of imminent war." As a matter of fact, Grey never seriously considered pressing Russia for peace. From the beginning of the crisis Nicolson insisted that Russia must be handled with gloves. On the 24th of July he contended that: "Our attitude during the crisis will be regarded by Russia as a test and we must be most careful not to alienate her." [68]

The desirability of promising British neutrality in the event of war was clearly seen by the Manchester *Guardian* in the crisis of July, 1914, and thus forcefully stated in editorials of July 28th and July 30th:

Not only are we neutral now, but we could and ought to remain neutral throughout the whole course of the war.

We have not seen a shred of reason for thinking that the triumph of Germany in a European war in which we had been neutral would injure a single British interest, however small, whereas the triumph of Russia would create a situation for us really formidable. If Russia makes a general war out of a local war it will be a crime against Europe. If we, who might remain neutral, rush into the war or let our attitude remain doubtful, it will be both a crime and an act of supreme and gratuitous folly.

Far the most brilliant and forceful plea for British neutrality was made by A. G. Gardiner in the London *Daily News* for August 1st. After pointing out in masterly fashion the real issues in the case and the dangers to England from a Russian victory, he concluded with words, whose truth and sagacity history has since amply vindicated:

Let us announce our neutrality to the world. It is the one hope. There is no other. Let us make it clear that unless and until British interests are attacked, we will have no part in this world-insanity, that we will not shed a drop of English blood for the Czar or Servia, that our one obligation is the interests and peace of this land, and that we refuse to recognize any other. We can save Europe from war even at this last moment. But we can save it only by telling the Czar that he must fight his own battles and take the consequences of his own action.

If the British government does this, it will do the greatest service to humanity in history. If it does not do it, it will have brought the greatest curse to humanity in history. The youngest of us will not live to see the end of its crime.

5. *Grey, Germany and the Diplomatic Efforts to Settle the Crisis*

We shall next examine Grey's proposals for conferences, conversations and mediation, with the results of these suggestions. In doing so we should keep in mind the usual assumption that these were all original with Grey and that Germany alone rejected all of them. In his memoirs Grey, with astonishing mendacity, refers time and again to the fact that Germany rejected a European conference, and vigorously contends that this wrecked all chances for peace.[69] He does not reveal the fact that Russia, for all practical purposes, rejected the proposal, and that Sazonov announced that he would have nothing to do with anything which would limit his freedom of action against Austria.[70]

In considering Grey's plans for a diplomatic settlement of the crisis we should understand that only those proposals made before July 30th are of any significance, as the Russian mobilization prevented any chance for a pacific settlement after that date. Grey's first plan to avert war in 1914 was made as early as July 20th. It was that of direct conversations between St. Petersburg and Vienna. We have pointed out that this was promptly rejected by Poincaré (*British Documents,* Nos. 67, 76). Grey's second plan for a diplomatic settlement of the crisis in 1914 was proposed to Paul Cambon on July 24th, as soon as he learned the terms of the Austrian ultimatum. It is contained in Number 10 of the British *Blue Book* and was to the following effect:

I would say that I thought the only chance of any mediating or moderating influence being exercised was that Germany, France, Italy and ourselves, who had no direct interests in Servia, should act together for the sake of peace, simultaneously in Vienna and St. Petersburg.

This plan for the mediation of the Austro-Russian quarrel was forwarded to Berlin on the same day as Number 11 of the *Blue Book*. Von Jagow accepted this proposal, as is evident in Number 18 of the *Blue Book:*

If the relations between Austria and Russia became threatening, he (von Jagow) was quite ready to fall in with your suggestion as to the four Powers working in favour of moderation at Vienna and St. Petersburg.

As far as we can discover, France never approved this plan for the mediation of the Austro-Russian dispute, and on the 27th Sazonov sharply refused to consider any proposal whatever for the limitation of the freedom of Russian action against Austria. On the 28th France informed Sazonov that it would not be a party to any diplomatic proposition designed to exercise a moderating influence on Russia. The first of Grey's proposals, then, was agreed to by Germany, but rejected explicitly or by implication by Russia and France.

Grey's next proposal was put forward on July 26th, when he suggested that there should be a conference of the French, Italian and German Ambassadors in London, together with himself, for the purpose of "discovering an issue which would prevent complications." [71] We have just pointed out that both Germany and Russia declined to favor a conference. Germany said that it would be equivalent to haling Austria before an arbitration court, which could not be done without her consent.[72] Russia refused to approve such a plan because she would tolerate no interference with her freedom of action towards Austria. We have referred above to Sazonov's bluff in proposing a conference at London on July 31st, a day after the mobilization had been ordered, in order to gain more time for the Russian mobilization measures.[73] In this way Grey's plan for a conference of ambassadors came to naught. Grey's tendency to revert frequently to the German rejection of his conference plan is in interesting contrast to his complete failure to mention his own coldness towards the promising Italian plan for a conference of the nations, and towards Colonel House's plan in 1916.[74]

We may now consider the fate of the direct

conversations.　In doing so we must call attention to the utterly misleading statements of Grey in his memoirs concerning the significance of the German rejection of the proposed conference and his reaction to this decision on the part of Germany in 1914.　In one place he says of the Germans: [75] "The complacency with which they had let Austria launch the ultimatum on Serbia was deplorable, and to me unaccountable; the blocking of a conference was still worse." Again: [76] "From the moment that Bethmann-Hollweg vetoed a conference, without qualification, without condition or reservation suggested on which a Conference might be agreed to, I felt that he would not be allowed to make a peaceful end to the negotiations." Finally: [77] "Germany ceased to talk of anything but the Russian mobilization.　I could do nothing to stop that. The rejection of a Conference struck out of my hand what might have been a lever to influence Russia to suspend military preparations." He neglects to mention the fact that Russia was equally set against a conference on July 26th and 27th.

By far the most damaging fact relative to Grey's above denunciation of Germany's action in rejecting the conference of ambassadors lies in the fact that on July 28th Grey expressed himself as believing that the German plan of direct conversations between Vienna and St. Petersburg—actually his own first proposal—was preferable to his scheme of a conference. He stated in two telegrams on the 28th: [78]

As long as there is a prospect of direct exchange of views between Austria and Russia, I would suspend every other suggestion, as I entirely agree that this is the most preferable method of all. . . .

It is most satisfactory that there is a prospect of a direct exchange of views between the Russian and Austrian Governments.

This "most preferable method" was, as we pointed out at length in the fifth chapter, a German substitute and was pressed with vigor upon Austria from the 28th to the 31st of July. It was also formerly approved by Sazonov, though early rejected by Poincaré. German adherence to this plan only ceased when the Russian general mobilization had become well advanced.

Equally disastrous to Grey's recent allegation that Germany blocked all plans for a diplomatic settlement are the facts about the fifth method proposed, namely, mediation between Austria and Serbia. Grey made this suggestion on July 29th, namely, that Austria occupy Belgrade and the adjacent territory and then hold up her military measures until mediation had been attempted between her and Serbia.[79] It so happens that this was the identical plan—the pledge-plan—which had been outlined by the Kaiser on the previous day and sent on to Austria with vigorous German suggestions that Austria adhere to it.[80] Further, on July 28th and 29th the Austrian Ambassador in St. Petersburg explicitly informed Sazonov that Austria would respect the territorial integrity and sovereignty of Serbia.[81] Finally, on the 31st, Austria announced her willingness to discuss with Russia the terms of the ultimatum to Serbia.[82] Hence, far from rejecting all of Grey's proposals Germany rejected only one, in which action she was accompanied by Russia. She proposed and warmly seconded what Grey admitted to be a better plan than his conference method. Again, she was the author and forceful sponsor of Grey's other scheme, namely, that of mediation between Austria and Serbia, as well as of the specific grounds of this mediation. As late as just before midnight on July 30th George V telegraphed to Prince Henry of Prussia: [83]

My Government is doing its utmost, suggesting to Russia and France to suspend further military operations, if Austria will consent to be satisfied with occupation of Belgrade and neighboring Serbian territory as a hostage for satisfactory settlement of her demands, other countries meanwhile suspending their war preparations. Trust William will use his great influence to induce Austria to accept this proposal, thus proving that Germany and England are working together to prevent what would be an international catastrophe.

While England, as we now know, was not pressing either France or Russia for restraint in any serious fashion, and while Germany had been executing the plan suggested by George V for two days, this telegram indicates at least the formal unanimity of the British and German governments up to a time which was hours after the order for Russian general mobilization had been dispatched.   In other words, when the Russian mobilization was ordered, Germany and England were apparently in full accord and enthusiastically coöperating to advance those diplomatic negotiations best designed to preserve the peace of Europe.   As Loreburn says: [84]

This was an acceptance by Germany of Sir Edward's own suggestion—an event of enormous importance, for London and Berlin were at one.   We must appreciate that London and Berlin were at one on 30th July in a plan which would have preserved peace, if we are to realize the full horror of what followed.

Unfortunately the *Livre Noir,* the *Falsifications of the Russian Orange Book,* and the British documents had not appeared when Loreburn wrote, and he could not know who was responsible for these later horrors.   We, today, are in no doubt. England's inseparable ally approved the fatal Russian general mobilization, and Grey, instead of standing with Germany for peace, deserted Germany and cast his lot with the aggressors.

In the light of the above demonstration that Germany had accepted and urged the Austrian adoption of the more practicable plans for peace before July 30th, and that Austria had assured Russia that she would respect the territorial integrity and sovereignty of Serbia by July 28th, we can readily understand with what levity Grey viewed his own telegram to the British Ambassador at Berlin on July 31st: [85]

I said to the German Ambassador this morning that if Germany could get any reasonable proposal put forward which made it clear that Germany and Austria were striving to preserve European peace, and that Russia and France would be unreasonable if they rejected it, I would support it at St. Petersburg and Paris, and go to the length of saying that if Russia and France would not accept it his Majesty's Government would have nothing more to do with the consequences.

Austria and Germany had met Grey's conditions by the 30th, but he did not keep his word. If he had, war might quite possibly have been prevented. By the 31st the pressure of Cambon had become too heavy for him, and by August 1st he did not even make adequate use of the information that Austria had at last acceded to the most persistent Russian demand, namely, a willingness to discuss directly the terms of the ultimatum to Serbia.[86] By the close of the 31st he had succumbed to Cambon, Crowe and Nicolson and had begun his campaign to prepare English opinion for entry into the war by his first move in the Belgian imposture.[87]

6. Grey Surrenders to the War Makers

The next matter to be considered is the all-important subject of the gradual capitulation of Grey to the assaults of Sazonov, Cambon, Crowe, Nicolson and Poincaré. The conditional agreement of England to aid France in the event of a European war rested, as we have seen, upon the Grey-Cambon correspondence of November 22, 1912. That was, as Grey said on August 3, 1914, "the starting-point for the Government with regard to the present crisis." [88] This was confirmed on August 2, 1914, but, as we shall show below, it had ceased to be binding by the next day, as Germany agreed to refrain from those acts which bound England to intervene according to the note of August 2nd.

The campaign to wear down Grey's resistance to the importunities of France and Russia began early. On the 24th Buchanan telegraphed to Grey that Sazonov "hoped that his Majesty's Government would not fail to proclaim their solidarity with Russia and France." [89] This pressure, encouraged by Crowe and Nicolson, was kept up unceasingly until Grey began to break on July 30th. On July 29th Sazonov sent his famous telegrams announcing the first Rus-

sian order for mobilization and exhorting Benckendorff and the French authorities to get after
Grey at once and get England committed to the
military policies of France and Russia.[90] On
the next day Viviani telegraphed to Cambon to
begin working on Grey, and Izvolski informed
Sazonov to that effect. On the 30th the ten
kilometer withdrawal imposture was staged by
France and Grey's attention was called to it (if,
according to Campbell, he did not himself suggest it). On July 30th Grey took his first important positive step towards the abyss. In answer to Cambon's query he admitted that it was
time to discuss the bearing of the Grey-Cambon
correspondence of 1912 upon the present crisis.
This is not mentioned in the British *Blue Book*.[91]
On the 31st Cambon's efforts were supplemented
by Viviani's appeals for an English decision to
stand by France, and particularly by Poincaré's
direct telegram to George V asking him to make
a declaration that England could be counted in
on the side of France and Russia. All of
these appeals were hypocritically based upon the
allegation that such a decision would make for
peace by restraining Germany, though all requests from the 29th onward were made after
the Russian decision upon the measures which
were certain to provoke war.[92]

The concentrated assault on the 31st was too
much for Grey. He broke down under the pres-

sure and, though he would not yet give Cambon any definite promise, he began to prepare the ground for the decision.   He knew that he would have the greatest difficulty in swinging England for war to support France on the basis of an agreement which he and Asquith had repeatedly stated to the House of Commons did not exist. Some high moral issue must be sought, and only the possibility of a German invasion of Belgium seemed to present itself for this purpose. Hence, on the 31st he telegraphed to the British Minister in Brussels: [93]

You should say that I assume that the Belgian Government will maintain to the utmost of her power her neutrality, which I desire and expect other Powers to uphold and observe.   You should inform the Belgian Government that an early reply is desired.

Belgium replied at once: [94]

Belgium expects and desires that other Powers will observe and uphold her neutrality, which she intends to maintain to the utmost of her power.

On the same day Grey inquired of the French and German governments what their attitudes would be with regard to the invasion of Belgium. The French, quite naturally, replied that they would respect it.[95]   It was a diplomatic joke of the first order for Grey to propound this question to France, as nothing could have been fur-

ther from French intentions than to take a step
so obviously in the face of British opinion at a
time when all hinged on British support. It
was equivalent to Senator Butler asking Frank
Stearns to declare himself for Calvin Coolidge
in the presidential campaign of 1924. Germany
would not commit herself in reply to Grey's
question, so Grey felt very comfortable and quite
hopeful of being able to use the Belgian issue
to arouse British opinion against Germany. He
met something of a reverse the next day, however, when he learned from the German Ambassador that Germany would not invade Belgium
if England would declare her neutrality. This
would have upset his plans completely, and Grey
coldly refused the German proposal.[96] It prevented him, however, from having courage to declare himself for France on August 1st.

On the 2nd of August the pressure from
France and Russia was augmented by that in
England. Grey had been importuned to intervene by Nicolson and Crowe in the Foreign Office (see especially *British Documents,* Nos. 101,
369 and enclosure), and now he was besieged by
Bonar Law, Maxse and others of the "war gang"
in the Conservative Party. On the night of
August 1st the "war hawks" among Conservatives were brought together in a secret conference by Leo J. Maxse, editor of the *National Review* and the most vocal and detestable of British
chauvinists—a man wholly comparable in his

views to General Bernhardi, Ernst Haase, Karl Peters, Déroulède and Barrès. They formulated the following letter, which was taken to Asquith and Grey early in the afternoon of August 2nd: [97]

DEAR MR. ASQUITH,—

Lord Lansdowne and I feel it our duty to inform you that in our opinion, as well as in that of all the colleagues whom we have been able to consult, it would be fatal to the honour and security of the United Kingdom to hesitate in supporting France and Russia at the present juncture and we offer our unhesitating support to the Government in any measures they may consider necessary for that object.

Yours very truly
A. BONAR LAW.

At least Maxse, Law, *et al.* were frank in their statement of the grounds of British intervention. As Loreburn says: [98] "Not a word in it, observe, about Belgium. To support France and Russia: that was the thing to be done." The land legislation and Irish Home Rule were probably uppermost in their minds.

We may pause here to indicate that Grey not only secretly and arbitrarily brought England into war, but he also committed party treason in addition. The Liberal Party was at this time engaged in the most important program of social legislation in the history of government, and was, in particular, attacking the land problem for the first time in a serious fashion. [99] Perhaps their most relentless and implacable enemy in England at the time was this same Andrew Bonar Law. At a time when, according to Churchill, a majority of the Liberal Cabinet were against Grey, and when Morley, Burns and Trevelyan were about to resign, Grey deserted his own party and its interests and joined hands with his enemies. His act was symbolic of the effect of the War upon the Liberal Party as a whole: it killed it as a real political force in England, in the same way that Woodrow Wilson's entry into the World War destroyed the Democratic Party as an active and constructive force in American political life. And the British loss was a far more serious one, as the English Liberal Party was a much more powerful factor in world progress in 1914 than the Democratic Party, even in the early days of Wilson's administration. The Manchester *Guardian* clearly pointed out in 1914 that to enter the War meant the destruction of the Liberal Party in England: "It is a war to the knife between it and Liberalism. Either it kills us or we kill it."

This ultimatum of the British reactionaries brought action from Grey at once. He acceded to Cambon's demand and handed him the long-awaited document to the effect that: [100]

I am authorized to give an assurance that, if the German fleet come into the Channel or through the North Sea to undertake hostile operations against French coasts or shipping, the British fleet will give all the protection in its power.

This assurance is, of course, subject to the policy of his Majesty's Government receiving the support of Parliament, and must not be taken as binding his Majesty's Government to take any action until the above contingency of action by the German fleet takes place.

To Lord Bertie in Paris he reiterated the statement: [101] "It did not bind us to go to war with Germany unless the German fleet took the action indicated." This is particularly important to remember, because, on the next day, and before Grey's speech, Germany offered to refrain absolutely from all attacks upon the French coast if England would refrain from intervention. Moreover, Lichnowsky made the astonishing suggestion that Germany might be willing to respect the integrity of France and the French colonies in the event of war. This shows that Grey was not legally bound after August 3rd by his letter to Cambon on November 22, 1912; he was not even bound by his agreement of August 2, 1914. Nor can he find justification in the Belgian issue, for he gave Cambon his promise before Belgium had even been threatened by Germany, and after Germany had proposed to keep out of Belgium if England would remain neutral. Premier Pashitch's letter to his chief of staff on July 31st, indicates that he had British assurance of intervention if France and Germany entered the war.[102]

The above facts show that there was nothing which Germany could have done in 1914 to keep

England out of the War. Germany was pressing upon Vienna the diplomatic plans most highly approved by Grey on July 30th, when the Russian mobilization was ordered that made war inevitable. This fatal mobilization was encouraged and supported unconditionally by France, and Grey persisted in coming to the aid of France, though all the foundations of his obligation to do so had evaporated before he made his speech asking Parliament for permission to support France. Not only did Grey refuse to stand with Germany for peace through diplomatic pressure of the sort which he had himself warmly seconded; he also refused to attempt to dissuade Russia from mobilization; and he likewise refused to refrain from attacking Germany after Germany had proposed not to invade Belgium, had agreed not to attack the French Channel ports, and had asked Grey to formulate any set of conditions for British neutrality.[103]

As to the motives for this absolute and adamant determination to enter the War, we are probably safe in saying that with Grey, Asquith and Haldane it was primarily a conviction of national interest, as well as a sense of obligation of honor to support France. Unquestionably, with the reactionary clique led by Maxse, Law, Carson, and the Harmsworth press, it was chiefly a desire to crush Germany, and to forestall the Liberal land reforms and Irish Home Rule program with the aid of France wholly secondary.[104]

The degree to which Grey was torn by conflicting convictions, his partial appreciation of Germany's efforts for peace, and his qualms about the wisdom of his commitments to France are all well brought out in his telegram to Sir Edward Goschen on July 30th. In this he told Goschen to inform Bethmann-Hollweg that if any way could be found to get through the 1914 crisis without war, Grey would see to it that a European organization including Germany would be created in the place of the alliance of Russia, France and England against Germany. In other words, when it was too late Grey both saw and admitted the futility and failure of his balance of power scheme.[105] As Dr. Henderson says of this significant passage in the telegram to Goschen: [106] "Grey himself, in the end, we know, saw the enormity of what he had done. As he stood naked and shivering before the spectre of death, he repented, and said to the Germans":

If the peace of Europe can be preserved, and the present crisis safely passed, my own endeavor will be to promote some arrangement to which Germany could be a party, by which she could be assured that no aggressive or hostile policy would be pursued against her or her allies by France, Russia, and ourselves, jointly or separately.

But the Russian mobilization had already been let loose, and Cambon was shortly afterwards to overcome Grey. Not until after the four years of carnage and then seven years of blind diplomacy of revenge and recrimination among former allies was Europe, at Locarno, to realize even in part the vision which Grey held up for a moment on July 30, 1914, and then allowed to drop into the mire of the Franco-Russian will for war.

7. Why Grey Threw England into the War

In his recent memoirs Grey takes occasion to justify his attitude towards intervention in 1914. He puts first the agreements with France, but on the basis of English interests rather than technical obligation. It is significant that he admits that Cambon, quite wisely, stressed England's interests rather than her obligations to France throughout the period of his pestering Grey from July 30th to August 2nd.[107] Grey's attempt to justify his conduct towards Germany is, quite inevitably, entirely misleading and evasive. He charges time and again that Germany rejected his plan for a conference, and implies that this was the only diplomatic proposal during the crisis.[108] He exploits again the threadbare and preposterous untruth that Germany was overwhelmingly more powerful than the Entente in a military sense.[109]   He holds that France recognized this enormous superiority of Germany and stood in abject dread of war: [110]

France, indeed, dreaded war, and did all she could to avoid it.   French minds were probably more preoccupied with the awful peril of war to France than with the dread of war as a general catastrophe.   The immense growth and strength of Germany had smothered all French intention to attempt a *revanche.*

Apparently forgetful of the above he tells us some forty pages further on in the same volume: [111]

It must be remembered that both British and French military opinion of the highest order held (in 1914) that the French Army and the British Expeditionary Force would together be able to resist successfully a German attack, even if France and Britain were alone and unsupported by Russia.

When we remember that Poincaré was telling Izvolski two years before, prior to the enormous Russian army increases, that the French General Staff held that France and Russia alone could whip Germany and Austria,[112] we may doubt the intensity of the fear of Germany entertained by Poincaré, Millerand, Delcassé, Viviani, and Messimy.

Not only was Germany powerful; according to Grey she was equally bellicose.   To clinch this he cites the opinion of President Wilson's representative, Colonel Edward M. House, who had just come from Germany to England in July, 1914, and confirmed Grey's opinion of the belligerent state of the German psychology: [113]

Earlier in the summer Colonel House had been in London, and I had seen him then. He had just come from Berlin, and he had spoken with grave feeling of the impression he had received there; how the air seemed full of the clash of arms, of readiness to strike. This might have been discounted as the impression which would naturally have been produced on an American seeing at close quarters a continental military system for the first time. It was as alien to our temperament as to his, but it was familiar to us. We had lived beside it for years; we had known and watched its growth ever since 1870. But House was a man of exceptional knowledge and cool judgment.

Since Grey published in his memoirs this alleged opinion rendered by Colonel House, von Jagow, German Foreign Secretary in 1914, has published the following letter of Colonel House to the Kaiser on July 8, 1914: [114]

London, July 8, 1914.

Sir!

Your Imperial Majesty will doubtless recall our conversation at Potsdam, and that with the President's consent and approval I came to Europe for the purpose of ascertaining whether or not it was possible to bring about a better understanding between the Great Powers, to the end that there might be a continuation of peace, and later a beneficent economic readjustment which a lessening of armaments would insure. Because of the commanding position your Majesty occupies, and be- cause of your well-known desire to maintain peace, I came, as your Majesty knows, directly to Berlin.   I can never forget the gracious acceptance of the gen- eral purposes of my mission, the masterly exposition of the world wide political conditions as they exist to-day and the prophetic forecast as to the future which your Majesty then made. I received every reasonable as- surance of your Majesty's cordial approval of the President's purpose, and I left Germany happy in the belief that your Majesty's great influence would be thrown in behalf of peace and the broadening of the world's commerce. . . .

I have the honor to be, Sir, with the greatest respect, your Majesty's very obedient Servant,

EDWARD M. HOUSE.

In the recently published *Intimate Papers of Colonel House,* edited by Professor Charles Sey- mour, we find a complete substantiation of this letter published by von Jagow.   In fact, in his papers Colonel House is even more decisive in declaring his convictions as to the pacific philos- ophy and program of the Kaiser, and he confirms the thesis of the present writer that the Kaiser was opposed to war because he recognized that it was to the interest of Germany to continue peaceful methods.   House, on the other hand, describes George V as "the most pugnacious monarch loose in these parts."

Grey also attempts to excuse his conduct in 1914 on the basis of the assertion, similar to that exploited by Poincaré, Viviani and Asquith, to the effect that Germany's peace efforts in 1914 were of no significance because Bethmann-Hollweg had no power whatever, the general staff being in control from the first.[115]   We now know that Bethmann-Hollweg was in absolute control of the situation until at least twenty hours after the order had been issued for the Russian general mobilization.   But the supreme absurdity in Grey's apologia comes in his statement of just why, after all, he knew that Germany wanted war in 1914.   In answering this question he makes the most preposterous statement which has thus far been uttered among the diverse reasons which have been put forward for holding Germany guilty in 1914.   Not even James M. Beck has delivered himself of such puerile nonsense.   Grey's reason is as follows: [116]

The precedent of 1870 was ominous; we all knew how Prussian militarism had availed itself of this time and season of the year to strike.   The same time and season of the year were now approaching.

This passage appears to the writer to be easily the nadir point of drivel to which the Entente mythology has descended, compared with which Mr. Morgenthau's Potsdam Conference is a dignified and credible tale.

But after all his diversified quibbling, Grey comes back to the fact that the real reason for his entering the War was because he felt that it was for the best interests of England to do so. In a long, and one of the most eloquent, passages of his memoirs Grey sets forth why he believes that it was to the interest of England to enter the war in 1914: [117]

Paris would have been taken according to the German calculation. Paris very nearly was taken; there was nothing to spare. If there had been lacking anything, French or British, that was used to stop the retreat and accomplish the battle of the Marne, the Germans would have reached Paris; the absence of the British Expeditionary Force would have made a difference that would have been fatal. How long France would have been able to hold out after Paris fell is matter for military conjecture. Her fleet having to contain the Austrian Fleet in the Mediterranean could not have kept the Atlantic and Channel sea communications open. France would have been cut off from foreign supplies of iron and coal, of which some of her most valuable supplies would have been in German hands, as indeed they actually were even after the battle of the Marne. The end was certain. Huge defeats of Russian armies would have followed; and, with no prospect of recovery in France, those elements in Russia that were always susceptible to German influence would have asserted themselves. Russia would have made peace in no very long time; especially if Germany, having gained the day, had been wise enough to make the terms appear easy. Then Germany would have been supreme on the Continent. Belgium would have been under her heel. The fear of the fate of Belgium would have been before the eyes of every neutral State; the position of Italy, who had refused to join the other two members of the Triple Alliance in the war, would not have been pleasant.

Consider what the position of Britain would have been. We should have been isolated; we should have had no friend in the world; no one would have hoped or feared anything from us, or thought our friendship worth having.

We should have been discredited, should have been held to have played an inglorious and ignoble part. Even in the United States we should have suffered in good opinion. Those Americans who were outspokenly pro-Ally and who wanted the United States to join the Allies at once much earlier than their own country eventually did, would have despised us. We would have lost what pro-British sympathy there was in the United States, and we should have gained nothing there: the feeling that was indifferent about us would have remained indifferent; the feeling that was anti-British would have been anti-British still. Every neutral country would have held that we had turned our back on a clear obligation to Belgium and done this in spite of the Belgian appeal and of the fight she herself was making against overwhelming odds.

We should have been hated. Even after the Franco-

Prussian War of 1870 we incurred much odium for having stood aside. I think the odium was then quite unreasonable, but the *tertius gaudens* is always hated. Our intense unpopularity on the Continent at some previous times has been due largely to the opinion that we were always taking a hand and never taking a side. In those days we had boasted of a "splendid isolation"— in other words, of having no friend. Of late years we had found the position of having no friend to be unsafe; we had made friends. If we had stood aside now, we should again have had no friends. France and Russia would not have loved Germany after the war, but in one thing they would have been ready to join with her, and this would have been in a policy directed against Britain, who had stood aside while they suffered. In Germany militarism and navalism would have been supreme. The Socialism in Germany of which we heard so much, counted for nothing on the outbreak of war. For a time, after a triumphant war, it must have been still more subordinate; if it had become troublesome, its energies would have been turned into patriotic channels once more, this time in war against Britain. And that war we should certainly have had to face. Germany would have wielded the whole diplomatic strength of the Continent. For a time we might have struggled on ingloriously, squeezed and thwarted everywhere. There would have been weakness, moreover, inside the Empire. What the Dominions would have thought I do not venture to say, but quite a substantial section of British opinion would have regarded with shame the conduct of this country in standing aside; some of our self-respect would have gone. Finally, when the German fleet was

ready, war would have been forced on us, and we should
have been found dispirited, half beaten before the war
began. By that time the full range of the big gun, the
extended use of the submarine, would have been known;
the French shores would have been in unfriendly hands,
and the Channel would have been closed to us. Can
anyone say that this picture is remote from probability? If anyone thinks so, let him read the second edition of von Bülow's book and the *Memoirs and Letters
of von Kiderlen Waechter,* and consider German feeling and the part played by German militarism in policy
before the war. Then let him picture to himself faithfully what German militarism and its policy would have
meant for us after a war from which Germany had
emerged supreme.

Grey thus comes to the same ultimate conclusion which Dr. Ewart has arrived at in his
monumental treatise in dealing with the causes
for England's entry into the war: [118]

British self-interest was the reason for the form of
the Belgian treaty in 1839; for entente relations with
France and Russia; for support of these powers in various crises; for military and naval conventions with
France; for naval arrangements with Russia; for Sir
Edward Grey's letters to the French ambassador of
22 November, 1912, and 2 August, 1914; and for entering upon the war. . . .

Speaking generally, then, we say that the United
Kingdom joined in entente relations with France
and Russia, and entered the war because her inter-

ests pointed a course in opposition to Germany. . . .

The action of the United Kingdom in 1870 was inconsistent with the idea of existing obligation to defend Belgian neutrality.

British opinion in 1887 repudiated liability to withstand the passage of German armies through Belgium.

Sir Edward Grey's attitude in 1914, as revealed in the diplomatic correspondence, was inconsistent with the idea of the existence of treaty obligation to defend Belgian neutrality.

It is clear therefore that the United Kingdom was under no treaty obligation to interfere in the war. . . .

Though usually well hidden beneath many assertions of disinterested motive—hidden sometimes from the asserters themselves—British self-interest was the reason why British troops fought in Flanders and elsewhere. It was not because Serbia was right and Austria-Hungary wrong. The merits of the quarrel between these two countries were unconsidered and deemed to be irrelevant. It was not because of obligation to France —although obligation existed. And it was not because of obligation to Belgium—for there was none. It was because British interests were at stake.

Professor Charles Austin Beard, in a lengthy review of Grey's memoirs, comes to a similar conclusion: [119]

The most extraordinary feature of Viscount Grey's whole survey is the practical indifference shown to anything outside of the British Empire which does not impinge immediately and obviously on British interests.

8. What Grey's Folly Cost England

It might be worth while to scrutinize briefly the validity of Sir Edward's catalogue of the calamities which would have come to England if she had not entered the War on the side of France and Russia, and to present a brief review of the disasters which actually accompanied England's participation in the conflict. In the first place, there is no proof whatever that things would have actually turned out as Grey predicts if England had not gone into the War. Instead of German animosity and an ultimate war to the death between England and Germany, the result would much more likely have been German gratitude and an Anglo-German Entente which would have dominated the Eastern Hemisphere. The military crowd in France and Russia would have been thoroughly discredited, and the Russian Revolution would have come sooner than it did. Grey fails completely to mention the point made by the Manchester *Guardian,* namely, the disastrous results to England of a decisive and early Entente victory which would have strengthened the Russian autocracy, given Russia the Straits, and increased the Russian menace to the British Empire in the Near East. America would have gone in its opinion as England did, because our European news came chiefly through the Harmsworth papers. Without the English navy to blockade German ports, we might have sold munitions to both groups of combatants, and hence loved them both, with our affection distributed in direct proportion to our sales. If the German navy had been able to blockade the French ports, we should have sold our products primarily to the Central Powers, and would have loved them as we actually did the Entente after 1914. Still further, Grey fails to state that if he had declared for strict English neutrality as early as July 24th there might not have been any war at all.

But all of the above is highly hypothetical. We have no means of knowing just what would have happened if England had not intervened, but we do know what did happen to England because she did come in. The catalogue of these losses and disasters seems to the present writer much more impressive than the highly hypothetical list of potential ills which possibly might have fallen to the lot of England if she had refrained from hostilities. To follow Sir Edward's precedent in the scale of values we may first mention the destruction of England's material prosperity caused by the War. In 1914 English manufacturing and trade had reached a high level of development, unemployment was relatively slight, and the excellent system of social legislation was offering protection and security to the laboring classes. England was in better condition economically and socially than at any previous time in her history.

As the result of the War, with its destruction of the prosperity of other countries and the growth of the Ghandi movement and similar tendencies towards the boycott of British goods, England descended to a lower level of economic misery than at any earlier period of her historic development. The aftermath of the Napoleonic Wars was far less severe in its economic incidence.[120] More than a million have been unemployed, and have been kept alive by government allowances which have enormously increased the operating expenses of the government. The War, indeed, has brought England to a situation where it will be faced for generations by the alternative of widespread unemployment, poverty and misery or wholesale emigration to other parts of the world. The poverty, misery, unemployment, sickness, sorrow and other incidental effects of the War and the period since have served greatly to lower the morale of the English people.[121] Incidentally, it may be remarked that the War destroyed for the time being the purchasing power of England's best continental customers, Germany and Russia, in the interest of her least important customer among the major states, France.

To this loss of prosperity must be added the enormous increase in the public debt of England,

together with the terrific advance in the burden
of taxation to pay off the war expenses—a burden of taxation which must be met by a country
on a much lower level of financial power than
was maintained in 1914. England's pre-War
debt was only £700,000,000. In 1919 it stood at
£6,750,000,000.[122] It must, further, be remembered that the financial incidence of the War fell
particularly hard upon England, as she has been
the one major European power which has attempted to keep her exchange up to par, and has
avoided the seductive temptation of inflation.

Next to the economic losses of England we
may put the loss of life.[123] The known and assumed dead from England who fell in the World
War are estimated at 938,904. If we follow the
London *Morning Post* and give each a capitalized valuation of £828, the economic loss of
the English dead amounts to £695,420,512.
Though Sir Edward would probably refuse to
recognize such an item, it might be timidly suggested that there are certain incidental features
of this toll of dead, such as the sorrow, suffering
and dependency of bereaved relatives which must
be added to the economic loss of England on the
battlefield. In addition to the dead, there were
617,740 English soldiers seriously wounded and
1,441,394 wounded in differing degrees. It
must be borne in mind that, aside from economic
waste and the psychological suffering, this loss

of English manhood in death and serious maim-
ing means a great biological lesion in the English
nation. The best physical types of England
have been removed in considerable part by the
War. All the eugenic proposals that Francis
Galton, Karl Pearson and their disciples could
propose and institute in a century or more were
far more than offset by the biological incidence of
the War upon England.

In international relations the War ended with
equally unfortunate results for England. The
Triple Entente was completely disrupted. Russia was lost by internal corruption and revolution. France was lost through the continuation
of her aggressive plans for the destruction of
Germany after the Armistice, in which, be it said
to her everlasting credit, England at last refused
to participate.[124] How much better it would
have been for England, France and the world if
England had "ditched" the Poincaré gang in
1913 instead of ten years later! Instead of
the probable German gratitude and good-will,
which would have resulted from British non-
intervention in 1914, there has developed in Germany a far more deep-seated hatred of England
than existed before the War.

Again, the War brought to England the greatest humiliation in her history. In the place of
the purely mythological German hegemony on

the Continent has appeared the actual French hegemony. Instead of the inferior German navy, which never in any menacing degree challenged the naval supremacy of England, we have the actual enormous preponderance of the French aircraft. For the first time in her history, England is no longer free from invasion. Likewise, for the first time in her national existence she has come to the point where she dare not assume a wholly independent position in foreign policy because of the fear of invasion by a foreign country. She has been compelled to acquiesce in many aspects of French foreign policy on the Continent, of which she heartily disapproved, because she did not dare openly to break with France. The country, to protect whose Channel ports England made the above-mentioned enormous sacrifices, has become the most dangerous enemy England has ever known in her history, compared with which the French menace in the time of Napoleon was negligible. In the spring of 1924 many well-to-do parents in London had made arrangements with people in the country to take their children in the event of war with France and the consequent French air-raids upon London. Then, while there was much anti-English sentiment in Germany in 1914, the attitude of the average German towards England in 1914 was one of the warmest affection, not to say adulation, as compared with the sentiments entertained by the average Frenchman towards the English in 1927.

Finally, the War had a most unfortunate reaction upon the British Empire by stimulating nationalistic and independence movements everywhere. The temporary enthusiasm for united action, which was generated early in the War, has now suffered a great relapse, and few intelligent and informed observers doubt that the War greatly weakened the cohesive influences in the British Empire. Many of the most penetrating students of the problem even go so far as to state that the War meant the beginning of the end for the Empire.

Last, and not least, the War bore out the dire predictions of the Manchester *Guardian* in 1914 that it was an alternative of keeping out of the War or destroying the Liberal Party. To the writer this seems in many ways the most serious loss which England sustained during the War. In the writer's opinion the Liberal Party and its policy and achievements from 1905 to 1914 marked the highest level to which the socio-political development of mankind has ever attained. It was the one government which seemed to give proof that democracy might prove capable of coping with the complex problems of the post-Industrial Revolution age. Compared with it, the American government, even under

President Roosevelt, was crude, undeveloped and ineffective. Now it appears to be gone forever. The Labor Party is not yet prepared or powerful enough to take over the political and economic life of England, and the country seems committed indefinitely to the amiable and dignified futility of the Tories.

Such is the debt which, by his own confession, England owes to her late Foreign Secretary, Viscount Grey. These are the cold facts to be opposed to his nebulous and dubious hypotheses which were quoted above. George V is said to have remarked to Walter Hines Page shortly after the outbreak of hostilities: "My God, Mr. Page, what else could we do?" [125] If Mr. Page were still in our midst the King now might well remark: "My God, Mr. Page, what else could we have done which would have been worse for England?" And still Lord Grey is more revered in England today than in 1914. Even Mr. A. G. Gardiner and the Manchester *Guardian,* who bitterly attacked him in 1914, now hold that his weak, dishonest and evasive memoirs constitute the vindication of his career. These memoirs seem likely to create a "Grey Myth" of even more heroic proportions than the "Page Legend" in America.

As to the primary responsibility of Grey, Crowe and Nicolson for pushing England into the War there can be no doubt. When, in 1915,

Sazonov was inclined to criticize Grey for his policy in regard to Italy Benckendorff telegraphed to Sazonov on April 6, 1915: [126]

I should like to be able to help modify your severe judgment of Grey in view of the services he has rendered us since the beginning of the crisis. Let me add for your own most personal information that there is a feeling which almost never quits Grey and that to some extent is justified—namely, that, in the moment of the indecision of the English public and of all the ministers, it was Grey above all who dragged England into the war, and that for this reason he always has a feeling of the most profound personal responsibility quite apart from that of the Cabinet. Still I don't see any symptom that his energy of decision is affected by it.

Indeed, Grey admits his personal responsibility in his memoirs and allows the reader to pass judgment upon him on the basis of the wisdom of the decision.* He unquestionably carried the day by his famous speech of August 3rd, together with his later exploitation of the Belgian issue. Dr. Ernest F. Henderson thus describes Grey's speech in what appears to the writer to be an admirable characterization—stressing the remarkable combination of fundamental deception and ostensible moral earnestness: [127]

It was a masterly speech, one of the most masterly ever delivered. Sir Edward actually succeeded in mak-

* The new British documents show Grey much more loath to enter the conflict than Nicolson or Crowe.

ing black seem white to the majority in that House—
said what he did not mean and meant what he did not
say: built up a structure on no foundation—knocked
the props away himself—and let it hang dangling in
the air. A masterly speech! The last and greatest
achievement of Sir Edward's persuasive eloquence.
His evident deep emotion, his undoubted earnestness
and sincerity, his certainty that he was right, won him
the victory.

As bearing upon the discrepancy between the
theory of democratic Britain, with its assumed
Parliamentary control of foreign policy, and the
actual autocracy and secrecy of Grey and his associates, we may here appropriately call attention to the fact that the mobilization of the British Expeditionary Force was ordered on August
3rd before Grey had received Parliamentary approval of his policy of intervention and before
Belgium had been invaded.

While scholars may differ widely upon the subject, it seems to the present writer that the "verdict of history" will be in harmony with the
words of a critic speaking from the floor of the
House of Commons after Sir Edward had finished his speech: [128]

I regret very much that at the end of eight years the
best you can say of the policy that has been pursued—
of the Triple Entente—is that it should have landed us
in a war like this!

9. *Grey's Psychology in 1914*

There is an interesting problem connected with the development of Grey's psychology during this period; the question of how the man who loved peace in the abstract allowed himself to get into war in the concrete with no adequate cause, and ended by justifying his conduct. The writer has examined the various critiques of and apologies for the conduct of Sir Edward Grey in 1914, and the following interpretation seems to him the most plausible and probable: Grey was a man of peace in the sense of being for peace as long as it preserved the *status quo* and protected the integrity and entirety of British imperial interests. It must be recognized that it is easy to be for peace when a country has attained to the "lordship of the world," and merely desires to be maintained securely in this position. When anything seemed likely to challenge British interests Grey was as alert as Izvolski and Poincaré. A number of things prevented him from taking in 1914 the statesmanlike stand which he had assumed in the Balkan crisis of 1912–13. He hesitated and vacillated in his policy and attitude until the situation had developed so far towards a general European war as to be difficult to recall or control. Not until August 1st, apparently, did Sir Edward come to see that peace could be maintained only by restraining the Rus-

sian mobilization. He refused to take any positive steps to obstruct this. This made war between Austria and Germany and France and
Russia inevitable, and Grey knew that this would
force him, sooner or later, to reveal the nature of
his secret negotiations with France and Russia.
His guilty feeling in this regard, caused by his
previous denials of any such arrangements, led
to an inflation of his compensatory mechanisms
and the resulting ardent desire to justify his acts
and prove them the desirable policy for Britain.
His sensitiveness on this point made him quite
unwilling to concede for a minute the right to
question his statesmanship and personal rectitude. His *amour-propre* was still further affected by the resignation of Morley and Burns
from the Cabinet and his criticism by others in
the Cabinet and the House of Commons. Under the circumstances he had to go through with
the war policy to save his face. The conflict between his underlying desire for peace and his
aversion to the concrete horrors of war, on the
one hand, and his injured pride and sense of
power and responsibility which led to war, on
the other, made him more than usually "muddle-
headed" in the crucial periods of the crisis, especially after July 30th. A steady determination
to go to war if France did, no matter under what
conditions, was the only fixed idea which Grey
preserved throughout the crisis—the only point

on which there was no vacillation.   This rendered him unusually susceptible to the suggestions and control of those who, like Maxse, Law, Crowe and Nicolson, were in no sense confused, but knew just exactly what they wanted and precisely how they expected to get it.   Once the decision for war had been made, Grey was hard put to it for some noble moral issue to soothe his conscience on the matter of his secret diplomacy and the adoption of a method which was repugnant to his finer sensibilities and deepest convictions. This he found in the German invasion of Belgium, and he quite naturally exploited this heaven-sent opportunity to the utmost.

V. SIR EDWARD GREY AND THE BELGIAN IMPOSTURE

No legend with respect to the causes of the War is more firmly established, and at the same time more absolutely without foundation in fact, than the assumption that Great Britain entered the War because of the German invasion of Belgium.   The British ultimatum to Germany on August 4th stated that: "His Majesty's Government feel bound to take all steps in their power to uphold the neutrality of Belgium and the observance of a treaty to which Germany is as much a party as ourselves."   In his speech on

August 6, 1914, Asquith contended that the object of England's entry into the War was: [129]

To fulfil a solemn international obligation, an obligation which, if it had been entered into between private persons in the ordinary concerns of life, would have been regarded as an obligation not only of law but of honor, which no self-respecting man could possibly have repudiated.

Again, in his apology, *The Genesis of the War*, he repeats the same point of view: [130]

The German Government had deliberately outraged, by one and the same act (the German invasion of Belgium), two deep-seated sentiments, which alike in Great Britain and Ireland, are always alive and ready to show themselves alert: the sense of the sanctity of treaty obligations; and the feeling that it is impossible for people of our blood and history to be content to stand by, and help keep a ring while a big bully sets to work to thrash and trample to the ground a victim, who has given him no provocation, and who is his equal in everything but size and physical strength.

We have already stated Grey's view as expressed in the British ultimatum to Germany, though it is interesting to note that on August 2nd, in answer to a direct question by Paul Cambon, Grey had stated that he could not yet tell whether the Cabinet would decide that an invasion of Belgium was a valid cause for British intervention.[131] On August 3rd, in his great speech before the

House, he took the view that the Belgian issue was of the highest importance and a binding obligation upon England: [132]

The treaty is an old treaty—1839—and that was the view taken of it in 1870. It is one of those treaties which are founded, not only on consideration for Belgium, which benefits under the treaty, but in the interests of those who guarantee the neutrality of Belgium. The honour and interests are, at least, as strong to-day as in 1870, and we cannot take a more narrow view or a less serious view of our obligations, and of the importance of those obligations, than was taken by Mr. Gladstone's government in 1870.

In spite of the fact that two days before he had had a definite proposal from the German Ambassador to the effect that Germany would keep out of Belgium if England would remain neutral, Grey devoted a large share of his speech to an appeal for British intervention in case Germany invaded Belgium. It was the first public launching of the barrage of propaganda designed to obscure the real reason for intervention. In his memoirs he continues unflinchingly his thesis that England was legally bound to enter the War to defend Belgium and that this was a leading cause of British participation.[133] A similar view was expressed by Lloyd George in 1915: [134]

Our honour as a nation is involved in this war, because we are bound in an honorable obligation to defend the independence, the liberty, the integrity of a small neighbour that has lived peaceably; but she could not have compelled us, being weak. The man who declines to discharge his debt because his creditor is too poor to enforce it, is a blackguard.

Likewise, George V, in his speech to Parliament on September 18, 1914, said: [135]

After every endeavor had been made by my government to preserve the peace of the world, I was compelled in the assertion of treaty obligations deliberately set at naught, and for the protection of the public laws of Europe, and the vital interests of my Empire, to go to war.

We shall now proceed to show how completely lacking in any foundation in fact are all of the above contentions by distinguished Englishmen. We have even decided that it is best not to treat the Belgian issue as an integral part of the British diplomacy in the crisis of 1914, as it had no primary influence on the British decisions. Grey agreed to participate entirely irrespective of Belgium, and he refused to agree not to participate in case Belgian neutrality was respected. The only relation that Belgium had to British intervention was that Grey refused to promise Cambon definitely that England would intervene until he had reasonable assurance that Germany would invade Belgium (after her neutrality proposal had been coldly rejected by

Grey) and that Belgium would resist. This would provide the lofty moral issue which would inflame the British public against Germany, and quickly lead them to forget that England was actually going into the War because of secret promises to France, the nature and existence of which Grey had repeatedly denied, and had partially obscured even in his speech of August 3rd. He tells us himself in his memoirs he would have tried to put England into the War irrespective of Belgium, and that he would have resigned if he had failed.[136] In our refutation of Grey's Belgian imposture of 1914 we shall not rely upon German critics or British socialists, but upon the documents and the analyses of the legal facts by the two most distinguished British lawyers who have examined the problem, the Earl of Loreburn, former Lord Chancellor of England, and Dr. J. S. Ewart, one of the ablest of Canadian jurists.

In the first place, we may point out that there was no treaty obligation whatever binding England to protect the neutrality of Belgium. Such an obligation was alleged by Grey and his associates to reside in the treaty of 1839, but this only bound the various signatory powers not to violate Belgian neutrality themselves. It did not in any way bind them to intervene to protect Belgian neutrality.[137] Loreburn has summarized these facts in succinct fashion: [138]

Very few people will be found to deny that we have great interests in preventing a great military Power, be it Germany or be it France, from securing a mastery of the Belgian coast. Nor can it be denied that the spectacle of some military bully devastating that small kingdom, while we passively looked on across the narrow seas, would be regarded as a dishonor and an affront to the United Kingdom. In these circumstances it does not much signify whether or not we were in 1914 bound by Treaty to defend Belgium against invasion. For the sake of historical accuracy, however, it is right to say that we were not so bound either by the Treaty of 1839 or by any other instrument. All that we did in 1839 was to sign, together with Austria, France, Prussia, Russia and Holland, an agreement that Belgium should be a perpetually neutral State. We bound ourselves, as did the others, not to violate that neutrality, but did not bind ourselves to defend it against the encroachment of any other Power. That is the plain effect of the document.

The distinguished English historian, G. P. Gooch, in the latest authoritative treatment of the subject in the third volume of the *Cambridge History of British Foreign Policy*, comes to the same conclusion as Loreburn:

The Guarantee of 1839, as Palmerston pointed out, gave a right, but did not impose an obligation to defend Belgian neutrality. Gladstone's Treaties with France and Prussia in 1870 were only necessary because that of 1839 did not automatically invoke action.

Gladstone, in 1870, far from contending that the treaty of 1839 obligated England to intervene to protect Belgian neutrality, actually recognized that it did not, and secured the consent of France and Prussia to a new treaty binding them not to violate Belgium during the course of that particular war under penalty of British intervention. The British intervention under such circumstances was to be limited solely to operations in Belgium. The treaty was to lapse upon the cessation of hostilities in the Franco-Prussian War, and conditions were to revert to the situation under the treaty of 1839. There was, thus, no precedent in Gladstone's action for the conduct of Grey in 1914, and Gladstone held that the treaty of 1839 did not require British intervention.[139]   He acted solely from the dictates of what he believed to be British interests. In 1887, when war between France and Germany seemed possible, British opinion was decidedly against the obligation of Great Britain to intervene to prevent the passage of German troops through Belgium. Dr. Ewart well summarizes the relevant facts in regard to the false statement of Grey and the British Cabinet in 1914 that England was under a definite treaty obligation to protect Belgium against foreign invasion:[140]

1. The Belgian treaty (really treaties) of 1839 contains no obligation to defend Belgium or Belgian neutrality.

2. The action of the United Kingdom in 1870 was inconsistent with the idea of existing obligation to defend Belgian neutrality.

3. British opinion in 1887 repudiated liability to withstand the passage of German armies through Belgium.

4. Sir Edward Grey's attitude in 1914, as revealed in the diplomatic correspondence, was inconsistent with the existence of treaty obligation to defend Belgian neutrality.

5. It is clear therefore that the United Kingdom was under no treaty obligation to intervene in the war.

6. Sir Edward Grey did not desire Belgian neutrality. He refused to agree to British neutrality on condition that Germany refrain from invasion of Belgium; and he urged Belgium to resist.

7. Before the German invasion of Belgium had commenced or been threatened, Sir Edward Grey, by his letter of 2 August, had made neutrality impossible.

8. Although for rallying purposes, Mr. Asquith told the public that they were fighting in pursuance of high moral duty, the efficacy of that sort of appeal disappeared under the stress of protracted war and was discarded.

9. British self-interest was the reason for the form of the Belgian treaty in 1839; for *entente* relations with France and Russia; for the support of these powers in various crises; for military and naval conventions with France; for naval arrangements with Russia; for Sir Edward Grey's letters to the French Ambassador of 22 November, 1912, and 2 August, 1914; and for entering upon the war.

Not only international lawyers and historians,

but every English statesman who faced the Belgian issue—Palmerston, Lord Derby, Gladstone and Salisbury—all agreed that the treaty of 1839 did not bind England to defend Belgian neutrality.

Another point of importance is the current assumption that neither France nor England has ever considered so base an act as the violation of Belgium, this being something which only a Teuton could contemplate. As a matter of historic fact Napoleon III tried to *annex* Belgium after the Austro-Prussian War of 1866, and in the spring of 1914 the King of Belgium expressed himself as more fearful of a French than a German invasion, and often complained of the nuisance of French spying on Belgian territory. From 1906 onward the British tried in vain to secure Belgian consent to the landing of a British expeditionary force on Belgian soil in the event of war, and then arrived at a determination to land the troops whether Belgium gave her consent or not. The Franco-British military plans in 1911, 1912 and 1913 were based upon the assumption of an advance through Belgium. In 1914 Germany "got the jump on them" because of the delay which Grey believed necessary in the process of bringing England into the War. This necessitated an alteration of the plan for the French offensive, and the attack was shifted from Belgium to

Alsace. In spite of the fact that as early as 1906 the French and British had known of the German plan to invade Belgium under pressure of sufficient military necessity, the French had not fortified the Belgian frontier to any significant extent, which proves that they presumed on repulsing the Germans on Belgian soil.[141] In any event the French and English would probably have allowed Germany to take the first step, so as to place the odium of the initiative upon Germany and turn the opinion of the world against her. To be sure, these facts do not justify the German invasion, and no reputable German from Bethmann-Hollweg down has ever contended that they did. What they do prove is that, in the words of Montgelas: [142] "It is not honest indignation, but pharisaical presumption on the part of England and France to represent the German plan of campaign as an unparalleled crime."

The official demand of Great Britain on July 31st that Germany and France declare publicly their attitude towards Belgium was purely hypocritical stage-play on the part of France and England. England knew that Germany would go through Belgium unless England promised neutrality, and France had been carefully coached by both French and English statesmen as to how she should respond. A country which would stage the ten kilometer withdrawal imposture and advise secrecy in Russian mobilization to influence England favorably would never have considered for a moment executing the supreme stupidity of invading Belgium before British participation had been either assured or absolutely precluded. The attempt to brand Germany as criminal because she did not give an unconditional negative to England's question is absurd. She would have been most foolish to surrender this one great potential lever on British neutrality without trying to secure some reciprocal British assurance. The astute procedure was to be non-committal in regard to Grey's question about Belgian neutrality on the 31st, and then attempt, through direct negotiation, to get England to promise neutrality if Germany would respect Belgian territory. This was exactly what Germany proceeded to do. On August 1st Prince Lichnowsky, German Ambassador at London, proposed to Grey that England remain neutral on condition that Germany keep out of Belgium. Upon Grey's refusal, he then asked Grey to formulate the conditions under which England would remain neutral. Grey refused this also. For this information we do not have to rely upon the explicit and wholly credible German sources,[143] but upon Sir Edward Grey's own telegram to Sir Edward Goschen, British Ambassador in Berlin. On August 1st Grey telegraphed to Goschen: [144]

He (Lichnowsky) asked me whether, if Germany gave a promise not to violate Belgian neutrality, we would engage to remain neutral.

I replied that I could not say that; our hands were still free, and we were considering what our attitude should be. All I could say was that our attitude would be determined largely by public opinion here, and that the neutrality of Belgium would appeal very strongly to public opinion here. I did not think that we could give a promise of neutrality on that condition alone.

The Ambassador pressed me as to whether I could not formulate conditions on which we would remain neutral. He even suggested that the integrity of France and her colonies might be guaranteed.

I said that I felt obliged to refuse definitely any promise to remain neutral on similar terms, and I could only say that we must keep our hands free.

How far Grey's hands were actually free in the light of his commitments and his psychology we have made clear earlier in the chapter. Loreburn has perfectly grasped the significance of the above telegram: [145]

If language means anything, this means that whereas Mr. Gladstone bound this country to war in order to safeguard Belgian neutrality, Sir Edward would not even bind this country to neutrality in order to save Belgium. He may have been right, but it was not for the sake of Belgian interests that he refused.

On August 27th Grey was asked whether he had ever submitted the offer of Lichnowsky to the

Cabinet for consideration. His answer was characteristic. He stated that the offer was purely personal and unofficial on the part of Lichnowsky, but he belied this statement by the fact that he gave a formal and official answer to Lichnowsky, telegraphed this answer officially and formally to the British Ambassador in Berlin, and submitted the German proposal to the Cabinet the next morning before the decision to inform Cambon that the agreement of November 22, 1912, still held with the British government. He also stated that he had formulated the conditions upon which England would remain neutral and had communicated these to the German Ambassador and to the House of Commons. But he informed Goschen that he had not done so, and there is no evidence in any speech or document to support his contention that he ever formulated the conditions of British neutrality.[146] In his memoirs Grey admits that he would have resigned if he had not been able to bring England into the War on the side of France even if Belgium had not been invaded.

After he had committed England to war on August 2nd, the one desire which was uppermost in Grey's mind was that Germany would invade Belgium, that Belgium would resist this invasion, and that Belgium would appeal for assistance to the Entente.[147] This would provide a second "brave and innocent little country" to aid the

British propaganda, Russia having intervened to protect the first "brave and innocent little country." The writer would yield to no one in his sincere belief in the bravery and innocence of Belgium, but it was not Belgian innocence and bravery which interested Sir Edward Grey early in August, 1914. After August 2nd, if there was anything in the world which Grey feared and desired to avert, it was the possibility that Germany might respect Belgian neutrality, or, if she did invade Belgium, that the Belgian attitude would be such that the Belgian issue would not constitute highly potent material for inflaming the British populace.

Grey's great anxiety after August 2nd lest Belgium would *not* be violated appears in his telegrams. As early as the 31st he informed the Belgian government that he assumed that the Belgians would resist a German invasion "to the utmost of their power." On August 3rd he was thrown into a panic when he learned that the Belgian government appealed to England merely for diplomatic intervention against Germany and had declined the aid of the French troops offered them to help repel the expected German invasion.[148] Belgium had also given definite information that it preferred to attempt to resist Germany unaided in a military way by the other powers. As this was after the expiration of the time-limit in the German ultimatum to Belgium, the situation was alarming for Grey. He might have to take the desperate chance of putting England into the War without the enormous psychological advantage of the Belgian appeal for military aid. [149] Determined not to lose this indispensable phase of propaganda for his policy, he practically went to the extreme of demanding that Belgium ask for the military aid of the Entente. His proposal in the following telegram to the British Minister in Brussels is certainly as near to the point of intimidation as he could have gone without insulting Belgian pride: [150]

You should inform Belgian Government that if pressure is applied to them by Germany to induce them to depart from neutrality, His Majesty's Government expect that they will resist by any means in their power, and that His Majesty's Government will support them in offering such resistance, and that His Majesty's Government in this event are prepared to join Russia and France, if desired, in offering to the Belgian Government at once common action for the purpose of resisting use of force by Germany against them, and a guarantee to maintain their independence and integrity in future years.

The Belgian government took the hint and replied: [151] "The Belgian Government are firmly determined to resist by all the means in their power. Belgium appeals to Great Britain,

France and Russia to coöperate as guaranteeing
Powers in the defence of her territory. There
should be concerted and joint action, to oppose
the forcible measures taken by Germany against
Belgium." As soon as this reply was received
from Belgium Grey breathed easily for the first
time since August 2nd, and confidently dispatched his ultimatum to Germany. The next
morning Asquith stated with great effect in the
House of Commons: [152]

> The House has read, and the country has read, of
> course, in the last few hours, the most pathetic appeal
> addressed by the King of Belgium, and I do not envy the
> man who can read that appeal with an unmoved heart.
> Belgians are fighting and losing their lives. What
> would have been the position of Great Britain to-day in
> the face of that spectacle, if we had assented to this in-
> famous proposal? [Prolonged applause.]

Asquith carelessly neglected to state that the
Belgians were losing their lives and having their
territory violated because Grey needed a lofty
altruistic motive for his determination to advance
the aims of the Franco-Russian Alliance.

In the light of such facts as that Belgium and
the Entente knew of the German plan of invasion from 1906 onward; that Great Britain had
been negotiating with Belgium for years in the
vain effort to secure Belgian consent to the landing of British troops in Blgium to repel this in-

vasion; that the Belgian King had said as late as the spring of 1914 that he feared a French invasion more than a German; that Germany had explicitly proposed to keep out of Belgium if England would remain neutral, and had been repulsed by Grey in this proposal; that Belgium preferred to resist alone in order to preserve her precedent of independence to the last; and that Grey himself extracted the Belgian appeal for British intervention from the Belgium government, the following statement from Grey's memoirs may be allowed to stand without comment: [153]

By the end of the week, on August 1, we had before us the announcement of the Belgian Government that Belgium would, if invaded, defend her own neutrality to the utmost of her power; that made the question straight and simple. Belgium at this stage made no appeal to the guaranteeing Powers. In this she acted properly and wisely. Such information as has come to my notice goes to show that up to the last moment, the Belgian Government did not believe that any Power intended to violate the Treaty of Guarantee. To appeal to the Powers would then have implied a suspicion that she did not entertain: to ask help from some of them, and not from all, would have laid her open to charges of siding with some against another, and thus departing from neutrality before this was threatened. But the announcement that, if her neutrality was assailed, she intended to defend herself, was important. If she were to acquiesce voluntarily, or even under duress, in the passage of German troops, we should be entitled to send troops to vindicate the neutrality and resist the violation of it; but it was clear that an appeal from her for help, when she was herself fighting for what we were pledged to defend, would be peculiarly strong and moving. How could we possibly resist it?

If it be asserted that Moltke had secretly drawn up the ultimatum to Belgium on July 26th, it may be answered that the Belgians had already begun to mobilize against the Germans by that time, and that by February, 1914, the English had determined the rate of exchange for payment of British soldiers fighting in Belgium.

The lawlessness of England during the World War in regard to the commercial rights of neutrals was far more serious and extensive than the German invasion of Belgium, while the British bullying of Greece during the period of the World War would thoroughly match Austria's attitude towards Serbia or the German attitude towards Belgium. During the War, in the effort to relieve Antwerp, France and England endeavored to violate Dutch neutrality. During the period of the War no country did more to make international law a "scrap of paper" than did Great Britain.[154] Finally, the one true and perfectly authenticated "atrocity" in the World War, and the situation which produced by far the greatest suffering and death among the civilian population was the illegal blockade of Germany, continued for months after the Armistice. Not only was this by far the most horrible and tragic indignity perpetrated on non-combatants during the World War, but it was also the one for which no plea of military necessity could be offered in extenuation or defense. For the perpetuation of this blockade Great Britain was very largely responsible. It could be justified only on the ground of weakening Germany and lessening future German competition through starving off some 800,000 German women and children. Indeed, it was defended on this basis by distinguished Englishmen. In fact, a noted English scholar who accepted a chair in the most honored of American universities at the close of the War is known by the writer to have advocated in a lecture before a leading women's college in this country the starvation of German babies. Yet even the unspeakable Prussians had food moving into Paris twenty-four hours after its capture in 1871. Of course, England could plead the right of self-preservation, but she cannot make such a plea in extenuation without fully admitting the validity of the similar German plea in regard to the invasion of Belgium or submarine warfare.

VI. ASQUITH AND GREY IN SELF-JUSTIFICATION

In the chapters on Russia and France we examined the apologies offered by Sazonov, Poincaré and Viviani in the light of the assumption that statesmen who allege that they were fighting purely in self-defense and had done everything possible to avert war would not need to falsify in their account of the events of the July crisis in 1914.   Such men should stand immaculate upon a pyramid of irrefragable facts. We indicated that with respect to straightforwardness and factual accuracy the apologetic works of Sazonov, Poincaré and Viviani left much to be desired.   Of all the major participants in the heroic tragedy of 1914 the two men with the highest reputation for veracity and command of relevant facts are Asquith and Grey, though their responses in the House of Commons before the War when interrogated on the matter of the British commitments to France should have demonstrated their subtlety in evasive foot-work.   We shall here examine the merits of the apologies by Asquith and Grey only very briefly, and by means of a catalogue of some of their more important statements concerning the crisis of 1914.   In large part we shall rest content by merely setting forth their views and allowing them to stand condemned out of their own mouths.   We shall, of course, in this way omit the even more damning case which could be established through a list of their "sins of omission."

In his *Genesis of the War,* published late in 1923, Asquith presents the following contentions: [155] that Sazonov from the first urged conciliatory methods on Serbia in the highest good faith; that Sazonov was willing at any time to discuss the Austro-Serbian issue with Austria in any form; that Russia was the first to propose direct conversations between Austria and Russia; that Russian mobilization was caused by the false report in the Berlin *Lokalanzeiger;* that Germany rejected all British proposals for naval limitation with derision; that Colonel House informed the British in July, 1914, of the ominous and unique military preparations and bellicose psychology in Germany; that the German army bill of 1913 came before the other similar bills and forced the other states to take defensive measures; that Kautsky's book is the most illuminating and valuable of the books published on war guilt since the new documents have been brought to light; that Tschirschky prodded Austria into action against Serbia; that Austria delayed her ultimatum to Serbia until Poincaré left Russia because she feared that Poincaré would suggest peaceful diplomatic measures for settlement of the dispute; that Germany urged Austria to declare war on Serbia; that Austria rejected all mediation proposals and that none of these originated in Germany; that Grey's offers, suggestions and appeals, fully supported by France, were rendered fruitless by Germany's opposition; that Germany opposed all suggestions for a diplomatic settlement of the crisis, and that this was throughout the attitude of the Kaiser; that the pledge-plan when proposed by the Kaiser was a potent form of incitement to war (p. 289), but when proposed by Grey it was a noble stroke for peace (p. 295) ; that the merest hint of restraint from Berlin would have sufficed to curb Austrian aggression, but that this hint never came, Germany rather urging Austria into hostilities with Serbia and the World War; that it was the German ultimatum which broke up all diplomatic efforts for peace; that Germany acted with great haste in precipitating hostilities after she learned of the Russian mobilization; that while England had an obligation of honor to support France, she entered the War chiefly because of the Belgian issue, being unwilling to "make a ring" in which a great brutal bully might trample his victim in the dust and gore. We cannot close this summary of Asquith's contributions to the *Kriegsschuldfrage* without mentioning the fact that chapters xiv-xvii of this book constitute the final refutation of the myth that England, France and Russia were caught unawares by the German octopus in 1914— pounced upon in a moment of the most profound expectation of universal and permanent peace.

The distinguished English scholar, Frederick Cornwallis Conybeare, when describing the attack upon Alfred Loisy by Pius X, remarked that because of its thoroughness and its presentation of exactly the reverse of scientific truth the papal condemnation would constitute an admirable summary of modern biblical scholarship if one forgot that the list of scholarly conclusions there catalogued were regarded as errors by His Apostolic Eminence.[156] The same would apply to the statements contained in the four chapters in Grey's memoirs devoted to the crisis of 1914 and its problems.[157] His list of alleged facts concerning the period and its issues constitutes an almost perfect summary of the reverse of the actual truth in the circumstances. This will appear in the following brief survey. In regard to Russia he tells us that Izvolski and Russia were deliberately humiliated by Germany in 1908 through the annexation of Bosnia and Herzegovina; that Sazonov worked hard to force a conciliatory policy in Belgrade; that the Russian general mobilization was not an unreasonable or unnecessary precaution; that it was a purely preparatory measure and in no sense meant war; that Austria mobilized before Russia; that Sazonov agreed heartily to Grey's conference plans; and that Germany mobilized before sending her ultimatum to Russia.

With respect to France he contends that there was no longer in 1914 any desire for revenge or for the recovery of Alsace-Lorraine; that the French had no interest in a Balkan quarrel; that no country in Europe was more determined to

avoid a European quarrel over the Balkans; that
French statesmen and people alike in 1914 were
terrified by the thought of war; that Paul Cambon lived in a veritable nightmare lest France
might become involved in war; that the French
realized that the odds against the Entente in a
European war were simply overwhelming; that
France went to the most extreme limits of pacific diplomacy to avoid war in 1914; and that she
was technically and legally bound by a treaty to
aid Russia in the specific circumstances of 1914.

In the matter of German guilt and turpitude
he contends that Germany before 1914 was deliberately plotting world dominion; that Germany
refused all proposals for naval limitation; that
Colonel House informed him that Germany was
everywhere in the clutches of a most aggressive
and arrogant military gang; that 1914 was the
year consciously chosen for war by Germany because this was a particularly favorable year for
her; that there was no good-will towards England in Germany; that Germany's army was far
the largest and most powerful in the world; that
Germany recognized this overwhelming superiority of her armies and expected an easy victory
over the Entente in a few months; that Germany
alone vetoed Grey's plan for a conference of
nations, and hence destroyed all diplomatic
methods of settling the dispute; that the Kaiser
made no effort to secure a diplomatic settlement

of the crisis in 1914; that Bethmann-Hollweg's actions in 1914 had no significance whatever because the army was in control of matters in Germany from the beginning of the crisis; that Germany was bent upon the diplomatic humiliation of the Entente; that Germany was determined upon a European war from the outset; that when things began to look like a European war in 1914 Austria weakened and tried to avert the conflict, but "Germany then precipitated war and told Austria that as an ally she could not get out."

In defending England's procedure in 1914 he alleges that he could do nothing to restrain Russia; that England determined to participate because she could not endure the thought of the German fleet steaming down the Channel and attacking the ports of an ally; that England had recognized a treaty obligation to defend Belgian neutrality in 1870; that there was no possibility of England's remaining neutral in 1914 because she could not stand aside and allow Belgium to be violated, and the Germans would under no conditions keep out of Belgium; that Belgian neutrality could be secured only by war; and that in his speech of August 3, 1914, he consciously kept to matters of hard prosaic fact and refused throughout to appeal to the feelings of the House.

While on this subject of the assumption of the consistent and limpid honesty and candor of Sir

Edward Grey it might be well to point out once more that it was he who invented the notorious Berlin *Lokalanzeiger* myth.[158] By December, 1914, the news had leaked out in Entente countries that the Russian mobilization had been the first in the crisis. Grey recognized the danger of this fact to Entente propaganda, so he stated that though this was true the Russian priority was due to the fact that the Russians heard of the false report published in the Berlin paper concerning the German mobilization and gave out the Russian mobilization order in hasty and terrified self-defense. Sazonov was so well aware of the preposterous falsity of this assertion that even he refused to use it as an excuse for Russia. Nearly two years later, at a conference of foreign journalists, Grey once more brought forth the old myth and gave it an even more forceful and attractive statement. From this time onward it worked itself into the fabric of the Entente mythology, and since the War even Sazonov has possessed the effrontery to exploit this legend.

One of the chief points against Grey's reputation for candor and veracity brought out in the recently published British documents is the fact that, in spite of his frequent assertions in his memoirs that he knew in 1914 that Germany was determined upon war, the documents prove that he was well aware that Germany did not wish a

European war and that he was fully informed as to the fatal military acts of Russia and France at every step.[159]

The conclusion to which one is inevitably led by a study of the career of Sir Edward Grey is that he was not a consummate Machiavellian diplomat such as Izvolski, Delcassé, Poincaré and Paul Cambon, but is one of the foremost examples in history of the disaster which may befall a state when its foreign policy is entrusted to an eminently well-meaning, and generally honest man, but a naïve, ignorant, stupid and vacillating diplomat. Grey was afflicted by a childish fear and suspicion of Germany and an equally blind and sentimental trust in the innocence and goodness of France which made him incapable of discriminating between the *Politik* of men like Caillaux and Delcassé.[160] He wished for peace, but allowed himself to be exploited by those who worked for war. There can be no doubt that he stood for peace as late as July 24, 1914, but he followed a course which inevitably placed his country in the War. He doubtless believed as late as his speech of August 3rd that he had done all he could consistent with England's honor to avoid war. Having undoubtedly a rather far-sighted sentimental vision of peace, he was quite incapable of taking practical steps to secure this end. He vainly tried to muddle through the crisis of 1914 and to settle problems as they arose.

In this he was unsuccessful, partly because of indecision, partly because of the complexity of the
issues, and partly due to the pressure put upon
him by his more bellicose subordinates, Nicolson
and Crowe. The new British documents fully
prove Crowe to have been the *bête noir* of the
British Foreign Office in 1914. As early as
July 24th Crowe urged Grey to throw England
in with Russia and France.

The rather thorough analysis of the career of
Grey in this chapter has not been produced by
any bitterness towards a great scoundrel, but
rather by the desire to illustrate how a good man
may be brought to a deplorable course of conduct
through bad company and personal inadequacy
to the tasks imposed upon him. We do not believe that Grey was even fundamentally dishonest. Though he has falsified innumerable
times from 1914 to the completion of his memoirs, there is no doubt that he regarded each falsification as justified by its service to some
larger end. He trusted those who betrayed him.
There is no greater bit of ironic tragedy in
literature than the passages in his memoirs
where Grey testifies to the high character and
ideals of Paul Cambon and the confidence and
affection in which he was held by Grey.[161]

As to how Grey's reputation is affected by the
complete publication of the British documents on
the crisis of 1914, honest, informed and discern-

ing readers are likely to conclude that it is essentially unchanged. It is certain now that he was much better informed as to the details of the crisis than we had earlier believed, especially in regard to the aggressive and fatal Russian military measures and the hypocritical French diplomatic ruses. He obviously did not stumble into war through ignorance of what his allies were up to. Yet, at the same time, the full documents prove him much more loath to bring England into war than was earlier apparent. He moved very slowly, and might even have kept England neutral but for the vicious influence of Cambon, Crowe and Nicolson. Further, it must be conceded that Grey comes out of the documents in a much more credible manner than he does out of his own memoirs. A fallible human may be forgiven for succumbing to the difficulties which faced Grey in 1914 much more than he can be pardoned for the hypocrisies, evasions and misstatements of *Twenty-Five Years*.

One of the most interesting questions as to Sir Edward Grey is as to why the man who brought to England the greatest and most unnecessary disaster in her history should be one of the most beloved men in English history. In the first place, he was a famous athlete and sportsman, which won for him the sentimental admiration of the English people. Dr. Henderson says on this point: [162]

Grey was a great sportsman—spent long days alone, tramping along by trout-streams and watching the birds. He had written a treatise on angling: knew all the twists and turns of that sport; how to choose the shady places and keep silent so as not to alarm the fish; how to prepare his bait, how to fling it; how, always with that calm imperturbability, to play his fish and how finally to land him. Grey's other love was tennis —not lawn-tennis but the real time-honored game. In this he had earned the championship,—held it for at least two years.

Various writers attribute Grey's influence over the House of Commons to their knowledge that he was a great sportsman. "England had not lost her sporting instincts," says one of them, "lightly to abandon hope of a great fly-fisher and a prize tennis man."

Grey also possessed the unusual combination of dignity and gravity joined to the charm of youthful appearance. His manner was impressive and convincing without dogmatism or arrogance. He was also aided by the fact that he had a distinguished family tradition behind him. Dr. Henderson ironically states the significance of these factors: [163]

But Grey had other qualities besides his sportsmanship, qualities that made for confidence, love and trust. His appearance was singularly youthful, almost boyish: we hear of his "boyish and beardless face." At his first appearance in the House as Under-Secretary of Foreign Affairs in 1892 his personal charm, added to a curious impression of reserve, "gained for him almost at a bound the confidence of the House." He was beardless and boyish "yet magisterially serious"; gave an "impression both of race and of high intellectual distinction"; some one recognized in his face "the type of countenance of the rulers of England at the end of the 18th century." Not the type of countenance of George III, let us hope, but of Pitt, say, or Fox. He was modest, not egoistic or vain but tactful and urbane. In time he earned the reputation of being a true patrician in politics, of being untouched by any ordinary meannesses, of never being treacherous, or self-seeking or ambitious for his own personal advancement. He refused a peerage because he was sure of his position, could afford not to be a lord, preferred the House of Commons to the House of Lords. Altogether a fine, handsome, winning straightforward sort of man! Theodore Roosevelt once said that a visit to Grey was the crowning experience of a three months' tour.

Further, Grey was a man of marked scholarly interests and achievement. His knowledge of Greek won for him the friendship and confidence of Gilbert Murray. The latter in appreciation wrote the most effective defense of Grey which has yet been attempted, an apology which has led many to think that Grey must be a great and honest man, even though they feel that his own words and works seem to lead to an opposite conclusion.[164] It is hard for many to conceive that a man like Murray could be mistaken in his judgment. Grey's interest in English literature, particularly the works of Wordsworth, won for him the undying admiration of Walter Hines Page, and greatly aided Grey in distracting Page's attention from his duties as American Ambassador, commissioned to defend our rights as a neutral power.[165]

Then, Grey possessed unusually convincing oratorical powers. He was lucid and direct in expression, with an intimacy and appearance of candor and fairness which carried conviction and disarmed criticism. As Henderson says:[166]

> When he speaks in Parliament it makes no difference what Grey's subject may be, his "exposition" of that subject will be "so luminous, reasonable, moderate and judicial that soon it appears almost impossible to dissent from the speaker's conclusions." Always and ever he "seems to be the embodiment of common-sense."

The impression made by his oratory is attested by the following passage from a review of his memoirs by A. G. Gardiner of the London Daily News, in which Gardiner describes the effect upon him of Grey's speech of August 3, 1914, a speech actually full of errors and misstatements, partially conscious and partially due to ignorance:[167]

> In my experience—and I have been familiar with the oratory of the House of Commons since the days of Gladstone—there has been no speaker of distinction in our time whose method was so plain and unadorned, or

who sustained his argument with such unanswerable force as Lord Grey. He has the gift of what one may call naked oratory beyond contemporary precedent. The secret of his power is indicated in his reference to his momentous speech in the House of Commons on August 3rd, 1914. No one who heard that speech will ever forget it. The last hope was gone. Europe was plunged into the abyss of war—war on a scale such as the world has never seen. He rose in a House shaken with the agony of the moment, torn with the bitterest dissensions, the bulk of his own supporters gloomily distrustful of the policy that was sweeping the nation into the general vortex. He sat down—and I speak as one who has been publicly critical of his diplomacy—with the House silent, sorrowful but convinced. It was that speech and it was his personality that carried the nation into the war at once and with practical unanimity.

Grey's reputation as a statesman and diplomat, established by the above-mentioned traits, seems likely to be perpetuated, even enhanced, by the stylistic powers manifested in his memoirs. They display much of the same power exhibited in his oratory. The style is clear and lucid. The reader is apparently taken into Grey's intimate confidence. There is a great show of frankness and candor. The views of opponents are presented, if only to be proved wrong-headed and mistaken. He admits himself in error occasionally on irrelevant matters, but always shows how he was dead right on vital issues. He deals in sweeping generalities, avoiding embarrassing details. The alternatives to his policies appear by implication dishonorable and discreditable. A critical reviewer, Dr. Henderson, admits that "in his memoirs Grey lives up to his reputation. The work may become an English classic; it may be read and admired a thousand years hence. It will crystallize the English legend." [168] The estimable P. W. Wilson, reviewing the memoirs in the New York *Times,* holds that: "His story is startling in its candor. . . . There is a winning quality which can hardly fail profoundly to influence public opinion throughout the world." Mr. Harry Hansen, writing in the Chicago *Daily News,* pronounces them "The most important disclosures of the inside of the war so far published. . . . Frank, open, direct." Mr. Gardiner, forgetting his *Daily News* editorial of August 1, 1914, waxes even more enthusiastic: [169]

He writes as he speaks, with the same simplicity, honesty, directness. You may doubt his wisdom, but you cannot doubt the high and chivalrous quality of character that shines through his utterance. You cannot doubt the nobility of his aims nor the large humane disinterestedness with which he pursues them. This candor disarms criticism. If he thinks he was wrong here or there he says he was wrong. If he has changed his view of a given situation in the light of fuller knowledge, he admits it.

Not only in England, but also in America the memoirs have been accorded the widest popularity. They seem likely to have as large a circulation as the letters of Mr. Page. They are likely to far more than offset all the work of all the historians in the English-speaking world who have been laboring for years to dispel myth and legend and lay before the world the facts concerning the genesis of the foremost tragedy which has befallen the planet. It is chiefly because of this dangerous and menacing prospect that the writer has believed it wise to give much more space to an analysis of Grey's part in the crisis of 1914 than has been allotted to the account of the genesis of the War in the other countries involved. In diplomacy Grey was not the aggressive and dominating figure that some of his colleagues in the Triple Entente unquestionably were, but in the field of legend-building and epic-mongering he is likely to prove, with the possible exception of Mr. Page, the most potent and disastrous influence which has come down from the days of 1914.[170]

Many who read this rather thorough and frank statement of British responsibility for the World War and of British conduct in the War may suspect the writer of being affiliated with pro-Irish sympathizers and other haters of the British Empire. In reality, the writer has, because of his published discussions of the causes of the American Revolution and the War of 1812, been accused by these very pro-Irish elements of being obviously in the pay of the Sulgrave Foundation and other organizations subsidizng propaganda favorable to Anglo-American union. The writer is a firm believer in the cause of Anglo-American accord and amity as a first step towards world peace, but in these pages he is not primarily interested in that subject. We are here concerned with the facts regarding the guilt of Grey and his advisers in 1914.

Indeed, it is desirable to emphasize that the treatment of Grey in this chapter is not an anti-English interpretation. It is in essential accord with the views of distinguished Englishmen, not party rivals from the Tories or Laborites, but from Grey's own party. We have in mind such men as Lord Loreburn and E. D. Morel, eminent Liberals of 1914, and, if we may judge from his actions instead of his words, John Morley. Equally critical have been the estimates of the great Canadian student, Dr. J. S. Ewart, and the candid Frenchman, Pevet. Compared with books like Jellicoe's *Playing the Game,* and Morhardt's *Les Preuves* my account of Grey is a veritable eulogy. We should further stress the fact that the English nation should not be held responsible for Grey's acts in 1914. The more enlightened among the Conservatives, the majority of his own party, and all of the Laborites would have opposed his diplomacy tooth and nail had they known of its nature and progress. They were not informed until England had slipped into the abyss prepared by Grey, Asquith and Haldane. This latter fact disposes incidentally of the myth that democratic political institutions in Britain brought assurance of open diplomacy, any more than French republicanism produced "open covenants openly arrived at." [171]

VII. CONCLUSIONS

(1) The key to British action in the crisis of 1914 must be found in the facts of the Anglo-French Entente which was worked out between 1901 and 1914. England in 1914 was determined to go to war if France did, and France decided to stand firmly with Russia in measures bound to provoke war.

(2) From 1906 to 1912 England carefully worked out plans for military and naval cooperation with France against Germany. A verbal agreement to aid France against Germany in case of war was also provided. On November 22, 1912, Grey committed himself in principle to aid France in the event of an attack by Germany, his commitment involving a reference to the joint plans for armed action formulated by the military and naval authorities in the two countries. Both Asquith and Grey re-

peatedly denied these facts when questioned concerning them in the House of Commons.

(3) Anglo-Russian relations were never cordial nor popular in England. They were important in connection with the crisis of 1914 chiefly because of England's relations with France and the firm support of Russia by France. England made war to support a "Russian quarrel" because France was determined to support Russia, and England was resolutely devoted to France.

(4) Anglo-German relations between 1898 and 1912 oscillated, due to Holstein's opposition to an Anglo-German understanding, the British support of France in Morocco, the German naval plans, and the fact that Grey would never modify his relations with France or Russia in behalf of a more cordial understanding with Germany. From 1912 to 1914 Anglo-German relations grew progressively better. The naval rivalry was temporarily adjusted, and the conflict over the Bagdad Railway eliminated. A powerful group in the Liberal Party showed impatience concerning the Entente and favored closer relations with Germany. Anglo-German affairs were more promising in June, 1914, than they had been in fifteen years prior to that time.

(5) The possibility of an Anglo-German *rapprochement* alarmed the French and Russians, and they decided to precipitate a Euro-

pean conflict, if possible, before England could escape from the Triple Entente. They pounced upon Grey in the spring of 1914 and initiated negotiations for an Anglo-Russian naval convention.

(6) In the crisis of 1914 Grey was for peace in the abstract, but had no definite and clear-cut policy from the outset, vacillated and hesitated, and actually encouraged both groups. He led the French and Russians to feel that they could count on English aid, and he made the Austrians and Germans believe that they could depend upon British neutrality.

(7) Grey was absolutely determined to bring England into the War on the side of France if France entered the conflict. The complete British documents show that Grey learned from Buchanan as early as July 25th of the impending Russian mobilization, and on the 31st of the general mobilization. He made no serious attempt to curb France or Russia, and when their action brought on war he refused to let England stand aside.

(8) The only way in which England could have prevented the World War in 1914, if at all, would have been to promise her complete neutrality from the outset. But Grey would not promise to remain neutral even though Germany would agree to keep out of Belgium, refrain from attacking the French ports, and guarantee the integrity of France and her colonies. Grey

absolutely refused to formulate the conditions of English neutrality, though Germany requested him to do so, and though he falsely informed the House of Commons that he had done so. He justified his refusal on the grounds that England must keep her hands free, though he knew that they were not free at the time because of Anglo-French agreements.

(9) Grey succumbed to the pressure of Cambon, Crowe, and Nicolson at a time when England and Germany were in full accord as to the best diplomatic methods of settling the crisis, and when Germany, at England's request, was acting vigorously to carry these methods into execution.

(10) England was not technically or specifically bound to come into the War on the side of France in 1914 by the agreement of November 22, 1912, or August 2, 1914, as on August 3, 1914, Germany offered not to attack the French ports if England would remain neutral.

(11) Grey's basic reason for bringing England into the War was because he believed it to England's interest to stand with France, but subsequent events prove that he made a colossal blunder in this respect.

(12) He admits that he was personally responsible for bringing England into the War, and that he would have resigned if he had not done so whether Belgium had been invaded or not.

(13) The whole Belgian issue in 1914 was pure imposture as far as Grey and England were concerned. It was a fortunate subterfuge which Grey exploited to the limit as a high moral issue wherewith to inflame the British public against Germany. England had no treaty obligation to protect Belgian neutrality. Germany proposed to keep out of Belgium if England would remain neutral. After August 2nd Grey most ardently desired to have Germany invade Belgium, and he extorted the Belgian appeal to the Great Powers from the Belgian government through his own initiative.

(14) Grey's career is not the record of a great scoundrel, but is interesting rather as an illustration of the disasters which may befall a country which entrusts its destiny to a well-meaning but vacillating and indecisive man, and an ignorant, stupid and naïve diplomat. The tragedy of Grey is also an example for all posterity of the evil effects of bad company upon a diplomat, and of the pernicious influence of the permanent staff of Foreign Offices. Had Grey relied upon and confided in men like Earl Loreburn and John Morley instead of Crowe and Nicolson, the history of England, Europe and the world would have been far different and far happier.

(15) Grey's recently published memoirs are inaccurate and evasive, and present a picture of the crisis of 1914 almost exactly the reverse of the

actual facts. They discredit the man far more than his acts of 1914. Yet they will become immensely popular and constitute the basis for an enduring Grey legend.

(16) With the publication of the complete British documents for 1914 the verdict of history as to Grey and England in relation to the World War may be definitely formulated. It is in full accord with the courageous words of the distinguished English scholar, Frederick Cornwallis Conybeare, contained in a letter written to a leading American historian on August 4, 1922:

> Grey was doubtless as much of a hypocrite in the week before the War as he had been for eight years before that. We attacked Germany for three reasons: (1) to down her navy before it got any larger; (2) to capture her trade; (3) to take her colonies.

SELECTED REFERENCES

Asquith, H. H., *The Genesis of the War; The Diary of Lord Bertie of Thame;* Beard, C. A., *Cross-Currents in Europe Today;* Beazley, R., "Lord Grey's Account of Things," in *Foreign Affairs* (English), December, 1925; Buchanan, G., *My Mission to Russia and Other Diplomatic Memories;* Churchill, W., *The World Crisis, 1911–1914;* Ewart, J. S., *The Roots and Causes of the Wars;* Gooch, G. P., *Modern Europe, 1878–1920;* (Ed.) *The Cambridge History of British Foreign Policy;* Gooch and Temperley (Eds.) *Official British Documents on the Origins of the War,* Vol. XI; Grey,

Viscount E., *Twenty-Five Years, 1892–1916;* Haldane, Viscount R. B., *Before the War;* Henderson, E. F., *The Verdict of History: the Case of Sir Edward Grey;* Jagow, G. von, *England und der Kriegsausbruch;* Jellicoe, E. G., *Playing the Game;* Loreburn, Earl, *How the War Came;* Lutz, H., *Lord Grey und der Weltkrieg;* Meyer, E., *England;* Montgelas, Mo., "Lord Grey als Staatmann und Geschichts-schreiber," in *Die Kriegsschuldfrage,* May–July, 1926; Morel, E. D., *Truth and the War; The Secret History of a Great Betrayal;* Murray, G., *The Foreign Policy of Sir Edward Grey;* Norman, G. H., *A Searchlight on the European War;* Oman, C. W. C., *The Outbreak of the War;* Pevet, A. H., *Les Responsables de la guerre;* "De Sarajevo à Bruxelles," in the *Kriegsschuldfrage,* July, 1924; Renouvin, P., *Les Origines immédiates de la guerre;* Sanger, C. P., and Norton, H. T., *England's Guarantee to Belgium and Luxemberg;* B. de Siebert and G. A. Schreiner, (Eds.) *Entente Diplomacy and the World;* Willis, I. C., *How We Went Into the War.*

FOOTNOTES AND FURTHER REFERENCES

[1] Cf. Irene Cooper Willis, *How We Went into the War.*

[2] E. F. Henderson, *The Verdict of History: the Case of Sir Edward Grey,* p. 192.

[3] Viscount Grey of Fallodon, *Twenty-Five Years,* 1892–1916, Vol. I, pp. 303, 316.

[4] Earl Loreburn, *How the War Came,* p. 17.

[5] Ibid., pp. 72–3.

[6] Ibid., pp. 73–4; *Cambridge History of British Foreign Policy,* Vol. III, pp. 305 ff.

[7] *Twenty-Five Years,* Vol. I, p. 74; Vol. II, p. 2.

[8] Loreburn, op. cit., p. 216.

[9] *Twenty-Five Years,* Introduction, pp. xxii–xxiii.

[10] Loreburn, op. cit., pp. 75–81; J. S. Ewart, *The Roots and Causes of the Wars, 1914–1918,* Vol. II, p. 846.

[11] Loreburn, op. cit., pp. 98–9, 98 ff.; *Cambridge History of British Foreign Policy*, Vol. III, pp. 467 ff.

[12] *Twenty-Five Years*, Vol. II, p. 312.

[13] Henderson, op. cit., p. 204.

[14] W. Churchill, *The World Crisis, 1911–1914*, Vol. I.

[15] F. Stieve, *Isvolsky and the World War*, p. 90.

[16] E. D. Morel, *The Secret History of a Great Betrayal*, pp. 5–6.

[17] Ibid., pp. 15–16.

[18] C. A. Beard, *Cross-Currents in Europe To-day*, pp. 54–5.

[19] W. C. Bridge, "England's War Preparations," in the *Kriegsschuldfrage*, July, 1924, pp. 268–9.

[20] Morel, op. cit., p. 17. On Northcliffe see the famous "Open Letter" by A. G. Gardiner in the London *Daily News*, December 5, 1914.

[21] Loreburn, op. cit., pp. 101–2.

[22] Ewart, op. cit., Vol. I, p. 128.

[23] Ibid.

[24] Ibid.

[25] Ibid. Cf. Loreburn, pp. 102 ff.

[26] Morel, op. cit., p. 3.

[27] *Twenty-Five Years*, Vol. II, pp. 16–17.

[28] Morel, op. cit., p. 3.

[29] *Cambridge History of British Foreign Policy*, Vol. III, pp. 404–5.

[30] Ewart, op. cit., pp. 877 ff.; Siebert and Schreiner, *Entente Diplomacy and the World*, pp. 44–93.

[31] Ewart, Vol. I, pp. 44 ff.; Beard, op. cit., p. 49.

[32] Siebert and Schreiner, op. cit., p. 525.

[33] Stieve, op. cit., pp. 89–90.

[34] Beard, op. cit., pp. 43–50; Stieve, op. cit., pp. 194 ff.; Henderson, op. cit., p. 184.

[35] Cf. Loreburn, op. cit., pp. 105 ff.

[36] Ibid., pp. 183 ff.

[37] G. P. Gooch, *Modern Europe, 1878–1920*, pp. 198, 302, 328; and J. Haller, *Die Ära Bülow;* Fischer, *Holsteins Grosses Nein;* Brandenburg, *Von Bismarck zum Weltkriege;* T. Wolf, *Das Vorspiel;* Eckardstein, *Ten Years at the Court of St. James.*

[38] Gooch, op. cit., pp. 439–44; Ewart, op. cit., p. 166.

[39] Ewart, op. cit., pp. 846 ff.; Gooch, op. cit., Chap. xiv.

[40] *Cambridge History of British Foreign Policy*, Vol. III, pp. 456 ff.

[41] Siebert and Schreiner, op. cit., p. 615.

[42] Stieve, op. cit., p. 78.

[43] Morel, op. cit., p. 12.

[44] Ibid., p. 14.

[45] M. Montgelas, *The Case for the Central Powers*, pp. 109–10.

[46] Morel, op. cit., p. 21.

[47] E. M. Earle, *Turkey, the Great Powers and the Bagdad Railway,* pp. 258–71.

[48] Stieve, op. cit., pp. 194 ff.

[49] E. Judet, *Carnets de Georges Louis,* Vol. II, pp. 178–9; cf. *The Progressive,* January 1, 1926, p. 130.

[50] Morel, op. cit., pp. 22–24, 27–8.

[51] *British Documents on the Origins of the War,* No. 340.

[52] Loreburn, op. cit., p. 183.

[53] Ewart, op. cit. pp. 131 ff.

[54] Loreburn, op. cit., pp. 185, 192.

[55] *British Blue Book,* No. 1.

[56] Ewart, op. cit., p. 113.

[57] *British Documents,* No. 284.

[58] Ibid., No. 282.

[59] *Twenty-Five Years,* Vol. I, p. 325.

[60] Loreburn, op. cit., p. 191.

[61] *British Blue Book,* No. 5; *British Documents,* No. 91.

[62] Ibid., No. 112. Cf. H. Lutz, "Lord Grey's Responsibility for Russia's Mobilization," in New York *Times Current History Magazine,* May, 1925.

[63] Loreburn, op. cit., pp. 191–2.

[64] Dickinson, *International Anarchy,* pp. 454–5.

[65] Ewart, op. cit., pp. 131–7.

[66] *Falsifications of the Russian Orange Book,* p. 17.

[67] *Twenty-Five Years,* Vol. I, p. 320, Vol. II, p. 23.

[67a] *British Documents,* Nos. 419, 426, 447, 453, 460.

[68] *British Documents,* Nos. 101, 125, 347, 367.

[69] *Twenty-Five Years,* Vol. I, pp. 308–9, 311, 314, 320; Vol. II, p. 23.

[70] Ewart, op. cit., pp. 1074–6.

[71] *British Documents,* No. 140.

[72] Ewart, op. cit., p. 1074.

[73] Ibid., pp. 1074–6, 1123.

[74] M. Morhardt, *Les Preuves,* pp. 249 ff.

[75] *Twenty-Five Years,* Vol. I, p. 311.

[76] Ibid., p. 314.

[77] Ibid., p. 320.

[78] *British Blue Book,* No. 67; *British Documents,* Nos. 203, 218.

[79] Ibid., No. 285.

[80] *The Outbreak of the World War,* pp. 273–4.

[81] Mongelas, op. cit., p. 162.

[82] Ewart, op. cit., pp. 1104–5, 1112–13; Montgelas, op. cit., pp. 184–7.

[83] S. B. Fay, "New Light on the Origins of the World War," in the *American Historical Review,* October, 1920, p. 51; *Outbreak of the World War,* p. 378.

[84] Loreburn, op. cit., p. 157.

[85] *British Documents,* No. 340.

86 Montgelas, op. cit., pp. 185–7.

87 *Twenty-Five Years*, Vol. I, pp. 319–20; Ewart, op. cit., p. 137.

88 *Twenty-Five Years*, Vol. II, p. 312.

89 *British Documents*, No. 101.

90 M. F. Schilling, *How the War Began*, p. 50; *Falsifications of the Russian Orange Book*, pp. 38–9.

91 Henderson, op. cit., p. 203.

92 Loreburn, op. cit., pp. 205–6; *British Blue Book*, No. 124.

93 *British Blue Book*, No. 115; British Documents, No. 351.

94 Ibid., No. 128.

95 *Twenty-Five Years*, Vol. I, pp. 319–31.

96 Ewart, op. cit., p. 135; Loreburn, op. cit., pp. 236–8.

97 Loreburn, op. cit., pp. 209–11; L. J. Maxse, "Retrospect and Reminiscence," in *National Review*, August, 1918.

98 *British Blue Book*, No. 115; *British Documents*, No. 351.

99 Cf. C. J. H. Hayes, *British Social Politics*.

100 *British Documents*, No. 487.

101 Ibid.

102 *Twenty-Five Years*, Vol. II, pp. 316–17; Henderson, op. cit., p. 203; *British Blue Book*, No. 123. For the Pashitch letter of July 31st see *Die Kriegsschuldfrage*, November, 1926.

103 *British Documents*, No. 448.

104 Ewart, op. cit., Chaps. v, xv, xvi, xix; Grey, *Twenty-Five Years;* H. H. Asquith, *The Genesis of the War;* I. C. Willis, *How We Went into the War.*

105 *British Documents*, No. 340.

106 Op. cit., p. 183.

107 *Twenty-Five Years*, Vol. I, pp. 329–30.

108 See references in footnote 69 above.

109 *Twenty-Five Years*, Vol. I, pp. 302, 321; Vol. II, p. 24.

110 Ibid., Vol. II, p. 22.

111 Ibid., p. 68.

112 Stieve, op. cit., p. 106.

113 *Twenty-Five Years*, Vol. I, p. 313.

114 G. von Jagow, *England und der Kriegsausbruch*, pp. 76–8.

115 *Twenty-Five Years*, Vol. I, pp. 311–14; Vol. II, p. 26.

116 Ibid., Vol. I, p. 313.

117 Ibid., Vol. II, pp. 36–9.

118 Ewart, op. cit., pp. 145–6, 198–9, 444.

119 C. A. Beard, "Viscount Grey on War Guilt," in *New Republic*, October, 7, 1925, p. 174.

120 Mrs. H. A. L. Fisher, *Then and Now.*

121 Cf. G. A. Greenwood, *England To-day;* A. Siegfried, *Post-War Britain;* and the various volumes on England in the Carnegie Endowment *Social and Economic History of the World War.*

122 This material on the losses of England in the War, as estimated by the London *Morning Post*, is reprinted in Ploetz's *Manual of Universal History*, new edition, pp. 744 ff.

[123] Ibid.

[124] A. Fabre-Luce, *La Crise des alliances.*

[125] Gooch, *Modern Europe,* p. 558.

[126] Quoted by E. F. Henderson in a letter to the writer, and in part in the New York *Nation,* October 28, 1925, p. 490. The original is in the Italian Archives.

[127] Henderson, *The Verdict of History,* p. 198.

[128] Ibid., pp. 206–7.

[129] Ewart, op. cit., p. 131.

[130] Asquith, op. cit., p. 320.

[131] *British Documents,* No. 487.

[132] *Twenty-Five Years,* Vol. II, p. 318.

[133] Ibid., Chaps. xvi–xviii, passim.

[134] Loreburn, op. cit., p. 242

[135] Ewart, op. cit., p. 188.

[136] *Twenty-Five Years,* Vol. I, pp. 303, 316.

[137] The whole question of the Belgian treaty of 1839 and its implications and guarantees is treated in masterly fashion from both the genetic and the analytical viewpoints in chapter fourteen of Dr. Ewart's monumental *Roots and Causes of the Wars, 1914–1918.*

The textual basis of the so-called obligation to defend Belgian neutrality is found in Article II of the Treaty of 1839 to the following effect: "Her Majesty the Queen of the United Kingdom of Great Britain and Ireland, His Majesty the Emperor of Austria, King of Hungary and Bohemia, His Majesty the King of France, His Majesty the King of Prussia, and His Majesty the Emperor of all the Russians, declare that the articles mentioned in the preceding article [i e. including the crucial statement that "Belgium shall form an independent and perpetually neutral state."] are considered as having the same force and validity as if they were textually inserted in the present Act, and that they are thus placed under the guarantee of their said Majesties."

[138] Op. cit., pp. 227–8.

[139] Ibid., pp. 229–31; Ewart, op. cit., pp. 429–31.

[140] Ewart, op. cit., pp. 131–2, 198, 443–4.

[141] Beard, op. cit. 50–54; Loreburn, op. cit., pp. 81–84, 87–89; Montgelas, op. cit. pp. 224–5; A. Pevet, "De Sarajevo à Bruxelles," in the *Kriegsschuldfrage,* July, 1924; Belgian documents in the addition to the *German White Book,* in J. B. Scott (Ed.), *Diplomatic Documents Relating to the Outbreak of the European War,* Part II, pp. 837–60; and in the larger collections by Bernhard Schwertfeger; Fox, op. cit., Chap. xv.

[142] Op. cit., p. 225.

[143] *Outbreak of the World War,* pp. 444, 452, 461.

144 *British Documents*, No. 448.
145 Op. cit., p. 238.
146 Ewart, op. cit., pp. 135–7.
147 Ibid., pp. 134 ff.
148 *British Blue Book*, No. 151; cf. *British Documents*, No. 551.
149 Ewart, op. cit., p. 138.
150 *British Documents*, No. 580.
151 *Belgian Grey Book*, No. 40.
152 Ewart, op. cit., p. 140.
153 *Twenty-Five Years*, Vol. II, pp. 9–10.
154 C. H. Grattan, "The Walter Hines Page Legend," in *American Mercury*, September, 1925; M. Caracciolo, *L'Intervento della Grecia nella guerra mondiale e l'opera della diplomazia alleata;* A. Pevet, *Les Responsables de la guerre*, pp. 476–7; S. Brooks, *America and Germany, 1918–1925;* J. K. Turner, *Shall It Be Again?* Chaps. xv, xvi, xxiii.
155 Op. cit., Chaps. xix–xxvii.
156 F. C. Conybeare, *History of New Testament Criticism*, p. 177.
157 Op. cit., Chaps. xvi–xix.
158 Montgelas, op. cit., pp. 215–17.
159 *British Documents*, passim.
160 *Twenty-Five Years*, Introduction, and Chaps. xvi–xix; *Un Livre noir*, Vol. II, p. 309.
161 *Twenty-Five Years*, Vol. I, pp. 328–9; Vol. II, pp. 240–42.
162 Op. cit., pp. 9–10.
163 Ibid., pp. 10–11.
164 G. Murray, *The Foreign Policy of Sir Edward Grey.*
165 B. J. Hendrick, *The Life and Letters of Walter Hines Page*, Vol. II, pp. 103 ff., 305 ff.
166 Op. cit., pp. 11–12.
167 *Saturday Review of Literature*, October 31, 1925.
168 New York *Nation*, October 28, 1925, p. 490.
169 Loc. cit.
170 Cf. C. A. Beard, "Viscount Grey on War Guilt," in *New Republic*, October 7, 1925. For an illustration of the epic in the making see Gardiner, loc. cit.; and compare this with his great editorial in the London *Daily News* for August 1, 1914.
171 This matter of the alignment of British opinion and parties on the matter of entering the War, together with the relevant newspaper comment, is described in Irene Cooper Willis's important book, *How We Went into the War.* The most vigorous criticism of Grey and British foreign policy has been written by an English lawyer, E. G. Jellicoe, in his *Playing the Game.* Compared with this book, Loreburn's work seems almost an apology for Grey.

CHAPTER IX

THE ENTRY OF THE UNITED STATES INTO THE WORLD WAR

I. THE TRANSFORMATION OF AMERICAN SENTIMENT TOWARDS GERMANY, 1870–1914

THE causes for the entry of the United States into the World War are many and varied. The case is more complicated than with respect to Russia, France and England. Nor was one person almost solely responsible for the attitude of the United States. It is quite evident that Walter Hines Page must be assigned a greater degree of guilt and responsibility than any other single "American," but he was not uniquely responsible. Colonel House presses him hard for first honors.

The approach to any interpretation of the entry of the United States into the World War must rest upon a review of the relations between Germany and the United States in the generation before the World War. The change in our sentiment towards Germany between 1870 and 1914 has been made the subject of an illuminating book by Dr. Clara E. Schieber.[1] In 1870 we were overwhelmingly on the side of Prussia in the Franco-Prussian War, and were very friendly with the German states.[2] Prussia was also the first European country to accept the sacrifices involved in the Bancroft treaties recognizing American naturalization as a renunciation of German citizenship. By 1914 there was more adverse sentiment towards Germany in this country than was directed against any other European state.[3] The reasons for this transformation are numerous.

There was unquestionably some development of antipathy on account of post-Bismarckian autocracy and militarism. The Kaiser's utterances on these and other matters were of a striking character, much like those of Mr. Roosevelt in this country, and hence made good copy for the newspapers.[4] Very important was the growth of trade rivalry. Both Germany and the United States underwent a tremendous economic and commercial development prior to the World War, and this led to competition for the markets of the world. Many believe this to be the most important and deep-seated cause of the growing coolness between the two countries.[5] The imperialism associated with this commercial expansion brought numerous clashes in foreign policy. There was some trouble over Samoa between 1872 and 1889. The conduct of Admiral von Diederichs in the Philippines in 1898 was distinctly unfriendly to this country, and in marked contrast to that of the commander of the British

fleet in these waters at the time.[6] The procedure
of Germany in China at the time of the occupation of the Shantung peninsula and in the Boxer
Revolt alarmed the representatives of American
interests in China.[7] Germany was also making a
notable economic conquest of Latin American
markets in the decade before the War, and
stirred the envy of American merchants and
investors. Then there was a definite clash
over Venezuela during Roosevelt's administration.[8]

Another very important factor lay in the fact
that the American papers relied for much of their
material on German affairs upon the Harmsworth papers in England which were even notoriously anti-German.[9] The articles of the Ger-
manophobe, F. W. Wile, in the New York *Times*
powerfully promoted American suspicion of Germany. By the opening of the present century
the anti-German current was definitely setting in
in this country, and the various efforts to counter-
act it through the visit of Prince Henry in 1902,
the gift of the statue of Frederick the Great in
1905, the exchange professorships, and the interpretation of German culture by Hugo Münster-
berg were inadequate to the task. We were already very strongly pro-Entente before Printsip
began his target-practice in the spring of 1914.[10]

Yet the anti-German feeling was more prevalent in lay circles than in the acts and policies of
the government. The American State Depart-

ment in 1914 was officially friendly and formally correct in its attitude towards Germany, though it must be remembered that there were certain unofficial, and perhaps written, understandings with Great Britain likely to influence our action in any European crisis in which Great Britain was involved.

There was, of course, some strong anti-English sentiment in Hibernian circles, but the anti-German sentiment was far stronger than any other American attitude towards a major European state. There were some prominent men who maintained independent judgment and failed to capitulate to the Harmsworth policies. Among these were Roosevelt,[11] Nicholas Murray Butler and W. H. Taft. The New York *Times* for June 8, 1913, ran a special section devoted to the celebration of the twenty-fifth anniversary of the accession of the Kaiser. Among other things it contained eloquent testimonials of prominent Americans and Englishmen bearing upon the contributions of the Kaiser to the advancement of the culture and well-being of the German Empire and the world, laying special stress upon the Kaiser's work in advancing the cause of world peace. Roosevelt led off with the statement that he had received more aid from the Kaiser in ending the Russo-Japanese War than he had obtained from any other person. Perhaps the most striking example of moral courage and independent opinion was the letter written for this issue by President Butler of Columbia University which we quote in full:

To THE EDITOR OF THE NEW YORK *Times:*—

It was either a satirist or a cynic who said that European politics might best be described as the science of misunderstanding. No personality is so likely to be misunderstood as one called to occupy high position and so placed as to be unable to make explanation or defense when misinterpreted or personally attacked. It may safely be said that this is particularly true of a sovereign, especially of a sovereign in these twentieth century days.

The German Emperor, who is now about to complete the first quarter century of a most eventful reign, will only be correctly understood when history is called upon for its calm, dispassionate judgment, and when those intimate revelations of mind and of character that private records contain are added to that which is made public as it occurs.

To be hereditary ruler, monarch, of millions upon millions of highly intellectual, industrious, and ambitious people, is in itself, at this period of the world's history, an achievement of the first magnitude. To be monarch of such a people in a period of industrial and intellectual unrest, of economic and territorial expansion, and of unprecedented commercial development, avoiding armed conflict with other nations and preserving order and progress at home, rises almost to the heights of the miraculous. To be a King who rules, who shares in the task of government, and who represents the national life and the national aspiration, requires ability and character of the first order.

Such a monarch must be at once a man of action and

a student; he must be at once of judicial temperament and abounding in sympathy and imagination; he must have both sound ideas and true ideals; he must really care, and care profoundly, for the economic welfare, the happiness, the comfort, and the morality of his people; he must guide their thought and their action constantly forward, yet he must not get out of touch with the great mass of the population or fall out of step with their daily tramp.

It must be left for history and the public revelation of that knowledge which is now confined to the few to support the statement that the German Emperor, in his reign of twenty-five years, has done all these things and has manifested all these traits. If the German Emperor had not been born to monarchy, he would have been chosen monarch—or Chief Executive—by popular vote of any modern people among whom his lot might have been cast.

NICHOLAS MURRAY BUTLER.

Former-President, now Chief Justice, Taft took the following strong position in the New York *Times* for June 6 and 8, 1913:

The truth of history requires the verdict that, considering the centrally important place which has been his among the nations, the German Empire has been for the last quarter of a century the greatest single individual force in the practical maintenance of the peace of the world."

Another important factor is to be found in the contrast between the attitudes of Mr. Page and

Mr. Gerard towards the countries in which they were resident as the representatives of the United States when the War came. As we shall point out later in more detail, Mr. Page so conducted himself that even Mr. Wilson once pronounced him more English than the English themselves. Gerard offered no such services to the German cause. The German attitude and activities growing out of the German efforts to retaliate against the illegal British blockade were a frequent cause of irritation to Mr. Wilson, and Mr. Gerard was not a second Page continually soothing Wilson with respect to troublesome German acts. In fact, Gerard was notably anti-German, and his administration of his duties was frequently so maladroit as to cause Mr. Wilson no little irritation.[12] But Wilson in most cases transferred his dislike from his Ambassador to the country with which he was dealing. Hence, there was a situation in which the Ambassador to England was doing everything possible to prevent this country from getting indignant with England, while the Ambassador to Germany behaved in quite a different fashion.

II. ENGLISH VIOLATION OF NEUTRAL RIGHTS IN ITS RELATION TO THE GERMAN SUBMARINE WARFARE

The alleged reason why the United States entered the War was, of course, the resumption of unlimited German submarine warfare,[13] but to have any understanding of the deeper causes we must get at the causes for the German submarine warfare in general, as well as its resumption in January, 1917. Here we are on firm ground. There is no doubt that the German submarine warfare was developed as a counter movement against the English violation of international law in regard to blockade, contraband and continuous voyage. By practically destroying, in these respects, the rights of neutrals, which had been worked out in a century of the development of international law, Great Britain was virtually able to shut off all imports into Germany from foreign countries, not only directly but also through neutral ports. It was to retaliate against this that Germany initiated her submarine warfare, which certainly cannot be regarded as in any sense more atrocious in fact or law than those English violations of neutral rights which had produced the submarine campaign. By practically acquiescing in these British violations of international law we not only lost most of what we had gained in the past in the way of establishing neutral rights on the seas, but also set a precedent which will prove an extremely nasty and embarrassing stumbling-block in the course of future negotiations in the event of war.[14]

In addition to these English violations of inter-

national law which vitally affected Germany as
well as neutrals, there were many special examples of British lawlessness, such a the intercep-
tion of our mails, the use of the American flag on
British ships, the seizure and search of United
States officials below the rank of minister while
traveling to and from their continental posts, and
the capture of ships like the *Dacia* (by the
French at the instigation of Page and the British), which had been legally transferred from enemy countries to American owners.[15] If the
United States had held England strictly to international law upon the threat of severance of diplomatic relations or even war, as we did in the
case of Germany and as we unquestionably
should have done in the case of England, the
German submarine warfare would not have been
necessary and probably would not have been utilized. So we may say with absolute certainty
that it was the unneutrality, lack of courage, or
maladroitness of the Washington authorities in
regard to English violations of international law
which produced the German submarine warfare
that actually led us into war.[16] It must be
remembered, however, that the resumption of
German submarine warfare, like the Belgian
question in England, was the excuse and not the
real reason for our entering the War. President
Wilson and Colonel House had decided that we

would come in at least a year before the submarine warfare was resumed by Germany.[17]

The gist of the whole matter, then, appears to be that Mr. Wilson failed himself to observe the neutrality he enjoined upon his country at the outbreak of the War.   By permitting England but not Germany to violate international law promiscuously he inevitably invited those reprisals which occurred.   He then found in the action which he thus stimulated those ostensible causes for the war which he idealized after April, 1917.

The above contentions are well brought out in the following letter of Mr. Bryan to President Wilson, which also makes it clear that Germany was willing to listen to the American suggestions as to negotiations about submarine warfare, while Great Britain refused to consider for a moment any discussion of the British blockade: [18]

April 23, 1915.

My Dear Mr. President:

In a note to you this afternoon I stated that Mr. Lansing would take your instructions to Old Point Comfort and prepare a tentative draft or note in the Thrasher case, during his stay there.

As I have not been able to reach the same conclusion to which you have arrived in this case, I feel it my duty to set forth the situation as I see it.   The note which you propose will, I fear, very much inflame the already

hostile feeling against us in Germany, not entirely because of our protest against Germany's action in this
case, but in part because of its contrast with our attitude toward the Allies. If we oppose the use of sub-
marines against merchantmen we will lay down a law
for ourselves as well as for Germany. If we admit the
right of the submarine to attack merchantmen but condemn their particular act or class of acts as inhuman
we will be embarrassed by the fact that we have not
protested against Great Britain's defense of the right
to prevent foods reaching non-combatant enemies.

We suggested the admission of food and the abandonment of torpedo attacks upon merchant vessels. Germany seemed willing to negotiate, but Great Britain
refused to consider the proposition. I fear that denunciation of one and silence as to the other will be construed by some as partiality. You do not make allow-
ance for the fact that we were notified of the intended
use of the submarine, or for the fact that the deceased
knowingly took the risk of traveling on an enemy ship.
I cannot see that he is differently situated from those
who by remaining in a belligerent country assume risk
or injury. Our people will, I believe, be slow to admit
the right of a citizen to involve his country in a war
when by exercising ordinary care he could have avoided
danger.

The fact that we have not contested Great Britain's
assertion of the right to use our flag has still further
aggravated Germany and we cannot overlook the fact
that the sale of arms and ammunition, while it could not
be forbidden under neutrality, has worked so entirely
for the benefit of one side as to give to Germany—not

justification but an excuse for charging that we are favoring the Allies. I have mentioned these things to show the atmosphere through which the Thrasher note will be received by Germany.

Believing that such a note as you propose is, under the conditions that now exist, likely to bring on a crisis, I venture to suggest an alternative, namely, an appeal to the nations at war to consider terms of peace. We cannot justify waiting until both sides, or even one side, asks for mediation. As a neutral we cannot have in mind the wishes of one side more than the wishes of the other side. . . .

With assurances, etc., I am, my dear Mr. President,

Very truly yours,

W. J. BRYAN.

On the point that the failure of the United States to deal with both belligerents in identical fashion helped to bring on the War, Germany stated her position in the note of February 18, 1915, in which she said that "They (the Germans) rely on the neutrals who have hitherto tacitly or under protest submitted to the consequences, detrimental to themselves, of England's war of famine to display no less tolerance toward Germany, even if the German measures constitute new forms of maritime war, as has hitherto been the case with the English measures." This demand for impartiality of treatment was proper, but that the State Department did not consider it so is evident from Secretary Lansing's note to the German Government on May 8, 1916, as follows: "In order, however, to avoid any possible misunderstanding the Government of the United States notifies the Imperial Government that it cannot for a moment entertain, much less discuss, a suggestion that respect by German naval authorities for the rights of citizens of the United States upon the high seas should in any way or in the slightest degree be made contingent upon the conduct of any other Government affecting the rights of neutrals and noncombatants. Responsibility in such matters is single, not joint; absolute, not relative." This position of Secretary Lansing was unsound and improper. He could hardly demand that one belligerent obey the laws of war and tolerate repeated violations by the other. The toleration of British violation induced and made necessary the German departure. At an earlier stage in the war, our State Department seems to have admitted some such doctrine, but as we gradually departed from neutrality, the view changed and it was deemed proper to hold one belligerent to strict compliance with the laws governing neutrality and to permit the other widely to depart therefrom. At one time Lansing denounced the British measures as "illegal and indefensible" but he did nothing to support the use of these harsh but just words.

In considering the problem as to why Mr. Wil-

son and his associates were unwilling to intervene
to coerce England and restrict her lawlessness
on the seas, we can be sure that there were many
and varied factors involved. Unquestionably
the most powerful influence was the virulent
pro-English attitude of Ambassador Page, who
persistently and openly fought against Mr.
Bryan and Mr. Lansing in the efforts of the
latter to protect American rights against the
arrogance and maritime anarchy of Great
Britain. The sad and humiliating story of
Page's reprehensible activities in this regard is
admirably summarized in the article by Mr. Grattan in the *American Mercury* for September,
1925—an article which was carefully read and revised by one of the world's foremost authorities
on the international law of neutral rights.[19]

The following is a fair sample of Mr. Page's
"patriotic" procedure as the accredited representative of the United States at the court of St.
James, entrusted with the responsibility of protecting the rights of his country. Our government had mildly protested against the flagrant
violation of international law by the English,
but Page, instead of presenting a forceful case
to Sir Edward Grey, went through the form of
reading it to Grey and then asked Grey to co-
operate with him in formulating an effective
reply *to our own State Department.* The
offense of Benedict Arnold seems highly com-

parable.   Both worked earnestly and directly to
promote the cause of Anglo-American unity.
This astonishing conduct of Page is revealed
by Sir Edward Grey in his recently published
memoirs.   One of the significant cases he re-
counts as follows: [20]

Page came to see me at the Foreign Office one day and
produced a long dispatch from Washington contestng
our claim to act as we were doing in stopping contraband going to neutral ports.   "I am instructed," he
said, "to read this dispatch to you."   He read and I
listened.   He then said: "I have now read the dispatch, but I do not agree with it; let us consider how it
should be answered."

This was too much even for the editorial writers of the New York *Times,* certainly a group
as much committed to the theory of the lamb-like
innocence of Poincaré and the divinely-guided
rectitude of Sir Edward Grey as it would be possible for any equally large assemblage of cultured
men to be.   The *Times* writer comments as follows upon Page's behavior as a "second Nathan
Hale": [21]

For a parallel to this action the records of diplomacy
would probably be searched in vain.   An ambassador
is right in doing all he can to help maintain friendly
relations between his own Government and the one to
which he is accredited. . . . But an ambassador's first
duty is, after all, to the government which he represents.

If he disagrees with its policy, he must keep still about it while in office abroad. Should his dissent be too strong for him to endure, he can always resign. But to act as Ambassador Page did was to follow a course for which it would be difficult to find a precedent and which could not be made common in diplomatic practice without demoralizing and disastrous consequences.

When Page did take his duties as Ambassador seriously Grey was able to divert his attention from "intercepted cargoes to the more congenial subject of Wordsworth, Tennyson, and other favorite poets." [22]

One of the most fair and judicious estimates of Page as Ambassador is contained in the following concluding paragraphs of Bainbridge Colby's review of the third volume of Mr. Page's letters in the *Saturday Review of Literature* for December 5, 1925:

I had occasion during one of the darkest hours of the War to visit England on an official mission and when I took my leave of the President at the White House he said to me: "Now be an American. Our men only last about six months in England and then they become Anglicized." The President referred to the subtle and encompassing and penetrating charm which is English. I think Page fell a victim to it. He took absolutely the English view of the controversies that arose during the War about our neutral rights. He saw with the vividness of close proximity the great issue of freedom as opposed to autocracy. It impaired his intellectual refraction. It distorted the angles of his vision. His sincerity is beyond question and his popular success in England was unmistakable, but he had ceased to be a serviceable spokesman of the President or a dependable Ambassador of the United States.

Hence Colonel House and his unofficial mission. Hence the estrangement of Page from the President,— and a Presidential silence that was considerate but knowing; followed by a course that was independent of his Ambassador, but right.

Incidentally, Mr. Wilson's remark to Colby furnishes an excellent illustration of the Scriptural statement as to the ease with which one detects the mote in the eye of another without discerning the beam in his own. Colby's judgment of Page is thoroughly shared by Colonel House in his recently published memoirs.

If we had possessed at London a competent, fair-minded and judicious Ambassador the story of American foreign policy from 1914–1919 would have been far different from what it was.

In a letter to the New York *Nation* for November 25, 1925, Mr. Arthur Garfield Hays contends that Mr. Page was not so anti-American as he seems from his letters. Mr. Hays believes that a most exaggerated impression of Mr. Page's pro-British attitude has been created by the editorial work of Mr. Burton J. Hendrick. When we recall that Mr. Hendrick was largely responsible for the book of Mr. Morgenthau containing the Potsdam Conference myth, we might be inclined to take considerable stock in Mr. Hays' thesis, were it not for the fact that Lord Grey makes out quite the same case against Page in his memoirs. Moreover, the well-known results of Mr. Page's conduct of his office during the controversy over neutral rights were not due to Mr. Hendrick. Again, Mr. Hays wrote before the third volume of Page's *Life and Letters* had appeared in which Mr. Page stands self-convicted as an open opponent of Mr. Wilson, Colonel House and the State Department.

Added to Page's primary responsibility was the naïve Anglo-mania of Secretary Houston, who had great influence with Mr. Wilson as an individual and as a member of his cabinet. Then, there was the very real pro-British sentiments of Mr. Wilson. Though Mr. Wilson's Anglo-mania was relatively slight and benign as compared with that of Mr. Page, it was unquestionably robust, and all of his writings from his youth onward reveal the fact that Mr. Wilson knew little or cared little about the culture of any other European country save that of England. All of his great heroes in literature and political science were English authors.[23] These diverse facts and influences prevented Mr. Wilson from ever sending the strong note he had drafted in protest against English violations of our rights, and also prevented him from thoroughly backing up Mr. Lansing in his struggle against Mr. Page and the British authorities in the vain effort to defend American rights against Great Britain.[24]

Our attitude as to the settlement of claims against the Entente and against Germany has been as lacking in impartiality as our conduct in enforcing the recognition of international law as between these two groups. The claims against Germany, even when judged by standards entirely outside of international law, boil down to $180,000,000. In part to vindicate these claims we entered a war that cost us about $30,000,000,-000. The claims against the Entente, even when based strictly on international law, greatly exceed $180,000,000. Nevertheless, though eight years have passed since the termination of hostilities, our Department of State has never made the slightest move to bring about a settlement of these large claims against the Entente.

III. THE PRESSURE FOR WAR BY AMERICAN BUSINESS AND FINANCE

Next we should note the powerful pressure of the great American financial interests and their subsidized press. From the beginning the international banking houses of the United States had taken a distinctly unneutral attitude, favoring investment in the bonds of the Allied countries, and discouraging or refusing investment in the paper of the Central Powers. This immediately gave us a strong financial stake in the cause of the Entente, and this stake grew larger with each year of the war. Likewise, American industry inevitably became violently pro-Ally. This was due to the fact that the British illegal blockade unlawfully cut off our sales of war materials to the Central Powers and made our enormous war profits dependent upon the purchases made by Great Britain, France, Russia and Italy. Upon the prospects of their success in the War and their ability to prolong the conflict depended the relative amount of American profits and the probability of our receiving payment for the goods we sold to these Entente powers.[25]

The writer is no fervent believer in the universal validity of the economic interpretation of history or in the correctness of the attempts which have been made to demonstrate that the United States went into the World War solely because of our investments in and sales to the Allied countries, but unquestionably from 1915–1918 the enormous power of American finance and industry was directed wholly toward the defense of the Allied powers and the support of their subtle propaganda.[26] In most cases this did not rest upon any original sympathy with these countries, but upon the actual nature of the economic realities of the moment. Had we invested primarily in the bonds of the Central Powers, and had we been selling most of our goods to these same powers, there is no doubt that American finance and industry would have been as flagrantly pro-German as it was pro-English and pro-French in 1915, 1916 and 1917.

Interesting in this connection is Gabriel Hanotaux's statement, never denied by the Americans involved, that former Ambassador Myron T. Herrick, Ambassador William Graves Sharp and Robert Bacon, all intimately related to great international banking houses in the United States, gave France every encouragement in September, 1914, that the United States would ultimately be brought in to aid the Allies, though they frankly admitted there was as yet little or no sentiment for intervention in this country.[27]

The problem of the American bankers in regard to Allied credit became acute at the close of 1916. The ability to raise further loans for the Entente countries from private credit was practically at an end by January, 1917, and the Wall Street bankers were in despair. Their only hope of relief lay in the possibility of shifting the burden from their own shoulders to the back of the United States treasury. This feat could only be achieved by having the United States abandon the pretense of technical and formal neutrality and enter the conflict as a co-belligerent. The German submarine note of January 31, 1917, was therefore a veritable god-send to the international bankers of this country. It crowned with success their earlier efforts to bring about American intervention. At the time the United States declared war Great Britain had overdrawn her account with American bankers to the amount of $400,000,000. As the British fiscal agent admitted, the immediate American deposit of this sum with J. P. Morgan "saved the British from a collapse in their credit." One does not have to adopt the theory of diabolic possession in interpreting this aspiration or this conduct on the part of the leading bankers, many of whom were high-minded and pacifically inclined individuals. They had simply become very heavily involved in a complex net of international finance which seemed likely to disintegrate with disastrous results to themselves and their clients if we did not enter the World War. As is usual in the business world, they put their professional interests and commitments ahead of their personal opinions, preferences and convictions. In an article in the Anglo-American number of the Manchester *Guardian* (January 27, 1920) Mr. Thomas Lamont set forth the facts as to the attitude of his firm before America's entry into the War with a blunt honesty and candor, as commendable as it is rare:

At the request of certain of the foreign Governments the firm of Messrs. J. P. Morgan and Co. under-

took to coördinate the requirements of the Allies, and
then to bring about regularity and promptness in fulfilling those requirements.   Those were the days when
American citizens were being urged to remain neutral
in action, in word, and even in thought.   But our firm
had never for one moment been neutral: we didn't know
how to be.   From the very start we did everything we
could to contribute to the cause of the Allies.   And
this particular work had two effects: one in assisting
the Allies in the production of goods and munitions in
America necessary to the Allies' vigorous prosecution
of the war; the other in helping to develop this great
and profitable export trade that our country has had.

One does not have to follow Upton Sinclair in
every phase of his argument to be aware that
American newspapers follow the dictates of
American finance and industry very closely and
very faithfully.   Hence, the American press had
become by 1915 and 1916 almost uniformly and
intolerantly pro-Ally, and in its editorials and its
handling of the news scathingly attacked Mr.
Wilson's neutral efforts.   In some cases Englishmen actually took over the control of some of
the leading American dailies.   Northcliffe spent
vast sums of money to secure extensive control
over the sentiment of the American press.   In
the case of the Providence *Journal,* the propaganda efforts of the editor were so extreme and
flagrant, that in the case of faked material pre-

pared for *World's Work,* the government had to intervene, and force strategic moderation. The story of Entente triumph over the American press is proudly narrated by Sir Gilbert Parker in Harper's *Magazine* for March, 1918.[28]

IV. AMERICA AND ENTENTE PROPAGANDA

This favorable attitude of the American press toward the Entente Powers was an enormous advantage to the latter. We were made to feel that the Entente was fighting the cause of the small and weak nations against the ruthlessness of a great bully. We were inevitably led to believe that the War had been started through the deliberate determination of Germany to initiate her alleged long-cherished plan to dominate the planet, while the Entente had proposed diplomatic settlement from the beginning and had only taken up arms in self-defense with the utmost reluctance. This theory of the German provocation of the War and the German lust for world dominion was played up in the newspapers and distributed in pamphlets of the National Security League and the American Defense Society [29] until the danger from Germany struck terror into the hearts of Americans, and citizens of Peoria, Illinois, and Council Bluffs, Iowa, lived in daily dread of a German submarine at-

tack; as a few years later they searched under
their beds nightly for the Bolshevik there secreted.

Then, the United States was peculiarly at the
mercy of the falsified atrocity pictures and other
propaganda poured into this country by the
Allies, who were at the same time able to keep
from public knowledge the German counter-
propaganda as well as German proofs of the falsity of these atrocity pictures, recently so conclusively demonstrated by Ferdinand Avenarius.[30] These circumstances made it much
easier for the pro-Ally groups to inflame American opinion and swing the country for war.

While in America during the War Northcliffe
made the following significant remark to a distinguished American professor: "Much as I
like the Americans, for a people who have
boasted of their freedom and democracy, I had
never expected to behold on their part so craven
a spirit of submission. So far as exercising real
independence of judgment and action with respect to the war is concerned, I can think of only
one people with whom to compare the Americans, namely, the Chinese."

Further, the Germans were singularly awk-
ward and unhappy in their utterances. The
more exuberant among them openly voiced their
aspirations as to territorial aggression and aggrandizement, while the Allies carefully re-

stricted their similar plans to closely hidden secret treaties, and concentrated their publicity upon their unselfish and disinterested struggle for ideals and the peace of the world.[31]

Finally, there is the question of the *Lusitania,* one of the matters most exploited by friends of the Entente in their efforts to drive Mr. Wilson into the War. It is debatable as to whether the *Lusitania* was violating international law by carrying a heavy cargo of munitions of war. But it is beyond question that as a naval auxiliary, as a British ship warned of her danger in the war zone, and as a warship carrying munitions, she lost about all of her immunities as a merchant ship. Her passengers likewise assumed the risks inherent to their danger in accepting passage on the boat. If, in addition, she was armed she unquestionably lost all of her privileges as a peaceful merchant ship, and was not even entitled to a warning before being attacked. While any humane person would naturally deplore the loss of life incidental to the sinking of the *Lusitania,* it is necessary to insist here that the sinking of a score of ships such as the *Lusitania* in no way compared as an inhuman atrocity with the illegally produced British blockade of Germany which brought disease or starvation to hundreds of thousands of innocent German non-combatants.[32]

As few persons have any real knowledge of the

facts in the *Lusitania* case it may be useful here to set forth some of the essentials. The passengers on the *Lusitania* had not only been warned of their danger by Germany two weeks before the ship sailed, but their sailing on this ship was actually in violation of our own statutes. The salient facts were set forth by Senator La Follette in a speech of September 20, 1917, in St. Paul: [33]

Four days before the "Lusitania" sailed, President Wilson was warned in person by Secretary of State Bryan that the "Lusitania" had six million pounds of ammunition aboard, besides explosives, and that the passengers who proposed to sail on that vessel were sailing in violation of a statute of this country, that no passenger shall travel upon a railroad train or sail upon a vessel that carries dangerous explosives. And Mr. Bryan appealed to President Wilson to stop passengers from sailing upon the "Lusitania."

The Senate attempted to impeach La Follette for this speech, but Dudley Field Malone, Collector of the Port of New York, confirmed the truth of the statements of Bryan and La Follette concerning the cargo of the *Lusitania* and the matter was adroitly and speedily dropped.

The British have denied that the *Lusitania* was armed, but before they can substantiate this claim it will be necessary for them to disprove the following revelation taken from the New York *Tribune* of June 19, 1913:

The reason why the crack liner *Lusitania* is so long delayed at Liverpool has been announced to be because her turbine engines are being completely replaced, but Cunard officials acknowledged to the *Tribune* correspondent today that the greyhound is being equipped with high power naval rifles in conformity with England's new policy of arming passenger boats. So when the great ship, the third selected by the Government for armament, next appears in New York Harbor about the end of August she will be the first British merchantman for more than a century sailing up the Lower Bay with black guns bristling over her sides.

In fact, the *Lusitania* was registered in the British navy as an auxiliary cruiser. Finally, the rapid sinking of the *Lusitania* was something unforeseen by naval engineers or the German naval authorities. She was expected to remain afloat for hours after being torpedoed.[34]

As early as May, 1915, when the *Lusitania* was torpedoed it was evident to Germany that the United States could not be depended upon to defend the rights of neutrals by curbing English violations of international law.

v. "HE KEPT US OUT OF WAR"

The case of Woodrow Wilson is singularly like that of Sir Edward Grey, namely, that of a man who loved peace but was drawn into war by a false conception of the facts and issues involved. There is no doubt that he was a pacifist at heart, but he viewed the conflict as one in which

England was upholding the cause of civilization. This led to his determination to enter the conflict if the entry of the United States should become essential to a British victory and if it was possible to put the country in as a unit. His policy, then, was one of combining a hope for an Entente victory with the preparation of the country for war in the event that England could not win without our assistance. There is no doubt that Wilson was as determined to enter the conflict as was Roosevelt, but he was far more subtle and adroit in his method of getting the country ready to support him in that move. When Wilson put the country into the War he had given the impression of having been a long-suffering and much abused pacifist who had resolutely stood out against war until no other alternative presented itself. This made the country convinced that it was really fighting in self-defense, something far different from what would have been the case if we had followed Roosevelt's advice and jumped headlong into the conflict after the sinking of the *Lusitania.*[35]

On August 11, 1914, Mr. Wilson issued his proclamation of neutrality, embodying a most commendable spirit of fairness. He stated in part:

We must be impartial in thought as well as in action; we must put a curb on our sentiments as well as upon

every transaction that might be construed as a preference of one party to the struggle before another. . . .
Every man who really loves America will act and speak
in the true spirit of neutrality, which is the spirit of
impartiality and fairness and friendliness to all concerned.

That Mr. Wilson was never in fact really neutral is attested to by numerous competent authorities. The letter of Mr. Bryan cited above
proves that he had one set of concepts and procedure for Great Britain and the Entente, and
quite another for the Central Powers. Even
more authoritative and convincing on this point
is the letter contributed to the New York *Times*
for January 29, 1925, by Thomas Watt Gregory,
the former Attorney-General in the administration of Woodrow Wilson:

To the Editor of the New York *Times:*

I have recently spent two months in Great Britain
and was greatly surprised to find there a growing tendency to minimize the contributions of the United
States to the winning of the World War, and a curious
misconception of Woodrow Wilson's attitude toward
that war. This misconception seems to have been
steadily growing since the late President retired from
office, and is largely accounted for by the fact that during these four years a number of his political opponents
have written and spoken to English audiences. In
many instances they have been severely critical, and in
some instances frankly abusive. The impropriety and

cruelty of aiming poisoned shafts at a slowly dying man—of whom, at least, it must be said that he fell in the harness, sacrificing his life, his health, his happiness —all but his fame—in valiantly battling for what he believed to be the salvation of mankind—is manifest. The friends of Mr. Wilson have too often remained silent when the truth should have been told and misrepresentations corrected.

Sometimes through ignorance, and sometimes through malice, the War President has been charged with having had no sympathy with the Allies, with having improperly delayed the entry of the United States into the war, and with having failed to vigorously prosecute that war.

A single incident furnishes a complete refutation of the first charge. Up to the time that Germany began its atrocious submarine warfare culminating in the sinking of the *Lusitania* we had far less cause for complaint against her than we had against Great Britain; the latter had repeatedly seized on the high seas our vessels bound for neutral ports; it had appropriated these vessels and their cargoes; it had opened our mail and prevented its delivery; it had ignored our protests, and in some instances had for weeks and months even failed to acknowledge their receipt. These were substantially the same acts that brought on the War of 1812.

While these conditions existed, a Cabinet meeting was held, at which several of Mr. Wilson's advisers expressed great indignation at what they considered violation of our international rights, and urged a more vigorous policy on our part.

After patiently listening, Mr. Wilson said, in that

quiet way of his, that the ordinary rules of conduct had no application to the situation; that the Allies were standing with their backs to the wall, fighting wild beasts; that he would permit nothing to be done by our country to hinder or embarrass them in the prosecution of the war unless admitted rights were grossly violated, and that this policy must be understood as settled.

Like all true-hearted Americans, he hoped that the United States would not be drawn into the war; but he was of Scotch and English blood, and by inheritance, tradition and rearing at all times the friend of the Allies.

As to the second charge that Mr. Wilson improperly delayed our entry into the war, all well-informed men whose minds work honestly know that the wisest thing he ever did was to refrain from recommending to Congress a declaration of war until a practically united country was behind the recommendation.

No greater mistake could have been made in a country organized like ours than to have declared war over the protest of a large body of our citizens or a large minority of the Congress; such action could have resulted only in disaster.

During the first two years of the war undoubtedly a large majority of our people and of Congress favored our keeping out, and this was the overwhelming sentiment of the people of the middle and western portions of the country. As time passed and the situation became more tense, Mr. Wilson repeatedly investigated and weighed public opinion, and kept himself fully advised of the situation in and outside of Congress.

Unanimity came with the repudiation by Germany

of her pledge as to restricted submarine warfare and the publication of the Zimmerman note. Mr. Wilson then acted at once, and a united country sprang to arms.

No greater slogan was ever uttered by human lips than his call of a peace-loving people to war. He signaled to the Allies across the Atlantic to hold the lines, for we were coming; he promised 2,000,000, 4,000,000, 10,000,000 men, if needed, and all the moral and material resources of the country without stint.

T. W. GREGORY.

Houston, Texas, Jan. 23, 1925.

Mr. Tumulty interprets Mr. Wilson's attitude in exactly the same fashion. Writing of the scene after the President's delivery of his message advising the declaration of war, Mr. Tumulty says: [36]

I shall never forget that scene in the Cabinet Room beween the President and myself. He appeared like a man who had thrown off old burdens only to add new ones.

It was apparent in his talk with me that he felt deeply wounded at the criticism that for months had been heaped upon him for his seeming unwillingness to go to war with Germany. As he discussed the step he had just taken, it was evident to me that he keenly felt the full solemnity and tragedy of it all. Turning to me, he said: "Tumulty, from the very beginning I saw the end of this horrible thing; but I could not move faster than the great mass of our people would permit. Very few understood the difficult and trying position I have been placed in during the years through which we have just passed. In the policy of patience and forbearance I pursued I tried to make every part of America and the varied elements of our population understand that we were willing to go to any length rather than resort to war with Germany. As I told you months ago, it would have been foolish for us to have been rushed off our feet and to have gone to war over an isolated affair like the *Lusitania*. But now we are certain that there will be no regrets or looking back on the part of our people. There is but one course now left open to us. Our consciences are clear, and we must prepare for the inevitable—a fight to the end. Germany must be made to understand that we have rights that she must respect. There were few who understood this policy of patience. I do not mean to say this in a spirit of criticism. Indeed, many of the leading journals of the country were unmindful of the complexities of the situation which confronted us."

The President then took out of his pocket an old and worn newspaper clipping, saying: "I wish to read you an analysis of my position and my policy by a special writer for the *Manchester Guardian*, who seemed, without consulting me or even conferring with me, to know just what I am driving at."

This special writer, commenting upon the Wilson policy, had said:

"Mr. Wilson's patience, now derided and criticized, will inevitably be the means by which he will lead his people by easy stages to the side of the Allies. By his methods of patience and apparent subservience to Germany, he will convince the whole American people that no other course save war is possible. This policy of Wilson's, now determined on, will work a complete transformation in his people. It will not evidence itself quickly or overnight. The moral preachment of Wilson before and after war will be the cause that will finally bring his people to the side of the Allies."

A crucial aspect of the causes of the American entry into the World War is the problem of what changed Mr. Wilson from an ostensible and far-sighted neutral into a vigorous partisan of the Allied propaganda. In 1914 he had proclaimed that the United States must be neutral in thought as well as action, and that the assumption of the unique guilt of one or another nation was absurd, the war having sprung from a multitude of complex causes. By 1917 he was maintaining that Germany alone brought on the War and that the very safety of the United States depended upon the crushing of German militarism.

In the first place, we must remember that Woodrow Wilson was a human being affected by the news, editorials and propaganda that played upon the minds of his fellow-citizens. When we recall that a large number of American historians and political scientists who were much superior to Mr. Wilson in intellectual capacity and professional standing completely succumbed to this same propaganda we need not wonder that he was affected by it to some considerable degree. In the next place, we should note the importance of his strong British sympathies which we have pointed out above. Also there was the long-continued pressure of Mr. Page, which most certainly must have had a tremendous influence upon Mr. Wilson, in spite of his occasional irritation at Page's excesses, and his exclamation at one time to the effect that Page was more British than the British themselves. Colonel House's memoirs now show us that he was converted to the war policy months before Wilson. In the light of his close relations with Wilson at the time there can be little doubt that House was a powerful factor after 1915 in swinging Wilson for war. The distinctly anti-German bias and pro-British sympathies of Wilson, Houston, Page, House and other Southern confidants of Wilson, have led some writers to hold that Wilson was motivated in part by resentment at the decisive part played by the Germans in preserving the union during the Civil War. They contend that Wilson made war on Germany to "avenge Appomattox."

Again, there was the matter of natural human pride and sensitiveness to criticism. Some of the most powerful American individuals and newspapers had become violently pro-Ally early in the War and directed withering and scandalous criticism against Mr. Wilson's ostensibly broad-minded and statesmanlike program of neutrality. Particularly notorious was the atti-

tude of men like Theodore Roosevelt and George
Harvey.   Harvey's attack upon Wilson was far
more bitter and vindictive than that of many radicals and pacifists who were condemned to long
terms   in   federal   penitentiaries.   Roosevelt
greatly angered Wilson by such speeches as "The
Shadows of Shadow Lawn," and by phrases like
"weasel words."   Even Elihu Root enormously
irritated and humiliated him by his speech in
which he asserted rather contemptuously in regard to Wilson: "First he shakes his fist and
then he shakes his finger!" [37]   Further, there
was the matter of Mr. Wilson's courtship and
his marriage with the second Mrs. Wilson.   The
psychology of the long-suffering, non-resisting
pacifist was not well adapted to the conventional
behavior patterns, attitudes and technique of the
suitor and bridegroom.   Mr. Lawrence points
out how Wilson's first apparent changes in the
way of advocating preparedness synchronized
very exactly with the period of his courtship and
second marriage.   There is no doubt that the
second Mrs. Wilson was more irritated by and
resentful of the criticism of her distinguished
husband's pacific endeavors than was he himself.[38]

Then, it is certain that Wilson's vanity
was enormously inflated by the remarkable popularity of his "swing around the circle" in ad-
vocacy of preparedness late in 1915, so well described in the tenth chapter of David Lawrence's

True Story of Woodrow Wilson. This contrasted most strikingly with the denunciations of his "too proud to fight" speech and his other efforts to appear neutral. Wilson was ever sensitive, like other human beings, to popular acclaim, and by the beginning of 1916 it was apparent that popularity was to be found on the side of preparedness, even if the country was not ready for war. Any striking change in German policy, like the resumption of submarine warfare, or any example of German resentment, like the Zimmermann telegram, could be relied upon to carry the American people from preparedness to the next step of actual war.

It has been generally supposed that Mr. Wilson was strongly pacific up to February, 1917, and was won over to war solely by the information that the resumption of submarine warfare had been decided upon by the German authorities. This view is now shown to be completely fallacious. Sir Edward Grey has revealed this fact in his memoirs, and it has been amply confirmed in the third volume of Page's letters, and by Colonel House in his memoirs.[39] In the winter of 1915–16 Wilson sent Colonel House to Europe with a plan for peace, the rejection of which by Germany would carry with it the probable entry of the United States into the War on the side of the Entente. It is most significant that even though the peace proposals of Mr. Wil-

son embodied terms for Germany which only a
thoroughly defeated nation could have been expected to accept, still Germany seemed willing
to negotiate if the Entente would consent to such
a procedure. Yet Lloyd George brusquely
turned down any suggestion of negotiations for
peace at this time. The following is the essential
portion of this plan:

Colonel House told me that President Wilson was
ready, on hearing from France and England that the
moment was opportune, to propose that a Conference
should be summoned to put an end to the war. Should
the Allies accept this proposal, and should Germany refuse it, the United States would probably enter the war
against Germany.

Colonel House expressed the opinion that, if such a
Conference met, it would secure peace on terms not unfavorable to the Allies; and, if it failed to secure peace,
the United States would leave the Conference as a belligerent on the side of the Allies, if Germany was unreasonable. Colonel House expressed an opinion decidedly favorable to the restoration of Belgium, the
transfer of Alsace and Lorraine to France, and the
acquisition by Russia of an outlet to the sea, though
he thought that the loss of territory incurred by Germany in one place would have to be compensated to her
by concessions to her in other places outside Europe.
If the Allies delayed accepting the offer of President
Wilson, and if, later on, the course of the war was so
unfavorable to them that the intervention of the United
States would not be effective, the United States would

probably disinterest themselves in Europe and look to their own protection in their own way.

At a luncheon with Sir Edward Grey, Lord Robert Cecil and Page, Colonel House expressed Wilson's purpose even more explicitly: "The United States would like Great Britain to do whatever would help the United States to aid the Allies." [40]

Grey rejected this plan for a conference, but without any apparent consciousness of the fact that he had been guilty of any such crime as he assigns to the German government for their rejection of his conference plan in 1914. As usual, Sir Edward was rendered yeoman service in his struggle against the United States by Mr. Page, who, Mr. Hendrick informs us, had "by this time lost faith in the wisdom of President Wilson's leadership." He even refused to go with House to a conference with British officials on the subject of the peace plan of Mr. Wilson, and roundly denounced House and the President for their meddling in British affairs.[41]

But this British rebuff did not lead Mr. Wilson to lose courage in his efforts to put the country into the War. His next step was taken in this country. Early in April, 1916, Wilson called into consultation Champ Clark, Congressmen Claude Kitchin and H. D. Flood, and sounded them out to see if they would support him in a plan to bring the United States into the

War on the side of the Allies. This was the famous "Sunrise Conference" described later by Gilson Gardner in *McNaught's Monthly* for June, 1925.[42] These men sharply refused to sanction any such policy, and Mr. Wilson allowed the campaign of 1916 to be fought out on the slogan, "He kept us out of war." Wilson did not dare to risk splitting the Democratic Party over entry into the War before the campaign of 1916 was successfully ended. Once elected, he could count on even virulent Republican enemies like Lodge to offset any Democratic defection in Congress over the war problem.[43]

Gilson Gardner, who has made a special study of this question of the famous "Sunrise Conference," thus describes the meeting of Wilson with the leaders of the Democratic Party in Congress: [44]

As the story was told to me, this early morning conference at the White House was attended by Representatives Clark, Flood and Kitchin. It was at this conference that President Wilson announced his intention to put the United States into war and to do so immediately. Clark, Flood and Kitchin were shocked at Wilson's announcement and declared that it was impossible; that the people did not want this country put into war, and that any effort on Wilson's part to force such a result would be met by them with a very bitter fight. Wilson threatened, and said that any man standing in the way would be politically destroyed if he started to carry out his purpose. There were heated words, and the conference broke up with a declaration by these leaders that they would resist the President to the utmost in any such effort.

The attitude taken at this time by Champ Clark raises an interesting question as to what would have happened to this country and the world if Mr. Bryan had not interfered at Baltimore in 1912 and Champ Clark had been nominated and elected President of the United States. The writer has discussed this problem with some of the best informed men in the country and he has yet to find any one who does not feel that Clark would have stood out resolutely against war. Some have agreed with this, but have held that we should also have missed the remarkable reform legislation of the first Wilson administration. Of this we cannot be sure, as the Democrats would probably have enacted some part of this program without the Wilson leadership. But, in any event, it can scarcely be doubted that the disasters which came to the country as a result of our entry into the War far outweighed any advantages which have come from the Wilsonian legislation. Hence, it would seem that one of the strange ironies of history lies in the fact that when the Great Commoner strode down the aisle amidst the hisses of delegates at the Baltimore Convention he was launching the first

act in the great drama which was to put the
United States into the most costly war in our history and to bring the country into the darkest
and most hopeless period of political and economic reaction which we have yet experienced.
This, indeed, was a tragic achievement for the
apostle of the Prince of Peace and the leading
figure in American political and economic radicalism for a generation!

With Mr. Wilson in office as President it was
a great blow to the United States when John
Bassett Moore resigned from the State Department.   Had Wilson been able to retain the greatest international jurist of the age his betrayal
of American traditions and self-interest would
have been clearly pointed out to him, and he
would have received a definite and unbiased conception from a genuine international statesman
as to what the War actually involved from the
standpoint of the issues of international law and
world statesmanship.

Mr. Wilson was convinced after the failure of
the "Sunrise Conference" that there was no hope
of getting the country into the War until after
the election.   He quite well sensed the value of
making the campaign on a pacific platform.
The sentiment of the country was for peace, and
if he was elected as an exponent of peace and
then went into war the country as a whole would
believe that he had done his best to "keep us out

of war." He would have a united country behind him. Hence, he sent Governor Martin
Glynn of New York and Senator Ollie James of
Kentucky to the Democratic National Convention at St. Louis in June, 1916, with instructions
to make keynote speeches which would emphasize
Mr. Wilson's heroic efforts to keep us out of
war. Glynn praised the pacific efforts of Mr.
Wilson in the following fulsome phrases: [45]

This policy may not satisfy those who revel in destruction and find pleasure in despair. It may not satisfy the fire-eater or the swashbuckler but it does satisfy
those who worship at the altar of the god of peace. It
does satisfy the mothers of the land at whose hearth
and fireside no jingoistic war has placed an empty
chair. It does satisfy the daughters of the land from
whom bluster and brag have sent no loving brother to
the dissolution of the grave. It does satisfy the fath-
ers of this land and the sons of this land who will fight
for our flag, and die for our flag when reason primes the
rifle, when Honor draws the sword, when Justice
breathes a blessing on the standards they uphold. . . .
The paramount issue of this campaign is that the
United States is constrained by the traditions of its
past, by the logic of its present, and by the promise of
its future, to hold itself apart from the conflict that
now devastates the nations across the seas.

Equally eloquent was the eulogy of this same
program of peace by Senator James: [46]

Four years ago they sneeringly called Woodrow Wilson the school-teacher; then his classes were assembled within the narrow walls of Princeton College. They were the young men of America. To-day he is the world teacher, his class is made up of kings, kaisers, czars, princes and potentates. The confines of the schoolroom circle the world. His subject is the protection of American life and American rights under international law. The saving of neutral life, the freedom of the seas, and without orphaning a single American child, without widowing a single American mother, without firing a single gun, without a shedding of a single drop of blood, he has wrung from the most militant spirit that ever brooded above a battlefield, along with an acknowledgment of American rights and an agreement to American demands. (*Vigorous cheering and applause for twenty minutes.*)

Thus was fashioned the famous slogan *"He kept us out of war"* which reëlected Woodrow Wilson to the presidency almost a year after he and Colonel House had decided that "The United States would like Great Britain to do whatever would help the United States to aid the Allies." It has sometimes been said in defense of Mr. Wilson that he did not personally invent the slogan "He kept us out of war." Yet he not only allowed it to be used as the very keynote of his campaign in 1916, but also personally directed the nomination and campaign policies which formulated this slogan. If one is still in-

terested in the moral character and political
integrity of Woodrow Wilson the following exhibit should prove illuminating and convincing.
A month after he had sent Colonel House abroad
to tell Grey that he could count on the entry of
the United States into the War on the side of the
Entente just as soon as Wilson could swing public opinion for such an act, and when Wilson
knew that American public opinion was still distinctly against intervention, he said the following in a speech at Milwaukee on January 31,
1916:

Governments have gone to war with one another.
Peoples, so far as I can remember, have not, and this is
a government of the people, and this people is not going
to choose war.

After the election, Germany, convinced, quite
correctly, that the United States had in practice
given up the pose of neutrality and intended to
get into the War as soon as possible, decided to
resort to a revival of unrestricted submarine warfare as a last hope and expedient. This decision
was taken quite as much through a popular demand for such action in Germany as through any
sinister and secret plotting of von Tirpitz or other
officials. A starving people were demanding an
early release from their suffering and despair
through a rapid termination of the War. Having been the victims of illegal starvation and cut

off from even neutral foodstuffs, they assented
to the necessity of unrestricted submarine warfare which Tirpitz and others had assured them
would bring the War to a speedy close. The
United States had helped along this step in that
our unwillingness to restrain Allied illegality
forced Germany to seek reprisal and relief
through the pursuit of desperate methods.
Many believe that joy reigned in the White
House when the German note of January 31,
1917, announcing the resumption of submarine
warfare, reached this country. Whether this is
true or not, there can be no doubt of the universal
and complete rejoicing in Wall Street.

The propaganda favorable to war in the United
States was greatly aided, and in a most timely
fashion, by the revelation of the *Zimmermann
Telegram* to Mexico. The British had captured
it three months before they made its contents
public, late in February, 1917. They carefully
waited until the most opportune time and then
"sprung" it at a highly appropriate moment to
inflame American opinion. The Zimmermann
proposition was foolish, but it must be remembered that it contained a plan which was *only* to
be put into operation in the event that the United
States entered the War, and Germany wished
above all else to keep us from coming into the
conflict. But the announcement of the resumption of submarine warfare and the publication

of the Zimmermann note turned the trick. From the close of February, 1917, there was no doubt that the United States would enter the War. Within less than a month after his second inauguration Mr. Wilson was recommending war to Congress, with the lofty exhortation to his country that "God helping her, she can do no other." We were fairly launched on the great crusade to make the "world safe for democracy" with the appropriate and efficient aid of the armies of the Tsar of Russia and the Mikado of Japan.

Some have held that a powerful factor affecting Mr. Wilson's decision was his conviction by 1916 that he could not lead world policy through pacific methods but might assume world leadership if he threw the United States into the War and was thereby able to dominate the war aims of the Allied powers and the United States. Many of the facts in his conduct in the spring of 1916 and thereafter lend much plausibility to this hypothesis. The writer believes, however, that it was his pro-British sympathy more than anything else which led Mr. Wilson into his decision by the close of 1915 that we must enter the World War unless the English objectives could be realized through a negotiated peace.

The well-nigh complete psychic confusion generated in the mind of Woodrow Wilson by the conflict between his basic conceptions of international relations, his pro-British sympathies, his desire to avoid war and yet save England, and his disillusionment after the war for idealism is admirably brought out in the following selections from his speeches which have been brought together in the appendix to John Kenneth Turner's valuable work:

No people ever went to war with another people. Governments have gone to war with one another. Peoples, so far as I can remember, have not, and this is a government of the people, and this people is not going to choose war . . . Speech of Woodrow Wilson, January 31, 1916.

The great fact which stands out above all the rest is that this is a people's war. . . . Flag Day Address, 1917.

We find ourselves fighting again for our national existence . . . Independence Day, 1918.

America was not immediately in danger . . . America was not directly attacked . . . September, 1919.

I challenge you to cite me an instance in all the history of the world where liberty was handed down from above. Liberty always is attained by the forces working below, underneath. . . . Published statement, in *Saturday Evening Post*, May 23, 1914.

We are to be an instrument in the hands of God to see that liberty is made secure for mankind . . . June 5, 1917.

First of all it must be a peace without victory. . . . Victory would mean peace forced upon the loser, a victor's terms imposed upon the vanquished . . . Only a peace between equals can last; only a peace the very principle of which is equality and a common participation in a common benefit . . . January 22, 1917.

Force will not accomplish anything that is permanent . . . June 30, 1916.

Force, force to the utmost, force without stint or limit, the righteous and triumphant force that shall make right the law of the world . . . April 6, 1918.

The German power must be crushed . . . December 4, 1917.

Have you heard what started the present war? If you have I wish that you would publish it, because nobody else has. So far as I can gather, nothing in particular started it, but everything in general . . . October 26, 1916.

The war was begun by the military masters of Germany . . . Flag Day Address, 1917.

This war, in its inception, was a commercial and industrial war. It was not a political war . . . September 5, 1919.

The German bankers, the German merchants and the German manufacturers did not want this war. They were making conquest of the world without it, and they knew it would spoil their plans . . . September 9, 1919.

The German nation had no choice whatever as to whether it was to go into that war or not, did not know that it was going into it until its men were summoned to the colors . . . September 11, 1919.

In the last analysis, my fellow-countrymen, as we in America would be the first to claim, a people are responsible for the acts of their government . . . Germany was self-governed. Her rulers had not concealed the purposes they had in mind . . . September 4, 1919.

VI. THE EFFECT OF AMERICAN INTERVENTION

A very important element in adequately debunking us of wartime illusions is a consideration of the actual results for the world of the American entry into the World War. We have conventionally believed that it was a great boon to civilization and that it saved the world from German domination and the imposition of German militarism and tyranny upon the planet as a whole.[47] The facts are almost exactly the reverse of this picture. In 1916 and 1917 Germany was ready for peace on very moderate and constructive terms, certainly terms far more fair and more to the advantage of the world at large than those imposed at Versailles two years later. In fact, if the American papers had been able or willing to get hold of and print the full German terms of peace and to portray accurately the state of the German mind in 1916 and 1917, there is no likelihood that Mr. Wilson or any one else could have forced the United States into the World War.[48] There is little probability that Germany could have conquered the Allies if America had not intervened. The best that Ludendorff hoped for after 1916 was enough success to force an honorable peace. Germany

would have welcomed an honorable peace; it was
the Allies who were bent upon the destruction of
Germany even after they knew that a just peace
could be secured by negotiation. What the
American entry did was to encourage the Allies
in the wastes and savagery which led to Versailles, the blockade of Germany after the Armistice, and the outrages in the Ruhr. The
highly precarious foundation upon which Europe
stands today with almost a sure guaranty of future war, as well as the outbreak of Bolshevism,
which was due to the prolongation of the War
after the Russian people desired to withdraw,
may both be traced to the results of American
intervention. Our entry was, thus, a menace to
both the "Reds" who met punishment as a result
of the Palmer inquisition, and the conservatives
who were thrown into a panic by Bolshevism.

One of the main activities of the Allied censorship and propaganda in this period consisted in
keeping from the United States any adequate
knowledge of the very real desire for peace in
Germany at this time and the highly reasonable
and statesmanlike nature of the German proposals. These really sincere efforts of the Germans were portrayed as but insidious German
propaganda designed to divide the Allied Powers. The chief reason why the Entente statesmen did not accept these German terms and end
the War, with all its attendant miseries and

losses, two years before the armistice, was their knowledge of the evident breaking down of American neutrality and their ever-brightening hope that the United States would ultimately come into the conflict on their side. Mr. Page's support of the British cause practically destroyed in England all fear of American protests against the Entente violations of neutral rights and made England quite unwilling to consider any peace proposals at the close of 1916. Had the British believed that the United States meant its protests seriously they would most certainly have listened with some patience to the peace proposals, but Page gave assurance that we were really their ally and that they had nothing to fear from us. Had Mr. Wilson dismissed Mr. Page early in the War and replaced him by an honest, courageous, far-sighted and well-informed Ambassador, and preserved a strict neutrality on the part of this country, there seems little doubt that the War would have come to an end by December of 1916, and would have been settled by a treaty of peace infinitely superior in every way to that which was worked out in 1918–19 and imposed by the victors at Versailles.

Page and Wilson must in part bear the responsibility not merely for the expense, losses and miseries brought to the United States by the World War but also for the destruction in Europe following 1916 both in war and in the ar-

rogant and atrocious policies of France and
England, particularly the former, since the
Armistice and the Peace Treaty.[49] Already, as
Mr. Gregory complains in his letter cited above,
England had begun to forget or to minimize our
contributions to winning the War, while the
hatred of the United States in France exceeds
anything which has existed since the French denunciation of the United States during the
Spanish-American War. The absurd and base-
less contention that the Allies really saved the
lives of countless millions of Americans, as well
as preserving our national independence and preventing us from becoming a slavish dependency
of Potsdam, has been made the foundation for
a serious proposal that we should cancel the
Allied indebtedness to the United States. Such
mythology is on a par with the "corpse-factory"
fabrications of the war period itself. There may
be valid grounds for debt cancellation, but this
alleged justification is one of the most notable
serio-comic propositions in the history.[50]

Added to the material and financial expenditures of the United States, due to our participation in the World War, are the political
corruption and incompetence which it has generated, the raids upon American liberty by Palmer
and his associates and successors, and the general
decline of morale in American public and private
life which has been unparalleled by any earlier

developments in the history of our country. Democracy did not cure war, but the War cured democracy in the United States—an outcome foreseen with eager anticipation by the American plutocrates in 1917.

As another phase of our entry we should not fail to remember the notorious debauching of American traditions with respect to enemy-owned property by the Alien Property Custodian which set a very menacing precedent for some future war when the United States might be the loser by such procedure.[51]

If we honestly face the facts we shall probably have to agree that the entry of the United States into the World War was an almost unmitigated disaster, not only to us but to Europe. We shall ultimately understand that Woodrow Wilson's greatest message to the world was not his war propaganda or his disregarded Fourteen Points, but his much ridiculed proclamation that the only possible peace was a "peace without victory."

The degree to which Mr. Wilson was compelled to develop psychic blindness, amnesia and anæsthesia in order to "stomach" Entente idealism towards the end of the war is well brought out by his refusal to recognize the existence of the Secret Treaties until concretely faced by them at the Paris Peace Conference. Though they were published in the winter of 1917–18 in the New York *Evening Post* and elsewhere, though the editor of that paper personally put them in

the hands of Secretary Tumulty with the promise
of the latter that he would call them to the attention of Mr. Wilson, and though Walter Lippmann contends that he is certain that Mr. Wilson personally knew of their existence and nature, yet when the latter left for Paris at the close
of November, 1918, he professed to be in complete ignorance of these documents which Mr.
Balfour had been careful not to disclose when
on his mission to this country.

Perhaps the best epitaph on the whole episode
of America and the World War, as well as the
finest proof of the futility of intervention, is contained in the statement of Mr. Wilson to James
Kerney on December 7, 1923, relative to the policy of Poincaré: "I should like to see Germany
clean up France, and I should like to see Jus-
serand and tell him so to his face." [52]

VII. CONCLUSIONS

(1) The United States was more friendly towards Germany than towards any other major
European state in 1870. By 1914 we were more
antagonistic towards Germany than towards
any other major European state. This transformation of American sentiment was caused
primarily by trade rivalry, clashes in imperialistic adventures, and the fact that most of the
American news concerning Germany came
through the notoriously anti-German English

papers controlled by Harmsworth (Northcliffe).

(2) It is conventionally believed that the resumption of unrestricted German submarine warfare early in 1917 was the real and only reason why the United States entered the World War. Such is not the truth. Mr. Wilson had decided to intervene as soon as he could swing the American people to this view more than a year before January, 1917. The German submarine warfare was a legitimate retaliation against the British violations of international law with respect to such matters as contraband, continuous voyage and blockade, against which Mr. Wilson refused to protest with adequate persistence and firmness. The pro-British sympathies of Mr. Wilson were far outdistanced by those of Walter Hines Page, Ambassador of the United States in London, whose maladministration of his duties was a chief obstacle to American impartiality in dealing with the belligerent nations after 1914.

(3) The *Lusitania* was a registered auxiliary cruiser in the British navy and was carrying 5400 cases of ammunition when she left New York on her last and fatal trip. The passengers had been warned of their danger by the German government two weeks before the departure of the boat, and their sailing on the boat was in violation of the laws of the United States. The commander of the German submarine which

sank the *Lusitania* did not know the identity of
the vessel when he discharged the first torpedo,
but when he discovered it he refrained from any
further attack.   The *Lusitania* should under ordinary circumstances have remained afloat for an
ample period to discharge all passengers safely.

(4) American finance and business were very
strongly pro-Entente and pressed hard for intervention on the side of the Allies.   Their attitude influenced the American press, which was
very generally under the sway of the Entente
propaganda.

(5) Mr. Wilson, while in favor of peace as
against war in the abstract, decided to enter the
War on the side of the Entente as soon as he was
convinced that England could not win decisively
without American aid.   This decision on his part
was arrived at before the close of the year 1915.
In January, 1916, he sent Colonel House abroad
to inform Grey that the United States would enter the War as soon as he could bring American
opinion to that point.   A month after the departure of Colonel House, Wilson emphatically
declared in a speech at Milwaukee that the
United States would not intervene in the World
War.   In April, 1916, he attempted to get the
Democratic leaders in Congress to aid him in
throwing the country into war, but they firmly
refused to support him in any such action.

(6) Mr. Wilson planned the 1916 campaign

for reëlection on the basis of an appeal to the pacifist sentiments of the country for a double purpose. He decided that non-intervention was still the more popular view in the doubtful political areas of the country, and that if he was elected on the pacifist platform there would be far less suspicion attached to his ultimate announcement of our decision to intervene.

(7) The resumption of German submarine warfare was a great German political blunder, comparable to the invasion of Belgium, and it played directly into the hands of President Wilson and the Wall Street bankers who wished the United States to finance the Allied Powers, in the same way that the German blunder in invading Belgium played into the hands of Sir Edward Grey.

(8) The intervention of the United States was an unmitigated disaster for both America and the world. Germany could not have decisively defeated the Entente if America had not intervened. She was eager by 1916 for a just negotiated peace. It was the ever brighter prospect of American intervention which encouraged the Entente to reject the peace proposals of Germany, President Wilson and the Pope. American intervention unnecessarily prolonged the War for two years, with all the resulting savagery, misery and increased economic burdens. It made possible the abomination of Versailles,

which has postponed the beginning of European readjustment for a decade and produced almost as much loss, misery and hatred as the War itself. The desolation and despair brought about in Europe by the prolongation of the War is what established Lenin in Russia and Mussolini in Italy.

(9) American intervention reacted disastrously upon the United States through its increase of our public debt and governmental expenses, its practical destruction of the effects of the Wilsonian liberalism and reform legislation, its promotion of the decline of public morale and political honesty and competence, and its contribution to the creation of an unprecedented atmosphere of intolerance, unreasoning conservatism and complacency in the face of unexampled public corruption and incapacity.

(10) The pathetic futility of the intervention of the United States is well expressed by the statement of Mr. Wilson shortly before his death that he would like to see Germany make war upon France and defeat the latter decisively. In spite of our intervention in behalf of the Entente we are today much more hated in England, France, Italy and Russia than in Germany.

(11) After it is too late to retrieve our losses in men, money and morale, thoughtful Americans have at last come to recognize that, in the words of Bruce Bliven: " 'We have been played

for a bunch of suckers,' used to pull the English and French chestnuts out of the fire.''

SELECTED REFERENCES

Bassett, J. S., *Our War with Germany;* Bausman, Frederick, *Facing Europe; The Memoirs of William Jennings Bryan;* Dunn, R. W., *American Foreign Investments;* Gardner, G., "Why We Delayed Entering the War," in *McNaught's Monthly,* June, 1925; Grattan, C. H., "The Walter Hines Page Myth," in *American Mercury,* September, 1925; Grey of Fallodon, *Twenty-Five Years;* Hale, W. B., *The Story of a Style;* Hendrick, B. J., *The Life and Letters of Walter Hines Page;* Keim, J., *Forty Years of German-American Political Relations;* Lawrence, David, *The True Story of Woodrow Wilson;* McMaster, J. B., *The United States in the World War;* Schieber, C. E., *The Transformation of American Sentiment Towards Germany, 1870–1914;* Seymour, C., *Woodrow Wilson and the World War;* (ed.) *The Intimate Papers of Colonel House;* Tirpitz, A. von, "The German Navy in the World War"; in *These Eventful Years,* Vol. II, Chap. xiii; Tumulty, J. F., *Woodrow Wilson as I Knew Him;* Turner, J. K., *Shall It be Again?;* Villard, O. G., "The Nakedness of Colonel House," in New York *Nation,* Avril 14, 1926; White, W. A., *Woodrow Wilson, the Man, His Times, and His Task;* Young, E. W., *The Wilson Administration and the Great War.*

FOOTNOTES AND FURTHER REFERENCES

[1] C. E. Schieber, *The Transformation of American Sentiment towards Germany, 1870–1914.* Boston, 1923, xvi, 294 pp. Cf. also

Jeanette Keim, *Forty Years of German-American Political Relations.*

2 Schieber, op. cit., Chap. i.

3 Ibid., Chaps. v, vii.

4 Ibid., pp. 98, 134, 159, 209–21.

5 Ibid., pp. 186 ff.

6 Ibid., pp. 111 ff.

7 Ibid., pp. 89 ff.

8 Ibid., Chap. iv.

9 This information comes to me from various American newspaper men of high repute, and has been confirmed in detail by Mr. H. L. Mencken.

10 Schieber, op. cit., Chaps. v–vii.

11 J. B. Bishop, *Theodore Roosevelt and His Time,* Vol. I, pp. 384–6; Vol. II, pp. 245 ff., 270 ff.

12 Cf. J. W. Gerard, *My Four Years in Germany.* My information as to the irritation of Wilson with Gerard comes from direct but confidential sources. See Gerard's article in the New York *Times Current History Magazine,* March, 1926.

13 J. S. Bassett, *Our War with Germany;* J. B. McMaster, *The United States in the World War,* Vol. I; C. Seymour, *Woodrow Wilson and the World War.*

14 J. L. Garvin (Ed.) *These Eventful Years,* Vol. I, Chap. xiii (Chap. by Admiral von Tirpitz); J. K. Turner, *Shall It Be Again?* Chaps. xiii–xviii, xxiii. Cf. the letter of Sir Percy Scott in the London *Times,* July 16, 1914.

15 B. J. Hendrick, *The Life and Letters of Walter Hines Page,* Vol. I, pp. 390 ff.; C. Hartley Grattan, "The Walter Hines Page Legend," in *American Mercury,* September, 1925; *The Memoirs of William Jennings Bryan,* Chap. xiv.

16 As above, and J. K. Turner, *Shall It Be Again?* Chaps. xi–xviii.

17 Grey of Fallodon, *Twenty-Five Years,* Chap. xxiii; B. J. Hendrick, op. cit., Vol. III, Chap. x.

18 *The Memoirs of William Jennings Bryan,* pp. 396–7.

19 C. Hartley Grattan, "The Walter Hines Page Legend," loc. cit.; the only intelligent effort to defend Page known to the writer is the letter by Arthur Garfield Hays in the New York *Nation,* November 25, 1925. For Colonel House's views of Page as ambassador see C. Seymour, *The Intimate Papers of Colonel House,* Vol. I, pp. 104 ff. For a moderate German analysis of Page see the penetrating articles by Georg Karo in the *Kriegsschuldfrage* for August and September, 1926.

20 Grey of Fallodon, *Twenty-Five Years,* Vol. II, p. 110.

21 New York *Times,* August 9, 1925.

22 Hendrick, op. cit., Vol. II, p. 306.

23 W. B. Hale, *The Story of a Style*, Chap. ii; Woodrow Wilson, *An Old Master and Other Political Essays*, and *Mere Literature;* C. E. Merriam, *Americal Political Ideas, 1865–1917,* pp. 381 ff.; D. F. Houston, *Eight Years with Wilson's Cabinet.*

24 *The Memoirs of William Jennings Bryan*, pp. 409 ff.; T. W. Gregory, in New York *Times,* January 29, 1925; see below pp. 616 ff.

25 The factual confirmation of the above statement is contained in R. W. Dunn, *American Foreign Investments,* and G. B. Clarkson, *Industrial America in the World War;* the best interpretation of the relation of finance and business to the American attitude towards the World War is contained in J. K. Turner, *Shall It Be Again?* Chaps. xxvii–xxxvii. See also L. E. Rowley, *War Criminals.*

26 Turner, op. cit.; and references in footnote 28 below.

27 G. Hanotaux, *Études diplomatiques et historiques pendant la Grande Guerre,* especially pp. 109 ff., and Turner, op. cit., pp. 260–61.

28 Isaac R. Pennypacker, in *American Mercury,* November, 1925, p. 357; cf. Upton Sinclair, *The Brass Check;* speech of Congressman Callaway, in *Congressional Record,* 64th Cong., 2nd Sess., pp. 2947–8; G. Parker in *Harper's Magazine,* March, 1918; and speech of M. A. Michaelson, *Congressional Record,* May 26, 1921, pp. 1–2.

29 Cf. National Security League pamphlets: *America's Peril from Germany's Aggressive Growth,* by H. E. Barnes and W. H. Gardiner, and *The Tentacles of the German Octopus in America,* by E. E. Sperry; and American Defense Society pamphlets: *Germany's War Plans,* and *America's Peace Essentials* by W. H. Gardiner; also the Red, White and Blue Series sent out by George Creel's Committee.

30 F. Avenarius, *How the War Madness Was Engineered; The Secrets of Crewe House,* etc.

31 Compare W. Archer, *Gems of German Thought;* W. R. Thayer, *Out of their Own Mouths;* and S. Grumbach, *Das Annexionistische Deutschland* with Sir Edward Grey, *The Conflict for Human Liberty;* and the war time addresses of Woodrow Wilson.

32 Turner, op cit., pp. 100 ff., 199–214.

33 Ibid., p. 101.

34 *These Eventful Years,* Vol. II, pp. 325–6.

35 The accuracy of the above interpretation of Wilson's policy will be established upon the basis of materials to be cited below. By far the ablest indictment of Wilson along this line is contained in J. K. Turner's *Shall It Be Again?* which, in spite of its animus and bias, is one of the ablest books yet writ-

ten upon the entry of the United States into the World War.

36 J. F. Tumulty, *Woodrow Wilson as I Knew Him,* pp. 256–8.

37 See *George Harvey's Weekly;* and T. Roosevelt, *Fear God and Take Your Own Part,* and his speeches in the campaign of 1916, especially "The Shadows of Shadow Lawn."

38 D. Lawrence, *The True Story of Woodrow Wilson,* Chaps. x–xi.

39 Grey of Fallodon, *Twenty-Five Years,* Vol. II, Chap. xxiii; and Hendrick, op. cit., Vol. III, Chap. X; C. Seymour, *The Intimate Papers of Colonel House,* Vol. II, pp. 82 ff.

40 *Twenty-Five Years,* Vol. II, p. 127; Hendrick, op. cit., Vol. III, p. 279.

41 Hendrick, op. cit., Vol. III, pp. 281 ff.

42 Gilson Gardner, "Why We Delayed Entering the War," in *McNaught's Monthly,* June, 1925.

43 Turner, op. cit., Chap. i–viii.

44 W. A. White, *Woodrow Wilson,* p. 329.

45 Tumulty, op. cit., p. 185; Turner, op. cit., p. 43; *Congressional Record,* June 15, 1916; and 64th Cong., 1st Sess., Appendix, p. 1203.

46 Tumulty, op. cit., p. 185.

47 Probably the worst exhibits of this sort of mythology, and also the most influential, are the books by J. M. Beck, *The Evidence in the Case; The War and Humanity;* and *The Reckoning.*

48 For the German peace offer of 1916 see below p. 687.

49 Turner, op. cit., and Grattan, in *American Mercury,* September, 1925.

50 Cf. T. S. Wauchope, "What the French Think of Us," in *American Mercury,* December, 1925; and H. E. Barnes," America Hated by her Former Allies," in *Current History,* November, 1926. See also the amusing propaganda of Mr. Frederick Peabody on debt cancellation, based on the contention that France fought our battles and saved us from invasion. The realistic viewpoint on debt cancellation may be found in F. Bausman, *Facing Europe;* and in the Alexander Hamilton Institute *Business Conditions Weekly* for December 25, 1926.

51 Z. Chafee, *Freedom of Speech;* L. F. Post, *The Deportations Delirium of 1920;* M. E. Ravage, *The Story of Teapot Dome;* F. Schönemann, *Die Kunst der Massenbeeinflussung in der vereinigten Staaten von Amerika;* B. Bliven, "The Great Coolidge Mystery," in *Harper's Magazine,* December, 1925; J. B. Moore, *International Law and Some Current Illusions,* Chap. I, esp. p. 22.

52 D. Lawrence, *The True Story of Woodrow Wilson,* p. 354.

CHAPTER X

THE PROGRESS OF THE REVISIONIST
VIEWPOINT

I. SUMMARY STATEMENT OF THE REVISIONIST
POSITION AS TO WAR GUILT

WE have now devoted a series of chapters to the question of war responsibility in each of the major states involved. We may here briefly summarize the general situation in what may be regarded as a brief statement of the revisionist point of view as it appears to the present writer. The general European system after 1870, based as it was upon nationalism, militarism, secret alliances, and imperialistic aims, naturally inclined Europe toward war. The system does not, however, explain why war came in 1914, as the same general European situation had been prevailing for many years prior to that time, though certain problems had become more acute in the years immediately preceding the World War, particularly in the Near East and Morocco.

The Franco-Russian Alliance concluded by 1894 was transformed into an offensive organization following 1912 through the coöperation of Izvolski and Poincaré. Both recognized that the chief objects of Russian and French foreign policy, the seizure of the Straits and the return of Alsace-Lorraine, could be realized only through a general European war. From 1912–14 their joint plans involved a manipulation of the Balkan situation in such a fashion as to be able to take advantage of any crisis likely to provoke a European war, an arrangement to get England so involved that she would be bound to come in on the side of France and Russia, and a great increase in military preparations in France and Russia.

It was decided that Serbia would be the most favorable area in which to create the desired incident in the Balkans. In the early spring of 1914 prominent officers in the Serbian General Staff laid a plot for the assassination of the Archduke, Franz Ferdinand. The Serbian civil government was aware of the plot for at least a month before its execution, but made no adequate effort to stop the plot or to warn Austria. Prominent Russians were also aware of the plot, but the degree of the complicity of Russia is as yet uncertain.

When the assassination came, the French and Russians recognized that the impending clash between Austria and Serbia would constitute a highly appropriate episode over which to bring about the desired conflict. The year 1914 was a particularly desirable year for the Entente because there was imminent danger that England might develop more happy relations with Germany, and that the French Radicals might be able to secure the repeal of the French Army Bill. Poincaré went to St. Petersburg, and, before knowing the terms of the Austrian ultimatum, renewed his pledge of two years earlier to support Russia in a war over the Balkans, and indicated that the probable Austro-Serbian conflict would meet the conditions demanded by the French in supporting Russia in intervention in the Balkans.

The Franco-Russian procedure in 1914 was to indicate a show of conciliation and concessions on the part of Serbia, and apparent Franco-Russian willingness to settle the dispute through diplomacy, while secret Franco-Russian military preparations were to be carried on which would ultimately make a diplomatic settlement quite impossible. Hence, Russia urged Serbia not to declare war on Austria, and, to insure a sufficiently conciliatory Serbian reply to Austria the Serbian response to the Austrian ultimatum was drafted in outline in the French Foreign Office. Russia did not desire to have Serbia precipitate matters prematurely by a declaration of war on Austria, because this would have affected European opinion, particularly English opinion, unfavorably and would also have brought about military activities altogether too rapidly for Russia, whose mobilization over a vast area would necessarily be slow as compared with that of Austria and Germany.

On the 24th of July, the moment Russia and France learned of the terms of the Austrian ultimatum to Serbia, they began that dual program of a diplomatic barrage combined with secret military preparations which had made a European war inevitable by the afternoon of July 30th. Russia sent a diplomatic message to Serbia counselling moderation, but at the same time decided upon the mobilization of the four great military districts of Central and Southern Russia as well as of the Russian fleets. Russian money in Germany and Austria was also called in.

On the same day Viviani telegraphed to the French Foreign Office that the Austro-Serbian situation was likely to develop serious European complications, and the French troops in Morocco were ordered home. Both countries began systematic military preparations for war on the 26th of July. By the 29th the time had come when Russian military preparations had gone far enough to warrant a general mobilization, and the Tsar was persuaded to consent to this order. A telegram from the Kaiser, however, induced him to revoke the order, but the next day Sazonov and the army officials once more extracted from the Tsar his reluctant consent to the order for general mobilization. The French and the Russians had understood for a generation that once Russian general mobilization was ordered there would be no way of preventing a general European war. General Dobrorolski has told us with great candor that the Russian authorities in 1914 fully realized that a European war was *on* as soon as the mobilization order had been sent out of the general telegraph office in St. Petersburg late in the afternoon of July 30th.

The French authorities had been thoroughly informed as to the nature and progress of the Russian military preparations, but they made no effort to restrain them, though the French well knew that these military activities were bound to render a European war inevitable. They actually urged the Russians to speed up their military preparations, but to be more secretive about them, so as not to alienate England or provoke Germany to counter-mobilization. On the night of July 31st the French government went still further and finally decided for war, handing this information to Izvolski about midnight of the 31st. France was, thus, the first country to declare itself for war in the European crisis of 1914.

The Austrian statesmen in 1914 decided that the time had come when it would be necessary to control the Serbian menace, and they consciously planned an ultimatum to Serbia of such severity that it would be practically impossible for Serbia to concede all of these demands.   The plan, then, was to make a show of diplomacy but to move toward certain war.   This program was much like that of France and Russia, save for the fact that *Austria desired to provoke nothing but a local punitive war while the plans of France and Russia envisaged a general European conflict.* This is the most important point to be borne in mind when estimating the relative war guilt of Austria as against that of France and Russia.

Germany, formerly friendly to Serbia, was alarmed by the assassination of the Archduke and the resulting menace to her chief ally.   Germany therefore agreed to stand behind Austria in the plan of the latter to execute her program of punishing Serbia.   The answer of the Serbians to the Austrian ultimatum, however, impressed the Kaiser as satisfactory, and from that time on he was opposed to further military activity on the part of Austria against Serbia.

In coöperation with Sir Edward Grey, Germany began on the 27th of July to urge upon Austria direct negotiations with Russia and the mediation of her dispute with Serbia.   Austria at first refused to listen to this advice and declared war upon Serbia on the 28th.   Germany then became alarmed at the rumored Russian military preparations and vigorously pressed Austria for a diplomatic settlement of the dispute.   Austria did not give way and consent to this until the 31st of July, which was too late to avert a general European war because the Russian mobilization was then in full swing. Germany endeavored without success to secure the suspension of military activities by Russia, and then, after unexpected hesitation and deliberation, declared war upon Russia.

The Russian general mobilization, undertaken with the full connivance of the French, was ordered at a time when diplomatic negotiations were moving rapidly toward a satisfactory settlement of the major problems in the crisis. Hence, the Russian general mobilization not only initiated military hostilities, but was also the sole reason for the failure of diplomatic efforts.

England was for peace provided France was not drawn into the conflict, but was determined to come into the War in case France was involved. As France decided from the beginning to stand with Russia for war, and as England refused to attempt to restrain either France or Russia, England was inevitably drawn away from her encouragement of the German efforts towards a diplomatic settlement of the crisis and into the support of the military aggression of France and Russia. She made her decision to enter the War after Germany had proposed to keep out of Belgium and to refrain from attacking France if England would remain neutral. In fact, Germany even suggested that she might guarantee the integrity of France and the French colonies in the event of war if England would promise neutrality. The Belgian issue in England was a pure subterfuge, exploited by Sir Edward Grey to inflame British opinion against Germany and to secure British support of his war policy.

The United States entered the War in part because the British blockade of the ports of the Central Powers led us to have our chief financial stake in the Entente, and partly because of the pro-British sympathies of Ambassador Page and President Wilson, which made it impossible for them to attempt to hold England strictly to international law on the seas. (The English violations of international law in regard to neutral rights provoked the German submarine warfare in retaliation. This submarine warfare furnished the ostensible excuse for the American entry into the conflict. Yet, nearly a year before the resumption of submarine warfare, Mr. Wilson had secretly conveyed to England his intention to enter the war on the side of the Entente if Germany would not accept terms of peace which only a conquered state could have been expected to concede.)

(In estimating the order or guilt of the various countries we may safely say that the only direct and immediate responsibility for the World War falls upon Serbia, France and Russia, with the

guilt about equally distributed. Next in order—
far below France and Russia—would come Austria, though she never desired a general European war. Finally, we should place Germany
and England as tied for last place, both being opposed to war in the 1914 crisis. Probably the
German public was somewhat more favorable to
military activities than the English people, but,
as we have amply explained above, the Kaiser
made much more strenuous efforts to preserve the
peace of Europe in 1914 than did Sir Edward
Grey.

II. AUTHORITIES ON WAR GUILT AND THE REVISIONIST POSITION

Readers who have followed these chapters to
the present point will doubtless agree that if the
foregoing restatement and reinterpretation of
the issues and problems in war guilt are correct
it will be necessary to reconstruct our whole orientation with regard to the causes of the World
War and the present international issues which
are intimately related to that matter. Yet it
would be legitimate for readers not well grounded
in modern diplomatic history and not acquainted
with the sources of our knowledge in the circumstances to inquire as to how they are to be sure
that the revisionist interpretation is the correct
one, and as to how they are to be certain that
they are not being misled by propaganda com-

parable to that which they accepted as the truth in 1914–1918. The most direct and explicit answer is that complete assurance in the situation can only be obtained by a personal perusal of the new documentary evidence, not an impossible task for any educated and energetic person.

Certain considerations may, however, be brought forward as cogent evidence as to the reliability of the revisionist position. The editor of the New York *Times Current History Magazine* submitted the writer's article in the issue of May, 1924, to ten reputable historians. Only two dissented from the general interpretation; and these two could not be called experts on the specific problem, and offered no documentary basis for their dissent. This symposium of historical opinion on war guilt was carried in the June, 1924, number of *Current History Magazine,* and the writer commented upon the symposium in the July issue, in particular answering the criticisms of Professors Morse and Anderson. The writer's controversies with Professors Hazen, Turner, Davis, Eastman, Dickinson and Schmitt may be consulted in the *New Republic* for March 19, April 9, May 7, 1924 and October 20, 1926, the Springfield *Weekly Republican* for February 26, 1925, *The Progressive* for December 1, 1926 and the *Canadian Forum* for July, 1925, May, 1926, and August, 1926.

It is also quite evident that one who is dependent for his daily bread upon his reputation for accuracy and veracity as an historian could scarcely risk appending his name to any grossly erroneous presentation of historical material, particularly if this presentation be, as in the present case, opposed to the general opinion of the country. An *unpopular* falsification is still hazardous in the United States. The writer is willing to state that no trained and unbiassed historian has yet given evidence of having examined the new documents in a thorough fashion without having become distinctly converted to the revisionist point of view. It must be remembered that the general reputation of an historian in no way qualifies him to speak authoritatively upon the question of war guilt unless he has studied the specific documents concerned. A failure to recognize this fact was responsible for the mistake of asking Professor Albert Bushnell Hart to comment upon the writer's article in the May *Current History Magazine* (1924), as well as for Professor Hart's consent to make that comment.

Not all revisionists would agree in every particular with the statement of the new point of view contained in this book, but it is the writer's opinion that few, if any, would dissent from the general interpretation and the major outlines of the picture. To show the general unanimity of the views of reputable scholars from whatever land or group they are drawn we shall here submit the conclusions of representative revisionist scholars from Germany, France and the British Empire, such as Montgelas, Renouvin, Morhardt, Fabre-Luce, Ewart and Dickinson.

The most important German work on the immediate causes of the World War is the *Leitfaden zur Kriegsschuldfrage* (translated into English under the misleading title of *The Case for the Central Powers*) by Count Max Montgelas. Professor Fay describes this book as one "generally acknowledged by competent scholars as perhaps the ablest, clearest and fairest volume on war responsibility which has been written in Germany." Montgelas, whose knowledge of the facts of the crisis of 1914 is not even approached by any other living authority, presents at the close of his analysis some seventeen conclusions, which, Professor Fay suggests, it would be difficult for Poincaré and his supporters to refute. The essential conclusions of Montgelas are the following: [1]

The world war was not decided upon at Potsdam on the 5th of July, 1914; Germany merely assented to Austria's going to war with Serbia.

The possibility that the Austro-Serbian war, like others—the Boer, Moroccan, Tripolitan, and Balkan wars—might lead to further complications, was well weighed, but the risk was thought very small, in view of the special provocation.

After the publication of the Serbian reply, Germany no longer thought war was advisable, even against Serbia, and only favored strictly limited military operations, which were considered justifiable, even in London. . . .

An understanding had almost been reached by the methods Germany had been the first to propose, namely, direct discussions between Vienna and St. Petersburg, and limiting the military operations against Serbia, when the Russian mobilization suddenly tore the threads asunder.

, The leading men knew just as well in Paris and St. Petersburg as in Berlin, that this mobilization must inevitably lead to war.

Viviani telegraphed to London on the 1st of August that the one who first orders general mobilization is the aggressor, and he saddled Germany with this responsibility, knowing that the accusation was false. . . .

France not only did not advise Russia against ordering general mobilization, but gave surreptitious advice as to how she could carry on her military preparations secretly without provoking Germany to take timely counter-measures. . . .

Russia was the first power to order general mobilization. France was the first power to inform another power officially of her decision to take part in a European war.

England was never as firm in advising moderation in St. Petersburg as Germany in giving this advice to Vienna.

Unlike other British diplomats, Sir Edward Grey only realized the meaning of the Russian mobilization when it was too late, and St. Petersburg was no longer willing to put a stop to it.

Germany's premature declaration of war on Russia was a political error, which can be accounted for by the immense danger of the position on two fronts; her declaration of war on France was a pure formality.

The decisive event was not this or that declaration of war, but the action which made the declaration of war inevitable, and this action was Russia's general mobilization.

England declared war on Germany because she did not consider it compatible with her interests that France should be defeated a second time. Belgian interests, and the treaty of 1839, which Lord Salisbury had been prepared to sacrifice in 1887, were the reasons adduced to make it popular.

Over and above this, the naval agreement of 1912 with France compelled England to abandon her neutrality before Belgium's neutrality was violated.

The French work most comparable to the German guide to war guilt by Montgelas is *Les Origines Immédiates de la Guerre* by Professor Pierre Renouvin. In a review of this book in the New York *Nation* for November 18, 1925, Montgelas summarizes the chief positions established by Renouvin in the course of his work. A perusal of this thoroughly honest and competent summary will demonstrate the general similarity of the major facts in the situation as presented by Montgelas and Renouvin, though they differ more widely in their conclusions: [2]

For some years Professor Renouvin has been lectur-

ing at the Sorbonne on the origins of the World War.
As a result of his careful study of the diplomatic crisis
of 1914 he now presents the students of this vexed problem with a well-informed and most readable book. It
may be called the sanest and most up-to-date volume
which has come out of France.

These are the most important of the facts which, owing to the evidence produced by Renouvin, must be considered henceforth as indubitably established:

1. The Serajevo attempt was plotted and organized
by Colonel Dragutin Dimitrijevich, chief of the Intelligence Department of the Serbian General Staff. The
indirect complicity of the Serbian Government is proved
by their toleration of the Pan-Serbian agitation against
Austria-Hungary. One can hardly doubt that the eminent French scholar would have admitted as well the
direct responsibility of the Belgrade authorities if he
had known the latest revelations made by Ljuba Jo-
vanovich, Minister of Finance in the Pachich Cabinet.

2. At the Potsdam conference on July 5 "The Euro-
pean War seems not to have been part of the program."
It goes without saying that the myth of the Crown
Council is completely repudiated.

3. The Wilhelmstrasse did not join the Ballhausplatz
in working out the ultimatum to Serbia. In Berlin they
knew only the probable contents of that fatal document,
and it must be borne in mind that the Entente cabinets
also had succeeded in obtaining pretty exact information.

4. In the beginning Chancellor von Bethmann, relying
on the reports received, was entitled to believe that England and France would not be opposed to the "localiza-

tion" of the conflict. Grey's first proposal of *médiation à quatre* between Austria and Russia "suited the main thought of Austro-German policy, as it did not imply any interference with the Austro-Serbian issue. Bethmann-Hollweg was ready to accept it." This disposes of the legend that Grey's first proposal contained the idea of a conference in London, and of the accusation against Germany that she rejected the *médiation à quatre*.

5. The Serbian answer can be judged very severely. In Renouvin's opinion, a close examination of the note shows that it contains many "conditions and restrictions."

6. Grey's sudden proposal of a conference on July 26 was designed to settle the Austro-Serbian, not the Austro-Russian quarrel.

7. On July 27 the Berlin Cabinet agreed to direct conversations between Vienna and Petersburg and transmitted to Count Berchtold Grey's proposal to accept the Serbian reply either as satisfactory or as a basis for discussion. But next day, the Wilhelmstrasse having got a favorable impression of the Serbian reply and Austria having launched her declaration of war, Germany on her own initiative advised Vienna to limit her military operations to Belgrade and the neighborhood.

8. The highly interesting chapters on the mobilizations in Russia and Austria completely overthrow what has hitherto been the common opinion in the Entente countries. Founding his narrative on a minute inquiry into all the available evidence, Renouvin demolishes the very basis of the Versailles impeachment by his pitiless

chronology. Renouvin's account suffices to stigmatize forever the main war lie that Austria's general mobilization was anterior to Russia's.

9. Chancellor von Bethmann made vigorous efforts to arrive at a peaceful solution by diplomatic means at a time when in Russia military arguments were overriding all other considerations.

10. On the other hand, censure is due the way in which Austria carried on her direct conversations with the Petersburg Cabinet. She should have accepted Grey's last proposal; and General von Moltke, who quite rigidly insisted on Austria's mobilization, mistakenly meddled with diplomacy by telling the Austrian military attaché in Berlin that Vienna had better not accept Grey's suggestion.

11. What finally does Renouvin think about Germany's declarations of war? Even here his thesis does not agree with French and English war propaganda, for he writes: "It seems to be the point of view of [all] the general staffs and of [all] the governments" that declaration of war is "a mere formality."

All this has been well known for a long time to impartial historians. The novel thing is that it should be frankly accepted by a French scholar who is lecturing on the origins of the Great War in what may be called a semi-official position and who is not afraid of contradicting the fabulous compositions published by French and British statesmen or of revealing the falsehoods of the French *Yellow Book*.

It must be added, however, that history will not in the same degree approve of Renouvin's last chapter containing his "conclusions." There he says that the Central

Powers "remained tenaciously faithful to the plan of localization" and that Germany, by permitting Austria to declare war upon Serbia, "accepted voluntarily the possibility of Russian intervention and of a European war." Those statements overlook the facts that Germany renounced the program of strict localization as early as July 27 by transmitting to Vienna the English suggestion to treat the Serbian note either as satisfactory or as a basis for discussion, and that on the very day of Austria's declaration of war the Berlin Cabinet made the proposal to "Stop at Belgrade," which is universally considered to have been the sanest expedient under prevailing circumstances.

Dealing with the Russian general mobilization, Renouvin dares not squarely draw the conclusion that it meant war. He admits that the negotiators of the Franco-Russian alliance in 1892 had openly declared: "*La mobilisation, c'est la declaration de la guerre.*" But he adds that this referred to the mobilization of Russia's and France's adversaries, not to their own. The author may be reminded that he himself has said that Russia's mobilization "could not but provoke a reply from Germany." This reply could be no other than German mobilization. If Russian mobilization necessarily provokes German mobilization, and if German mobilization is equivalent to a "declaration of war," then Russian mobilization, too, must be equivalent to war. Renouvin further criticizes the hasty actions of German diplomats after the receipt of the official news that the whole of the Russian army and navy had been mobilized. Nobody will deny the blunders committed in those days in Berlin, but if Russia's mobilization

meant war the course of events would have been the same
without those blunders.

Finally, Renouvin says: "In July, 1914, the military
provocation was the result of a diplomatic provocation;
Austria's declaration of war (on Serbia) is the link between both." It must be observed that the origin of the
catastrophe does not lie in any diplomatic action in
July but in the murder in June. With regard to that
crime so much fresh evidence has come to hand that the
opinion about responsibility must be revised. Professor Renouvin has done so much toward clearing the way
for truth that it may be hoped that loyalty to his country will not make him shrink from drawing the inevitable conclusions.

Next to the book by Renouvin perhaps the best
French work on the immediate causes of the War
is *Les Preuves. Le Crime de Droit Commun.
Le Crime Diplomatique,* by M. Mathias Morhardt, President of *La société d'études docu-
mentaires et critiques de la guerre,* an eminent
French publicist, one of the staff of the Paris
Temps, and a worthy upholder of the cause of
justice and truth in France since the days of the
Dreyfus Case. It will be evident from the following paragraphs that the views of Morhardt
do not differ on any essential point from those
of Montgelas: [3]

The archduke and heir to the Austrian throne and his
wife were assassinated at Sarajevo, June 28, 1914.
The assassins came from Belgrade where they had close

relations with the Serbian officials and officers.   It was
at Belgrade that they received from the hands of these
officers the arms necessary for the accomplishment of
their sinister work.   These Serbian officials and officers
not only gave them arms; they supplied the money necessary for the trip to Sarajevo.   Still more, they
taught these young men how to use the arms they gave
them: ordnance bombs of the arsenal of Kragujevac
and Browning revolvers of the Serbian army.   Finally,
it was due to the complicity of the agents of the Serbian government that the orders were given to aid the
assassins in crossing the frontier.   At the head of the
plot thus formed was Colonel Dmitriévitch, chief of the
intelligence division of the general staff, one of the best
known ranking officers of the Serbian army. . . .

From the day after the double assassination at Sarajevo the chauvinistic Serbian press glorified the assassins by the title of "Martyrs."   It published about
them and their existence in Belgrade circumstantial evidence which shows that they were well known in that
vicinity.   Nevertheless, the government of Belgrade
made no inquest, investigation or arrest.   Twenty-four
hours later, it declared to the Austrian representative
that "it had done nothing about this affair. . . ."

It is also fully proved that, from the point of view of
principles of international law, her material and moral
responsibility being deeply involved in the double assassination at Sarajevo, Serbia, whose officers and officials
had just brought about the assassination of the archduke, owed to Austria-Hungary a complete, immediate
and decisive reparation.   It has been seen that Serbia
not only did not take the initiative in this matter, which
elementary decency dictated, but that, when, twenty-

five days later, Austria endeavored to impose upon her specific conditions, by the ultimatum of July 23, she evaded the issue in a response both arrogant and unbecoming, by eleven successive stipulations. Moreover, better to show her real intentions, three hours before returning to the Austrian representative her so-called "conciliatory" reply, Serbia, certain of the blind adherence of the powers of the triple entente, mobilized 400,000 men of her army while her government abandoned Begrade and retired to Nich.

Although the charges of Austria-Hungary, the attitude of the Serbian press and of the Belgrade government had not at that time established in an incontestable manner, the heavy responsibility of Serbia in the drama at Sarajevo, the authors of the double assassination and their accomplices had multiplied their confessions. The Serbian government itself proclaimed its own guilt by the official glorification of the assassins.

It was, however, in order to assure Serbia of the impunity to which no European statesman could have legitimately accorded her the least right, that Russia mobilized all her forces on land and on sea, July 30, 1914, at 4:00 P. M.

All the governments of Europe knew that "general mobilization means war!" The Russian general mobilization constituted, on the highest authority, an act of aggression. We have on this point the cumulative testimony of Czar Alexander III, of Czar Nicholas II, of King George V, William II, and M. Raymond Poincaré. And we also have the declarations of General de

Boisdeffre, of General Obroutcheff, of General Dobrorolski, of M. Maurice Paléologue, of M. René Viviani,
of Sir Edward Grey, of Lloyd George, etc., etc. Moreover, it was not because Russia mobilized that Germany
declared war. Threatened in her security, and even
in her existence by the Russian general mobilization,
Germany first demanded that Russia suspend her
mobilization, as proclaimed by Nicholas II in his declaration, and it was because Russia refused . . . that
the war became inevitable.

The governments of the triple entente are the less
justified in alleging their good faith since Italy, on July
26th suggested to them an ingenious method which permitted the maintenance of peace by giving full satisfaction to Austria and at the same time protecting the self-
respect of Serbia. This proposition was disdainfully
brushed aside by the British government as well as by
the Russian and French governments.

Finally, without repetition, let us recall that Germany after July 28th, exercised a vigorous pressure on
Austria in order to maintain peace. At the demand of
the British government, she even compelled her ally to
enter into direct negotiations with Russia. But Russia, by suddenly mobilizing July 30, when full negotiations were going on, and when neither her security nor
honor were threatened, struck a fatal blow at these last
and supreme efforts to maintain peace.

It is apparent that this French writer is more
critical of the Franco-Russian group than Montgelas. In regard to certain details he goes even

farther than the author of this book would regard as justifiable. Yet his general position is unassailable.

We may take from another French student, Alfred Fabre-Luce, the best summary of the revisionist viewpoint yet submitted:[4] *"The acts of Germany and Austria made the war possible, those of the Triple Entente made the war inevitable."* It is worth while to note that Fabre-Luce is not a member of the group of French Socialist revisionists, but a brilliant young student of history, politics and diplomacy and a member of one of the wealthiest and most powerful of French families. His book, *La Victoire,* while less detailed than Renouvin or Morhardt on the immediate causes of the World War, is more comprehensive in scope and highly judicious in tone. In discussing the matter of summary conclusions on war guilt he refers to the list of conclusions by Montgelas, and criticizes only three out of the seventeen.[5] There is only one important error in his work, namely, where he follows Renouvin's lectures in holding that Bethmann-Hollweg gave up his hope of restraining Austria on July 30th and surrendered to the war party. Perhaps the best brief up-to-date summary of war responsibility by a Frenchman is the *Conférence sur les Responsabilités de la Guerre* by Gustave Dupin, which arrives at conclusions very similar to those set forth by the present writer. The able and courageous French student of war guilt and French war propaganda, Georges Demartial, has recently expressed himself in an important article in the New York *Times Current History Magazine* for March, 1926, as being in full agreement with the present writer in regard to the primary responsibility of Russia and France for the outbreak of the War. He says: *"We are convinced that we can no more accept the thesis of divided responsibility than we can accept that of the exclusive responsibility of Germany."*

The Poincaré myth has been more disastrously shattered in France than elsewhere. Morhardt's book holds Poincaré to have been more culpable than any other individual. Special works have been directed towards a specific refutation of Poincaré's apologies in his *Origins of the War,* his article in *Foreign Affairs* for October, 1925, and his memoirs. Lazare, in his *A l'Origine du Mensonge,* has subjected Poincaré's *Origins of the War* to a most scathing dissection, while Gustave Dupin has demolished the *Foreign Affairs* article in the *Revue de Hongrie* for December 15, 1925, and Dupin, Fabre-Luce and Margueritte have effectively discredited his memoirs. Demartial's *L'Evangile de Quai d'Orsay* is a devastating revelation of the French official lies in 1914.

What Professor Fay has described as "the

most considerable and, in many ways, the best book on the subject of war guilt which has appeared in English" is *The Roots and Causes of the Wars, 1914–1918,* by Dr. John S. Ewart, one of the most distinguished of Canadian jurists. It will be seen from his summary that Dr. Ewart is in agreement with both Morhardt and Montgelas on all important issues: [6]

1. France was responsible for the western root of the war—Alsace-Lorraine.

2. Responsibility for the eastern root—the Balkan situation—must be shared, in chief measure by the great powers (1878); secondly, by Austria-Hungary (1908); and thirdly, by the parties to the treaty of Bucharest (1913). To the effect of the actions in these respects must be added: (1) national Jugo-Slavian ambition and propaganda; (2) national Austro-Hungarian reaction; (3) German interest in the preservation of Austro-Hungarian integrity; (4) Russia's pursuit of her "historic mission."

3. Responsibility for precipitation of hostilities must be attributed (1) to Serbia, because of her unneighborly conduct; (2) to Austria-Hungary, because of continuation of her truculent attitude after receiving Serbia's reply; and (3) and chiefly—conclusively— to Russia, because of interruption of negotiations for a peaceful settlement.

By all means the most competent and up-to-date book which has been written in England on the question of responsibility for the World War is G. Lowes Dickinson's *International Anarchy.*

The following citation of his conclusions will show that he is in almost complete agreement with the summary of the question set forth above (pp. 654–62 by the present writer: [7]

Little Serbia stood on the verge of satisfying her national ambitions at the cost of the peoples and civilizations of three continents.

For years the little state of Serbia had been undermining the Austrian Empire . . . What was the Empire to do in self-defense? One can conceive a world in which Austria would not have wished to hold down a nationality against its will. But that would not be the world of history, past or present. Never has an empire resigned before the disruptive forces of nationality. Always it has fought. And I do not believe that there was a state in existence that would not, under similar circumstances, have determined, as Austria did, to finish the menace, once for all, by war . . . With every year that passed the Austrian position would get worse and the Serbian better. So at least the Austrians thought, and not without reason. They took their risk according to the usual canons in such matters. They may be accused of miscalculation, but I do not see that they can be accused of wrong by any one who accepts now, or who accepted then, the principles which have always dictated the policy of states. . . . German diplomacy was cumberous, stupid, and dishonest. Granted, it was! But German policy was such as any state would have accepted in her position. The powers of the Entente say that the offense was Germany's backing of Austria. Germans say that the offense was Russia's backing of Serbia. On that point, really, the whole controversy turns. To my mind the German position is the more reasonable.

Why was the war not localized, as Austria and Germany intended and desired? There is only one answer to this: because Russia did not choose to allow it. Why not? . . . The answer is that she wanted Constantinople and the Straits; that she wanted access to the Mediterranean; that she wanted extension of territory and influence; that she had a "historic mission"; that she must make herself secure; in short, the whole farrago of superstitions that dominate all States under the conditions of the armed anarchy. . . . France entered for the sake of the balance of power and to recover Alsace-Lorraine; and her technical success in waiting till the declaration of war came from Germany does not alter the position. It had been known for at least two years past, it was reaffirmed more than once during the crisis, that if Germany came in against Russia, France would come in against Germany . . . At any rate since 1912 France would have entered when Russia did. And does any one who has perused the previous chapters, and who realizes the state of Europe, believe that Russia would not have started the war a year or two later? . . . And England? . . . She had military and naval commitments to France which were like a suction-pipe to draw her, whether she would or no, into the war. And that approximation to the other two powers of the Entente was made for no other reason than the maintenance of the balance of power. We had become more afraid of Germany than of our traditional enemies, France and Russia. After all of our commitments to France it would have been base to desert her. Agreed! But what were the objects for which those commitments were made?   Our own power, our own empire, our own security.

The judicious and broad-minded English historian, G. P. Gooch has thoroughly aligned himself with the revisionists.   The most decisive exponent of revisionism in England is the distinguished historian, Raymond Beazley, who greatly aided Morel, and whose forthcoming book will be the classic English study of war responsibility.

What should be the most adequate work on the facts of pre-war diplomacy will soon be published by Professor Sidney Bradshaw Fay, the historian who first aroused the world to the significance of the new documentary material from the German and Austrian archives through his notable articles in the *American Historical Review* in 1920–21.   His judgment as to the guilt of Serbia, France, Russia and England could not be definitive at that time, because neither the Serbian revelations, the *Livre Noir,* the Stieve collection of Russian documents nor the British documents had been published.   We shall leave Professor Fay to state his own conclusions.

At least passing reference should be made to such American writers as Francis Neilson and Albert Jay Nock, who, even before the publication of the new documents, showed the serious weaknesses in the Entente Epic.   Judge Frederick Bausman's *Let France Explain* was the first

thorough American repudiation of the war-time
mythology, while, in his *Cross-Currents in
Europe Today,* Charles Austin Beard presented
the first American survey of the problem of war
guilt based on all the evidence save the recently
published English documents. Much was expected of Professor Bernadotte Schmitt as a
leader of American revisionism on the basis of
his remarkable article in the *American Historical
Review* for April, 1924, but his articles in the
New York *Times Current History Magazine* for
March, 1926, and in *Foreign Affairs* for October,
1926, show that our anticipations were premature
and quite unjustified. Professor Schmitt has
now definitely aligned himself with the "bitter-
enders" and "straw-clutchers," such as Charles
Downer Hazen, Frank Maloy Anderson, Edward Raymond Turner and William Stearns
Davis. In the *Progressive* for December 1,
1926, and *Evolution* for February 15, 1927, the
writer has indicated at great length the personal
handicaps and the professional historiographical
limitations under which Professor Schmitt op-
erates as a student of contemporary diplomatic
history.

Two of the leading "die-hards," Professors
Davis and Turner, have recently attempted to
defend the war-time epic in the light of the new
documentary material—Professor Davis in Part
III of his *Europe since Waterloo,* and Professor
Turner in his article in the New York *Times*

Current History Magazine for February, 1927.
The pathetic hopelessness of such efforts is
readily apparent to all who have perused these
unconscious obituarial notices by Professors
Davis and Turner. Their contributions, far from
rehabilitating the Entente idealism, actually constitute the most powerful arguments for revisionism yet launched in the United States.

III. CONCLUSIONS

(1) There is practical unanimity among students of the problem of the responsibility for the
World War as far as the facts are concerned,
though there is some divergence in generalizing
as to the significance of those facts.

(2) The situation is not one, as is widely believed, in which some writers who have examined
thoroughly the new documentary evidence hold
to the view of war responsibility which generally
prevailed from 1914 to 1920, while others
take what is called the "revisionist" standpoint. There is no competent and honest authority on the problem of war guilt who is not
a "revisionist."

(3) There is no competent and informed historian in any country who has studied the problem of the genesis of the World War in a thorough fashion who does not regard the theory of
war guilt held in Articles 227 and 231 of the Versailles Treaty to be wholly false, misleading and
unjust.

(4) The recently published British documents on the crisis of 1914 offer a full confirmation of the revisionist point of view on war guilt.

SELECTED REFERENCES

"Assessing the Blame for the World War," in New York *Times Current History Magazine*, June, 1924, pp. 452–62; Barnes, H. E., "Seven Books of History against the Germans," in *New Republic*, March 19, 1924; "Assessing the Blame for the World War," in New York *Times Current History Magazine*, May and July, 1924; "Bernadotte Everly Schmitt and the War Guilt Controversy," in *The Progressive*, December 1, 1926; Demartial, G., and Schmitt, B., "France's Responsibility for the World War," in New York *Times Current History Magazine*, March, 1926; Dupin, G., *Conférence sur les responsabilités de la guerre;* Fabre-Luce, A., *La Victoire*, Chaps. i-ii; Fay, S. B., "New Light on the Origins of the World War," in *American Historical Review*, 1920–21; "Who Started the War?" in *New Republic*, January 6, 1926; Gooch, G. P., "Recent Revelations on European Diplomacy," in *Journal of the British Institute of International Affairs*, January, 1923; Margueritte, V., *Evolution*, 1926—; Schmitt, B. E., "July, 1914," in *Foreign Affairs*, (American), October, 1926; Wegerer, A. von, (ed.) *Die Kriegsschuldfrage*, 1923-.

FOOTNOTES AND FURTHER REFERENCES

[1] M. Montgelas, *The Case for the Central Powers*, pp. 200–203.
[2] M. Montgelas, "A French View of War Origins," in New York *Nation*, November 18, 1925.
[3] M. Morhardt, *Les Preuves*, pp. 291–97.
[4] A. Fabre-Luce, *La Victoire*, p. 232.
[5] Ibid., pp. 68–9.
[6] J. S. Ewart, *The Roots and Causes of the Wars*, p. 1173.
[7] Dickinson, op. cit., 429, 463–6,

CHAPTER XI

LIQUIDATING WAR-TIME ILLUSIONS

I. WAR ILLUSIONS AND WAR REALITIES

IN the preceding chapters the writer has pointed out how important it is for an adequate outlook upon contemporary problems of war and peace to assimilate in an intelligent and discriminating fashion what we now know about the actual causes of the late World War. Nothing could constitute a more complete exposure of the dishonesty and unreliability of diplomats and statesmen, who are, as Francis Neilson pointed out,[1] if anything, even more potent in the creation of wars than general staffs and war departments. We now know that practically the entire body of Entente "war aims," including even the melodious rhetoric of President Wilson, was mainly false and misleading, setting up a verbal barrage behind which were hidden the most sordid and selfish plans of unscrupulous diplomats and foreign ministers.[2] The acceptance of this view about the Entente position of course in no way carries with it any enthusiastic support of the diplomacy or viewpoint of the Central Powers, but we do not need debunking on German prop-

aganda in the United States. If we can but understand how totally and terribly we were "taken
in" between 1914 and 1918 by the salesmen of
this most holy and idealistic world conflict, we
shall be the better prepared to be on our guard
against the seductive lies and deceptions which
will be put forward by similar groups when urging the necessity of another world catastrophe
in order to "protect the weak nations," "crush
militarism," "make the world safe for democracy," "put an end to all further wars," etc.

II. WHO PROLONGED THE WAR?

We are now quite fully aware of the actual
facts in regard to the bringing on of the recent
World War through the plotting of Poincaré,
Delcassé, Izvolski and Sazonov, aided and
abetted by the Francophiles and Slavophiles in
the British government. There are, however, a
number of other problems and situations which
require and deserve investigation and elucidation.
One of the most significant would be a consideration of who prolonged the War unnecessarily.
Here, again, there is no doubt that the chief
guilt fastens itself upon the Allied Powers, and
particularly upon Lloyd George and Clemenceau.[3] The United States played her part in
obstructing the plans for an early peace through
the Anglomania of Ambassador Page and

President Wilson. By preventing the United
States from compelling Great Britain to observe
the rights of neutrals they practically destroyed
American neutrality, and by doing all they could
to bring America into the War they encouraged
the Entente Powers to count upon our ultimate
entry into the conflict. This made the bitter-
enders among the Allies the more unwilling to
consider the peace proposals of either the Central Powers or President Wilson.[4] Still further, Page openly and vigorously fought Colonel
House when he brought President Wilson's
peace proposals to Great Britain, and encouraged Grey to stand adamant for the prosecution
of the War.[5] It is certain that in 1916 or 1917 a
negotiated peace, embodying principles and adjustments far better adapted to the welfare of
man than the Versailles pact, could have been
arranged through the collaboration of Mr. Wilson, Caillaux and the Pope, with the coöperation
of the German government, but for the steadfast
position of Lloyd George, Clemenceau and certain other Entente statesmen who were bent
upon the destruction of the Central Powers.

The following terms represent the specific
German peace offer of December, 1916, which
may be profitably compared with the Treaty of
Versailles:

The complete restoration of Belgium.

The evacuation by Germany of all territory captured

in northern France during the progress of the war.

The establishment of Poland and Lithuania as independent kingdoms.

The retention of Serbia by Austria-Hungary and the restoration to Bulgaria of all territory lost by that country in the second Balkan war.

The restoration to Austria of territory captured by Italy in the neighborhood of the Adriatic Sea.

The restoration to Germany of all her colonial possessions in Africa, the Far East and other parts of the globe.

The retention of Constantinople by Turkey.

In due time it will probably be seen that the wisest utterance of Woodrow Wilson was not his fourteen points, but his conception of "peace without victory." The responsibility for the unnecessary and disastrous prolongation of the terrible holocaust, which involved the expenditure of vast sums of money and the loss of millions of lives in Europe, to say nothing of the debauching of American morale through our entry into the World War, is almost as heavy as that which rests upon Poincaré, Delcassé, Izvolski and Sazonov for the initiation of the conflict.[6]

III. THE WAR TO CRUSH MILITARISM

Another illuminating line of study and exposition would seem to lie in a contrast between Entente "war aims" and the actual objects and

results of the War. We were told that the
World War was fought to end all war and to
crush German militarism. Yet the world was
left in 1918 more bellicose in psychology than in
1914. There was a succession of wars in Europe
from 1918 to 1921, sometimes as many as a score
of separate wars being in progress. Further, a
large number of new states were created to constitute so many more causes of nationalistic out-
bursts, political ambition, and ultimate wars.
Patriotic savagery was stimulated to a far
greater degree than after the conflicts of 1870
and 1878.[7]

While German militarism has been for the
time being crushed, it has been replaced by the
even more dangerous militarism of France, whose
arrogant and aggressive policy since the War has
done more to stimulate a revengeful and militaristic psychology in Germany than anything
else which has happened to that country since
Napoleon's occupation in 1806. At the same
time, France has advanced and financed the
cause of militarism not only at home, but also
in the new states of central and southern Europe,
so that at the present time the militaristic psychology, as well as the military equipment outside of Germany, Austria and Russia, is more
vigorous and extensive than at the outbreak of
the World War. One of the great objects of
winning the War was to make no longer neces-

sary the enormous expenditures for armaments and other wastes. Nevertheless, to insure her military supremacy upon the Continent, France has not only doubled her indebtedness of 1918, but has practically led into bankruptcy a number of lesser European states as partners in her militaristic system. The increase of debts and armaments since 1918 has been appalling, and for this France and England must be held to be almost solely responsible.[8] The following compilation by the Foreign Policy Association of New York indicates the startling increase of the French public debt, not only since 1914, but even since 1919:

SUMMARY OF THE FRENCH PUBLIC DEBT—1914–1925

Date *	Total Debt
	Francs
	(Gold)
Aug. 1, 1914	27,704,330,634
	(Paper)
Dec. 31, 1918	151,122,338,054
Dec. 31, 1919	240,242,109,503
Dec. 31, 1920	300,108,315,306
Dec. 31, 1921	329,002,482,500
Dec. 31, 1922	379,501,076,812
Dec. 31, 1923	418,227,272,727
Dec. 31, 1924	426,388,083,185
Dec. 31, 1925	519,623,589,539

The following statistics gathered by the Federal Council of the Churches of Christ indicate the nature and extent of this insane continuation of excessive expenditure for armaments at the present time:

MILITARY BUDGETS

Country	Year	Army	Navy	Air	Total
Albania	1923	$ 1,017,229			$ 1,017,229
Argentina ..	1924	23,285,512	$16,540,806		39,826,318
Australia ..	1924	5,210,546	10,142,212	$ 798,012	16,150,770
Austria	1924	7,857,142			7,857,142
Belgium ...	1924	24,562,629			24,562,629
Bolivia	1924	2,958,285			2,958,285
Brazil	1924	17,304,597	9,513,750		26,818,347
Bulgaria ...	1924	1,134,000			1,134,000
Canada	1924	10,036,237	1,515,500	1,250,000	12,801,737
Chile	1923	7,948,032	8,177,407		16,125,439
Colombia ..	1824	2,986,123			2,986,123
Costa Rica .	1924	130,264			130,264
Cuba	1924				10,959,799
Czecho-					
Slovakia .	1924	68,999			68,999
Denmark ..	1924	6,440,000	4,240,000		10,680,000
Ecuador ...	1924				2,720,846
Esthonia ...	1923				4,844,036
Finland	1924				10,395,000
France	1924	172,076,462	48,327,139	(?)	220,403,601
Germany ...	1924	107,100,000			107,100,000
Great Britain	1924	268,342,470	290,109,199	94,245,120	652,696,789
Greece	1924				40,567,814
Guatemala .	1924				1,584,247
Haiti	1924				1,045,310
Honduras ..	1924				2,173,543
Hungary ...	1923	2,629,015			2,629,015
India	1923	182,500,000			182,500,000
Italy	1924	72,533,978	29,397,433	15,162,000	117,093,411
Japan	1924	7,913,000	9,770,300		17,683,300
Jugoslavia ..	1924				39,120,020
Latvia	1924				5,605,365
Lithuania ..	1923				5,176,682
Mexico	1923				63,238,095
Netherlands.	1924	25,251,895	17,153,605		42,405,500
Nicaragua ..	1923				145,827
Norway	1924	6,020,742	2,291,034		8,311,776
Paraguay ..	1923				470,252
Peru	1924	4,420,729	1,300,796		5,721,525
Poland	1924				85,102,964
Portugal ..	1924	7,420,886	3,733,980		11,154,866
Roumania ..	1924				17,873,503
Russia	1923	96,921,930	8,830,140		105,752,070
Salvador ...	1924				664,205
Santo Do-					
mingo	1924				1,124,827
Spain	1924	51,976,783	24,624,460		76,601,243
Sweden	1924				40,012,400

MILITARY BUDGETS (*continued*)

Country	Year	Army	Navy	Air	Total
Switzerland .	1924				15,733,361
Turkey	1924				24,340,880
United States	1924	257,274,768	297,097,250		554,372,018
Uruguay ...	1924				7,027,556
Venezuela ..	1924				2,400,000

IV. THE WORLD SAFE FOR DEMOCRACY

We were solemnly informed that the World War was also being fought to make the world "safe for democracy," and particularly to insure the existence, safety and stability of democracy in Germany. The end of the World War saw even the architect of that phrase acquiescing in the sending of American troops to crush out the existence of the Bolshevik government in Russia, which represents the most radical democracy anywhere in the world. Even more serious is the fact that the Entente policy since the War has almost destroyed the strong sentiment and movement for democracy in Germany, which could easily have triumphed in that country but for the effective indirect coöperation of Poincaré with the party of Ludendorff and the militaristic monarchists. There can be no doubt that Poincaré contributed more than any other force or influence to the election of von Hindenburg, as well as to many other much more serious symptoms of autocracy and reaction in Germany. Since the War, "friends of democracy" in Europe and the United States have looked with horror upon Bolshevik Russia, but have co-operated with enthusiasm with Mussolini, un-doubtedly the most brazen autocrat that western Europe has known since Napoleon III. In Greece, Spain, Hungary, Rumania and Bul-garia *Fascism* has made nearly as much head-way as in Italy. A dictatorship is also imminent in Belgium and Poland, and there has been much talk of a similar development in France as an aid to the solution of her financial crisis. In-deed, democracy seems in greater peril in Eu-rope than at any time since 1848. Of course, there are valid arguments for a dictatorship, but we are here interested in indicating how the War failed to advance the cause of democracy. Even the United States, which was supposed to be in-terested, far beyond any other country, in making the War a great crusade for democracy, has un-dergone a veritable orgy of reaction since 1917, so that individual liberty and the freedom of ex-pression are to-day in greater jeopardy amongst us than at any other time since the period of the Alien and Sedition Laws of 1798.

But we must go still further and recognize the fact that even though the World War had most notably promoted the development of democracy, and secured its complete domination on the planet, that would in itself be no guaranty of sub-sequent world peace. When the Allied propa-ganda was in full bloom it was a basic thesis that the War had been caused by autocracy, in spite of the fact that the most autocratic of the greater powers of the world was one of the Triple Entente. Democracy was held to be a sure panacea against war. The facts which we now possess about war guilt completely explode this view of democracy as a defense against war when taken alone. Professor George H. Blakeslee, in the following paragraph, shows how the facts of modern history prove the futility of relying upon democracy as an adequate assurance of peace unless we combine with it real world organization: [9]

During the past century the great democracies have been making war, threatening war, and preparing for war, much of the time against each other. Their history shows clearly enough that if their neighbors had also been democratic this change alone would not have prevented wars. Nor is the outlook for the future encouraging. Democratic nations are still willing to fight to defend their national interests and policies; they demand their due share of over-sea trade, concessions and colonies—if they are a commercial or expansionist people—no less insistently because they are democratic. But the interest and policies of one nation conflict with those of another; what one democracy regards as a due share of over-sea trade, concessions, and colonies is an undue share to its rival. Each democracy becomes an excited partisan of its own view, ready to back it by force of arms; and the natural result is, as it always has been, wars and rumors of wars. There are enough conflicts in national policies today to lead to a dozen future conflicts, even if all the world should be democratic. There is Japan's insistence upon controlling China; our own Monroe doctrine, when interpreted in a domineering or selfish spirit; England's Persian gulf policy; the anti-oriental policy of the United States and the British self-governing colonies; the expansionist policy of all the Balkan states; and the entente policy, formulated at the Paris conference, of discriminating against the trade of the central powers after the present war shall be over. Unless present conditions are changed, the democratic nations of the world, with their conflicting interests, would find it difficult to maintain world peace for the next century, even if they wished to maintain it. History, present conditions, and the logic of the situation show that democracy alone will never make the world safe. It is only by a definite concert of states that we may secure a reasonable promise of obtaining a permanent international peace and of becoming a non-militaristic world.

V. THE TRIUMPH OF IDEALISM

Yet a third alleged purpose of the Allies was to bring about among the peoples of the world the triumph of idealism over selfish imperialism and territorial ambitions. But the Bolsheviks and the Versailles Conference revealed the existence of the notorious Secret Treaties embodying as sordid a program of territorial pilfering as can be found in the history of diplomacy. It appears that the chief actual motives of the Entente in

the World War were the seizure of Constantinople and the Straits for Russia; not only the return of Alsace-Lorraine to France, but the
securing of the west bank of the Rhine, which
would have involved the seizure of territory his-
torically far longer connected with Germany
than Alsace-Lorraine had ever been with France;
the rewarding of Italian entry into the War by
extensive territory grabbed away from Austria
and the Jugo-Slavs; and the sequestering of the
German imperial possessions, the acquisition of
the German merchant marine and the destruction
of the German navy in the interest of increasing
the strength of the British Empire.[10]

The officials of the United States have boasted
that they did not secure one inch of territory, but
we did snatch from the spoils enemy property
approximately equal in value to the German indemnity levied on France in 1871. Professor
John Bassett Moore thus sarcastically describes
the combination of hypocrisy, sophistry and
casuistry which underlay the juristic exegesis
whereby the Alien Property Custodian was authorized to execute his noble defensive crusade
against the Hun in our midst:

In the original statute the function of the alien property custodian was defined as that of a trustee. Subsequently, however, there came a special revelation,
marvelously brilliant but perhaps not divinely inspired,

of the staggering discovery that the foreign traders and manufacturers whose property had been taken over had made their investments in the United States not from ordinary motives of profit but in pursuance of a hostile design, so stealthily pursued that it had never before been suspected, but so deadly in its effects that the American traders and manufacturers were eventually to be engulfed in their own homes and the alien plotters left in grinning possession of the ground. Under the spell engendered by this agitating apparition, and its patriotic call to a retributive but profitable war on the malefactors' property, substantial departures were made from the principle of trusteeship.

To this, of course, must be added the enormous profits of American manufacturers and bankers in supplying the Allies with munitions and credit. We must not forget that some of the most vocal apostles of idealism were among the most notorious of profiteers, and that the intolerant and noisy organizations of "idealists" were subsidized and supported by those same groups, an investigation of the perfidy and corruption of which was blocked by the now Vice-President Dawes. We must pass over with the merest mention the Entente idealism since the autumn of 1918, as exemplified in the continuation of the blockade of Germany after the armistice, the intervention in Russia, the policy of France in the Ruhr and the occupied regions along the Rhine, and the operations of Great Britain and France in India, Egypt, Persia, Morocco, Syria and China.

VI. WORLD ORGANIZATION

Probably the most seductive of all the Allied war aims was the promise that the conflict would emerge with the creation of a world organization, based upon fairness and justice and designed to make impossible, henceforth, the waging of another war. It would be a "league to enforce peace" and to promote sentiments of international brotherhood. By 1920 it was apparent that the United States, the country that had shouted most loudly during the War for such a league, would feel compelled to refrain from joining this organization because it was linked up with an atrocious peace treaty, while Germany, Austria and Russia were arrogantly excluded from the opportunity of securing membership should they have clamored for admittance. What ultimately came out of the movement was essentially an Anglo-French organization, namely, a *league of victors* rather than a league of nations. The saving factor in the situation was that England gradually became unwilling further to tolerate the French desire utterly to destroy Germany and wreck Europe, with the result that the League of Nations has gradually been able to make a number of notable contributions to peace, because France and England could not agree upon the policy of aggression.[11]

While every honest friend of peace should desire to see the League of Nations grow not only in strength but also in membership, it is complete folly to expect that the mere union of a number of selfish, corrupt and war-like states can in itself create a world organization entirely divorced from selfish aims, and exuding a sentiment of Christ-like sweetness. The banding together of a safe-blower, a forger, a pick-pocket, a "stick-up man," a "house-prowler," a blackmailer, a "con" man, a mail-order crook and a "bunko artist" would scarcely constitute an organization for the elimination of crime, even though they incorporated and adopted the by-laws of the National Society for the Prevention of Crime. It will not be necessary to stress the fact, before an intelligent group of readers, that the League of Nations will function as an organ and agency of peace only so far as we bring about a change of heart upon the part of the constituent governments. No league of nations can ever go forward to become a great world force unless a pacific and constructive spirit dominates the foreign offices and public opinion of these same nations. Georges Demartial, the eminent French publicist, has well stated the view of the inevitable futility of the League of Nations if it does not abandon the war hatreds, the war-time theories of war guilt, and the fiction of Article 231 of the Treaty of Versailles:

But it may be said, does not the League of Nations exist to prevent war? A humorous suggestion! If war becomes of rarer occurrence it will be because war itself has become too cruel and devastating, because of fear of aerial warfare and of the consequences of failure, and not because of the hypocrites of Geneva. France was represented there by Viviani, who said of the war that, "It was the final and decisive clash of the dark powers of evil with the radiant powers of good." England was represented there by Lord Balfour, who said: "It was the war of Heaven against Hell." The men who represent the different peoples there today are hardly less biased. Imagine the butchers of St. Bartholmew at the head of a League of Religions! I will believe in the League of Nations when it has painted on the walls of the Assembly hall a picture representing the judges of Versailles crouching over Germany, each with an upraised dagger in his hand, and with the following inscription below: "Admit that you are sole cause of the war or we will finish you off."

The overthrow of the arch-militarists in France, the development of a European point of view recently at Locarno, and the admission of Germany to the League, give more ground for optimism than anything else which has happened in a decade, but we must not forget the rosy hopes for world peace which pervaded western society from 1910 to 1914 and represented another war as unthinkable.

VII. DISARMAMENT

Equally futile is it to talk about disarmament without such a change of international outlook as would naturally involve both the spirit and fact of disarmament. As long as peoples think in terms of arms and wars and have recourse to arms to settle international disputes, even real and thoroughgoing disarmament would be of little or no significance. With our modern technical proficiency in the manufacture of munitions we could within six months equip armies with a far more formidable set of instruments for destruction than were known to Napoleon or General Grant.[12] We ought to be even less misled by the fake Disarmament Conference at Washington in 1920 which, however much it may have achieved temporarily in the diplomatic settlement of the Far East, was a pure burlesque as far as disarmament is concerned. The only equipment about which there was any agreement as to disarmament and abandonment was those forms of armament which had already become hopelessly obsolete. It was equivalent to a group of sportsmen in 1925 agreeing to dispense with flint-lock muskets in their fall shooting exercises. We must accustom ourselves to referring causes of international dispute to leagues of nations and world courts, or else disarmament will be no more than a meaningless, if not dangerous, rhetorical illusion. We should not, of course, overlook the fact that a mere assembling of a conference on disarmament, however futile its achievements, was in itself a gesture of high psychological significance in the field of international relations and diplomatic discussion. It was certainly some advance over the international astronomical conference which Graham Wallas suggested might have to be the first step in the development of world organization.[13]

Professor Parker Thomas Moon has prepared an interesting comparison of the armies of the major world powers before and after the World War: [4]

ARMIES OF THE GREAT POWERS

	1914	1922	Population 1922
Germany	812,000	100,000	60,000,000
Austria		30,000	6,428,000
Hungary	424,000	35,000	8,000,000
Italy	318,000	210,000	39,000,000
Russia	1,300,000	600,000	132,000,000
France	846,000	736,000	41,000,000
Great Britain	250,000	225,000	41,000,000
U. S. A.	105,000	145,000	106,000,000
Japan	250,000	250,000	60,000,000

ARMIES OF THE SMALLER POWERS

	1914	1922	Population 1922
Poland		275,000	27,000,000
Czechoslovakia		150,000	13,600,000
Yugoslavia	58,000	127,000	12,000,000
Greece	60,000	150,000	5,500,000
Rumania	130,000	200,000	17,000,000

COST OF ARMAMENTS AFTER THE WAR

	1913–14	1922
British Empire	$661,000,000	$1,073,000,000
France	349,000,000	461,000,000
Italy	181,000,000	123,000,000
Japan	96,000,000	367,000,000
Total	$1,287,000,000	$2,024,000,000

VIII. SECURITY

Another objective of the War was to "right the wrong of 1870," namely, the seizure of Alsace-Lorraine and the billion dollar indemnity levied upon France. This wrong was "righted" by attempting to levy an indemnity of fifty billion dollars on Germany; by wresting from Germany, in behalf of Poland, territory which was far more an integral and vital part of Germany than Alsace-Lorraine had ever been of France; by seizing the German colonies in the interests of the British, French and Japanese Empires; by preventing German Austria from executing the natural and desirable junction with Germany; and by most unfairly and unjustly depriving Bulgaria of territory to recompense Serbia, Greece, and Rumania for their contributions to the Allied cause during the War.

Another cornerstone of Entente propaganda was the assertion that the War was fought to protect humanity against those who made "scraps of paper" out of sacred treaties, but the Entente made a "scrap of paper" out of the Fourteen Points and the Armistice terms by the Treaty of Versailles, and allowed France to make a "scrap of paper" out of the Treaty of Versailles through the Ruler invasion.

One of the persistent, and yet one of the most

insidious phases of the Entente propaganda since the War has been the constant reiteration that the security of Europe and the world is identical with the security of France. Our present knowledge of the French part in the War of 1870, the menacing French spirit of revenge following 1871, the French diplomatic intrigues and aggressive aims in the Franco-Russian Alliance, the relatively unparalleled French militarism and military expenditures in 1914, the prominent part played by France in precipitating the War, and the domination of Europe by French aggression and militarism since 1918 should be sufficient to convince even the most biased Francophile Americans that we cannot found the slightest expectation of European peace upon any plan which gives France either security or ascendency in Europe at the expense of other countries. There can be no security for Europe which does not rest upon a general European organization which will insure the security, as well as hold in restraint the military tendencies of France, Germany or any other country. It must be emphasized, of course, that when we speak critically of France in this place, as well as elsewhere in this book, we refer to the France of Déroulède, Barrès, Daudet, Delcassé, Poincaré and other exponents of revenge, war and militarism, from whatever parties and groups drawn. France, under

men like Combes, Painlevé, Caillaux and Herriot, would be not only as good, but, in the opinion of the present writer, a little better than other
European states.[15]

We have not here laid stress upon the militarism or secret diplomacy of Germany, primarily because few Americans have harbored any
illusions on this subject, unless it be an unfair
impression of the relative amount and menace of
German militarism as compared with that of
France and Russia. The writer is no apologist
for German *politik,* but a fair and candid study
of European diplomacy, nationalism and militarism since 1870 has gradually but certainly
shown us how impossible it is to maintain the old
thesis that Germany was not only primarily responsible for the World War but was also the
chief source and stimulus of the savage patriotism
and excessive armaments of Europe in the forty
years before the calamity of 1914. The writer
does believe, however, that one of the few real and
substantial positive gains of the World War is
to be found in the breaking of the power of the
narrow but powerful clique of extreme and arrogant militarists in Germany, and it is one of the
chief counts against Poincaré that his savage
post-War policy in regard to Germany has given
this group in Germany a greatly increased popularity and prestige.[16]

IX. THE DELUSIONS AND MYTHOLOGY OF WAR
PROPAGANDA

The conclusion of these few very casual, desultory and almost platitudinous remarks on the contrast between myth and fact in connection with the World War and after, is that they prove beyond the possibility of contradiction or doubt the highly relevant fact that war cannot be ended by more war any more than a drowning man can be resuscitated by pouring more water down his throat. The type of mind and intellectual attitudes which are developed for and by war are those which bring to the fore practically all of the baser traits of human nature and intensify hatred and savagery, while reducing the potency of those mental operations which are conducive to pacific adjustments and mutual toleration. It is only by attacking war head on, and making clear its multifarious contributions to human brutality and waste, as well as by proving the futile and unnecessary nature of every war, that we can make headway, if at all, against modern militarism and the war spirit.[17]

It may have been worth while on this basis to point out with more than usual frankness the imbecilities and disasters of the late World War, because this is a particularly instructive instance for those now alive. It was not only a struggle through which we have all lived, but also the one which was most exploited as an example as the one uniquely necessary, idealistic and justice-promoting conflict of all history. If we show how totally we were deluded on all these points, it may help us in the future to guard against being led astray by the same groups when they are interested in provoking another world conflict.

It has doubtless been a consideration of the above points which has led a few courageous spirits among us, like Harry Emerson Fosdick, Sherwood Eddy, Kirby Page and others to express doubt as to whether they would ever again support or sanction another war. But it is necessary to carry this salutary disillusionment beyond the few to the mass of students of the coming generation who will be those who must take the leading part in opposing a military policy and in substituting for savage patriotism a broad international point of view. And if we may judge by the symptoms of the last decade, students will primarily need to look for truth and guidance to themselves rather than to their professors of history and diplomacy, many of whom will probably tenaciously continue to remain devotees of the Rip Van Winkle and Pollyanna schools of historiography.[18]

X. THE LESSONS

The really important aspect of the above material is not, of course, merely the satisfaction of our curiosity as to the historical facts regarding War origins, but the important bearing which these facts have on public and international policy at the present time. As the prevailing European international policy is still based upon the assumption of unique German responsibility for the War it is evident that the facts in the situation demand the repudiation of this program and the adoption of a more fair and constructive policy. The Dawes Report, and the discussion which it has promoted, in common with most of the analyses of the Reparations problem, rests upon altogether fallacious premises which alike invalidate the content of the proposal and the machinery of enforcement. The whole logical and juristic foundation of the notion of reparations from Germany, in so far as it differs from the age-old policy of punitive levies on conquered peoples, is the assumption of the complete and unique responsibility of Germany for the origin of the World War and the misery, suffering and economic losses which it entailed. This assumption is fully embodied in the provisions of the Treaty of Versailles relating to reparations, and even Poincaré was once incautious enough to admit that proof of divided responsibility for the outbreak of the great conflict carried with it a disappearance of the case for German reparations. The Dawes Plan, and any current American and European agreements as to its enforcement, while immensely better than the Poincaré policy, are comparable to efforts to reduce the fine of a man, known by all to be innocent.

What we need to do is to adopt a broad, constructive and far-sighted policy. The guilt for the World War having been distributed, the expense of indemnifying the sufferers should likewise be distributed. The United States might well use its undoubted financial power to induce France and England (the latter would probably gladly welcome the proposal) to forgo all notion of any reparations from Germany and to adopt the program of a mutual sharing with Germany of the burdens of reconstruction and rehabilitation. The United States could with great propriety indicate its good-will and intentions in the circumstances by cancelling the debts of the European powers on the above condition. Once England and France gave some such evidence of international honesty and decency, one of the chief obstacles and objections would be removed to our joining the League of Nations. We may agree with Fabre-Luce that, though the wartime slogan that America and the Entente entered the War solely for the purpose of ending all war was at the time pure hypocrisy, yet we shall have lost both the War and the peace if we do not take steps to make this constructive slogan an achieved reality. The beginnings of any such move must be found in an appreciation of the facts concerning the origins of the World War. Hence the truth in the following statement by John Kenneth Turner:

Instead of being a dead issue, our late war is the livest issue of the day, and it will remain an issue so long as future war is in the reckoning. Its lessons hold not only the secret of averting future war, but also the solution of other public questions of a pressing nature.

SELECTED REFERENCES

Bakeless, J., *The Origin of the Next War;* Baker, R. S., *Woodrow Wilson and the World Settlement;* Bausman, F., *Let France Explain; Facing Europe;* Brailsford, Henry N., *After the Peace;* Buell, R. L., *International Relations;* Chafee, Z., Hall, N. F., and Hudson, M. O., *The Next War;* Clarke, J. H., *America and World Peace;* Demartial, G., *La Guerre de 1914. Comment on mobilisa les consciences;* Ebray, A., *La Paix malprope; Chiffons de papier;* Fabre-Luce, *La Victoire; La Crise des alliances;* Fisher, I., *League or War;* Gibbons, H. A., *Europe since 1918;* Hudson, M. O., *The Permanent Court of International Justice;* Irwin, W., *The Next War; Christ or Mars;* Jagow, K., "Die Friedensverträge als politischer Werkzeug," in *Deutsche Politik,* 1926; Knight, M. M., "Liquidating Our War Illusions," in *Journal of International Rela-*

tions, April, 1922; Lippmann, W., *The Stakes of Diplomacy*; Miller, D. H., *The Geneva Protocol*; Nitti, F. S., *Peaceless Europe*; *The Decadence of Europe*; Mowrer, P. H., *Balkanized Europe*; Neilson, F., *How Diplomats Make War*; Page, K., *War: Its Causes, Consequences and Cure*; *An American Peace Policy*; Ravage, M. E., *The Malady of Europe*; Schwertfeger, B., *"Der Tiger": die Kriegsreden Clémenceaus*; Stannard, H., *The Fabric of Europe*; Street, C. J. C., *The Treachery of France*; Turner, J. K., *Shall It be Again?*; Wallas, G., *Our Social Heritage*; Williams, R., *The League of Nations Today*; Willis, I. C., *How We Went into the War*; *How We Got On with the War*; *How We Got Out of the War.*

FOOTNOTES AND FURTHER REFERENCES

[1] F. Neilson, *How Diplomats Make War.*

[2] J. K. Turner, *Shall It Be Again?*, Chaps. xix–xxvi.

[3] See B. Schwertfeger, *Deutschlands Schuld am Weltkriege;* and *"Der Tiger": die Kriegsreden Clémenceaus.*

[4] C. H. Grattan, "The Walter Hines Page Legend," in *American Mercury*, September, 1925; Grey of Fallodon, *Twenty-Five Years*, Vol. II, Chap. xxiii; see also Chap. IX, above.

[5] B. J. Hendrick, *The Life and Letters of Walter H. Page*, Vol. III, Chap. x.

[6] Cf. D. Lloyd George, *Is It Peace?*

[7] M. E. Ravage, *The Malady of Europe;* P. S. Mowrer, *Balkanized Europe;* M. H. H. Macartney, *Five Years of European Chaos.*

[8] See below, pp. 697–8; and H. G. Moulton and C. Lewis, *The Financial Problem of France.*

[9] G. H. Blakeslee, "Will Democracy Alone Make the World Safe?" in *Journal of Race Development*, 1918.

[10] R. S. Baker, *Woodrow Wilson and the World Settlement*, Vol. I, Part I.

[11] A. Fabre-Luce, *La Crise des Alliances;* H. J. Carman, "Franco-British Rivalry and the Entente Cordiale," in *Historical Outlook*, November, 1923.

[12] W. Irwin, *The Next War.*

[13] G. Wallas, *Our Social Heritage.*

[14] P. T. Moon, *Syllabus on International Relations,* pp. 80–81.

[15] See the criticism of France in F. Bausman, *Let France Explain;* C. J. C. Street, *The Treachery of France;* D. Lloyd George, *Is It Peace;* and F. Nitti, *The Decadence of Europe.* France is defended by André Tardieu, *The Truth about the Treaty;* and Lucien Graux, *Histoire des violations du traité de Paix.* The most judicious analyses are to be found in A. Fabre-Luce, *La Crise des alliances;* and J. Bardoux, *Lloyd George et la France.* Probably the most statesmanlike plan for European security was that drawn up by J. T. Shotwell, D. H. Miller and T. H. Bliss and described in D. H. Miller, *The Geneva Protocol.*

[16] See above, Chap. iii, and J. S. Ewart, *The Roots and Causes of the Wars,* Chaps. iii, xv–xvii.

[17] Cf. W. Irwin, *The Next War;* J. K. Turner, *Shall It Be Again?;* P. Gibbs, *Realities of War; Now It Can Be Told; More That Must Be Told;* J. Dos Passos, *Three Soldiers;* L. Stallings, *Plumes.*

[18] See the remarks of A. L. P. Dennis at the Foreign Policy Luncheon in New York City, March 14, 1925, in New York *Times,* March 15, 1925; the letter of A. P. Dennis in the New York *Tribune* for May 9, 1925; the remarks of A. E. Morse and F. M. Anderson in New York *Times Current History Magazine,* June, 1924; the letters of W. S. Davis in the Springfield *Republican* for February 5, 1925 and the Springfield *Weekly Republican* for February 26, 1925; the letter of E. R. Turner in the *New Republic* for April 9, 1924; the review of Hazen's *Europe since 1815,* Ibid., March 19, 1924; R. W. Seton-Watson, *Serajevo;* review in London *Times,* September 30, 1926; J. W. Headlam-Morley in the London *Observer* for October 3, 1926; W. S. Davis, *Europe since Waterloo,* Part III; and the article by E. R. Turner in *Current History,* February, 1927. Typical samples of "pussy-footing" revisionism are Mack Eastman, "New Myths for Old," in Canadian *Forum* for April and May, 1926; and Bernadotte Schmitt, "July, 1914," in *Foreign Affairs* (American) October, 1926.

APPENDIX I

THE LITERATURE OF WAR GUILT

OUTBREAK OF THE WORLD WAR. German Documents collected by Karl Kautsky and edited by Max Montgelas and Walther Schücking. New York, 1924, 688 pp.

THE AUSTRIAN RED BOOK. Edited by R. Goos. London, 1922. 3 Vols.

UN LIVRE NOIR. Diplomatie d'avant guerre d'après les documents des archives Russes. Edited by René Marchand. Paris, 1922–23. 2 Vols. 372, 591 pp.

DER DIPLOMATISCHE SCHRIFTWECHSEL ISWOLSKIS, 1911–1914. Edited by F. Stieve. Berlin, 1924. 5 Vols.

ENTENTE DIPLOMACY AND THE WORLD, 1909–1914. By B. de Siebert. Edited by G. A. Schreiner. New York, 1920. 762 pp.

BRITISH OFFICIAL DOCUMENTS ON THE ORIGIN OF THE WAR, 1898–1914. Edited by G. P. Gooch and H. Temperley. London, 1926 ff. 11 Vols.

"New Light on the Origins of the World War," by Sidney B. Fay, in *American Historical Review,* July and October, 1920; January, 1921.

"Serbia's Responsibility for the World War," by Sidney B. Fay, in New York *Times Current History Magazine,* October, 1925; "The Black Hand Plot that Led to the World War," by Sidney B. Fay, Ibid., November, 1925.

DIE GROSSE POLITIK DER EUROPAEISCHEN KABINETTE, 1871–1914. Edited by J. Lepsius, A. M. Bartholdy and F. Thimme. Berlin, 1922. About 30 volumes have appeared.

DEUTSCHLANDS AUSSENPOLITIK. By Veit Valentin. Berlin, 1921. 418 pp.

ERINNERUNGEN. By Otto Hammann. Berlin, 1918–21. 3 Vols.

BILDER AUS DER LETZEN KAISERZEIT. By Otto Hammann. Berlin, 1922. 163 pp.

DEUTSCHE WELTPOLITIK, 1890–1912. By Otto Hammann, Berlin, 1924. 280 pp.

VON BISMARCK ZUM WELTKRIEGE. By Erich Brandenburg. Berlin, 1924. 454 pp.

A HISTORY OF MODERN EUROPE, 1878–1920. By G. P. Gooch, New York, 1923. 728 pp.

FRANCO-GERMAN RELATIONS, 1871–1914. By G. P. Gooch. London, 1923. 64 pp.

THE SECRET TREATIES OF AUSTRIA-HUNGARY, 1879–1914. By A. F. Pribram. Edited by A. C. Coolidge, Cambridge, Mass., 1922–23. 308, 271 pp.

AUSTRIAN FOREIGN POLICY, 1908–1918. By A. F. Pribram, London, 1923. 128 pp.

THE CASE FOR THE CENTRAL POWERS. By Max Montgelas. New York, 1925. 255 pp.

RUSSLANDS EINTRITT IN DEN WELTKRIEG. By G. Frantz. Berlin, 1924. 306 pp.

ISVOLSKY AND THE WORLD WAR. By F. Stieve. New York, 1925. 254 pp.

FALSIFICATIONS OF THE RUSSIAN ORANGE BOOK. Edited by G. von Romberg. New York, 1923. 77 pp.

ICH SUCHE DIE WAHRHEIT. By Wilhelm, Kronprinz. Berlin, 1925, 396 pp. (English translation, 1926.)

LORD GREY UND DER WELTKRIEG. By Hermann Lutz. Berlin, 1926. 421 pp.

KAISERLICHE KATASTROPHENPOLITIK. By Heinrich Kanner. Vienna, 1922. 468 pp.

DER UNTERGANG DER DONAU-MONARCHIE. By Julius von Szilassy. Berlin, 1922. 425 pp.

AUS MEINER DIENSTZEIT, 1906–1918. By Conrad von Hötzendorf. Vienna, 1922–23. 4 Vols.

POINCARÉ A-T-IL VOULU LA GUERRE? By Gouttenoire de Toury. Paris, 1921.

JAURÈS ET LA PARTI DE LA GUERRE. By Gouttenoire de Toury. Paris, 1923. 234 pp.

THE ORIGINS OF THE WAR. By Raymond Poincaré. London, 1922. 230 pp.

AU SERVICE DE LA FRANCE. By Raymond Poincaré. Paris, 1926.

L'EVANGILE DU QUAI D'ORSAY. By Georges Demartial. Paris, 1926. 190 pp.

LA GUERRE DE 1914. COMMENT ON MOBILISA LES CONSCIENCES. By Georges Demartial. Paris, 1922. 325 pp.

LES RESPONSABLES DE LA GUERRE. By Alfred Pevet. Paris, 1921. 520 pp.

LES PREUVES. LE CRIME DE DROIT COMMUN. LE CRIME DIPLOMATIQUE. By Mathias Morhardt. Paris, 1924. 340 pp.

LA VICTOIRE. By A. Fabre-Luce. Paris, 1924. 428 pp. (English translation, THE LIMITATIONS OF VICTORY. New York, 1926.)

CONSIDÉRATIONS SUR LES RESPONSABILITÉS DE LA GUERRE. By Gustave Dupin. Paris, 1925.

CONFÉRENCE SUR LES RESPONSABILITÉS DE LA GUERRE. By Gustave Dupin. Paris, 1925. 39 pp.

LES CARNETS DE GEORGES LOUIS. By E. Judet. 2 Vols. Paris, 1925.

LA RUSSIE DES TSARS PENDANT LA GRANDE GUERRE. By Maurice Paléologue. Paris, 1922. 3 Vols. (English translation, AN AMBASSADOR'S MEMOIRS, 3 Vols. 1924–5.)

LA CONDAMNATION D'UN RÉGIME. By René Marchand. Paris, 1922. 151 pp.

LES CRIMINELS. By Victor Margueritte. Paris, 1925. 356 pp.

A L'ORIGINE DU MENSONGE. By Lazare. Paris, 1925. 272 pp.

LES ORIGINES IMMÉDIATES DE LA GUERRE, 28 JUIN-4 AOUT, 1914. By Pierre Renouvin. Paris, 1925, 226 pp.

HOW THE WAR BEGAN. The Diary of Baron Schilling, Chief of the Chancellery of the Russian Foreign Office in 1914. London, 1925. 122 pp.

DIE MOBILMACHUNG DER RUSSISCHEN ARMEE, 1914. By S. Dobrorolski. Berlin, 1922. 52 pp.

ERINNERUNGEN. By W. A. Suchomlinow. Berlin, 1924. 526 pp.

LES CAUSES DE LA GUERRE. By M. Bogitschevich. Paris, 1925. 254 pp.

DIE ERMORDUNG DES ERZHERZOGS FRANZ FERDINAND. By S. Stanojević. Frankfort, 1923. 66 pp.

THE MURDER OF SERAJEVO. By L. Jovanovitch. London, 1925. 15 pp.

THE SERAJEVO CRIME. By Edith Durham. London, 1925. 208 pp.

SARAJEVO. By R. W. Seton-Watson. London, 1926, 303 pp.

COME SI SCATENO LA GUERRA MONDIALE. By Corrado Barbagallo. Rome, 1923. 166 pp.

THE SECRET HISTORY OF A GREAT BETRAYAL. By E. D. Morel) with the aid of Raymond Beazley). London, 1922. 47 pp.

HOW THE WAR CAME. By Earl Loreburn. London, 1919. 340 pp.

HOW WE WENT INTO THE WAR. By Irene Cooper Willis. London, 1919. 179 pp.

THE GENESIS OF THE WAR. By H. H. Asquith. London, 1923. 304 pp.

THE WORLD CRISIS, 1911–1914. By Winston S. Churchill. London, 1923. 2 Vols.

MY MISSION TO RUSSIA AND OTHER DIPLOMATIC MEMORIES. By Sir George Buchanan. London, 1923. 2 Vols.

THE DIARY OF LORD BERTIE OF THAME: 1914–18.

Edited by Lady Algernon Gordon Lennox. New York, 1925. 2 Vols.

TWENTY-FIVE YEARS (1892–1916). By Viscount Grey of Fallodon. New York, 1925. 2 Vols.

THE INTERNATIONAL ANARCHY, 1904–1914. By G. Lowes Dickinson, New York, 1926. 505 pp.

THE ROOTS AND CAUSES OF THE WARS, 1914–1918. By Sir J. S. Ewart, New York, 1925. 2 Vols.

THE PAN-GERMAN LEAGUE. By Mildred S. Wertheimer. New York, 1924. 256 pp.

THE LIFE AND LETTERS OF WALTER HINES PAGE. By Burton J. Hendrick. New York, 1922, 1926. 3 Vols.

THE INTIMATE PAPERS OF COLONEL HOUSE. Edited by Charles Seymour. Boston, 1926. 2 Vols.

THE VERDICT OF HISTORY: THE CASE OF SIR EDWARD GREY. By E. F. Henderson. Monadnock, N. H., 1924.

LET FRANCE EXPLAIN. By Frederick Bausman. London, 1922. 264 pp.

FACING EUROPE. By Frederick Bausman. New York, 1926. 330 pp.

SHALL IT BE AGAIN? By John Kenneth Turner. New York, 1922. 448 pp.

HOW DIPLOMATS MAKE WAR. By Francis Neilson. New York, 1915.

THE MYTH OF A GUILTY NATION. By Albert J. Nock. New York, 1922. 124 pp.

CROSS-CURRENTS IN EUROPE TODAY. By C. A. Beard, Boston, 1922. 278 pp.

I. INTRODUCTORY

Never before in the whole history of historical writing has there been so rapid and complete a change in the opinions of historians concerning an event of major importance as has been witnessed in the revision of our conceptions concerning the causes of the outbreak of the World

War in August, 1914. There were a few brave souls, like Morel, Bertrand Russell, Francis Neilson, and others, who, during the War, refused to accept at its face value the Entente propaganda concerning the sole and diabolical guilt of Germany in the precipitation of the great calamity which broke out in the summer of 1914. Yet the views of these men rested very largely upon intuition rather than demonstrable facts. It has been due only to the unprecedented rapidity of the publication of the documents in the foreign offices of Germany, Austria and Russia that we have been able to discover the actual facts in the same generation as that which witnessed the late world conflict. Previously such documents have normally been kept secret from forty to one hundred years, so that the mythology which passed current during a war could not be inadequately overthrown until the time of the grandchildren of those who had participated.

But the mere documents themselves, such as those edited and published by Kautsky, Goos, Marchand, Stieve, Siebert, and Gooch would have been of little significance had not alert historians made use of them immediately upon their appearance. The first scholar to attempt to assimilate the new evidence and to indicate its significance for the problem of war guilt was Professor Sidney B. Fay, of Smith College, who published the results of his preliminary investigations in three notable articles in the *American Historical Review,* beginning in July, 1920. He was able to explode the myth of the alleged Potsdam Conference of July 5, 1914, at which the Kaiser was supposed to have revealed his plot to force a European war. Professor Fay demonstrated that the initiative in the punishment of Serbia was taken by Austria, and that Germany, late in July, 1914, made earnest efforts to restrain Austria when it began to appear as if the Austrian punitive expedition into Serbia would bring in its train a general European war. The incriminating evidence against Russia and France was not, however, at this time available, and while Professor Fay was able to demonstrate that it was the premature Russian mobilization which produced the German declaration of war, he was still able to regard France as a state which had done all it could to preserve the peace of Europe in 1914. Since 1920 additional material has enabled a large number of historical scholars to carry forward the task begun by Professor Fay, until we are now relatively certain as to the major facts involved, and Professor Fay himself promises us in the near future a definitive appraisal not only of the documentary evidence, but also of the chief books and monographs which have thus far been produced on the question of responsibility for the World War. In two recent lucid and scholarly articles in the New York *Times Current History Magazine* Professor Fay has not only given us the best summary of the evidence establishing the full Serbian responsibility for the assassination of the Archduke, but has also indicated the masterly command of the data of war guilt which we may expect in his forthcoming book.

One cannot expect to understand the issues of 1914 unless he is familiar with the diplomacy of the period following 1870. Fortunately, the post-war publication of documents has been of as much assistance here as in respect to the immediate cause of the War. The great German set, *Die Grosse Politik,* which is now being issued in a large number of imposing volumes (approximately fifty), embodies most of the more important documents in the German foreign office since 1870, and has necessitated a complete recasting of our views on European diplomacy in the forty years before Sarajevo. This material has been worked over by a number of enterprising scholars, among them Valentin, Rachfahl, Hammann and Brandenburg in Germany, and Gooch in England. Gooch's book is the only reliable guide yet available in English, and constitutes an indispensable introduction to the problem of war guilt for those who can only follow the argument in English. Gooch reveals the steady tightening of the Franco-Russian Alliance, and its transition into an aggressive policy guided by Poincaré and Izvolski after 1912. England, after having been rebuffed in her advances to Germany by the naval policy of Tirpitz, and the anti-English attitude of Holstein, was driven into ever closer relations with France, and even into the unpopular agreement with Russia which cemented the Triple Entente. The German ambitions in the Near East threw her into ever closer relations with Austria and made it more and more necessary for her to support the efforts of Austria to maintain her integrity in the face of the nationalistic movements in the Balkans.

Europe became divided into two "armed camps," each of which grew ever more disinclined to give way before the demands of the other. The stage was being set so that such an inflammable episode as that of the murder of Franz Ferdinand in June, 1914, could precipitate the entire continent into a life and death struggle. With the exception of a somewhat inadequate presentation of the case against Sir Edward Grey, and his Russophile under-secretary, Sir Arthur Nicolson, Gooch's book is a model of fairness, and the author exhibits unusual capacity in the way of being able to combine complete mastery of detail with clear and forcible presentation of the larger issues and policies involved. The fact that the more damaging evidence against France and Russia, as well as the evidence of Serbian responsibility for the assassination of the Archduke, had not appeared when Gooch wrote his book makes his judgment as to the relative order of responsibility archaic. Gooch has also contributed much of the material in the third volume of the *Cambridge History of British Foreign Policy* dealing with the British aspects of the back-ground of the war. Gooch has further given us an admirable brief survey of the history of Franco-German relations since 1870, interpreted in his usual lucid and impartial fashion. In connection with the diplomacy of the generation before the war, mention should be made of the notable work of Professor Pribram on the secret treaties of Austria-Hungary, which has been brought out in an excellent English edition under the supervision of Professor A. C. Coolidge, of Harvard University.

II. GERMANY AND AUSTRIA

We shall not here make any effort at a summary of the many important German and Austrian monographs on war guilt, as it would still be assumed by many in the United States that such works must more or less naturally and inevitably be biased in favor of the Central Powers. We cannot, however, overlook the admirable brief summary of the revisionist point of view by Count Max Montgelas. This book was unfortunately christened in the English edition. The original German title of *Leading Threads in the Problem of War Guilt* was much more accurately descriptive of the content than the English version entitled *The Case for the Central Powers*. About half of the book is devoted to an excellent brief summary of the diplomacy from 1907 to 1914. This is followed by a systematic analysis of the main elements in the crisis of July and August, 1914, together with a thorough criticism of many of the more important myths and legends connected with the Entente indictment of Germany during the War and Peace Conference periods. On pages 200–203 he gives some seventeen conclusions on the matter of war guilt, which represent one of the best and most accurate statements of the conclusions of revisionist scholarship to be found anywhere.

While Montgelas puts the primary responsibility upon

Russia, because of her precipitate general mobilization, and clearly shows how this action was encouraged by France, he does not hesitate to criticize German policy where the facts lead him to the conclusion that Germany was in error. He fully recognizes, for example, that the German invasion of Belgium was both a violation of international law and a serious diplomatic blunder, and he is honest enough to point out that the strong probability that the French would have invaded Belgium if Germany had not, constitutes no adequate justification of the actual German invasion. Montgelas' book is easily the best brief statement of the revisionist point of view which has thus far come out of Germany, and it is unfortunate that its German authorship will probably prevent it from receiving the attention and respect from English-speaking readers to which its high quality entitles it.

Among the mass of works which have come out of Germany on the question of war guilt a few others must be mentioned, such as the very competent book of Dr. G. Frantz on the all-important Russian military activities at the outbreak of the War; Dr. F. Stieve's excellent analysis of Izvolski's correspondence; and Baron Romberg's exposure of the falsifications of the *Russian Orange Book* issued early in the War as a vindication of Franco-Russian conduct in July and August, 1914. Frantz's work is unquestionably the best monograph on Russia's part in producing the World War which has thus far been written. He makes rather a stronger case against Sazonov than has hitherto been accepted among revisionist historians. Stieve demonstrates the primary responsibility of Izvolski for the direction of the forcible Russian policy leading to the diplomacy of 1914, and Romberg shows that in the original *Orange Book* all of the telegrams indicating collusion between France and Russia in the effort to bring on mobilization and the War were carefully excluded. He proves that

the only telegram indicating a French desire for caution
was one in which the French advised secrecy and adroit-
ness, so that Germany and England would not discover
the mobilization plans, but at the same time urged even
greater Russian activity in the actual military preparations.

The most interesting, as well as the most recent, important German book on war guilt has been prepared by the
ex-Crown Prince. While the Crown Prince was probably
aided by competent historical scholars, the book is a generally reliable and technical work, indicating a mastery of
the latest documents and monographs and exhibiting a
broad viewpoint and great moderation and restraint. The
author demolishes the official French work on war responsibility by Bourgeois and Pagès, *Les Origines et les Responsabilités de la Grande Guerre.* So competent and convincing is the work that it has been very favorably received in
Germany by political groups fiercely antagonistic to the
old Hohenzollern régime. The best work on British pre-
war diplomacy is that of Hermann Lutz, editor of the German edition of the complete British documents of 1914.

The most important organ in Germany for promoting
scholarship in the war guilt problem is the monthly journal,
Die Kriegsschuldfrage, edited by Herr Alfred von Wegerer.

In Austria, along with the editorial work of Roderich
Goos and Professor Pribram, the most important works
bearing on war origins are the important monographs of
Heinrich Kanner and Julius von Szilassy, and the memoirs
of Conrad von Hötzendorf, the Austrian Chief of Staff in
1914. Kanner looks upon such forces as nationalism, militarism and imperialism as basic in bringing on the World
War. He exaggerates greatly, however, the alleged incitement of Austria by Germany. Szilassy takes the same
general position, but shows how Berchtold was influenced
by aggressive subordinate associates in the foreign office,

though there are some who dispute this view and contend
that Berchtold himself exhibited more than usual energy
and decision in the July crisis. Hötzendorf, with very
unusual frankness, reveals the determination of the forceful group in the Dual Monarchy to have a last reckoning
with the Serbian nationalists, in the hope of finally ex-
tinguishing this menace to the integrity of Austria-
Hungary. The general significance of these works is that
they put an end for all time to the allegation that the
initiative in the fatal crisis of 1914 with respect to the
punishment of Serbia came from Germany rather than
Austria.

The Dutch have created a commission to study the
causes of the war which publishes an excellent journal edited by Dr. N. Japiske.

III. FRANCE

One of the most reassuring and satisfactory aspects of
the study of war guilt by honest and impartial historians
has been the courageous effort of liberal French scholars
to contribute their share to the establishment of the truth
concerning this important problem, even though the results
of their researches might prove extremely damaging to
their own country. In fact, it has required much more
courage on the part of French historians to present an
honest picture of the war guilt question than has been the
case with German historians, because the new documents
destroy the validity of the indictment of Germany and constitute the basis for an inevitable case against France and
Russia. In the light of these facts it is reassuring to be
able to call attention to so impressive a list of books by
capable French authors who accept the revisionist position.
The struggle for truth in France began with such things
as the brochures of Gouttenoire de Toury, making serious

charges against Poincaré, and eliciting from the latter his apology entitled, *The Origins of the War.* About the same time Georges Demartial made use of some of the new evidence and indicated the necessity of a serious revision of our wartime views. A more thoroughgoing indictment of French policy, based upon wider acquaintance with the newer literature, was brought out a year later by Alfred Pevet. Pevet's book represents a vigorous onslaught upon the Franco-Russian militarists, calls for a complete reconstruction of our notions of war guilt, and concludes with a scathing demonstration of the hypocrisy of the Allied charge of complete German responsibility for the outbreak of the War, which the Germans were compelled to sign at the Versailles Peace Conference. In 1922 Demartial published his second work—an illuminating analysis of the methods used by Poincaré and his associates in duping the French people into accepting the fiction of a defensive war. He is now bringing out a monumental work on the Russian mobilization.

In 1924 Mathias Morhardt, of the Paris *Temps,* one of the leaders in the movement for truth about war origins in France, published the most damaging indictment of France which has yet appeared. While fully admitting that it was the Russian mobilization which actually precipitated the War, he emphasizes the fact that the Russians would never have dared to move without the insistent encouragement of Poincaré. Establishing to his own satisfaction the primary personal responsibility of Poincaré for the World War and everything which it brought with it, Morhardt inquires why Poincaré is loath to accept the honor of having done more to alter the face of civilization than any other human being who has ever lived. He answers that while Poincaré was not averse at the beginning of the conflict to admitting responsibility, the long duration of the War, with the consequent losses and burdens imposed upon France, made him fearful of facing the responsibility for his own acts. In addition to the convincing marshalling of evidence against Poincaré, the other notable aspects of Morhardt's book are his demonstration of the low political status and barbarous methods of Serbia, the relative inadequacy of the Serbian answer to the Austrian demands, and the unwillingness of the Allies to accept the constructive Italian plans of mediation and arbitration in July, 1914. Morhardt's conclusion is especially statesmanlike when he declares that "it is not true that France and Germany are doomed to fight eternally. . . . What is true is that France can live in peace, side by side, with Germany. It is only necessary to wish to do so."

Even more valuable and rather more moderate in tone is the notable book by Alfred Fabre-Luce, which is the most comprehensive work on the broad question of war guilt which has thus far been published in France. This book not only embodies an excellent analysis of the outbreak of the War, but, like Monteglas's work, contains a concise, impartial, and illuminating survey of the antecedent European diplomacy. He demonstrates very adequately that the history of contemporary European diplomacy offers in no sense a one-sided indictment or a white-washing of either the Triple Alliance or the Triple Entente. Coming to the immediate problem of war guilt he is in essential agreement with Morhardt as to the facts but contends that the responsibility for the War was divided between the Entente and the Central Powers. He declares that after Poincaré's visit to Russia there was only a very slight possibility of averting the war. His epigrammatic conclusion that "the acts of Germany and Austria made the war possible; those of the Triple Entente made it inevitable," is probably as competent a summary of the actual facts as has thus far been achieved. The book exhibits the most judicious and open-minded attitude of any work on war guilt yet published in France, if not in the world. Particularly satisfactory and constructive is Fabre-Luce's plea for some form of international organization which will make another European war impossible. While showing the hypocrisy of the original Entente claim that the World War was a war against war, he presents an effective plea for a type of contemporary diplomacy which will actually make the great conflict turn out to have been such in its results, whatever it causes. We are now very fortunate in having available an English translation of this extremely valuable book under the title, *The Limitations of Victory*.

Excellent work has been done by G. Dupin in summarizing the newer information concerning war guilt. His *Conférence sur les responsabilités de la guerre* is probably the best brief summary of the more decisive revisionist position.

Ernest Judet has recently edited the diary of Georges Louis, who was the pacifically inclined French minister at St. Petersburg, recalled by Poincaré to be replaced by the master mind of contemporary French secret diplomacy and aggressive intrigue, Delcassé. This work contains a large amount of interesting intimate material, much of which strengthens the case against Poincaré, Delcassé and others in charge of French diplomacy from 1912–1914. Like the *Livre Noir* it presents a picture of an ever closer and more determined Franco-Russian policy. When Delcassé was needed in Paris he was replaced by Maurice Paléologue, who thoroughly shared Delcassé's point of view. In his diary Paléologue has given us a vivid, if naïve, picture of the aggressive attitude of Poincaré on his fateful St. Petersburg visit in the latter part of July, 1914, as well as of the great enthusiasm for war at the Russian court. René Marchand has not only prepared the great French edition of the Russian archival material in the *Livre Noir*, but has also summarized the significance of his documentary researches for the assessment of responsibility for the

World War. Even French men of letters have become interested in the problem of war guilt and Victor Margueritte
has brought out a relatively competent and extremely
trenchant work in which he accepts the revisionist point of
view and indicts all of the European powers involved in
the conflict. The book is particularly valuable for its attack upon the forces making for war in general, such as
capitalism, patriotism and militarism. M. Margueritte and
M. Charpentier have recently founded a monthly journal,
Evolution, comparable to Herr Wegerer's *Kriegsschuldfrage.*

Lazare's brilliant work rivals that of Morhardt as the
most striking French critique of Poincaré and the military
clique in France in relation to war guilt. It is specifically
by far the most effective demolition of Poincaré's *Origins
of the War* which has thus far been published. The publication of Poincaré's memoirs under the title, *Au Service
de la France,* will call for a resumption of Lazare's critical
labors. The most scholarly Frenchman who has devoted
his attention to a serious study of war guilt is Pierre Renouvin, and in his recently published book we may discover
the definitive French statement of the case, interpreted in a
somewhat more conservative fashion than in the works of
such writers as Morhardt and Pevet. The works of Fabre-
Luce and Renouvin admirably supplement each other, as
Fabre-Luce gives most of his space to the events preceding and following the War, while Renouvin sticks close to
a most detailed analysis of the diplomatic crisis of the mid-
summer of 1914. For this particular subject Renouvin's
book is the most competent work which has yet appeared,
and will only be superseded by that of Professor Fay.
There are only four notable major errors of fact or interpretation. He does not possess the latest information on
the responsibility of Serbia for the assassination of the
Archduke. He holds that Germany favored the local war
of Austria against Serbia to the end. He quite erro-

neously asserts that Germany reverted to the war policy
and ceased restraining Austria on July 30. And, finally,
he fails to state with directness the fact that Russian mobilization inevitably meant war. The best indictment of
the Treaty of Versailles has been written by Alcide Ebray.

IV. RUSSIA

On Russia the most important materials thus far published in regard to war guilt are the diary of Baron
Schilling, the work of Dobrorolski on the fateful Russian
mobilization of 1914, the memoirs of Suchomlinov, the
Russian minister of war in 1914, the complete German
edition of Izvolski's correspondence, an analysis of which
has been made by the German editor, Dr. F. Stieve, and
the monograph of Dr. G. Frantz. The diary of Baron
Moritz Fabianovich Schilling, chief of the chancellery of
the Russian foreign office in 1914, constitutes one of the
most valuable sources for a definite knowledge of the succession of events and policies in Russia through the time
of the fatal general mobilization order. Not even the interesting foreword by Sazonov is adequate to explain away
the inherent and implicit indictment of the Russians in
their acts and decisions during this period. Dobrorolski's
work is of great importance as showing the determined and
steady Russian preparations for war from the moment the
general staff and the civil government learned of the terms
of the Austrian ultimatum to Serbia. He demonstrates
that for all practical purposes the war was actually on,
as far as the Russian militarists were concerned, by the
24th of July, and that the details as to the date of the
Tsar's alleged ordering, countermanding and reordering of
the mobilization are matters of greater military than
diplomatic import. Dobrorolski frankly admits that the
Russian order for general mobilization was the real beginning of the World War, and that the Russians fully realized

this fact. To use Dobrorolski's own words relative to the
final order for general mobilization:

"This once fixed there is no way backwards. This step
settles automatically the beginning of war. The affair had
now (early in the evening of July 30th) begun irretriev-
ably. The order was already known in all of the larger
towns of our huge country. No change was possible. The
prologue of the great historic drama had begun."

Dobrorolski's work and those of Frantz and Schilling
are the indispensable sources for the details involved in
the much-discussed problem of the Tsar's attitude and acts
in the crisis of the decision upon mobilization.

Suchomlinov's work contains a large amount of intimate
personal detail concerning the Russian military and diplomatic situation in July, 1914, but the notorious unreliability
of the author makes one uncertain as to how much credence
should be given to any specific statement. It would appear, however, from his work and that of Dr. G. Frantz,
that at the last moment Suchomlinov lost his nerve, and the
determination on war was carried along successfully by
Sazonov, Grand Duke Nicholas, and Izvolski. Izvolski's
correspondence offers the most complete summary of evidence concerning his primary responsibility among the Russians for the fatal determination upon a European war to
realize Russia's ambitions in the Near East. By all odds
the most important works on Russia's guilt in bringing
on the World War are Dr. Stieve's account of the collaboration of Izvolski and Poincaré up to 1914, and Dr. Frantz's
admirable monograph upon Russia's activities and policies
in the July crisis of 1914. Stieve's work has, fortunately,
appeared in English translation.

V. SERBIA

Extremely important information in determining the
problem of responsibility for the War has recently come

from Serbians. The courageous book of Dr. Bogitshevich is full of cogent information on Austro-Serbian and Russo-Serbian relations before 1914. Early in 1923 Professor Stanojevic published a work on the assassination of Franz Ferdinand, which revealed the fact that the plot for the murder of the Archduke was laid by the chief of the intelligence division of the Serbian general staff. Within the last year even more startling information has been brought forward by a prominent Serbian, L. Jovanovitch, and by Bogitshevich, Colonel Simitch and Leopold Mandl who have very definitely implicated not only the Serbian military authorities, but the Serbian civil government as well.

We now know that, in spite of his vigorous denials in 1914, Premier Pashitch of Serbia knew of the plot for the assassination of the Archduke at least three weeks before it was executed, and made no adequate effort to prevent its taking place or to warn the Austrians of the danger to the Archduke in his impending visit to Sarajevo. These writers have still further shown that Dimitrijevitch, the author of the plot, was put to death by means of a judicial murder by the Serbian government in 1917, lest he might divulge the facts concerning the guilt of the Serbian government in the premises. The most recent and comprehensive summary of the guilt of Serbia in the plot for the assassination of the Archduke is contained in the extremely important recent book by Miss Durham, and in the articles by Professor Fay in the October and November, 1925, numbers of the New York *Times Current History Magazine*. The case for the Serbs has been presented in the work of R. W. Seton-Watson, which has proved a flat failure, misleading and unconvincing.

VI. ITALY

One important book has come out of Italy on the problem of war origins, namely, that by Dr. Corrado Barbagallo.

Excellent work on war origins has also been executed in Italy by Augustino Torre and Alberto Lumbroso.

VII. ENGLAND AND CANADA

In England the war epic was first undermined through the vigorous attacks upon Sir Edward Grey by Morel, Loreburn and Miss Willis. While it has generally been held that their judgment of Sir Edward Grey is much more harsh than the facts would warrant, it must nevertheless be recognized that the more complete evidence confirms the general outlines of their indictment. The endeavor to justify the policy of the Liberal Ministry in England in 1914, by Asquith, and later by Grey himself, is an even more feeble attempt than the apologia of Poincaré. To an astounding degree they have had the audacity to parade once more the mythology of 1914 to 1917, thus seriously compromising their reputation for both intelligence and veracity. In refreshing contrast to the sorry quibbling and evasion of Asquith and Grey is the candor of Winston Churchill who, as First Lord of the Admiralty, admits that he and his associates anticipated war with Germany, and from 1912 onward prepared for it both in equipment and spirit.

Of special importance are the memoirs of Sir George Buchanan, the British Ambassador at St. Petersburg in 1914, and of Lord Bertie, the British Ambassador in Paris at the same period. Buchanan reveals in a convincing fashion the Russian will for war, and indicates his own efforts to restrain the Russians. But it is apparent that his attempts in this direction were seriously handicapped by the activities of Sir Edward Grey and Nicolson, and the relations of both of them with Benckendorff. Lord Bertie's diary contains a similar indication of the French enthusiasm for war, but is perhaps most significant as demonstrating the eagerness of Izvolski, and his enthusiastic boast in early August, 1914, that he was the author of the war which had just burst forth.

Sir Edward Grey's much vaunted and praised apology is a sad performance as far as defending his part in the crisis of 1914 is concerned. The best that can be said for it is that he is a more noble and dignified evader of the truth than Asquith. He admits, however, that he was impatient at the suggestion that he should restrain Russia from taking the steps that would inevitably lead to war, and that he would have resigned if he had not been able to drag England into the War to fulfil his promises to Cambon that he would come to the aid of France. It is doubtful if even elementary honesty can be claimed for a writer who states that the chief reason why he felt sure that Germany was determined upon war in 1914 was the fact that it was the *same season of the year* at which the Franco-Prussian War began. Even favorable reviewers have admitted that Grey possessed no vision beyond the interests and limits of the British Empire, and his oft-praised efforts to promote the peace of the world appear to be nothing else than the effort to protect England in her position of world supremacy. It is a matter greatly to be regretted that E. D. Morel was not spared long enough to dissect Grey's ostensibly frank and honest exposition of his career in the Foreign Office. What would have remained of Grey after such an analysis one can well comprehend by perusing Morel's brief but trenchant work, *The Secret History of a Great Betrayal.*

Unquestionably the best book which has been published on the diplomatic history of the decade prior to 1914 is the recent work of the courageous British internationalist, G. Lowes Dickinson. With the exception of an emotional tenderness for Sir Edward Grey, the book is almost a model of exact scholarship, lucid exposition, critical poise and constructive outlook.

In general it may be said that Gooch and Dickinson have been the only Englishmen to produce a systematic and scholarly survey based upon the documents published since 1918, Professor Oman's effort being premature. Of particular significance is the recent determination of the British government to allow Gooch and Temperley to edit and publish the secret documents in the British archives, dealing with the period from 1908 to 1914. The volume on 1914 has just been published. It is to be hoped that the publication of this material may smoke out the French, and compel them to open their archives in self-defense.

The thorough and detailed two-volume work of Dr. Ewart considers the various specific reasons for the entry into the War on the part of the major powers involved; then investigates the general diplomatic background of 1914 in the international relations of the world from 1870 onward; and concludes with a highly judicious analysis of the specific crisis of 1914. Dr. Ewart appears as an honest, sincere and industrious person who has been "fed up" on the Entente propaganda of 1914 and the following years. His book embodies a thoroughgoing acceptance of the revisionist point of view and a smashing demolition of the Entente epic. He places the responsibility for the outbreak of the War squarely upon the Russian mobilization, though it is probable that he does not go as far as the facts warrant in his indictment of Poincaré and his associates. The book is weak only with respect to the author's ignorance of some of the German monographs, of the work of Dobrorolski on the Russian mobilization, and of the above-mentioned revelations concerning the complicity of the Serbian authorities in the murder of the Archduke. It is significant, however, that all of this neglected material would only tend to make the author's indictment of France, Russia and Serbia just so much more thorough and convincing.

VIII. UNITED STATES

In the United States, with the exception of the articles
of Professor Fay, which are now being expanded into
a magisterial treatment of the question of war guilt, there
has been no systematic work produced on the immediate
causes of the World War. There have been, however, a
number of very significant contributions to specific phases
of the problem. Among these, one of the most interesting
is Dr. Mildred Wertheimer's excellent and thorough study
of the Pan-German League. It was once believed that
Germany had a comprehensive and well studied plan to
annex the world, and that the organization which was
engineering this plot was the Pan-German League. The
French propagandist, André Chéradame, in particular,
wrote a number of alarmist volumes, attempting to demonstrate how the peace of the world was being jeopardized
by this noisy group of German super-patriots. Dr.
Wertheimer has made an analysis of the origins, membership, activities and influence of the Pan-German League
on the basis of a first-hand study of the documents and
extensive personal investigation in Germany. Her work
refutes all of the war-time illusions by showing that the
Pan-German League was simply the German manifestation of the universal tendency toward obsessed nationalism
and patriotism on the part of a small group of earnest
souls in every modern state. Its membership was relatively insignificant, and it had little or no influence upon the
official policy of the German government. The fiction of
the menace of the Pan-German League has thus been dissipated parallel with the dissolution of the thesis of the
German will for war and world domination. At the same
time, one must not overlook the fact that the frenzied
patriots in every country constitute one of the greatest
of menaces to the peace and stability of the world, and the

Pan-German League, while not any worse than the French League of Patriots, was a dangerous nuisance far beyond its numerical strength. The great error lay in attempting to find in it something uniquely German and uniquely menacing. In his scholarly article in the *American Historical Review* for April, 1924, Professor Bernadotte E. Schmitt has given us the best summary of the development of the great counter-alliances in Europe from 1870 to 1914. In the New York *Times Current History Magazine* for March, 1926, Professor Schmitt presents a representative summary of the extreme conservative interpretation of the revisionist position as to war guilt.

The letters of Ambassador Page and the memoirs of Colonel House are of real importance with respect to the problem of war guilt and the entry of the United States into the War. (Page took a highly pro-British attitude towards the causes and issues of the War and opposed the efforts of the State Department of the United States to hold Great Britain strictly to international law with respect to neutral rights on the seas. It was this failure which invited the German submarine warfare in reprisal and furnished the ostensible cause for the entry of the United States into the War) The journal of Colonel House is of quite a different feather. His visits to Europe before and during the War gave him ample opportunity to observe the trends and currents in politics and diplomacy, and he reports his observations and convictions with clarity and insight. Incidentally, he offers his own opinion in refutation of the conventional American view that the Kaiser was ardently in favor of war in 1914. The work presents the conclusions of one of the best informed Americans of the War period on international relations, and proves Colonel House to have been on many matters a man with a level head and keen judgment. He seems, however, to have been converted to the war policy some months before President Wilson.

Dr. Ernest Flagg Henderson, in the preliminary section of a series of studies of the leading characters involved in the responsibility for the World War, has presented a very thorough and convincing indictment of Sir Edward Grey. He shows how Grey's involvements with France and Russia practically made it inevitable that Grey and Asquith would attempt to force England into any European conflict in which France and Russia should be aligned against Germany and Austria. They had made secret military and naval agreements, binding for all practical purposes, with both France and Russia, and there is no doubt that they would have made an effort to swing the cabinet for war, even though Belgium had not been invaded. This work is supplemented by the German treatise of Herr Lutz.

When Henderson's indictment is combined with Hermann Lutz's demonstration that on July 25 Sir Edward encouraged Sazonov to feel that England would support the Russian general mobilization, it becomes apparent that Grey's responsibility for the War ranks easily above that of the Kaiser, though, of course, far below that of the Franco-Russian militarists. It must be remembered, further, that Grey made no such effort to restrain France and Russia as did Bethmann and the Kaiser to hold back Austria, though there is little probability that France and Russia would have risked their aggressive policies without a pretty definite feeling that England could be counted upon to come in to support them.

Judge Bausman's work is a devastating attack upon the myth of a defensive and pacific France. While, by its main concentration upon but a single phase of the aggressive European diplomacy of the past half century, the book gives a somewhat distorted and one-sided interpretation, it

is generally accurate in statements of fact, and constitutes
a very convincing refutation of the sentimental view common in America of the self-denying generosity, sweet temper and pacific nobility of the recent leaders of *La Belle
France*. It is interesting further to point out that the
more recent French writers on the question of war responsibility and French policy agree with Bausman's general position, and Gouttenoire de Toury, Dupin, Morhardt
and Lazare present an even more damaging indictment of
Poincaré and his clique.

The two standard works on America's part in the World
War, namely, those by Professors Bassett and McMaster,
are of little value as a study of the *causes* of America's
entry into the World War because they were written before
it had been possible to formulate in adequate fashion the
revisionist point of view. The first serious effort at a
corrective was embodied in the sprightly volume of John
Kenneth Turner. Accepting the doctrine of economic
determinism, he attempts to explain the American entry
on the basis of the desire to protect American investments
in foreign bonds, and to continue the large profits inhering
in the sale of munitions to the allied countries. The financial manufacturing classes in this country feared a German victory if we did not enter, and this would have
prematurely terminated our profit-making sales and jeopardized our investments in Allied paper. While this is
doubtless an over-simplified explanation, there can be no
doubt that it possesses far greater validity than the conventional thesis that we entered in behalf of the abstract
rights of mankind or for the protection of the world against
the lust of Germany for the conquest of the planet. It
can scarcely be alleged that we entered purely for the
sake of protecting our rights as a neutral state, because
during the three previous years we had acquiesced without
effective protest in the most flagrant violations of our

neutral rights by Great Britain. A brilliant young American writer, Mr. C. Hartley Grattan, has best summarized the case against the conduct of Walter Hines Page in an article on the "Walter Hines Page Legend" in the *American Mercury* for September, 1925. By all odds the best work we have as yet on the entry of the United States into the World War is Judge Bausman's *Facing Europe,* which deals with both the issues at stake and the leading personalities involved.

We should not close this section without some mention of the courageous book of Mr. Francis Neilson and the interesting brochure of Mr. Albert J. Nock, which were about the first efforts in America to expose the quite obvious weaknesses of the war-time epic of a single guilty nation, as well as of Professor Beard's trenchant analysis in his work on post-war Europe which has not received one-tenth of the attention it deserves. It is significant that Neilson and Nock were able to riddle this illusion of unique German guilt even before the vast mass of new documentary material had been published.

Industrious German scholars have recently provided us with an excellent bibliography of the literature of war responsibility which is published by the *Deutsche Verlagsgesellschaft für Politik und Geschichte in Berlin.* Readers who desire to follow the latest literature which is appearing on war guilt will find most useful Professor W. L. Langer's bibliographies which are published in *Foreign Affairs.*

INDEX

Algeciras Conference, 81

Alliances, the Great, 66 ff.

Alsace-Lorraine and World War, 76, 84, 384 ff.

American business, pro-Entente, 608 ff.

American Defense Society, propaganda of, 613

American intervention in World War, disastrous effects of, 639 ff.

Anderson, Frank Maloy, 663

Angell, Norman, 24

Anglo-French relations, 1898-1914, 129 ff., 453 ff.

Anglo-French responsibility for Russian aggression in 1914, 370, 390 ff.

Anglo-French war preparations, 461 ff.

Anglo-German naval arrangement, 1913, 47, 482 ff.

Anglo-German *rapprochement* alarms French and Russians, 485 ff.

Anglo-German relations to 1914, 45 ff., 478 ff.

Anglo-Russian naval negotiations, 134 ff., 471 ff.

Anglo-Russian relations to 1914, 129 ff., 471 ff.

armaments,
after World War, 690, 701
before 1914, 54 ff.
comparative in 1914, 54 ff.

Arnold, Benedict, compared to Walter Hines Page, 603 ff.

Artamanov, 169, 314

Asquith, Herbert Henry (British Prime Minister),

denies agreement with France, 467 ff.

unsuccessful attempt to justify policy pursued in 1914, 561 ff.

assassination of Franz Ferdinand, 161 ff.

atrocity factory, French, 294

atrocity myths, refutation of, 292 ff.

Austria-Hungary,
degree of responsibility of for World War, 153 ff.
determines to punish Serbia, 175 ff.
finally consents to negotiate on Serbian issue, 214 ff., 508
opposed to mediation of issue with Serbia, 212 ff.
purpose of in 1914 crisis, 217 ff.
secret plans of in July, 1914, 178
ultimatum of to Serbia, content and purpose of, 190 ff.
Serbian reply to, 199 ff.

Austrian *Red Book,* 38

Avenarius, Ferdinand, 292, 613 ff.

Bacon, Robert, 610

Balkan Wars, effect on World War, 64 f., 85

Balkanizing of the Franco-Russian plot, 110 ff.

Barbagallo, Corrado, 731

Barrès, Maurice, 383

Bassett, John Spencer, 738